REPARATION

AUSTRALIA
LBC Information Services—Sydney

CANADA and USA
Carswell—Toronto

NEW ZEALAND
Brooker's—Auckland

SINGAPORE and MALAYSIA
Thomson Information (S.E. Asia)
Singapore

REPARATION

William J. Stewart

LL.B, LL.M., Solicitor

Partner, MacMillans, Glasgow

W. GREEN/Sweet & Maxwell Ltd
EDINBURGH
2000

Published in 2000 by W. Green & Son Ltd
21 Alva Street
Edinburgh EH2 4PS

Typeset by LBJ Typesetting Ltd, Kingsclere
Printed and bound in Great Britain by
Athenaeum Press Ltd, Gateshead, Tyne and Wear

No natural forests were destroyed to make this product;
only farmed timber was used and replanted

A CIP catalogue record for this book is available from the British Library

ISBN 0 414 010 248

TO

LAWRENCE WILLIAM WALTER STEWART

PREFACE

This is a new book. It is not a new edition of Professor Walker's valuable book on Delict, or even less an update of Glegg.

This is intended to be (at least) a useful book. The literature on the law of tort and the Scots law of delict is now so large that some lengthy discussions have been avoided by reference to fuller treatments. Important or useful contributions from the literature have been noted for the benefit of the scholar and the practitioner seeking more subtle arguments.

The book is special, in the sense that it has no extensive general part such as occupies half of Professor Walker's text. This is for two reasons. First, Professor Walker's general map is accepted and still used subject to the upheaval of the fair, just and reasonable test in negligence. Secondly, Scots law has grown considerably. Unreported cases are now also available to all practitioners and academics through *Greens Weekly Digest* and the Scottish Courts website, further extending resources available. There is even a specialist series of law reports. While it is often said Courts website, further extending resources available. While it is often said that Scotland has a principled system, it can equally be said that for a very long time it had scant case law and therefore a general part was necessary to make up the gaps in the customary law expressed in the cases. The volume of decision now means that case law fits less easily into simple maxims. The focus therefore needs to be on the growing "special" part which then begins to have its own, rather detailed principles, descending in places into bodies of rules. As a result, it might be found that this book, more than any of its predecessors (such as Glegg and Guthrie Smith) has a very small proportion of references to English cases as they are no longer needed to fill gaps, if ever they were. The drawback of this for the reader, especially perhaps the practitioner, is that all of the English cases that are useful are not mentioned and so reference to leading English texts is essential in appropriate cases. Another feature of the end of the last century is that the quality of the Scots decisions has increased, particularly in the sheriff court, and it has been thought proper to cite extensively from such cases, knowing that the practitioner will appreciate the status of such decisions. Many judicial opinions of the last quarter of a century have rendered discussion and citation of older authorities otiose and unnecessary. There has been legislation in the last few decades relating to areas such as products, animals and employers and it is only proper to accept this for what it often is—an attempt to simplify the law. Thus, in this book, the detailed antecedents of repealed common law are essentially ignored or treated very briefly.

I am grateful to my wife, who having cut her teeth on the *Scottish Contemporary Judicial Dictionary*, provided much needed and extensive research and administrative assistance on this work. Thanks to Bill McBryde for setting me off on this voyage. Jim Logie very kindly and very diligently read the first draft, making helpful comments and assisted me yet again in revision of the text for publication. Thanks also to Pino Di'Emidio for his research work on some footnotes and to James Boyd for his help on some missing references. During my time as Convenor of the Library of the Royal Faculty of Procurators in Glasgow I spent many a happy hour working in the library, commanded by the very helpful Alan McAdams. I cannot be more obliged than to Karen Taylor of Greens for seeing the project through. Thanks to my former colleagues at the University of Strathclyde for their support in this project up until 1993. Finally, thanks are as always due to my partner, G.P. Macmillan for supporting this project over the last seven years by steering our firm on his own during my occasional study breaks.

The law is stated as at January 1, 2000.

W.J. STEWART
DALMARNOCK

CONTENTS

TABLE OF CASES

TABLE OF STATUTES

TABLE OF STATUTORY INSTRUMENTS

TABLE OF EUROPEAN AND INTERNATIONAL MATERIAL

TABLE OF ABBREVIATIONS

Bankton
Andrew McDouall, Lord Bankton, *An Institute of the Laws of Scotland in Civil Rights* (1751–53, reprinted by the Stair Society, Vols 41–43, 1993–95).

Bell, *Comm.*
G.J. Bell, *Commentaries on the Law of Scotland and the Principles of Mercantile Jurisprudence* (7th ed. by J. McLaren, 1870, reprinted 1990).

Bell, *Prin.*
G.J. Bell, *Principles of the Law of Scotland* (10th ed. by W. Guthrie, 1899, Reprinted 1989).

Clerk and Lindsell, *Law of Torts*
J.F. Clerk and W.H.B. Lindsell, *Law of Torts* (17th ed. by Brazier *et al*, 1995).

Ersk.
John Erskine of Carnock, *An Institute of the Law of Scotland* (8th ed. by J. B. Nicholson, 1871, reprinted 1989).

Glegg, *The Law of Reparation in Scotland*
A.T. Glegg, *The Law of Reparation in Scotland* (1892).

Gloag & Henderson, *Introduction to the Law of Scotland*
W.M. Gloag and R.C. Henderson, *Introduction to the Law of Scotland* (10th ed. by W.A. Wilson and A.D.M. Forte, 1995) (except where another edition is specified).

Guthrie Smith, *The Law of Damages*
J. Guthrie Smith, *The Law of Damages: A Treatise on the Reparation of Injuries as Administered in Scotland* (2nd ed., 1889).

Hume
Baron David Hume, *Lectures on the Law of Scotland 1786–1822* (Stair Society, G. Paton ed., 6 vols, 1939–59).

McKechnie
H. McKechnie, "Delict and Quasi-Delict" in *Introduction to Scottish Legal History*, Vol. 20 (Stair Society, G. Paton ed., 1958).

Mack.
Sir G. Mackenzie, *The Institutions of the Law of Scotland* (1684).

McKenzie & Evans-Jones
D.W. McKenzie and R. Evans-Jones, "The Development of Remedies for Personal Injuries and Death" in *Civil Law Tradition* in *Scotland* (Stair Society, R. Evans-Jones ed., 1995).

Macphail, *Sheriff Court Practice*
I.D. Macphail, *Sheriff Court Practice* (2nd ed. by C.G.B. Nicholson and A.L. Stewart, 1998).

Markesinis, *The German Law of Torts*
B. Markesinis, *The German Law of Torts: A Comparative Introduction* (2nd ed., 1990).

Paisley Papers
P.T. Burns, S.J. Lyons, "*Donoghue v. Stevenson* and the Modern Law of Negligence" in *The Continuing Legal Education Society of British Columbia* (1991).

Smith, *Short Commentary*
T.B. Smith, *Short Commentary on the Law of Scotland* (1962).

Stair	James Dalrymple, 1st Viscount Stair, *Institutions of the Law of Scotland* (Tercentenary (6th) ed. by D.M. Walker, 1981).
Stair Memorial Encyclopedia	Sir Thomas Smith *et al.*, eds, *The Laws of Scotland: Stair Memorial Encyclopedia* (1987–).
Walker, *Delict* (2nd ed.)	D.M. Walker, *The Law of Delict in Scotland* (2nd ed., revised 1981).
Walker, *Delict*	D.M. Walker, *The Law of Delict in Scotland* (2 vols, 1966).
Walker, *History*, Vol. I	D.M. Walker, *A Legal History of Scotland, Volume I: The beginning to A.D. 1286* (1988).
Walker, *History*, Vol. II	D.M. Walker, *A Legal History of Scotland, Volume II: The Later Middle Ages* (1990).
Walker, *History*, Vol. III	D.M. Walker, *A Legal History of Scotland, Volume III: The Sixteenth Century* (1995).
Walker, *History*, Vol IV	D.M. Walker, *A Legal History of Scotland, Volume IV: The Seventeenth Century* (1996).
Walker, *History*, Vol. V	D.M. Walker, *A Legal History of Scotland, Volume V: The Eighteenth Century* (1998).
Weir, *A Casebook on Tort*	A. Weir, *A Casebook on Tort* (9th ed., 2000).
Zimmerman, *Obligations*	R. Zimmerman, *The Law of Obligations: Roman Foundations of the Civilian Tradition* (1990, reprinted 1996).

CHAPTER 1

TERMS, HISTORY AND THEORY

Introduction

Practitioners reading this book may be assumed to know quite a bit about **1–1** the history, development and theory of reparation. Such wisdom is called upon hardly at all in daily, weekly or monthly practice. So this is a condensed treatment for use in the unusual cases where a more fundamental analysis is needed. It may also be helpful to students or comparatists consulting the book.

Terms

Reparation

"Reparation" is still the name that practitioners use for cases where they **1–2** seek damages for wrongdoing.[1] Stair speaks of "delinquence" but the title of his treatment is "Reparation, where of deliquencies and damages thence arising".[2] Bankton talks of crime and delinquence and the title is headed "Reparation arising from Crimes or Delinquencies".[3] Bell speaks of reparation of injuries.[4] The post-institutional books before Professor Walker's *Delict* are called *Reparation* and *Damages*. Glegg in an interesting footnote defending his use of "reparation" as the title of his book admits it is defective because it describes the right by the remedy. "Delict" was rejected because of the criminal connotations, connotations which are no longer widespread. The main objection Glegg noted is relevant today: "it has been improperly applied to damages for breach of contract; but here it is used in its proper sense, *Reparatio injuriarum*."[5] *Reparatio injuriarum* is a term used as recently as 1991.[6] Glegg was cited to the court in *Miller v. Glasgow District Council*,[7] The context of the debate was the application of statutory rules on prescription to an obligation to re-instate. Counsel was trying to narrow the meaning of the word "reparation" so that the case would not be struck by prescription. An observation of Sir Thomas Smith

---

[1] It is the title of the Greens Bulletin on the subject, and a series of specialist law reports. It is also the title of a Scottish Legal Aid Board publication giving guidance to practitioners.

[2] Stair, I,ix,pr. Grotius, his near contemporary fellow natural law civilian used "maleficium". Stair at I,ii,2 says "The obligation of delinquence then, is that whereunto injury or malifice doth oblige, as the meritorious cause thereof." Mackenzie used the similar anglicisation "malifices" III,i,4.

[3] Bankton, I,x,pr.

[4] Bell, *Comm.*, i, Part II, Chapter 18.

[5] Glegg, *The Law of Reparation in Scotland*, p. 3, n.1.

[6] *Middleton v. Douglass*, 1991 S.L.T. 726.

[7] 1989 S.L.T. 44.

was also cited in support.[8] The court accepted (on the basis of the authorities to which they were referred) that the word is used in the statute in the sense: "*reparatio injuriarum* and is a pecuniary remedy which the law of Scotland affords for a loss caused by a wrong. It is not a remedy which the law of Scotland affords for breach of contract. A breach of contract, if established, attracts an award of damages, the damages being the remedy for the breach of contract."[9]

This view was not the only one. Gloag & Henderson[10] was cited to the court to the effect that in relation to prescription the word included breach of contract. Authority decrees the answer, but what is the correct view? Some support for the "breach of contract" line can be found in the fact that at one time it was thought that reparation for delinquence was based on a contract between the wrongdoer and the pursuer. Bankton says:

"A crime is an unlawful act that merits punishment. The obligation thence arising to punishment and reparation may be said to proceed from the party's consent; for one, by contracting the guilt of a crime, tacitly subjects himself to Punishment, which, he is presumed to know, is its natural consequence, and to the Damage occasioned thro' his fault."[11]

The same theme is evident in Hume's Lectures:

"In the Civil law, the commission of a crime is likened, accordingly, to a contract, and it is said of the offender "*quod delinquendo contraxisse videtur.*"[12]

It could then be possible that "reparation" as a general term predates any sharp modern distinctions of the law of obligations and historically is applicable to both. It is also well appreciated (although differently articulated at various times) that there are two aspects to a contractual obligation. This is sometimes put as a matter of there being primary and secondary obligations—the primary obligation being the expected performance and the secondary obligation being to pay damages for breach. While the use of reparation for the primary obligation would be clearly wrong (payment or performance being more appropriate in most cases) the term does not seem out of place in relation to the secondary obligation. Stair accepts as much when he says that although all there is reparation for delinquence, there can also be "reparation arising from contracts".[13] Further because Scots law admits the existence of concurrent liability, it is curious that the simple choice by the pursuer of how he frames his case could change the name of the remedy he has obtained.

---

[8] Smith, *Short Commentary*, p. 648.
[9] *Miller*, at 47.
[10] *Introduction to the Law of Scotland* (9th ed. W. Green, 1987).
[11] Bankton I,x,1.
[12] Hume iii, 120; And see also Stair I,ix,3.
[13] Stair, *ibid.*

Delict, Quasi-Delict

In the universities and now often in the courts and in practice the reason **1-3**
for there being liability is discussed in terms of "delict". The etymology of
the word is from the Latin *delictum*—a fault or a crime.[14] Delict was not a
commonly used term in early Scots law.[15] Stair and Bankton favoured
delinquence and reparation. By the time of Erskine "delinquency" was still
preferred—crimes and delicts being treated later in the book.[16] Hume in his
lectures adopted *Obligations ex delicto* as a title.[17] He also utilises "quasi-
delict" for some of the old Roman cases and a number of instances of
vicarious liability.[18] In Bell's Principles a different use of words can be
detected.[19] Bell's division depended upon the idea of delict as deliberate
harm: "Quasi-delict is an intentional interference with rights of another so
as to cause him to suffer loss, for want of care."[20] The distinction can be
seen in older decisions.[21] Another understanding of the denotation of the
two terms is that delict refers to personal wrongdoing and quasi-delict to
imputed fault.[22] For Bell actionable wrongs comprised both "an offence
committed with an injurious, fraudulent, or criminal purpose"[23] as well as
the case of "gross negligence or imprudence, though it should bear no such
character of fraud, malice, or criminal purpose as to subject the person to
criminal cognisance, is, as a ground for an action for damages, held as a

---

[14] "'Delinquo', supine delictum means "to be lacking" or "fail". It was already used in
classical Latin to mean "fail in one's duty, offend" — P. Birks, "The Concept of a Civil
Wrong" in *Philosophical Foundations of Tort Law* (Owen ed, 1995) p.39, n.28. The adjective is
delictual. "Delictal" sounds better and it is wondered whether delictual has grown out of
contractual. It is noted in *Salmond and Heuston on Tort* that the word "delictal" may have
been invented by Salmond, see p.14, n.53. J.J. Gow, "Is Culpa Amoral?" 1953 J.R. 17 at 30
has "quasi-delictal".

[15] H. McKechnie, "Delict and Quasi-Delict" in *An Introduction to Scottish Legal History*
(1958, Stair Society, Vol. 20), p. 265. Professor Walker has traced the use of a number of
quainter terms in the early years. "Cro", "Kelchyn" and "enach" he tells us are Irish and
"galbnes" Welsh. Walker, *History*, III, 724. They both mean compensation for a killing, fine
for a killing, amends for a fault or trespass. "Assythment" has been used right into the
twentieth century but this native remedy is named from the middle English "assithe". Walker,
History, III, 724 "Kinbut" is anglo-saxon. Walker, *History*, III 724. Compensation to the
Kindred. "Slains" is used because letters of slain were the receipt for the payment which
excluded punishment. It seems that the root of the term is not "slay" as might be expected but
the Irish "slainte" meaning health or safety, or, in context, "freedom from suite". Walker,
History, III, 724.

[16] Ersk., III,i,12.

[17] Hume ii, 14.

[18] Hume ii, 16.

[19] Bell, *Prin.*, s. 543.

[20] Bell, *Prin.*, s. 544.

[21] *Palmer v. Wick and Pulteneytown Steam Shipping Company Ltd* (1894) 2 S.L.T. 91:
"Delicts proper embrace all breaches of the law which expose their perpetrator to criminal
punishment. The term quasi-delict is generally applied to any violation of the common or
statute law which does not infer criminal consequences, and does not consist in the breach of
any contract, express or implied. Cases may and do often occur in which it is exceedingly
difficult to draw the line between delicts and quasi-delict. The latter class, as it has been
developed in the course of the present century, covers a great variety of acts and omissions,
ranging from deliberate breaches of the law, closely bordering upon crime, to breaches
comparatively venial and involving no moral delinquency." (1894) 21 R. (H.L.) 39, *per* Lord
Watson at 43 based on the unsuccessful appellants' submissions.

[22] Zimmerman, *The Law of Obligations*, p.19.

[23] Bell, *Prin.*, s. 544.

delict, to the effect making the person guilty of the imprudence or negligence liable to indemnify the person who suffers by the fault."[24] Some judicial disapprobation of the distinction between delict and non-criminal quasi-delict appears as long ago as 1860.[25] The term quasi-delict is still used today.[26]

Professor Walker suggested that it would be appropriate to reserve the term quasi-delict for cases involving the old Roman remedies and that is now something with which few people would disagree.[27]

Actio Injuriarum

1–4 Discussion of the term *actio injuriarum* is no longer so difficult thanks to the sustained efforts of, among others, Professor T.B. Smith.[28] The *actio injuriarum* in Roman law and in the civilian tradition itself refers to claims based on assault and affront rather than Aquilian loss wrongfully caused. In Scotland there had been, in a sense, an abuse of terminology which much to Smith's annoyance had been "tolerated and encouraged in the Scottish Courts." Scots lawyers called the relatives' action in respect of the death of a victim caused by culpa of the defender an *actio injuriarum*. The "mis-use" was eventually corrected judicially and is no longer encountered in its erroneous sense.[29]

History

Ancient Rome

1–5 Scots law has as an intellectual root, the Roman law. It is not a pure civilian system like France or Germany. It retains native sources. The influence of the last two hundred years has been that of the English common law.[30] The

---

[24] Bell, *Prin.*, s. 553.

[25] In *Western Bank v. Douglas* (1860) 22 D. 447 at 475, it was said by the Lord Justice-Clerk (Inglis): "Some writers in our law have made a distinction between delicts and quasi-delicts as a ground for a civil action of reparation , giving the former name to those graver offences which might form the object of criminal proceedings, and the latter to those which will only found a claim for pecuniary reparation of damage sustained. But this distinction is of little importance to the present case, for we are of opinion that the same measure of reparation is due, on the same conditions, and by the same form of action, whether the cause of action be the one kind of delict or the other. *Crassa negligentia equiparatur dolo.*"

[26] See Lord Fraser in *Junior Books v. Veitchi Co.*, 1982 S.L.T. 492 at 494 It appears in statutes: Civil Jurisdiction and Judgments Act, Art. 5 (3) Sched. 4. The same language is found in the associated European Convention making it possible that a private international law case will require some civilian analysis; Private International Law (Miscellaneous Provisions) Act 1995, s. 9; P. Stein, "The *actio de effusis vel dejectis* and the Concept of Quasi-delict in Scots Law" [1955] 4 I.C.L.Q. 356; See the instances noted in W.J. Stewart, "Smith's Question Mark, Walker's exhortation and quasi-delict", 1990 J.R. 71.

[27] Walker, *Delict*, p. 28. This is obviously subject to the use when compelled by statute (see n. 26 above); Zimmerman says the two uses merged in France in the 19th Century, *Zimmerman* p.20.

[28] T.B. Smith, "Designation of Delictual Actions: Damn Injuria Damn", 1972 S.L.T. (News) 125; "Damn injuria again", 1984 S.L.T. (News) 85.

[29] *McKendrick v. Sinclair*, 1972 S.L.T. 110 (H.L.); and also in the Court of Session, 1971 S.L.T. 17 and 234.

[30] To this extent it is very similar to South Africa but the Roman-Dutch roots are much more visible and vibrant there. W.J. Kamba, "Concept of duty of care and Aquilian liability in Roman-Dutch law", 1975 J.R. 252.

principal aspect of Roman law relevant to reparation is the *lex Aquilia*.[31] It was in three chapters or paragraphs.[32] The third chapter provided: "In the case of all other things apart from slaves or cattle that have been killed, if anyone does damage to another by wrongfully burning breaking or spoiling his property, let him be condemned to pay to the owner whatever the damage shall prove to be worth in the next thirty days."[33] There are hugely interesting debates about the text and meaning of these passages but these must be left to the Romanists to enjoy.[34] It is what was done with the *lex Aquilia* by the Roman jurists and the lawyers ever since that interests contemporary lawyers. One of the first things it did or was taken to have done was to require something to have been done illegally or wrongfully.[35] This idea of wrongfulness depended of course on a view of what was lawful and tends to circuity.[36] However the jurists went a step further and gave wrongfulness a new signification. *Injuria* was interpreted as comprehending damage caused in a blameworthy fashion—the key Latin word used being *culpa*.

Before Stair in Scotland

But that is to anticipate. Moving from ancient Rome to early Scotland our **1–6** oldest major law book, *Regiam Majestatem*, it has been said "has practically nothing to teach us" of delicts.[37] Professor Walker in his *History* says: "Harms and wrongs were no doubt common enough in Scotland at this time but there was no law of delict because there could be no enforcement of reparation."[38] Later, in the fourteenth and fifteenth centuries a law of "wrongs" appears where there is a civil aspect to elements of crime.[39] In the

---

[31] The clearest reference to it in the institutional writers is Bankton, I,x,40. The *lex Aquilia* was a statute and so those who today refuse to consider statutes as part of the theoretical structure of reparation for wrongdoing have this impressive precedent to contradict. It replaced the existing law (or perhaps derogated from it): see the treatment of delict at the time of the XII Tables in H.F. Jolowicz, *Historical Introduction to the Study of Roman Law* (2nd ed., Cambridge University Press, 1954), with corrections, 170–178. It is normally dated about 287 B.C. but there is scholarly debate about even this.

[32] The first provided that if anyone unlawfully killed a slave or servant-girl belonging to someone else, or a four-footed beast of the class of cattle he would be condemned to pay the owner the highest value that the property had attained in the preceding year. D 9,2,2 pr.(Gaius) The second is less exciting and in any event was not known to the civilian jurists, only coming to light in 1816, Zimmerman, *Obligations*, p. 954 The second paragraph provides an action for the amount in question against an adstipulator [a kind of guaranteeing trustee] who released the debtor in fraud of his principal. Gaius Inst. III, 215–216.

[33] D.9.2.27.5 (Ulpian) trans. Kolbert.

[34] Zimmerman, *The Law of Obligations*, pp. 957–969.

[35] D.9.2.5.1 (Ulpian).

[36] An obvious case is self-defence where the defender kills the pursuer's ambushing slave D.9.2.4.pr.(Gaius).

[37] T.M. Cooper (ed.) *Regiam Majestatem and Quoniam Attachiamenta* (Stair Society, 1947), p. 10.

[38] Walker, *History*, I, p. 344. Professor Walker puts *Regiam Majestatem* between 1285 and 1320, *History*, I, pp. 114–117. He does note two chapters from the Leges Quatuor Burgorum which are apparently delictual. Walker, *History*, I, p. 344. In one edition of this old law there is a tariff giving the price of blood an injuries but its source is not clear. *Regiam Majestatem*, Stair Soc. IV, 40.

[39] Walker, *History*, II, p. 612 Professor Walker expresses the view that in these times wrongs were redressed by the brieve anent breach of the king's protection which "seems accordingly to have been the Scottish counterpart of the English writ of trespass." Walker, *History*, II, p. 614.

fifteenth century assythment (the relatives claim against a killer), Lawburrows[40] and Spuilzie[41] were all known. In the sixteenth century it is clear
from Balfour's Practicks that there was a vibrant law of delict probably
appropriate to the times.[42]

Stair, Erskine and Bell

1–7 Stair's treatment is not entirely revolutionary for the detailed rules he
expounds are not surprising to a reader of Balfour. He does, of course, try
to rationalise this liability. He saw delinquence as a separate source of
obligation. He rejected the fourfold division of Justinian's Institutes,
namely *furtum, rapina, damnum, injuria.* Instead he says: "it shall in general
suffice here to consider, that, according to several rights and enjoyments,
damages and delinquencies may be esteemed." These are then set out in
categories: (1) life, members and health; (2) liberty; and the delinquencies
against it are restraint and constraint; (3) fame, reputation, and honour,
"which is also in some way reparable"; (4) "our content, delight, or
satisfaction; and especially by the singular affection to, or our opinion of,
the value or worth of any thing that owners have, in which consideration it
is said, that every thing is to every man as he esteemeth it"; and (5) goods
and possession. After taking this rights or interest based approach which
appears to be an attempt at synthesis he reverts to a practical listing of
nominate delicts:

> "We come to the obligations by delinquence, which are civilly cognosc-
> ible by our custom, according to their known names and titles in our law;
> which though they do rather signify the acts or actions, whereby such
> obligations are incurred or prosecute, than the obligations themselves,
> yet will they be sufficient to hold out both . . . These are either general,
> having no particular name of designation; and such are pursued under
> the general name of damage and interest. Which hath as many branches
> and specialties, as there can be valuable and reparable damages; besides
> those of a special name and nature, which are chiefly these, assythment,
> extortion, circumvention, spuilzie, intrusion, ejection, molestation,
> breach of arrestment, deforcement, contravention, forgery, which comes
> in more properly in the process of improbation (IV, 20, *infra*)".[43]

That is not however all that there is. Some very special cases of negligence
exist but even then they are not considered as such, merely as other

---

[40] See Chap. 5 below.

[41] See Chap. 6 below.

[42] Assythment features considerably. Balfour, *Practicks*, 516. Professor Walker has examined
the remedy in this period and offers an example of a letter of slains — the formal document
buying off the vengeance. Walker, *History*, III 725–729. See Balfour, *Practicks*, for copious
authority on spuilzie and ejection protecting property (465–476); liability for and in respect of
animals (490); wrongful detention (178); and damage to coalheughs (493); feature. It is
interesting to note that there is a provision concerning liability of judges. The marginal note
mentions negligence and the passage itself does refer to fault in the non-execution of office
(284).

[43] Stair, I,ix,6.

recognised cases of civil reparation.[44] It may be that Stair was in the tradition of the *ius commune* in formulating a general reparation action.[45] Evidence of its frequent use has not yet materialised. Strong evidence of such a theme being current in these times—no doubt from the *ius commune* is clear in Erskine, writing in the eighteenth century. He expressed a general principle:

> "every one who has the exercise of reason, and so can distinguish between right and wrong, is naturally obliged to make up the damage befalling his neighbour from a wrong committed by himself. Wherefor every fraudulent contrivance, or unwarrantable act, by which another suffers damage, or runs the hazard of it, subjects the delinquent to reparation."[46]

But it is not even then clear that cases were decided from this principle. Bell in the early nineteenth century entitles his chapter 18 "Of reparation of Injuries." He expresses a rights based general rule:

> "The rights of individuals, either to property or to personal liberty, safety, or reputation, are not only protected by penal law, but in civil law they furnish, when invaded, ground of action for reparation".[47]

He explains that delict is committed with an injurious, fraudulent or criminal purpose. The law only seeks indemnification rather than punishment.[48] He covers the liability of the master.[49] He then deals with quasi-delict:

> "Gross negligence or imprudence, though it should bear no such character of fraud malice, or criminal purpose as to subject the person to criminal cognisance, is, as a ground for an action for damages, held as a delict, to the effect of making the person guilty of the imprudence or negligence liable to indemnify the person who suffers by the fault. These by lawyers are called quasi-delicts."[50]

The examples he gives are of ship collisions (property damage), keeping a dangerous dog, the use of diligence and the carelessness of public officials.[51]

---

[44] (1) an accessory action against those who fail in their duty in executing captions; IV,xlvii,21; (2) another is the liability of magistrates for prisoners who escape thus depriving the creditor of the benefit of *squalor carceris*. Liability was elided if it could be shown that provident diligence could not prevent the escape: escape with the traditional file was not a good excuse because the prisoners ought to have been searched. This liability may be based on breach of the statutory duty imposed by the Act of Sederunt, June 14, 1671 rather than any traditional Scots law; (3) the clerk of bills was liable to a charger for taking insufficient caution and to a suspender if he refused sufficient caution. Again this was required by Act of Sederunt Feb 18 1686. McKechnie cites Stair, II,iii,67 as another example but it is obscure.

[45] McKenzie and Evans-Jones "The Development of Remedies for Personal Injuries and Death" in *Civil Law Tradition in Scotland* (Evans-Jones ed., 1995).

[46] III,i,13.

[47] Bell, *Prin.*, s. 543.

[48] *ibid.*, s. 544.

[49] *ibid.*, s. 547.

[50] *ibid.*, s. 553.

[51] *ibid.*, s. 553.

Later he treats of delict as a means of protection of the person and character. Everyone has an absolute right to the safety of his person and whenever invaded has a right to damages.[52] Assythment for homicide is recognised.[53] Reparation for injuries by negligence is clearly recognised.[54] He notes that rapid travel on land and water brought about most of these cases. Insufficiency of vehicles, overloading or furious driving are examples. Solatium for pain and distress is part of the claim.[55] Personal violence is such an invasion of right that it requires justification. Damages are not only for injury but also for the affront.[56] Other known heads of claim noted are seduction[57] and wrongous imprisonment.[58] Character is protected in the civil courts both for damage and solatium.[59]

Roman Law again: Civilian Culpa

1–8 It is at this stage that there must be another digression into the civilian tradition because it can be seen that the institutional writers all show some tendancy to express a general principle. Intellectually the ancient Roman law was at the times of Stair, Erskine and Bell being reformed. The most significant development in the civilian world is on "culpa". Culpa in the sense of blameworthiness appears in the *Digest* as a supplement to the *injuria* of *damnum injuria datum*.[60] Ulpian's examples are cases where the act is *ex facie* wrongful as infringing the potential pursuer's rights but which are not within the Aquilian liability because the defender is not blameworthy—the lunatic and the infant being examples.[61] This idea grew out of and could easily assimilate the various defences to an injuria based action—self-defence, necessity and consent for example.[62] But what was this blameworthiness denoted by *culpa*? MacCormack puts the point clearly:

> "*Culpa* is to be translated as fault and not negligence. Where a jurist presents the facts of the case and draws the conclusion that there has, or has not, been *culpa*, he is not asking, do these facts constitute negligence? His approach is to ask, do these facts constitute a fault? From this one may infer that where *culpa* is used as a criterion of liability in a general context without the addition of facts which explain what is meant, it should be taken as fault. The texts frequently state that a person is liable under the *lex Aquilia* for *dolus* and/or *culpa*. Such statements do not contrast loss brought about through intention and loss brought about through negligence. The mention of *dolus* in no way shows that *culpa* is negligence. As in other contexts it means fault,

---

[52] Bell, *Prin.*, s. 2028.
[53] *ibid.*, s. 2029.
[54] *ibid.*, s. 2030.
[55] *ibid.*, s. 2031.
[56] *ibid.*, s. 2032.
[57] *ibid.*, s. 2033.
[58] *ibid.*, s. 2034.
[59] *ibid.*, s. 2043.
[60] D.9.2.5.1(Ulpian)
[61] For a broader and deeper discussion see P. Birks, "The Concept of a Civil Wrong" in *Philosophical Foundations of Tort Law* (Owen ed., 1995), pp. 42–45.
[62] Zimmerman, *The Law of Obligations*, pp. 998–1004.

specifically fault not falling within the ambit of *dolus*. Whether *culpa* is taken as negligence or as fault is important. To say that someone is at fault implies that he has behaved in some way that he should not have behaved but leaves open the nature of the behaviour. To say that someone has been negligent implies that he has acted in a careless fashion and that he ought to have foreseen that what he did would cause damage."[63]

Carelessness was a way in which fault could be established.[64] "Under the *lex Aquilia* even the slightest degree of fault counts".[65] The crucial point is also made, "there is fault when what could have been foreseen by a diligent man was not foreseen."[66] Sometimes *culpa* includes *dolus* and sometimes it is excluded.[67] This traditional view has been restated as recently as the last decade of the twentieth century by Lord President Hope:

"*Culpa* which gives rise to a liability in delict may take various forms. In *Stair Memorial Encyclopaedia*, Vol. 14, "Nuisance", para. 2087, it is stated that the usual categories of *culpa* or fault are malice, intent, recklessness and negligence. To that list there may be added conduct causing a special risk of abnormal damage where it may be said that it is not necessary to prove a specific fault as fault is necessarily implied in the result: See *Chalmers v. Dixon, per* Lord Justice Clerk Moncreiff at (1876) 3 R. 464."[68]

Zimmerman, summarising the further development of the *actio*, states that: "by the end of the seventeenth century . . . the modern law in action no longer reflected the Aquilian delict of the *corpus juris*."[69] The end of the seventeenth century is a critical time for Scots lawyers being the time in which Stair was working on the Institutions.[70] Foreseeability was an aspect

---

[63] Zimmerman, *The Law of Obligations*, p. 202.

[64] *ibid.*

[65] D.9.2.44.pr.

[66] D.9.2.31.

[67] Zimmerman, *The Law of Obligations*, p. 201.

[68] *Kennedy v. Glenbelle*, 1996 S.L.T. 1186.

[69] Zimmerman, *The Law of Obligations*, p. 1018. He explains that Thomasius put the matter as strongly as saying that the action then current bore as little resemblance to the *lex Aquilia* as a bird to a beast — that an action for damage done was hiding behind an Aquilian mask. Note Zimmerman's verdict is that historically Thomasius was wrong but purely dogmatically he had a point, p.1031.

[70] There is very little of liability for lack of care before Stair. Professor Walker finds what we would now describe as case allowed on relevancy, where the dispute was whether the defender was negligent or whether it was heavy weather that caused the loss of a ship as long ago as 1492, Walker, *History*, II, p. 737 (when of course the world was flat). He also finds a questionable Scots Privy Council case in 1566: *Dick v. Grizzel* in which a person injured by an accidentally dropped plank was compensated by £20. Zimmerman, *op. cit.*, summarises that natural law school of which Stair is one of the least well-known members as moving away from looking at the injured party to looking at the injuring party and their duty, above, p. 1033.

of the necessary imputability.[71] Thus for a system to have an action for recovery of damage based on the *lex Aquilia* it need not be called that.[72]

But so far as Scotland is concerned the Romanist trail eventually runs cold. Much scholarly work has been done to help unravel the historical development.[73] So far as property damage is concerned Stair's "Damage and Interest" can be seen as a manifestation of a civilian Aquilian remedy for damage to property, which being based on *culpa* would be activated by negligence. The picture which emerges in relation to personal injuries and death is one where the native remedy of assythment is eventually overtaken in the nineteenth century by a civilian general principle of loss wrongfully caused based on the *lex aquilia*, but by accident wrongly called the *actio injuriarum*.[74] It has been argued that the civilian strand runs deeper.[75]

A native remedy: assythment

1–9 One final excursus is required to represent properly the history of Scots law and to explain the older cases to the practitioner forced to excavate. The ancient laws of Scotland provided for assythment. Criminal wrongdoers could escape their penalties including death if they paid off the relatives.[76]

---

[71] Zimmerman, *op. cit.*, p.1034.

[72] Nor need it any longer comply with any of the rules applicable to that remedy at any particular time. However, in systems which codify the view of the remedy at the time of codification is entrenched and whether or not better rules or more efficient or more just rules can be arrived at may become a matter of legislation rather than permissible judicial development. One major divergence is that German law on one view still differentiates fault and unlawfulness whereas the French do not. Markesinis, *The German Law of Torts*, p. 58. There is justification for that approach because the German Code specifies certain protected interests. If Scots law treated Stair as "the codification that never was" then the enumerated rights would provide a foundation for a similar approach in Scots law. This is a preliminary enquiry for then it must be established that there was intention to harm or a lack of reasonable care. Yet by interpretation it is argued that the imputability idea should mean that lack of care itself can constitute the wrongfulness. Markesinis, *op. cit.*, p. 60.

[73] D.M. Walker, "The Development of Reparation." 1952 J.R. 101; R.A. Black, "Historical Survey of Delictual Liability in Scotland for Personal Injuries and Death" [1975] 8 C.I.L.J.S.A. 46,189,316; [1976] C.I.L.J.S.A. 57; H. McKechnie, "Delict and Quasi-delict" in *Introduction to Scottish Legal History* (Paton ed., Stair Society), Vol. 20.

[74] T.B. Smith, " Damn injuria again", 1984 S.L.T. (News) 85.

[75] McKenzie and Evans-Jones, "The Development of Remedies for Personal Injuries and Death" in *Civil Law Tradition in Scotland* (Evans-Jones ed., 1995), in which it is said that the general civilian aquilian action recognised early on by Stair in relation to property damage, existed alongside assythment applying to personal injuries and death. Thus, the civilian heritage goes much further back. The significance of this is that Scots law may well have recognised liability for negligent personal injury for some considerable time before *Gardner v. Ferguson*, unreported. The first reported case Black points out is *Innes v. Magistrates of Edinburgh* (1798) Mor. 13189, 13967. The cases cited by McKenzie and Evans-Jones are *Lady Leith Hall v. Earl of Fife* (1768) Mor. 13904 and *Denistoun v. Smith* (1698) 4 B.S. 426; *Macdonnell v. Macdonald*, 2 Dow. 66.

[76] The Assise Regis David of the 12th century provided in Chapter 14 that an attempt to strike a blow resulted in a penalty to the king of four cows and a payment to the man he missed of one cow. If he made contact but drew no blood he paid the King six cows and the man struck two cows. If he drew blood the king got nine cows and the victim three cows. If the victim was slain the king got 29 cows and a colpindach. Walker, *History*, I, p. 98. At the stage of the 29 cows Professor Walker very practically asks: "What if the defender had not so many cows?". A colpindach is a young cow or ox. Earlier historical predecessor are traced in Walker, *History*, III, pp. 723–724. Various Acts of the 15th Century infer something of a developed system. Walker, *History*, II at pp. 616–618 citing the Remissions Act 1425, the Public Peace Act 1449 and the Remissions Act 1457.

In the sixteenth century the institution is more secure and it seems that the King could not remit the obligation to compensate the relatives.[77] It is by an Act of Parliament of 1600 that, according to Professor Walker the the remedy becomes more mature.[78] The seventeenth century saw many instances of assythment in cases of homicide and mutilation.[79]

According to Professor Walker it is in the eighteenth century that assythment began to denote reparation for intentional or negligent injury.[80] What was left, whatever it was called, was an action for damages by members of the family for solatium and loss of support based on nearness of relationship and the mutual obligation of support.[81] Collaterals were not allowed this claim as they had in cases of assythment. After another attempt by collaterals to claim the law was reformed.[82] Assythment faded away for all practical purposes in the nineteenth century. So far as the modern concept that negligence depends upon breach of a duty to take care Erskine does indeed mention the idea of duty in his treatment: "Wrong may arise, not only from positive acts of trespass or injury, but from blameable omission or neglect of duty."[83] Lord President Dunedin said in *Clelland v. Robb*[84] "Negligence per se will not make liability unless there is first of all a duty which there has been a failure to perform through that neglect."

---

[77] So much so that ambassadors between Scotland and England meeting to discuss the execution of Mary, Queen of Scots asked what satisfaction could be offered to the Scottish King and it was apparently replied that it was for the kin to discuss that matter. This bold negotiating tactic apparently resulted in the English leaving and giving nothing at all. Walker, *History*, III, pp. 723–727. Citing D. Moysie, *Memoires of the affairs of Scotland*, pp. 60–61 and pointing out, p.745, n. 348 that the claim was in any event doubtful the act taking place outwith Scotland and being a judicial act. Still the English were presumably not so misguided as to be offering satisfaction when there was not some claim. Generally there seems to have been an encouragement for bargaining or what would now be called ADR by appointing commissioners and by making remission conditional on satisfaction being agreed.

[78] Moysie, *op. cit.*, p. 729.

[79] Professor Walker records that in several cases it was awarded without reference to criminal liability. Walker, *History*, IV, p. 696. Assythment was mentioned by Stair as a nominate delict: "assythment, as it signifies the reparation made, so it insinuates the obligation to repair damage, sustained by slaughter, mutilation or other injuries in the members or health of the body; but it is chiefly pursued by the wife, children or nearest of kin of parties slain. In other cases it is competent to the party mutilate or hurt, but otherwise prejudged by the mutilation or hurt. And though the private interest be only for reparation of damage and loss; yet our custom applyeth much of that, which is penal therein to the injured. And, therefor, consideration is had of the ability and estate of the offender, and the assythment is accordingly modified, all circumstances being considered; and that either against the principal offender or the accessories." I,ix,7.

[80] Walker, *History*, V, pp. 721–723; citing *Gardner v. Ferguson*, Campbell Collection, Session Papers, lxxix, No.8; *Innes v. Edinburgh Magistrates* (1798) Mor. 13189, 13967 and the famous *Black v. Cadell* (1804) Mor. 13905, affd. Mor. Vol. 23,33. The analogy with assythment was not however adopted by the widow in *Black*, McKechnie, *op. cit.*, p. 274. After this time assythment proper faded into the new action for reparation for personal injuries or death itself drawing inspiration from the *lex aquilia*. It has been suggested that *Black* was not so innovatory as it seemed and that it was in fact Stair who set up two parallel systems, that of assythment and a general action. See Mckenzie and Evans-Jones, *op. cit.*, pp. 186–289. The argument is of interest but they have been able so far to find only three markers in the cases *Lady Leith Hall* (1768) Mor. 13904; *Denistoun v. Smith*, 4 B.S. 426; *Macdonnell v. Macdonald*, 2 Dow. 66. This results in their disputing McKechnie's reading (at p. 274, n. 26) which has heretofore been generally accepted.

[81] *Eisten v. NBR* (1870) 8 M. 980.

[82] *McKendrick v. Sinclair*, 1972 S.L.T. 110.

[83] III,i,13.

[84] 1911 S.C. 253.

Now

1–10 The nineteenth and twentieth centuries brought us to the position we know today. As Bell signalled industrialisation brought ever more cases of liability and many recognitions of liability.[85] Nonetheless, Scots lawyers were sufficiently conservative not to allow the injured consumer to recover from the negligent manufacturer, a form of liability only recognised by force of the House of Lords. The English recognition of negligence and the already entrenched Scots doctrine of *culpa* meant that the twentieth century saw in Scotland as elsewhere[86] many more cases of alleged liability for negligence and the struggle to define and contain it. Yet again it was the House of Lords, this time in an English appeal, *Hedley Byrne v. Heller*,[87] that opened the way to recovery for economic losses and even that case was treated with extreme caution, in Scotland, for a while. The twentieth century marked an increase in legislation and, since the Second World War especially, legislation designed expressly to reform the law of delict. The sources of such legislation are various and include party political imposition, law reform committees, pressure group lobbying, the European Union and the statutory Scottish Law Commission. The decline in any civilian influence is now complete.[88]

What the law does

1–11 Such is the volume and range of writing on delict and tort at the end of the twentieth century that even this obvious section requires some defence. Two modern English academics comment:

> "Generally, however, although conventional texts do give some attention to competing accounts of tort's function, usually in an introductory chapter . . . the themes there identified are not commonly integrated into textual discussion of individual cases throughout. In other words the textbook proceeds on the assumption that case law can usefully be examined without particular reference to torts competing goals. Thus at the very outset, it becomes clear that the reinterpretation of negligence as accident compensation is at odds with the textbook approach, for while the former views negligence as a means to an end, the latter proceeds on the basis that ends are, for the most part irrelevant."[89]

---

[85] J. McLaren, "Nuisance Law and the Industrial Revolution—Some Lessons from Social History" [1983] 3 O.J.L.S. 155.

[86] M. Horowitz, *The Transformation of American Law 1780–1860* (1977).

[87] [1964] A.C. 465.

[88] But there may be a renaissance afoot — while this book was being completed the Law Faculty at Edinburgh University began a codification project.

[89] J. Conaghan and W. Mansell, *The Wrongs of Tort*, (Pluto Press, London, 1993), p. 86 . However, the evidence adduced by Conaghan and Mansell is hardly compelling. The main case cited is that of AIDS victims infected by infected blood rather than intravenous blood use or homosexual activity. Another is pressure in medical cases to introduce no-fault with a bill in 1991. They argue: "all this adds up to a greatly increased level of excitement arising from public debates about accident compensation. This combined with the emotive effects arising from media focus on recent mass disasters — the Hillsborough disaster (1989), the Zeebrugge ferry accident (1987) and the King's Cross fire (1988) has once more heightened public awareness so that the issue of accident compensation has re-emerged as a respectable matter for debate. Yet this political resurgence of an apparently dead issue is barely reflected in tort textbooks." p.101.

The need for *damnum* in aquilian cases meant and means that compensation is unlikely to be lost from sight.[90] So far as new heads of compensation are concerned it is now usually considered better that such is achieved by the legislature if for no other reason than that economic or constitutional issues which arise can be better dealt with by a commission or a committee taking evidence from persons other than the parties involved in a litigation.

Deterrence

The threat of having to pay damages if a course of conduct is followed **1–12** deters persons from following that course. Reparation operates to control the behaviour of actors in society in advance. The function of delict as deterrence is normally unseen. In the realm of intentional conduct and intentional harm it is at its most powerful. It is true that the deterrent function in some cases has been better fulfilled by the criminal law or special statutory schemes. The rich man refrains from punching the poor man not for fear of having to pay a few hundred pounds of damages for assault but because he might be sent to jail. In cases of unintentional harm the deterrent effect is more subtle. In most cases of negligent harms the actor does not want to cause the harm and may indeed be upset so to have done. The obligation to pay for the harm makes even the ordinary citizen consider the idea of risk management. Liability insurance does not always destroy this useful effect of the law of delict. The insurers provide a different function—they spread the cost of harm, hoping for a profit but open to making losses.[91] They prevent a lottery where a failure to pick up the banana causes the householder to be liable for a very expensive case of paraplegia. They very seldom immunise the actors of any consequences; they make the insured pay an excess, or worse a double deductible. There are no penal damages in Scotland, nor exemplary damages.[92]

Deterrence is an important aspect of negligence too. A recent expression of the traditional view can be seen in the judgment of Henry, L.J. in the Court of Appeal in *Frost v. Chief Constable*.[93] Deterrence, he said, was part of the public policy behind tort law. Prevention was better than cure and potential defendants should face up to their safety responsibilities before rather than after an accident.[94] Stapleton has demonstrated that the idea of deterrence is perhaps quite deeply entrenched in the modern law.[95] What

---

[90] See para. 1–8 above.

[91] Which ironically they may seek to recover in delict actions: *Henderson v. Merrett* [1995] 2 A.C. 145.

[92] See Clerk and Lindsell, *Law of Torts*, para. 27–66 for the position in England. This is a rule which might be reviewed from time to time. It is a power which should be used sparingly and only by a judge (or a jury subject to review for excess)—it gives the community, though the court the chance to deal with cynical and ruthless bad people. Some societies would baulk at such a power being given to a court. Scottish society might not find this difficult because in the criminal law we allow our courts to declare new crimes. *Grant v. Allan*, 1988 S.L.T. 11; or develop existing crimes: *H.M. Advocate v. Khaliq*, 1984 J.C. 23.

[93] [1997] 1 All E.R. 540.

[94] *ibid.* at 567. See also Lord Hoffmann in *Stovin v. Wise* [1996] A.C. 923.

[95] J. Stapleton, "Duty of Care: Peripheral Parties and Alternative Opportunities for Deterrence." [1995] 111 L.Q.R. 301. For an argument at an even higher level of theory see R. Wright, "Right Justice and Tort Law" in *Philosophical Foundations of Tort Law* (Owen ed., 1995).

she has identified is the theme in modern cases denying liability, even where the harm caused could be described as reasonably foreseeable, a theme founded on the idea of "alternative means of protection." She shows that in cases of denial of liability in the face of what might be expected to be liability, deterrence is an issue. Looked at in this way doctrines of *volenti non fit injuria* and contributory negligence also show deterrence at work— deterring careless behaviour on the part of the pursuer.[96] In economic loss cases the pursuer must often show that it was reasonable to rely upon the information carelessly given which has caused the loss.[97] Imposing too much liability can result in over deterrence. This is the argument often used in professional negligence cases: doctors will do too many, perhaps unnecessary tests. The idea of deterrence may also be a factor in letting some potential defenders escape in order to make sure that liability is focused towards another party whose conduct it is sought to deter, perhaps the negligent builder rather than the busy local authority.[98]

Compensation

The Common Law

1–13 Stair explained that in relation to wrongs to man the measure of damages, the response, is what we would now call compensation:

> "In reference to man is the obligation of repairing his damage, putting him in as good condition as he was in before the injury; and this only is man's part for himself."[99]

Damages for wrongdoing are not designed to punish but to indemnify.[1] This clearly marks the separation of the civil remedy for wrongdoing from crime.[2] Again compensatory. There are however, moves to minimise the role of delict in compensation.[3] There are two main ways in which even a strict liability delict system can be replaced. The first is by some form of insurance.[4] First party insurance if compulsory and comprehensive would obviate the social need for compensation litigation.[5] But not everyone could

---

[96] Stapleton, *op cit.*, p. 305.

[97] *ibid.*, p. 306.

[98] *ibid.*, p. 317; See the cases discussed in Chapter 10.

[99] I,9,2.

[1] For the inflicting of punishment is for God, in so far as it is authorised or allowed by him; but it is not for, or from man to himself: "Revenge is mine; and I will repay it, saith the Lord." (Rom, xii,19) . . . So in delinquence the power of exaction of reparation of his damage is man's for himself, but the power of exacting punishment is in God. I,9,2.

[2] For Erskine the separation is accepted and delict obliges the wrongdoer to "make-up to him the damage he suffered by the wrong." 3,1,12. By the time of Bell it is very sharply divided and compensation is the focus: "Criminal law looks to the prevention of delict by punishment, example, and terror without any view to indemnification; while civil jurisprudence, looking only to indemnification, without regard to punishment or example, raises for this purpose, by construction of law, an obligation to repair the damage occasioned by the delict." Bell, *Prin.*, s. 544.

[3] This is now virtually a subject of study in its own right. The issues and the context are examined fully in P. Cane, *Atiyah's Accidents Compensation and the Law* (4th ed., Weidenfeld and Nicolson).

[4] *ibid.*, Chap. 12.

[5] P.S. Atiyah, "Personal Injuries in the Twenty-First Century: Thinking the Unthinkable" in *Wrongs and Remedies in the Twenty-First Century* (Birks ed., 1996), p. 1.

afford it.[6] This explains why there are alternatives. For example, there is compulsory third party insurance for employers ensuring that if the law supports the worker in his case against his employer there is money to pay the award and the social function of compensation is achieved.[7] Third party insurance is often socially cheaper. It is generally cheaper for the producer of a risk to find insurance for that risk which they understand and can more easily quantify, than it is for each potential victim to negotiate a separate first party policy. Some State systems already exist and it might be thought that these could be extended to replace delictual liability entirely, reduce it to a safety net or patch up perceived inadequacies.[8]

Generally, the courts do not pay attention to whether or not the defender is insured.[9] However, in negligence cases where it is being asked whether or not it is fair, just and reasonable to impose a duty, the availability of insurance is sometimes thought to be a proper issue for investigation.[10]

State Systems

The state has provided a compensation scheme for workers for a very long time. More recently it provides for compensation for victims of crime where it is usually the case that the wrongdoer is not worth suing in a civil action. The motor car is almost universally present but a large number of people do not pay for the compulsory insurance they should, so a non-state system exists to compensate some victims who cannot find an insured defender. These topics are discussed in a later chapter.[11]

Satisfaction

Practitioners today will be as aware as their ancient predecessors that often **1–14** the client is not concerned just with compensation, but with having their anger at the defenders conduct assuaged. However, a theme of the civil law of wrongs is that of satisfaction and the non-patrimonial award in Scotland called solatium for personal injury (and its statutory analogue in death cases) may be better thought of as distinct from compensation.[12] Assythment was a buying-off of vengeance. While unfashionable among the economic theorists, there is still a demand for satisfaction.

Inter-relation with other subjects

It is not intended to examine every possible interface and only those of some practical or theoretical importance are considered here.

---

[6] B. Hepple, "Negligence: The Search for Coherence" [1997] 50 C.L.P. 69 at 85.

[7] Atiyah, *op. cit.*, Chap. 13.

[8] See generally D.R. Harris, et al *Compensation and Support for illness and Injury* (Oxford, 1984); Report of the Royal Commission on Civil Liability and Compensation for Personal Injury, Cmnd. 7054 (1978).

[9] See, *e.g.. Davie v. New Merton Mills Ltd* [1959] A.C. 604 at 626–627.

[10] See, e.g. *Smith v. Eric S. Bush* [1990] 1 A.C. 831, *per* Lord Griffiths at 858; *Marc Rich & Co A.G. v. Bishop Rock Marine Co Ltd* [1996] 2 A.C. 211, *per* Lord Steyn at 236 *et seq.*

[11] See Chapter 19.

[12] Markesinis, *The German Law of Torts*, p. 682; Zimmerman, *The Law of Obligations*, p. 1027 noting that Grotius was influential in bringing about compensation for non-pecuniary loss based on the canonist doctrine of restitution.

Contract

1–15 Stair clearly separates delict and contract and in a way that is fundamental
to an understanding of Scots law.

> "Amongst obligations obediential we have placed these which are by
> delinquence; because they arise without any convention, consent, or
> contract, either particularly or only by virtue of any positive law; and,
> therefore they must needs have their original from the authority and will
> of God, and of our obedience due thereto. For though they do proceed
> from our fact, and from our will, whence that fact is voluntarily
> committed, yet it is not from our contracting will; and therefore, these
> obligations do not receive their effect, and measure, or extent, by our
> will."[13]

Thus a great divide is established between aspects of voluntary human
conduct. This is a divide which has been challenged by scholars and is not
so clear as it appears.[14] This is too great a debate to be discussed here.
However, it should always be remembered that the Scots law of contract
has adhered to this idea of a contracting will. In so doing it is less
susceptible to the tort=contract argument.[15] Two famous Scottish cases
discussed in their context later in the book illustrate how delict can look
like contract and contract can look like delict.[16] Delict looks like contract
where the duty imposed is to compensate in the measure of a disappointed
expectation; contract looks like delict when a third party can sue (on a *ius
quaesitum tertio*) on the basis of the intention of the contracting parties to
benefit him.[17] In both cases it is submitted that Scots law has got the
division just right and has done so on the basis of the idea of a contracting
will which is a very special kind of voluntary human act.[18] The most
common problems are cases of overlapping or concurrent liability. The case
of doctors and other professionals has made it look as if there is no
problem but these cases can be explained by a principle whose status and
origin is not entirely clear, *spondet peritiam artis*[19] that a person who
professes a skill must answer for the failure to deliver it.[20] Cases of carriage
are easier and do suggest that Scots law was within a general civilian

---

[13] 1,ix,pr.

[14] G. Gilmore, *The Death of Contract* (Ohio State, 1974). P. Atiyah, *Rise and Fall of the
Freedom of Contract* (Oxford, 1979).

[15] Although systems with a civilian heritage like Scots law must concede that the Roman law
of contract grew out of a notional delict, Zimmerman, *op. cit.*, pp. 4–5.

[16] *Junior Books v. The Veitchi Co.*, 1982 S.L.T. 492; *Robertson v. Fleming* (1861) 4 Macq. 167.
The suggestion made by English writers today is that an expansion of contractual liability to
cover *ius quaesitum tertio* would prevent unnecessary and conceptually difficult developments
in tort. See, e.g. B.A. Hepple, "Negligence: The Search for Coherence" [1997] C.L.P. 69 at
89–90. It has not happened that way in Scotland thus far.

[17] For a recent examination, albeit a case that failed, see *Strathford East Kilbride Ltd v. HLM
Design Ltd*, 1997 S.C.L.R. 877 in which no intention to create a *jus quaesitum tertio* could be
found.

[18] Albeit one which, due to the objective theory of contract, can be obscured.

[19] *et emperitia culpae enumeratur.*

[20] See Chaps 10 and 12.

tradition of allowing concurrent liability.[21] Now that English law has accepted concurrent liability even in claims for economic loss for negligence[22] it can be said that Scots law most certainly accepts concurrent liability and will do so even in a contractual matrix.[23]

Unjust Enrichment

Until recently unjust enrichment would have been thought rather **1–16** peripheral in a discussion of delict, for restitution was called for a long time "quasi-contract".[24] Even now the issues are not all clear. The main point is that the law of property is so strong that it looks after itself.[25] To recover property that is still the pursuer's own is the law of property in operation. However, if property has transferred and it has become the defender's only the law of restitution (the response to unjust enrichment) can compel the defender to make the property over. The main areas of interaction are (1) the recovery of property wrongfully taken; and (2) restitution for wrongful breach of contract generally.[26] So far as traditional property is concerned, the law of Scotland either prevents unjust enrichment through its law of property or provides restitutionary remedies; and in respect of soft property[27] is as yet undeveloped and indeed hostile.[28] There is the yet unravelled canonist thread which runs through Scots law and in that system restitution for a wrong was the natural starting point because the commission of the delict was a sin.[29] Spuilzie is the prime example in Scots law.[30] Indeed it is remarkable that while it would be generally agreed that breach of a delictual obligation results on the defender having to make *restitutio in integrum*, the association with restitution has passed largely unremarked.[31]

---

[21] This has been generally ill-articulated. But it is possible to align Scots law more with a German model, where concurrent liability is allowed. In German law liability itself is constrained to certain interests, a line which has not been taken in Scots law in such a dogmatic fashion This is in direct contrast to a French model where concurrent liability is not generally allowed. An explanation for this French position can be found in J. Gordley, "Contract and Delict: Towards a Unified Law of Obligations", (1997) 1 E.L.R. 345.

[22] *Henderson v. Merrett* [1995] 2 A.C. 145. See P. Cane, "Contract, Tort and the Lloyd's Debacle" in *Consensus Ad Idem* (Rose ed., 1996).

[23] See Chap. 10.

[24] W.J. Stewart, *The Law of Restitution in Scotland* (W. Green, 1992), and supplement.

[25] *ibid.*; K. Reid, "Unjustified Enrichment and Property Law" 1994 J.R. 167.

[26] Stewart. *op. cit.*; J. Blackie, "Enrichment and Wrongs in Scots Law" [1992] *Acta Juridica* 23; J. Blackie, "Enrichment Wrongs and Invasion of Rights in Scots Law" in *The Limit of the Law of Obligations* (Visser ed., 1997).

[27] Like some intellectual property.

[28] *Teacher v. Calder* (1899) 1 F. (H.L.) 39; *Exchange Telegraph v. Guilianotti*, 1959 S.C. 19.

[29] Zimmerman, *The Law of Obligations*, p. 1021.

[30] See Chap. 6.

[31] Gordley, *op. cit.*, has recently set out the fundamental historical and intellectual relationship. It was, he pointed out, Aristotle who said that the obligation to compensate follows from the restitution principle. He deemed that one who injures another gains, p. 348, n. 9, citing the Nichomachean Ethics, V,i,1132). Then, via Aquinas, the late scholastics influenced the natural lawyers of whom Stair was one. One practical illustration may be spuilzie itself. Gordley cites Aquinas' application of the principle to the taking of a horse—the owner should get the lost rental he would have made from the horse, although, differing in this respect from spuilzie, Aquinas would have reduced the amount by a factor to reflect the contingency that the rents would perhaps not have been obtained, p. 345.

Property

1–17 In Scotland there is a strong and distinct law of property and so delict does not have to protect ownership as tort appears to in England. So far as Scots law is concerned much of the substance of the law is rather lost in the law of interdict. In practice the overlap arises in cases of infringement of property interests,[32] and to an extent in intellectual property cases. Occupiers' liability is another phase of the same relationship. The idea that there is no liability from the ownership of property is of the order of a principle discussed below.

Public Law

1–18 Reparation for delict is a branch of private law. The "farming out" of government functions to private or partly private bodies taken with the Crown Proceedings Act[33] are two major developments which have meant that the state in some shape or form finds itself in arguments about reparation. The landmark case in negligence, *Dorset Yacht v. The Home Office*[34] brought the state more closely into the scope of liability as some of their functions were now thought justiciable and remain so. New procedures for judicial review allowing a claim for damages for results of an unreasonable or wrongful decision has the look of delict. When the Inner House then made it clear that judicial review was not exclusively a matter of reviewing public bodies, it even more so resembles a new area of delict— that of wrongful administration.

Crime

1–19 As stated above, Stair made a clear division between these two areas of law which had hitherto been extremely closely related although obviously links remain. What has most certainly gone is any penal aspect of damages in Scotland for delict. Because it is sometimes said that "all crimes are delicts", which has the sound of principle about it, the remainder of this topic is dealt with further below.[35]

Constitutional Law

1–20 The delicts which control intentional harms are essentially bastions of the constitution. In Scotland as in England our Claim of Right and Bill of Rights are not documents upon which the citizen regularly has recourse to protect any civil rights that he may have. The Constitution depends upon the fact that people are free to do what is not prohibited and delict is one of the major prohibitions. As Fraser put it in the first half of the century:

> "The British subject has no rights which are guaranteed by the constitution. For the protection of his rights to personal freedom, as of all his other rights, the British subject must look to the ordinary law, par-

---

[32] See Chap. 5.
[33] See para. 2–22 below.
[34] [1970] A.C. 1004. See Chap. 10.
[35] See para. 1–32.

ticularly parts of it dealing with crimes and delicts, and not to any constitutional guarantees. It is an important feature of these branches of the law that they afford protection whether the citizen's rights are wrongfully invaded by a private person or a public official."[36]

Delict as much as crime regulates what we may or may not do the one to the other. Verbal injury is one of the most obvious examples. If free speech is indeed pivotal to civilisation, then in Scotland it is largely verbal injury which regulates it.[37]

This aspect of delict must never be forgotten. Rules which seem unfortunate in the context of compensation or insurance or risk may well have significance in maintaining the balance of freedoms in society.[38]

The European Convention on Human Rights has now been incorporated **1–21** to an extent into Scots Law.[39] Part of the enforcement mechanism of such Human Rights will be by way of reparation actions for infringement of the rights conferred.[40] It is likely that such actions will be not infrequent and will expand the constitutional function of the law of reparation.

Principles of Liability

The courts will always tend to approach cases from the point of view of **1–22** remedies but in cases not obviously covered by precedent, will refer to the theoretical writings or broad dicta in other cases to assist. The purpose of this section is to set out the broad principles which have in cases been said to apply. Some of these may be a priori principles but many are inductively arrived at—synthesised from previous cases. To spare the reader the repetition which can occur when a general part and a special part are stated, this is a condensed treatment.

There is no general agreement among commentators as to the effect of statute upon principle. Some consider statute to be *sui generis* and thus of no effect upon principles. However, if the principles concerned are inductive, then statute should arguably be fed into the algorithm to produce a new modulated principle. This, it is submitted, is the better view.

Neither is this section a matter of the intellectual desire for rationalisation; indeed that is expressly eschewed. It is a collection of certain rhetorical foci: arguments that have been taken in the past from a high level of generality to obtain a particular result, and arguments which can be

---

[36] W.L.R. Fraser, *Constitutional Law* (Hodge, 1938), p. 179. See also pp. 194 and 200.

[37] There are many ways in which free speech is punished without legal redress; see Chap. 8.

[38] P.Q.R. Boberg, *The Law of Delict* (Jutta, 1989), says "the law of delict . . . is close to the core problem of balancing individual freedom against collective security — a balance that it seeks to achieve by tempering broad principles of liability with limiting interpretations of wrongfulness, fault and causation. It follows that a proposition should never be propounded without due regard to its social implications, and that the merit of a rule depends on its functional effects rather than the purity of its ancestry.", pp. 26–27.

[39] The Human Rights Act 1998 comes into force in October 2000. Meantime s. 29(2)(d) and s. 54 of the Scotland Act 1998 make Human Rights law supreme in relation to devolution issues. See Chap. 11.

[40] It is likely to develop at least at first along the lines of Euro-rep (see Chap. 11.), *viz.* the content being supra national and the enforcement and application through the reparation system. The subject is treated in more detail, in Chap. 11.

taken again. To do otherwise would be to ignore one of the most
prominent intellectual movements of the second half of the twentieth
century—modernity.[41] Modernity is to be contrasted with the situation
prevailing before:

> "In terms of the history of the social sciences, the latter quarter of the
> nineteenth century was characterised in no uncertain manner by neo-
> kantianism. The revival in question was aimed at rehabilitating the
> Kantian concept of science as a system, unified essentially by the idea of
> a system, rather than by any more realistic or historical classification of
> its social matter. The most notable and far-reaching effects of this revival
> were to be the constitution of the sciences of linguistics and of law."[42]

1-23 One great debate in the Scottish legal literature, particularly relevant to this
chapter produced a statement which certainly appears to be redolent of
modernity and, being written not long after the Second World War, might
be thought to be so. Professor Gow said discussing nuisance in Scots law:

> "The cry that 'intelligent application' will lead to a wilderness of
> uncertainty is the refuge of the intellectually indolent. Certainty is an
> admirable quality, but a slavish adherence to it inevitably produces
> stupidity, which is not. The greatest evil which uninspired Austinian
> jurisprudence has inflicted on Scots law is the belief that a legal system is
> somewhat akin to Euclidean geometry, complete and self-sufficient, a
> gigantic exercise in abstraction. The truth is otherwise. The life of law is
> uncertainty, the climate in which it flourishes is competitive, and its task
> may be interpreted as a never-ending series of compromise and recon-
> ciliation. Law is neither abstract nor ornamental, but concrete and
> dynamic."[43]

That seems very similar to the position reached by the contemporary legal
theoretician Professor Goodrich:

> "To begin with, the very existence of the legal system as a system is,
> more than anything else, the product of educational practice. From the
> founding of the law schools, the Western legal tradition has consistently
> placed the task of the systematic conceptual elaboration and justification
> of the legal order in the hands of the university. The discipline of law as
> a science, a comprehensively textual discipline, is not a product of
> philosophical research nor of professional or practical knowledge, it is
> fundamentally no more than a pedagogy—an authoritarian mode of
> teaching."[44]

1-24 While principles are more abstract and more generalised than rules, not
every statement which is abstract or general is a principle, certainly not

---

[41] Summarised, explained, developed and applied in the context of law in P. Goodrich,
Reading the Law (Blackwell, 1986); *Legal Discourse* (Macmillan, 1987); *Languages of Law*
(Weidenfeld, 1990).
[42] Goodrich, *Legal Discourse, op. cit.*, p. 11.
[43] J.J. Gow, "Is culpa amoral?" 1953 J.R. 17, pp. 31–32.
[44] Goodrich, *Legal Discourse, op. cit.*, p. 207.

necessarily a legal principle and even less a valid legal principle in the sense of either being descriptively accurate as to the past or predictively valid as a determinant of future legal decision. Law in the courts is about argument and conflict and decision. Any reference to a principle is part of an argument intended to persuade. While its name may be the same from case to case, the content of the principle in any given case may well be different. The view generally taken in this book and in this chapter is summarised in the following passage:

"Under this view [law as practical wisdom] principles are not ends in themselves; they are merely devices by which human beings seek to achieve the good life. The goals and values of life are many and diverse. They are often incompatible, as even modern natural lawyers recognise and yet do not feel that they are being unprincipled in so doing.[note omitted] Principles are useful, even essential, in helping us to resolve legal and moral dilemmas but they are not themselves ultimate."[45]

Add to that that legal science works in much the same way as the natural sciences (as opposed here to mathematics) on the basis of working hypotheses as to the nature and scope of principles—new cases and new articles supplying new material for the formulation of new principles. Accordingly, it is submitted, there is not an underlying principle or set of principles to be found. Nor is there any one theory which will explain the law. There is a central core of theory which is particularly applicable to reparation. It is the principle of corrective justice. Outlined by Aristotle, it was developed by Grotius and Pufendorf and later by Kant.[46] Gordley, speaking of the Natural Lawyers in this tradition, including Grotius, a great influence on Stair, says:

"They used an Aristotelian principle of corrective justice—that no one should gain through another's loss—to explain liability both for taking anothers property and for causing another harm. They gave a unified explanation of causation and fault: one could not say a person was the cause of another's harm unless he chose to harm him by acting intentionally or negligently. They thought that to avoid negligence, a person must weigh the costs and benefits of a course of action, but they did not think the purpose of the law of negligence was to give him the proper incentives to do so."[47]

The idea of prudence in Aristotle is still familiar. This involves accepting small evils to produce great goods.[48] It is addressed to contingencies of action.[49] The prudent person considers probabilities and what happens in most cases.[50] This theory more than the *Digest* texts on the *lex Aquilia*

---

[45] G.C. Christie, "The Uneasy Place of Principle in Tort Law" in *Philosophical Foundations of Tort Law*, (Owen ed., 1995), p. 127.
[46] Owen, "Why Philosophy Matters to Tort Law" and J. Gordley, "Tort Law in the Aristotelian Tradition" in Owen, *ibid.*
[47] Gordley, *ibid.*, p. 131.
[48] *ibid.*, p. 146.
[49] *ibid.*
[50] *ibid.*

explains why there is a core need for causation and a link between pursuer and defender.

1–25   There are other theories. Strict liability can be accommodated within various theories.[51] But that is on first blush an example of a different approach, perhaps a distributive approach. It is possible to accept that there are many and different theories underlying various aspects of delictual liability. Most practitioners would find this perfectly acceptable.[52]

There are the anti-theory schools. As mentioned at the start of this chapter most modernists reject general principles.[53] At best it might be accepted that the rules reflect the will of the most powerful. One theme is that the reader is the ultimate arbiter of the text and the author or scriptor has no say or part.[54] Law in the courts is authoritarian and the readings of the judge and those predicated by the formal sources are privileged.

There is a law and economics school, active since the second half of the last century. Its influence, even theoretically, has been in negligence and it is discussed briefly in that part of this book. It is possible that the system which has in the past operated to deal with culpable individuals can be hijacked or adapted to become a loss distribution or compensatory system.

1–26   Finally, the view taken in this book is consonant with that taken by the Lord Justice-Clerk in writing a preface for a book on delict in 1998:

> "The subject [delict] might suggest the image of a large mansion to which many additions have been made over the years in response to changing conditions in society. Some but not all of its rooms are interconnected—haunted no doubt by the benign ghost of the reasonable man. Some rooms are plain: others are richly elaborate. Some are thronged and familiar: others rarely visited."

It would be impossible to develop a coherent theory of architecture that would predict how the next extension to this large mansion would look. It would not be possible to fully understand exactly why the lights come on in the conservatory fountain without a knowledge, not only of architecture, but also of plumbing and electrics. So too this book cannot and will not try to explain why every rule exists, nor try to erect a coherent theory, even with exceptions, where one simply cannot be produced.

Alterum non laedere

1–27   To harm no one. This was one of Justinian's three precepts of the law.[55] Scots law has settled upon the view that it is perfectly permissible to harm others and to destroy their property. The clearest example of this is

---

[51] *ibid.* p. 150.

[52] It is even possible to find a justificatory foundation for such a position—Complementarity. I. England, "The Idea of Complementarity as a Philosophical Basis for Pluralism in Tort Law" in Owen, *op. cit.*, p. 183.

[53] See above.

[54] Save of course to suffer the reviews and collect the meagre royalties.

[55] Inst I,i,3; originally Ulpian's dictum: D. 1,1,10,1. It was revived to an extent by the natural lawyers such as Pufendorf, *De jure naturale et Gentium Lib* III, Cap 1,1. See Zimmerman, *The Law of Obligations*, p. 1032, n. 224. On the face of it such a rule requires strict liability; see Zimmerman, *op. cit.*, p. 1033. The natural lawyers began to mitigate that view by reference to imputability, duty and the foreseeability of wrong; Zimmerman, *op. cit.*, p. 1033.

economic torts where the courts have deliberately left business people to do their worst, subject to the control of excess.[56] However, there is some mention of the doctrine of *aemulatio vicini*: the prohibition of the venting of spite on neighbours.[57] This balances the apparent breach of the *alterum non laedere* precept, even in the economic sphere. Perhaps the best way of looking at the precept is that it operates at a very high level of generality and that "harm" in this context requires definition in the broad circumstances. If this view is taken, there are no exceptions because loss, injury or damage caused without breach of duty are excluded. The precept is of limited descriptive value and little or no predictive value.

Rights and Interests will be protected

It has been seen that Stair spoke in terms of certain rights being **1–28** protected.[58] Those which are not recognised are not reparable.[59] Such an approach is not a Roman law doctrine but comes from the civilian tradition. It found at its peak and present significance in its incorporation in the German Code:

> "A person who wilfully or negligently injures the life, body health, freedom, property, or other right of another contrary to law is bound to compensate him for any damage arising therefrom."[60]

New issues test these apparently clear and principled divisions. Thus, the Germans have had to consider whether nervous shock relates to health.[61] Economic loss (non-derivative) is generally unrecoverable because of the wording of the code entrenching eighteenth century thinking.[62] The apparently wide "other rights" applies only to absolute rights like patents and not relative rights like contractual rights.[63] It should also be appreciated that if one is following this kind of analysis, right and interest cannot necessarily be equiparated.[64] Although even for civilians duty, right and interests are different paths in the same enquiry.[65]

The practical value of such a scheme would be if there were new cases where new interests were either recognised. There are two good examples of an explicit interest based approach. In *Henderson v. Chief Constable, Fife Police*[66] a female worker was asked to remove her bra in the cells for her own safety, the concern being that she might do herself a mischief. Lord Jauncey said:

---

[56] J. Adams, "Is there a Tort of Unfair Competition?" [1985] J.B.L. 26; H. Carty, "Intentional Violation of Economic Interests: The Limits of Common Law Liability" [1988] 104 L.Q.R. 242. See Chap. 7.

[57] See Chaps 5 and 7.

[58] Professor Walker points out that such an approach was hinted at in the *Digest* and appeared in Grotius and Van Leeuwen. Walker, *History*, IV, p. 695.

[59] That can be seen carried through to Bell who speaks in terms of rights being protected.

[60] Markesinis, *The German Law of Torts*, p. 10.

[61] *ibid.*, pp. 35, 95–109.

[62] *ibid.*, pp. 37–43, 148–239; Zimmerman, *The Law of Obligations*, p. 1037, nn. 255 and 256.

[63] Markesinis, *op. cit.*, pp. 51–58.

[64] *ibid.*, p. 56.

[65] P.Q.R. Boberg, *The Law of Delict* (Jutta, 1989), pp. 31–32.

[66] 1988 S.L.T. 361.

"such removal must amount to an infringement of liberty. I see no
reason why the law should not protect the individual from this infringement just as it does from other infringements".

Yet another important dictum appears in *Micosta S.A. v. Shetland Islands
Council*[67]. The case was unusual in that the wrong alleged was a deliberate
misuse of a statutory power by a public body. Lord Ross, approving a
statement of general principle by Professor Walker[68]:

"The validity of a claim such as that made by the present pursuers does
not depend upon there being any precise Scottish authority. There is no
such thing as an exhaustive list of named delicts in the law of Scotland. If
the conduct complained of appears to be wrongful, the law of Scotland
will afford a remedy even if there has not been any previous instance of
a remedy being given in similar circumstances. As Professor Walker puts
it at p. 9: 'The decision to recognise a particular interest, and consequently to grant a remedy for its infringement, is a question of social
policy, and the list recognised has grown over the years. In considering
whether or not to recognise particular interests the courts have had
regard to such factors as the moral obliquity of the defenders' conduct,
the capacity of the parties to bear the loss, and the consistency of
recognition with what is conceived to be public policy.' In my opinion,
deliberate misuse of statutory powers by a public body would be
actionable under the law of Scotland at the instance of a third party who
has suffered loss and damage in consequence of the misuse of statutory
powers, provided that there was proof of malice or proof that the action
had been taken by the public authority in the full knowledge that it did
not possess the power which it purported to exercise."[69]

1-29 Another much more significant example might be the *Crofter* case[70] in
which conspiracy was developed to protect business interests but also
respecting other legitimate interests.[71] However, it is not obvious that case
or the others in the area of economic delicts are truly the reflection of a
general protection of economic interests rather than discrete delicts which
have that effect. The thinking has essentially all been done in England and
so it would not be surprising if an interests based approach was not
intended. In a penetrating review, Weir concludes that the Germans
require immorality, the French, unreasonableness and the Americans
impropriety—all signs of a more general interests based approach. But the
English law, which the Scots law follows but seldom leads, does not, he tells
us, take that path but a more conduct-orientated regime.[72] As will be seen
in a later chapter, one interest which might have been expected to be
afforded protection has not. That is privacy.[73] It would be expected for

---

[67] 1986 S.L.T. 193.
[68] W.J. Stewart, *Delict* (2nd ed., W. Green, 1993), p. 878.
[69] *Micosta* at 198. The English tort considered was misfeasance in public office.
[70] *Crofter Hand Woven Harris Tweed Co. v. Veitch*, 1942 S.C.(H.L.) 1. Discussed in Chap. 7.
[71] See Chap. 7.
[72] T. Weir, *Economic Torts* (1997), Chap. 3.
[73] L. Blom-Cooper, "The Right to be Let Alone" [1989] J.L.S. 402; A.J. Bonnington,
"Privacy: Letting the Right Alone", 1992 S.L.T. (News) 289; G.T. Laurie, "Privacy, Paucity
and the Press", 1993 S.L.T. (News) 285; D.L. Carey Miller, and H. Lardy, "Calcutt II:
Comments from a Scots Perspective", 1993 S.L.T. (News) 199; M.A. Hogg, "Privacy: A
Valuable and Protected Interest in Scots Law", 1992 S.L.T. 349.

social reasons. Its failure to thrive in England can easily be ascribed to the force of precedent.[74] A principled system based on rights and interests could easily have recognised such an interest or right but it has not happened in Scotland, casting doubt perhaps on the extent to which this principle is an effective source of remedies. Such a basic theory has predictive value. It is principled in the sense that new cases in the same branch can be decided on the basis of a general rule. It is practically flexible if and only if new interests can be recognised relatively quickly.[75] The introduction of European Human Rights law could become a foundation for the recognition of new wrongs.[76]

The difficulty with the interests theory is that it conflicts and overlaps **1–30** with another—that of focusing on wrongful conduct as opposed to a result. The modern law of negligence which underlies the bulk of litigation is founded on conduct. Take the case of a punch in the nose: is this actionable because the defender caused an infringement with the pursuer's personal bodily integrity or because it is actionable to carelessly injure a person and must *a fortiori* be actionable to deliberately punch him? The answer must be both. That means that where the law has in the past recognised a legally protected interest or chooses to do so at some time causation and remoteness and not conduct are the main questions. If the conduct is culpable, then that may form the basis of liability. It will be seen that the interest theory allows for a superimposed additional test of culpability. It is indeed tempting to rationalise the different theories by making interest infringement the basic threshold test and superimposing a requirement of conduct fault. That is not necessarily how the law has gone nor how it need go.

No liability without fault

The notion of fault is now thought to mean breach of legal duty and not to **1–31** have any real moral connotation.[77] "No liability without fault" appears as an oft cited maxim but its status as a principle is not secure.[78] It is perhaps tied to certain political and economic theories.[79] Certainly it is not neutral. *Culpa* is often translated as fault and so discussion of this maxim is closely related to what has gone before. The rise of fault only (as opposed to discussions of *culpa*) coincides with the Victorian mercantile era. It is also possible that prominence of the maxim has been over exaggerated. Elliot says that:

> "During this formative period of our law of negligence Scotland was fortunate in having Lord President Inglis to preside over the First or

---

[74] Albeit, ironically, it was an English case which founded the article that founded the tort in England: *Prince Albert v. Strange*, 2 De G. & Sm. 652.

[75] Less than a generation and more than a general election!.

[76] See Chap. 11.

[77] W.A. Elliot, "What is Culpa?", 1954 J.R. 6; J.J. Gow, "Is Culpa Amoral?", 1953 J.R. 17; W.W. McBryde, "The Advantages of Fault", 1975 J.R. 32.

[78] G. MacCormack, "Culpa in the Scots Law of Reparation", 1974 J.R. 13.

[79] For England Hepple says: "A mixture of Kantian moral philosophy and the economic dogma of laissez-faire provided and intellectual climate sympathetic to the notion of 'no liability without fault'" [1997] C.L.P. 69 at 72.

Second Division of the reconstituted Court of Session for a period of over thirty years (1858–90). On every possible occasion he sought to hammer home the principle of culpa as the basis of quasi-delictual liability and to stress that there could be no such liability unless negligence or culpa of some description were proved."[80]

So it is possible that the law was pushed into a position which it might otherwise not have taken. For the better or the worse it is hard to say. The maxim had to labour against older ideas and perhaps the case of nuisance is the best illustration of the ebb and flow of ideas. The decision in *R.H.M. Bakeries v. Strathclyde Regional Council*[81] is a hearty vindication of the "no liability without fault" principle and in its negative form because the case exculpates in the absence of fault. It took *Kennedy v. Glenbelle*[82] to give some flesh to the idea of fault.

However, the present state of the law is that there is a huge amount of liability without fault. As will be seen statute has built upon the few existing cases of common law strict liability[83] to create a situation where strict liability is coming to be the norm[84] and this "no liability without fault" principle may well require to be reformulated unless restricted to a small area of common law liability. It is probably no longer necessary to refer to the maxim for its meaning is too slippery to be of value. It is better to examine the conduct complained of and the interest infringed. In the great Scots debate both writers were justly sceptical of the maxim:

"For long enough Scots lawyers have been accustomed to proclaim, with a somewhat irritating complacency, that the basic principle is that there is no liability without fault."[85]

And Elliot:

"Clearly Scots law would be lagging behind if it sheltered too blindly behind the phrase 'no liability without fault' when it is patently obvious that certain activities, though not unlawful per se, are yet so potentially harmful that one is morally to blame for any resulting damage and no care short of not carrying on the activity at all will suffice."[86]

All crimes are delicts

1–32 In the formative period of Scots law delicts or crimes were the paradigm cases of liability, quasi-delicts which were not crimes but were compensatable were the supplementary category. Now everything is reversed. Most

---

[80] Elliot, *op. cit.*, p. 21.

[81] 1985 S.L.T. 214. See Chap. 5.

[82] 1996 S.L.T. 1186. See Chap. 5.

[83] Edictal liability for carriers, innkeepers and stablekeepers is now attenuated; see Chap. 7. For animals replaced by statute, see Chap. 22 and as will later be seen nuisance, thought to be a wrong of strict liability, has been reinterpreted as not being such; see Chap. 5. The diversion of the natural course of a stream is an existing head at present; see Chap. 5.

[84] Especially so if proposals to introduce strict liability in motoring cases are implemented.

[85] Gow, *op. cit.* at p. 28.

[86] Elliot, *op. cit.*, p. 25.

criminal issues are treated in the criminal courts although from time to time, dissatisfaction with the public prosecution service leads people to take their own civil actions. Nonetheless, the principle really ought to hold based on these foundations. The trouble is that the last century has seen so many new crimes and crimes involving none of the dole required for a true delict—parking on a double yellow line for example. Dole still exists as a requirement for a number of crimes in the still independent criminal jurisprudence of Scotland and so the principle might be restricted to all crimes for which dole must be established. It is submitted that is the safest course. Indeed it might be wondered what is to be gained in continually speaking of dole and *dolus* in Scots law unless there is a useful cross-fertilisation across the "subject boundaries." Many other crimes which do not require dole are statutory and the law of delict has already developed techniques, albeit not a coherent theory, to deal with cases where it is suggested that there is a delictual duty based upon a statutory duty.[87] Many statutory crimes now can be committed carelessly. However, negligence or at least reckless neglect has for a long time been a basis for criminal liability—even culpable homicide.[88]

It is most certainly possible to raise a civil action regardless of the **1–33** disposal of a criminal action. In *Mullan v. Anderson*[89] the wife of a murdered man sued the alleged murderer who had been acquitted on a not proven verdict. It was argued that the action was contrary to public policy, especially so as the defender was unlikely to be able to pay. This plea was rejected. In the early case of *Young v. Mitchell*,[90] it was held that a civil action was incompetent on the basis of *res judicata* where, under legislation then applicable, an employee had prosecuted an employer for breach of contract, one penalty being a fine or imprisonment and the case being brought under the Summary Procedure Act applicable. Lord President Inglis was convinced by the fact that the same parties were involved, which would not be the case with HMA prosecutions. He also referred to what we would now call the mischief of the Act—the need to dispose of the question summarily.[91] Lord Deas was brief and simply considered that the doctrine applied to the case in hand.[92] The decision in a criminal trial can be decisive in a civil case. In practice it often is where a running down or collision case is argued on the basis of section 10 of the Law Reform (Miscellaneous Proceedings) (Scotland) Act 1968.

Malice

In the last century this word could be taken as equivalent to dole as distinct **1–34** from *culpa*. So a malicious delict would be an intentional one as opposed to a negligent one. Now its main role is in relation to defamation and abuse of

---

[87] See Chap. 11.

[88] *H.M. Advocate v. Kirkpatrick*, Hume, Crime, Vol. 1; *H.M. Advocate v. McLure* (1848) 1 Ark. 448; *H.M. Advocate v. Wilson* (1852) 1 Irv. 84; *H.M. Advocate v. McDougall*, unreported; R.S. Shiels, "The Ibrox Disaster of 1902", 1997 J.R. 230; *Paton v. H.M. Advocate*, 1936 J.C. 19 seems to be responsible for the divergence of criminal and civil negligence. It might not have seemed such a divergence at the time when *Donoghue* had not filtered through to general cases and *Hunter v. Hanley* had not dealt with gross negligence.

[89] (1996) Rep. L.R. 47.

[90] (1874) 1 R. 1011.

[91] *ibid.* at 1014.

[92] *ibid.* at 1105.

process. As will be seen,[93] malice in the sense of intention rather than spite is presumed in defamation but a defence of qualified privilege will be lost on proof of malice, even if not established in relation to the particular defamatory statement. In legal process cases the idea is that the pursuer may have to show malice and want of probable cause; sometimes a bald averment of malice is sufficient and sometimes actual averments inferring actual malice are required.

Malitas non indulgendum is a maxim which has been considered in Scots cases closely related to the doctrine of *aemulatio vicini*.[94]

Spite suggests motive for an intention and is hardly ever relevant. However, in the field of the economic delicts, there is scope for looking at motive and malice in that common sense might well be significant.[95]

No liability ex domino solo

1–35 There is no liability merely from ownership of land. This principle has been expressed a number of times and there is some force to it in a society that respects property. Some heads of liability have existed both in the civilian tradition and in Scotland.[96] In recent years environmental law has arisen as a discipline, based mainly on statute, but building upon certain rules of the common law.[97] That body of law does create liabilities solely from ownership of land. Planning law most certainly prevents owners doing what they want with their property but may also impose positive duties. Planning conditions may do so too.[98] Liability of occupiers is well recognised but that supports the principle that by making the occupier liable the owner is more likely to be acquitted if he is not in occupation. However, the general principle of liability for lack of care can bring liability upon a landowner as much as anyone else and so there will be liability for dangerous premises. Indeed, one of the foundation cases of the Scots law of negligence[99] was followed in a later case in such a way as make it clear that the rule was not to be treated like an immunity. In *Hislop v. Durham*[1] a young woman took a detour across the pursuer's lands by way of a private road. She was drunk. The Lord President (Boyle) charged the jury that if the pit was, as a matter of fact, insecurely fenced, then merely by being the proprietor the defender would be liable. The issue expressly stated the defender admitted he was the proprietor.[2]

Volenti non fit injuria

1–36 This is a defence (or a non-constitutive factor) in various areas of the law. It operates in the law of delict and is dealt with in the section on defences.[3] Suffice to say that the principle that one who is willing suffers no loss, is no

---

[93] Chap. 8.
[94] See Chap. 5.
[95] See Chap. 7.
[96] W.M. Gordon, "Householders Liabilities" (1982) 27 J.L.S. 253.
[97] G. Cross, "Does only the Careless Polluter Pay?" [1995] 111 L.Q.R. 445. J. Steele, "Private Law and the Environment: Nuisance in Context" (1995) J.L.S. 236.
[98] See generally N. Collar, *Planning* (2nd ed., W. Green, 1999).
[99] *Black v. Cadell* (1804) Mor. 13905.
[1] (1842) 4 D. 1168.
[2] The verdict was for the pursuer.
[3] T. Ingman, "A History of the Defence of *Volenti Non Fit Injuria*", 1981 J.R. 1.

longer of universal applicability.[4] It is abrogated within the common law of delict but it is also abrogated and excluded by statute in various spheres of activity.[5]

Causation and Liability

Early systems tend to focus on results. The *lex Aquilia* did and so causation **1–37** as a more abstract notion was not required. But it now features in most systems and there are many theoretical problems. It can now be said that normally it will have to be shown that the pursuer caused the loss or injury complained of. Statute can attenuate or remove that requirement. As discussed above where the law is that infringement of an interest is actionable, causation is the principal inquiry. Following the approach of this book rather than discuss causation in three or four different places, the full discussion appears in the context of negligence.[6]

---

[4] N. Shaffer, "Volenti Non Fit Injuria", 1965 S.L.T. (News) 133.
[5] For a modern and thoughtful re-analysis see, C.G.S. Tan, *"Volenti Non Fit Injuria*: An Alternative Framework" [1995] Tort L.R. 208.
[6] See Chap. 10.

CHAPTER 2

PARTIES TO ACTIONS

GENERAL RULES

A pursuer must sue for all loss in a single action. There is an exception in **2–1**
the Administration of Justice Act 1982, s.12. This permits a pursuer to come
back to court to make a claim for further compensation if, but only if, in
the original action (i) the defender is a public authority or is otherwise
indemnified[1]; and (ii) it is admitted or proved that the pursuer may develop
some serious disease or suffer some serious deterioration in his physical or
mental condition.[2] If this is established, the court may award damages
immediately on the basis that the injuries will not get worse, and allow a
later application should the pursuer's condition deteriorate. The court may
specify the period within which the application must be made.[3]

If a number of parties have a claim arising from the same incident or **2–2**
affront they must raise separate actions.[4] However a joint claim is permissible where two people have suffered the same harm and have a joint
interest, such as where common property is damaged.[5] If in doubt it is
wisest to raise separate actions and seek conjoination. That is in a way the
test of whether on the basis of convenience A can sue B for a number of
wrongs in the one action. In *Yoker Housing Association Ltd v. McGurn
Logan Duncan & Opfer*,[6] it was held that considerations of common sense
combined with careful case management would allow actions against
different defenders on different grounds so long as there was a practical
connection.[7] On the other hand in *Hook v. McCallum*[8] a female servant
raised an action for slander against her mistress and her husband concluding for a lump sum of damages for separate slanders, one uttered by the
wife and one by the husband at different times. It was held incompetent.[9]

---

[1] s. 12(1)(b): statutory instrument may designate a responsible authority, s. 12(6).
[2] s. 12(2)(a).
[3] See Chap. 23.
[4] *Killen v. Weir* (1905) 7 F. 526.
[5] *Revey v. Murdoch* (1841) 3 D. 88; *Hawkes v. Mowat* (1862) 24 D. 701.
[6] 1998 S.L.T. 1334.
[7] In *Western S.M.T. v. Magistrates of Greenock*, 1957 S.L.T. (Notes) 22, the pursuer sued the
defenders as roads authority for payment of damages in respect of three separate occasions in
which three buses were damaged on a particular stretch of road, alleging the nature of
construction of the road had caused the problem. The court considered that as the parties
were the same and the accidents had happened at about the same place and time, it was
convenient and economic to deal with the cases together. The ground of fault was the same. If
a motion to conjoin had been made it would have been granted.
[8] (1905) 7 F. 528.
[9] *Barr v. Neilsons* (1868) 6 Macph. 651 followed.

2–3   It is of course competent to sue two potential joint wrongdoers. In the *Ellerman Lines Ltd v. The Clyde Navigation Trustees*[10] two separate actions were brought by owners of two steamships which collided on the River Clyde which were heard together. The first defenders were the trustees on the basis that they had responsibility for the negligence of those in charge of a tug which was said to have crossed the river in a manner which was in contravention of the bye laws and regulations relating to navigation. The second defenders were John Brown & Co. Ltd, Shipbuilders who were alleged to have moored a partly constructed battleship in a way that obstructed navigation. Each defender argued that the action was irrelevant. The Inner House upheld the sheriff's granting of an appeal against dismissal at first instance. Lord President Dunedin said:

> "if he [the pursuer] is able to show that they are joint delinquents, he will get a joint and several decree against both, which he may make good against either, leaving the person so distressed to make good his claim of relief, if he can."[11]

TITLE TO SUE

2–4 This is a procedural issue. It strikes at the pursuer.[12] It represents a kind of defence but is more a recognition of certain "obvious" non-constitutive factors. The plea applies across the law and not just to the law of delict. The traditional picture can be seen in *D. and J. Nicholl v. Dundee Harbour Trs.*[13] The action was one for interdict upon a statutory duty, but it is nonetheless interesting for the analysis by Lord Dunedin of what at the time of the First World War was considered to constitute title and interest. A rival trader sought to interdict the statutory ferry company from plying for pleasure hire. This was held under the law then applicable to be *ultra vires*. The question was whether the rival traders had title and interest. A rival trader simpliciter has interest but no title.[14] Lord Dunedin accepted that there was no definition of title to sue and was not disposed to give one himself:

> "for a person to have such title he must be a party (using the word in its widest sense) to some legal relation which gives him some right which the person against whom he raises the action either infringes or denies. The simplest case of all is where a person is owner of something. That legal relation of ownership gives him the right to sue all actions which deal with the vindication or defence of his property. Next in simplicity comes contract, where the relation of contract gives the one party a right to insist on the fulfilment of the contract by the other. Generally speaking, persons who are not parties to the contract cannot sue upon it, but this rule suffers an exception when there has been created what is known as a *jus quaesitum tertio*."[15]

---

[10] (1909) 1 S.L.T. 249.
[11] *ibid*. at 251; see also Lord McLaren at 252.
[12] There is a mirror plea, less often encountered, title to defend.
[13] 1914 2 S.L.T. 418.
[14] *ibid*. at 420.
[15] 1914 2 S.L.T 418 at 421.

Early cases cited under this rubric are not always helpful in formulating any general position albeit the cases themselves may be useful authorities in assisting particular parties.[16] However, the plea being procedural tells us very little about the rights and obligations involved. For example prior to the Damages (Scotland) Act 1976, the question of who could sue and for what in respect of the death of a person was a major question of title to sue; now, however, it is no longer considered as such, the law having fundamentally changed.[17] If there is doubt as to what the legal rights are, title to sue can be an issue.[18] In *Gunstone v. Scottish Women's Athletic Association*[19] there was no claim for damages and this was noted by Lord Prosser.[20] He granted *decree de plano*, but it is submitted that he did so because the case although not clearly involving a patrimonial interest was based on a contract.[21] There is a view that in Scots law all contracts involve a patrimonial interest or they would not be contracts at all. The only remarkable thing about the case is the acceptance that office-holding in a voluntary association is a material interest. Cases such as this should not be overpled. The case can be cited for authority for what might be considered the true principle—that the courts will not concern themselves with mere academic matters but will consider a live issue if it is relevant and competent. Lord Prosser in this case commented:

"I do not consider that out-of-date expressions such as 'patrimonial' are likely to be of much use as a test of true interests which the courts

---

[16] As early as *Bow v. Patrons of Cowans Hospital* (1825) 4 S. 280, it was expressly declared that one guild brother could sue the charity constituted for his benefit, this case being a declarator and claim for financial loss. Although it is not clear whether this was an alternative conclusion, Lord Glenlee doubted that the petitory conclusion for money was justified. *Rodgers v. Incorporation of Taylors* (1842) 5 D. 295, is not strong authority but the Inner House did reverse *in hoc statu* a finding against the pursuer of no title or legal interest to challenge the decision of the defenders to cut her annuity. This case is not a full consideration of reparation for delict and is typical of findings under this rubric that should not be carried further than is appropriate. See also *Baird v. Mags of Dundee* (1865) 4 M. 69; *Bruce v. Aiton* (1885) 13 R. 358.

[17] See the "in-law" cases discussed in Chap. 18. Of these *Monteith v. Cape Insulation Ltd*, 1998 S.L.T. 456 (O.H.); 1998 S.C.L.R. 940 (I.H.) started on a plea that certain averments were irrelevant and ought not to be remitted to probation.

[18] See for example *Comex Houlder Diving Co. (No.2) v. Colne Fishing Co. Ltd*, 1992 S.L.T. 89. The language of interest was used relatively recently in *Furmston*, 1987 S.L.T. (Sh. Ct) 10. The sheriff continued a petition of liquidation to allow the petitioner to consider his position. The case does not establish any general principle on interest. The creditor had not been paid at the time of raising the petition but was paid just before proof. The sheriff said: "if a contributory must show an interest in winding up the company it seems inescapable that a creditor must also: indeed a fortiori because a shareholder, even fully paid-up, surely maintains some interest in the progress of his company, whereas the ex-creditor can lay claim to nothing more than curiosity. The present petitioner has been paid in full; he therefore stands to gain nothing from the outcome of his petition; ergo it must fail." There is a real danger in such a rule, where a defender in an action raised to vindicate a right, is met with payment in full. The pursuer's only interest is to obtain a ruling that, for example, he was assaulted, but the amount of his claim having been met it might be said he has no interest.

[19] 1987 S.L.T. 611.

[20] *ibid*. at 615E.

[21] *ibid*. at 614J.

should protect; and if civil rights such as rights under contract are affected, I should regard little more as enough to show a true interest."[22]

It is submitted this is a better way of expressing what the court does—it looks to the rights of the parties and if the pursuer is potentially the beneficiary of a right in law then there is title and interest. The "potential" part is argued under relevancy.[23] An example is *P. Boyes (Contracts) Ltd v. Mardum Investment Co. Ltd*[24] where the pursuers set up a pension scheme for the benefit of its directors and were advised by financial advisers on the appropriate form of pension scheme. The company provided the initial finance for the scheme and acted as trustee under the scheme. The company sued the defenders because a better scheme could have been set up. The pursuers' averments of loss included a sum which, if invested in the existing pension scheme, would have provided benefits comparable to those obtained under the alternative scheme. It was held that the pursuers had suffered no loss since the benefits under the pension scheme were not payable to the company itself, and the pursuers were under no legal obligation to make up for the benefit of the participants any alleged shortfall in the scheme. But this was decided on a careful consideration of the legal rights involved, delictual and contractual, and an excursus on subrogation—not on any doctrine of title to sue.[25]

PARTICULAR PARTIES

2–5 The purpose of the following sections is to set out cases where the nature of the party suing will have an effect on the success or otherwise of an action, whether effect is given to the speciality by a plea of title to sue or otherwise. Some of the specialities are better considered as immunities but they are dealt with here for convenience.

The Life Cycle

2–6 The paradigm litigant is a human being. Following the treatment in a recent student family law book,[26] an exposition in terms of biology seems to beg less questions than that which would normally be expected. It is fair to

---

[22] 1987 S.L.T. 611 at 614K. For cases mentioning "patrimonial" see *Robinson v. Scottish Amateur Athletic* (1900) 7 S.L.T. 356 at 357; *Murdison v. SFU* (1896) 23 R. 449. See also, in a different context, G. Gretton, "Trust and Patrimony" in *Scots Law into the 21ˢᵗ Century* (MacQueen ed., 1996), p. 182.

[23] *Hester v. MacDonald*, 1961 S.L.T. 414 is an example of what could be called a title to sue point actually being decided and pled on competency.

[24] 1994 S.L.T. 1298.

[25] A plea of no title and interest was taken in the passing-off case of *William Grant & Sons Ltd v. Glen Catrine Bonded Warehouse*, 1995 S.L.T. 936, and again it is submitted that the case was truly decided upon an analysis of the rights involved—what was the scope of the wrong of passing-off. However, the convenience of the plea was more obvious in this case. Passing-off protects what can be considered as a soft property right. Goodwill is in a loose sense property. Thus, it was useful to ask if the pursuer "owns" it. On the other hand, it soon became apparent that being soft property, it was not possible to refer back to the law of property to answer the question and the familiar circularity of the title to sue point emerged (at 945).

[26] A mode of exposition suggested and used by Edwards and Griffiths, *Family Law* (W. Green, 1997). The cycle chosen here will be objectionable to those who do not consider marriage or parenting part of the cycle, although this text is probably on safe ground, even in a post-modern era in accepting birth and death as extreme nodes on the cycle.

say that many of the issues decided by the courts, sometimes decided on a purely juridical or jural basis, involve ethical and moral issues which in turn challenges the basis of the decisions. At the time of writing it is thought that generally such issues are best left to the legislature or the Law Commission where broader views may be canvassed.

The Nasciturus Doctrine

Birth is an obvious stage at which a bright line might be drawn. A person is **2–7** certainly a person when alive out from the womb, whether naturally or untimely plucked. It is all the time prior to birth which is difficult for political, religious and moral reasons. For those reasons it is best not to be coy in this text and say that there are at least two very strong views which have been dominant for some time, that human life begins at conception; and the other, that life begins at some later stage.[27] Scotland has no statutory regime expressly covering litigation by or for things not yet born.[28] The Scottish Law Commission[29] did not consider it necessary to legislate considering that Scots law would permit recovery if the thing became a child. The English legislated.[30] The basis of the Scottish Law Commission's view that no legislation was required was the *nascituri* doctrine often discussed in such cases. The maxim or brocard is *nasciturus pro iam nato habetur quotiens de eius commodo agitur*. The doctrine is set out in Bankton as follows:

"A child in the mother's womb is esteem'd as already born, in all things that concern its own interest, but is not reckoned among children in relation to questions to the advantage of parents from a certain number of children. By our law, rights may be granted in favour of children *nascituri* of any particular person, tho' not begotten at the time, and upon their existence they are entitled thereto, in the same manner as if they had been born at the date of the rights."[31]

The doctrine had already received judicial approval in a succession case.[32] The Scottish Law Commission position was criticised at the time.[33]

---

[27] That difference in belief or view or analysis became very focused in the U.K. by the decriminalisation of some forms of abortion by the Abortion Act 1967. The Act lays down an arbitrary line for potential abortion. Many of the points discussed today were canvassed in D. Bogie, "Personality in relation to the Law of Abortion", 1967 S.L.T. (News) 145. He points out that for the stoics and Baron Hume, the foetus was *"pars ventris"* or *"portio viscerum"* or *"pars viscerum matris"*.

[28] Foetus is the term most normally used in legal discussions but strictly speaking denotes the three to nine month period after conception, before which the term denoted by the scientist is embryo.

[29] *Liability for Antenatal Injuries*, (Scot. Law. Com. No. 30 (1973)).

[30] Congenital Disabilities (Civil Liability) Act 1976. This was after the report of the English Law Commission Report on *Injuries to Unborn Children* (Law Com. No. 60 (1974)).

[31] I,i, 7.

[32] *Elliot v. Joicey*, 1935 S.C. (H.L.) 57 at 70, *per* Lord Macmillan. The Canadian case of *Montreal Tramways v. Leveille* [1933] 4 D.L.R. 337 is often cited. See also *Reid's Trustees v. Dashwood*, 1929 S.L.T. 619; *Allan's Trs v. Allan*, 1949 S.L.T. (Notes) 3; *Cox's Trs v. Pegg*, 1950 S.L.T. 127. In *Dunbar of Kilconzie, Petr*, 1986 S.L.T. 463 the House of Lords refused to extend the doctrine in a rather esoteric and unprecedented heraldry case.

[33] A. Rodger, "Antenatal injury", 1974 J.R. 83.

The foetus's right to continued incubation in the womb

2–8 In *Kelly v. Kelly*,[34] a husband sought to interdict his wife from aborting their foetus.[35] It was accepted that interdict would be available to a person's representative to prevent damage being caused to that person if it would result in an award of damages. If abortion had been an actionable wrong the father could have sued. However, because the foetus itself had no right to continued existence while in the womb it could not be represented as a matter of law.[36] The question was considered to be one of law and not of policy.[37] That must be doubted. On the legal point all that was said was that there had been no authority adduced for protection. Nonetheless, the court then went on to consider other matters in what it is submitted was an inadequate degree of detail.[38] To protect the foetus might cause problems with the "right" to terminate a pregnancy according to the act. It might be suggested that the law should balance the interests identified rather than ruling one out altogether, although in most cases the decision would favour the mother, particularly because under the United Kingdom abortion legislation, the health of the woman is one of the key grounds for termination. Another point was that if abortion could be interdicted then so could other harmful acts like smoking or certain sports. This seems obvious but, even if there were a right, it would hardly be enforced on the point of a mother playing a game of squash. It is however, harder to make the point to the extent of allowing intravenous drug use, or worse the use of a drug known to produce a serious birth defect such as thalidomide. The difficulty is in agreeing that this is a necessary legal or jural result, rather than a policy decision. Statute is often seen as superimposed on the common law, and if that were applied here it is clear that if the law takes any view it is against termination.[39] From a title to sue point of view, it should be noted that *Kelly* was at the instance of the father, in England wardship was attempted and it is no doubt possible that some other person may be thought to have some jurisdiction in these matters. This is an important point because the woman's "right to terminate", even if protection of a foetus were possible, could not be vindicated by the public at large or a section of it, such as anti-abortion activists. The imposition of liability would protect the biological father's interest in his potential offspring.

A person, born alive, injured while a foetus

2–9 Moving on from the right, which the foetus does not have, to remain in the womb or be allowed to be born in due course, to cases where there is injury to the foetus, the law has settled. Many of the cases are decided against the

---

[34] 1997 S.L.T. 896.

[35] *ibid.* at 897: "from instructing, consenting or submitting to a termination of pregnancy". Interdict was also sought against those who would have actually carried out the act.

[36] *ibid.* at 901. The decision in *Hamilton v. Fife Health Board*, 1993 S.L.T. 624 discussed below at para. 2–10 was influential in the overall approach to the legal point. Reference was made to a number of English and Commonwealth authorities. See *inter alia Paton v. British Pregnancy Advisory Service* [1979] 1 Q.B. 276; *B v. Islington Health Authority* [1991] 1 Q.B. 638; *Borowski v. Att. Gen for Canada* (1987) 39 D.L.R. (4th) 731; *F (in utero)* [1988] 2 W.L.R. 1297; *Dehler v. Ottawa Civic Hospital* (1979) 101 D.L.R. (3d) 686.

[37] *Kelly* at 901C.

[38] *Kelly* at 901F.

[39] As the court accepted under reference to Gordon, *Criminal Law* (2nd ed.), para. 28–01.

background of the Damages (Scotland) Act 1976. Section 1(1) provides that where a person dies in consequence of personal injuries sustained by him as a result of an act or omission of another person, then the person responsible for that death will also be liable to pay damages to any relative of the deceased as long as the person responsible would have been liable to pay. The law is considered in detail in *Cohen v. Shaw*.[40] The pursuer claimed, *inter alia*, for damages on behalf of a child born alive after the death of its father. Lord Cullen[41] allowed a jury trial. He accepted that the *nascituri* doctrine could apply unless it were excluded by statute. The 1976 Act did not exclude it.[42] The definition of relative in Sched. 1, para. 1(b) includes a person who "was" a child of the deceased. Lord Cullen took this to mean that the focus was on the time of the death in which case the claimant would not have been a child.[43] It has to be asked again whether this is truly a decision of juristic necessity or a policy decision.

Parents' claim for the death of person injured while a foetus

The law was extensively canvassed in *Hamilton v. Fife Health Board*.[44] A **2–10** child died three days after birth. The parents alleged it was due to fault. They were parents of the deceased in terms of the Damages (Scotland) Act 1976. However, the claims being based on statute, the other requirements had to be met. The important point of interpretation was that the Act applies "where a person dies in consequence of injuries sustained by him." Lord Prosser held that this was not satisfied. His view was that the injuries were not "sustained" by the child but by the foetus.[45] It was accepted by the pursuers that prior to being born a "child" is not a person. It was accepted by the defenders that the *nascituri* principle is recognised in Scotland, subject to the limitation that the fiction operates "only for the purpose of enabling the child to take a benefit to which, if born it would be entitled" and cannot be invoked in the interests of any third party. On a close reading of the Act, Lord Prosser concluded that Parliament had not intended a foetus to be a person capable of sustaining personal injuries. In addition he held the section to be unambiguous and that it did not accordingly require to be interpreted according to the mischief rule. In any event he could see no mischief being cured by the Act. This, perhaps unlike *Kelly*, is indeed a juristic approach and one entirely justified because the Damages (Scotland) Act 1976 was intended to be a statement of who could sue in respect of fatal injuries. Shortly afterwards the first instance hearing

---

[40] 1992 S.L.T. 1022.

[41] Who, as Lord Justice Clerk, delivered the opinion of the Court in *Kelly v. Kelly*, 1997 S.L.T. 896. See para. 2–8 above.

[42] This decision consolidates the Law Commission view. It is also supported by earlier cases which made such awards but without discussion. *Moorcraft v. W. Alexander & Sons*, 1946 S.C. 466; *Leadbetter v. N.C.B.*, 1952 S.C. 19; *Riddell v. James Longmuir & Sons Ltd*, 1971 S.L.T. (Notes) 33. Professor Norrie argued that it may not have been necessary to apply the fiction at all. K. McK. Norrie, "Liability for injuries caused before birth", 1992 S.L.T. (News) 65, especially at 66.

[43] Norrie's argument appears to be that the word "was" is not indicating a *punctum temporis* but rather is required grammatically to reflect the fact that the father is dead.

[44] 1992 S.L.T. 1026; 1993 S.L.T. 624 (I.H.).

[45] Norrie objected to this decision on the basis that a foetus, not being a legal person, cannot sustain injuries, n. 43 at p. 67.

of *Hamilton McWilliams v. Lord Advocate*[46] was decided. In this case the defender founded on *Hamilton*, and sought dismissal. Lord Morton of Shuna considered that the section had to be interpreted in the context of the whole section. Furthermore, he considered there was precedent for considering the Report of the Scottish Law Commission.[47] In accepting and adopting a large passage from the Law Commission Report, Lord Morton considered that the 1976 Act could not have intended to change the law, which was that in principle Scots law would allow the claim, without need to refer to the *nasciturus* fiction. The conflict was resolved when the Inner House reversed *Hamilton* on appeal. Injuries caused to a foetus are personal injuries and "properly and sensibly" described as "personal injuries" even although when inflicted the "victim" did not enjoy legal personality. "To suppose that only one who enjoys legal personality can sustain 'personal injuries' is to attach an artificial legal meaning to the adjective 'personal' in s. 1(1)."[48]

A further comment was offered by his Lordship which may be intended to explain this point:

> "there are many examples in history of adult, sentient human beings being denied human status and legal personality and of limited liability companies and even of non-human animals being accorded rights and responsibilities normally appropriate only to human beings."[49]

However that can be argued the other way. Slaves in Rome being adult and sentient could not sue for personal injuries—indeed to flog another's slave was to commit a delict against the slave's owner.[50] Noxal surrender, by which slaves (and at one time children) would be handed over to the victim of their wrongdoing, occurs in an action against the owner or father and is in a way a method of damage limitation for slave owners and fathers. Limited companies generally can sue because they have legal personality and so the quotation above begs the question. The court stated that the case depended not on a fiction but on the neighbour doctrine of *Donoghue*. This begs the question because there is no neighbour until the foetus is born alive. While the decision may well be generally acceptable, it remains the case that the reasoning in these cases is not sufficiently convincing to prevent further argument in different cases raising the same policy issues.

Parents claim for the birth of a healthy child

2–11 A similar issue to the two discussed above arises where the child is born normal—like the majority of the population—but contrary to the wishes of the parents and in breach of the standard of care which ought to have been met by the professional undertaking a sterilisation. The parents are faced with costs they deliberately did not want. In *Allan v. Greater Glasgow Health*

---

[46] 1992 S.L.T. 1045.

[47] See generally on this topic G. Maher, "Statutory Interpretation and Scottish Law Commission Reports", 1992 S.L.T. (News) 277.

[48] 1993 S.L.T. 624 (I.H.), *per* Lord McCluskey at 629.

[49] *ibid.*

[50] Gaius, III, 222.

Board,[51] Lord Cameron had opined that such a claim was justiciable and could result in damages. In doing so he followed the path of English decisions.[52] This seemed a secure position.[53] However, the position has now been settled by *McFarlane v. Tayside Health Board*,[54] which must be taken as the law. The case arose from an unwanted pregnancy which resulted from an error by the consultant surgeon who had informed the pursuer that "your sperm counts are now negative and you may dispense with contraceptive precautions". At first instance Lord Gill decided that such a claim must fail. He excluded the pain and suffering caused by the pregnancy itself as a head of claim as it is outweighed by the benefit of bringing a life into the world. Lord Gill took a firm view that the birth of a healthy child was simply not actionable. It was not a personal injury. In any event it was such a good thing that it could not be measured in damages as a bad thing happening. On reclaiming the decision was reversed.[55] In the House of Lords, for Lord Slynn the case was one of economic loss notwithstanding that it arose from what he held to be an actionable pregnancy. The doctors did not assume responsibility for this economic loss. People who want to do that should recover by an appropriate contract. Lord Steyn's speech is one of the most radical in respect of delict theory in a century. He based his decision on distributive justice although he would have, if required, dismissed the claim on the basis of the fair, just and reasonable text in economic loss. Lord Hope accepted most of the key points for the pursuer. Patients are entitled to expect reasonable care and pregnancy through natural methods can be an injury or a wrong and contraception is a legitimate aspect of freedom of choice. This meant that the claim for solatium for having the child and the financial loss while having the child were valid. However, the costs of raising the child could not be recovered as being an economic loss. It was not fair, just or reasonable to impose liability for these costs. Lord Clyde expressed his opinion as being based on remoteness of damage rather than duty or no duty.

At least the position is settled with all arguments having been canvassed. Should the matter be reviewed again, perhaps with a view to legislation, then it is submitted that assuming the upbringing claim is that of the mother, then it is generally accepted that the pregnancy in this context is a personal, physical injury and the other losses are not excluded by a duty of enquiry (this accepts Lord Clyde's point). However, it is respectfully submitted that at the next stage either losses directly and naturally consequent upon the wrong or reasonably foreseeable, whatever test of remoteness of damage is employed, should thus be recoverable. Finally, it is

---

[51] November 25, 1993.

[52] *Emeh v. Kensington, Chelsea and Westminster Area Health Authority* [1985] 1 Q.B. 1012; *Thake v. Maurice* [1986] 1 Q.B. 644; *Allen v. Bloomsbury Health Authority* [1993] 1 All E.R. 651. *Jones v. Lanarkshire Health Board*, 1990 S.L.T. 19 seems to be a similar case although as it was a procedural decision the fundamentals are not discussed in the report.

[53] See A. Stewart, "Damages for Birth of a Child" (1995) J.L.S. 298 and the sequel after the Outer House decision A. Stewart, "Live Issue—Damages for Wrongful Birth" (1996) J.L.S. 443. L. Sutherland, "Damages for the Birth of a Healthy Child", Rep. B. 14–3.

[54] 2000 S.C. (H.L.) 1.

[55] *McFarlane v. Tayside Health Board*, 1998 S.C.L.R. 126. *Anderson v. Forth Valley Health Board*, 1998 S.C.L.R. 97 decided before the reclaiming motion in *McFarlane* but reported after *McFarlane* was decided, is to the same effect as the successful reclaiming.

submitted that a point not sufficiently developed in the case is that there is a legal principle which justified the decision and it is one which has in recent times apparently over-ridden established doctrine in the law of negligence: *spondet peritiam artis*—the doctors got it wrong and they must pay for their want of skill. That principle pre-dates duty of care enquiries and has been strongly applied in relation to solicitors.[56] It is submitted that doctors should have to pay and for those, such as Lord Steyn, who worry about redistribution, the doctors can insure—there is no indeterminate liability and the losses are likely to be of an order already insured for catastrophic injury. Better liability encourages doctor and hospital management to put in place sensible risk management techniques to clarify the extent to which reliance can be placed on their statements.

Parents' claim for the birth of an abnormally expensive child

2–12 If a child is born alive and, through lack of care, disabled, and thus different from the way it would have been born but for the carelessness, it seems obvious that it will, over its life, be much more expensive to raise. The question is then whether the parents should have a claim for the increased cost. It has been so held in England. The fact that a legal abortion might have been allowed has been held in England not to break the causal link.[57]

A person's claim for having been wrongfully allowed to be born

2–13 Another question is the action of a child born in some way different from the norm to claim *in its own right* for damages for a wrongdoing, such as the failure of the medical practitioner to advise or advise in sufficient time for the parents to consider deciding to seek a legal abortion. The difficulty is expressed by Norrie: "there have been times when we all were, in fact, non-existent but we have never *experienced* that state."[58] Causation is another important issue, but that is not a matter of title to sue. Norrie's conclusion that " a child's action based upon the denial of a 'right' to have had its life prevented has, and ought to have, no chance of success," is sound. The issue was tested in *P's C.B. v. CICB*.[59] A child was born, it was alleged, as a result of an incestuous rape by her maternal grandfather on her mother. She was born with severe congenital mental and physical abnormalities. Her curator bonis applied for a payment from the CICB.[60] The Board refused the claim and the curator bonis applied for judicial review. The legal background to the claim was the statutory phrase "personal injuries". Nonetheless, the case is valuable for a wide-ranging examination of cases from Scotland, England, the Commonwealth and the United States. Lord Osborne's decision is expressed in terms such that it is reasonable to say that the ratio might be wider than the narrow point of interpretation of the scheme. He essentially agreed that a definition of injury depends upon a "pre-injury state which is capable of assessment and comparison with the post-injury state."[61] In the case before him it was clear that the child had not and could not have had any life other than "a defective state".[62]

---

[56] See Chap. 12. *White v. Jones* [1995] 2 A.C. 207.
[57] *Emeh v. Kensington, Chelsea and Westminster Area Health Authority* [1985] 1 Q.B. 1012.
[58] K. McK. Norrie, "Wrongful Life in Scots Law: No Right, No Remedy", 1990 J.R. 217.
[59] 1997 S.L.T. 1180.
[60] See Chap. 1.
[61] *P.'s C.B.*, 1997 S.L.T. 1180 at 1199.
[62] *ibid.*

Children

The foetus, which after these many hazards, is born becomes a child and **2–14** thus entitled to all the protections due to a human being. People who are not adults are nowadays called children in many statutory contexts. However, that word has many different connotations and statutory inflexions. The law of delict was not altered by the Age of Legal Capacity (Scotland) Act 1991, so technically there is still a difference between pupils—boys under 14 and girls under 12; and minors—non-pupils under 18.[63] It is submitted that a pupil may be liable in civil law for his or her own delicts in Scotland but probably subject to a minimum age of seven.[64] The basis for this distinction is the civilian distinction within "pupils", that of the infans.[65] Thus an infans will not be liable but an older pupil will be. The rationale might be if the infans cannot speak it cannot concoct a crime or delict. However, since the advent of negligence it is not necessary to have an intention to harm, so it might be said that there can be liability. However, as there is often no liability for a pure omission, the infans must still be held to have known or that it should have known the consequences of its conduct. It should have reasonably foreseen something. It is submitted this cannot hold as a basis of distinction. Either the infans is liable for intention and negligence, or neither. The argument becomes complicated by the issue of contributory negligence because children are forever being injured. But this is mere verisimilitude.

The Age of Legal Capacity (Scotland) Act 1991 did not intend to change **2–15** the legal position of children so far as liability in delict is concerned. It has however introduced a regime governing, *inter alia*, reparation litigation. Children aged 16 or over can give consent to medical treatment.[66] Children under 16 can consent to a procedure or treatment so long as the doctor considers the child can understand the nature and consequences of the treatment. Non-therapeutic research is excluded. The Act governs the bringing or defending of or taking any step in civil proceedings.[67] If 16 or over the minor can proceed without a *curator ad litem*. A minor needs the concurrence of their guardian. The right of a minor to set aside transactions does not apply to civil proceedings,[68] although discharges granted can be set aside until the minor reaches 21. It is possible to apply to the sheriff by way of summary application asking the court to ratify the settlement in which case it cannot be set aside. It is submitted that this position is not satisfactory. Too much can go on in the course of a litigation to prejudice the minor—an example being the deletion of some aspect of the case or the decision not to call evidence in support of it in which case it would be lost. All that can be said is that in the court process there is a lawyer who

---

[63] s. 1(3)(c).

[64] *Somerville v. Hamilton* (1541) Mor. 8905.

[65] See for example the German Civil Code: 828. A person who has not completed his seventh year of age is not responsible for any damage which he does to another. A person who has completed his seventh but not his eighteenth year of age is not responsible for any damage which he does to another, if at the time of committing the damaging act he did not have the understanding necessary to realise his responsibility. The same applies to a deaf mute.

[66] s. 1(1)(b).

[67] s. 9.

[68] s. 3(3)(d).

although probably brought into the case by the parents must look after the interests of the minor. The Children (Scotland) Act 1995 gave effect to the international desire to protect the rights of children. A person under the age of 16 has legal capacity to instruct a solicitor in connection with any civil matter where that person has a general understanding of what it means to do so and a person of 12 or older is presumed to have that general understanding.[69] Such a person has legal capacity to sue in civil proceedings.[70]

Married people

2-16 The child may in due course marry another person. Marriage to this day constitutes a change in the status of a person. Historically women were disadvantaged in delict cases. The nineteenth and twentieth centuries saw the legal regime changing with the political and social "emancipation" of women.[71] Some important changes have only come about towards the end of the century. A married woman in minority is not under the curatory of her husband.[72] A spouse is not liable for the act or omission of the other unless on a basis other than marriage such as agency, employment or as a joint wrongdoer. The Law Reform (Husband and Wife) Act 1962, s. 2 removed the difficulties which formerly existed from the doctrine of the common law that husband and wife were one person which prevented them suing each other.[73] The court may still exercise a discretion to dismiss an action if it is shown that no substantial benefit would accrue to either party if the action continued.[74] A spouse may be able to claim losses of the nature of personal services sustained by the other spouse, in a claim of their own.[75] A spouse suffering the loss has no title to sue.[76] So, if a wife is injured in a car accident, a claim may be made in the wife's action for the cost to her husband of paying for a housekeeper.[77]

2-17 A spouse has no title to sue for the enticement of the other spouse.[78] This used to be a ground of action.[79] The position now is that a man who, by a moment's inattention, drives a car poorly and deprives me of my wife's society by running her down will pay large damages, but the man who schemes to do so by running away with her, will not. The difference can be justified by the fact that in the case of enticement the woman, now recognised to be well able to exercise her own judgment, decides to go—in a fatal car accident she has no choice.

2-18 In the law of damages there have been two decisions, one in an English[80] case and one in a Scottish case which have practical effects in many

---

[69] s. 2(4A) of the 1991 Act inserted by the 1995 Act.

[70] s. 2(4B).

[71] Married Women's Property (Scotland) Act 1881; Married Women's Property (Scotland) Act 1920.

[72] Law Reform (Husband and Wife) Act 1984, s. 3.

[73] See *Harper v. Harper*, 1929 SLT 187; *Gormanley v. Evening Citizen Ltd*, 1962 S.L.T. (Sh. Ct) 61; *Bush v. Belling*, 1963 S.L.T. (Notes) 69.

[74] The Scottish Law Commission recommended this last anomaly be removed: Scot. Law Com. No. 135, paras 10–1—10–8.

[75] Administration of Justice Act 1982, ss. 7–9.

[76] s. 8(2) and (4).

[77] See Chap. 18.

[78] Law Reform (Husband and Wife) Act 1984, s.2(2).

[79] See *Stedman v. Stedman* (1744) Mor. 13909.

[80] *Hunt v. Severs* [1994] 2 A.C. 350.

ordinary cases. In the Scottish case *Kozikowska v. Kozikowski*[81] the case turned on the terms of the Administration of Justice Act 1982, s. 8 which provides that a person who has sustained personal injuries may recover from the wrongdoer damages representing reasonable remuneration for any necessary services rendered to the injured person by a relative as a consequence of the injury. The injured person has a duty to account to the relative for damages recovered on this ground. In *Kozikowska* a wife sued her husband and a roads authority for damages in respect of injuries suffered when her husband's car skidded on an icy road. The wife's claim included a claim for necessary services rendered to her by her husband and by their children. Lord Coulsfield, following the English case, held that it was incompetent for the wife to recover from her husband remuneration in respect of his own services.

Parents

Parents are not as such liable for the delicts of their children.[82] They can **2–19** however be vicariously liable or liable themselves for putting an inadequate person in charge of dangerous things.[83] An averment that the driver of a car was the defender's 19–year-old son was irrelevant absent "employment" or that the son was an improper or inadequate driver.[84] Issues were allowed on an allegation of putting a 14–year-old in charge of a horse of which it was said he was incapable of handling.[85] Parents can sue children just as children can sue their parents.[86] Parents and children are "relatives" for the purposes of the Administration of Justice Act 1982 and in terms of the Damages (Scotland) Act 1976

Dead people

Dead men can't sue. Actions by relatives for wrongs causing death are now **2–20** governed by the Damages (Scotland) Act 1976.[87] In the other direction a deceased person's estate can be sued in delict for wrongs done.[88] The claim

---

[81] 1996 S.L.T. 386.

[82] *Davie v. Wilson* (1854) 16 D. 956; *Mckay v. McLean*, 1920 1 S.L.T. 34. Compare the position under the German Civil Code: 832 "A person who is bound by law to exercise supervision over a person on account of minority, or of his mental or physical condition, is bound to make compensation for any damage which the latter unlawfully does to a third party." The duty to compensate does not arise if he fulfils his duty of supervision, or if the damage would have occurred notwithstanding the proper exercise of supervision. The same responsibility attaches to a person who takes over by contract the exercise of supervision. Thus the parents of a seven-year-old child who got hold of easily available matches were liable, although not the parents of a 15-year-old playing football. Markesinis, *The German Law of Torts*, p. 662 .

[83] See Chap. 3.

[84] *Mckay v. McLean*, 1920 1 S.L.T. 34.

[85] *Brown v. Fulton* (1881) 9 R. 36.

[86] *Wood v. Wood*, 1935 S.L.T. 431.

[87] See Chap. 18. There is a Roman law maxim sometimes encountered: *actio personalis moritur cum persona*. It is not of itself of any assistance today. See generally *Bern's Ex. v. Montrose Asylum* (1893) 20 R. 859.

[88] See, *e.g. Bourhill v. Young*, 1942 S.C.(H.L.) 78 It is worth mentioning *Thomson v. Duggie*, 1949 S.L.T. (Notes) 53 in case anyone else has the same idea. There was a collision between a motor ship called *Resplendent* and another motor ship, *Marinia*. The master of the *Marinia*

that the person had before they died transmits to a certain extent to the executor, including pain and suffering.[89] Defamation is more interesting because traditionally people take insults upon their kin or clan seriously. In *Broom v. Ritchie & Co.*[90] a widow on her own behalf and for her children sought damages for defamation for the publication in the press of a false statement that her late husband had committed suicide.[91] She claimed solatium only. The defenders pleaded, *inter alia*, no title to sue. The Lord Ordinary (Kincairney) sustained the plea primarily on the basis of there being no clear principle on which the case was based, and only some very old doubtful authority to support it. The pursuer reclaimed and the Court adhered to the Lord Ordinary's judgment. The Lord Justice-Clerk (Mac-Donald) said that "an aspersion on a person after death cannot, I hold, give right to anyone else to recover damages as for a wrong done to the deceased."[92] However, it was thought that a slander against the character of a deceased person which by necessary implication injured others, *e.g.* stamping his children as bastards, would be different and would give right in persons to sue for the effect on their status or patrimonial interests.[93] But this case was for solatium only.[94] In *Agnew v. Laughlan*[95] the pursuer sought reduction of a sheriff's order under which his now deceased wife had been detained in an asylum, and of certain certificates by medical practitioners. He brought the action both as an individual and as tutor of his son. The sheriff's order was said to be wrongfully obtained and the doctor's certificates were said to be false and inaccurate. The wife had just given birth and died a few days later. After a procedure roll debate held by the Lord Ordinary (MacKintosh) that the pursuer had no title to sue as the document sought to be reduced had long since been spent and inoperative. The action was dismissed. Any prejudice to the pursuer or to his son attaching to the family was too vague and remote to found a patrimonial interest. Any stigma attending to relatives of the deceased because she was put in an asylum was irrelevant. The right to sue for defamation was the deceased's alone and no claim for defamation arises after the death of the defamed.[96]

2–21   The dead person's body is of course no longer his. Interference with it (unless permitted by the Human Tissue Act 1961) is probably wrongful unless authorised by the next of kin who themselves probably only have the body for disposal and cannot sell it, for example.[97]

---

died suddenly some time after the accident and before action was raised. The owners of *Resplendent* brought an admiralty action *in personam* against the widow of the master of *Marinia* in which they claimed damages for loss due to the fault of her husband. The pursuers complained that the widow, or her solicitor, had failed to disclose who were the true representatives of the deceased. Lord Birnam dismissed the case.

[89] So far as the latter is concerned as a result of reforms in 1993. See Chap. 18.

[90] (1904) 6 F. 942.

[91] It being remembered that then, much more so than now, suicide carried a stigma and indeed was a crime in England.

[92] *Broom, op. cit.* at 945.

[93] It being remembered too that now there are no bastards in Scotland.

[94] Note that Lord Young agreed with the result but not with the reasoning of the Lord Ordinary or the other judges of the Division. He thought the claim irrelevant on the facts.

[95] 1948 S.L.T. 512.

[96] A rule retained when the law was reformed by the Damages (Scotland) Act 1993.

[97] *Pollock v. Workman* (1900) 2F 354.

The Crown, its Judges, its Government and the State

The Crown and the Parliaments

The Sovereign is immune from action. At common law the Crown is not **2–22** vicariously liable for the actings of its agents or employees but the liability of the Crown is now governed by the Crown Proceedings Act 1947, which generally makes the Crown liable.[98] The Crown is liable both as an employer and as an occupier.[99] The Crown is bound by statute if express or by necessary implication.

Scotland has its own devolved Parliament.[1] Prior to the key provisions coming into force, actions against the Crown had to be raised against the Lord Advocate. He required the prior authority of whomsoever he represents.[2] This could not be challenged by a private party.[3] The Secretary of State for Scotland was called as the defender in cases where one of his departments was involved.

In terms of the new regime, the Lord Advocate and the Solicitor General for Scotland are now Scottish law officers to the Scottish Executive. The Advocate General for Scotland become the adviser to the United Kingdom Government on Scottish legal matters. Between May 20, 1999 and July 1, 1999 any action which would previously have been raised against the Lord Advocate as representing the Crown was raised against the Advocate General for Scotland.[4] Actions which would have been raised against the Lord Advocate in United Kingdom matters are raised against the Advocate General for Scotland.[5]

The Armed Forces

In respect of injuries suffered by members of the armed forces the law is **2–23** special. By section 10(1) of the Act there was no liability in delict if the injuries were certified as pensionable. In *Adams v. War Office*,[6] certification was made but no pension was actually awarded.[7] The Crown Proceedings (Armed Forces) Act 1987 prevented this apparent injustice:

"Section 10 of the Crown Proceedings Act 1947 shall cease to have effect except in relation to anything suffered by a person in consequence of an act or omission committed before the date on which this Act is passed."[8]

---

[98] Previously it was necessary to seek declarator of the wrong and seek *ex gratia* damages.

[99] s. 2(1) and the Occupiers' Liability (Scotland) Act 1960, s. 4.

[1] Scotland Act 1998.

[2] Crown Suits (Scotland) Act 1857, ss. 1 and 2.

[3] 1857 Act, s. 3.

[4] Between May 20, 1999 and July 1, 1999 any action against the Scottish Ministers including the Lord Advocate in that capacity should be raised against the Lord Advocate. After July 1 actions within the competence of the Scottish Parliament and Ministers are raised either against the Ministers or the Lord Advocate.

[5] Scotland Act 1998 (General Transitory, Transitional and Savings Provisions) Order 1999 (S.I. 1999 No. 901); Scotland Act 1998 (Commencement) Order 1998 (S.I. 1998 No. 3178); Transfer of Property (Scottish Ministers) Order 1999 (S.I. 1999 No. 1104).

[6] [1955] 3 All E.R. 245.

[7] A Scottish example, from before the 1987 Act is *Brown v. Lord Advocate*, 1984 S.L.T. 146 in which the Lord Advocate represented the Ministry of Defence. A certificate was lodged and the action held to be incompetent. It would also have been held irrelevant.

[8] May 15, 1987.

The Secretary of State can revive the effect of section 10 if it appears necessary or expedient to do so by reason of any imminent national danger, any great emergency or for the purposes of any warlike operations in any part of the world outside the United Kingdom. Perhaps surprisingly, no such order was made when the Gulf War against Iraq broke out. Thus the Crown did not have this defence when sued by a soldier who claimed that the Crown was vicariously liable for the fault of his fellow soldier in not arranging a safe system of work as he fired a howitzer at the Iraqis.[9] In *Derry v. Ministry of Defence*,[10] it was held that section 10(1) of the Crown Proceedings Act applied to protect the Crown from a claim based on an allegation that the military doctor failed to diagnose the plaintiff's cancerous condition. Because the condition predated the act or omission the state was protected. The persuasive argument that it was the omission to diagnose properly that led to a loss of a chance of better treatment seems to have failed mainly because it is difficult to fit the common law concept of a loss of a chance into the statutory language of the 1947 Act which talks of a thing suffered.

Local authorities

2–24 Local authorities have been sued in delict for a very long time. Cases now are raised against the appropriate statutory body. Frequent reorganisation of local government means that for all practical purposes the responsible bodies will be creatures of statute and liable to that extent. At present actions are in the main likely to be directed towards the "new" unitary authorities who are sued in their statutory name. Practitioners must always be on their guard at or around the time of such reorganisation as can be seen from the case of *Stephen v. North of Scotland Water*.[11] The pursuer was allegedly injured at work. He had been employed by Grampian Regional Council. However, their function in this regard was later transferred to the defenders. The pursuer's lawyers were instructed with little time to go before the expiry of the triennium. They had enough time to sue the correct defenders but got it wrong misconstruing or failing to construe the difficult legislation and suing Aberdeenshire Council instead. The pursuer's argument that under section 17 of the Prescription and Limitation Act 1973, the time did not start to run until the person responsible came into legal existence failed. But they were, on the basis that they missed the time-bar by only eight days allowed to proceed with the action. Until these reforms actions were raised sometimes against the district authorities and sometimes against the regional councils. Earlier actions were against the magistrates or other officers depending on the status of the organisation.[12] Local authorities are treated more kindly at present in the law of negligence at least where they are acting as a public body.[13]

---

[9] *Mulcahy v. MOD* [1996] T.L.R. 39. However it was held there was no duty to provide a safe system of work at war.

[10] [1998] T.L.R. 364.

[11] June 30, 1998.

[12] A perusal of the table of cases will show just how many cases involve such parties as pursuers and defenders.

[13] See Chap. 10.

In a particularly principled decision it has been held in England that a local authority cannot sue for defamation at all.[14] The reason is to allow criticism of the authority an important civil right. Lord Keith followed with approval some American decisions, one as old as 1923, in coming to the conclusion that English law would not permit such an action[15]: "Every citizen has a right to criticise an inefficient or corrupt government without fear of civil as well as criminal prosecution". It was appreciated that the truth might be known, but no evidence available to substantiate it and thus the immunity was necessary to allow criticism to be made. Lord Keith agreed with Lord Goff in *Guardian Newspapers (No.2)*[16] that so far as the law of England was concerned it was in concert with Article 10 of the European Convention of Human Rights. So far as Scotland is concerned this approval of the European convention and the use of the words United Kingdom in the judgment suggest that a similar result would be reached in a Scottish case. At present the law is probably the same as for any other corporation and it might be that recovery would be allowed of all but solatium.[17]

Judges

Judges have extensive immunities. In *Haggart's Trs v. Lord President* 2–25 *(Hope)*,[18] the pursuers were the trustees of an advocate who had raised an action for damages against the Lord President in respect of certain remarks of censure made from the bench about the conduct of his practice. These remarks were alleged to be motivated by malice and to injure John Haggart in his practice. However, the whole court had agreed with the Lord President. In another case, the Lord President was alleged to have said: "I have never seen such low wit, vulgar abuse, scurrility, and buffoonery, as in these answers. It is painful to think the Bar of Scotland has furnished a man capable of writing such a paper."[19] A further action was raised and the two conjoined. The Lord Ordinary (Pitmilly) granted absolvitor on basis that an action could not be maintained against a judge of the court; allegations of malice could not render it competent, in any event the averments of malice were irrelevant. The pursuer reclaimed and then died. The trustees insisted in the action. The Court adhered to the interlocutor of Lord Ordinary although Lord Craigie thought that the Lord Ordinary went too far in his view on competency and malice. The other judges also gave reasoned opinions, several being in agreement with the Lord Ordinary. Several said that judges of the court might well be answerable in other circumstances, especially in a private capacity, but also that the court might be able to censure those who practise before it. A further appeal was taken to the House of Lords who dismissed the appeal. Lord Gifford said that an action for damages is not maintainable against a judge for words delivered from the bench in the exercise of judicial duty. If it was otherwise—this would

---

[14] *Derbyshire County Council v. Times Newspapers Ltd* [1993] T.L.R. 87.

[15] Supreme Court of Illinois: *City of Chicago v. Tribune Co.* (1923) 139 N.E. 86.

[16] [1990] 1 A.C. 109.

[17] The English position before *Derbyshire County Council* was to this effect: *Mayor of Manchester v. Williams* [1891] 1 Q.B. 94; *Bognor Regis U.D.C. v. Campion* [1972] 2 Q.B. 169.

[18] (1824) 2 Shaw's App. 125.

[19] *ibid.* at 131.

subvert due administration of justice. The judges had a public responsibility but it did not follow how this action could be maintained.[20] On the other hand in the House of Lords in *Allardice v. Robertson*[21] the House held affirming the judgment of the Court of Session, that a justice of the peace is not protected against an action of damages for verbal slander made maliciously in delivering judgment against a party to a trial before him. Many of the other protections available to judges are considered below.[22]

2–26 The law of the European Union has provided that the Government shall be responsible to its citizens for failure to carry through properly or at all certain community laws.[23]

Unincorporated bodies

2–27 An unincorporated body can sue in its own right although some patrimonial interest need be averred and proved.[24] An unincorporated body as defender will be liable to the extent of any property held in trust for all the members and to the extent of the members interest in the body, *e.g.* a club subscription.[25] In *Campbell v. Wilson*[26] the pursuer was a member of the Scottish Society for the Protection of Wild Birds, an unincorporated society. The defender was a naturalist who wrote to the press complaining of the actions of the SSPWB in releasing birds at a time of year when they could not find adequate food. The pursuer sued for damages. She did not aver she was present when the birds were released. The defender pleaded no title or interest to sue. The Lord Ordinary (MacKay) dismissed the action. The SSPWB was of unlimited size; if the pursuer could sue so could every other member, even though they had not taken part in the release of the birds.[27] It is more likely that a particular office bearer will be personally liable, or all members approving a certain course of conduct will be liable. Although there is a body of authority the position is less clear than would be ideal, especially as many clubs are run by individuals without the benefit of legal advice. The former rule that a club cannot be sued in its own name—actions required to be raised against the club and the office bearers[28] has been departed from by Rules of Court. Arguably, all that does is to allow a decree to be enforced against club assets. It has already allowed an action of interdict against nuisance to be raised against a golf club and it was thought that suitable parties could be found to answer for any breach.[29] It does rather assume that a club has title to defend to that extent.[30] It may be questioned whether a member has a right to sue for

---

[20] (1824) 2 Shaw's App. 125 at 143.
[21] (1830) 2 W. & S. 102.
[22] See Chap. 8.
[23] See Chap. 11.
[24] *Highland Dancing Board v. Alloa Printing Co.*,1971 S.L.T. (Sh.Ct) 50.
[25] *Gibson v. Smith* (1849) 21 Sc.J. 331.
[26] 1934 S.L.T. 249.
[27] It was said that *Brown v. D.C. Thomson Co.*, 1912 S.C. 359 did not justify an action such as this one.
[28] *Somerville v. Rowbotham* (1862) 24 D. 1187.
[29] *Borland v. Lochwinnoch Golf Club*, 1986 S.L.T. (Sh. Ct) 13.
[30] Although the case failed and was by a visitor rather than a member, the point was not taken in *McQueen v. Ballater Golf Club*, 1975 S.L.T. 160.

injuries or wrongs by the association. Analogies with partnership suggest a case might well fail.[31] In *Graham and Simpson v. Hawick Common Riding Committee*,[32] the pursuers sued for declarator under the Sex Discrimination Act 1975 and for "nominal" damages of £1. The defenders were a committee but it was not clear of what. A plea of no title to sue was repelled and that course approved on appeal. The Sheriff Principal did not find it necessary to comment on the English cases *Prole* and *Robertson* although he could see some force in the view that, if an association consists of its own members and has no independent existence, then on the basis that a person cannot sue himself, those decisions might well be followed in Scotland.[33] However, where the personal wrong of individuals can be established they are personally liable. In *Matthew v. Perthshire Cricket Club*,[34] the pursuer sued "the Perthshire Cricket Club, and the officials and Committee of the Club, for damages in respect of personal injuries sustained by him through the collapse of a grand stand on the North Inch of Perth on August 1, 1903."[35] In *East Lothian Angling Association v. Haddington Town Council*,[36] the pursuers who held permissions to fish in the Tyne were unable to sue the Burgh for polluting the river and causing damage to the fish they actually fished and economic loss by the loss of permits to fish. It was held that the association did not have title to sue having an insufficient interest in the fishing.[37] In *Milne v. Duguid*,[38] Sheriff Kelbie reviewed the authorities, applied *Prole* and held that a member of an unincorporated association could not sue an association. However, he allowed proof before answer on a case against a member who was being sued on the independent ground of his activities as greenkeeper.

Partnerships

Partnerships are considered to have quasi-personality, so it may be the case **2–28** that a firm can only sue if the alleged wrong is done to it as a quasi-person rather than to an individual partner.[39] Partners are jointly and severally liable.[40] They are so liable for the matters set out in the Partnership Act 1890:

"Where, by any wrongful act or omission of any partner acting in the ordinary course of the business of the firm, or with the authority of his

---

[31] See para. 2–28 below. For England see *Robertson v. Ridley* [1989] 2 All E.R. 474, doubted by Clerk and Lindsell, *The Law of Torts*, para. 10–11 and distinguished in *Jones v. Northampton Borough Council* [1992] 156 L.G.Rev. 23. See also *Prole v. Allen* [1950] 1 All E.R. 476 and *Shore v. Ministry for Works* [1950] 2 All E.R. 228.

[32] 1997 S.C.L.R. 917.

[33] *ibid.* at 932.

[34] (1904) 12 S.L.T. 635.

[35] More marginal (being before the Division on exceptions) is *Glass v. Leitch*, (1902) 5 F. 14, in which a case for damages based on the collapsing of structure was brought against the race committee who acted gratuitously and had a lease of the premises.

[36] 1980 S.L.T. 213.

[37] See generally D. Brodie, "The Common Members Rule" Rep.B. 24–2.

[38] 1999 S.C.L.R. 512.

[39] See the "peculiar" case of *Melville v. Cummings*, 1912 S.C. 1185.

[40] 1890 Act, s. 12.

co-partners, loss or injury is caused to any person not being a partner in the firm, or any penalty is incurred, the firm is liable therefor to the same extent as the partner so acting or omitting to act."

The scope of the partnership business determines the scope of the liability.[41] The whole issue was canvassed in recent times in the Inner House in the case of *Kirkintilloch Equitable Co-operative Society Ltd v. Livingstone*,[42]. In this case there was an allegation of negligence by a member of a firm of accountants who acted as auditor. The fee was paid to the firm and members of the firm assisted in the audit. However, neither the partners nor the firm were entitled to be appointed as auditors under the appropriate legislation. It was argued that accordingly the work was not within the ordinary course of business of the partnership. It is clear from the opinion of Lord President Clyde that s. 10 of the Act provides two alternative modes of liability: "ordinary course" and "authority" cases. In *Kirkintilloch Co-op* the acts were within the scope of the business and in any event the averments as to authority were sufficient. Section 11 also makes provision for liability in the following cases, namely: (a) where one partner acting within the scope of his apparent authority receives the money or property of a third person and misapplies it; and (b) where a firm in the course of its business receives money or property of a third person, and the money is misapplied by one or more of its partners while it is in the custody of the firm. The firm is liable to make good loss.

An Extra Division considered this section in *New Mining and Exploring Syndicate Ltd v. Chalmers & Hunter*.[43] This was a case against a partner in a firm of solicitors in respect of the transactions of his partner who was secretary to the pursuers. The issue in the case was the same one as in *Kirkintilloch Co-op*, whether the money obtained by the fraudulent partner was within the partnership business. In this case it was held that it was not. The firm were not secretaries to the company and were not its law agents. The Inner House upheld the decision to assoilzie the defenders.

2–29   What of the position where one partner wants to sue or defend but the others do not? It has been held that where two of three partners disclaimed, the remaining partner had no title to sue.[44] In another, sheriff court case, albeit one of contract, where one of four partners, three of whom had disclaimed, was held to have no title to sue.[45] It was explained that where there were only two partners this rule could not apply, either party having title to sue.[46]

2–30   It was held by in the first division, in *Mair v. Wood*,[47] that a partner injured by the negligence of his co-partner cannot sue the firm. Lord President Clyde accepted that a partner could in principle sue and confusio would not operate initially but would restrict the claim to the amount of the claim minus the "suing partner's" share. However, negligence was a

---

[41] *Lloyd v. Grace Smith* [1912] A.C. 716.
[42] 1972 S.L.T. 154.
[43] 1911 2 S.L.T. 386.
[44] *Marquis of Bredalbane v. Tobernochy Quarry Co.* (1916) 33 Sh. Ct Rep. 154.
[45] *Hutcheon & Partners v. Hutcheon*, 1979 S.L.T. 61.
[46] *ibid.* at 63–64.
[47] 1948 S.L.T. 326.

different matter because *culpa tenet suos auctores*. It has to be suggested however that the law of vicarious liability has now moved on so much in its ordinary sphere of employment that the decision could usefully be reviewed.[48] There is some support in Erskine:

> "It also proceeds from the mutual confidence inherent in this contract, that the several partners are not always obliged to use that middle kind of diligence which prudent persons employ in their own affairs; they are secure if they manage the company's concerns as they would do their own. If, therefore, a partner should fall into an error in management, for want of a larger share of prudence or skill than he was truly master of, he is not answerable for the consequences. He did his best; and the other partners have themselves to blame that they did not make choice of a partner of greater abilities."[49]

That is however different from actionable negligence. In *Blackwood v. Robertson*[50] in an action of payment by a consulting engineer against his former partners, the defender partners counter-claimed for damages in respect of alleged negligence on the part of the pursuer as a result of which the partnership suffered loss. It was held by Sheriff Macvicar that a partner might in serious cases be made liable to his fellow partners for loss occasioned to the partnership business by his lack of care or skill, but that a minor blunder would not give rise to a right of action and so a proof before answer was needed. He also considered the counter-claim contractual, contrary to the argument before him which was delictual. In the earlier case of *Parker v. Walker*,[51] the facts were similar to *Mair*. A marine engineer was employed as a member of the crew of a motor fishing boat engaged in trawl-fishing. He was injured in the course of his employment. He sued the owners. Fish salesmen sold the catch and thereafter divided the net profits into two equal shares, one for the crew and one for the boat. The crew's share was divided equally among members. The defenders argued that the crew, including the pursuer and his fellow-member, against whom he averred negligence, were not employees of the owners but were partners or joint adventurers with them in a fishing venture. A proof before answer took place. Lord Walker decided the arrangement was a joint venture. He went on to hold that the owners were under a duty to provide safe gear.[52] In *Bruce v. Clapham*[53] the question was the liability of the crew of a fishing boat for the negligence of the skipper. The boat was operated as a joint adventure. It was held *obiter* that even if the parties were in a joint

---

[48] It is accepted in Walker, *Delict*, p.81 and in Clerk and Lindsell, *The Law of Torts*, para. 4–53.

[49] III, iii, 21.

[50] 1984 S.L.T. (Sh. Ct) 68.

[51] 1961 S.L.T. 252.

[52] Lord Grieve commented: "At the hearing on evidence, counsel for the pursuer did not maintain that the defenders were under a duty to provide a safe system for working the gear. Whether that surrender of part of his record was necessarily dictated by the proposition that a firm cannot be liable to one partner for the fault of another, as established by *Mair v. Wood*, 1948 S.C. 83, 1948 S.L.T. 326, I do not pause to consider. In my opinion, the pursuer cannot succeed on a ground not ultimately maintained." *ibid*. at 255.

[53] 1982 S.L.T. 386.

adventure, the injured workman joint adventurer would have been an employee quoad the Captain.[54]

Trade Unions

2–31 Trade unions[55] are unincorporated bodies. Their ability to sue and be sued is subject to constraints and immunities as befits organisations which have essentially come to have constitutional significance in the twentieth century from having been primarily illegal combinations in the nineteenth.[56] Article 23(4) of the Universal Declaration of Human Rights declares "Everyone has the right to form and to join Trade Unions for the protection of his interests." The more practical European Convention on Human Rights provides in Article 11 the right to form and join trade unions for the protection of his interests, but this is subject to restrictions necessary in a democratic society in the interests of national security or public safety, for the prevention of disorder or crime, for the protection of health or morals or for the protection of the rights and freedoms of others. Thus delict which protects and enforces the interests of persons must treat trade unions specially. A trade union is an organisation which consists mainly or wholly of workers whose principal purpose includes the regulation of worker/employer relations.[57] Workers and employers are specially defined.[58] A trade union is not an incorporated body by statute.[59] A union may sue or be sued in its own name and any judgment is enforceable against any property which is held in trust for its benefit. The economic, political and near constitutional importance of trades unions is reflected in the history of legislation adjusting the legal position of trades unions as defenders. Trade unions are liable for any negligence nuisance or breach of duty resulting in personal injury to any person or from any breach of duty imposed in connection with the ownership, occupation, possession, control or use of property.[60] There is a general immunity in respect of "an act done by a person" in respect of acts done "in contemplation or furtherance of a trade dispute." There is protection against an action based on inducing a breach of contract or interfering (or inducing another to interfere) with its performance[61]; and where there is a threat that a contract (whether or not the threatener is a party to it) will be broken or its performance interfered with or that the threatener will induce another to break or interfere with a contract.[62] An agreement between two or more persons to do or procure the doing of any act in contemplation or furtherance of a trade dispute, if the act is one which, if done without any such agreement, would not be actionable, is protected.[63]

---

[54] This view is all the more interesting as Lord Grieve was counsel in *Parker*. Lord Grieve was happy the result was in accord with common sense.

[55] The proper plural hardly ever used is trades union.

[56] See the review in *Wilkie v. King*, 1911 S.C. 1310.

[57] Trade Union and Labour Relations (Consolidation) Act 1992, s. 1.

[58] ss. 30, 295, 296.

[59] s. 10(1).

[60] Employment Act 1982, s. 15.

[61] s. 131(a).

[62] s. 131(b).

[63] s. 13(4).

For all of these immunities to apply the acts must be in contemplation or **2–32** furtherance of a trade dispute. This is defined in the 1974 Act. The dispute must be between workers and their employers (not with other workers) which relates wholly or mainly to and not just connected with, one or more of the following statutory factors:

(a) terms and conditions of employment, or the physical conditions in which any workers are required to work;

(b) engagement or non-engagement, termination or suspension of employment, or the duties of employment of one or more workers; allocation of work or the duties of employment as between workers or groups of workers;

(d) matters of discipline;

(e) the membership or non-membership of a trade union on the part of a worker;

(f) facilities for officials of trade unions; and

(g) machinery for negotiation or consultation, and other procedures, relating to any of the foregoing matters, including the recognition by employers or employers' association of the right of a trade union to represent workers in any such negotiation or consultation or in the carrying out of such procedures.

There has been at least one discussion of this concept in a Scottish case. In *Square Grip Reinforcement Co. v. MacDonald*[64] officials and members of the union attended building sites where contractors known to be customers of the company were operating and induced workers there to refuse to offload lorries carrying materials supplied by the company, and to threaten that if the lorries were offloaded all the workers on the site who were members of the union would cease work. The customers were forced to refuse to take delivery of the company's materials, and so to break their contracts with the company. It was held that there was a "trade dispute". The conduct, which was an inducement to break a commercial contract, was not protected by the legislation. There are many English cases.[65] A political protest is not a trade dispute.[66] Picketing is expressly declared to be lawful, and often it would be anyway. On occasion the protection is needed where the conduct constitutes perhaps a trespass or a nuisance.[67] The following conditions must be met—the picket must be at or near his place of work (unless a union official) and be there for the purpose only of peacefully obtaining or communicating information, or peacefully persuading any person to work or abstain from working.[68]

---

[64] (O.H.) 1968 S.L.T. 65. A case under the earlier Trade Disputes Act 1906 and Trade Disputes Act 1965.

[65] See Craig and Miller, *Employment Law in Scotland*, Chap. 11.

[66] *Mercury Communication Ltd v. Scott-Garner* [1984] I.C.R. 74 and the *Post Office Engineering Union* [1984] Ch. 37. See also *Express Newspapers Ltd. v. McShane* [1980] A.C. 672; *Dupont Steels Ltd v. Sirs* [1980] 1 W.L.R. 142.

[67] See *Thomas v. N.U.M (South Wales Area)* [1985] 2 W.L.R. 1081.

[68] See *Timex Electronic Corporation v. Amalgamated Engineering Union, The Scotsman*, April 14, 1993.

"Secondary action", *i.e.* action taken against someone not a party to the dispute will not, generally, attract the immunity. The immunity has been restricted in respect of interference with contracts to contracts of employment only. Interference with other contracts is not protected in this way as, for example, a charterparty.[69] Secondary action is permitted only to attack the supply of goods between the employer in dispute and the employer of workers who are supplying goods. The Trade Union Act 1984 made it necessary to hold a secret ballot before taking certain strike action which would require the immunity as a defence against the delict of interference in contract.

2–33   There are many cases of trade union members suing their organisation and that is ruled by ordinary principles governing actions by members against their association. Thus, a trade unionist was fined and was held to have title and interest to challenge the resolution but the action was not one for reparation.[70]

Incorporated Bodies

2–34 Incorporated bodies whether incorporated by Royal Charter, under the Companies Acts or otherwise, may sue and be sued in their own name so long as the wrong is one done to the organisation. An incorporated body being a legal person cannot have hurt feelings and therefore cannot be awarded solatium. It can however be injured in its reputation.[71] In *Waverley Housing Management Ltd v. British Broadcasting Corporation*,[72] the defenders argued that the pursuers' action should be dismissed as the company could not sue for solatium. It was held that while indeed a company cannot sue for solatium, the pursuers could maintain the action by way of general damages for future loss of business, although not for damages based on particular contracts or diminution of turnover. Although shareholders may lose money by damage to company property it is the company who must sue.[73] Again, because incorporated bodies have no actual physical body, technically they are always vicariously liable. No distinction is made between *ultra vires* and *intra vires* acts.[74] It must be determined when suing a corporation that it is indeed the corporation and not the individuals in their own right who have done the wrong.[75] However dependent on the wrong, the actual wrongdoer is likely to be as liable as the corporation if the wrong is also a corporation wrong.[76] Directors of a company may be held personally liable where in the conduct of the company's affairs they have broken a statutory duty owed to the pursuer. Every case depends upon the duty in question and it would not be right for

---

[69] *Merkur Island Shipping Co. v. Laughton* [1983] A.C. 570.

[70] *Spowart v. TGWU*, 1926 S.L.T. 245.

[71] *Solicitors of Edinburgh v. Robertson* (1781).Mor. 13935; *Dumfries Fleshers v. Rankine*, Dec. 10, 1816, F.C.; *North of Scotland Bank v. Duncan* (1857) 19 D. 881; *Glebe Sugar Refining Company v. Lusk* (1866) 2 S.L.R. 9; 3 S.L.R. 33.

[72] 1993 G.W.D. 17–1117.

[73] *Scottish Australian Emigration Society v. Borland* (1855) 18 D. 239; *Dunnett v. Mitchell* (1887) 15 R. 131.

[74] *Houldsworth v. City of Glasgow Bank* (1880) 7 R. (H.L.) 53.

[75] *Gordon v. Metaline Company* (1886) 14 R. 75.

[76] *Dunbar v. Presbytery of Auchterarder* (1849) 12 D. 284.

the law of delict routinely to pierce the veil of incorporation. However, one recent instance can be found in *Quinn v. McGinty.*[77] The pursuer sued a director of his employer company for his failure to comply with the statutory obligation to insure in terms of the Employer's Liability (Compulsory Insurance) Act 1969. The sheriff found against him but the Sheriff Principal allowed the action. Whether discussed as title to sue or relevancy a shareholder has generally no right to sue for loss of profits due to injury to that shareholder himself, even where he is the largest shareholder and earns most of its profits.[78]

Insane persons

It all depends what is meant by "insane". A recent case on prescription had **2–35** to consider the term in relation to the protection from the effects of prescription on an insane pursuer and the discussion therein gives a better view of what is thought to be alienation of reason in current Scots law.[79] Ultimately the law is likely to look at its own view of the voluntariness of the conduct. It might be that the recent liberalisation of the criminal law on automatism would provide some guidance, especially in cases where it is the defender's voluntary conduct which brings about an insane state. The tests in the criminal cases are that the external factor must not be self-induced, that it must be one which the accused was not bound to foresee, and that it must have resulted in a total alienation of reason amounting to a total loss of control of his actions in regard to the crime with which he is charged.[80]

When reparation was about deliberate harm then those who could not **2–36** form such an intention through alienation of reason had to be exempted from liability. Thus the law in the *Digest* would be correct in Scots law in such cases: "accordingly the question is asked whether there is an action under the *lex Aquilia* if a lunatic causes damage. Pegasus says there is not, for he asks how there can be any accountable fault in him who is out of his mind; and he is undoubtedly right."[81] This is supported by the reasoning in *Waugh v. James K. Allan Ltd.*[82] In that case the defenders' driver who was suddenly disabled by an attack of coronary thrombosis ran down a pedestrian. Lord Reid said "One must have great sympathy with the appellant who has suffered so severely through no fault of his own, but I find it impossible to blame the driver." It is voluntary human conduct which is regulated by delict. Practically, it can be seen from *Waugh* that there can be liability if the person knew or ought to have known his condition would develop.[83]

---

[77] 1999 S.L.T. (Sh. Ct) 27.

[78] *Young v. Ormiston*, 1936 S.L.T. 79; *Fox v. P Caulfield & Co Ltd*, 1975 S.L.T. (Notes) 71.

[79] *Bogan's C.B. v. Graham*, 1992 S.C.L.R. 920.

[80] See *Ross v. H.M. Advocate*, 1991 S.L.T. 564; *Ebsworth v. H.M. Advocate*, 1992 S.L.T. 1161; *Cardle v. Mulrainey*, 1992 S.L.T. 1152.

[81] Dig. IX 2,5,2,

[82] 1964 S.C. (H.L.) 102.

[83] See *Roberts v. Ramsbottem*, [1980] 1 All E.R. 7, where a man was held liable although he had been in a state of automatism, but on the basis that he should have taken steps to prevent himself causing harm to others. And generally by comparison, see the German Civil Code:

Insolvent persons

2–37 Bankruptcy takes the estate into the hands of the trustee *tantum et tale*. It has been said that:

> "It may not be necessary here to define absolutely how much remains of radical title in a bankrupt who has been sequestrated . . . but I am not prepared to say, that along with the radical interest there does not remain to some effect the radical title also, and there are many instances in which the bankrupt may intervene in fortification of the title of the trustee."[84]

So far as natural persons are concerned, the debtor has title and interest to sue for personal wrongs such as assault, unintentional personal injury or defamation.[85] The trustee in bankruptcy has title and interest to sue and if the bankrupt recovers compensation, the damages go to the estate.[86] It may be that a person whose estates are insolvent has no title to sue unless he can show that the trustee and the creditors have abandoned a claim.[87] However section 32 of the Bankruptcy (Scotland) Act 1985 allows the debtor to keep his income, placing the onus on the trustee to make a claim upon it. This income is a kind of patrimony and it might be that an action relating to it should not be affected by the rules of title to sue; the rules depriving bankrupts of title to sue was probably based on the law which vested his entire estate in the trustee. Even under the 1913 Act a different view has been expressed, although on the general issue of title to sue, doubting *Grindall*.[88] In *Watson v. Thompson*[89] the trustee in bankruptcy was held entitled to be sisted as a party in a claim for solatium by the debtor.[90] The right was no longer personal after the action has been raised. A bankrupt has title to sue for the reduction of the decree which led to his sequestration, where his trustee makes clear that he does not intend to proceed with such an action. A formal abandonment by the trustee is not required before the bankrupt may proceed.[91] The latest analysis is to be found in the Inner House decision, *Coutts' Trustee v. Coutts*.[92] A trustee

---

BGB 827—a person who does damage to another in a condition of unconsciousness, or in a condition of morbid disturbance of the mental activity, incompatible with a free determination of the will, is not responsible for the damage. If he had brought himself into a temporary condition of this kind by spiritous liquors or similar means, he is responsible for any damage which he unlawfully causes in this condition in the same manner as if negligence were imputable to him; the responsibility does not arise if he has been brought into this condition without fault, Markesinis, *The German Law of Torts*, p. 11. Note the defender might still have to make equitable compensation to the extent his supervisor is not compelled to indemnify (para. 832) providing it does not leave the defender without the means of living his normal life (para. 829). Means includes however the availability of insurance. Markesinis, p. 662.

[84] *Graham v. Mackenzie* (1871) 9 M. 798 (I.H.), *per* Lord Justice-Clerk (Moncreiff) at 800.
[85] *Muir's Trs v. Braidwood*, 1958 S.C. 169.
[86] *Jackson v. MacKenzie* (1875) 3 R. 130.
[87] *Grindall v. John Mitchell (Grangemouth) Ltd*, 1984 S.L.T. 335.
[88] *Dickson v. United Dominions Trust Ltd*, 1988 S.L.T. 19.
[89] 1990 S.L.T. 374.
[90] Affirmed 1992 S.C.L.R. 78; 1991 S.L.T. 683.
[91] *Watson, ibid*.
[92] 1998 S.C. 798.

sought a declarator that the debtor's right to solatium in a claim vested in the trustee and that the trustee should receive that sum. The debtor was injured, then sequestrated, then he raised his action and was automatically discharged and he then settled his action. It was held in the First Division that once the action was raised it lost its personal character and vested in the trustee.[93]

So far as insolvent incorporated bodies are concerned it is essential that **2–38** if a liquidator has been appointed the permission of the court is sought to maintain the action. It has been held that where a joint liquidator is being sued in delict there is no need to convene the other liquidator.[94] In terms of the applicable legislation, the actions cannot proceed against the company without the permission of the court.[95] The court which should be approached is the one dealing with the liquidation and not the one where the reparation action is taking or is to take place.[96] The court looks at the matter from the point of view of expediency and the interests of third parties, such as the pursuer, as an important factor.[97] The liquidator can waive any objection.[98] Without leave the action is incompetent.[99]

A receiver has power to bring and defend any action or other legal **2–39** proceedings in the name of and on behalf of the company.[1] In *Miles J Callaghan Ltd v. Glasgow DC*,[2] it was pointed out that the action should be raised in the name of the company with an indication that the receivers were bringing it. The company is the pursuer. A failure to do so led to an action for count reckoning and payment being dismissed.[3]

Assignees

Once it has been accepted, as it has been in Scotland, that a right of action **2–40** vests on the wrong, the right to recover can be assigned *mortis causa* or *inter vivos* subject to the usual rules on assignation.[4] Thus, a victim can settle a claim by selling an assignation to one of several defenders who can then use the assignation to pursue the other defenders.[5] A party without title to sue may acquire such by way of assignation.[6] Care must be taken though to consider the authorities which suggest that a person who has been paid out has nothing to assign—view that is probably incorrect. A full examination of assignation, reviewing the older authorities, took place in *Purden's Curator Bonis v. Boyd*.[7] Two straightforward rules were also therein stated:

---

[93] Under reference to *Watson, ibid.*
[94] *Highland Engineering Ltd v. Anderson*, 1979 S.L.T. 122.
[95] Insolvency Act 1986, s. 130(2).
[96] *Martin v. Port of Manchester Insurance*, 1934 S.C. 143; *Coclas v. Bruce Peebles & Co* (1908) 16 S.L.T. 7; *D.M. Stevenson & Co. v. Radford & Bright Ltd* (1902) 10 S.L.T. 82.
[97] *Coclas, ibid.*
[98] *Hill v. Black*, 1914 S.C. 913.
[99] *Radford & Bright Ltd v. Stevenson* (1904) 6 F. 429.
[1] Insolvency Act 1986, Sched. 2, para. 5.
[2] 1988 S.L.T. 227.
[3] *Ritchie and Redman v. EFT Industrials Ltd*, 1997 S.C.L.R. 955.
[4] *Traill & Sons Ltd v. Actieselskabat Dalbeattie Ltd* (1904) 6 F. 798; *Purden's C.B. v. Boyd*, 1963 S.L.T. 157.
[5] *National Coal Board v. Thomson*, 1959 S.C. 353, at 356; *Esso Petroleum Co Ltd v. Hall Russell & Co. Ltd*, 1988 S.L.T. 874 at 885.
[6] *Nacap v. Moffat Plant*, 1987 S.L.T. 221 at 224.
[7] 1963 S.L.T. 157.

(1) if a person other than an alleged joint-wrongdoer pays a sum to obtain an assignation of the injured person's claims for damages, he can sue for the full sum which the injured person could have recovered; the sum which he paid is irrelevant; and

(2) if the injured person claims and receives compensation from an alleged wrongdoer and then sues a joint-wrongdoer, his action is competent (in the absence of a full discharge which releases the defender)—but as he cannot be allowed to receive compensation twice, the sum which he has already received must be deducted from the damages which would otherwise be payable.[8]

In case of damage to the property of others[9] the issue of assignation is practically very important. An assignation should come before the action is raised to demonstrate the title to sue.[10] In *G.U.S. Property Management Ltd v. Littlewoods Mail Order Stores Ltd*[11] a recent decision of the House of Lords, a building owned by Rest Property Co. Ltd ("Rest") was damaged by building operations being carried out on a neighbouring property. Rest was a wholly-owned subsidiary of a company which transferred its properties to a newly created, wholly-owned subsidiary company—the pursuers. Rest conveyed the building in question to the pursuers for a figure representing its book value. After that Rest assigned to the pursuers all claims competent to them arising out of the building operations. The pursuers raised an action of damages against the neighbouring proprietors and those involved in the building operations. Not unsurprisingly, the Inner House agreed that the action should be dismissed both because of the title to sue having been with Rest and because, the building having been transferred at book value, there was no loss. The House of Lords reversed this decision. As a general rule the owner of a property damaged by delict did not by parting with it to another lose his title or interest to pursue a claim for damages. In this particular case the depreciation in value and the cost of reinstatement of the building were alternative approaches to estimating the damages, the appropriate measure requiring evidence.

Property

2–41 In a way property cases seem the best cases for consideration of title as one can have title to property and this linguistically is linked to title to sue. However, the connection is co-incidental. It is possible to have title to property and no title to sue and vice versa. However, most of the time title to property will offer title to sue. The difficult cases are now really matters of law as for example the economic loss cases discussed below.[12] The same issues arise in relation to heritage.[13] As long ago as *Cowan & Sons v. Duke of Buccleuch*[14] several riparian proprietors of different lands by a river

---

[8] *ibid.* at 160.
[9] See Chap. 10.
[10] *Symington v. Campbell* (1894) 21 R. 434.
[11] 1982 S.L.T. 533.
[12] See Chap. 10. See also *Golden Sea Produce Ltd v. Scottish Nuclear plc*, 1992 S.L.T. 942.
[13] *e.g. Dundee District Co. v. Cook*, 1995 S.C.L.R. 559 and the many cases collected in S. Robinson, *Interdict* (2nd. ed. Butterworths, 1994).
[14] (1876) 4 R. (H.L.) 14.

raised action against several firms of paper manufacturers with works at different sites. They were held entitled to bring such an action. It was competent as the pursuers were jointly interested in preserving the stream from pollution alleged to result from actings of all defenders. The conclusions were for declarator and interdict.[15] It is by no means certain that if the claim had been for damages such a convenient course would have been permitted.

Members of the Public

The whole idea of the plea of title to sue and the requirement of interest is **2–42** to keep members of the public out of the courts in matters that do not concern them. Universal suffrage and the welfare state have brought about a situation towards the end of the twentieth century that there is a perceived wide community of interests, perhaps not obtaining at the time the earlier cases were decided. If the law of delict protects infringement of legal interests, if the rest of the law has come round to recognising wider interests then more people may have title and interest than before in certain cases. Nonetheless, the policy of keeping the courts free to deal with live issues is still strong as can be seen from judicial review cases where the courts are open in principle to many more claimants over many issues including the challenge of government decisions. Yet the courts will not deal in matters that are when they come before the court, academic. *Scottish Old People's Welfare Council*[16] is a good example. The petitioners were challenging the Secretary of State's decision as erroneous in law and *ultra vires*. There was no claim for damages but the possibility of claiming damages exists in Scottish judicial review. In this case the petitioners were considered too remote to challenge the circular. It was however accepted in that case by both sides that members of the public might have title and interest to sue. The problem in this case was that the complaint although sincere and public spirited was against a circular about benefits and nobody had claimed under the circular at that stage.

There are cases where members of the public have been allowed to sue. Encroachment on the land of another is a delict and can be interdicted. This has been done on the basis of an action by an individual member of the public protecting a public right. In *Sanderson v. Lees*[17] a surgeon was entitled to sue even although not a golfer himself, but a member of the club using the links in question, he was a burgess and an inhabitant of the burgh. The magistrates wanted to sell part of the links for building. It was accepted that the public had possession from time immemorial. The basis of the case was not a servitude right but encroachment on possession (as opposed to ownership). Lord Ivory thought that if the magistrates wanted to establish a prior title of ownership they would need to bring a declarator citing all their constituents. There is a constitutional ring to the decision for it is in Curriehill's opinion as much about "a legal right to be protected in the enjoyment of their ancient privileges."[18]

---

[15] The unanimous decision of the Second Division was affirmed in the House of Lords which was reluctant to take a different view as a question of procedure and practice.

[16] 1987 S.L.T. 179–186.

[17] (1859) 22 D. 24.

[18] *ibid*. at 31. See also *Marquis of Bute v. McKirdy and MacMillan*, 1937 S.C. 93; *Cowie v. SRC*, 1985 S.L.T. 333; *Love-Lee v. Cameron of Lochiel*, 1991 S.C.L.R. (Sh. Ct) 61.

Diplomats and Visiting Forces

2–43 The Diplomatic Privileges Act 1964 implementing the Vienna convention on Diplomatic Relations 1961 protects a number of parties from actions. Immunity is conferred by agreement. The United Kingdom must have approved the individual. The head of mission and diplomats are generally immune,[19] but not in respect of their own houses, private succession matters or personal, professional or commercial activity. Administrative and technical staff are immune but not for acts outside the course of their duties. Service staff are immune in respect of acts carried out in the course of their duties. Families are protected in the same way.[20] There are detailed rules as to the duration of the protection.[21] The protection can be expressly waived.[22] A protected person who raises an action is not immune from a counterclaim.[23]

The State Immunity Act 1978 provides that the Diplomatic Privileges Act 1964 applies to Heads of State, members of their family forming their households and their private servants. Foreign States have general immunity including from defamation but are not immune from actions for personal injury, death or damage. Economic loss cases do not obviously fit into this catalogue. Commercial transactions are not protected.[24] Being widely defined it covers financial and professional activities, or many things outside the exercise of sovereign authority.[25] The extent of the immunity of a Head of State was litigated under English law in *R. v. Bow Street Metropolitan Stipendiary Magistrate, ex parte Pinochet Ugarte (No. 3)*.[26] It was sought to extradite a former Head of State for various crimes allegedly committed when he was in power. At the time of the proceedings he was in the United Kingdom for medical treatment. It was held that the former head of state could be extradited in respect of a limited number of charges. He was entitled to immunity in respect of charges of murder and conspiracy to murder but it was permissible to extradite in respect of torture after the date when the head of state lost his immunity.

Foreign states are liable as occupiers in respect of heritage unless the case relates to the embassy or similar property. Section 13 (6) of the Act provides, *inter alia*, (as respects Scotland): "(b) the property of a State shall not be subject to any diligence for enforcing a judgment or order of a court or a decree arbitral or, in an action in rem, to arrestment or sale". This was litigated in *Forth Tugs Ltd v. Wilmington Trust Co.*[27] before the First Division. The claim was one of salvage but was a personal claim as would be a reparation plea. The salvors raised an action against, among others, the United States of America for those salvage services. The pursuers claimed jurisdiction on the basis, *inter alia*, of the United States of

---

[19] Art. 31(1).
[20] Art. 37(1)(2).
[21] Art. 39.
[22] Art. 32(1) and (2).
[23] Art. 32(3).
[24] s. 3.
[25] s. 3(3).
[26] [1999] T.L.R. 222.
[27] 1987 S.L.T. 153, reviewing the authorities.

America's admitted ownership of heritable property in Edinburgh—the Consulate General. The USA argued that heritable property in Scotland belonging to a sovereign state which was used for purposes other than commercial purposes could not be attached in an attempt to enforce a judgment against that foreign state, by reason of s. 13(6)(b), and the state was accordingly not subject to the jurisdiction of the Court of Session. It was held that the court did have jurisdiction and it was not necessary that the court need be satisfied that any decree would be effective. There is no general immunity in relation to patents.[28] There are detailed rules on separate entities such as news agencies or tourist agencies or airlines and the like. One such issue has been litigated in Scotland. In *Coreck Maritime GmbH v. Sevrybokholodflot*[29] it was held that the defenders, (i) having undergone the process of privatisation to the extent that there were private stockholders holding a majority of the stock in the company; (ii) being a commercial company with its own legal personality intended to be controlled by a board of directors; and (iii) substantially free of government control and exercising no governmental functions, could not be regarded as an organ of the Russian Federation. Immunity may be waived.[30]

The Immunity of Armed Forces of foreign states is covered by the Visiting Forces Act 1952 creating a general immunity in their favour.

---

[28] s. 7.
[29] 1994 S.L.T. 893.
[30] s. 2.

CHAPTER 3

VICARIOUS LIABILITY

Introduction

The basic rule of the law is *culpa tenet suos auctores*.[1] So in *Grieve v. Brown*[2] **3–1** where there was a debate as to whether liability should fall on a contractor employed by the owner of a house or the occupier, the maxim was a guide to decision:

> "An employer may in certain circumstances be liable for the fault of an independent contractor, but the rule is not universal or so clear as in the case of the servant acting within the scope of his authority. But in my view, whether the employer be liable or not, the independent liability of the contractor to the person injured for the consequence of his negligence appear to me to be a *fortiori* of that of the servant. *Culpa tenet suos auctores*."[3]

To an extent the maxim begs the question of who is really responsible for the harm.[4] The doctrine is well established in Scots law.[5] In *Baird v. Hamilton*[6] the doctrine was accepted but nonetheless it was considered from various points of view. Baird entrusted the running of his horse and cart filled with dung leaving Paisley to a lad of seventeen or eighteen. The lad was not an unfit person and had not previously caused harm. Unfortunately he allowed the cart to run down the defender's daughter. He was not at the horse's head but straggling along beside it. The pursuer pled *culpa tenet suos auctores* and pointed out there was no *culpa*. Lord

---

[1] Fault binds (only?) its originator.

[2] 1926 S.L.T. 498.

[3] *ibid.*, *per* Lord Sands at 500.

[4] Stair says "He doth that causeth do" Stair I,ix,5: speaking of delinquence by command. In modern vicarious liability there is usually no command as such. There are early cases in 1590 and 1623 which foreshadow the doctrine: Walker, *History*, III, p. 695 Bankton after discussing noxal surrender says: "By the present custom, if damage is done by children in family, or servants, in the offices or business in which they are employed, their father or master is liable to repair it; but otherwise, the children or servants are only answerable themselves for the damage done, without the parent's or master's authority; and if with it, the parent or master only, and not the children or servants who were bound to obey." Bankton I,x,47. This is not the same as the modern doctrine which covers unauthorised acts. Not only that, the servant or employee remains liable under the modern doctrine: *Lister v. Romford Ice & Cold Storage Co.* [1957] 1 All E.R. 125. See also G. Junor, "The Employer Solicitor's Right of Relief?", 1998 S.L.T. (News) 275.

[5] See "the fox must pay his own skin." *Wood v. Fullerton* (1710) Mor. 13960. For a discussion of the rationale and theory of the doctrine see G. MacCormack, "*Culpa Tenet Suos Auctores*: The Application of a Principle in Scots Law", 1973 J.R. 69.

[6] (1826) 4 S. 790.

Robertson found liability in policy, the modern justification for the rule: "It is necessary for the safety of the lieges that masters should be bound to employ servants of such character as will conduct their carts with safety to the public."[7] He also mentioned the necessary refinement—that the damage must be done "in performance of some work committed to him by the master."[8] The doctrine developed in the shadow of another doctrine, common employment,[9] and so older cases should be regarded with considerable caution. Common employment was abolished by the Law Reform (Personal Injuries) Act 1948.

Independent Contractors

3–2 It is useful to begin with this type of case which can be seen as being at the end of a spectrum of cases. It is from consideration of the case of the independent contractor that cases of the existence of vicarious liability are sometimes consciously or sub-consciously judged. In *D.& F. Estates Ltd v. Church Commissioners*[10] Lord Bridge said[11]: "It is trite law that the employer of an independent contractor is, in general, not liable for the negligence or other tort committed by the contractor in the course of the execution of the work."[12] On the principle *culpa tenet suos auctores*, the example given by Lord President McNeil in *Mackenzie v. Goldie*[13] holds if a contractor points out to a proprietor that work instructed may cause damage and the proprietor insists that he goes ahead, the contractor who does so may also be liable. In another often cited case *Woolfson v. Forrester*,[14] it was held that an owner was not liable to a tenant whose house was flooded by water getting into a pipe installed by plumbers; they were independent contractors. Simply labelling a person an independent contractor is unlikely to avoid vicarious liability.[15] There are exceptional cases where there appears to be vicarious liability but these are essentially cases where the defender is liable for his own breach of duty the most obvious case being where someone puts, "an improper person to do some act which, if done by an improper person is likely to result in mischief."[16] The exceptional cases are cases of non-delegable duties where, in fact, the duty is still that of the defender and cannot be passed on to another.

---

[7] (1826) 4 S. 790 at 799.

[8] *ibid.*, *per* Lord Justice-Clerk (Boyle) at 800 who also noted the public policy point: "I hope that our decision will lead to much greater caution on the part of owners of carts and carriages in the choice of those to whom they instruct them." Lord Pitmilly focused on the fact that the workman was "doing an act which he was specifically hired and employed by his master to perform", at 799. Lord Alloway refers to the law of Europe for support and finds the same principle applicable in case of coach passengers and the liability of ship owners for damage to other vessels caused by their crews, at 800.

[9] From the decision in *Bartonshill Coal Co. v. Reid* (1858) 3 Macq. 266.

[10] [1988] 3 W.L.R. 368.

[11] *ibid.* at 387.

[12] A similar expression of opinion can be found in *Stephen v. Thurso Police Commissioners* (1876) 3 R. 535 at 538.

[13] (1866) 4 M. 277.

[14] 1910 S.C. 675.

[15] *Fergusson v. Davidson Partners (Contracts) Ltd* [1976] 1 W.L.R. 1213.

[16] *Woolfson v. Forrester*, 1910 S.C. 675.

Exceptional Cases

Employees

The most common is the employer's duty of care for his workman.[17] While **3–3** on one view the case of *Davie v. New Merton Mills*[18] may have inclined against this view on one reading, the House of Lords has confirmed the non-delegable nature of the duty in an English appeal.[19]

Statutory Duties

One of the leading Scots cases is *Stephen v. Thurso Police Commissioners*.[20] **3–4** The pursuer was injured when he fell into a heap of rubbish which was unfenced and unlit after nightfall. The defenders responded that they had contracted out street cleaning powers to a third party who was liable. It was held that the terms of the contract were such that defenders had complete control over execution of operations and remained liable. The third party was not an independent contractor. The defenders were liable under the rule *qui facit per alium facit per se*.[21] The sub-contract did not lay a duty to fence and light obstructions on the third party. That obligation remained with defenders.[22] Similarly, in *MacMillan v. Wimpey Offshore Engineers and Contractors*[23] where the pursuer sustained a head injury from an employee and it was held that a statutory duty can avoid the need for vicarious liability to be established. The regulation applicable in the case[24] imposed a direct duty and so it was it unnecessary to aver and prove the course of employment.

Dangerous Operations

There are not all that many Scots cases but the idea is recognised.[25] In **3–5** *Anderson v. Brady and Ross Ltd*[26] it was held that the employer of independent contractors could not escape liability when workmen were killed during demolition operations. *Anderson* was distinguished, it is submitted with justification, in *McKenzie v. Peter McAinsh Ltd*[27] in which a man fell off a tree while employed by timber merchants. His case against the forestry commission was dismissed. The danger or hazard arose from the particular operation itself and not from the basic operation of cutting timber. In another case, work in a house which involved creating a hole by lifting floorboards was not inherently hazardous.[28] The law of nuisance must

---

[17] See Chap. 14.

[18] [1959] A.C. 604.

[19] *McDermid v. Nash Dredging* [1987] 3 W.L.R. 212.

[20] (1876) 3 R. 535.

[21] Where one does a thing through the instrumentality of another he is held as having done it himself.

[22] *Per* Lord Justice-Clerk (Moncrieff) at 538–9.

[23] 1991 S.L.T. 515.

[24] Mineral Workings (Offshore Installations) Act 1971.

[25] *Paterson v. Lindsay* (1885) 13 R. 261 is a good example of a dangerous operation—blasting—but it is one of ordinary vicarious liability for a servant. On appeal in the sheriff court *Rylands v. Fletcher* was in the mind of the court. The Inner House decided on fault.

[26] 1964 S.L.T. (Notes) 11.

[27] 1975 S.L.T. (Notes) 34.

[28] *Grieve v. Brown*, 1926 S.L.T. 498. See also *Hamilton v. Wahla*, 1999 G.W.D. 25–1217, in which a tenant who instructed overtly hazardous works was liable to his neighbours for property damage.

not be forgotten and in a nuisance case the neighbouring proprietor will be liable even although he had the work done by a sub-contractor. This is a case of primary liability rather than vicarious liability albeit it looks very much like it.[29]

Employees

3–6 The basic position at the time of writing is that there is vicarious liability on grounds of policy for persons said to be employees for the purposes of the doctrine. The law of contract distinguishes between the independent contractor and other persons. Not every person calling himself an employee is the type of person to whom vicarious liability may be attracted. It is a matter of fact and degree. *Short v. J. & W. Henderson,*[30] is often cited, but it is a Workman's Compensation Act case. It was accepted that the following factors were right for consideration, but that conditions even then were rendering them suspect: "(a) the master's power of selection of his servant; (b) the payment of wages or other remuneration; (c) the master's right to control the method of doing the work; and (d) the master's right of suspension or dismissal".[31] Indicators of employment in other statutory contexts are not decisive but may be of relevance.[32] It has been held that although often facts and circumstances have to be known for a legal decision to be taken, as the matter is essentially a matter of law, where the case can be decided on documentary evidence it ought to be.[33]

Skilled Employees

3–7 Until the middle of the twentieth century, the fact that doctors and nurses, to take prominent examples of a type of case, exercised professions, although paid wages, mitigated against their employers being held liable. If the employer cannot understand what is being done he can hardly have instructed the wrongdoer. In *Reidford v. Magistrates of Aberdeen*[34] an action against managers of a hospital complaining of the failure of nurses to administer prescribed medicines and to make use of laxatives was held irrelevant by the sheriff, with whom the Inner House agreed. Lord President Clyde based his opinion on the distinction between the Roman categories of *locatio operis* and *locatio operarum*. The nurses were comparable to other professional persons and not subject to the order of their employers, the defenders, who were not liable.[35] With the passage of time

---

[29] See *Cameron v. Fraser* (1881) 9 R. 26.

[30] 1946 S.C. (H.L.) 24.

[31] *ibid. per* Lord Thankerton at 33.

[32] *e.g. O'Kelly v. Trusthouse Forte plc* [1984] Q.B. 90; *Nethermere (St. Neots) Ltd v. Taverna* [1984] I.C.R. 612; *Mcleod v. Hellyer Bros. Ltd* [1987] I.R.L.R. 232. See *Harvey on Industrial Relations and Employment Law* for up to date examples. English law has canvassed an organisation or integration test and a multiple approach: see Clerk and Lindsell, paras 5–08— 5–10.

[33] *Davies v. Presbyterian Church* [1986] 1 W.L.R. 323, an English employment law case which held that on the documents a minister was not employed by his church under a contract of service.

[34] 1933 S.L.T. 155.

[35] *Dow v. McNeill*, 1925 S.C. 50 was referred to with approval. *Lavelle v. Glasgow Royal Infirmary*, 1932 S.C. 245 and 1931 S.C.(H.L.) 34 was considered. *Reidford* itself was reconsidered in the leading case of *Macdonald* discussed below.

vicarious liability has become seen as a policy of applying responsibility to those whose activity tends to cause harm. On one theory the hospital has a non-delegable duty to the patients. That theory appears in a case which is also authority for holding a health board liable. In *Reid v. Greater Glasgow Health Board*,[36] a mental patient sued for injuries sustained in an abortive suicide attempt. She was successful in desiderating that windows such as the one she jumped through should have been secured. It was held the risk was a foreseeable one and the precaution necessary was a simple one that would not disrupt the hospital. There had been a previous incident both at the locus and elsewhere. The nurse on duty explained in evidence that she thought that the risk was a possible one and that the precaution could be taken. This looks like a case not of vicarious liability for the nurses' omissions but for the failure of the authority to take reasonable precautions.[37]

It is important to check as at the date of the episode complained of whether a health board or a hospital trust was in control. Most NHS hospital staff are covered by Crown indemnity meaning that the trust or health board is liable.[38] With aspects of health becoming "privatised" it is important to be sure that a vicarious liability situation is actually in point. This will not be the case necessarily with private medical care and the individual wrongdoers should be sued. It is significant that the case establishing liability for doctors and hospital staff, *Macdonald v. Glasgow Western Hospitals*,[39] proceeded not by way of over-ruling previous contrary authorities, but by declaring them to be outmoded by a fundamentally different situation.[40] They may, therefore, be taken to stand and the thinking of Lord President Cooper—that the authorities in this regard may be treated as outmoded due to changes in circumstances of national health care can be applied to *Macdonald* itself. As private medical care is usually contracted for, cases may well turn around the contracts in question in the first instance. While the NHS was in a sense underwritten by the government, private medical concerns may or may not be subject to regulations governing their creditworthiness and checks should be made or steps taken to ensure that a final judgment will be realisable. Most hospital doctors are members of friendly societies which operate like, but are not insurance companies.[41] Vicarious liability was accepted by a hospital board for one of its hospital doctors in *Kay's Tutor v. Ayrshire and Arran Health Board*.[42] The vicarious liability of a health board for a health visitor was allowed to

---

[36] 1976 S.L.T. (Notes) 33.

[37] See also the unusual case decided by the Inner House, *Sorman v. Royal Scottish National Institution*, 1961 S.L.T. 217; and *Hunter v. Magistrates of Glasgow*, 1969 S.L.T. (Notes) 35 in which it was sought to make a registrar liable but again the pursuer directed her case against the hospital board as well as the city as being vicariously liable for the midwives involved. The report is only on the fundamental relevancy of the case against the doctor and is of no wide significance.

[38] NHS Circular 1989 (PCS/32).

[39] 1954 S.L.T. 226.

[40] *ibid., per* Lord President Cooper at 235. The main cases are *Lavelle v. Glasgow Royal Infirmary*, 1932 S.L.T. 179 and *Reidford v. Magistrates of Aberdeen*, 1932 S.L.T. 179.

[41] *MDU Ltd v. Dept. of Trade*, [1979] 2 W.L.R. 686. The same applies to dentists; see generally, R.H. Dickson, *Medical and Dental Negligence* (T & T Clark, 1997).

[42] 1987 S.L.T. (H.L.) 577.

proceed to a proof before answer and the position of general medical practitioners was canvasseed in *Bonthrone v. Secretary of State for Scotland*[43]:

> "It was accepted on behalf of the pursuers that, prior to the coming into force of the 1972 Act, it would not have been possible to maintain that a hospital board, the predecessor of the health board, was vicariously liable for the actings of a general medical practitioner, albeit it was so liable for the actings of a doctor employed in a hospital. In my opinion the law on the matter is correctly stated in Martin on *The Law Relating to Medical Practice* at p. 100 to the effect that, while the Secretary of State is responsible through his agents for the treatment of the National Health Service patients in hospital, he is not responsible for their treatment by general medical practitioners for whom arrangements have been made to provide general medical services under s. 34 of the Act of 1947."[44]

3–8 There are not that many cases on nurses. *Dow v. McNeil*[45] was a claim by a nurse for compensation for injury sustained while looking after a child. The award was made after an arbitration under the Workmen's Compensation Act 1906 on the basis that the nurse was a "workman" within the meaning of section 13. In *Skinner v. Glasgow Corporation*[46] it was admitted that the defenders were responsible for a teacher in their employ. Many of the cases collected under solicitors' negligence in fact involve the negligence of solicitors working for other solicitors as is the case in relation to surveyors and accountants.[47]

Scope of the Employment

3–9 Assuming the wrongdoer to fall within the category of "employee", the acts or omissions must have been carried out within the scope of the employment. A leading statement of the law is the dictum of *Kirby v. National Coal Board*.[48] There the Lord President, following *Goh Choon Seng v. Lee Kim Soo*[49] and *Canadian Pacific Railway Company v. Lockhart*,[50] said:

> "Vicarious responsibility for the act of a servant will only attach to the master if the act of the servant is done within the scope of the employment. It is probably not possible, and it is certainly inadvisable, to endeavour to lay down an exhaustive definition of what falls within the scope of the employment. Each case must depend to a considerable extent on its particular facts. But, in the decisions, four different types of situation have been envisaged as guides to the solution of this problem. In the first place, if the master actually authorised the particular act, he

---

[43] 1987 S.L.T. 34.
[44] *ibid.*, at 43–44.
[45] 1924 S.L.T. 767.
[46] 1961 S.L.T. 130.
[47] See generally the cases in Chap. 12.
[48] 1958 S.C. 514.
[49] [1925] A.C. 550.
[50] [1942] A.C. 591.

is clearly liable for it. Secondly, where the workman does some work which he is appointed to do, but does it in a way which his master has not authorised, and would not have authorised had he known of it, the master is nevertheless still responsible for the servant's act is still within the scope of his employment. On the other hand, in the third place, if the servant is employed only to do a particular work or a particular class of work, and he does something outside the scope of that work, the master is not responsible."[51]

More recently there is apparent a marked reluctance to comment on what may or may not fall within this phrase prior to hearing the facts: "This leaves the question as to whether the pursuers have averred sufficient to show that Deeney was acting within the scope of his employment. Many words have been written in attempting to delimit the meaning of that phrase and we do not propose to add to the collection."[52] At a practical level courts have sometimes taken a strict view of what a pursuer must aver to maintain a vicarious liability case. In *McGowan v. Mein*[53] the deceased was run over by a vehicle driven by the first defender. The second defenders argued successfully that an averment that the act was in the course of the employment was not sufficient where they also averred that the workman was allowed to use the van to and from work and that the accident happened when the driver was driving home from work but failed to say that the worker was obliged to use the car. This seems unnecessarily restrictive. A proof before answer is more likely to be the proper course.[54] In *Jamieson v. Adamant Stone and Paving Co. Ltd*[55] the pursuer was injured by falling through planking—a case of vicarious liability for a workman for the actings of another workman. Lord Stott said: "If Watt (the fellow workman) had thought about it he should have realised that the planking could be unsafe for the pursuer as for himself and in failing to take any action to check the pursuer from going out on the planking he must, I think, be regarded as having been in breach of his duty of care, care which was owed by him to his company's employee."[56] As might be expected there have been a number of Scottish cases on this essentially factual enquiry. The following is a treatment of a number of cases illustrating the applicability of the idea and at the same time answering a number of practical questions.

Deviation from allocated task

In *Thomson v. British Steel Corporation*[57] the issue was the question of **3–10** liability where the worker is not driving as a driver and is indeed not driving as part of his daily tasks. Three co-workers were killed in a car accident.

---

[51] *Kirby v. National Coal Board*, at 532.

[52] *ibid., per* Lord Sutherland expressing the opinion of the Court in *Taylor v. City of Glasgow District Council*, 1997 Rep.L.R. 17 at para. 4–08.

[53] 1975 S.L.T. (Sh. Ct) 10.

[54] *e.g. Roberts v. Matthew Logan*, 1965 S.L.T. (Notes) 93; and see the distinction in *R.J. McLeod (Contractors) Ltd v. SSEB*, 1982 S.L.T. 274 discussed below at para. 3–11.

[55] 1970 S.L.T. (Notes) 41.

[56] *ibid.* at 43.

[57] 1977 S.L.T. 26.

The representative of one passenger sued the employers of the driver. The employees were employed at three centres: A, B and C. The men normally worked at A. They lived close to A. The accident happened when the employees were travelling from working at B back to A. This was allowed by the employers. In particular, the employers allowed the employees to use their own cars to move around especially when resident at the other centres. The employers were held to be vicariously liable. The case is valuable for Lord Maxwell's review of the authorities (mainly English) and the themes in the cases. The fact that the passengers were fellow employees was a factor to be taken into account, but not nearly decisive. (There may be other cases where that fact carries greater weight). In this case as the journey started on a Friday and the employees were not going to work at A, it was fairly argued that in this case they were just going home. The Lord Ordinary was tempted to make a distinction between the outward journey and the return journey but considered that in fact the opposite conclusion was correct—if the employer sent the man out then he was responsible for the journey back. It was accepted that in general a journey to work is not within the scope of the employment unless the mode of travel is set by the employer.

3–11   In *Williams v. A. & W. Hemphill Ltd*,[58] the pursuer was returning to Glasgow from a Boys' Brigade camp at Benderloch, Argyll, in a lorry which had been hired from the defenders. The lorry had been hired by the Boys' Brigade company, of which the pursuer was a member. It was being driven by the defenders' employee, Ross. On the same day a company of Girl Guides, who had also been camping at Benderloch, were returning to Dollar by train. The shortest route from Benderloch to Glasgow was by Loch Lomond, but at the request of some of the boys on the defenders' lorry, Ross drove the lorry to Stirling station in order that the boys from the Boys' Brigade might meet girls from the Girl Guides at those places. In Stirling, after a further request from the boys, Ross agreed to drive the lorry to Dollar in order that the boys might again meet the girls. At a bend in the road near Dollar the lorry swerved off the road and crashed into a field.

> "His duty was, by implication, to drive by the most direct route. When the accident happened, he had not yet completed his overall duty of driving the boys and baggage to Glasgow, but he was on a part of the road where he would not have been if he had carried out his orders. He should not have gone anywhere near the place of the accident, and his employers, had they been asked, would certainly not have permitted him to go there. Was he still acting within the scope of his employment so as to make his employers vicariously liable for his negligence? It is a question of fact and degree in each case whether the deviation is sufficiently detached from the master's business, to constitute a frolic of the servant unconnected with the enterprise for which he was employed ... Had the driver in the present case been driving a lorry which was empty or contained nothing of real importance, I think that so substantial a deviation might well have constituted a frolic of his own. The

---

[58] 1966 S.C. (H.L.) 31.

presence of passengers, however, whom the servant is charged qua servant to drive to their ultimate destination makes it impossible (at all events, provided that they are not all parties to the plans for deviation) to say that the deviation is entirely for the servant's purposes. Their presence and transport is a dominant purpose of the authorised journey, and, although they are transported deviously, continues to play an essential part . . . The more dominant are the current obligations of the master's business in connection with the lorry, the less weight is to be attached to disobedient navigational extravagances of the servant . . . In the present case the defenders remained liable, in spite of the deviation, for their driver's negligence."[59]

That this case has set down the approach to these problems is demonstrated by a consideration of the later case *Angus v. Glasgow Corporation*[60] in which the Inner House held that a driver who went home to pick up his spare spectacles was acting in the course of his employment. However, this case is more interesting because in the Outer House the explanation about the glasses had been rejected. In the Inner House Lord Emslie indicated that even if it had been a case of the driver going home to dodge a bit more work he would have been in the course of his employment.[61] Lord Cameron agreed.[62] In the later case of *R. J. McLeod (Contractors) Ltd v. SSEB*,[63] a case of property damage rather than personal injury and thus void of any suspicion of sympathy for widows and orphans, the employers were held to be vicariously liable where their driver had been authorised to take the vehicle home, but had taken a fellow worker home and then visited his mother in law. If he had gone home first Lord Wylie would have held that he was outwith the scope. This case should be seen close to the border because the employee came close to admitting and the Lord Ordinary found that the visit to the mother in law was unauthorised. It is most likely to be the fact that the employers were happy for the van to go to the employee's home which resulted in their being held vicariously liable. In a case where an army driver waiting to pick up an army van drove off for some food at a cafe, his deviation was not exclusively on his own business and so the army were vicariously liable.[64]

---

[59] 1966 S.C. (H.L.) 31, *per* Lord Pearce at 44–46.

[60] 1977 S.L.T. 206.

[61] *ibid*. at 214.

[62] *ibid*. at 218. However, Lord Avonside was less enthusiastic about *Williams*, saying at 219: "The decision of the House of Lords in the Scottish case of *Williams v. A. & W. Hempill Ltd*, is relevant to the present case and I see no point in exploring earlier Scottish or English cases. That decision is to my mind, an extraordinary decision, but one to which I must pay conventional deference. . . the question of the effect of the deviation seems to be that each case depends for solution on its own facts and that it is a question of fact and degree in any case whether a deviation was sufficiently detached from the employer's business to constitute a 'frolic' of the servant unconnected with the enterprise for which he was employed. . . each case must be viewed on its own facts." See also Lord Avonside's general approach in the earlier case of *Roberts v. Matthew Logan*, 1966 S.L.T. 77. He was not alone at the time: see Professor Walker's book review, 1967 S.L.T. (News) 171: "a specimen of a hard case making bad law. But this again is arguable."

[63] 1982 S.L.T. 274.

[64] *Stewart's (Edinburgh) Holdings Ltd v. Lord Advocate*, 1966 S.L.T. (Sh. Ct) 86.

Deliberately harmful conduct

3–12 The next few cases illustrate the applicability of the concept of vicarious liability to more deliberate conduct by employees. The difficulty is that few employers permit deliberately harmful acts and so it is almost always going to be the case that the act is outwith the precise rules of the employment. The scope of the employment is wider. In *Bell v. Blackwood Morton & Sons Ltd,*[65] the Inner House upheld a decision finding vicarious liability where a worker jostled another in the rush down the only staircase to get home. The employers had expressly prohibited rushing. The defenders argued specifically that the scope of employment was restricted to situations in which the servant was doing something he was employed to do. Lord President Clyde considered that proposition unwarranted by authority and contrary to principle. Lord Sorn related the fact that the employer owed a duty of care to the employee at the time in delict as relevant to the separate vicarious liability question. In *Peden v. Strathclyde Regional Council*[66] the pursuer, an employee of the defenders, wanted to use the toilet. Another employee resisted saying the toilet was locked. There was a struggle over the keys. The other employee recovered the keys but partly to cover her own position with her employers. It was argued that the case was irrelevant as it had not been specified what duty the employee was carrying out and in any event the employee was acting for her own good. A proof before answer was allowed but no jury trial. In *Power v. Central SMT*[67] the pursuer was injured getting off a bus. Motion for a new trial was granted where the Lord Ordinary had directed the jury that if they found that the conductress had rung the bell too soon to get the bus to move deliberately out of spite towards the pursuer, then the defenders were liable. The pursuer's argument was that the quarrel that caused the conductress's animosity arose out of a matter intrinsic to the employment, namely whether the pursuer had a valid ticket. However, the proposition that a master is liable for any act of his servant done while engaged at his work even if this act is wrongful or it may be criminal was rejected.[68]

3–13   Turning to fraud, in England cases of fraud by an employee are treated differently from other cases. In *Generale Bank v. Export Credit Guarantee Department*[69] it was held in the Court of Appeal that an employer was not liable for the deceit and fraud of an employee where the acts were not within his actual or ostensible authority.[70] Lord Johnston at first instance in *Taylor v. City of Glasgow*[71] reviewed the authorities. The pursuers were purchasers of houses from a development company. They said that they entered into their contracts relying on completion certificates and building warrants. However, they said that these were fraudulently issued by a

---

[65] 1960 S.L.T. 145.
[66] 1995 G.W.D. 4–202.
[67] 1949 S.L.T. 302.
[68] *per* Lord President Cooper at 303. *Lloyd v. Grace Smith & Co* [1912] A.C. 716 was distinguished.
[69] [1997] T.L.R. 441.
[70] It was accepted in this English case that the doctrine of vicarious liability applies differently in fraud as opposed to negligence and trespass: *Armagas Ltd v. Mundogas* [1986] A.C. 717.
[71] 1996 Rep. L.R. 69.

council employee. It was argued there could not be liability where the employee exceeded his authority. Lord Johnson considered various prior authorities although there was not fundamental review stretching back into history.[72] He considered *Lloyd* to be clear and authoritative and that it had been accepted, although not necessarily, as the law of Scotland in *Central Motors*. He was impressed by the highly persuasive decision in *Uxbridge Permanent*. But most of all he was impressed by a passage in the speech of the Scots Lord of Appeal Lord Keith in *Armagas*:

"At the end of the day the question is whether the circumstances under which a servant has made the fraudulent representation which has caused loss to an innocent third party contracting with him are such as to make it just for the employer to bear the loss. Such circumstances exist where the employer by words or conduct has induced the injured party to believe the servant was acting in lawful course of the employer's business. They do not exist where such belief although it is present, has been brought about through misguided reliance of the servant himself, when the servant is not authorised to do what he is purported to do when what he is purporting to do, is not within the class of acts that an employee in his position is usually authorised to do and when the employer has done nothing to represent that he is authorised to do it."[73]

From this Lord Johnson considered his task to be "to ascertain the general scope of the powers and duties conferred on the employee by the employer within his terms of employment such as are represented as such to the world and secondly, whether what is actually done, falls under that umbrella albeit an obvious excess of authority occurs when a criminal act is perpetrated."[74] The defenders reclaimed.[75] Lord Sutherland, giving the opinion of the court stated that since *Lloyd* it had not been necessary to show that the employer received any benefit from the fraud, and that since *Uxbridge Permanent Building Society v. Pickard*[76] it has not been necessary to show that the employers and the defrauded party have been in some contractual relationship.[77] That much having been accepted, the case was argued very subtly on the difference and meaning of actual and ostensible authority in delict. If the case was based on ostensible authority the fact that the developers were interposed between the alleged fraudster and the pursuers might have made a difference—if you do not see someone it is hard to show them something. The pursuers' case was "perilled" on actual authority. Upon that matter the facts were important as to whether issuing certificates was his job or whether the alleged fraudster was a mere cog down the line of authority. This, the Court decided, was a matter of proof before answer not safely decided upon averment.[78] Finally, in regard to this

---

[72] *Lloyd v. Grace Smith & Co, cit. supra; Armagas, cit. supra; Central Motors (Glasgow) Ltd. v. Cessnock Garage Motor Co.*, 1925 S.C. 796.
[73] *Armagas Ltd* [1986] A.C. 717 at 782.
[74] 1996 Rep. L.R. 69 at 71.
[75] *Taylor v. City of Glasgow*, 1997 Rep. L.R. 17.
[76] [1939] 2 K.B. 248.
[77] *Taylor v. City of Glasgow*, at para. 4–07.
[78] *ibid.*

case, it recognises the concept familiar to criminal practitioners of the fraudulent scheme. If it turned out to be the case that the council employee and the developers were "in it together", then the fact that the developers "passed on" the fraud was irrelevant so far as constituting a *novus causa interveniens*.

In *Ward v. Scotrail Railways Ltd*[79] it was held that the employers could not be vicariously liable for alleged sexual harassment by one employee of another.

3–14   An employer can be liable vicariously liable in verbal injury for the statements of an employee.[80] The issue was canvassed in the House of Lords, reversing the decision of the Inner House, in *Riddell v. Corporation of Glasgow*.[81] The pursuer was the wife of a Glasgow ratepayer who sued for slander by a tax collector employed by the defenders to collect police assessments. She alleged the collector had stated that a receipt produced by the ratepayer was forged. The defenders were not liable because it was no part of the collector's duty to explain opinions as to the genuineness or falsity of any receipt. The level of his post was relatively humble. It was not within the scope of his authority to communicate any opinion on behalf of the defenders.[82] Lord Shaw of Dunfermline thought that to allow this case would undermine the maxim *qui facit per alium facit per se*.[83] In *Craig v. Inveresk Paper Merchants Ltd*,[84] the pursuer alleged that the defenders' representatives were saying that the pursuer was going out of business and that customers should buy from the defenders. It was held after proof that this conduct did occur but that vicarious liability could not be brought home to the employer. It was accepted they were in the course of their employment when they committed the verbal injuries in the sense that the representatives were entitled to speak to the customers and solicit custom. It may be that Lord Leechman demanded too much by saying that the pursuer had to prove an authority conferred to discuss rival businesses.

*Multiple Employers—***Pro hac vice**[85]

3–15 Where an employee is hired by one employer, the primary employer, and working to the direction of another, the secondary employer, questions arise as to which of the two is liable for the wrongdoing. This is difficult in law and in practice. It is difficult in law because the very basis of vicarious liability has not been ultimately defined. It is difficult in fact because workmen just go and do their work for whoever tells them what needs done—they are not always sure who is in control. When there is an accident there is often a reluctance among the insurers representing the employers to accept full responsibility. *Moir v. Wide Arc Services Ltd*[86] is a particularly clear and typical case. Moir was employed by Wiggins Teape (UK) Plc. He and a fellow employee Morris helped Gabriel, an employee of the

---

[79] 1999 S.C. 255.
[80] *Ellis v. National Free Labour Association* (1905) 7 F. 629.
[81] 1911 1 S.L.T. 341; Inner House 1910 1 S.L.T. 358.
[82] *ibid., per* Lord Chancellor at 342.
[83] *ibid.* at 343.
[84] 1970 S.L.T. (Notes) 50.
[85] For this turn (job).
[86] 1987 S.L.T. 495.

defenders Wide Arc, in an operation in which, as a result of the fault of Gabriel, the pursuer was injured. The work took place on the premises of Wiggins Teape. It was held that the defenders were liable for their employee and that he had not been transferred *pro hac vice*. The general rule against transfer was upheld. The great English case often relied on is *Mersey Docks and Harbour Board v. Coggins and Griffith (Liverpool) Ltd.*[87] So well established is the rule that a case can be dismissed on relevancy as in *Kerr v. Hailes (Plant) Ltd.*[88] In this case the pursuer sued his own employers as being vicariously liable for a crane driver on hire with his plant from another company. He failed, even although the contract between the employer and the plant company made it clear that the driver was to be the employee of the pursuer's employer. So far as the Lord Ordinary (Wylie) was concerned the absence of a power over the crane driver's use of the controls meant that the onus against transfer could not apply. The case is probably correct only because the accident happened because of the use of the controls rather than direction by the main employer. A general averment that a crane and its driver were at all material times under the management and control of the defenders has been held irrelevant.[89] Nonetheless it is submitted that only the most extreme case could safely be disposed of as a matter of relevancy. In one of the leading modern Scots cases, *Park v. Tractor Shovels*[90] the pursuer alleged that the first defenders were vicariously liable for the negligence of a worker (Hatten) on the basis that they accepted him as a volunteer and by doing so took him into their employment. It was accepted that it was theoretically possible that although Hatten was acting within the scope of his employment with the second defender, he was at the time of this accident in the temporary employment of the first defenders. However, Lord Cowie stated:

"Having stated that possible argument, I have no hesitation in rejecting it. In the present case, in the light of my decision that Hatten was acting within the scope of his employment with the second defender when this accident occurred, he was in my opinion in the same category as a crane driver operating his crane in connection with work being done by the first defenders; that being so the burden of proof of showing that responsibility for his actings shifted from the second defender to the first defenders falls on the pursuer. It is a heavy burden and can only be charged in a quite exceptional circumstances . . . It is quite clear on the facts of the present case that that burden has not been discharged and accordingly in my opinion the responsibility for Hatten's actings remains with the second defender as his general employer . . . Having reached that decision it seems to me that that disposes of any question of joint liability on the part of the defenders based on vicarious responsibilty. In my opinion it is not merely a tenet of the Christian faith that a man cannot serve two masters, but that it applies also to the legal doctrine of vicarious liability."[91]

---

[87] [1947] A.C. 1.
[88] 1974 S.L.T. (Notes) 31.
[89] *Boyle v. Glasgow Corporation*, 1978 S.L.T. (Notes) 77. See also *Kerr, ibid.*
[90] 1980 S.L.T. 94.
[91] *ibid.* at 100–101.

Pro hac vice employment is a difficult matter to establish at proof. In *McAllister v. Oban Transport*[92] proof failed where lorry drivers helped unhook skips and were paid at casual rates for this work by the skip operators and not their own primary employers. There are at least two Scots cases where *pro hac vice* has been established.[93] In *McGregor v. J. S. Duthie & Sons*[94] two passengers in a lorry were injured by the fault of the driver who was in the general employment of a partnership who had contracted to saw timber for a company. By agreement the driver drove a lorry belonging to the company from the site to a railway station when required by the company, and the partnership was reimbursed for his wages by the company. The driver delivered timber on the company's instructions to the station. On his normal route back he stopped as instructed by one of the partners to pick up two passengers, who were expected in due course to become employees of the partnership, on work for the company. At the time of the accident one of the partners was actually sitting beside the driver in the cab of the lorry. The passengers brought actions against the company and the survivor of the partnership claiming damages for the driver's negligence. The sheriff-substitute assoilzied the surviving partner and found that at the time the driver was in the *pro hac vice* employment of the company. The company appealed. The Inner House held that in the very special circumstances the pursuer had discharged the onus of showing that the driver was in the *pro hac vice* employment of the company. In *Sime v. Sutcliffe Catering (Scotland) Ltd*,[95] Lord Caplan found *pro hac vice* employment established in a situation quite often found nowadays, where the catering in the pursuer's normal place of work was being provided by an outside contractor rather than her general employer.

Other Particular Cases

Company Directors

3–16 In *Scobie v. Steele & Wilson Ltd*[96] a pedestrian was injured when he was in collision with a motor vehicle owned by a limited company which, at the time of the accident was being driven by one of the directors of the company. The pedestrian brought an action claiming damages against the company. The company contended that the pursuer had not made a relevant case of vicarious liability inasmuch as the doctrine of vicarious liability applied only in the case of an employee or servant of a company, and a director not being a servant of a company, could not therefore involve the company in vicarious liability: "if it is relevantly averred that a company director is driving a company vehicle with the knowledge and on the authority of the company upon company business, and through his negligent driving is involved in an accident, the company may be made vicariously liable for that negligence. That seems to me commonsense and sound law."[97]

---

[92] 1971 S.L.T. (Notes) 51. *Malley v. L.M.S. Railway Co.*, 1944 S.C. 129 and *Mersey Docks & Harbour Board v. Coggins & Griffith* [1947] A.C. 1 were applied.
[93] This may be more than in England.
[94] 1966 S.L.T. 133.
[95] 1990 S.L.T. 687.
[96] 1963 S.L.T. (Notes) 45.
[97] *ibid., per* Lord Cameron at 45.

That is the alleged vicarious liability of the company for the director. While a director causes the company to do things, directors are not generally liable for the acts of the company because of the concept of corporate personality—the director is the controlling mind rather than instructing.

Police Officers, Procurators Fiscal, assistants and deputes

By statute the chief constable is vicariously liable for his officers, who **3–17** traditionally being officers rather than employees would not have been his responsibility. There are many cases in which liability has been established or accepted. One example is *Wilson v. Chief Constable*[98] in which two officers and the more senior were sued and one, the junior officer was assoilzied. It was admitted that the chief constable was "vicariously liable for the negligent acts and omissions of police officers in the course of their duty."[99]

The officer can be sued as an individual.[1] In *Cropper v. Chief Constable, Dumfries & Galloway*[2] the first defenders argued that under the detailed provisions of the Police (Scotland) Act 1967, the Secretary of State should be liable instead because the officer being seconded to the Scottish Crime Squad was on "central service" as defined. It was held that this was not central service and accordingly the second named defender was let out. It seems if the officer had been on central service the first named defender would have to have been let out. So, it is not always the case that the chief constable is the correct target of vicarious liability for a police officer. In another case it was decided that the chief constable's vicarious liability is not sufficient to make him responsible to find lawburrows for the acts of his officers, although if it were alleged that he actually instigated harm he could be made liable.[3]

It has been held that a procurator fiscal, for the time being, is not in the same position a chief constable, that is liable for his deputes or assistants.[4] A named individual must be cited.

Agents

Independent contractors and employees can in fact be agents of a principal, **3–18** as indeed can partners be for their firm. By agent in this section is meant the person obliged under the contract of agency or mandate (gratuitous agency). The law is essentially simple. The actual wrongdoer is of course liable. The principal is not normally liable unless he instructed the act.[5] In the unlikely event that the act is ratified by the principal he is liable for it.[6] Scottish authority is scant on the more difficult issues such as where the act

---

[98] 1989 S.L.T. 97.
[99] 1989 S.L.T. 97 at 98. See also *Downie v. Chief Constable, Strathclyde Police*, 1998 S.L.T. 8.
[1] *Laverie v. Murray*, 1964 S.L.T. (Notes) 3.
[2] 1998 S.L.T. 549.
[3] *Handy v. Bowman*, Dundee Sheriff Court, September 22, 1986.
[4] *McLaren v. Procurator Fiscal for the Lothians and Borders*, 1992 S.L.T. 844.
[5] This was accepted in *Crawford v. Adams* (1900) 2 F. 987 in which the active issue was more the agent's responsibility.
[6] See the very unusual *Buron v. Denman* (1848) 2 Ex. 167.

is outside the agent's authority but within his ostensible authority. These concepts were developed within the law of contract. Their use in delict is questionable in view of the attitude of the law of delict to the vicarious liability of employees. The most interesting and helpful discussions are in cases where employees are acting, or alleged to be acting as agents with a view to expanding the employer's liability particularly in the case of fraud.

The Crown and Crown servants

3–19 This topic is dealt with above.[7]

Partnership and joint adventure

3–20 This topic is dealt with above.[8]

Family Cases

3–21 This topic is dealt with above.[9]

Landlord and Tenant

3–22 In principle there is no vicarious liability for a tenant absent instruction to the tenant by the landlord. Liability in nuisance may result in a primary liability upon the landlord for the actings of his tenants. In *Caledonian Railway Co v. William Baird & Company*,[10] the pursuers owned a stream of pure water. The defenders erected a village for miners employed by them. It was alleged that drainage from the miners' village was polluting the stream. The pursuers established nuisance at first instance. This was upheld on appeal.[11]

Owner and Visitor

3–23 In principle there is no vicarious liability without instruction. There may be primary liability for nuisance, or for negligence along the lines of the third party intervention cases.[12]

Roman Quasi-Delicts

3–24 The Roman quasi-delicts, with the exception of the judge who makes the cause his own, have the effect of making the defender liable for the conduct of another. They are discussed elsewhere in this book.[13]

---

[7] For an example see *Keetings v. Secretary of State for Scotland*, 1961 S.L.T. (Sh.Ct) 63 in which a prisoner was unable to sue the crown for the actings of another prisoner in shaking the scaffolding upon which the pursuer was standing. The Crown was not vicariously liable.

[8] See paras. 2–27–2–30.

[9] See paras. 2–16–2–19.

[10] (1876) 3 R. 839.

[11] *ibid.*, *per* Lord Justice-Clerk (Moncrieff) at 844–845 who regarded the miners as being truly only servants of the landlord—they were under his control. Lord Gifford concentrated on control—the defenders were proprietors, they drew rents and let the property. The drainage system was devised and upheld by them.

[12] See Chap. 10. See *Buchanan v. Alexandra Golf Club*, 1916 1 S.L.T. 353 discussed in Chap. 5.

[13] See Chap. 5.

Chapter 4

LIFE, LIMB AND LIBERTY

Introduction

The core of this chapter concerns wrongs done to the person—primarily to **4–1** the body. The scope of the chapter is wider and deals with issues beyond the physical space occupied by the human frame—at the very least to the extent of considering other more debatable wrongs. So far as Roman roots are concerned it should be appreciated that the law did not concern itself with injuries to free men—the legal treatment applied only to slaves and the like because the person of a freeman could not be valued.[1] Later systems provide tariffs for particular classes of individuals rather than individuals themselves.[2] Tariffs are still attractive to legislators, indeed CICA deals with application for criminal injuries on the basis of a tariff. Stair, after recognising the obvious "life, members and health"[3] considered liberty to be an interest protected by the law: "Next to life is liberty; and the delinquencies against it are restraint and constraint: and though liberty itself be inestimable, yet the damage sustained through these delinquencies are reparable."[4] However, that does not mention personality or privacy which are different but related matters. This description relates more to wrongful detention.[5] Bell states "Everyone who lives under the protection of the law has an absolute right to the safety of his person; and wherever this right is invaded there is in civil law a provision for redress of injury, as well as in penal law a punishment for the crime".[6] The ancient remedy of assythment had developed to cover cases of mutilation.[7]

The modern case *Henderson v. Chief Constable, Fife Police*[8] is important because Lord Jauncey decided the case on wide grounds. The facts were not special, relating to the arrest and detention of strikers, but one head of claim was less usual. A female worker was asked to remove her bra in the cells, the concern being that she might do herself a mischief. Lord Jauncey's dictum is a fine example of the law of delict acting as part of the structure which defends what are often called civil liberties:

"I should perhaps add that the researches of counsel had disclosed no Scottish case in which it had been held that removal of clothing forcibly

---

[1] Not however a problem for Stair who recognised that such was priceless but still reparable—I,ix,3.

[2] The *Leges Inter Brettos et Scotos* which Walker says dates back possibly to the 10th century but probably the 11th century. Walker, *History*, I, 27.

[3] Stair I,ix,3.

[4] Stair I,ix,3.

[5] See Chap. 3.

[6] Bell, *Prin.*, s. 2028.

[7] See generally Chap. 1.

[8] 1988 S.L.T. 361.

or by requirement could constitute a wrong but since such removal must amount to an infringement of liberty I see no reason why the law should not protect the individual from this infringement just as it does from other infringements".[9]

4–2 Nonetheless it is still the case that the focus of the law is on nominate delicts. Where the harm is unintentional and the act complained of is not obviously aggressive the law of negligence is likely to apply. The scope of the law of negligence is so wide that it has the potential to subsume nominate delicts. It should also be appreciated that injury to the person can be by way of words and the civilian *actio injuriarum* redressed injury to the person by word and indeed by act. It is not the case that an overall theory of protection exists. The most obvious gap at the time of writing is the person's desire for privacy. As this is litigated most commonly in relation to the publication of private matters it is dealt with elsewhere,[10] but again this is arguably part of the ever fluid idea of personality or liberty. Many of the rules herein discussed will have to be reconsidered as a result of the incorporation into Scots law of European Human Rights law.

ASSAULT

4–3 This must be the most straightforward instances of reparation.[11] There need be no complex analysis of duty of care. To say that a person is liable for an assault because he acted in breach of a duty not to do so is an unnecessary complexity. The basis of the action is the unwarranted interference with the person. In modern times most people will complain of such conduct to the police and obtain satisfaction through the offender being punished by the criminal courts. Under the Criminal Procedure (Scotland) Act 1995[12] criminal courts can make compensation orders and do so regularly, particularly in trivial assaults. Where the injury is serious and the defender of means or insured then a civil action is much more likely. Just as in the criminal law, motive is unimportant.[13] In *Reid v. Mitchell*,[14] farm workers at play harmed one of their number. It was held that "technically he assaulted him, although he did it playfully and without any bad intention, for if a man playfully attacks another to make him engage in sport, I am of the opinion that that is an assault, and if harm results that is an actionable wrong."[15] However, in the criminal law *mens rea* is important and dole is required for assault. So an accidental blow is not a crime and not assault. The case of transferred intent which raises difficult questions when dole is required does not trouble the modern law of delict because *culpa* can cover the

---

[9] 1988 S.L.T. 361 at 367.

[10] See Chap. 8.

[11] Liability to compensate as part of the fine for blood "bloodwite" has been known since the Assize Regis David, c. 14. Walker, *History*, II, pp. 535, and 619; III, pp. 730–731.

[12] ss. 249–253.

[13] For a good example in nominate delicts see Chap. 4. For a good example from the criminal law see *Lord Advocate's Reference* (No. 2 of 1992), 1993 S.L.T. 460.

[14] (1885) 12 R. 1129.

[15] *ibid.*, *per* Lord Young at 1132. The case was pled not as assault but as carelessness, recklessness or negligence.

case.[16] If the person does agree to become involved in sport, unlike the pursuer in *Reid*, then *volenti non fit injuria* as a defence can meet the case so far as based on *injuria*. In the Justinianic law the acquilian action was denied if the act was carried out for glory rather than wrongdoing.[17] Arguably that would still apply to such amateur sports as remain at the start of the twenty-first century. Certainly there is a reluctance to bring the law into consensual sport and this idea of glory is an interesting alternative analysis to the consent approach.

So common is litigation based on negligence founded on the aquilian **4–4** idea of wrongfully caused loss, it is sometimes forgotten that assault owes much to the *actio injuriarum* and that proof of physical injury or loss is not required. This is clear from *Ewing v. Mar*.[18] It was alleged that the defender had ridden at the pursuer putting him in danger of his life and had insulted the pursuer by spitting at him and on him. Lord President Boyle's charge to the jury could hardly state the law more plainly:

"Now, I have no hesitation in telling you, that if a man on horseback rides at a foot-passenger, so as to place him in danger, and in reasonable alarm, that is assault in law, although the foot-passenger may not have been thrown down or actually ridden over. In like manner, it is assault to discharge firearms, or even to point them at a person, though he should not be wounded."[19]

In relation to the spitting, the Lord President continued: "it is quite settled that to spit upon a person is an assault, and a gross and opprobrious insult . . . to spit at a person is also an assault, though it should not actually take effect on his person, provided you are satisfied that the parties were so near each other that it might have done so, or probably did so."[20]

A true accident is not actionable. A woman was unsuccessful when she **4–5** fell after remonstrating with a policeman. All he did was to release himself from her and she probably overbalanced and fell in that she was a rather heavy elderly woman and had a basket over one arm and a parcel in the other. The sheriff did not think there was any real violence.[21]

Causation arises as an issue. A person who allegedly kicked a boy was **4–6** assoilzied, the death being caused by a fall, the boy surviving for over two years.[22] In negligence it is appreciated that causation and remoteness of damage are connected and it is more likely in cases of assault that chains of events would be dealt with on the basis of remoteness. Some authority for that might be found in *Scorgie v. Lawrie*,[23] where it was held that although paralysis of a pupil's thumb was caused by a blow with the cane, it was not attributable to the fault of the headmistress. *Ewart v. Brown*[24] is even

---

[16] See para. 1–8 above.
[17] The wrestler case: Dig. IX.2.7.4.
[18] (1851) 14 D. 314.
[19] *ibid*. at 315.
[20] *ibid*. The pursuer recovered damages of one farthing.
[21] *Hall v. Watson* (1896) 12 Sh. Ct. Rep. 117.
[22] *Milne v. Thomson* (1841) 5 D. 759.
[23] (1883) 10 R. 610.
[24] (1882) 10 R. 163.

clearer in that the schoolmaster who hit a boy on the head with a pointer was held liable for damages for being at fault in hitting him but not for his subsequent illness.

Defences

General

4–7 General defences in the law of delict apply.[25]

Self-defence

4–8 Where parties are involved in a brawl and there is at least an implication of a degree of self-defence at some stage, there is no defence where one party clearly becomes an assailant, as where one man hit another with a bottle at a time when he had ample opportunity to disengage.[26]

Justification

4–9 Conduct which would otherwise be actionable is not actionable where the defender acts in accordance with law. Thus, there is no action where a person is thrown off a bus or train so long as no unnecessary violence is used;[27] or out of a shop when no longer present on the basis of the arrangement upon which he entered.[28] Reasonable force may be used to eject a trespasser.[29] The police do not have a special immunity in relation to assault, but where they are using force in the exercise of their duty it is necessary to aver that the conduct is outwith the scope of his duty.[30] *Mason v. Orr*[31] purports to lay down some guidance in such cases. Mason was bundled down his own stairs from his own pavement as an officer tried to clear the pavement of Mason and his workforce who were watching a royal visit. The Lord Ordinary allowed an issue, but on reclaiming the case was held to be irrelevant. Lord McLaren in whose opinion the rest of the division concurred said:

> "To make a relevant case of assault on the part of a police officer on duty it appears to me to be necessary to aver either (1) that the order which the officer was seeking to enforce was unlawful, that is, not within the scope of his duty; or (2) that the pursuer was willing to comply with the order, in which case the use of force would be unnecessary; or (3)

---

[25] See Chapter 20.
[26] *Marco v. Merrens*, 1964 S.L.T. (Sh. Ct) 74.
[27] *MacRaild v. North British Railway Co.* (1902) 10 S.L.T. 348.
[28] *Highland Railway Co. v. Menzies* (1878) 5 R. 887; *Aphthorpe v. Edinburgh Street Tramways Co.* (1882) 10R. 344. *Wallace v. Mooney* (1885) 12 R. 710.
[29] *Wood v. North British Railway* (1899) 2 F. 1.
[30] *Lennox v. Rose* (1824) 2 S. 650; *Wallace v. Mooney* (1885) 12 R. 710.
[31] (1901) 4 F. 220.

that the force used was manifestly in excess of the requirements of the case."[32]

Although there is clear authority that it is necessary to aver and prove malice and want of probable cause when suing the police, that applies where the conduct complained of is, on the face of it, within the competence of the officer concerned.[33] However, where it is not there is no need to aver malice and want of probable cause.[34]

Well before the era of prisoners' rights a case of assault was upheld **4–10** against a governor, but it was emphasised that in such cases the pursuer had to show that the extraordinary powers held were exceeded.[35]

Taking a gun from a trespasser by force has been held to be justifiable.[36] **4–11**

Stewart v. Thain[37] is authority for saying that an apparent assault is **4–12** justified if it is in the context of reasonable chastisement. Even in more robust times excess has not been protected as where a teacher set about a pupil with a stick and leather thongs, striking the pupil in the face and arms until he bled.[38] The defence is available to parents of children and to others having a position of authority and responsibility over the child such as teachers,[39] and probably cohabitants.[40] What is or is not considered reasonable is a matter for the court and clearly there is likely to be uncertainty as a result.[41] In the case of teachers the defence has been limited to exclude the use of implements.[42] The Scottish Law Commission have recommended restriction of the parent's defence. Clause 4 of the Draft Family Law (Scotland) Bill provides, *inter alia*: (1) In any proceedings (whether criminal or civil) against a person for striking a child, it shall not be a defence for the person to establish that he or she struck the child in the purported exercise of any parental right if he or she struck the child—

---

[32] *ibid.* at 223. See also *Baillie v. Edinburgh Magistrates* (1906) 14 S.L.T. 344. The test is the balance of probabilities: *Anwar v. Chief Constable*, Unrep., September 20, 1995; *Ward v. Chief Constable*, 1991 S.L.T. 292; *Mullen v. Anderson*, 1993 S.L.T. 835; *Anderson v. Chief Constable*, Unrep., Jan. 20, 1987; *Gilchrist v. Chief Constable*, Unrep., Glasgow Sheriff Court, Jan. 7, 1988, although the view that the evidence has to be of "more than ordinary persuasive weight" only means that the officer is assumed, as any other citizen, to be honest and truthful until the evidence is heard tested and scrutinised. There have been far too many cases in which the police have not been believed in recent years for any general rule to be acceptable. *Downie v. Chief Constable, Strathclyde Police*, 1998 S.L.T. 8; *Airnes v. Chief Constable, Strathclyde Police*, 1998 S.L.T. (Sh. Ct) 16; *Rae v. Chief Constable, Strathclyde Police*, 1998 G.W.D. 8–406.

[33] *Ward v. Chief Constable, Strathclyde Police*, 1991 S.L.T. 292.

[34] *Robertson v. Keith* (Seven Judges) 1936 S.L.T. 9. It is submitted that this is also established by *Mason v. Orr* (1901) 4 F. 220, where the Lord Ordinary had thrown out the argument: "This is an action for damages for assault, and if assault be well averred there is no need for an averment or an issue of malice or want of probable cause." This argument was not taken further although it was suggested that there needed to be "an averment to make him responsible analogous to the averment of malice in a case of wrongful apprehension" at 222.

[35] *McFarlane v. Young* (1824) 3 Mur. 408, 415.

[36] *Aitchison v. Thorburn* (1870) 7 S.L.R. 347.

[37] 1981 S.L.T. (Notes) 2.

[38] *Muckarsie v. Dickson* (1848) 11 D. 4.

[39] *Stewart v. Thain*, 1981 S.L.T. (Notes) 2.

[40] *Byrd v. Wither*, 1991 S.L.T. 206.

[41] *B. v. Harris*, 1990 S.L.T. 245; *Peebles v. MacPhail*, 1990 S.L.T. 245.

[42] Education (No. 2) Act 1986 which abolished corporal punishment in the public sector and the Education Act 1993 for the private sector.

(a) with a stick, belt or other object of whatever description; or (b) in such a way as to cause, or to risk causing—(i) injury; or (ii) pain or discomfort lasting more than a very short time."[43]

Consent

4–13 If assault is an unwarranted touching then if someone agrees to be touched they have the necessary authority and there is no wrong. It is possible to imply that in many of the ordinary touchings of ordinary life. Sport raises interesting problems because the issue is often one of the extent of the authority conferred, for example a footballer agrees he might have his shoulder dislocated by a shoulder charge but not that he will have his nose broken by a punch.[44] Medical cases are a good example because the motive involved in medical treatment is usually of the highest order but nonetheless without authority even that is an assault. In the case of *Thomson v. Devon*[45] a man was incarcerated in a prison. He was inoculated in accordance with the usual practice. He sued for damages on the basis that he had not wanted to be inoculated. The court must have considered consent was necessary as his claim was rejected on the basis that his conduct in proffering his arm was sufficient to indicate that he had consented to the treatment. If consent were not a defence there would have been no need to analyse the prisoner's actings as implied consent.

4–14 *Moyes v. Lothian Health Board*[46] is one of the clearest considerations of the issue of the quality of any consent given in a reported Scots case.[47] A patient suffered a stroke while undergoing angiography. The case failed at proof. The risk involved in the treatment was about 0.2 per cent. An allergy to one of the chemicals used doubles the risk and the pursuer had alleged that the doctors knew or ought to have known she suffered from this. It was not proved that this was the case and in any event, if it had been it was not proved it was the cause. The case is important because of the *obiter* expressions of the Lord Ordinary's view of the law on informed consent. The first observation was that if there were say five factors, each of which increased the risk involved in an operation—one standard risk and four special ones—then the doctor could not be exculpated if in failing to advise of the four special factors, injury came about through the standard risk which was warned. Causation, he thought, was satisfied. This is in line with the common sense view of causation—the patient can say that he would not have had the operation at all if all the risks were known. The issue was relevant in *Moyes* because there was also an allegation of a special risk of a history of migraine. The following views were expressed on informed consent:

---

[43] The SLC Report on *Family Law* (Scot. Law Com. No. 135), p. 156.

[44] For England see *Bravery v. Bravery* [1954] 1 W.L.R. 1169; *R. v. Coney* (1882) Q.B.D. 534. See the extensive review of authority in the Law Commission paper, *Criminal Law: Consent and Offences against the Person*, 1944 No. 134.

[45] (1899) 15 Sh. Ct Rep. 209.

[46] 1990 S.L.T. 444. See also *Bonthrone v. Secretary of State for Scotland*, 1987 S.L.T. 34 which raises other and much broader issues.

[47] See generally, L. Sutherland," A Relationship of Mutual Trust" Rep. B. 5–4; for England, P.M.D. Grundy, A.P. Gumbs, "Bolam, Sidaway and the Unrecognised Doctrine of Informed Consent: A Fresh Approach" [1997] J.P.I.L. 211.

"as I see it the law in both Scotland and England has come down firmly against the view that the doctor's duty to the patient involves at all costs obtaining the informed consent of the patient to specific medical treatments. When the patient entrusts himself to the doctor he expects, and is entitled, to be kept fully informed about decisions which have to be taken and which may concern his welfare but the paramount expectation is that the doctor will do what is best to care for the patient's health. In general it will be consistent with that primary responsibility that the doctor should acquaint the patient with the risks facing him and that becomes particularly critical when the risk is a severe risk for, as Lord Bridge observes in *Sidaway* [[1985] A.C. 871] in such a case the patient may want to be able to decide whether he should submit himself to a significant risk or even a secure second opinion. However, I can read nothing in the majority view in *Sidaway* which suggests that the extent and quality of warning to be given by a doctor to his patient should not in the last resort be governed by medical criteria. The risks inherent in a particular operation or procedure, the manner in which the operation may affect or damage a particular patient, the medical need for the operation and the ability of the patient to absorb information about his situation without adding damage to his health, are all matters where the doctor, with his own clinical experience of other practitioners, is best able to form a judgment as to what the patient can safely be told in the exercise of medical care. Nor is it practical or necessary that the patient should be told every risk."[48]

He went on to say that in this case a 0.2 per cent risk fell within the area of competence of doctors to consider; it was not a substantial risk like a 10 per cent risk as had been mentioned in *Sidaway*.

Notifiable Diseases

For the good of the community a person having a notifiable disease or 4–15 carrying an organism capable of causing one can be treated without his consent on the order of a justice of the peace or sheriff.[49]

Provocation

The law of Scotland accepts that provocation can mitigate damages. As 4–16 early as *Anderson v. Marshall*[50] Lord President Hope charged the jury in the following terms:

"No verbal provocation whatever can justify a blow . . . But, as verbal provocation is a good ground for mitigating damages, and as the pursuer does not come before you with clean hands, I should conceive that

---

[48] *Moyes v. Lothian Health Board, op. cit* at 449.
[49] Public Health (Scotland) Act 1897. The diseases are: acute encephalitis, acute meningitis, acute poliomyelitis, anthrax, cholera, diphtheria, dysentery (amoebic or bacillary), food poisoning, infective jaundice, lassa fever, leprosy, leptospirosis, malaria, marburg disease, measles, ophthalmia neonatorum, paratyphoid fever, plague, rabies, relapsing fever, typhus, viral haemorrhagic fever, whooping cough, yellow fever.
[50] (1835) 13 S. 1130.

sufficient reparation would be made in this case by a small award of damages "[51]

In *Ross v. Bryce*[52] the pursuer had driven up to the defender's house at night after drinking. He came off the worse in a fight that ensued and claimed damages for his injuries. The defender himself was uninjured. The sheriff principal upheld the sheriff and allowed a reduction in damages to take account of the provocation. However, it is perhaps unwise to accept the statement in that case that the rationale for so doing is that liability is based upon *culpa* and that the pursuer must come with clean hands.[53] That depends very much upon what is meant by *culpa*. The mental state of the defender, as has been pointed out, can be quite blameless. The notion of fault has to be technical and in those circumstances the hands of the parties may be equally clean in that moral sense.[54] In *Rutherford v. Chief Constable, Strathclyde Police*[55] the policeman did not admit the assault and so did not try to establish provocation. The Lord Ordinary (Maxwell) said that he thought there was a problem which would one day have to be resolved as to the test to be applied in determining whether provocation by physical violence amounts to a complete defence to a civil claim for damages for assault or merely mitigates damages.[56] In this case the issue turned on onus—it was for the officer to prove provocation and he had not tried to do so. It is submitted that *Ross* correctly states the law; that provocation can never exculpate but can mitigate. Renewing a quarrel after it has subsided will prevent a party claiming provocation.[57] The response to the provocation must be commensurate.[58]

PHYSICAL DETENTION

4–17 Preventing a person moving around is actionable and sounds in damages for the affront caused. This point of principle is confirmed by the Second Division in *MacKenzie v. Cluny Hill Hydropathic Co. Ltd*[59] in which the pursuer was prevented from leaving a room for 15 minutes. The apparently attractive *de minimis* argument was rejected until, if at all, after proof. Lord Low said:

> "I have no doubt that a wrong and in my view not a trifling wrong, has been averred. It is averred that the manager detains this lady in his room for fifteen minutes after the assault had been committed, and refused to

---

[51] The jury awarded one shilling. Earlier a theatre manager had been held liable for assaulting a person who hissed at a performance: *Seymour v. McLaren* (1828) 6 S. 969. See also *Falconer v. Cochran* (1837) 15 S. 891.

[52] 1972 S.L.T. (Sh. Ct) 76.

[53] This kind of statement is encountered in the older authorities: *Young v. Allison* (1820) 2 Mur. 231.

[54] See contra in England *Lane v. Holloway* [1968] 1 Q.B. 379.

[55] 1981 S.L.T. (Notes) 119.

[56] *ibid.* at 120.

[57] *Robertson v. Hill* (1824) 3 S. 383.

[58] *Brown v. Gibson-Craig* (1834) 13 S. 697. *Seymour*, n. 51 above.

[59] 1907 S.C. 200.

let her go until she made an apology. If that be true it was an outrage, and a relevant case has been stated."[60]

It is important to distinguish between cases of unlawful arrest simpliciter **4–18** and cases where there was a power or warrant to arrest but one which turned out to be ineffective. In the former case there is no need to aver malice and want of probable cause; in the latter case the pursuer must prove malice and want of probable cause.[61] In *Robertson v. Keith*,[62] the Lord President (Normand) said: "It is not doubtful that any unwarranted and unlawful proceedings by a public officer resulting in injury to anyone will subject him to liability, and that in such a case proof of malice or want of probable cause is not required of the pursuer."[63] In *Leask v. Burt*[64] where a man was arrested without warrant and many months after the alleged offence, the case was relevant without averment of malice. In *Shields v. Shearer*[65] the police arrested under a statutory power and without a warrant and the House of Lords held that malice need not be established. This was followed by Lord Ross in *Dahl v. Chief Constable*[66] after a full review of the authorities. The pursuer was taken from her house to a police station and released after two hours. Lord Ross, it is submitted, analysed the problem correctly. It is not enough to say that the arrest is unwarranted, it must also be averred that it is illegal in the sense of not being within other legal powers.[67] It is therefore submitted that the decision of Sheriff Principal Cox in *McKinley v. Chief Constable*[68] is correct. The police got it wrong when they, with some reason, thought they had a power of arrest in a matrimonial interdict case but did not. It was conceded the arrest was unlawful in this sense. The defenders could not insist upon the pursuer showing malice and want of probable cause.

Cases of store detectives detaining persons suspected of shoplifting could **4–19** fall within this head if there were no reasonable grounds for the suspicion and no need to detain. The wrongful detention is enough to constitute the delict. There is no need to establish defamation of character. If Lord Jauncey was correct in *Henderson v. Moodie*,[69] then this is simply a species of conduct interfering with liberty. In that case it was also accepted that unnecessary handcuffing was actionable. Indeed, the most common cases relate to arrest, usually by police officers. The law here takes on a constitutional nature. If the police officer is clearly in exercise of his duty then there is a need to aver and prove malice and want of probable cause.[70] It is of course the case that the constitutional structure of the United

---

[60] *ibid.* at 204.
[61] This point was made in *McKinney v. Chief Constable, Strathclyde Police*, 1998 S.L.T. (Sh. Ct) 80 and rejected by Lord Kingarth in *Woodward v. Chief Constable, Fife Constabulary*, 1998 S.L.T. 1342.
[62] 1936 S.C. 29.
[63] *ibid.* at 41.
[64] (1893) 21 R. 32.
[65] 1914 S.C. (H.L.) 33.
[66] 1983 S.L.T. 420.
[67] *ibid.* at 422.
[68] 1998 Rep. L.R. 82.
[69] 1988 S.C.L.R. 77.
[70] *Young v. Magistrates of Glasgow* (1891) 18 R. 825.

Kingdom is changing, particularly by the incorporation of European human rights law which may require reconsideration of the malice and want of probable cause protection given to the police.

4–20 There are innumerable examples of common law authority to detain and cases of police action are the most common. The authorities are usefully reviewed, and the overlap with the statute expressly made the subject of decision, in the relatively recent decision of the Second Division in *B. v. F.*[71] In that case, a petition for judicial review and for reparation, the petitioner complained that he had been unlawfully detained. The statutory unlawfulness is admitted in an affidavit by one of the key doctors involved.[72] In a case like this reparation is one of these areas of life in which the law of delict is no mere compensation adjusting mechanism, but rather the focus for vindicating constitutional rights. Lord Davidson supported the doctors: "If one invokes the metaphor of statute as a rug which covers the common law floor, then, where the common law relied upon has its base in necessity, it is easier to suppose that there is a hole in the statutory rug and that the floorboards of the common law show through."[73] In the Inner House the detention was held illegal. The doctors went too far in a spirit of paternalism:

> "Having regard to these authorities, I am satisfied that at common law a private person is entitled without an express warrant to confine a person who is mentally disordered where it appears that he is liable to do mischief to himself or others. In the present case, however, none of the respondents were purporting to act as private individuals, but the first two respondents were acting as medical practitioners and the third respondents as the managers of the hospital. In my opinion, so far as medical practitioners and hospital managers are concerned, their powers to confine mentally disordered persons are to be found in the Mental Health (Scotland) Act 1984. The Act of 1984 contains a detailed and comprehensive code of provisions dealing with the care and control of

---

[71] 1987 S.L.T. 681.

[72] *ibid.* at 684–685: "Over the four days leading up to and including Saturday 9 November there were ample clinical grounds for continued detention of the petitioner in hospital. Were he to have been released on 9 November there seemed to me reason to fear for the safety of his family, to predict further deterioration in his mental illness (by reason of both his inaccessibility to anti-psychotic medication and the adverse effects of any aggressive interactions and possible police arrest) and to fear physical injury to himself as a result of his impaired judgment, disinhibition and general over activity. I feel it would have been utterly irresponsible of me, as his responsible medical officer, to stand by and watch the petitioner discharge himself from care against advice. I was aware of the illegality of this action but feel at a loss to know how the ethical and legal requirements could have been reconciled. I feel that such a clinical situation is not uncommon in dealing with clinical conditions such as manic-depressive illness where relapse may be rapid and unpredictable. To follow the other administrative option, of applying for s. 18 in every case of manic-depressive illness during the first week of short-term detention regardless of clinical condition, seems to me clinically undesirable in view of the potentially disturbing impact on the patient—and probably unworkable in view of the burden of work. Since the commencement of the Mental Health (Scotland) Act on 30 September 1984 we have implemented s. 26 on 48 patients in the Argyll and Bute Hospital. Faced with the choice between protection and care of the patient, and abiding by the letter of the Mental Health Act, I chose the former option—a decision which was arrived at after very careful consideration, and which I felt to be ethically imperative."

[73] *ibid.* at 686.

mentally disordered persons. In my opinion, the powers of medical practitioners and hospital managers in relation to the care and control of mentally disordered persons are to be found in the Act of 1984, and not in the common law."[74]

So this supports a very limited common law power. The curiosity is that medical men appear to be worse off than the ignorant, but a close reading of the opinions shows that it is because medical men have extra powers that their powers are expressly contained. Indeed, the history of the legislation showed a concern that individual doctors could detain a person overly long by repeated use of emergency powers.[75] The decision was not an easy one as evidenced by the fact that Lord Dunpark changed his draft opinion.[76] The Lord Justice Clerk and Lord Dunpark thought there was a lacunae which parliament should address and they also thought that had a common law power existed detention would have been justified, but on this Lord Robertson did not agree.

Statutory Authority

Merchant Shipping Act 1995, s. 105

A ship's captain is allowed to detain where necessary.[77]   **4–21**

Aircraft

Commanders of aircraft have statutory powers ever more requiring to be **4–22** exercised as a result of a recent phenomenon of "air-rage".[78]

Mental Health (Scotland) Act 1984

The relationship of the Act to the Common law has been discussed above.[79] **4–23** Another good example of the rigour with which the courts scrutinise these extraordinary powers is *Miborrow Petitioner*,[80] in which the detention was held lawful but the practical application of the Act in the circumstances of practice were minutely examined to see if the detention were unlawful. If it had been unlawful under the statute damages would have been due.

SEDUCTION

Case of "fylthy lust and desyr" have been known since 1562 but civil **4–24** actionability comes later.[81] The difference between seduction and fornication (or adultery in particular) is that in the latter there is genuine and full

---

[74] *ibid.*, *per* Lord Justice-Clerk Ross at 689. Considering *Glegg on Reparation* (4th ed.), p. 199; Lord Wark, "Prosecution (Malicious)" in Green's *Encyclopaedia*, Vol. 12, p. 238; Walker, *Delict* (2nd ed.), p. 682. Clerk and Lindsell, *Law of Torts* (15th ed.), p. 690.

[75] *ibid.*, *per* Lord Robertson at 692L.

[76] *ibid* at 697A.

[77] This is the position in English common law: [1953] 1 W.L.R. 682.

[78] Tokyo Convention Act 1963, s. 3.

[79] See para. 4–20.

[80] 1996 S.C.L.R. (Notes) 314.

[81] Walker, *History*, III, p. 732.

consent. Rape is itself actionable as an assault, but differs from seduction in that consent is never given at all in a case of rape. In seduction consent exists but it is vitiated by the trickery or wiles involved. An example from the twentieth century is *Murray v. Fraser*.[82] The pursuer was a headmaster's daughter and alleged that sexual intercourse with the defender, a family friend, took place on two occasions. She became pregnant. The case of seduction was established after proof, the concepts of ascendancy and dependency and fraud being to the forefront. That the girl was under 16 and on the evidence unaware of sexual matters seems to have been essential. Other examples of wiles are promises to marry not later implemented, courtship with apparent intention to marry and taking advantage of the woman's dependency as when she is in the man's employment. While there is an established body of law,[83] it is difficult to justify this head of liability. If the seducer does not obtain consent then the case is one of assault. If the consent is vitiated by the pursuer's lack of understanding then that should apply in medical cases which it does not at present.[84] There are three choices:

(i) seduction should not be a separate delict;

(ii) if it is, it must be a patronising sexist anachronism, like rape itself; or

(iii) uninformed or defective consent should not be a defence to any assault if it is to be allowed in this area of the law.

ENTICEMENT

4–25 This delict, the luring away of a spouse or other family member, does not strictly speaking fit within this chapter as relating to conduct towards other persons. However, it can be seen in a more contemporary way as a complaint against the pursuer's interest in family life. It amounts to a complaint that the pursuer cannot enjoy something—the society of the enticee. In its roots it is personal, verging on the proprietorial[85] and so, it is submitted, reasonably dealt with here. The paradigm case is that of the wife

---

[82] 1916 S.C. 623.

[83] In *MacLeod v. MacAskill*, 1920 S.C. 72 a case was held to be relevant at the instance of a 26-year-old woman who had gone to work as a housekeeper. Lord Dundas was reluctant to allow the case to proceed for there were no wiles alleged, no proposals of marriage, no threats of violence nor any gradual debauching. *Hislop v. Kerr* (1696) Mor. 13908 shows a reluctance to compensate every unfortunate woman: "The Lords found a woman being got with child was no ground of action for damages, else a hundred such processes would be taken up by whores." It was also thought that every promise or insinuation of marriage would be thought enough. In the instant case there was sufficient dole and induction of trust. There was reliance on the Judaic law. *Lanning v. Hamilton* (1748) Mor. 13909 was a case for loss of virginity which was refused. The majority view was that a woman who was not a prostitute would seek marriage; if that failed, the law of damages might encourage women to yield with a view to being rewarded with a "handsome portion." Women it was said in those days and until recently suffer "irretrievable loss of reputation" on yielding.

[84] See para. 4–14.

[85] See *Stedman v. Stedman* (1743) Mor. 13909, an action against an adulterer in which he was found liable in the expenses of divorce and an appeal—reference was made to the consequent loss to the pursuer's business.

enticed away from the husband,[86] but the delict may also have applied in reverse.[87] The law on seduction discussed above is not relevant to the married woman because, being married, the other man has nothing to offer. She, being married, cannot be fooled by wiles. So the action seemed an obvious one. The twentieth century marked the complete legal and political emancipation of women with economic emancipation following swiftly behind. Politically the right of a spouse to sue for the enticement of another spouse appeared akin to ownership and was repealed by statute.[88]

That does not mean that the idea of a wrong to a person's family was **4–26** abandoned. Indeed in a sense, in the latter half of the twentieth century the real or rhetorical entity of the single parent family grew up. Absent another spouse, the critical component of such an entity is a child. Therefore, theoretically the enticement of a child would remain as potential source of liability. On the other hand the law respects the interference with contracts and if it protects partnership and employment it seems curious that it does not protect familial obligations. The case of the child seems easier. Professor Walker expressed the view:

"It is probable that any third party who entices a pupil or minor child to leave his parent or other person having lawful custody of him is liable in damages. A claim may lie even against a parent not entitled to custody who seeks to entice the child out of the custody of the parent lawfully entitled thereto. In English law the basis of the action is for depriving the parent of the child's services, but in Scots law the basis of the claim is probably interference with the natural parental rights to custody and upbringing."[89]

That view was tested in *McKeen v. Chief Constable, Lothian and Borders Police*[90] in which a father complained that police intervention had unwarrantably deprived him of his child's society, coming as it did in the middle of a custody dispute with the mother, his wife. Lord Morton of Shuna rejected the claim and did so, it is submitted, on wider grounds than was necessary for dealing with the narrower point:

"The part of the pursuer's averments of loss which I consider to be clearly irrelevant is the pursuer's claim to have, as a result of the police officers' actings, lost the society and company of the child. The only support for the existence of a right to sue for damages for depriving a parent of the custody of a child is a passage in Professor Walker's *Delict* (2nd ed) at p. 173. The cases to which Professor Walker refers do not appear to me to support his view and I do not consider that the fact that in *Delaney v. Stirling* [(1893) 20 R. 506] the question of competency was not raised in the case, which was dismissed on other grounds, is any support for the existence of such a right to sue for damages. There are situations in which a parent is deprived of the society and company of a

---

[86] *Adamson v. Gillibrand*, 1923 S.L.T. 328.
[87] *McGeever v. McFarlane*, (1951) 67 Sh. Ct Rep. 48.
[88] Law Reform (Husband and Wife) (Scotland) Act 1984, s. 2(2).
[89] Walker, *Delict*, (2nd ed.), p. 713.
[90] 1994 S.L.T. 93.

child in circumstances such as an accident in which the child is so seriously injured that it cannot communicate with anyone and requires institutional care. I was referred to no case in which such a claim has been advanced. The Administration of Justice Act 1982 provided for awards of damages to include compensation for services rendered to the injured person, but there is no suggestion of a right to a relative to sue for loss of society and company except in the special circumstances of a death. Apart from personal injury cases there are, of course, many situations in which parents dispute custody or one parent or others deprive a parent of the custody of a child for differing periods of time. If there is such a right as is sought in this case, it is surprising that there is no reported decision of a case in which any pursuer advanced such a claim. In my opinion, such a right does not exist at present. If such a right as is sought were to be recognised in the law of Scotland, it is my opinion this could only be done by legislation and it may well be that there are many social reasons why the recognition of such a right would be thought inappropriate."[91]

At the time of writing it has to be admitted that both Professor Walker's statement and the opinion of Lord Morton in relation to the parents and children so far as the law is concerned has changed as a result of the intervention of the United Nations, brought to fruition in the Children (Scotland) Act 1995. The broad thrust of these changes is from rights to responsibilities. Rights are very close to interests. Some of these new legal responsibilities bring about remedies and rights. The juridical point is whether a responsibility implies an interest. In this context it is submitted it does. The more subtle relation of residence and contact juridically blurs the distinction between custody and access which was essential for Professor Walker's point. It is submitted that by reasonable analogy with a now reorganised body of law Professor Walker's view on the major premise is correct.

BREACH OF CONFIDENCE

4–27 Breach of confidence is dealt with elsewhere in this book.[92] It is noticed here because it can be argued that our secrets are part of our personality, our lives or our liberty. Sometimes the revelation of the secret causes no loss. It would accordingly be cases from this area of the law that would be prayed in aid to justify a case where there is no patrimonial loss. Alternatively, where the defender gains from the wrong an analysis based on restitution for wrongs may be appropriate.

PRIVACY

4–28 Just as secrets are perhaps part of personality so it can be argued is the right to be let alone—the interest in a free space. The delicts discussed in this chapter are largely about intrusions upon physical liberty. Invasion of

---

[91] *McKeen* at 95–96.
[92] See Chap. 7.

privacy can now be achieved by invisible and harmless electronic means, without assault or trespass, but the hurt can still exist to the person whose privacy has been invaded. For convenience this topic is treated elsewhere[93] because most considerations of this possible protected interest take place in the context of restraints upon the press. Obviously European human rights law may bring about developments in this particular area.

HARASSMENT

As long ago as the nineteenth century there was statutory protection from a **4–29** form of harassment which remains in force. The Conspiracy and Protection of Property Act 1875, s. 7 provides as follows:

> "Every person who, with a view to compel any other person to abstain from doing or to do any act which such other person has a legal right to do or abstain from doing, wrongfully and without legal authority: (1) uses violence to or intimidates such other person or his wife or children, or injures his property; or (2) persistently follows such other person about from place to place; or (3) hides any tools, clothes or other property owned or used by such other person, or deprives him of or hinders him in the use thereof; or (4) watches or besets the house or other place where such other person resides, or works, or carries on business, or happens to be, or the approach to such house or place; or (5) follows such other person with two or more other persons in a disorderly manner in or through any street or road, shall, on conviction thereof [be liable to certain penalties]."[94]

By a much more recent statute, the Protection from Harassment Act 1997, in Scotland, every individual has a right to be free from harassment and, accordingly, a person must not pursue a course of conduct which amounts to harassment of another and: (a) is intended to amount to harassment of that person; or (b) occurs in circumstances where it would appear to a reasonable person that it would amount to harassment of that person.[95] Conduct includes speech.[96] Harassment of a person includes causing the person alarm or distress.[97] A course of conduct must involve conduct on at least two occasions: s. 8(3). It is not otherwise defined and the matter will be for the courts. *Khorasandjian v. Bush*[98] showed the English courts trying to adapt nuisance to conduct which might be considered to be an illustration of harassment, namely the repeated making of telephone calls, but it was later held that this was erroneous so far as nuisance was concerned and had perhaps been an attempt to fill the gap later plugged by the 1997 Act.[99]

---

[93] Chap. 8.
[94] A case to answer under this statute was upheld in the High Court on appeal as recently as *Galt v. Philp*, 1984 S.L.T. 28.
[95] s. 8(1).
[6] Bell, *Prin.*, s. 2028.
[97] *ibid.*
[98] [1993] 3 W.L.R. 476.
[99] *Hunter v. Canary Wharf* [1997] 2 W.L.R. 684. See also para. 5–16 below.

The Secretary of State may certify that the conduct complained of related to national security, the economic well being of the United Kingdom or the prevention or detection of serious crime and so provide a defence.[1] Alternatively, it is a defence to show that the conduct complained of was pursued for the purpose of preventing or detecting crime.[2] The other defences are legal authority[3] and that the conduct was reasonable.[4]

---

[1] s. 12(1): the certificate is conclusive. A certificate which purports to be such a certificate is presumed to be such a certificate unless the contrary is proved: s. 12(3).
[2] s.8(4)(b).
[3] s.8(4)(a).
[4] s.8(4)(c).

CHAPTER 5

HERITAGE

Introduction

This chapter sets out the delictual obligations of persons who own or **5–1** occupy land, the obligations of persons towards landowners and related cases. In some cases, because of the development of the law of negligence, treatment in this chapter is by way of cross reference to later sections of the book. It is often said that there is no liability *ex dominio solo*.[1] Another maxim often encountered in this area of the law is *sic utere tuo ut alienum non laedas*.[2] It is, however, not really of much help because it does not say who or what is not to be harmed or damaged nor what care must be taken and thus what conduct is prohibited.[3]

Trespass

Trespass is a temporary intrusion on to the property of another. The term **5–2** encroachment is used where the intrusion is by other property. It is sometimes said that there is no law of trespass in Scotland but that is a proposition usually made in relation to the special case of a single crossing over land causing no damage.[4] In the modern case of *Brown v. Lee Constructions*,[5] albeit the case is one of interdict, it can be seen that a person's interest in the physical integrity of their property is likely to be protected. In *Brown* a home owner petitioned for interdict against builders to prevent their crane sweeping over his property. While the case turned to an extent on the possible danger from items falling it seems to recognise trespass as an actionable wrong.[6] In *Nisbett v. Hogg*,[7] the First Division upheld a finding of reparation based on averments and pleas of trespass but the award of reparation was for actual damage.

---

[1] See para. 1–35.

[2] As noted by Trayner, *Latin Maxims*, (4th ed., W. Green, 1993), p. 578: "So use your own property as not to injure that of another".

[3] See Zimmerman, *The Law of Obligations*, p. 1033, where *alterum non laedere* is noted as supporting both strict liability and fault liability and again at p. 1137, n. 317 where he describes the same phenomenon in England in regard to *sic utere tuo ut neminem laedas*.

[4] In England trespass is historically and theoretically at the centre of the law of torts. Professor Walker has indicated that there exists an early brieve based on a similar phrase in the English writ of trespass. He goes on to remind us that the style in *Quoniam Attachiamenta* says that the defender "did a trespass". He concludes that the brieve anent the king's peace was "well on its way to becoming a general remedy for harm to a man in his property". Walker, *History*, II, p. 614.

[5] 1977 S.L.T. (Notes) 61.

[6] *Shell UK v. McGillivray*, 1991 S.L.T. 667.

[7] 1950 S.L.T. 289.

In *Davidson v. Nicol*,[8] it was stated, adopting the now aged *Fraser on Master and Servant*,[9] that there "can be no liability—that is, vicarious liability—for trespass unless there is express command or the trespass is the necessary consequence of an order given." The complaint in this case was the incursion on to land to take away sand. In *Buchanan v. Alexandra Golf Club*[10] the pursuer, an agricultural tenant, sued the defenders who leased a golf course. The pursuer had crops in his field and the defenders allowed a large number of persons, including members of their club, ladies, youths and guests irrespective of standard to play their course. It was found that "many of the said players were in the habit . . . of trespassing by themselves or their caddies in the pursuer's said field for the purpose of recovering the said balls . . . misdirected."[11] This caused damage to the crops. He complained often. The defenders erected a notice and despite names of persons offending being passed on they did nothing. The sheriff substitute found that the driving of golf balls into the pursuer's said field, and the consequent trespass and damage, were the natural and probable results of the defenders' invitation to the club members and others to play golf and that this natural and probable result should have been foreseen by the defenders. He found the defenders liable.[12] The sheriff adhered.[13] Both the sheriff and the sheriff substitute were content to deal with the case on the basis of what would now be considered to be negligence—the foreseeability of harm. Of course writing now from a duty minded perspective the worry with this case is that some of the wrongdoers were not the defenders but third parties, and it transpires that the key authority discussed in *Buchanan* is the first of the now well-known third party intervention cases—*Scott's Trs v. Moss*.[14] In *Cousland v. Magistrates and Councillors of the Burgh of Kinghorn*,[15] the pursuer was again a tenant of land and the defenders were the proprietors of the "Kinghorn Golf Course." This time any member of the public was entitled to play on the course on payment of a small charge. There was a fence but the pursuer averred that this fence was not sufficient. It was averred that it should have been constructed much higher and wire netting put on it. Again there were detailed averments that crops were destroyed. Foreseeability was again the ground of argument: "The defenders . . . ought to have foreseen that, from the position of the teeing grounds, greens, and holes placed on said golf course, near to said march fence, a very large number of golf balls would fall on to Kilcruick land, and that in such an event it was natural that the persons to whom such golf balls belonged and their companions should go over into pursuer's fields to search for them, and thereby cause damage to the pursuer's crops." The sheriff substitute found for the pursuers accepting their argument which in this case too was based on *Scott's Trustees v. Moss*.[16] In *Cousland* it was

---

[8] 1949 S.L.T. (Sh. Ct) 66.
[9] 3rd ed., p. 274.
[10] 1916 1 S.L.T. 353.
[11] *ibid.* at 354.
[12] *ibid.* at 354.
[13] *ibid.* at 357.
[14] (1889) 17 R. 32.
[15] 1907 15 S.L.T. 791, not cited in *Buchanan*.
[16] (1889) 17 R. 32.

expressly argued that the only case was against the trespassers.[17] In both of these cases it is at least assumed, or conceded that temporary intrusions are trespasses and that they are wrong but the liability is truly, it is submitted, in negligence for failure to control the risk of damage-causing third parties.[18]

In the odd case of *A. v. B.'s Trustees*[19] a man took a tenancy of a flat and **5-3** committed suicide. The pursuers claimed nervous shock and material damage. Responsibility for the material damage was not an issue. The nervous shock was as difficult then as it has remained, but as the case was not one of negligence categorisation was difficult:

> "Here the difficulty is to say exactly what wrong this gentleman did—I mean legal wrong—which can be stated as the foundation of an action. Mr. Christie suggested trespass. Trespass in this case really means use of property *ultra vires* of the contract. This gentleman took these rooms for his lodgings. Well, I do not think the person who takes premises as furnished lodgings is entitled to turn them to uses other than occupation as a resident lodger . . . Is it one of the purposes of renting lodgings that they should be taken for the purpose of committing suicide? I think that it is not, and that in so using the lodgings in turning the bathroom into a slaughter-house, this man was performing a wrongful act, an act in breach of the contract under which he received possession of the premises. I am therefore prepared to. . . send the case to proof."[20]

In *Gibson v. Stewart*,[21] the First Division treated as trespass something **5-4** which would hardly be thought of as that today; the idea seems to be that if trespass is established the typical negligence issues do not. While the pursuer was driving up a loaning that led from the public road to the farmhouse of Airds, his horse shied at a heap of manure bags covered with a tarpaulin which had been placed by the defender in a corn field on the said farm immediately adjoining the loaning. The pursuer was injured. It was held that as the defender was alleged to have been in trespass in putting the bags where he did, the pursuer was entitled to an issue. The "wrongfulness" would appear to be the trespass rather than negligent fault.

Land being owned from the centre of the earth to the heavens trespass is **5-5** relevant for burrowing under land as much as it is for swinging a crane over it. The leading case is *Graham v. The Duke of Hamilton*.[22] This was a case of interdict. The complainer owned lands which had been feued to his predecessor in title by the Duke of Hamilton under a reservation of minerals. The Duke let out the coal in the lands belonging to the complainer and also that in other lands originally feued out but with a reservation of minerals. The mineral tenants took the coal from both estates and took by underground passage to their own lands. The tunnel ran under the complainer's lands. The Lord President (Inglis) said:

---

[17] Under reference to *Stirling Crawford v. Clyde Navigation Trs* (1881) 8 R. 826.

[18] See also *Ritchie v. Dysart Golf Club* (1909) 26 Sh. Ct Rep. 70; *Allan v. Calderbraes Golf Club* (1934) 50 Sh. Ct Rep. 86.

[19] 1905 13 S.L.T. 830.

[20] *ibid* at 831.

[21] 1893 1 S.L.T. 479. See also *Lindsay v. Sommerville* (1902) 18 Sh. Ct Rep. 230.

[22] (1868) 6 M. 965.

"If they [the defenders] are allowed to exercise that right until they have worked out the coal, all the complainer would have in the end would be a claim for damages for their having, without legal right, used this passage. Now, there may be no damage in any proper sense of the term. Indeed, it is pretty plain there will be none; and if the question of damages be submitted to a jury, the verdict would probably be nil. The value of the complainer's right, if he has it, the means he has of compelling them to pay for the passage of the coal. The fear is, that the right to demand payment for its passage through his mine may not be a legal right enforceable at law by action for damages; and his only safe course, therefore, is to refuse passage unless on payment."[23]

This appears to be confirmation of the inapplicability of aquilian liability where there is no damage. The Lord President arrived at a solution to the problem that such a rule creates—that a use may be made of the property of another without payment. The solution was to remit to a man of skill to fix a reasonable wayleave, which in the event of the complainer's case failing would be subject to repetition. If they would not pay they would be interdicted.[24] Lord Deas dissented. He described the result as "unprecedented" and one "which neither party has proposed".[25] This case is of great significance for the law of obligations. On one view what is being sought is restitution. Not restitution in its subtraction sense where A sends money by mistake to B, but in the sense of B being enriched unjustly by a wrong he does. If the conduct is wrong enough for an interdict it ought to be wrong enough for restitution. It must however, be appreciated that this clear analysis is modern and was not available in these terms to the court at the time. Lord Deas could agree that the conduct complained of must be disgorged but he saw the way to do that as being through delict:

"if he succeeds in his action he will have a claim against the respondents for the full amount of loss and damage which he has sustained by being so kept for a time out of payment of his wayleave. It is said that his claim will only be for damages *pendente lite*, and not for wayleave, and that he will be able to establish any damage. I do not understand that. If he has established sustained damages he will get damages, and if he has sustained none he ought to get none. It appears to me, however, that in the event of the complainer succeeding the wayleave which ought to have received in the interval will be the measure of damage due to him".[26]

The restitutionary measure would be the charge which could have been made. The reparation measure under our ordinary law would be the loss of the chance of the wayleave charge which might be the same.[27] Similar issues

---

[23] *ibid.* at 968.
[24] Lords Curriehill and Ardmillan concurred with the Lord President.
[25] *Graham*, (1868) 6 M. 965 at 969.
[26] *ibid.*, at 969. See also *Ramsay v. Blair*, 1876 3 R. (H.L.) 41 affirming 3 R. 25.
[27] It is noteworthy that the English court of appeal denied a similar claim in 1883 in *Philips v. Homfray* (1883) 24 Ch. D. 439. Professor Birks has argued strongly that English law should have admitted that claim. P. Birks, *An Introduction to the Law of Restitution* (Oxford, 1989), p. 323.

were considered in relation to trespass in *Lord Advocate v. Glengarnock Iron and Steel Company Ltd.*[28] The Lord Advocate was representing the Commissioners of Woods and Forests. The Commissioners claimed that the defenders were trespassing by taking coal other than authorised coal through the ground. The arrangement by lease was that the defender was to work the Crown minerals, but the complaint was that the defender also took his own coals. Although damages were claimed the pursuer in his condescendence said he was restricting his claim to damages calculated at 1d. per ton as a wayleave. The pursuer relied on *Gardner v. Beresford's Trs*[29] to say that the defenders were probably liable in violent profits. It is argued that the Crown did not have to show loss but if the Crown did it could because of the loss of opportunity to contract for wayleave.[30] The pursuer's case was dismissed because it was thought that there was not a trespass, the agreement between the parties envisaging that the Crown coal should be worked at the same time as the other coal. Accordingly the other statements in relation to liability are *obiter*. They are against restitutionary damages, the payment or reparation. Lord Low expressed a doubt that even if it had been an unlawful use, money would be due but refused to consider the matter.[31] Lord Ardwall was opposed to the idea that damages should be awarded without damage. Nor was he convinced by the Lord Ordinary's analogy with violent profits although the main reason for that was the absence of bad faith.[32] Lord Dundas also agreed there was no trespass because of the agreement. He expressed an opinion against a wayleave by reference to Lord Ardwall's arguments against the application of the law on violent profits. The modern Scots law does now offer restitution for the wrong of unlawful long term use and it is submitted it should do so in cases of trespass.

Finally it must be noted that trespass is criminal in many circumstances **5–6** in Scotland and it is always arguable at least that a criminal trespass should be civilly actionable. In *Shell U.K. Ltd v. McGillivray*[33] trespass was pled as the basis of an action for interdict The action was against workmen of contractors of the petitioners who were "occupying" oil installations where they worked. While it was (rightly) argued for the respondents that as the property was moveable the law of trespass did not apply, Lord Cameron of Lochbroom said,

> "In my opinion, the use of the word trespass has no particular significance in these petitions other than indicating that the actings of the respondents are averred to be wrongful acts of occupation of parts of property of which the petitioners have the exclusive right of occupation."[34]

He then proceeded on the basis that such was a delict.[35] The Trespass (Scotland) Act 1865 criminalises certain trespasses, being "an Act to

---

[28] 1909 1 S.L.T. 15.
[29] (1877) 4 R. 1091.
[30] On the authority of *Davidson's Trs v. Caledonian Railway Co.* (1895) 23 R. 45.
[31] *Gardner, ibid.* at 17.
[32] *ibid.* at 19.
[33] 1991 S.L.T. 667.
[34] *ibid.* at 669.
[35] *Phestos Shipping v. Kurmiawan*, 1983 S.L.T. 388.

provide for the better Prevention of Trespass in Scotland." The Act is important in making conduct "wrongful" but it has not been decided whether it can be founded on in a breach of statutory duty case.

> "3. Every person who lodges in any premises, or occupies or encamps on any land, being private property, without the consent and permission of the owner or legal occupier of such premises or land, and every person who encamps or lights a fire on or near any private road or enclosed or cultivated land, or in or near any plantation, without the consent and permission of the owner or legal occupier of such road, land, or plantation, or on or near any . . . highway, shall be guilty of an offence."

Premises for these purposes include any home, barn, stable, shed, loft, granary, outhouse, garden, stockyard, court, close or enclosed space. The Conspiracy and Protection of Property Act 1875, s. 7 provides, *inter alia*, as follows: "Every person who, with a view to compel any other person to abstain from doing or to do any act which such other person has a legal right to do or abstain from doing, wrongfully and without legal authority— (1) uses violence to or intimidates such other person or his wife or children, or injures his property"[36]

In the same way the Criminal Justice and Public Order Act 1994 requires persons to move when encamping on the land of others and failing to remove as soon as reasonable practicable when requested.[37] The difficulty in a civil action based on this statute could be that liability may only accrue from the time of the demand to move rather than from occupation.[38]

Wrongful occupation: ejection, intrusion and molestation

5–7 In the institutional law wrongful occupation is struck at by the wrongs known under the names of ejection and intrusion. Ejection is dispossession and intrusion occupation without ejection. They differ in this, that intrusion is the "entering in possession being for the time void, without the consent of the parties interested, or order of law", but ejection "is not only the unwarrantable entering of lands but the casting out of the then possessor."[39] The word ejection is still known in the context of the action of ejection but the delict of ejection was wrongfully entering land and throwing out the possessor.[40] Intrusion was entering vacant land without consent. These wrongs are no longer named as such but like spuilzie ought not to be forgotten. This is especially so where the pursuer's loss is financial. The focus of modern law teachers and hence practitioners on negligence means that non-recovery rules in negligence in respect of economic loss may erroneously be carried over to cases of intrusion and ejection. Following these ancient precedents and applying the general principle against deliber-

---

[36] See *Galt v. Philp*, 1984 S.L.T. 28.
[37] In *Neizer v. Rhodes*, 1997 S.L.T. 364, it was held that it was not incumbent on the Crown to show which of two potential occupiers was the true occupier.
[38] There are other provisions in the Game (Scotland) Act 1832 and the Night Poaching Act 1828. See *Stair Memorial Encyclopedia*, Vol. 11, "Game".
[39] Stair, I,ix,25.
[40] *Wishart v. Lord Arbuthnot* (1573) Mor. 605; *Calliston v. Errol* (1575) Mor. 3605.

ate infringement with recognised interests such cases are clearly cases of liability. Both are clear wrongs as can be demonstrated by two recent cases.[41] In *Axis West Developments Ltd v. Chartwell Land Investment Ltd*[42] the pursuers claimed reparation from the defenders because they had constructed a drainage pipe on the pursuers' land without the pursuers' consent. The Lord Ordinary allowed a proof before answer on quantum only. However, after reviewing the land ownership and title issues the Inner House granted dismissal. In *Property Selection and Development Trust Ltd v. United Friendly Insurance Plc*[43] the pursuers were heritable proprietors of adjacent subjects. The pursuers' subjects were destroyed by fire and they discovered rock anchors in their own subjects supporting the defenders' buildings. They sued for the losses involved in exploring and removing the rock anchors. The Lord Ordinary[44] held that the encroachment itself would not justify damages and that there had to be averments of *culpa*. With respect, it might not have been necessary to go that far. The argument in this case was that it was not the defenders who built the rock anchors. It could simply be said that they did not cause the result—conduct was irrelevant. The point would be live where the defenders had encroached and then it is submitted the *Kennedy* rules do not apply and subject to causation and remoteness the pursuers would be liable. The action was amended and debated of new before Lord MacFadyen. Because the pursuers failed to satisfy his Lordship that they had relevant averments sufficient to make it clear that the defenders were responsible for the workings. The reparation case had to fail.[45]

Cases where the occupation is not contractually permitted but is not *vi clam aut pecario* are more difficult. Here it is hard to characterise the case as wrongful or culpable. If it is culpable in the sense of lacking in care or negligent, then indeed general principle may allow the loss of rent to be recoverable. The approach of the modern law has been to treat this as a restitutionary claim.[46] Restitutionary analysis is, it is submitted, the better.[47] **5–8**

Molestation is sufficiently defined in Stair: **5–9**

"Molestation is the troubling of possession chiefly in and about marches of lands; the party injurer is obliged to refund the damage to the party injured, and the marches being cognosced, he will be decerned to desist, and cease from troubling in time coming; whereupon all personal

---

[41] The feudal law of property reaches further than personal wrongs, the most notable case being real burdens: *Lees v. North East Fife District Council*, 1987 S.L.T. 769; and servitudes: *Sutherland v. Pottinger*, 1989 S.L.T. 697; *Inverness Farmers Dairy v. Kinlochdamph Ltd*, 1989 G.W.D. 25–1106.

[42] 1999 S.L.T. 975.

[43] 1998 S.C.L.R. 314.

[44] Influenced by *Kennedy v. Glenbelle*, 1986 S.L.T. 1186..

[45] 1999 S.L.T. 975.

[46] Perhaps following the ancient tradition of spuilzie which applied to land and moveables and included reparation and restitution.

[47] *Glen v. Roy* (1882) 10 R. 239. *HMV Fields Properties v. Skirt 'n' Slack Centre of London*, 1987 S.L.T. 2; *Shetland Islands Council v. B.P. Petroleum Development*, 1990 S.L.T. 82; *Rochester Poster Services Ltd v. A.G. Barr Plc*, 1994 S.L.T. (Sh. Ct) 2; *G.T.W. Holdings Ltd v. Toet*, 1994 S.L.T. (Sh. Ct) 16.

execution is competent. It is also competent when possession is otherwise troubled. . . . the process by which molestation is determined is called a cognition."[48]

In contemporary usage, molestation interdicts are by persons seeking to stop other persons calling them on the telephone, approaching their house or verbally abusing them or perhaps also physically assaulting them. They have no connection with molestation proper. They are very common, being granted on a daily basis but leaving aside the verbal abuse and the assault the legal basis of such interdicts is difficult to discern.

Damage and Interest

5–10 Professor Walker reminds us that this remedy is in Hope's *Major Practicks* in which can be found collected six cases from 1610 onwards.[49] It is arguably Stair's "general action" although the extent to which it was in regular application is yet not clear.[50] It appears from Professor Walker's examples to have covered property damage and economic loss. One case he cites was that of a building falling on another, the well-known *Hay v. Littlejohn*.[51]

Nuisance

5–11 Nuisance is a Cheshire cat among delicts; so much of it has started to fade away that there is only a mysterious smile left behind. But it was definitely there before.[52] It is still an identifiable body of law no matter what view is taken of it.[53] The puzzle now is to what extent it should be dealt with in a book like this.[54] The following statements are uncontroversial and justify the inclusion of the subject in this book at this time:

(i) For some time it was thought that nuisance was a head of strict liability in Scots law. So there are many cases in the law reports which support that view. Practitioners, students and scholars need to be aware of the change in approach.[55]

(ii) It is accepted that a suitable nuisance case can be won by the pursuer having to prove less than would be so on a case pled based on negligence.[56]

(iii) Its core is about regulating the behaviour of landowners *inter se*.

---

[48] Stair, I,ix,28.

[49] Walker, *History*, IV, pp. 699–700.

[50] See D.W. McKenzie, R. Evans-Jones, "The Development of Remedies for Personal Injuries and Death" in. *Civil Law Tradition in Scots Law* (Evans-Jones ed., 1995).

[51] (1666) Mor. 13974, although McKenzie and Evans-Jones do not cite that case in support of their argument. The case is also known for a rejection of *damnum infectum*.

[52] T.B. Smith, *Short Commentary*, p. 531 acknowledged its existence as "a definite branch of the law of Scotland" and referred to its "recognition."

[53] N.R. Whitty, *Nuisance*, p. 2087.

[54] Instead of, for example, Gordon, *Land Law* (2nd ed., 1999).

[55] Whitty, *Nuisance*, para. 2087.

[56] "in some nuisance cases at least the onus of proof of specific fault is reversed." Whitty, *Nuisance*, para. 2107.

(iv) Cases of interdict do not require any serious consideration of the basis of liability for damages and so such cases may still appear to support a theory of strict liability but on the other hand may not be delict cases at all. They are certainly not necessarily reparation cases although some might be too.

(v) Damages is a response associated, *inter alia*, with delictual liability.[57]

Beyond that, even after two major decisions, there is still academic debate and analysis, attempting to locate all or bits of the doctrine.

Conduct

Before discussing the basis of liability in nuisance, it is necessary to say **5–12** what it is that is being talked about. The idea is that nuisance, contrary to the constitutional freedom of persons to do as they please with their own land, controls land use where the use is more than tolerable or *plus quam tolerabile*. Bell expressed this idea as follows:

"Whatever obstructs the public means of commerce and intercourse, whether in the highways or navigable rivers: whatever is noxious or unsafe, or renders life to the public generally, or to the neighbourhood; whatever is intolerably offensive to individuals in their dwellinghouses, or inconsistent with the comfort of life, whether by stench (as the boiling of blubber), by noise (as a smithy in an upper floor), or by indecency (as a brothel next door), is a nuisance".[58]

The commonly cited and still authoritative expression of the idea is that of Lord President Cooper:

"If any person so uses his property as to occasion serious disturbance or substantial inconvenience to his neighbour or material damage to his neighbour's property, it is in the general case irrelevant as a defence for the defender to plead merely that he was making a normal and familiar use of his own property".[59]

In modern times nuisance has been canvassed as an aspect of the law's protection of the environment.[60] For reasons to be discussed later that development may well also be coming to an end. The following Scots examples give meaning to the idea which is to be discussed. In *Shanlin v. Collins*[61] the pursuer sought interdict and damages complaining of the defenders' use of their property as a kennels. The defenders were found liable in damages and were interdicted. The maxim *lex non favet delictarum,*

---

[57] *Kennedy v. Glenbelle*, 1986 S.L.T. 1186 at 1188, *per* Lord President Hope.
[58] Bell, *Prin.*, s. 974; a civilian basis for a nuisance-like doctrine is detectable in the Institutional writers, especially Kames. For a full analysis see D. Johnston, "Owners and Neighbours: from Rome to Scotland" in *Civil Law Tradition in Scotland* (Evans-Jones ed., Supplementary Vol. 2, 1995).
[59] *Watt v. Jamieson*, 1954 S.C. 56 at 58.
[60] J. Steele, "Private Law and the Environment: Nuisance in Context" [1995] L.S. 236.
[61] 1973 S.L.T. (Sh. Ct) 21.

votis[62] was held not to be applicable in this case. A plea of *res judicata* was rejected as the noise complained of in this action was materially greater than in the earlier action. In *Maguire v. Charles McNeil*[63] the locality principle was considered by the First Division. The site occupied by the defenders had been used as a forge. They bought more adjacent property and installed heavy drop hammers which were alleged to be causing noise and vibration. The pursuers, churchmen and teachers complained. Lord President Clyde declared the locality to be "one of a familiar kind in a great centre of commerce such as the City of Glasgow".[64] He continued, "The doctrine of locality is a concession made by the law to that social necessity which (particularly in towns) drives people into close neighbourhood, not only with each other, but also with the work by which they earn their living". He explained that a considerable sacrifice is required in a society as "the price of the advantages which close neighbourhood to others, and to remunerative employment brings with it".[65] However, that did not mean that "the small but indispensable section of brain workers in the community must suffer torture without hope of protection, however close to the ears the industrial babel may be brought".[66] It was held that in this case the doctrine would not have applied but there had not been proof of sufficient inconvenience, although if there had been proof of noise at night that might have been different. In *Webster v. Lord Advocate*[67] the complaint was the noise of erecting the scaffolding for the grandstand of the Edinburgh Tattoo. While it was accepted that the Tattoo is "a spectacle appreciated by the public and a valuable publicity and commercial asset to the city", it was considered that it could be interdicted. The interesting point in this case was that the suggestion that the pursuer should simply keep her windows closed was rejected: "one of the nice things about summer is that you are able to open your windows". For a long time it has been accepted that it is not a defence to say that the pursuer has come to the nuisance. In *Fleming v. Hislop*[68] it was put thus: "It is clear that whether the man went to the nuisance or the nuisance came to the man the rights are the same".[69] The flexibility of the remedy is illustrated by a case involving a rave—a dance event hardly contemplated by a Tattoo attender.[70] A sheriff refused to allow a local authority an interdict to prohibit a "rave" dance event. It was a "one off" event. Only a few people might potentially be disturbed as 11 out of 14

---

[62] The law does not favour the wishes of the fastidious.

[63] 1922 S.L.T. 193.

[64] *ibid*. at 200.

[65] *ibid*.

[66] *ibid*. at 201.

[67] 1984 S.L.T. 13 and on appeal at 1985 S.L.T. 361.

[68] (1886) 13 R. (H.L.) 43.

[69] *ibid*., *per* Lord Halsbury at 49. This is so well established that counsel on both sides accepted the point in *Webster*. In E. Reid, "The Basis of Liability in Nuisance" 1997 J.R. 162, the interesting point is made that coming to the nuisance is perhaps only applicable in continuing nuisance cases and that it "is not clear whether the rule . . . would also apply in cases where the alleged basis of liability is the defender's negligent failure to a avert latent hazard. The suggestion has been made that in such circumstances the defence of *volenti non fit injuria* should be made available no matter whether the case is pled in negligence or negligent nuisance."

[70] *Cumnock & Doon Valley District Council v. Dance Energy Associates Ltd*, 1992 G.W.D. 25–1441.

local residents had accepted rehousing offers and the noise would last only a short period of time: this was not *plus quam tolerabile*. So this modern form of fun was permitted.[71]

Basis of liability

The basis of liability in nuisance would form an interesting topic for an 5–13 historical excursus[72] but the two big cases have rehearsed the history and closed off many of the older arguments. Nuisance appears to be an English import. *Aemulationem vicini*[73] has deeper roots but did not flourish as a response to the demands of litigants and as has already been seen in discussing trespass at the turn of the twentieth century, nuisance was considered by a sheriff to be an English response, negligence being a sufficient basis for decision.[74] In *RHM Bakeries (Scotland) Ltd v. Strathclyde Regional Council*[75] the parties, by their pleadings, made it necessary for a decision to be made as to whether liability in nuisance was a wrong of strict liability or whether fault needed to be averred and proved. A sewer collapsed and the pursuers who suffered property damage were unable or unwilling to state what it was the defenders should have done. Lord Fraser began with an examination of *Kerr v. Earl of Orkney*[76] which he considered had long been regarded as a landmark decision. He then revealed that the legal basis of the case had been misunderstood. The Earl of Orkney built a dam on his land in Ayrshire across a stream on which the pursuer had a mill about half-a-mile lower down. Four months after the dam had been completed, there were several days of heavy rain, the dam burst, the waters in the pond behind it escaped and the stream, augmented by those waters, swept away the pursuer's house and his mill. The defender was held to be liable in damages to the pursuer. For Lord Fraser the question was as to the exact basis on which he was found to be liable. It was *culpa* and not strict liability. A re-examination of most of the important Scottish cases[77]

---

[71] In another case celebrations based on an ancient grant of a charter in 1620 (based on an original of 1130), enlarged by prescriptive use, was not interdicted even although a business claimed that the fun now lasted two days or as was said "bedlam broke loose and passage along the streets became impossible". *Central Motors (St. Andrews) Ltd v. Magistrates of St. Andrews*, 1961 S.L.T. 290.

[72] The treatment by Whitty in the *Stair Memorial Encyclopedia* has found favour with Lord Hope more than once.

[73] See 5–22 below.

[74] *ibid*. There is a distant common ancestor in *Novel Disseisin* which was imported into medieval Scotland and to which the assize of nuisance was a supplementary real action. *Sedleigh-Denfield v. O'Callaghan* [1940] A.C. 880 at 902–903, *per* Lord Wright.

[75] 1985 S.L.T. 214; for cases decided not long before it struggling with the doctrinal problems see *MacNab v. McDeveitt*, 1971 S.L.T. (Sh. Ct) 41; *Lord Advocate v. Reo Stakis Organisation Ltd*, 1980 S.L.T. 237 (O.H.).

[76] (1857) 20 D. 298.

[77] *Lord Advocate v. Reo Stakis Organisation Ltd*, 1982 S.L.T. 140; *Campbell v. Kennedy* (1864) 3 M. 121; *Fleming v. Hislop* (1886) 13 R. (H.L.) 43.; *Giblin v. Lanarkshire County Council*, 1927 S.L.T. 563; *Gourock Rope Work Co. Ltd v. Greenock Corporation*, 1966 S.L.T. 125; *Hanley v. Magistrates of Edinburgh*, 1913 1 S.L.T. 420; 1913 S.C. (H.L.) 27; *Kerr v. Earl of Orkney* (1857) 20 D. 298; *Macaulay v. Buist & Co.* (1846) 9 D. 245; *McLaughlan v. Craig*, 1948 S.L.T. 483; *Miller v. Robert Addie & Sons' Collieries Ltd*, 1934 S.L.T. 160; *Moffat & Co. v. Park* (1877) 5 R. 13; *Rae v. Burgh of Musselburgh*, 1974 S.L.T. 29; *Samuel v. The Edinburgh and Glasgow Railway Co.* (1850) 13 D. 312; *Slater v. A. & J. McLellan*, 1924 S.L.T. 643; *Tontine Hotel (Greenock) Ltd v. Greenock Corporation*, 1967 S.L.T. 180; *Watt v. Jamieson*, 1954 S.L.T. 56.

and a consideration of academic writing[78] showed that liability to make reparation for nuisance was based on *culpa*, albeit it would look like strict liability in interdict. A possible cause was explained:

> "The doubt about whether *culpa* is the essential basis in Scots law for the liability of the proprietor of land to a neighbour arises from the fact that the English decision in *Rylands v. Fletcher* has sometimes been referred to as if it were authoritative in Scotland. In my opinion, with all respect to eminent judges who have referred to it in that way, it has no place in Scots law, and the suggestion that it has, is a heresy which ought to be extirpated."[79]

The theory having been set back on its true path there then followed the passage which caused immediate difficulties for practitioners and is still difficult to give its proper weight. Lord Fraser added two "comments":

> "The first is that the view that I have just expressed does not by any means imply that, in a case such as this, a pursuer cannot succeed unless he avers the precise nature of the fault committed by the defender which caused the accident. It would be quite unreasonable to place such a burden on a pursuer, who in many cases will have no knowledge, and no means of obtaining knowledge, of the defender's fault. As a general rule it would, in my opinion, be relevant for a pursuer to make averments to the effect that his property has been damaged by a flood caused by an event on the defender's land, such as the collapse of a sewer which it was the defender's duty to maintain, that properly maintained sewers do not collapse, and that the collapse is evidence that the defender had failed in his duty to maintain the sewer. The onus will then be on the defender to explain the event in some way consistent with absence of fault on his part. As a general rule the defences available will be limited to proving that the event was caused either by the action of a third party for whom he was not responsible, as the defender did in *Gourock Ropework Co. Ltd v. Greenock Corporation*, or by a *damnum fatale*. My second comment is that I do not believe that there is much difference, in the practical result between the law as laid down in *Rylands v. Fletcher* and the law as laid down according to my understanding of *Kerr v. Earl of Orkney*. On that matter, I accept the majority view expressed in the Thirteenth Report of the Law Reform Committee for Scotland, Cmnd. 2348 (1964), para. 22 where they say this: 'We agree that the theory of the common law is at present doubtful, but we are impressed by the argument that it seems to make little, if any, difference in the result whether one adopts what may be called the "absolute liability" theory or adheres rigidly to the fault principle'. But as the parties have chosen to litigate the question, and as they presumably consider it to be important to them, I think they are entitled to have it decided. In my opinion it should be decided in favour of the local authority."[80]

---

[78] Glegg, *Reparation*, p. 19, McKechnie "Reparation" in *Greens Encyclopaedia of The Laws of Scotland*, Vol. 12 and Walker, *Delict* (2nd ed.), pp. 975 *et seq*.

[79] *RHM Bakeries (Scotland) Ltd*, 1985 S.L.T. 214 at 217. *Rylands* is not doing too well in the Anglo-American world either: J.G. Fleming, "The Fall of the Crippled Giant (*Rylands v. Fletcher*)" [1995] 3 Tort L. R. 56.

[80] *ibid.* at 219–220.

For those only wanting to win cases this was an enigmatic smile indeed. This new *culpa*-based nuisance liability which was not all that unlike absolute liability was soon considered in subsequent cases.[81] In *Argyll & Clyde Health Board v. Strathclyde Regional Council*[82] a water main owned by the defenders burst causing damage to the pursuers. The pleadings indicated that the pursuers were unable to say precisely what factors caused the burst. They went on to say that water mains properly laid and properly maintained do not burst. Much emphasis was laid by the pursuers on the fact that the defenders knew or could have known much more about the location and condition of the pipe. It was held that the case lacked the specification necessary for the defenders to know the case being made against them—the facts from which the inference of negligence was to be taken were not set out. To have succeeded the pursuers would have to have said what maintenance was required. The case was dismissed without enquiry.[83] *Noble's Trustees v. Economic Forestry (Scotland) Ltd*[84] involved a claim for damage to a downstream property by construction works on upstream property. The claim was against contractors and the two owners of the upstream land. The nuisance claim against the proprietors was challenged. The challenge was upheld. It was thought (by Lord Jauncey) that this was tantamount to a claim *ex dominio* against which the law of Scotland is said to be opposed.[85] In *Borders Regional Council v. Roxburgh District Council*,[86] the foundations of the pursuers' subjects were undermined and suffered damage. This was alleged to be a result of the conduct of four defenders, a nuisance case being alleged against the first defender, the owner of the adjacent land. The argument for the pursuers was that the first defenders were "occupiers and proprietors" of the ground and that they were responsible for the work that was being done on their land. Lord Dervaird found that there was nothing in the pleadings in the case from which *culpa* could be inferred.[87]

Many of the post-*RHM Bakeries* authorities were reviewed in *G. & A. Estates Ltd v. Caviapen Trustees Ltd (No. 1)*.[88] This was another culvert

---

[81] See generally F. McManus, "*Culpa* and the Law of Nuisance", 1995 J.R. 462; F. McManus, "Bye-bye Rylands—Again!", 1995 J.R. 194.

[82] 1988 S.L.T. 381.

[83] Although not giving general guidance, Lord McCluskey thought that the pursuers could have taken expert advice as to how old pipes could be examined and could have taken evidence about the steps taken by other water authorities to inspect and monitor their pipes. Another careful decision which, it is submitted reached the correct balance, was *Trustees of Inverness Harbour Trust v. British Railways Board*, 1993 G.W.D. 14–952. In that case a railway viaduct collapsed causing damage to the pursuers. They sued as this *novum opus manufactum* had to be maintained "with the utmost measure of precautions". This was not specified and attempt was made to have the case dismissed. A proof before answer was allowed. It was accepted on both sides that the issue was *culpa*. The Lord Ordinary (Kirkwood) accepted that the precise duties could vary with the circumstances. In some cases there would be little practical difference between absolute liability and *culpa*.

[84] 1988 S.L.T. 622.

[85] See Chap. 1. This followed *Gourock Ropework Co v. Greenock Corporation*, 1988 S.L.T. 622, to the extent that a proprietor who has given up control to a contractor is no longer liable. The pursuers' attempt to distinguish it failed. It would have to have been shown that there was some actual fault in the proprietors as where there would be danger no matter what care is shown.

[86] 1989 S.L.T. 837.

[87] Lord Jauncey's view in *Noble's Trs* was approved.

[88] 1993 S.L.T. 1037.

case. The pursuers owned a piece of land. They instructed the building of a shopping centre on it. A burn had to be culverted. The pursuers then sold most of their land to the defenders with the shopping centre upon it, but they retained the entry pond and entry to the culvert. The work was then completed but then there was a flood of the whole shopping centre. The pursuers made a claim in contract with which this work is not concerned. The defenders counter claimed for nuisance and for absolute liability for diversion of a stream. A proof before answer was allowed on both cases.[89]

In *McQueen v. Glasgow Garden Festival (1988) Ltd*[90] the pursuer was injured when, as a spectator, she was injured by a metal fragment of a firework—a part of the mortar tube in which the firework shell was located. She sued the convenor of the festival, the conductor of the firework display and the manufacturer and supplier of the firework. The case against the manufacturer was abandoned before proof. The case against the conductor was rejected on all three heads. First, unnatural use of land was held to be inapplicable as it sounded like *Rylands v. Fletcher*. Secondly, the shell casing was not a *res* for the purposes of *res ipsa loquitur*. Perhaps more importantly the incident was not unexplained. It was due to the premature explosion of the firework, due to a fault in the firework. Thirdly, there was no duty to inspect the firework fuses for latent defects.

5–14   In *Kennedy v. Glenbelle Ltd*[91] building work was done on the pursuer's premises by the first named defenders on advice from the second named defenders who had been engaged by the first defenders. The Inner House agreed with the Lord Ordinary that a proof before answer was allowable in relation to averments of nuisance. The Lord President (Hope) took the opportunity to add his exposition of the law of nuisance. He accepted that *Caledonian Railway Co.* may be an exception to basic *culpa* position. The Lord President tried hard to clarify the nuisance/*culpa*/negligence relationship.

> "According to the law of Scotland liability in reparation for damages arises either *ex contractu* or *ex delicto*. There is no other basis on which a liability in reparation for damages can arise, according to our law. A claim of damages for nuisance is a delictual claim, as it does not depend for its existence on any contract. It arises where there is an invasion of the pursuer's interest in land to an extent which exceeds what is reasonably tolerable. The *plus quam tolerabile* test is peculiar to the liability in damages for nuisance. Where that test is satisfied and *culpa* is established, the requirements for the delictual liability are fulfilled. Liability in damages for negligence, on the other hand, depends on a failure to take reasonable care where there is a foreseeable risk of injury. That is another species of delictual liability, the basis for which also depends upon *culpa*. *Culpa* which gives rise to a liability in delict may

---

[89] The other important point about the case is that the claim for loss was measured by the costs involved in building a second culvert rather that simply repairing the flood damage. It would be difficult to justify this as an aquilian claim on the face of it. Lord Coulsfield considered that these costs could be treated as a direct and natural consequence of the fault in commencing the operation.

[90] 1995 S.L.T. 211.

[91] 1996 S.L.T. 1186.

take various forms. In *Stair Memorial Encyclopaedia*, Vol. 14, "Nuisance", para 2087 it is stated that the usual categories of *culpa* or fault are malice, intent, recklessness and negligence. To that list there may be added conduct causing a special risk of abnormal damage where it may be said that it is not necessary to prove a specific fault as fault is necessarily implied in the result".[92]

His Lordship then reviewed the authorities coming to note a distinction between "conduct which is deliberate, involving the intention to carry out the operation which proves inevitably to be harmful, and conduct which is negligent in that harm would have been avoided if due skill and care had been taken in the conduct of the operation." He made reference to *Noble's Trustees v. Economic Forestry (Scotland) Ltd*,[93] discussed above[94] and in particular to a passage of Lord Jauncey's:

"A landowner will be liable to his neighbour if he carries out operations on his land which will or are likely to cause damage to his neighbour's land however much care is exercised. Similarly will a landowner be liable in respect of carrying out operations, either at his own hand or at the hand of the contractor, if it is necessary to take steps in the carrying out of those operations to prevent damage to a neighbour, and he, the landlord, does not take or instruct those steps. In the former case the landowner's *culpa* lies in the actual carrying out of his operations in the knowledge actual or implied of their likely consequences. In the latter case culpa lies in not taking steps to avoid consequences which he should have foreseen would be likely to flow from one method of carrying out the operation."[95]

Lord President Hope then glossed Lord Fraser's quotation from Lord Atkin:

"Although Lord Fraser of Tullybelton added emphasis to the phrase 'some degree of personal responsibility is required' when quoting from Lord Atkin, I do not think that these words can be regarded as providing a complete guide to what is involved in the concept of fault in Scots law. The purpose of the quotation, as I understand it, was to underline the point that liability for nuisance did not arise merely *ex dominio* and without fault. The essential requirement is that fault or *culpa* must be established. That may be done by demonstrating negligence, in which case the ordinary principles of the law of negligence will provide an equivalent remedy. Or it may be done by demonstrating that the defender was at fault in some other respect. This may be because his action was malicious, or because it was deliberate in the knowledge that his action would result in harm to the other party, or because it was reckless as he had no regard to the question whether his action, if it was

---

[92] 1996 S.L.T 1186 at 1188.
[93] 1988 S.L.T. 662.
[94] See 5–13 above.
[95] *Noble's Trs*, at p 664A–B.

of a kind likely to cause harm to the other party, would have that result. Or it may be—and this is perhaps just another example of recklessness— because the defender has indulged in conduct which gives rise to a special risk of abnormal damage, from which fault is implied if damage results from that conduct. In each case personal responsibility rests on the defender because he has conducted himself in a respect which is recognised as inferring *culpa* by our law. So what is required is a deliberate act or negligence or some other conduct from which *culpa* or fault may be inferred."[96]

Lord Kirkwood had less to say on the theory but on this practical point said:

"In my opinion the reference to a 'degree of personal responsibility' was simply intended to emphasise that there was no liability *ex dominio* and that the party alleged to be liable had to be to some extent responsible for causing or continuing the nuisance founded on by reason of his use of the land or premises in question. However the use of the land or premises must give rise to wrongful interference with the neighbour's enjoyment of his property and that raises the issue as to whether or not *culpa* has been established. Accordingly I agree that before liability in damages for nuisance can be established there must be proof of a deliberate act or negligence or some other conduct from which *culpa* can be inferred."[97]

Lord Murray commented:

"In the passage from Lord Atkin's speech quoted by Lord Fraser the latter italicises the words 'some degree of personal responsibility is required'. The emphasis laid by Lord Fraser on those words may lend some superficial support to the view which the Lord Ordinary appears to adopt. Read in context I consider that Lord Fraser was not seeking to redefine *culpa* in the field of nuisance in Scots law on the basis of Lord Atkin's dictum. He may well have referred to that passage merely to illustrate that even south of the border there was no place for strict liability for nuisance arising *ex dominio*, some degree of personal responsibility being required to bring home liability. In Scotland where *culpa* is the ruling concept this would apply *a fortiori*. Counsel for the second defenders submitted that the Lord Ordinary had erroneously proceeded on the view that in addition to *culpa* arising from a deliberate act on the one hand or from negligence on the other hand there was a third ground on which it could arise in light of Lord Fraser's adoption of Lord Atkin's formula for liability in nuisance, this third ground being circumstances from which some degree of personal responsibility arises for the consequences of a particular use of land adversely affecting a neighbour. If the Lord Ordinary intended to substitute this notion of fault for *culpa* in the accepted sense, then I would respectfully differ from him.[98]

---

[96] *Kennedy v. Glenbelle Ltd*, 1996 S.L.T. 1186 at 1189.
[97] *ibid.* at 1191.
[98] *ibid.* at 1191.

Then the very practical point which had been causing trouble since *RHM Bakeries* was directly addressed because understandably in view of the cases, counsel for the second defenders complained about the averments in art. 9 of the condescendence because they did not mention fault and contained nothing from which fault, either in terms of negligence or a deliberate act, could be inferred. They were then lacking in specification. The pursuers argued that as the case of nuisance was not based on negligence but on an intentional or deliberate act.

That act was the deliberate removal of a section of the basement wall in the knowledge that, as this was a load bearing wall, the result of this interference with it would be to cause damage to the pursuers' property on the upper floors. It was not being suggested that the second defenders' action was malicious, in the sense that they were setting out to cause damage to the pursuers' property. But the action was a deliberate one, as it was done in the knowledge that damage would result from it. This was sufficient to show that they were at fault and thus liable in damages for the nuisance."[99]

That was sufficient *culpa*. The second defenders had instructed and directed hazardous works within the premises which they occupied at the material time, which they knew constituted an interference with the support enjoyed by each of the pursuers.[1]

The same approach can be seen in an older case of *Campbell v. Kennedy*[2] **5–15** much discussed in the leading cases. The pursuer Archibald Campbell, who had a shop on the ground floor of the building, sued the defender, the proprietor of a flat two storeys above the pursuer's shop. The claim was based on the damage sustained by the pursuer through the bursting or insufficiency of a water-pipe in the defender's flat: "all through the culpable carelessness or recklessness, or negligence of the defender or others (whose names and designations are to the pursuer unknown) for whom the defender is responsible". The defender admitted that some damage had been done to the pursuer's property "through the accidental escape of water in a house belonging to the defender," but denied that there was any negligence or want of care on his part or anybody for whom he was responsible. Lord Benholme appreciated the key problem:

"But I cannot help thinking that there was another matter of fact in his Lordship's view in pronouncing this judgement, which ought also to have been stated. I mean the fact of culpa, or negligence; and I would, therefore, propose to add the findings in fact, another finding, *viz.* 'That through the negligence of the defender, the said pipe had been allowed to remain in an insufficient or defective state'. Some such finding is necessary in order to make the findings in fact quadrate with the findings in law. It was not enough to say that the premises in which the defective pipe existed were the defender's property and that they were the cause of the damage. I have no doubt but that the Lord Ordinary held that, to

---

[99] *Kennedy v. Glenbelle Ltd*, 1996 S.L.T. 1186 at 1190.
[1] *ibid.*
[2] (1864) 3 M. 121.

infer responsibility for damage, there must be *culpa*. It may have been that the duties of property are so generally recognised, and that it is so well known, that one of these duties is to keep one's property in such a state that it shall not injure neighbours, that the Lord Ordinary may have felt justified in assuming that the fact of damage inferred negligence, and therefore, responsibility. But I think it is of great importance that there should be no mistake as to the true ground of liability".[3]

The facts of the case were so indicative of *culpa* that the court itself was prepared to add the necessary averment.

5–16   In England where the history of the law is different the question of who may sue has been the subject of recent judicial decision. In *Hunter v. Canary Wharf Ltd and London Dockyard Development Corporation*,[4] a 4–1 majority ruled that a mere licensee could not sue in nuisance and an earlier "molestation"[5] case was over-ruled to the extent that it had allowed a licensee to sue. The former Lord President Hope's comments in the majority in that case are likely to be influential in Scotland, but because he was clearly of the view that the law of England and the law of Scotland were different it is not easy to say how far his remarks should be carried over as applicable to Scots law on this point.

5–17   Taken together *RHM Bakeries*[6] and *Kennedy*[7] have brought about a revolution in thinking about nuisance. It is now less like the English law and there is more of an apparent civilian look to the doctrine. It is, of course, not necessary that a system chooses one way or another. Scots law lost any overarching commitment to a civilian system a long time ago. In a comparative examination of the German law Markesinis says:

> "But then came the extension in the medieval and modern law. For suppose your neighbour does not walk across your land under a claim of easement but merely sends fumes across your land or makes life unbearable by noise, can he not be said to be really claiming something in the nature of an easement to these things even though no such easement would be recognised by the law? On that factious reasoning you can claim the freedom of your land from his encroachment as if it had been an easement, and your action will be an *actio quasi-negatoria*, which will sound in property and not in delict. From the substantive point of view, what will be in issue will be the ambit of ownership, not the personal duty of your neighbour not to commit a delict of encroachment. Incidentally, this attitude of mind-led German law and some of its derivatives to restrict the remedy, if no fault were proved in the neighbour to a declaration or injunction. French and Swiss law, on the other hand, which do not take their classifications so seriously, have found it possible to award damages as well."[8]

If the French and Swiss could have their injunction and damages so could the Scots, even if the idea did come from England. Who now knows what

---

[3] *ibid.* at 124–125.
[4] [1997] 2 W.L.R. 684.
[5] *Khorasanjian v. Bush* [1993] 3 W.L.R. 476.
[6] *RHM Bakeries (Scotland) Ltd v. Strathclyde Regional Council*, 1985 S.L.T. 214.
[7] *Kennedy*, 1996 S.L.T. 1186.
[8] Markesinis, *The German Law of Torts*, p. 24.

forces led Scots lawyers to accept a delict called nuisance importing strict liability? In his dissent in *Canary Wharf*, Lord Cooke of Thorndon alluded to the fact that since the war land use has been closely controlled by planning legislation. While it is true this can properly be seen as public law he suggested that it could be seen as "denoting a standard of what is acceptable in the community."[9] The problem of title to sue will not go away.[10]

Defences

As nuisance is no longer considered a matter of strict liability then there is **5–18** no need to consider the traditional defences to strict liability. Nonetheless, the factual circumstances which constitute a nuisance are such that will usually raise an inference of fault and so far as defending a case is concerned Lord Fraser commented:

> "As a general rule the defences available will be limited to proving that the event was caused either by the action of a third party for whom he was not responsible, as the defender did in *Gourock Ropework Co. Ltd v. Greenock Corporation*,[11] or by a *damnum fatale*".[12]

It is a defence to show that the has consented to the nuisance or acquiesces in it.[13] A right to commit a nuisance is not acquired in the ten years of the positive prescription but the right to object may be lost by a particular pursuer after the 20 years of the long negative prescription.[14] It might be expected that post-*RHM Bakeries* and *Kennedy* that a claim for damages will be lost to a particular pursuer according to the rules of the five year short negative prescription. Some conduct which is a nuisance *ex facie* may be justified by statutory authority. But the conduct must fall directly within the authority and the statute must on construction be intended to protect from nuisance.[15]

The twentieth century will be noted, *inter alia*, as the century of the **5–19** powered aircraft. A wonder at the start of century, they became for many dwellers under their flight paths, a pest. While many of the victims are poor council dwellers who can barely afford the cost of air travel, one Lady Matilda Steel-Maitland took up the cudgels against three airline companies.[16] She claimed in respect of damage to her castle for damage caused

---

[9] *Hunter v. Canary Wharf Ltd and London Dockyard Development Corporation* [1997] 2 W.L.R. 684 at 722.

[10] See Whitty, *Nuisance*, para. 2134. Whitty would, it is submitted, correctly, have allowed the non-entitled spouse to sue. Under the Scottish legislation occupancy rights exist automatically for spouses. On the English legislation Lord Goff would not allow *locus standi*: *Hunter*, [1977] 2 W.L.R. 684 at 697.

[11] 1966 S.L.T. 125.

[12] *ibid*. at 129.

[13] *Hill v. Dickson* (1850) 12 D. 808; *Bargeddie Coal Co v. Wark* (1859) 3 Macq. 467; *Houldsworth v. Wishaw Mags* (1887) 14 R. 920; *Bicket v. Morris* (1866) 4 M. (H.L) 44.

[14] *Rigby & Beadmore v. Downie* (1872) 10 M. 568; *Harvie v. Robertson* (1903) 5 F. 338; *Central Motors (St. Andrews) Ltd v. Mags of St. Andrews*, 1961 S.L.T. 290.

[15] *Cooper & Wood v. North British Railway* (1863) 1 M. 499; *Ogston v. Aberdeen Tramway Co* (1896) 24 R. (H.L.) 8.

[16] *Steel-Maitland v. British Airways Board*, 1981 S.L.T. 110.

by vibration and by droplets of aviation fuel. She met the defence provided by Civil Aviation Act 1949, s. 40 (1) which provides that there is to be no liability in respect of normal flight (as defined) in nuisance. However, making up for this there is a provision in s. 40(2) which provides a right to damages in cases where material loss or damage is caused by an aircraft or by an article or (alarmingly) a person falling from a plane. In these circumstances there is no need to prove negligence or intention nor any other cause of action. There is mention of contributory negligence and sole fault and it may be assumed (but it is not clear) that a small amount of contributory negligence does not bar the defender entirely. The Scottish Court accepted a view which is certainly explicable against the background of English law, quoting from *MacNair's Law of the Air* (4th ed.) p. 107, in relation to the two provisions; "they represent a compromise or bargain which can be summed up as establishing no liability for technical legal injury (if any), but absolute liability for actual material injury".[17] Thus the case for interdict was unsuccessful but the case for damages was allowed to proceed to a proof before answer.

Diversion of the natural course of a stream

5-20 In *Caledonian Railway. Co. v. Greenock Corporation*[18] the defender altered the course of a burn by enclosing the burn in a culvert and filling in the valley through which the burn had flowed. He was held liable on the basis of what looked very much like strict liability. This case was considered by Lord Fraser in *RHM Bakeries*. He said: "it may be that the case should be regarded as laying down a special rule applicable only to the case of a person who interferes with the course of a natural stream. If so, it is contrary to a general principle of the law of Scotland and, in my opinion, the rule should not be extended beyond the facts of that case".[19]

Negligence and Dangerous Property

5-21 Negligence is treated separately in this book and the general duty to take reasonable care to avoid foreseeable harm applies to land owners as any other. The Occupiers' Liability Act is a statutory version of liability for lack of care, but the Act does not replace the general law. Thus even in cases where the precise terms of the Act might not apply, general principle may still apply. Most closely touching on the question of liability of the landowner are some of the cases of third party intervention discussed in detail later in this book.[20] Cases of bringing large numbers of people on to property causing loss can attract this kind of *culpa* liability and other examples have been seen above in connection with trespass.[21] In these cases the allegation is that the landowner knows or ought to have known that

---

[17] *ibid.* Quoted with approval by Lord Jauncey at 112.
[18] 1917 S.C. (H.L.) 56.
[19] It seems to have been accepted in principle in *G & A Estates Ltd v. Caviapen Trustees Ltd. (No. 1)*, 1993 S.L.T. 1037. In *Kennedy v. Glenbelle*, 1996 S.L.T. 1186 at 1188G it was also accepted albeit as a possibly anomalous case.
[20] See Chap. 10.
[21] *Scott's Trs v. Moss* (1899) R. 32. See the cases discussed under trespass above.

some step would have prevented third parties form utilising his land premises to harm the pursuer.[22] As can be seen in the more detailed discussion below the issue is whether the probability of the third party intervention is high on the scale of probability. An alternative view may be that in some cases, especially those involving a person's use of their home or premises, there cannot be liability.

Aemulationem Vicini

It is said to be wrong to act spitefully towards one's neighbour.[23] According 5–22 to Johnstone there are six important eighteenth century cases.[24] He considers that the reception of *aemulationem vicini* never faltered and became an established doctrine of Scots law. Its roots are in the ius commune rather than Roman law itself.[25] In one of the first modern cases, *Ritchie v. Purdie*[26] Lord Gillies said:

"It is a valuable rule of our law that a man cannot use his property in *aemulationem vicini*. He may attempt to do so by positive acts, and this is the most common form perhaps in which such an abuse of the right of property is attempted. But he may also attempt it, as in this instance, negatively, by endeavouring to retrain the rights of his neighbour, to this injury of that neighbour, and without any benefit whatever to himself. In this case, as well as in the other, the Court will refuse their sanction to the nimious and emulous enforcement of a right to the hurt of another."[27]

Indeed the case before the court was "the other way round". The court refused to allow a neighbour to interdict an alleged nuisance. The defender owned a flat or floor in No. 46, being the fourth storey from the foundation. The pursuer was proprietrix of a flat in No. 50, also on the fourth storey from the foundation. Her house was a few feet lower than the floor of Purdie's. There was an ascent of a few steps from the landing to the door of Purdie, which was situated in the mutual gable. Mrs Ritchie's house was described in the titles as "bounded on the east by the mutual gable between it and a tenement built by John Brough"; and it was disponed, "together with free ish and entry to the said dwelling-house and others, the common stair of the said tenement, and the privilege of the space or area at the foot of the common stair, which is declared to be the joint property of the whole

---

[22] The same law applies to moveables—in England a case failed against the owner of a van who left it with the keys in the ignition for the third party to take and in due course harm the plaintiff.

[23] The history development is chartered elsewhere; see D. Johnston, "Owners and Neighbours: from Rome to Scotland" in *Civil Law Tradition in Scotland* (Evans-Jones ed., Supplementary Vol. 2), p. 176.

[24] *Brodie of Letham v. Sir James Cadel of Morton*, March 22, 1707; *Fairly v. Earl of Eglinton* (1744) Mor. 12780; *Gordon v. Grant* (1765) Mor. 7356; *Dewar v. Fraser* (1767) Mor. 12803; *Ralston v. Pettigrew* (1768) Mor. 12808; *Glassford v. Astley* (1808) Mor. App No. 7.

[25] D. Johnston, "Owners and Neighbours: from Rome to Scotland" in *The Civil Law Tradition in Scotland* (Evans-Jones, ed. Supplementary Vol. 2), p. 197.

[26] (1833) 11 S. 771.

[27] *ibid.* at 774–775.

proprietors of the said tenement." Mrs Ritchie's husband was an elocution teacher and knocked a door out into the staircase so that his pupils could come and go. This case was an attempt to prevent the use of the property in this way. That attempt was what was considered to be in *aemulationem vicini*. The following from Lord Craigie represents the most emphatic statement:

> "I take the same view . . . It is a maxim of the law of Scotland, *malitiis non est indulgendum*; and the Court should not permit the malice of a neighbour to stop an operation beneficial to another party, and not injurious to any one."

In other words albeit there was a right to stop it, it was doing no harm and to stop it was contrary to the law. *More v. Boyle*[28] is an apposite case for contemporary conditions. The pursuers owned 88, 90 and 92 in a block of four. The defender owned number 86. The titles said nothing about water, drainage and other services. When the houses were built a water supply pipe was laid from the main supply pipe through the garden ground at the rear of number 86, through to the garden ground at the rear of numbers 88, 90 and 92. From this pipe where it passed through the garden ground there was a branch pipe with a stop-cock led at right-angles to supply each house. A leak occurred in the defender's property. The defender tried to get the pursuers to bear a proportion of the cost of repairing the leak. They refused so to do. The defender excavated the ground in his garden partially closing the water pipe supplying the pursuers' houses. Fourteen days later he closed the pipe and cut off the water supply completely. The claim for damages was put clear upon misuse of property in *aemulationem vicini*. Counsel for the defender argued that the doctrine of *aemulatio vicini* was no longer part of the law of Scotland under reference to *Mayor of Bradford v. Pickles*.[29] It was said, rejecting that argument:

> "In my opinion the dictum of Lord Watson in *Bradford v. Pickles* is inconsistent with principle as expressed by the institutional writers and as applied in numerous cases . . . Moreover in a case subsequent to *Bradford v. Pickles* the Court of Session recognised the existence in the law of Scotland of the doctrine of *aemulatio vicini* (*Campbell v. Muir*, 1908 S.C. 387; 15 SLT 737) Finally, I note that Lord Watson's dictum is doubted or rejected by Gloag and Henderson in their *Introduction to the Law of Scotland* (6th ed.) at p. 397; by Professor T.B. Smith in his *Short Commentary on the Law of Scotland* at p. 662; and by Professor Walker in his work on the *Law of Delict in Scotland*, Vol. II at pp. 992–994. In my judgment, therefore the clear weight of authority is that the doctrine of *aemulatio vicini* is still part of the law of Scotland in an appropriate case".[30]

Applying that to the instant case, it was noted that the defender could have achieved the same result by other means without causing the hardship

---

[28] 1967 S.L.T. (Sh. Ct) 38.
[29] [1895] A.C. 587 at 597.
[30] *More v. Boyle*, at 39–40.

which he did. The pursuers' case based upon the defender having acted in *aemulationem vicini* was held to be relevant.

Lawburrows

Early Scots law had a solution to problems of deliberate activity directed **5–23** against neighbours. A person who has been required to find caution (a sum of money or an insurance bond for a sum of money) not to harm another or his family, may, if he contravenes the non-molestation order be sued in an action of contravention of lawburrows for forfeiture of the caution.[31] The crave may seek imprisonment on the failure to lodge the bond.[32] This is not a process often used because there are so many other practical ways of obtaining the same result. An action of interdict as it has now developed is the most obvious. Another reason for its not being required is the applicability of the criminal law to many problems previously encompassed by lawburrows; breach of the peace being an important example. It has been unsuccessfully used in two tenement disputes between neighbours.[33] An unsuccessful attempt was made to have a chief constable find caution for the alleged behaviour of his officers, but it was held that lawburrows would only be granted in respect of the personal behaviour of the defender and not on the basis of his vicarious responsibility.[34] However, on the authorities it would cover active instigation where it could be shown the officers or other workmen were acting under orders.[35] In *Liddle v. Morton*,[36] a successful case, both parties accepted that the test was reasonable cause to apprehend injury. That is not a point without dispute, but it was not disputed in this High Court case.[37] The question was only whether that test had been met and it was held that it had.

Roman Quasi-Delicts

There are four cases in Justinian's *Institutes* of quasi-delicts. The category is **5–24** recognised as being miscellaneous and resting on no coherent foundation. The cases are important because it has not yet been decided by the Inner House to what extent these are instances of a special type of liability. Thinking about such cases now after the most authoritative rulings in *RHM Bakeries*, and *Kennedy v. Glenbelle* it is inconceivable that they could be seen as instances of strict liability. Instead they are, it is submitted, better considered to be instances where, if the facts meet the category, there is always an inference of *culpa* (not necessarily negligence) which the defender must meet. Only the two heads of liability relevant to heritable property are discussed here. They might be additional species of *culpa* or fall within *Kennedy culpa*.

---

[31] Lawburrows Acts 1429 and 1581.
[32] For an example see the report of *Liddle v. Morton*, 1996 S.L.T. 1143.
[33] *Morrow v. Neil*, 1975 S.L.T. (Sh. Ct) 65; *Porteus v. Rutherford*, 1980 S.L.T. (Sh. Ct) 129.
[34] *Bowman v. Handy*, Unrep., Dundee Sheriff Court, September 22 1986.
[35] See *Tahir v. Gosal*, Unrep., Glasgow Sheriff Court, May 16, 1974.
[36] 1996 S.L.T. 1143.
[37] Appeals are to the High Court of Justiciary.

Actio de positis vel suspensis

5-25 In *MacColl v. Hoo*[38] the owner of a motor car damaged by a slate which had been blown off the roof of a nearby house sought damages from the owner. Before the sheriff the pursuer was successful on the basis of "absolute liability". On appeal the sheriff principal held that the sheriff was mistaken to feel compelled to follow an earlier case of *Cleghorn v. Taylor*.[39] Looking back there is no doubt this is correct because *Cleghorn* was revised in *RHM Bakeries*. Considering Professor Walker's treatment the sheriff principal said:

> "The Roman actio, as the Professor points out, lay where a person kept something placed or suspended over a public way and it caused damage by falling. In such a case there was penal liability and an obligation to take down a thing which might do harm if it fell but no liability in reparation. Hume (Lect. III, 186) indicates that this head of quasi-delict is recognised in Scotland but the terms in which he writes are consistent with the doctrine that civil liability depends upon proof of negligence. In any event, in my opinion the modern view must prevail that there can be no liability without negligence, and it is significant that there is no decision (with the doubtful exception of *Cleghorn v. Taylor*) of any Scottish case which would support an absolute liability on the part of the proprietor of heritable property in any such circumstances. Accordingly in the absence of findings of which negligence on the part of the defender could be established, I am of the opinion that he must be assolizied."

This is entirely correct because the sheriff did indeed find that there was nothing from which fault could be inferred and the post-*RHM Bakeries* case law requires that. The view which found favour was that which had been urged in a critical and learned note of Professor Gordon.[40] The Professor examines another possible Roman source of a special liability:

> "Alternatively or additionally, he [Lord Wood] may have had in mind the Roman rules on *damnum infectum*. These latter imposed on a proprietor, the state of whose property threatened damage to a neighbour, an obligation to give a promise, with security, that he would make good any damage which did occur . . . If he [Lord Wood] were thinking of *damnum infectum*, which was indeed referred to in one of the cases quoted to the court, *Hay v. Littlejohn* (1666) Mor. 13974, Roman law required a neighbour to take preventative action in order to provide a remedy for damage if damage did occur. In *Hay v. Littlejohn* itself, where it was stated that the Roman rules on this matter did not apply and that the Scots law did not require such preventative action, it was nevertheless clearly held that the defender in that case, whose ruinous house (well named 'The Tower of Babylon') had caused the damage complained of, was at fault in not taking steps to prevent damage".

---

[38] 1983 S.L.T. (Sh. Ct) 23.
[39] (1856) 18 D. 664.
[40] "Householders' Liabilities" (1982) J.L.S. 253.

The article gives four reasons for the non-applicability of the Roman law: (1) the actio was for a penalty not damages; (2) the action lay against the occupier not the owner; (3) the Roman law did not apply to bits of a building falling off—that was covered by *damnum infectum*; (4) there is the possibility that the Roman action required the defender to have knowledge of the placing of the item.[41]

Actio de effusis vel dejectis

In *Gray v. Dunlop*[42] a Glaswegian boy had a pot of urine poured upon him 5–26 from the upper window of a lodging house. His father raised an action against the registered keeper[43] and occupier of the premises. In this case the Roman law was clearer than that in relation to the other action. An action *in factum* for double the damage law against the occupier of the house whence that which caused the damage had been thrown or poured. It was not necessary to show that he had been negligent in any way. *Culpa* was "conclusively presumed".[44] The sheriff substitute considered an argument based on Bankton[45] and rejected it.[46] He would have considered a case based on nuisance if there had been proof of a practice known or which ought to have been known.[47]

It can be noted that the conduct complained of under this head is deliberate, albeit the harm is unintentional. This is different from an accident or even from a case where through complete carelessness such as where something is left carelessly on a window sill which is shaken down and in falling injures someone below.[48]

Incorporeal Heritage

In theory it will be a wrong to intentionally destroy or interfere with a 5–27 person's incorporeal property. While there are statutory schemes for incorporeal moveable property, there is not for heritable incorporeals. The main instance of incorporeal heritable right is the lease. As against a wrongdoer the tenant is an assignee of the landlord's rights in so far as required, for example, to protect the subjects let by interdict.[49] So far as

---

[41] See also A. Watson, "The *actio de positis ac suspensis*", *Melanges Meylan*, 1(1963) 379; Birks, "The problem of Quasi-delict", 22 C.L.P. 164, both cited by the learned Professor. Professor Zimmerman comments that it is questionable whether there was strict liability: "perhaps this case was classified as quasi-delict because it was so closely related to the *actio de dejectis vel effusis* and because there did not have to be an injury for liability to arise."—*The Law of Obligations*, p. 17, n. 94.

[42] 1954 S.L.T. (Sh. Ct) 75.

[43] This phrase is used in the report which takes it from the pleadings. It is possible that as the premises were a lodging house there had to be a registered keeper, unlike the usual case where there would only be an owner or an occupier. A similar idea would be the public house which is licensed for use by an individual.

[44] Buckland, *Textbook of Roman Law*, p. 598, n. 22, quoted in Stein, "The *actio de effusis vel dejectis* and the Concept of Quasi-Delict in Scots Law" [1955[4 I.C.L.Q. 356. Zimmerman, *The Law of Obligations*, p.17 citing Ulpian D. 9.3.1.4.

[45] I, iv, 31.

[46] *Gray v. Dunlop, cit. supra*, at 76.

[47] *ibid.*

[48] *Robinson v. Reid's Trs* (1900) 2 F. 928 a case of a failing window sash which caused a pane of glass to fall on someone's head.

[49] *Fleming v. Gemmill*, 1908 15 S.L.T. 691.

damages are concerned in *East Lothian Angling Association v. Haddington Town Council*,[50] an angling association had had for a number of years written permission to fish for trout in parts of the River Tyne and its tributaries. The permission had been granted by the riparian proprietors concerned. As a result of the discharge of sewage into the river by the Burgh, the fishings deteriorated and the Association's sale of permits diminished. It was held that the pursuers had only a personal licence or permission to fish for trout and no real right or interest in the fishing and so had no right to recover damages for injury to the fishing. A permission or licence to fish did not carry with it a legally-implied assignation of the rights of the riparian owner to sue for damage to the fishings. The basic principle that a tenant has an action based on the landlord's right is supported by the decision of the Second Division in *Mull Shellfish Ltd v. Golden Sea Produce Ltd*[51] in which tenants of a seabed site leased from the Crown Estate Commissioners raised an action for damages which they attributed to damage to mussels and mussel larvae which they farmed at the site. The pursuers' lease provided that "subjects of let are let for the sole purpose of anchoring equipment for the rearing and cultivation of shellfish and for no other purpose". It was held that the express terms of the lease granted by the Crown to the pursuers necessarily implied that the pursuers had the right which the Crown alone would otherwise have enjoyed to attract free floating mussel larvae to settle upon the equipment which they were entitled to have at their sites.[52]

---

[50] 1980 S.L.T. 213.
[51] 1992 S.L.T. 703.
[52] See the cases discussed under secondary economic loss in Chap. 10.

CHAPTER 6

MOVEABLE PROPERTY

Introduction

Moveable property can be corporeal or incorporeal.[1] The treatment in this **6-1** book is based on corporeal moveables being the cases most likely to concern the ordinary practitioner although there is an outline treatment of incorporeal moveable property which is now the subject of many statutory rules and is considered a specialist field.

Scots law has given protection to interests in moveables for some time.[2] Spuilzie is the original indigenous wrong against moveables.[3] Professor Walker in *History* explains that two forms developed: the obvious lifting of another's property and a second more technical wrong. The second form relates to appropriation on a defective legal title.[4] Professor Walker identifies another wrong—wrongous intromission, distinguishable by the lesser degree of violence involved.[5] While there is a natural assumption to look for Roman law roots it has been shown that spuilzie may have much in common with the *actio spolii* of medieval law and canon law.[6]

What is attempted in what follows is to set out the principles and rules presently applicable. Erskine defines spuilzie as follows:

"Spuilzie is the taking away or the intermeddling with moveable goods in the possession of another, without either the consent of the other, or the

---

[1] See generally D. Carey-Miller, *Moveable Property in Scotland*, 1991.

[2] An Act of Robert I of 1318 prescribed what had to be specified in pleas relating to the seizure of cattle. Walker, *History*, II, p. 613. Early Scots law provided a remedy. Smith states: "The remedy for wrongful interference with possession of property . . . was in the remote past by the brieve of 'novel dissasine' but about 1400 it was replaced by the action for 'spuilzie'", *Short Commentary*, p. 648. See also Walker, "The Development of Reparation", 1952 J.R. 101. Brieves of Dissasine were still known in the mid-fifteenth century according to H. MacQueen, "Dissasine and Mortancestor in Scots Law" (1983) 4 *Journal of Legal History* 31.

[3] Although it was originally available in heritable cases as well. The Scottish National Dictionary provides a very full entry in respect of spuilzie. The principal meaning given is "to rob, despoil, plunder, lay waste (a person or a place)." One of the examples given is as follows: "Gin I had been meaning to spuilzie ye a', I micht hae taen a moon-lict flitting." Walker has charted the 15th century history of acts against robbery and spuilzie: Walker, *History*, II, p. 620 but matters become more complicated in the 16th century.

[4] Two of his examples are taking goods by virtue of unpaid rent—or poinding without a legal precept. Walker, *History*, III, pp. 734–736.

[5] The order was for repossession, a penalty of ten pounds, the lost profits and the expenses of process. *ibid.*

[6] According to Walker, the remedy dates from before the Decretal Saepe Contingit of Pope Innocent III of 1215 which actually extended the action available against a third party who received the thing (presumably now discussing moveables) with knowledge of the spoliation. Walker, *Delict*, compares spuilzie to the Roman *actio vi bonorum raptorum* The issue is surveyed in Savigny's *Treatise on Possession* (1803, Sweet) (6th.ed., 1848, trans. Perry).

order of law. When a spuilzie is committed, action lies against the delinquent, not only for restoring to the former possessor the goods or their value, but for all the profits he might have made of these goods, had it not been for the spuilzie."[7]

Spuilzie appears and is discussed throughout the rest of this chapter. The important things about the remedy is that it does not require legal possession as title to sue and that violent profits are allowed. Spuilzie effectively vanished although legal historians have not yet determined why or precisely when. Even if a general action for damage and interest was developing then it is hard to see what the attraction of it would be. Having been partially resurrected by Professor Walker,[8] the Scottish Law Commission commented on Spuilzie:

"Spuilzie was, or is the only possessory action recognised by Scots law in relation to moveables, and it is a matter of controversy as to whether, or to what extent, it has fallen into disuse . . . it combines elements of restitution and reparation. It asserts the principle '*spoliatus ante omnia est restituendus*'. It is partly penal in that the pursuer can himself estimate the value of the property of which he was deprived, and claim 'violent profit', *i.e.* such profit as could have been made from the moveables by use of utmost industry."

If something is used and returned undamaged, many modern practitioners have grave difficulty in stating the claim. If there is no harm done—there is no loss to specify. Sometimes it is easier if the pursuer has had to hire a replacement. Then it can be shown that there was a loss of use and it can be valued. Indeed such loss of use claims are familiar from aquilian cases where there is a delay in replacing the damaged article. Spuilzie provides an answer in violent profits without the need to establish a loss.

Too much importance need not be applied to Lord McLean's statement that on authority and on principle an action of spuilzie, in its modern form, was an action of reparation in which consequential damages could be claimed.[9] That dictum was in a case where the defender was relying on spuilzie; trying to say that the pursuer was restricted to violent profits rather than damages. The argument was rightly rejected by his Lordship.

A Practical Analysis

6–2 Problems fall into a number of categories and the lawyer's task is to ask what is the law. The categories of problems are essentially:

(1) Property destroyed

---

[7] Ersk., III,vii,16. Later, he says: "Spuilzie may, by the definition there given of it, be committed not only by strangers but even by the owner of the moveable goods carried off. This action when it is pursued recently and includes the violent profits, being penal, is elided by the defenders having a probable ground of excuse. Defences afford us protection except as to penal consequences of the action: they are utterly ineffectual in so far as concerns simple restitution and damages." IV,i,5.

[8] This was the topic of his first article: D.M. Walker, "Spuilzie", 1949 S.L.T. (News) 136.

[9] *MacKinnon v. Avonside Homes Ltd*, 1993 S.C.L.R. 976.

(2) Property taken

(3) Property used

(4) Property detained

These phenomena can be combined. Thus something can be taken, used, detained and then destroyed. A theory of liability can ignore these categories. The most developed theory of liability in delict today is negligence. It can theoretically be applied to all of these situations. If carried out intentionally these four categories represent four different modes of wrongdoing. They are likely to create four different losses but not necessarily so.

Property destroyed

So far as category (1) is concerned the *lex aquilia* principle of loss **6–3** wrongfully caused applies. In this case for a long time deliberate destruction has fallen clearly within the idea of wrongfulness. This does not depend in any way upon the law of negligence. Examples include the destruction of a horse[10]; the destruction of stakenets[11] and a simple failure to return without explanation raises an obligation to make reparation.[12]

However, the development of the law of negligence means that uninten- **6–4** tional harm is actionable as well. Here however, the idea of remotenesss of injury applies and it may be that some small inattention which could cause a bump to property does not trigger liability where it causes a calamity.[13]

Valuation is essentially based on loss. A valuable examination can be **6–5** found in *Lewis v. Laird Line Ltd.*[14] The pursuers founded on the maxim *contra spoliatorem omnia praesumuntur*[15] and on the analogous rule applicable in cases of spuilzie.[16] However, his Lordship was not prepared to hold that either of these special rules was applicable in proving the value of lost property in an action of damages founded on negligence.[17] It was explained that cost price was not the measure of damage for the loss of partly used or worn articles.

> "The pursuers founded on the rule established in collision cases that no deduction is made from the cost of repairs to the injured vessel on account of the increased value or the substitution of new for old materials (The "Gazelle," 2 W. Rob. 279). In like manner they maintained that they were entitled to the cost of replacing lost effects by purchasing new articles. I do not agree. I think that the general measure of damage for the loss of such articles is their market value. But I do not think that this measure could be fairly applied to a claim for the loss of personal apparel. In that case a distinction, for which I think there is a

---

[10] *Wilsons v. McKnight* (1830) 8 S. 398.

[11] *Grubb v. Mackenzie* (1834) 13 S. 717.

[12] *MacKinnon v. Avonside Homes Ltd*, 1993 S.C.L.R. 976.

[13] See Chapter 10.

[14] 1925 S.L.T. 316.

[15] All things are presumed against a wrongdoer.

[16] Under reference to Stair, I, ix.,18.

[17] Or as was then the term "quasi-delict".

great deal to be said, was drawn between claims by relatives of deceased persons and claims by the owners of the articles themselves. In the former class of claims the defenders' counsel very properly took no exception to the title to sue, but maintained, I think rightly, that the loss could not exceed what the articles would have brought on sale. But in the latter class I think it would not be fair to measure the damage of the owners themselves through the loss of partly used clothing at the very low price which such things would bring in the market. In dealing with such claims I have accordingly applied a percentage of depreciation based on the various considerations above mentioned, and on the special circumstances of each case."[18]

Loss of use is compensable as a head of damages in most cases whether deliberate or negligent.[18a]

6–6   Spuilzie is not appropriate in destruction simpliciter for, in such a case, there is no taking but the destruction is an actionable wrong in its own right.[19] The opinion has been expressed that even if spuilzie is available to a possessor then the damages in the event of non-return ought not to be measured at the value but rather by reference to the loss of possession, although this was expressed, with all respect curiously, as amounting only to a solatium.[20] Accidental destruction of property is generally not actionable as where a horse fell on a stake when being properly driven out of a field.[21]

Property of another taken

6–7   Taken means intentionally taken. Here there is no damage as such. The basis of the wrong being the appropriation of the property, the loss is the loss of the property and its use. There is sound and clear modern law on the topic. It is the kind of activity which would have been struck at by spuilzie and in modern times attracts an award of damages, albeit damage need not be proved. *Stove v. Colvin*[22] is the most important case. One group of Shetland islanders discovered a shoal of whales and managed to drive them to a bay. Another party joined in to help kill the whales. By custom they thus became entitled to a half share of the blubber. They turned up for their share but were turned off by the proprietor who was entitled to half of the fish. The proprietor was held liable for the loss. In a more recent case a counter-claim by a husband against his wife for damages for removal of furniture when they separated was allowed to proceed to proof and was held competent.[23] In *Gorebridge Co-operative Society Ltd v. Turnbull*[24] the pursuers clearly believed the defender to have stolen money and tokens from them. They raised an action against him for payment of money and delivery of the tokens with pleas appropriate only to an action for breach of

---

[18] *Lewis v. Laird Line Ltd*, 1925 S.L.T. 316 at 320.

[18a] See para. 18–9.

[19] *Millar v. Killarnie* (1541) Mor. 14723, a case of effective destruction—corn being cast upon sand.

[20] *Gemmell v. Bank of Scotland*, 1998 S.C.L.R. 144 at 147D.

[21] *Herriot v. Uthank* (1827) 6 S. 211.

[22] (1831) 9 S. 633.

[23] *Aitken v. Aitken*, 1954 S.L.T. (Sh. Ct) 60.

[24] 1952 S.L.T. (Sh. Ct) 91.

contract. The pursuers neither averred that the defender had possession of the money and tokens, nor averred that they had suffered loss and injury. It was held that the action failed as a "restitution" action and failed as an action of reparation based upon delict. The defender after all had been charged with the commission of this crime and sentenced to a term of imprisonment. He did, however, deny the commission of the theft. It was not disputed by counsel for the defender that the victim of a theft has a civil remedy for the recovery of stolen property or its value. The effect of the decision was merely that the civil remedy had to be crafted more finely— averments of the loss of the money would suffice. The tokens it is hard to comment upon—their value is not clear from the report and tokens often have only a nominal objective value.

At the time of writing the most extensive current discussion of spuilzie, in **6–8** this context, is to be found in the sheriff court decision of *Gemmell v. Bank of Scotland*.[25] Heritable creditors forcibly evicted the pursuers. They claimed damages for property they said was left behind and then not returned to them. The bank admitted that their agents removed the goods and disposed of them but said they were of little value. In that case it was complained by the defenders that there had been no allegation of an unlawful taking, the goods had been taken as a result of a warrant of ejection which it was accepted normally requires the subjects to be void and redd. The learned sheriff did not accept that the circumstances of this removal were sufficient to constitute the vitious dispossession required for spuilzie. At an earlier stage of his opinion the learned sheriff commented on this point:

"I read Professor Walker's treatment of spuilzie[26] as extending to virtually any action for the recovery of property and as having developed along with the law of theft, which no longer requires an unlawful taking. The institutional writers, however, all speak of unlawful taking. In my view, spuilzie has not developed in this way and whatever remedies may be available to persons whose property has been acquired by other people in ways other than unlawful taking, spuilzie is not one of them. 'Spuilzie' as Stair says (I,ix,16) is, 'the taking away of moveables without the consent of the owner or other lawful authority'."[27]

A similar view had been taken in relation to vitious dispossession earlier by Sheriff Craik in *Harris v. Abbey National Plc*[28] in which the goods had been disposed of on eviction by the lender's agents. That case was however decided, it is submitted unnecessarily, on the basis of an implied contract of gratuitous deposit.

Property of another used without permission

Usually a case in this category may involve a case under (2) above. **6–9** Rationally, it is possible for use to be made without there having been a taking—where a pawnbroker uses the pawned fiddle to earn money in the

---

[25] 1998 S.C.L.R. 144.
[26] Bell, *Prin.*, s. 676.
[27] *Gemmell v. Bank of Scotland*, at 146C.
[28] 1997 S.C.L.R. 359.

local orchestra. Whether *Pollock v. Workman*[29] is an example of this category is difficult to say. Damages were awarded where a person carried out a post-mortem without the permission of the deceased's son.[30] *Brown's Trustees v. Hay*[31] is clearer. Hay was an employee of a firm of solicitors who while involved with an estate discovered papers which he thought implicated the estate in false returns to the Inland Revenue. He was held liable in damages for the ultroneous use of the property, even although there was no actual loss and no taking. A defender who took possession of a car in a sale from a trustee of a garage proprietor which had not been included in the sale was held liable in damages to the owner of the car.[32] That case may come within this category because the taking was permitted. In *Cairns v. Harry Walker Ltd*[33] the owners of a ship were fined for an excise offence. The cause was the conduct of the steward in conjunction with the defenders. They were held to be liable for the wrongful and illegal use of the ship. Perhaps the most important cases for the development of Scots law in the twentieth century are the "other bottle cases". They are related to the great bottle case of *Donoghue v. Stevenson*[34] by the fact that the technology and circumstances of the time were less hygienic than today.[35] In *Wilson v. Shepherd*,[36] interdict was granted in a case where one trader allowed people to fill another's bottles with paraffin. In a later case the court refused to treat as wrongful the simple use of another trader's property.[37]

6–10   The hire-purchase cases may fall into this category. In such a case the goods are acquired legally by the defender. His use, initially authorised, ceases by contract to be so authorised. Thereafter he is wrongfully detaining the goods. In *F.C. Finance Ltd v. Brown & Son*,[38] a Daimler was let on hire-purchase. The defenders, in the knowledge that the car was subject to a hire-purchase agreement, sold it on the hirers' (West of Scotland Refractories Ltd.) instructions, as their agent, and applied the price to reduce the latters' account with the defenders. The finance company which owned the vehicle sued the dealer for the price. The defenders had thought that West of Scotland refractories would "clear off" the hire-purchase debt but they did not. At first instance a case argued as spuilzie failed. This appears to be because it was never clear that possession reverted to the pursuer owner whom it was also noted had never been in possession. On appeal it was noted that the same kind of circumstances had resulted in successful tort actions.[39] The sheriff principal with some

---

[29] (1900) 2 F. 354.

[30] See also *Hughes v. Robertson*, 1913 SC 394.

[31] (1898) 25 R. 1112.

[32] *Mackintosh v. Galbraith & Arthur* (1900) 3 F. 66.

[33] 1913 2 S.L.T. 379.

[34] 1932 S.C. (HL) 31.

[35] W.W. McBryde, "*Donoghue v. Stevenson*: The story of the 'snail in the bottle' case" in *Obligations in Context*, (Gamble ed., 1990), p. 13.

[36] 1913 S.C. 300

[37] *Leitch v. Leydon*, 1931 S.C. (H.L.) 1. See the parallel case of *A.G. Barr & Co. Ltd v. MacGheoghegan* decided in exactly the same way.

[38] 1969 S.L.T. (Sh. Ct) 41.

[39] Conversion was the tort. The cases were *North General Wagon & Finance Co. v. Graham* [1950] 2 K.B. 7, and *Moorgate Mercantile Co. Ltd v. Read* [1962] 1 Q.B. 701. Still good law in England: Clerk & Lindsell, *Law of Torts*, paras 13–67 and 13–82.

justification decided the case in favour of the pursuers on the basis of lack of care, although it must be said that he was perhaps ahead of his time in doing so then, the loss on one view being economic—a loss on the deal—rather than a loss to property, the car. He continued:

"It is unnecessary for me to consider spuilzie as a separate ground of action. Indeed it may be that the ground upon which I have decided supra is simply a spuilzie in its modern form, since it has been said that the essence of the wrong is to do any act in relation to goods which denies the complainer's title to own or possess them (Walker on Delict, p. 1004). The remedy seems to have much in common with the English doctrine of conversion as described in *North General Wagon & Finance Co. v. Graham*, and if denial of possession is essential to a spuilzie I should have held, following that case, that the pursuers became entitled to immediate possession as soon as the defenders were instructed by the hirers to sell the car."[40]

That dictum probably went too far in relation to spuilzie although it is a point of regret that despite a lot of effort since the explosion in "finance" that Scots law is not crystal clear on the topic. In *Mercantile Credit Co. Ltd v. Townsley*[41] the pursuers hired a motor vehicle to a hirer who was said to have disposed of the goods whilst they were still in the ownership of the pursuers. The pursuers said that this was a spuilzie and the case was so argued at first instance.[42] In the end it turned on an argument that the lack of care in discovering whether or not the goods were on hire-purchase was so bad as to amount to dole which it was assumed would be sufficient to infer liability. He allowed a proof before answer. On appeal to the sheriff it appears that the case had not been accepted as one of spuilzie at all. In any event the sheriff preferred to approach the matter from that of restitution. Thus if it could be shown that the sale was in *mala fidei* payment of the value would be due. On the averments it was held that there was not enough and this part of the case was lost. This seems sensible and simple. The only trouble is that we are then thrown back on the difficulty of the remedy of restitution in Scots law. If it is a kind of surrogate vindicatio then it can be left out of the law of reparation for delict. The measure of the claim is the value of the goods and not aquilian loss. *F.C. Finance Ltd v. Langtry Investment Co. Ltd*[43] covers the same factual territory. It was a case between two finance companies on agreed facts to see who had to carry the loss of an unauthorised transaction. The case was decided on the basis of negligence in the circumstances in not using the services of the hire purchase information service. It was not said that there was a general duty to do this merely that in the particular case it was something which ought to have been done. This case was decided after *Hedley Byrne*.

Property detained

Here the property is not destroyed, it is not taken and it is not used. **6–11** Damages have been awarded for the wrongful detention of property. A person who stopped a coach taking people to a funeral was held liable in

---

[40] *F.C. Finance Ltd v. Brown & Son*, at 44.
[41] 1971 S.L.T. (Sh. Ct) 37.
[42] Reference was made in the case to Professor Gow's *Law of Hire Purchase*, which for a long time was the only handy and thoughtful source on the special topic. See p. 232 *et seq.*
[43] 1973 S.L.T. (Sh. Ct) 11.

damages.[44] This head of liability is clearer in *Snare v. Earl of Fife's Trustees*.[45] In this case the defenders obtained a warrant on the basis that the pictures to be exhibited by the pursuer had been stolen or surreptitiously abstracted. The pursuer was allowed a trial claiming his losses from the absence of the paintings at his exhibition. In *Ferguson v. Peterkin*[46] a couple were staying in an Edinburgh hotel. The wardrobe mirror fell off. The defenders presented the pursuers with a bill for repair as well as for the stay. They tendered payment of the bill, eventually also by solicitor's letter. The defenders purported to detain the travellers' property including documents such as a passport and ration book under the hotel proprietor's lien. Of course the lien did not apply and the mistaken belief that it did, did not exculpate. The sheriff substitute (Garrett) found damages as a jury question. He stated the general rule as being computation by loss of profit, cost of hire or both. In this case he held there was no obligation to buy replacement clothing. On the basis of *Aarons v. Fraser*[47] he held that the court is entitled to award a substantial and not merely a nominal sum for illegal detention even where there is no evidence of specific loss.

6–12   Within this head can be comprised cases where a lawful title ceases and the goods are retained although often liability can be based upon breach of an implied term.[48] Where there is no contract it might be expected that the law applying to this problem should be governed by the same rules as (3) above. That seems to be vouched in *Aarons*. In that case furniture was sent to auctioneers, it was said on a sale or return basis. The defenders admitted at least that they agreed to allow free storage. The goods were sold by the pursuers to a third party. However that third party owed the defenders money and they retained the property against that debt. The pursuers cancelled their contract with the defender and called for delivery. They did not deliver but eventually tendered delivery. It is the cancellation of the contract that suggests that this case is a delict rather than a contract case. The Inner House held that although it was correct that the pursuer could not sue for the value of the goods as they were tendered, damages were due for the "wrongful detention". The Lord Justice Clerk (Aitchison) made it clear he thought a general award of damages, not attached to any particular loss, could be made regardless of whether the case was one of contract or delict.[49] Lord Anderson accepted that this was a prima facie wrong which imported an award of damages "and an award which is not entirely illusory."[50] Lord Murray was much more doubtful because for him liability in delict was anchored to the *damnum injuria datum* principle and he could find only the most trivial damnum.[51] In *VAG Finance Ltd v. Specialised Security (Scotland) Ltd*[52] the first defenders leased a motor vehicle from the pursuers subject to a lease purchase agreement. They sold the car to the

---

[44] *Crawford v. Mill* (1830) 5 Mur. 215.
[45] (1850)13 D. 286
[46] 1953 S.L.T. (Sh. Ct) 91.
[47] 1934 S.L.T. 125.
[48] *Stead v. Cox* (1835) 13 S. 1133.
[49] *ibid.* at 127.
[50] *ibid* at 127.
[51] *ibid.* at 128.
[52] Unreported, Glasgow Sh.Ct, July 8, 1994.

fourth defenders who sold the car on to a bona fide party protected by the Hire Purchase Act 1964.[53] It was argued the claim had to fail as the loss was one of pure economic loss. It was also argued that only fraud or *mala fides* could found a claim. It was held that on the authority of *Northwest Securities* and *F.C. Finance* a claim for negligence or recompense was available. It was alleged that the fourth defenders had contacted the pursuers in order to ascertain the outstanding debt as they were contemplating a kind of part-exchange deal with the first defenders whereby they sold the vehicle to the fourth defenders. A settlement figure was sought and given to discharge the lending but a cheque sent in a lesser sum. The sheriff held that this was not sufficient for a case based on *mala fides* or fraud. He allowed a case based on negligence and rejected the argument that the loss being an economic loss was excluded by the revised view of negligence in *Murphy v. Brentwood*. It is submitted the case on *mala fides* should have been allowed. The fourth defenders, having enquired how much was required to settle should not have sold on without protecting the owner's position. The *mala fides* case is relevant only to profit on the resale. The fraud case may well have been inadequately specified. The true point is that perhaps there was a wrongful interference case missing. The pursuers owned the goods, the fourth defenders knew that and they dealt with the goods deliberately. They are obliged therefore to make up the loss.

Scots Law and the English Law of Conversion

It is not unusual for the Scots practitioner to be asked by an English **6–13** correspondent to take out an action for conversion.[54] The Scottish courts have often disavowed any likelihood of adopting conversion.[55]

Crime and Delict

As can be seen from the discussion of *Gemmell v. Bank of Scotland*,[56] for **6–14** Professor Walker spuilzie is clearly wider in its scope than the law of theft at the time when the delict is being described by the institutional writers. The learned Sheriff, as noted above, disagreed with that view. Nonetheless, that point is worth looking at because it seems consonant with a law of wrongs that something considered to be wrong in a full criminal sense (a common law crime requiring *mens rea*) ought to be a delict in a common law system. This requires some brief examination of the present Scots law of crime.[57] Gloag & Henderson states: "The fact that a particular act which is done wilfully and which causes injury is a criminal offence at common law may, it is conceived, be regarded as a sufficient indication that it also

---

[53] s. 27.

[54] See Clerk and Lindsell, *Law of Torts*, Chap. 13.

[55] *North West Securities v. Barrhead Coachworks Ltd*, 1976 S.C. 68; *Moorgate Mercantile Co. v. Twitchings* [1975] 3 W.L.R. 286. See *Leitch v. Leydon*, 1931 S.C. (H.L) 1, *per* Lord Dunedin. In *First National Bank plc v. Bank of Scotland*, 1999 S.L.T. (Sh. Ct) 10, comment was made on the absence of the doctrine of conversion in Scots law in a case where the pursuers claimed the value of forged drafts from paying bankers because they had handled the drafts.

[56] 1998 S.C.L.R. 144.

[57] Sheriff Gordon is the author of the highly respected title *Criminal Law* so he was well aware of the criminal context.

constitutes a civil wrong".[58] Recently it has been said judicially: "There is no such thing as an exhaustive list of named delicts in the law of Scotland ... if the conduct complained of appears to be wrongful, the law of Scotland will afford a remedy."[59] The present criminal law has disavowed the need for an intention permanently to deprive the owner of his property. In *Milne v. Tudhope*[60] the taking away for a nefarious purpose was approved as a sufficient *mens rea* for the offence. In this case however, the furtiveness which could be said to distinguish theft from spuilzie was present. This was not so in the later case of *Kidston v. Annan*[61] where the complainer handed his television set over willingly for repair and then the repairer repaired the set without permission. The repairer refused to hand over the set without being paid. This was theft. Then, most recently, in *Black v. Carmichael*,[62] putting a restraining device on a motor car was held to be sufficient for theft. It is submitted that the criminal law has now clearly established a range of ways of committing wrongs to property interests, such that these ought to be recognised as civil wrongs bringing about a very similar result.

Restitution and Delict

6–15 Thus far we have looked at the wrong that is done when a person's right of property is interfered with. The court fixes a sum as damages. In the case of destruction it is clearly compensatory as is the case where property is taken. Use and detention can raise another issue. The loss may be small or negligible as where the defender uses one of the pursuer's fifty redundant motor vehicles. The law of obligations can analyse the problem in a different way. The wrong can be treated as a means by which the defender has been unjustly enriched. It has been seen that traditionally Scots law in the shape of spuilzie saw that the wrong of wrongful interference was best dealt with by restitution in the first instance. The remedy of violent profits while seen today as a way of protecting economic loss, which it is in cases other than real or constructive destruction, can be seen as stripping the wrongdoer of the gain of the interference. So far as heritage is concerned the law already, under the name of recompense, makes the defender pay.

Title to Sue

6–16 In principle a legally recognised interest in property ought to be necessary and sufficient. The problem is often precisely what interest is sufficient. Many of the spuilzie cases have raised this difficulty and as has been seen the issue is not free from doubt. The owner will normally have title to sue. Secondly, frequently a possessor will have title to sue against an owner. Novel Dissasine anciently was more concerned with the protection of tenants from their lords than against the world at large.[63] Spuilzie too was available.[64] But who is a possessor of moveables? It seems only the owner

---

[58] Gloag & Henderson, *Introduction to the Law of Scotland*, p. 496.
[59] *The Mihalis* [1984] 2 Lloyd's Rep. 525 at 543.
[60] 1981 S.L.T. (Notes) 42.
[61] 1984 S.C.C.R. 20.
[62] 1992 S.C.C.R. 709.
[63] MacQueen, *Conclusion*, pp. 38 *et seq.*
[64] Stair III,vii,16; Ersk., IV,i,15.

or a person who thinks he is the owner (and he may be in good or bad faith).[65] It is a real right, even though lesser than ownership.[66] Possession implies ownership and thus gives title to sue in spuilzie.[67] That ought to apply in the modern law where the basis of liability is not the existence of remedy but a civil wrong. Carey-Miller holds that "spuilzie will not be available to one who holds on the basis of a contract—such as loan or hire—from which one would infer a continuing acknowledgment of the right of ownership of another."[68] Guthrie-Smith instances the case of a pledgee being able to sue the owner.[69] In *McArthur v. O'Donnell*,[70] the sheriff substitute held that a hirer under a hire-purchase contract who had not paid all the instalments was entitled to sue for delivery against a third party into whose possession they had come. That, of course, is not to say that there is title to sue if the goods had been destroyed or damaged. The cases discussed above raised the question canvassed in England where possession is important—as to when in the hire-purchase type of case the possession ceases to be legitimate; the contract perhaps specifying termination on a failure to pay. We shall see later that the issue of title to sue has arisen in respect of negligent damage to moveables. Here it is important to determine whether the issue relates to remoteness of injury or remoteness of damage. Remoteness of injury does not arise in cases of deliberate wrongdoing. If A holds up a taxi for three income-earning hours then the argument that the taxi was only on hire-purchase cannot avail the defender who ought to be liable to the hire-purchaser. In theory he ought to be liable to the owner as well, but the owner suffers no loss at all. In the case of deliberate destruction the position should be the same but the case comes very close to the difficult negligence cases where the hirer is generally not entitled to sue.

Search and Seizure

A note is needed here because moveables are often interfered with by the **6–17** police in the course of investigation. Reparation for delict here takes on it constitutional function. The law is likely to develop quickly in new directions in view of the incorporation into Scots law of European human rights law. The law for the moment is still broadly as stated in *Laverie v. Murray*.[71] A police constable searched a mill which was on private ground and removed from the mill a driving belt. The owner of the mill subsequently brought an action against the constable claiming damages on the ground that the constable had acted illegally. Proof before answer was allowed. The defender admitted he took possession of the belt and that he did not have a warrant to do so. The policeman had occasion to see the

---

[65] Carey-Miller, *Corporeal Moveables in Scots Law* (1991), para. 1.13.

[66] *ibid.* para. 10.23, citing Stair, II,i,8.

[67] Stair, I,ix,17.

[68] Carey-Miller, *op cit.* para. 10–23.

[69] Guthrie-Smith, *The Law of Damages*, p.132.

[70] 1969 S.L.T. (Sh. Ct) 24.

[71] 1964 S.L.T. (Notes) 3. *Bell v. Black and Morrison* (1865) 3 M. 1079, is a good example of a traditional vindication of liberty from the nineteenth century, referring itself to earlier authority.

pursuer's mill standing on an unfenced piece of land of which the pursuer was neither the owner nor the lessee. He examined the mill and in the storage box attached to the machine was a belt like the belt which had been reported as stolen. Later, on the same day, he returned to the locus with an employee of the owners of the stolen belt who identified the belt in the box attached to the machine as the belt which had been stolen. He removed the belt to preserve evidence. After further inquiries the police were satisfied that the belt which the defender had taken from the pursuer's mill was not the belt which had been stolen. Lord Milligan assoilzied the defender. Lord Milligan summarised the position as being that it was clear that the police could in certain circumstances search for an article and take possession of an article without a warrant:

> "One of the circumstances in which they may do so is if there is "urgency". It may be a matter of urgency to confirm suspicions and it may also be a matter of urgency to take possession of an article if delay in either might result in the loss of evidence. It is, accordingly, necessary to consider whether it has been shown that there was sufficient urgency both in regard to search and in regard to removal of the belt to justify the defender's actings."[72]

It was held that in these circumstances the officer was justified in acting as he did. As expected this principle has been discussed many times and the discussions tend to be located in discussions of criminal procedure where the "illegality" of the search may result in its being excluded as evidence.[73]

SPECIAL CASES

The Praetor's Edict: Nautae, caupones, stabularii

6–18 As the name suggests this is an ancient head of liability. It is one of the cases of quasi-delict mentioned in the Institutes and in summary made the principals of a ship, inn or public stable responsible for theft or damage without proof of fault.[74] Its position in modern Scots law is seen in *Mustard v. Paterson*[75] in which the selection of the three trades was explained by the Lord Justice-Clerk (Alness) as arising from the opportunities for collusion between persons falling within the categories alluded to and their servants, guests, or others. Lord Anderson noted that while it could be said that the law of Scotland has adopted the edict, it had done so by copying and adapting the original doctrine. In *Mustard* it was stated that the defender can only escape liability by proving that the damage or loss arose from inevitable accident, or from the action of the King's enemies. The onus is on the defender to prove this. One interesting point argued in *Mustard* was that the edict was confined to a case of loss, and did not cover a case of

---

[72] *Laverie v. Murray, cit. supra.*
[73] See *Renton and Brown's Criminal Procedure Legislation* (looseleaf), paras 7.21 *et seq.*
[74] Buckland, p. 599.
[75] 1923 S.C. 142.

damage. It was said this was untenable, and unsupported by authority. That may be so for Scots law but Buckland states: "So far as theft was concerned it rested on a special edict but there seems to have been no edict for damnum."[76]

Nautae and the Carriers Act 1830

The strict liability outlined above applies to carriers of goods by sea and **6–19** carriers of goods by land. As explained above the demonstration of reasonable care is not enough. Theft is no defence.[77] Destruction by fire is the carrier's responsibility[78] Defences are *damnum fatale* or inevitable accident or the act of the Queen's enemies.[79] If the goods are damaged because of the way they were packed or addressed[80] or because they self-destruct through inherent vice[81], there is no liability.[82] While it has been held that carriers of passengers are not subject to the edict for injury to the passenger, the liability does apply to the passengers' luggage. In terms of the Carriers Act 1830, common carriers are not liable for the loss of certain specified items,[83] or any of them, contained in any parcel or package which has been delivered, either to be carried for hire, or to accompany the person of any passenger, when the value of such property exceeds £10, unless its nature and value have been declared at the time of delivery to the carrier and an increased charge paid, if required. The charge must be displayed by notice conspicuously in the carrier's office and a receipt must be given for it failing which the benefits of the Act are lost to him and the charge must be refunded. Other than that the Act precludes limitation of the carrier's liability.

Caupones and the Hotel Proprietors Act 1956

As a result of the Hotel Proprietors Act 1956 older authority concerning **6–20** what is or is not an inn and many other questions are now redundant.[84] The liability is as stated in the introduction above. It is essentially most strict. A good example of it is *Williamson v. White*.[85] A parcel was given to an innkeeper by a person who was not staying at the inn and who thus could not be said to be in contractual relations. The goods were left for a carrier

---

[76] Buckland, p. 599.

[77] *Ewing v. Miller* (1687) Mor. 9235; *Campbells v. North British Railway Co* (1875) 2 R. 433.

[78] Mercantile Law (Scotland) Amendment Act 1856, s. 17, applying only to carriers, not *stabularii* or *caupones*.

[79] Bell, *Prin.*, s. 235; Bell, *Prin.*, s. 239 on the effect of unexplained fire must be taken with *Sinclair v. Junor*, 1952 S.L.T. 181.

[80] *Caledonian Railway v. Hunter* (1858) 20 D. 1097.

[81] *Ralston v. Caledonian Railway Co.* (1878) 5 R. 671.

[82] *LNWR Co. v. Robert Hydson & Sons* [1920] A.C. 324.

[83] Gold and silver coin, or gold and silver in a manufactured or non-manufactured state, precious stones, jewellery, watches, clocks, or time-pieces, trinkets, bills, bank notes, orders, notes, or securities for payment of money, stamps, maps, writings, title deeds, paintings, engravings, pictures, gold or silver plate or plated articles, glass, china, silk in a manufactured or unmanufactured state, and whether wrought up or not with other materials, furs or lace (not being machine made).

[84] For examples of difficulties see *Scott v. Yates* (1800) Hume 207; *Watling v. McDowall* (1825) 4 S. 83.

[85] June 21, 1810, F.C.

who stayed at the inn. The parcel was taken off and put in a cellar. Although there was no intimation that the parcel contained money the innkeeper was liable. This Act is not a complete code for what it does is determine and moderate the applicability of the existing edictal liability. Thus it will still be necessary to consider the applicability of the edictal liability to the case in conjunction with the provisions of the Act. It replaced the earlier Innkeeper's Liability Act 1863. A hotel within the meaning of the Act is, and any other, establishment is not, deemed to be an inn; and the duties, liabilities, and rights which immediately before the commencement of the Act by law attached to an innkeeper as such, subject to the provisions of the Act, attach to the proprietor of such a hotel and do not attach to any other person. The proprietor of a hotel is under the same liability, if any, to make good to any guest of his any damage to property brought to the hotel as he would be under to make good the loss thereof. Leaving aside liability on any other ground (such as negligence) the proprietor is not liable except where: (a) at the time of the loss or damage sleeping accommodation at the hotel had been engaged for the traveller; and (b) the loss or damage occurred during the period commencing with the midnight immediately preceding, and ending with the midnight immediately following a period for which the traveller was a guest at the hotel and entitled to use the accommodation so engaged. Neither is the proprietor liable under the edict for any loss of or damage to any vehicle or any property left therein, or any horse or other live animal or its harness or other equipment. Where the proprietor is liable, his liability to any one guest cannot exceed fifty pounds in respect of any one article, or one hundred pounds in the aggregate, except where: (a) the property was stolen, lost or damaged through the default, neglect or wilful act of the proprietor or some servant of his; or (b) the property was deposited by or on behalf of the guest expressly for safe custody with the proprietor or some servant of his authorised or appearing to be authorised for the purpose, and, if so required by the proprietor or that servant, in a container fastened or sealed by the depositor; or (c) at a time after the guest had arrived at the hotel, either the property in question was offered for deposit as aforesaid and the proprietor or his servant refused to receive it, or the guest or some other guest acting on his behalf wished so to offer the property in question but, through the default of the proprietor or a servant of his, was unable to do so. This protection is only available if at the time when the property in question was brought to the hotel, a copy of the notice set out in the Schedule to this Act printed in plain type was conspicuously displayed in a place where it could conveniently be read by his guests at or near the reception office or desk or, where there is no reception office or desk, at or near the main entrance to the hotel.[86]

---

[86] The notice is in the following terms: "Schedule Notice Loss Of Or Damage To Guest's Property. Under the Hotel Proprietors Act, 1956, a hotel proprietor may in certain circumstances be liable to make good any loss of or damage to a guest's property even though it was not due to any fault of the proprietors or staff of the hotel. This liability however—(a) extends only to the property of guests who have engaged sleeping accommodation at the hotel; (b) is limited to £50 for any one article and a total of £100 in the case of any one guest, except in the case of property which has been deposited, or offered for deposit, for safe

Stabularii

The case of *Mustard v. Paterson*[87] is the leading modern authority on this **6–21** particular point. The pursuer entrusted a horse to the defender, who was the lessee of a stable, for some hours, in accordance with an existing arrangement. The horse was delivered by the pursuer to the defender in a sound condition, and was restored to the pursuer in such a state that, on the advice of a veterinary surgeon, it had to be put down. Based on a reading of the Institutional authorities as well as a hearing of arguments directed to the Roman law, it was held that a stabler was liable under the edict in Scots law. In this case the defender did not even try to meet the onus of proof imposed by the edict. It was suggested in argument by the defender that all he had to prove, in order to escape liability, was that he had taken all usual precautions. That view was rejected—if it had been sound, the edict would confer no advantage whatever upon a depositor. In *Laing v. Darling*,[88] the stabler was liable even although the horse was frightened by blasting carried out by another. It has been suggested strongly that a garage cannot by analogy be treated as a stable.[89] However, a garage within a hotel was held to be within the edict—or at least it was not disputed when a golfing lawyer's 1950 Armstrong Siddeley Coupe was melted.[90]

Edict Defences

An innkeeper was exculpated where stables burned down in a fire. Despite **6–22** the fact that there was a suggestion of neglect by the ostler, this was *damnum fatale*, a recognised defence.[91] That money was stolen by an employee was never a defence.[92] Housebreaking was held to be a defence under the edict as *vis major*.[93] The case of *Mustard* already discussed[94] contains a thorough statement of this defence to the edict:.

"I do not think that it matters whether the exceptions to liability are treated under two or three categories. It is generally recognised that the exception, act of God, as used in Roman and Scots law with reference to the edict, has a wider significance than that given to it in other branches of law. Lord Chancellor Westbury, in *Tennant v. Earl of Glasgow* (2 M. (H.L.) 22 at 27), explained that 'what are denominated in the law of Scotland *damnum fatale* occurrences [relate to] circumstances which no human foresight can provide against, and of which human prudence is

---

custody; (c) does not cover motor-cars or other vehicles of any kind or any property left in them, or horses or other live animals. This notice does not constitute an admission either that the Act applies to this hotel or that liability thereunder attaches to the proprietor of this hotel in any particular case".

[87] 1923 S.C. 142.
[88] (1850) 12 D. 1279.
[89] *Central Motors (Glasgow) Ltd v. Cessnock Garage & Motor Co.*, 1925 S.L.T. 563; concurred in by the Lord Ordinary (Strachan) in *Sinclair v. Junor*, 1952 S.L.T. 181 at 184.
[90] *Burns v. Royal Hotel (St. Andrews) Ltd*, 1958 S.L.T. 309.
[91] *McDonell v. Ettles*, Dec. 15, 1809, F.C.
[92] *McPherson v. Christie* (1841) 3 D. 930.
[93] *Watling v. McDowall* (1825) 4 S. 83.
[94] See para. 6–21 above.

not bound to recognise the possibility, and which, when they do occur, therefore, are calamities that do not involve the obligation of paying for the consequences that may result from them.' This interpretation of *damnum fatale* has not been accepted as determining whether a case comes within the exception to the edict or not. In *McDonell v. Ettles* (Dec. 15, 1809, F.C.) it was held that accidental fire in the stables of an inn causing injury to a horse which had been lodged there formed an exception to the edict. Cockburn C.J., in *Nugent v. Smith* (1 C.P.D. at 429), said: 'The Roman law made no distinction between inevitable accident arising from what in our law is termed the "act of God", and inevitable accident arising from other causes, but, on the contrary, afforded immunity to the carrier, without distinction, whenever the loss resulted from casus fortuitus or, as it is also called, *"damnum fatale"*, or *"vis major"*—unforeseen and unavoidable accident.' In the same case James L.J. said: 'The "act of God" is a mere short way of expressing this proposition. A common carrier is not liable for any accident as to which he can shew that it is due to natural causes directly and exclusively, without human intervention, and that it could not have been prevented by any amount of foresight and pains and care reasonably to be expected from him.' Accepting this view as sound (and I think it is) of the exception 'act of God' within the meaning of the edict as interpreted in Rome and Scotland, the appellant has, in my opinion, entirely failed to bring himself within the exception. He has not given any explanation of the circumstance that the pursuer's horse which was entrusted to him in a sound condition left that custody suffering from injuries that necessitated its being shot".[95]

In *Sinclair v. Junor*[96] a car in a garage for repair was destroyed by fire. The pursuer did not seek to base a case on the edict but nonetheless Lord President Cooper felt it necessary to deal with the issue of accidental fire. This does not mean these views are *obiter*.[97] So far as he was concerned in a case such as he was deciding based on deposit there could not be liability if there could not be liability under the stricter edict. An accidental fire, he considered, is one not started by the keeper nor one the result of culpable acts or omissions by him or those for whom he is responsible. The Lord President's view was that the onus was on the keeper to negate these two possibilities and in the case before him the first defender failed to do that much to the Lord President's regret. This passage is thus very special being an attempt to justify what was considered a difficult decision forced upon the court by the evidence which might not have been focused properly. Nonetheless, Lord Keith thought that *McDonell v. Ettles*[98] was only authority for the proposition that accidental fire is *damnum fatale* for the purpose of the edict. The Lord President pointed out that before *McDonell* it was thought that there was no excuse for fire. That case, he thought, was only to the effect that a defender could be exculpated if he were able to

---

[95] 1923 S.L.T. 21 at 26, *per* Lord Hunter.
[96] 1952 S.L.T. 181.
[97] It was an alternative case before the Lord Ordinary.
[98] Dec. 15, 1809, F.C. 460.

show that the fire were in fact accidental. All of this leaves us still curious as to arson. That does not fit into the two last categories. In *Burns v. Royal Hotel (St. Andrews) Ltd*[99] the issue was addressed by Lord President Clyde. With all respect this analysis seems the clearest.

There are three types of fire: intentional fires, negligent fires and accidental fires.[1] *Damnum fatale* only arises in the accidental case. The defender must establish under the edict the accidental fire. It is however stated there that the defender can escape liability by excluding intentional fire raising and their own or presumably their servant's negligence. Lord President Clyde did not agree with his learned predecessors view as it had no warrant. As stated above they cannot really be dismissed as *obiter* because they are really *a fortiori* arguments. It is clear too, that Lord Sorn felt that the issue was one of a shifted onus. This is a different thing from liability subject to a defence; not least because one can be decided as a matter of relevancy and the other only after proof. The only worrying thing about this case is the whole effort to reconcile it with the idea of negligence by the defender. The idea of the edict is that this need not be inquired into at all.

Animals

Animals are often valuable, but are not easily controlled. The law in this **6–23** area is contained within the Animals (Scotland) Act 1987. Where an animal strays on to any land and is not then under the control of any person, the occupier of the land may detain the animal for the purpose of preventing injury or damage by it.[2] Section 4(1) provides that in any civil proceedings against a person for killing or causing injury to an animal, it is a defence for him to prove: (a) that he acted—(i) in self-defence[3]; (ii) for the protection of any other person; or (iii) for the protection of any livestock. There are two other conditions: the person must be a person who, at the time of the injury or killing complained was a keeper of the livestock concerned (section 4(3)(a)); (b) the owner or occupier of the land where the livestock was present; and (c) a person authorised (either expressly or impliedly) to act for the protection of the livestock by such a keeper of the livestock or by the owner or occupier of the land where the livestock was present; and within 48 hours after the killing or injury notice must given by him or on his behalf at a police station or to a constable (section 4(1)(b)). There is an exception to the protection where the killing or injury (a) occurred at or near a place where the person was present for the purpose of engaging a criminal activity; and (b) was in furtherance of that activity. It will be noted that the Act does not say what the nature of the proceedings would be. It is submitted that the action is likely to be such as was discussed in 1 above where the animal is destroyed or injured or in category 2 where the animal is detained.

---

[99] 1958 S.L.T. 309.
[1] *ibid*. at 312.
[2] s. 3(1).
[3] A person killing or causing injury to an animal is regarded as acting in self-defence if, and only if, the animal is attacking or is about to attack and he has reasonable grounds for believing that there are no other practicable means of ending or preventing the attack. See *Fairlie v. Carruthers*, 1996 S.L.T. (Sh Ct) 56.

Statutory Authority

6–24 Some statutes, through their effect on the law of property, have the effect of protecting persons against delictual actions.[4]

INCORPOREAL PROPERTY

6–25 In principle the position should be the same in relation to incorporeal property as corporeal property. Clearly the first question is the property question. It is not possible to take a firm view on what is or is not incorporeal but there is a core of certainty. Incorporeal property rights created by statute incorporate their own systems of enforcement and protection. Questions of wrongs or damages in relation to these rights are today thought of as part of a legal speciality "intellectual property." The key statutes are United Kingdom statutes and the practitioner and the courts will make reference to U.K. cases and English books will be of very considerable assistance.[5] Common law principles still play a part. For the benefit of the practitioner analysing a problem raising these issues there follows a brief review of reparation and interdict claims under a selection of these statutes.[6]

Trade Marks

6–26 A registered trade mark is incorporeal property.[7] The Act purports to implement E.C. law. Thus it is possible Euro-rep issues might arise.[8] A trade mark is any sign capable of being represented graphically which is capable of distinguishing goods or services of one undertaking from those of another.[9] It can consist of words, including personal names, designs, letters numerals or the shape of goods or their packaging. To obtain the benefits of the Act the mark must be registered.[10] It is impossible to recover damages for the infringement of an unregistered mark[11] without prejudice to an action for passing-off. The main wrong is infringement which occurs where a person uses[12] the mark in the course of a trade—a sign which is identical with the trade mark in relation to goods or services which are

---

[4] See, *e.g.* Consumer Credit Act 1974; Innkeepers Act 1878; Civic Government (Scotland) Act; Sale of Goods Act 1979.

[5] Morcom, *A Guide to the Trade Marks Act 1994* (1994); Young, Watson, Thorley and Miller, *Terrell on the Law of Patents* (14th. ed., Sweet & Maxwell, 1994); Clark, Jacob, Cornish, May, Moody-Stuart, *Encyclopedia of United Kingdom and European Patent Law* (looseleaf) (Sweet & Maxwell); *Halsbury's Laws of England*, Vol. 35. For a full Scottish commentary, see *Stair Memorial Encyclopedia on the Laws of Scotland*, Vol. 18, "Intellectual Property".

[6] There are dangers in dabbling: F. Akers, "When Threats can Backfire" (1998) 43 J.L.S. 9–22.

[7] Trademarks Act 1994, s. 22. It can thus be assigned in whole or partially: s. 24.

[8] See Chap. 11.

[9] s. 1(1).

[10] s. 63.

[11] s. 2(2).

[12] According to s. 10(4) by affixing it to goods or their packaging, offers or exposes the goods or services for sale puts them on the market or stocks them, imports or exports them or puts the sign on business paper or in advertising.

identical with those for which it is registered.[13] Similar marks in identical fields or identical marks in similar fields are actionable if there is a likelihood of confusion on the part of the public.[14] It is possible to use the mark to identify goods as those of another so long as in accordance with honest practices in industrial or commercial matters; even then to be an infringement the use would have to take unfair advantage of the mark or be detrimental to it.[15] It is not an infringement for a person to use his own name or address, descriptive terms like purpose value or geographical origin, or to use it to denote the purpose of a product so long as in accordance with honest practice.[16] Title to sue is mainly with the proprietor although in some cases a licensee has title.[17] The remedies are damages, interdict or an account of profits. Statutory remedies such as erasure or obliteration of the mark; destruction of goods or delivery and disposal of goods are also possible.[18] Unlike the law of passing-off there is no need to show any misrepresentation nor is there any need to show a loss to goodwill.

One statutory remedy of which the non-specialist must be aware is the **6–27** action for groundless threats of infringement proceedings. Declarator, interdict and damages are available where a threat is made of an action for infringement unless the application of the mark is to goods or their packaging, the importation of goods to which or to the packaging of which the mark has been applied. It is not a threat to intimate the existence of the trade mark and express the intention that any infringer will be subject to enforcement.[19]

Patents

The present statutory regime is provided by the Patents Act 1977.[20] A **6–28** patent can be granted only for an invention which is new, involves an inventive step and is capable of industrial application.[21] The patent is granted by the Comptroller-General of Patents, Designs and Trade Marks. There is a register giving prima facie title to sue. For the purposes of this book the assumption is that the patent is granted and the question is whether there is a possible wrong. But the creation of the patent is critical to the ultimate decision of many cases for the patent is defined by its specification and claims. While it has been held in a Scottish case that construction of these critical parts is a matter for the court,[22] it is now the case that that interpretation ought to be in accord with the European

---

[13] s. 10(1).
[14] s. 10(2)(3).
[15] s. 10(6). See, *e.g. Teknek Electronics Ltd v. KSM International Ltd,* 1998 G.W.D. 5–253.
[16] s. 11(2). In *Allied Domecq Spirits & Wine Ltd v. Murray McDavid Ltd,* 1999 S.L.T. 157. Lord McFadyen expressed the opinion that in construing this subsection no or only the most cautious and guarded reliance should be placed on authority preceding the coming into force of the 1994 Act.
[17] s. 14; ss. 30 and 31.
[18] ss. 14–17.
[19] See F. Akers, "When Threats can Backfire" (1998) 43 J.L.S. 9–22.
[20] The Act both gives effect to three international conventions and the European Union system involving Community patents: see Copyright, Designs and Patents Act 1988.
[21] s. 1(1).
[22] *Lyle & Scott v. Wolsey,* 1955 S.L.T. 322.

Patent Convention which requires the interpretation to founded on the strict literal meaning of the words in the claim, the description and drawings being used only for resolving ambiguities. The claims are not to be interpreted as mere guidance. The claim should be interpreted providing a fair protection for the patentee with a reasonable degree of certainty for third parties. The House of Lords took a less than strict approach in *Catnic Components v. Hill & Smith Ltd.*[23]

6–29   There is an infringement if but only if the defender does any of the following without the proprietor's consent: (i) where the invention is a product he makes, disposes of, offers to dispose of, uses or imports the product or keeps it whether for disposal or otherwise; (ii) where the invention is a process, he uses the process or he offers it for use in the United Kingdom when he knows, or it is obvious to a reasonable person in the circumstances, that its use without the consent of the proprietor would be an infringement of the patent; (iii) where the invention is a process, he disposes of, offers to dispose of, uses or imports any product obtained directly by means of that process or keeps any such product whether for disposal or otherwise.[24] Private and non-commercial Acts, experimental acts and extempore preparation of medicine in a pharmacy are exempt. The basic remedy is damages or an account of profits. Interdict, declarator, delivery and destruction are also available. In *British Thomson-Houston Co. v. Charlesworth, Peebles & Co.,*[25] damages were allowed on a royalty basis. Actions have to be brought in the Court of Session. Matters which would allow a patent to be revoked because it should not really have been granted in the first place are available as defences.[26]

6–30   It is a wrong to threaten infringement proceedings without justification. It is not a threat to intimate the existence of the patent and express the intention that any infringer will be subject to enforcement.[27]

Copyright

6–31 The law is now set out in the Copyright, Designs and Patents Act 1988.[28] The right is about protecting works from copying or performance. It arises automatically without the need for registration. The maxim, "there is no copyright in an idea" must be regarded carefully[29] but that does convey rather well the key concept that it is copying something that is written down which is the core concept. Copyright exists in original literary, dramatic,

---

[23] [1982] R.P.C. 183. See also *Assidoman Multipack Ltd v. The Mead Corp.* [1995] F.S.R. 225.

[24] s. 60(1).

[25] 1923 S.C. 599.

[26] *Conoco Speciality Products (Inc.) v. Merpo Montassa Ltd,* 1992 S.L.T. 444; *Lyle & Scott v. Wolsey,* n. 22 above.

[27] Akers, *op. cit.*

[28] Note that by s. 172(2) a provision of the 1988 Act which corresponds to a provision of the previous law is not to be construed as departing from the previous law merely because of a change of expression. See *Redrow Homes Ltd v. Bett Brothers plc,* 1988 S.L.T. 648. Previous legislation is still very relevant as being directly applicable or in some cases persuasive by way of interpretation.

[29] *Ibcos Computers Ltd v. Barclays Finance Ltd* [1994] F.S.R. 275.

musical or artistic works[30]; sound recordings[31]; films[32]; broadcasts and cable tv programmes and the typographical arrangement of published editions.[33] Computer programmes are within the protection.[34] So are plans for houses.[35] Originality here means only that it originated from the author not that it was world-shattering. The owner is usually the author but where made by an employee in the course of his employment, it normally belongs to the employer unless otherwise agreed.[36] The basic period of protection is 70 years (50 for computer generated works) as a result of the Duration of Copyright and Rights in Performances Regulations 1995.[37] There are detailed rules for computing the period. There are complex provisions for international cases. Assignation is possible and subject to detailed rules. It is the owner or his licensee who may copy the work, perform it,[38] sell it on tape or video or adapt it and if anyone else does this is an infringement.[39] Copyright is not infringed by fair-dealing for the purposes of research or private study or for criticism, review or news-reporting and there are block licences in force in universities which may lead people in later life to underestimate the scope of copyright protection. Three dimensional representation of two dimensional work can be infringement.[40] To infringe, there must be copying of at least a substantial part and it can be difficult to determine on objective examination whether this has taken place. It is not an infringement to parody or use another writer's characters so long as the new work is itself original and not itself substantially similar. This whole investigation is a specialist area of law and the specialist texts need be consulted.[41] An infringement of copyright is actionable by the copyright owner.[42] In an action for infringement of copyright all such relief by way of damages, injunctions, accounts or otherwise is available to the plaintiff as is available in respect of the infringement of any other property right.[43] Where in an action for infringement of copyright it is shown that at the time of the infringement the defendant did not know, and had no reason to believe, that copyright subsisted in the work to which the action relates, the plaintiff is not entitled to damages against him, but without prejudice to any other remedy.[44] The court may in an action for infringement of copyright having

---

[30] *Howard Clark v. David Allan & Co. Ltd*, 1987 S.L.T. 271. This was a case under the 1956 Act in which Lord Jauncey held that prima facie design drawings for a new and original form of waterproof jacket fell within the phrase.

[31] *Phonographic Performance Ltd. v. McKenzie*, 1982 S.L.T. 272.

[32] *Milligan v. The Broadway Cinema Productions Ltd*, 1923 S.L.T. 35 re the screenplay of "Football Daft".

[33] s. 1.

[34] *Ibcos Computers Ltd v. Barclays Finance Ltd*, n. 29 above. And see the discussion in *Beta Computers (Europe) Ltd v. Adobe Systems (Europe) Ltd*,1996 S.L.T. 604.

[35] *Redrow Homes Ltd v. Bett Brothers plc*, 1988 S.L.T. 648; *Oliver Homes (Manufacturing) v. Hamilton*, 1992 S.L.T. 892.

[36] s. 11. See the facts of *Milligan v. The Broadway Cinema Productions Ltd* for an illustration of circumstances.

[37] S.I. 1995 No.3297.

[38] See *The Performing Rights Society Ltd v. Rangers F.C. Supporters Club*, 1974 S.L.T. 151.

[39] s. 16.

[40] s. 17(3); *Howard Clark v. David Allan & Co. Ltd*, 1987 S.L.T. 271.

[41] Laddie, Prescott and Vitoria, *The Modern Law of Copyright and Designs*, (2nd ed., 1994); Copinger and Skone, *James on Copyright*, (13th. ed. and supp., 1991).

[42] s. 96(1).

[43] s. 96(2).

[44] s. 97(1).

regard to all the circumstances, and in particular to: (a) the flagrancy of the infringement, and (b) any benefit accruing to the defendant by reason of the infringement, award such additional damages as the justice of the case may require.[45] This latter provision on damages has been interpreted in the Scottish case *Redrow Homes Ltd v. Bett Brothers plc*[46] in which it was held that the additional damages are additional only to damages and not an extra new remedy that can be claimed in addition to an account of profits.

Other Statutory Rights

6-32 All the foregoing are outwith even the sketchy treatment of incorporeal rights in this book but ought to be noted to complete the structure.

Moral rights

6-33 Introduced in the United Kingdom in the 1988 Act, these rights allow the author to be identified as such, to object to derogatory treatment and to object to false attribution.[47] The rights subsist for the copyright period but false attribution subsists for 20 years after death.

Design rights

6-34 These rights protect the designer of industrial goods. The provision is complex and its history convoluted. The 1988 Act essentially takes away previous protection, in some ways too strict, and gives a new protection. It declares that it is not an infringement of copyright in a design document or model recording or embodying a design for anything other than an artistic work or a typeface to make an article to the design or to copy an article made to the design.[48] So reverse engineering of an industrial thing is not protected by copyright but may be by the new design right.[49] The right applies without registration. It must be original and not commonplace. Spare parts makers have special protection where the product said to be infringing either "must fit" or "must match". The right applies for 15 years—much less than the copyright period and indeed lasts only ten years if a product is put out for sale. Infringement is by copying the design document or making articles to the design.

Registered Designs

6-35 Under the Registered Designs Act 1949, as amended by the Copyright Act 1988, protection may be given after registration to a design, being the features which appeal to the eye rather than the function. The right vests in the proprietor. Infringement is dealing with an article which meets the specification of the registered design. An example under the unamended legislation which included the word "solely" in relation to eye appeal is *G. A. Harvey And Company (London) Ltd v. Secure Fittings Ltd.*[50] The

---

[45] s. 97(2).
[46] 1998 S.L.T. 648. See also *Oliver Homes (Manufacturing) v. Hamilton*, 1992 S.L.T. 892.
[47] s. 86.
[48] s.51(1).
[49] s. 213.
[50] 1966 S.L.T. 12.

petitioners were the registered proprietors of a unit comprising in combination cold and hot water tanks. They alleged that the respondents had offered for sale an article to which the registered design, or one not substantially different from it, was to be applied. The design registered consisted of an upper cold water tank, rectangular in shape which had a top cover and rested on a tray; below there was a space and then there was a copper hot water cylinder resting on a tray, which was insulated by fibreglass slabs. It was all boxed in by a hardwood producing a rectangular shape identical with the upper shape, the two being connected by two pipes. Everything was put into a rectangular angle iron framework. The respondents maintained that the registration was invalid because, in order to work the unit could only be made in the shape registered, that the registered design lacked novelty, and that the unit offered by them would not necessarily present the same appearance. After proof interdict was granted it being held that the design registered was not dictated solely by function, nor that it lacked novelty. The respondents had not proved that the unit offered by them would have presented a different appearance.

Performers' rights

A performer's consent is required for the exploitation of his or her **6–36** performances. Infringement is by copying other than for private use.[51] The Copyright Tribunal can give consent where it is unreasonably withheld or the performer cannot be found.[52]

Recording rights

These are similar to the performer's rights save they are held by a person **6–37** having an exclusive recording contract.[53] Infringement is by copying other than for private use.[54]

---

[51] 1988 Act, s. 181.
[52] ss. 190, 149(9).
[53] s. 180.
[54] s. 186.

CHAPTER 7

BUSINESS

Introduction

It would be curious if a developed legal system protected a person against **7–1**
having his arm bruised or his vase broken but allowed his business to be
destroyed with impunity. As shall be seen there are some wrongs which
have the effect of protecting businesses. It is possible that they do so
because the law wants this result; equally it may be a coincidence. To this
extent these instances of liability could be good examples of the "interests"
theory of liability—especially because the wrongs against them are not met
by well-known ancient remedies.[1] Equally, some or all may be restraints on
disapproved conduct.[2] They require to be examined in context before a
view can be taken. Economic activities are a difficult area for legal
intervention because the nature of a free market is that the success of one
participant can necessitate the failure of another, although unfortunate for
the defeated entrepreneur, market theory considers that there are consequent gains for consumers in the market and indeed for producers and
workers. The further difficulty is that there is no such thing as a free
market. There are and always have been regulations to prevent the excess
of those who seek to maximise profit but who in so doing threaten the very
market upon which everyone depends.[3] There are important Scots cases but

---

[1] See Chap. 1. The German Civil Code most obviously reflects this particular "interest"
strand in civilian thinking. Art. 823I provides that a person who "wilfully or negligently injures
the life, body, health, freedom, property, or other right of another contrary to law is bound to
compensate him for any damage arising therefrom": Markesinis, *The German Law of Torts*, p.
10. This was extended in some cases to protect the rights of an established and operating
business (*ibid.* p. 54). However, the courts treat this rather restrictively (*ibid.* pp. 173 *et seq.*) A
different principle it seems informs German cases on the facts of our economic delicts—Art.
826 provides that a person is liable in damages if he deliberately causes harm to another in a
manner repugnant to good morals. Weir considers this a "morality" issue: see *A Casebook on
Tort* (8ᵗʰ ed., 1996), pp. 46–56. See also J. Holyoak and F. Mazzocchetti, "The Legal
Protection of Economic Interests", (1993) 1 Tort L. R. 185.
[2] Thomson sees conspiracy as a form of "conduct" wrong—a form of *culpa*: J.M. Thomson,
"An Island Legacy, the Delict of Conspiracy" in *Comparative and Historical Essays in Scots
Law* (Carey Miller and Myers ed., Butterworths, 1992), p. 149.
[3] See P.S. Atiyah, *The Rise and Fall of Freedom of Contract* (1979) dealing with the time
around 1770 and treating of the offences of regrating, forestalling and engrossing: p. 116 and
128 *et seq.* Professor Walker shows a similar history for Scotland: Walker, *History*, I, pp. 106
and 201. He points out that one early text the *leges Quatuor Burgorum* regulates, *inter alia*,
forestalling and regrating: pp. 202 and 342. The matter is charter in Walker, *History*, II, pp.
438 and 440. Walker also notes that when Balfour writes the offences were then still current:
History, III, p. 338. He goes on to summarise that "enterprise and competition were, however,
not favoured": p. 719. Walker, *History*, IV, p. 509 notes that despite the Forestalling Acts of
1535 and 1592, McKenzie's last noted case was 1592 and Hume's 1607.

for practical purposes the law of England is regularly observed.[4] This is partly *faut de mieux* and partly accident, because, as is discussed below, many cases involve trade unions whose activities are countrywide. English law is not the only answer and is not itself in an entirely happy state. In so far as the matters dealt with in this chapter affect competition between undertakings at a high level of operation the law of the European Union applies. At a lower level there is independent United Kingdom competition law which has now been brought into line with the philosophy of the European law.[5] For the present Scots lawyers at this time would be best advised to focus on the Scottish cases and the important English cases as first options, *faut de mieux*. The scope of this work precludes a full examination of the law of England save to the extent that it has shaped and determines our own law. The pleader utilising English authority must be aware of the debate and criticisms that exist in that system.[6]

7–2   It is a matter of observation that a large number of cases and particularly leading cases involve trade unions. This is not a coincidence. One of the things unions do is fight for their members against employers. It is "nothing personal" so the action is usually directed against businesses and the business interests of businesses. However, the traditional view is that this is coincidence and the law should be even-handed. It was put thus as long ago in Scotland as *Couper & Son v. Macfarlane*.[7] Lord Gifford said:

> "Of course, I do not enter in the slightest into the merits of the dispute between the employers and the workmen in the glass cutting manufacture in 1876. I do not know which party was right. And I do not care."[8]

The Lord Justice-Clerk (Moncreiff) dissenting said:

> "This action does not depend on any question of the freedom of whether masters or men to combine amongst themselves for any legitimate purpose, and it might just as well have been raised against a man who did not belong to a trades union, or against one who belonged to a masonic lodge, or to a temperance association, or to no association at all."[9]

PRINCIPLES

Non-intervention

7–3 In *Mogul Steamship Co. Ltd v. McGregor, Gow & Co.*[10] it was held not to be actionable for the defendants to put the plaintiffs out of business by undercutting their competitors, offering rebates to those exclusively dealing

---

[4] See Craig and Miller, *Employment Law in Scotland* (2nd ed., T&T Clark, 1996).
[5] Competition Act 1998.
[6] See Clerk & Lindsell, *Law of Torts*, Chap. 23.
[7] (1879) 6 R. 683. And see Atiyah, *op. cit.*, p. 410 dealing with the English case of *Hylton v. Eckersley* (1855) 6 El. & Bl. 47 requiring an even handed approach to unions and employers' associations.
[8] *ibid.* at 696.
[9] *ibid.* at 698.
[10] [1892] A.C. 25.

with them and restricting their own agents from dealing with competitors. Shortly afterwards it was held not to be actionable for defendants to offer to sell the plaintiffs pianos cheaper than their wholesale price.[11] This was permissible, even although at the time of the advertisement the defendant did not have any of the plaintiff's pianos in stock. In *Allen v. Flood*[12] a union official was held not to be liable for intimating to his employers that if certain workers (members of another union) were not dismissed, their union workers would not work. The workers were employed on a daily basis and were under no obligation to sign on for work the next day. The competition was not between businesses but between unions, however, the principles should be the same. Other judges were summoned to hear argument and offer guidance to the seven judge House of Lords. The division of opinion is considerable, as Weir points out[13] of the 21 judges who wrote on the case only eight were for the successful party.[14] The case is authority for freedom of action where there is no unlawful action nor unlawful means adopted. The critical fact was that the contracts were daily contracts. For some of the other judges whose opinion was the other way this was too legalistic an approach. In the middle of the twentieth century Lord Wright said in *Crofter Hand Woven Harris Tweed Co v. Veitch*[15]:

"We live in a competitive or acquisitive society, and the English common law may have felt that it was beyond its power to fix by any but the crudest distinctions the metes and bounds which divide the rightful or the wrongful use of the actor's own freedom, leaving the precise application in any particular case to the jury or judge of fact. If further principles of regulation or control are to be introduced, that is matter for the legislature. There are not many cases in which the Court has had to consider these problems. Actions of this character are not of everyday occurrence like actions for negligence."[16]

Not only was the court concerned not to interfere with commerce, but also to leave trades unions a considerable degree of freedom. The non-intervention in the name of freedom is as we shall see restricted, as Lord Wright put it in *Crofter*:

"It cannot be merely that the appellants' right to freedom in conducting their trade has been interfered with. That right is not an absolute or unconditional right. It is only a particular aspect of the citizen's right to personal freedom, and like other aspects of that right is qualified by various legal limitations, either by statute or by common law. Such limitations are inevitable in organised societies where the rights of individuals may clash. In commercial affairs each trader's rights are qualified by the right of others to compete."[17]

---

[11] *Ajello v. Worsley* [1898] 1 Ch. 274.
[12] [1898] A.C. 1.
[13] *A Casebook on Tort* (8th ed., 1996), p.595.
[14] "perhaps the most important (case) in the whole of the law of torts": R. Heuston, "Judicial Prosopography" (1986) 102 L.Q.R. 90 at 97.
[15] 1942 S.C. (H.L.) 1, discussed further at para. 7–33 below.
[16] *ibid.*
[17] *ibid.*

Aemulationem vicini

7–4 This doctrine has been discussed in relation to the use of heritage.[18] The idea can apply to the conduct of business. It represents a form of intervention short of judging what is or is not good business practice—the law only intervenes where it can be shown that conduct is not to further the interests of the defender's own organisation but to harm the pursuer. Bowen L.J. in *Mogul Steamship*[19] mentioned the doctrine. If this doctrine applies the malicious infliction of harm would be actionable, even if the conduct complained of is, on the face of it, lawful.[20] Professor Johnson notes that the earliest Scots cases did deal with competition rather than use of heritage, for example, the establishment of a new fair next to an existing one.[21] Thus this doctrine remains as a potential source of inspiration for judicial decision in the economic delicts, especially as there are so few precedents to get in the way.

Wrongful interference with trade; causing loss by unlawful means

7–5 The existence of such a broad principle justifying an action in tort and perhaps explaining some of the existing heads was pled and conceded in the House of Lords in *Lonrho plc v. Al-Fayed*[22] It was accepted in the House that the tort exists but that its definition was, and still remains, uncertain. It was briefly considered in a Scottish case which appeared to recognise the wider tort: *Shell U.K. Ltd v. McGillivary.*[23] Employees of contractors engaged in an industrial dispute conducted a "sit-in" on board offshore installations operated by a third party. The employees were on board the installations to carry out services which their employers had undertaken to supply to the petitioners, who were the operators of the installations. The sit-in interfered substantially with operations on the installations and the petitioners sought interdict and interim interdict to have the, by then former, employees of the contractors remove themselves. The employees argued that the petitioners had no right in law to require them to leave the installations and that their actings were subject to immunity under section 13(1) of the Trade Union and Labour Relations Act 1974. They also argued that the balance of convenience favoured the continuation of the sit-in. Lord Cameron of Lochbroom held that what was said in *Phestos Shipping Co. Ltd v. Kurmiawan*[24] was correct, namely Scots law "offers remedies for the unlawful occupation of property, be it heritable or moveable, even where that occupation is not affecting the owner's pocket". Lord Cameron

---

[18] Chap. 5.

[19] *Mogul Steamship Co. Ltd v. Mcgregor, Gow & Co.*, n. 10 above.

[20] A similar line has been taken in the USA: *Tuttle v. Buck* (1909) 119 N.W. 946. However, see the re-examination of that case in T. Weir, *Economic Torts* (1997), p. 72 *et seq.*

[21] D.E.L. Johnstone, "Owners and Neighbours" in *The Civilian Tradition in Scots Law*, (Evan-Jones and Mackenzie, ed., Stair Society 1995), p. 187, citing three consecutive decisions noted in Morrison's Dictionary, *viz. Falconer v. Laird of Glenberrie* (1642) Mor. 4146; *Farquarson v. Earl of Aboyne* (1679) Mor. 4147; *Mags of Stirling v. Murray* (1706) Mor. 4148.

[22] [1991] 3 W.L.R. 188. See generally, G.H.L. Fridman, "Interference with Trade or Business" (1993) 1 Tort L.R. 19 and 99.

[23] 1991 S.L.T. 667.

[24] 1983 S.L.T. 388, *per* Lord Dunpark at 391.

was of the opinion that the petitioners did have a prima facie case setting out a delict arising from unlawful occupation of property to which they have an exclusive right of occupation:

"The occupation in the present cases is continuing against the wishes of those who own or operate the platforms and the vessels and the respondents have neither right nor title to remain on board, following upon their dismissal from employment with their employers, not lease since the latter have no place of business aboard the platforms or the vessels. That being so, the occupation is wrongful . . . In my opinion, it remains the law that the tort of interference with business by the use of unlawful means, while it constitutes a delict, nevertheless if committed in contemplation or furtherance of a trade dispute will not be actionable . . . Counsel for the parties referred me to passages in the speech of Lord Diplock in *Lonrho Ltd v. Shell Petroleum (No. 2)*, the judgment of Henry J. in *Barretts & Baird (Wholesale) v. I.P.C.S.* and the opinions in *Lonrho plc v. Fayed* dealing with the issue of intent to injure. The proposition which I think can be deduced from those authorities is that the statutory immunity which would otherwise attach to acts by individuals which injure third parties not directly involved in a trade dispute between that individual and his employer or erstwhile employer, will be lost when it can be said that his acts are inspired by a desire to injure the third party as well as to further his ends in the trade dispute."

Some novel English cases may fall within this principle such as inducing a breach of a statutory duty[25] or interference with press freedom.[26]

This idea of a general wrong and special wrongs is not difficult if the **7–6** relationship is clear. At this stage of development, in England, it is difficult. Weir says: "I believe that the tort of inducing a breach of contract has now been absorbed into the general tort of causing harm by unlawful means. To the extent it has recently developed distinctive rules, because such absorption has been ignored, this development should promptly be put into reverse."[27]

FRAUD

Fraud can infringe any interest and is not solely related to business or **7–7** economic interests. Indeed "fraud" describing a motive and a purpose has the appearance of a conduct wrong. The most common occurrence of fraudulent conduct is to obtain an economic advantage. It is a machination or contrivance to deceive.[28] There is no substantial body of decisions. Many frauds involve bringing the other party into a contract and escaping with the proceeds. In such a case either the "fraudulent" defender is worth nothing or restitution on recision of the contract is sufficient. Fraud is a necessary

---

[25] *Meade v. Haringey LBC* [1979] I.C.R. 494.
[26] *Associated Newspaper Group v. Wade* [1979] I.C.R. 664.
[27] T. Weir, *Economic Torts* (1997), p. 28.
[28] Ersk., III,i,16.

ground of action where the defender brings the pursuer into a loss making contract with another party, innocent of all involvement in the fraud. In such a case the pursuer is unlikely to be able to escape the contract but retains its uneconomic burden. The essence of what constitutes fraud in law appears in the following dictum of Lord President Inglis in *Lees v. Tod*[29]:

> "A man making a statement on any subject which he believes to be untrue, though he does not know it to be false, is dishonest, but if he merely makes a statement which he does not actually believe to be true, that is a negative state of mind, and his honesty or dishonesty will depend on his relation to the facts which he states, and to the person whom he addresses. A statement on a matter of indifference both to the speaker and the listener, even though the speaker has no actual belief in the truth of the statement, provided he does not believe it to be false, will not infer dishonesty on his part. He is not seeking to mislead anyone. But a statement of facts made regarding a matter of interest both to speaker and listener stands in a very different position. If the speaker, having no actual belief in the statement, though not believing it to be untrue, volunteers the statement, inconsistent with facts, to a person interested in the statement, and likely to act on it, he is dishonest and guilty of deceit, because he produces, and intends to produce, on the mind of the listener a belief which he does not himself entertain. It has been said that if a person in such a position, having full means of information within his reach, turns his back on the light, and wilfully abstains from acquiring the requisite information, he ought to be answerable for the statement which he makes if it be contrary to fact. To this proposition I assent, because the person making the statement in the circumstances supposed can have no actual belief in its truth."[30]

An illustration of the technical and amoral nature of the wrong can be seen in *H & J.M. Bennett (Potatoes) v. Secretary of State for Scotland.*[31] The government department provided a certificate saying that certain potatoes were found or believed by the inspector to be free from potato cyct eelworm. The potatoes were sold by the pursuers to buyers not parties to the action who rejected the goods because they were infected. The tests carried out could not have determined whether the problem existed or not. At first sight the impression would be that this was an example of negligence. It is at least that (in the sense of carelessness) but the law on negligence makes the usual fraud losses/economic losses difficult. In this case by making the statement there had been an intentional act. Taking into account the wide definition of fraud, the official was guilty of fraud because he knew the certificate was not stating the true position, albeit another technical person might have read the certificate in a less stringent fashion. There was no need to establish an intention to cheat. In *Dunnett v. Mitchell*,[32] in the Inner House the delictual question arose because the

---

[29] (1882) 9 R. 807.
[30] *ibid.* at 854.
[31] 1986 S.L.T. 665.
[32] (1887) 15 R. 131.

action was at the instance of a partner in a company, where the company had already discharged its claims against the defender. The pursuer had entered the company, a joint stock company, to speculate on investment in the defender's timber and other operations in Norway. It was accepted that fraud had not been proved. The defender had an honest belief in what he put forward. Not only that, it appeared that he put forward his view on the basis of information obtained from reputable sources. Add to that that he told the investors to make their own enquiries and they did and agreed the representations were accurate. The case is also noteworthy for the title to sue point. Had it been necessary, three of their Lordships would have ruled against the individual having a better title than the company. In *Cullen's Trustees v. Thomson's Trustees*[33] guidance as to what constitutes fraud appears in the Lord President's (McNeill) charge to the jury. The questions are (1) were the statements made and promulgated; (2) were they false representations; (3) whether the defenders made and promulgated the statements fraudulently; and (4) whether the pursuer was induced by the representations. He added the following important practical point for the benefit of the jury: "A representation may be false by reason not only of positive mis-statements contained in it, but by reason of intentional suppressions, whereby the information it gives assumes a false colour, giving a false impression, and leading necessarily, or almost necessarily, to erroneous conclusions."[34] In *Western Bank v. Addie*[35] the pursuer's claim in the alternative for damages against the company for fraudulently inducing him to purchase its shares failed; the company was not to be held liable for the fraud of the directors. In *Brownlie v. Miller*,[36] another House of Lords case, it was held that a statement made by a seller's solicitor as to the state of a title was not fraud albeit it was inaccurate—it was more an opinion of law, held in good faith and nothing was held back which should have been revealed.

A case which shows facts upon which a causation problem could arise is **7–8** *Hillcrest Homecare Services v. Tartan Home Care Ltd.*[37] The averments were that the pursuers bought a nursing home from the defenders thinking that there were 16 residents when the true state of affairs was that there was never more than 11. It was alleged there would have been no purchase at 11 residents. The professional survey was based on similar information. There were detailed allegations of specific acts designed to convey the impression of there being 16 residents. Proof before answer was allowed. Averments that the surveyors were also defrauded clearly assisted, preventing there being a clear *novus actus interveniens* by the surveyor's negligence. In *Taylor v. Glasgow District Council*,[38] a number of proprietors of a tenement property sued the defenders in their capacity as the employers of an official who granted the property developers a completion certificate as

---

[33] (1865) 3 M. 935.
[34] *ibid.* at 936. See generally *Silverscreen Print plc v. Watters*, 1999 G.W.D. 8–399 for a case where the averments were insufficient to make out a case. The inference from the averments indeed suggested the opposite.
[35] (1867) 5 M. (H.L.) 80.
[36] (1880) 7 R. (H.L.) 66.
[37] Unrep., Oct. 18, 1995.
[38] 1996 Rep. L.R. 69; 1997 Rep. L.R. 17.

a part of an allegedly fraudulent scheme. Although the fraud did not induce a contract between the parties to the action, considerations of economic loss in negligence did not affect a case based on fraud. So where a financial claim can be proved on the basis of fraud it ought to be, to avoid the unnecessary application of rules from the law of negligence in the field of economic loss. Finally fraud is always a defence to an action as it was for the Romans—the *exceptio doli*. It is also, as shall be seen below, a factor in the newer theoretical way of looking at passing-off.

7–9   Although an English case *Smith New Court Securities Ltd v. Scrimgeour Vickers (Asset Management) Ltd*[39] is worthy of note. The case was based on fraudulent misrepresentations on the telephone. As a result of this fraud the plaintiffs paid 82.25p for shares which were really worth 78p on that day of that fraud. As a result of another unrelated fraud the share price tumbled and the shares were ultimately only sold for between 30p and 49p. It was held in the Court of Appeal that the damages were limited to the smaller gap between the value on the day and the price paid. This proceeded on the acceptance of the rule that there could be no restitutionary remedy. The effect of this was to reduce damages from about £10 million to over £1 million. The House of Lords allowed an appeal against that decision. While the decision is one on the tort of deceit in English law the following principles set out by Lord Browne-Wilkinson may well be of assistance in Scots law:

(1) the defendant must make reparation for all the damage directly flowing from the transaction;

(2) although such damage need not have been foreseeable, it must have been directly caused by the transaction;

(3) the plaintiff is entitled to recover the full price paid but must give credit for any benefits which he receives as a result of the transaction;

(4) the benefits include the market value of the property acquired but that need not be applied inflexibly if it prevented full compensation for the wrong;

(5) the market value would not be treated as a benefit where either the misrepresentation continued to operate after the date of the acquisition or where by reason of the fraud the plaintiff was locked into the property acquired;

(6) consequential losses were recoverable, and

(7) the plaintiff must take all reasonable mitigatory steps once the fraud was discovered.[40]

PASSING-OFF

7–10 There are many cases brought although few raise fundamental points. Again there are no significant differences between Scotland and England.[41] There are two identifiable approaches: the mechanical and the principled.

---

[39] [1996] 4 All E.R. 769.

[40] *ibid.* at 778–779.

[41] See *Lang v. Goldwell*, 1982 S.L.T. 309, *per* Lord Justice-Clerk Wheatley at 312: "There is ample authority for the proposition that the law of Scotland does not differ from the law of England in this field of law."

The mechanical arises because passing-off was a recognised form of wrong for a very long time and lawyers can simply fit cases into precedents. The scope of the claim would not expand because of the general principle of non-intervention. Tradesmen would expect to know what they might or might not do—lawyers and courts would be happy to answer such questions. The principled approach comes from the second half of the twentieth century when the success of the general principle of negligence has inspired such an approach in other areas of the law.[42]

The mechanical approach

7–11 The law here could not be plainer, albeit application to facts will cause the usual problems. This could be described as a statement of the basic law applicable to most commonly encountered problems. It is set out according to the statement of the law to be found in *John Haig & Co. v. Forth Blending Co.*[43] which although an Outer House case, summarises and restates the law in a very workable way. Some of the statements of the law are so apposite that they are simply quoted here. Some cases since illustrating, supporting or derogating from the guidelines are discussed. This case was about direct passing-off by get-up.

7–12 "(1) No man has a right to sell his goods as though they were the goods of another, or, to express this principle more fully, one man is not entitled to sell his goods under such circumstances, by the name, or the packet, or the mode of making up the article, or in such a way as to induce the public to believe that they are the manufacture of someone else."

7–13 "(2) In order to obtain redress in an action for passing off, the trader who sues must prove that his goods are known to and recognised by the public, or by a particular section of the public who deal in that type of goods, by a particular name, mark, get-up or other accompaniment, which is associated in their minds with his goods alone."

The main reason for the failure of the pursuer in *Baird & Tatlock (London) Ltd v. Baird & Tatlock Ltd*[44] was the point made in this guideline. Two partners broke up and set up their own operations and there was some evidence of confusion but there was no evidence that either side's products had acquired distinctiveness in the mind of the public. There had been a few misdirected orders but that was the fault of customers rather than the defenders.[45]

---

[42] Finally, this is an area where there has been a considerable Scottish contribution—not for jurisprudential reasons, but because the whisky produced here is (enviously) copied the world over. The vigilance of the Scottish Whisky Association has brought about a number of important cases both in Scotland and abroad.

[43] 1954 S.C. 35.

[44] 1917 1 S.L.T. 46.

[45] *ibid.* at 48. See also *Plotzker v. Lucas* (1907) 15 S.L.T. 186, "Irish Linen Company" was not sufficiently distinctive to attract protection. Neither was "Bile Beans" as a name for pills when at that time bean was a name used for pills: *The Bile Bean Manufacturing Co. v. Davidson* (1906) 14 S.L.T. 294.

7–14 "(3) The actings of the trader who is sued must satisfy the Court that there is a likelihood of the public or the particular section of the public being misled into thinking that the goods are the goods of the trader who sues. It is not essential that the trader who sues should prove actual instances of confusion having taken place, but, if such are proved the Court will more readily grant interdict."

This rule must be read subject to comments in *Dash Ltd v. Philip King Tailoring*.[46] In *Dash* it was argued that the confusion which was said to exist in the case was only such as to amount to the "possibility" of confusion whereas the *Haig* case required a "likelihood" of confusion. Lord McDonald, giving the opinion of the court, stated that the *Haig* case dealt with the similarity of goods rather than names. The Court did, however, consider that in the case before it, if the test were likelihood it had been met. There seems no reason why the principles expounded in *Haig* should not apply to names as much as get-up—the test should be the same whether a trader obtains another's sale by using a name or a get-up. "Likelihood," it is submitted, is still the better verbal formulation but the distinction having been made in relation to names by the Inner House great care will be needed in such cases. At the level of application this guideline makes it clear that it need not be the whole public who are confused. It may be a section of the public. Thus, it is the particular market which must always be looked at. An excellent example is *Scottish Milk Marketing Board v. Drybrough & Co. Ltd*.[47] The pursuers sold milk and the defenders sold beer. The pursuers sold their milk under a well-known brand "Scottish Pride", the defenders sold beer under precisely the same name "Scottish Pride". Lord Davidson said:

"For present purposes I am prepared to accept that the use of the words "Scottish Pride" in the petitioners' advertising campaign has been such as to make these words part of the goodwill of their products. But before they can obtain an interim interdict I am of opinion that the petitioners must satisfy the court that in the circumstances described by them there is a probability of confusion in the public mind which is likely to do damage to the petitioners' goodwill. . . It appears to me that the petitioners' basic problem is that their products are significantly different from the respondents' products . . . it is not immediately obvious that members of the public would be likely to confuse the petitioners' business with that of the respondents, or that the petitioners' goodwill is likely to be significantly damaged."[48]

The other focus which emerges from the cases is the geographic territory of the operation. Trade, at the time of writing, is spoken of as becoming global in the post GATT era. Even cases a century old were decided in a great mercantile era where distribution was essentially world wide and advertising through newspapers and the like very widespread. So in *Dunlop*

---

[46] 1989 S.L.T. 39.
[47] 1985 S.L.T. 253.
[48] *ibid*. at 255.

Pneumatic Tyre Company Ltd v. Dunlop Motor Company Ltd[49] the big English tyre company could not restrain the little garage proprietor in Kilmarnock who changed the occasional tyre.[50] More recently in *Paperchase Products Ltd v. Ridlington,*[51] one of the rarer cases decided after proof, Mr. Ridlington had a small shop in Ayr called "Paperchase". The pursuers were a big English company who had used that name before him and advertised widely and had a mail order business. Some of the defender's customers had become sufficiently confused to send invoices to the pursuers. One of the pursuer's witnesses was a bit confused by the similarity of the name but did think it odd that the fancy English firm would open in Ayr! The Sheriff granted interdict in what may have been a generous finding for the pursuers—or at least premature:

"In my opinion, the pursuers have clearly established the necessary factual ingredients for interdict, namely, that they have an established reputation and goodwill trading under the name Paperchase, and that the defender's actings, whether intended or not, are likely to deceive members of the public. Although it is true that the defender operates in a small way 400 miles north of London, the companies were trading under the same name and in very much the same area of the trade. Not only were two major firms in the trade itself confused, but Mr Barr, a commercial man in the same trade, assumed that the businesses were the same, although he found this a little surprising. The pursuers have not at present established any loss or damage or material prejudice, nor did they claim to do so. They only have a mail order business in Scotland at the moment but they are anxious to preserve future potential developments in Scotland, such as the opening of franchises in retail stores. They are entitled in law to protect this potential development and the goodwill attached thereto."[52]

This must be a marginal decision and could better have been met by the practical step adopted by the defender of adding a note that he had no connection with the big English firm.[53] It does not matter that the section of the public who might be confused is furth of Scotland, the best example of this being *John Walker & Sons Ltd v. Douglas McGibbon & Company Ltd*[54] in which Lord Avonside protected the citizens of the Republic of Honduras from the terrible fate of buying "McGibbon's Special Reserve" which contained local Honduran spirit mixed with the real thing. The defenders

---

[49] (1906) 14 S.L.T. 284; (1907) 15 S.L.T. 362; (1906) 8 F. 1146; 1907 S.C. (H.L.) 15.
[50] *See also Scottish Union & National Insurance Co. v. Scottish National Insurance Co Ltd* (1908) 16 S.L.T. 110, 671.
[51] 1980 S.L.T. (Sh. Ct) 56.
[52] *ibid.* at 59.
[53] The "no connection" solution was expressly sought in the petition in *Chill Foods (Scotland) Ltd. v. Cool Foods,* 1997 S.L.T. 38 which craved interim interdict against the respondents "trading in frozen foodstuffs under their company name unless and until they specifically and clearly dissociate and distinguish themselves from the petitioners in any canvassing for or soliciting of orders from and in any advertising of whatsoever nature directed at or which may be seen by persons or establishments which were, prior to August 1976, customers or suppliers of the petitioners".
[54] 1972 S.L.T. 128.

were knowingly assisting in the possible passing off and a proof before answer allowed.

7-15   "(4) A trader has no property in a trade name, trade mark or particular get-up. The object of the action is to protect the goodwill of the trader who sues. Goodwill, being invisible, is represented by visible symbols such as trade names, trade marks, get-up and other accompaniments associated with the goods of a particular trader. Every article which is sold by such a trade name or bears such a trade mark, get-up or accompaniment has behind it an element of the particular trade's goodwill and reputation, and a rival or second trader, by adopting that trade name, trade mark, get-up or accompaniment, or a substantial part of it, with the result that the public are misled into thinking that the goods of the second trader are the goods of the first trader, commits an actionable wrong and appropriates to himself part of the goodwill of the first trader."

There are many examples of this type of case and the use of names is the most common. In *Treadwell's Drifters Inc v. RCL Ltd*[55] the company that owned the whole recording and performance rights of a group "The Drifters" sued those using the name "The Sounds of the Drifters" but the action was dismissed on the technical incompetency that there were different types of actions against the different defenders. *Obiter*, Lord Osborne would have allowed the case to proof on the basis of the law as set out by Lord Oliver in *Reckitt & Colman Products Ltd v. Borden Inc*.[56] In *William Grant & Sons Ltd v. Glen Catrine Bonded Warehouse Ltd*,[57] the name argued over was "Grants" relating to whisky. Lord Abernethy held that the goodwill attaching to the name "Grants" was goodwill which belonged to every part of the group business of the petitioners and accordingly the subsidiary companies, having a stake in the goodwill, had a clear title and interest to sue—a fair extension of the ordinary case.[58] *International House of Heraldry v. Grant*[59] is a classic example. The pursuers traded under the name "International House of Heraldry" and obtained interim interdict *ex parte* against the use by the defenders of the trading name "International Art of Heraldry". The defenders argued on recall that their trading name consisted of words descriptive of the business. Lord Marnoch held that "International Art of Heraldry" was not a general descriptive name as it did not contain an obvious and self-explanatory description of the services or activities of the business in question and the slight difference in name was not sufficient to distinguish it from the pursuers.[60]

In *Orkney Seafoods Ltd, Petitioners*[61] the pursuers who produced top quality gourmet seafoods had traded under the trade name "Orkney

---

[55] 1996 S.L.T. 1048.
[56] *ibid* at 1062.
[57] 1995 S.L.T. 936.
[58] *ibid*. at 945.
[59] 1992 S.L.T. 1021.
[60] *ibid*. at 1021–22.
[61] 1991 S.L.T. 891.

Seafoods" for over 15 years. A number of traders in Orkney formed together in a group and traded in the same type of products under the trade name "Orkney Seafood Specialists". Lord Wylie held that there was a prima facie case that the close similarity in name was likely to confuse customers and potential customers, particularly overseas customers, of the first company and would lead to the passing off of the new group's products as the products of the existing company. In *Dash Ltd v. Philip King Tailoring Ltd*,[62] which as has already been noted the Inner House observed that *Haig* itself did not deal with names. The pursuers had shops trading as "Dash Man", "Dash Ladies" and "Young Dash". The defenders started trading as "Dasch For Men". The Inner House granted the reclaiming with the effect of reviving the interim interdict. In the similar case *Salon Services (Hairdressing Supplies) Ltd v. Direct Salon Services Ltd*[63] the result was different but on the same principle. The dispute arose when the defenders expanded into Scotland. It was held the difference in names was sufficient to avoid passing-off. The two companies had been in competition in England for some time and no confusion seemed to have arisen there.

In *Flaxcell Ltd v. Freedman*,[64] there was a close similarity between the names "Dickie Dirts" and "Dirty Dicks". Although the petitioners' predominant trading name was "Dickie Dirts"[65] there had been confusion in the past which had led the petitioners on occasion to trade under both names. The petitioners advertised under both names. They were listed under both names in the London telephone directory. It was averred that cheques and correspondence properly attributable to "Dickie Dirts" were frequently in error addressed to "Dirty Dicks". No explanation was offered for the respondent having chosen to trade under the name "Dirty Dicks", and, in all the circumstances, Lord Ross was satisfied that a prima facie case had been made out to the effect that the respondent's choice of that trading name was likely to confuse customers and potential customers.[66]

In one of the most often cited cases, *Chill Foods (Scotland) Ltd v. Cool Foods Ltd*,[67] Lord Maxwell granted interim interdict in favour of the longer established pursuers against the defenders. The similarity in names was sufficient to give rise to a considerable risk of confusion. In *James Burrough Distillers plc v. Speymalt Whisky Distributors Ltd*,[68] although the detail is not reported, Lord Coulsfield allowed a proof before answer over a disputed use of the word "Laphroaig".[69] It has long been established that simply using one's own name is not a defence to passing-off and that issue was canvassed in *O'Brien v. Watts*.[70] It was held that there was at least a prima facie case where the defender resigned as a partner in the pursuer's firm and opened an office in the same town under a name which incorporated

---

[62] 1989 S.L.T. 39.
[63] 1988 S.L.T. 414.
[64] 1981 S.L.T. (Notes)131.
[65] Derived it was said from rhyming slang.
[66] *Flaxcell Ltd v. Freedman*, at 131–132.
[67] 1977 S.L.T. 38.
[68] 1989 S.L.T. 561.
[69] See also *Highland Distilleries Co. Plc v. Speymalt Whisky Distributors Ltd*, 1985 S.L.T. 85 for "Bunnahabhain" single malt whisky and *William Grant And Sons Ltd v. William Cadenhead Ltd*, 1985 S.L.T. 291 for "Glenlivet".
[70] 1987 S.L.T. 101.

her maiden name O'Brien, namely O'Brien & Watts. The firm alleged that there had been examples of confusion among their clients and that the firm name had a substantial value to them. The defender argued that, since the name was her maiden name, she could only be interdicted from using it if the use was done with fraudulent intent, or with the deliberate intention of passing her business off as that of the firm. At the early stage of proceedings reported that particular question was not answered—it was enough that had that been the test, there were suspicious circumstances.[71]

Finally, the hardest to follow must be *Resartus Company v. Sartor Resartus Company*,[72] in which The Resartus Company had been carrying on business in Edinburgh for three years. They said they had been the first firm in Scotland to make a specialty of repairing, pressing and cleaning gentlemen's clothes. The respondents commenced the same business in Edinburgh at the end of May 1908, and sent out circulars to many of the pursuers' clients in which the name complained of was used. They argued that the name was obviously adopted for the purpose of deceiving the public and taking advantage of the reputation built up by the pursuers during the past three years. The respondents argued that the word "Sartor" sufficiently differentiated the two companies. The word "Resartus" was associated in the public mind with repair of clothes, and the respondents had used it in that sense.[73] Interdict was refused.

7–16   "(5). The get-up of goods comprises the size and shape of the package or container, labels and wrappers, the dress in which the goods are offered to the public. No trader, by adopting and using a particular style of get-up, thereby acquires a right to prevent a rival or second trader using the same or a similar get-up, unless the get-up of the first trader has become so associated in the minds of the public with the first trader's goods as to be distinctive of the goods of the first trader and no other. It is unusual that any single feature of the get-up of goods is so associated with particular traders' goods that a second trader cannot make use of it, but, if it is proved that a single feature of a trader's get-up is so peculiar that it above all else catches the eye and is retained in the memory of the purchasing public, and that the purchasing public recognise the goods of the trader by this one feature alone, then a second trader may be prevented from adopting this peculiar feature of the first trader's get-up and so misleading the public. A part of the article sold which is useful may, if peculiar, be part of the get-up of the goods and may become associated with and distinctive of a particular trader's goods."

The Scottish case *Alexander Fergusson & Co. v. Matthews McClay & Manson*[74] raised and answered an interesting question. The pursuers had

---

[71] See also *William Grant & Sons Ltd v. Glen Catrine Bonded Warehouse Ltd*, 1995 S.L.T. 936 where the law was extensively reviewed and applied. A trader new to the market but using a name it was entitled to was held to be capable of having passed-off.

[72] (1908) 16 S.L.T. 210.

[73] It is hard to say now whether that would indeed be the case, although if the market in question was that of gentlemen in Edinburgh it is certainly possible only so far as research shows by reference to the fact that *Carlyle's Sartor Resartus* published in 1833 would still have been well-known in 1908. My own edition in the Oxford Classics, printed in Edinburgh was first published in that popular series in 1902 and reprinted in 1903, 1906 and 1909.

[74] 1989 S.L.T. 795.

carried on the business of paint manufacturers and suppliers. They supplied paint called "Fergalex" which was supplied in tins with a distinctive get-up. They advised the suppliers of the tins that they were ceasing use of, and wished to have no more of, the tins. They continued to sell paint in the "Fergalex" tins which they still had. The defenders, who were also paint manufacturers, sold paint in "Fergalex" tins obtained from the same suppliers. In doing so, they applied labels to the tins which obscured the name "Fergalex" and substituted other brand names. Lord Dervaird, clearly recognising that delict protects goodwill instead of a particular name or get-up, held that since the pursuers no longer sold paint using the "Fergalex" get-up, other than the running down of remnant stock, they had no continuing interest therein to be protected, mainly because they were no longer the owners of goodwill of substantial value in relation to the "Fergalex" get-up.[75]

"(6) In dealing with ordinary cases where articles are sold to the public **7–17** whole and unopened you must look at the get-up as a whole, and you must treat the labels on the goods fairly in ascertaining whether or not the public is likely to be misled . . . but to place the articles side by side is not always the right test . . . the member of public who falls to be considered is a person with reasonable apprehension and proper eyesight."

Bostik Ltd v. Sellotape G.B. Ltd[76] is an interesting illustration because in this case it was held that there could be no passing-off where the confusion could only occur when the packet in question was opened up. Until then a shopper would not confuse the products. In *Highland Distilleries Co. Plc v. Speymalt Whisky Distributors Ltd*,[77] Lord Ross allied the practical test at the interim interdict stage:

"On the information placed before me, it appears to me that if a member of the public were to seek in the trade or from a retail outlet a bottle of single malt whisky described as 'Bunnahabhain', he might receive a bottle of the respondents' 'Bunnahabhain'. It is true that the respondents' label describes the whisky as 'from the Bunnahabhain Distillery, Islay', but the word 'Bunnahabhain' is in large letters and prominent, and in their wholesale wine and spirit list under 'Connoisseur's Choice Selected Malt Whiskies' there appears an entry described as 'Bunnahabhain, Islay'. In the same list, the petitioners' whisky is described as 'Islay: Bunnahabhain 12 Years Old'.[78]

That shows that the focus is on the ordinary reader of the material and that the "disclaiming" text may not have effect if the offending text is too prominent as compared with the disclaimer.[79]

---

[75] *ibid*. at 798.
[76] [1994] T.L.R. 14.
[77] 1985 S.L.T. 85.
[78] *ibid*. at 88.
[79] See also *Derwent Valley Foods Ltd v. Forth Valley Foods Ltd*, 1990 G.W.D. 7–402.

7–18 "(8)[80] If the goods of the trader have, from the peculiar mark or get-up which he has used, become known in the market by a particular name, the adoption by a rival or second trader of any mark or get-up which will cause his goods to bear the same name in the market is a violation of the rights of the first trader."

For an application in Scotland see *Carrick Jewellery Ltd v. Ortak.*[81] The complaint was against the use of "The Rennie Mackintosh Collection". The interdict, however, was only against the defenders using the stylised typeface and not the name "Rennie Mackintosh Collection." These words merely described a style. It was the typeface which had become known.

7–19 "(9) No trader, however honest his personal intentions has a right to adopt and use so much of his rival's established get-up as will enable any dishonest trader or retailer into whose hands the goods may come to sell them as the goods of his rival."

This is well established and one of the cases[82] supporting this proposition in *Haig* was relied upon in *John Walker & Sons Ltd v. Douglas McGibbon & Company Ltd*[83] in which the defenders, who were supplying whisky abroad where it was then allegedly set up for passing-off, argued that they had no responsibility for that. Lord Avonside disagreed.[84]

7–20 "(10) The actings of a trader who copies a rival's established get-up need not be fraudulent and he need have no intention of obtaining any benefit from his rival's goodwill and reputation—indeed he may be ignorant of his existence—but, if the result of his innocent actings is that the public are likely to be misled, he will be interdicted.[85] If, however, the Court is satisfied that the trader who is sued intended to obtain some benefit from his rival's established get-up and was thus fraudulent, the Court will be more ready to grant interdict."

An example of damages being awarded in England against an innocent party is *Gillette U.K. v. Edwenwest,*[86] in which the previous authorities were reviewed. The defendants in *Gillette U.K.* bought the copy razor head packs

---

[80] The seventh guideline is not of general application.
[81] 1989 G.W.D. 35–1624. See also *Rae v. Fullers Ltd*, 1990 G.W.D. 8–439.
[82] *R. Johnston & Co. v. Archibald Orr Ewing & Co.* (1882) 7 A.C. 219.
[83] 1972 S.L.T. 128.
[84] *ibid*. at 129.
[85] The earliest cases of passing-off are based on fraud but the need to prove fraud in an interdict case was conclusively negated in the Scots House of Lords case *Cellular Clothing Co. v. Maxton & Murray* (1899) 1 F. 29, *per* L.C. Halsbury at 31. Lord Kinnear expressed that rule in the early part of the last century: "I take the law to be well settled that if a new company has adopted, for the purpose of carrying on a business of the same kind as that of an already established company, a name so like theirs as to be calculated to mislead persons dealing with them into supposing that they are dealing with the other company, and in this way appropriates, although without any dishonest purpose, a part of the other company's business, that is a wrong which may be restrained by interdict": *Scottish Union and National Insurance Co. v. Scottish National Insurance Co. Ltd*, 1908 16 S.L.T. 671 at 672. See also *Highland Distilleries Co. Plc v. Speymalt Whisky Distributors Ltd*, 1985 S.L.T. 85.
[86] [1994] T.L.R. 135.

from an import/export company. This seems harsh and it may be the line of authority rejected in *Gillette U.K.* is preferable. The defendants, it should be noted, did not do the copying themselves.

The theoretical approach

This has its origins in *Erven Warnick B.V. v. Townend.*[87] That case was not a **7–21** traditional passing-off case and its importance for extended passing-off is discussed below. Lord Diplock considered passing-off to be a species of a broader wrong of unfair trading.[88] After an examination of the history of passing-off he said:

"it [is] possible to identify five characteristics which must be present in order to create a valid cause of action for passing-off: (1) a misrepresentation; (2) made by a trader in the course of trade; (3) to prospective customers of his or ultimate consumers of goods or services supplied by him; (4) which is calculated to injure the business or goodwill of another trader (in the sense that this is a reasonably forseeable consequence); and (5) which causes actual damage to a business or goodwill of the trader by whom the action is brought."[89]

His Lordship went on to explain that all five aspects must be present but that the presence of all five is not enough in itself. However, the presence of all five is enough:

"unless there is also present in the case some exceptional feature which justifies, on grounds of public policy, withholding from a person who has suffered injury in consequence of the deception practised on prospective customers or consumers of his product a remedy in law against the deceiver."[90]

Lord Fraser of Tullybelton said: **7–22**

"But the decision is in my opinion soundly based on the principle underlying the earlier passing-off actions, which I take to be that the plaintiff is entitled to protect his right of property in the goodwill attached to a name which is distinctive of a product or class of products sold by him in the course of his business. It is essential for the plaintiff in a passing-off action to show at least the following facts: (1) that his business consists of, or includes, selling in England a class of goods to which the particular trade name applies; (2) that the class of goods is clearly defined, and that in the minds of the public, or a section of the public, in England, the trade name distinguishes that class from other similar goods; (3) that because of the reputation of the goods, there is goodwill attached to the name; (4) that he, the plaintiff, as a member of

---

[87] [1979] A.C. 731.
[88] See generally J. Adams, "Is there a tort of unfair competition?" [1985] J.B.L. 26.
[89] [1979] A.C. 731.
[90] *ibid.* at 880.

the class of those who sell the goods, is the owner of goodwill in England which is of substantial value; (5) that he has suffered, or is really likely to suffer, substantial damage to his property in the goodwill by reason of the defendants selling goods which are falsely described by the trade name to which the goodwill is attached. Provided these conditions are satisfied . . . I consider that the plaintiff is entitled to protect himself by a passing-off action."[91]

Warnick has been cited, it is submitted correctly, in Scotland for the negative proposition that a misrepresentation on its own is insufficient to ground an action.[92] As shall be seen below the dicta in the case are not all reconcilable. From time to time other formulations are arrived at but as none are definitive and all are English they need not be rehearsed here.[93]

Extended passing-off

7–23   The Scottish case of *John Walker & Sons. Ltd v. Henry Ost & Co. Ltd*[94] supports this broader view in that the court accepted that a producer was entitled to protect his product from sales of non-scotch whisky on the basis that there would be damage to his sales where someone tasted the inferior product and decided not to try the real thing. This case need not be restricted to mere geographic appropriation but applies to the whole image of a product. *Erven Warnick B.V. v. Townend*[95] brought this line of authority to an end by validating all of the previous decisions. Thus later cases have been much easier for the established trader. In *Lang v. Goldwell Bros*[96] the issues were even wider. The petitioners sought to interdict the respondents from passing off as having been produced wholly in Scotland any alcoholic drink, containing in part whisky, which was not composed entirely of alcoholic beverages distilled, brewed or fermented in Scotland. The respondents sold "Wee McGlen", a Whisky Mac or mixture of whisky and ginger beer. The features complained of were that the label had a tartan background; that the words "A Whisky Mac" were printed on it. A newspaper advertisement contained reproduction of the bottle with the label showing and a caricature of a be-tartaned Scotsman to whom are attributed the words: "Haste ye back for another Wee McGlen. The drink the trade has been asking for—Whisky Mac in a baby bottle."[97] The Second Division allowed a proof before answer. The only reasoned opinion was given by the Lord Justice-Clerk (Wheatley):

> "[This] is not a classical case of passing off in that it is not said that the respondents are passing off their product as that of the petitioners. The

---

[91] *ibid.* at 755–756.

[92] *Treadwell's Drifters Inc v. RCL Ltd*, 1996 S.L.T. 1048.

[93] See Clerk & Lindsell, *The Law of Torts*, Chap. 25.

[94] [1970] 1 W.L.R. 917. Had it been necessary Lord Hunter would have accepted the doctrine of reverse passing-off. In *Argyllshire Weavers Ltd v. A. Macaulay (Tweeds) Ltd*, 1965 S.L.T. 21 at 33 following *J. Bollinger v. Costa Brava Wine Co. Ltd* [1960] 1 Ch. 262, [1961] 1 W.L.R. 277.

[95] [1979] A.C. 731.

[96] 1982 S.L.T. 309.

[97] See the cover of W.J. Stewart, *A Casebook on Delict* (2nd ed, W. Green, 1997).

petitioners' complaint is that the "set up" of the label on the bottle and of the advertisement is such as to mislead the public into thinking that the whole ingredients of 'Wee McGlen' are Scottish. It was said that the whole 'Scottishness' of the "set up" was liable to give this impression. The description of the contents of the product 'Ginger Wine Blended with Scottish Malt Whisky' in all the surrounding circumstances suggests or at least is liable to create the impression in the minds of the public that both the ginger wine and the malt whisky are 'Scottish'. This was not so, as the ginger wine was English, and the description was thereby misleading. Accordingly, when it became known that the reference to ginger wine was false and misleading the source of origin in all respects would fall under suspicion. This was liable to raise suspicion or cast doubts on the origin of the whisky as well, and diminish reliance on 'Scotch whisky', which would affect the goodwill of the petitioners' business . . . As hereinbefore noted, this is not a classical passing off case. Nor is it averred in terms that the misleading misrepresentation could cast doubts or suspicion on the authenticity of the Scottish malt whisky in the 'Wee McGlen' bottles. What is said is in general terms, *viz.* that the effect of the misrepresentation is that it is likely to endanger the reputation and goodwill which attaches to Scotch whisky because of its Scottish origin, since it is liable to dilute the distinctiveness of indications of Scottish origin when used in relation to alcoholic beverages. This, I suppose, could conceivably cover the Scottish malt whisky in the 'Wee McGlen' bottles. The *Warnink* case was said by petitioners' counsel to be a watershed in this branch of the law, just as the case of *Donoghue v. Stevenson* was a watershed in the law of negligence. I do not feel constrained to express any views on the validity of that comparison, whatever doubts I may have on its validity, since petitioners' counsel maintained that their averments cover the tests laid down in *Warnink* by Lord Diplock and Lord Fraser of Tullybelton respectively. Nor do I require to canvass the development of this chapter of the law, because that was exhaustively done in *Warnink*. The petitioners' complaint here is the damage to their reputation and goodwill by the respondents' alleged misrepresentation. The manner in which goodwill can be affected can occur in a variety of ways. . . . There is ample authority for the proposition that the law of Scotland does not differ from the law of England in this field of law. While it was accepted by petitioners' counsel that there were differences between the fourth and fifth characteristics adumbrated by Lord Diplock and the fifth characteristic adumbrated by Lord Fraser of Tullybelton, they submitted that their averments in art. 8 of the closed record, when read along with the other relevant averments in their pleadings, were sufficient to meet the requirements of either test. While, in my opinion, the petitioners' averments could have been more clearly and definitely framed in this regard, there is sufficient in them to satisfy these requirements, provided of course that the ultimate test of relevancy is satisfied."[98]

Interim interdict was granted in *Macallan-Glenlivet Plc v. Speymalt Whisky Distributors Ltd*[99] on a case involving the Macallan based on allegations that

---

[98] *Lang v. Goldwell Bros*, at 311—312.
[99] 1983 S.L.T. 348.

the reputation of the real product would be damaged by sales of the "inferior" product.

7-24   So far as whisky itself is concerned there is a definition of the drink in European Law.[1] It has been held in *Scottish Whisky Association v. Glen Kella Distillers*[2] that that regulation was intended not only to protect the public but also producers who would have title to sue for injunction for breach of the regulations. An injunction was granted where the defendants sold "white whisky". It was produced by redistilling ordinary whisky. It had not been re-matured after distillation. It would thus constitute passing off commencing an insidious process of erosion of the integrity and aura of true whisky. The regulation was founded upon, again in protection of Scotch Whisky in *Matthew Gloag and Son Ltd v. Welsh Distillers Ltd.*[3] The defendants sold a Welsh whisky called "Swyn y mor" with a big red dragon on the bottle. It said: "Welsh whisky . . . is a spirit unique in taste and origin—a superb blend of malt and grain whiskies blended and bottled by the Welsh Whisky Co. Brecon, Wales, U.K. Product of Wales, U.K. Blended in the Principality for the world to enjoy." It was not in dispute that the contents were Scotch whisky. It was held that this was extended passing-off on the basis of *Erven Warnick*[4] and *Bristol Conservatories Ltd v. Conservatories Custom Built Ltd.*[5] It was accepted that there had been a breach of the European regulation but it was argued that only consumers had a right of action under the regulation. On the basis of *Glen Kella*[6] and an unreported case *The Scotch Whisky Association v. J.D. Vintners*[7] Laddie, J found for the Scottish Whisky Companies.

7-25   It has been held that a puruser must claim either an account of profits or damages.[8]

7-26   As most cases involve interim interdict, matters arise which relate to that remedy, in particular the balance of convenience, which is outwith the scope of this text.[9] In *William Grant & Sons Ltd v. William Cadenhead Ltd*[10] it was held that delay in raising a passing off case was fatal. Although a general defence, two old cases show *ex turpi causa* being pled and it is not inconceivable that such might arise in the future.[11]

HARBOURING EMPLOYEES

7-27   It is a wrong for an employer to employ a worker when he knows that the worker is already under contract to another. In *Rose Street Foundry and Engineering Company Ltd v. John Lewis & Sons Ltd*[12] the Inner House

---

[1] Regulation 1576/89 [1989] O.J. L160/1.
[2] [1997] T.L.R. 186.
[3] [1998] T.L.R. 113.
[4] *Erven Warnick B.V. v. Townend* [1979] A.C. 731 discussed above at para. 7-21 *et seq.*
[5] [1989] R.P.C. 455.
[6] *Scotch Whisky Association v. Glen Kella Distillers* [1997] T.L.R. 186.
[7] [1998] C.L.Y. 352.
[8] *Treadwell's Drifters Inc v. RCL Ltd*, 1996 S.L.T. 1048, per Lord Osborne at 1060–61.
[9] See Scott-Robinson, "The Law of Interdict in Scotland" (2nd ed., Butterworth, 1994).
[10] 1985 S.L.T. 291.
[11] *The Bile Bean Manufacturing Co. v. Davidson* (1906) 14 S.L.T. 294, a successful action. *Plotzker v. Lucas* (1907) 15 S.L.T. 186 which was unsuccessful.
[12] 1917 1 S.L.T. 153.

reviewed the authorities in relation to this wrong. The pursuers sued their former employee Clark and his subsequent employers, the defenders. Interestingly the defenders complained that Clark had previously worked for them but had been induced by the pursuers to leave. When the matter came before the court the inducement issue was not live. The Lord Justice-Clerk (Scott-Dickson) reviewed and stated the law which is accurate today albeit there do not appear to be any reported Scottish cases: "I hold that the facts that A., knowing that B. is under a contract of service with C., takes B. into his service or continues to employ him during part of the period embraced in said contract and while C. desires implement thereof constitute "harbouring," and a legal wrong against the original employer".[13]

PROCURING BREACH OF CONTRACT

There is no authority on this narrow point concerning "procuring" in **7–28** Scotland although the word "procures" appears in *BMTA v. Gray*.[14] On the basis that Scots law has accepted inducing breach then it has probably accepted the more obviously wrongful conduct of procuring a breach. Indeed it appears to be the case that in England procuring and inducing are treated as one and the same.[15] This is, it is submitted, the preferable view. The conduct complained of in inducement cases is lesser than any procurement in the sense of vandalising machinery and so it is logical to locate this delict if it exists as a separate heading within Inducement. It is so identified in the leading English case *D.C. Thomson & Co. v. Deakin*[16] under the heading of other direct intervention.[17]

INDUCING BREACH OF CONTRACT

There are Scottish authorities to vouch for the proposition that it is a delict **7–29** knowingly to induce a party to breach a lawful and subsisting contract. In *Couper v. Macfarlane*[18] the employers locked out their workmen and hired men from England. The defender had given proper notice. It was alleged that he, with others, induced the English workers to break off. It should be noted that the allegations were of both threats and promises and that it was alleged that the defender acted as part of a combination. There is little doubt that before both the sheriff-substitute and the sheriff English authority was to the fore, albeit "smuggled in" through Fraser's *Master and Servant*. Lord Ormidale was emphatic that the law was as stated in the court below:

---

[13] *ibid.* at 155—156, relying, *inter alia*, on *Lumley v. Gye* (1853) 2 E. & B. 216 and *Dickson v. Taylor*, 1 Mur 141.

[14] 1951 S.L.T. 247.

[15] Clerk & Lindsell, *The Law of Torts*, para. 23–09.

[16] [1952] Ch. 646.

[17] McManus & Russell, *Delict* (Wiley, 1998) treat this as a separate wrong to be distinguished from inducing breach of contract, but of course the point they make that legal action preventing a breach is not wrongful is generally quite correct.

[18] (1879) 6 R. 683.

"it is enough to say that every master has a legal right and interest in the services of the workmen whom he has under engagement in his employment, and that every person who knowingly and designedly entices or seduces such workmen to break their engagements and desert their employment to the injury of the master , commits a wrongful act for which he is answerable in damages, it being always understood that the injury for which reparation is asked must be the natural and necessary consequence of the wrongful act complained of, and not merely remotely connected with it."

For Lord Gifford it was necessary for the seduction to be by illegal means.[19] On a careful reading of the evidence the Inner House took the unusual course of reversing the decisions below. Properly so. It appears that the witnesses testified that they were not induced and there was no way in which that evidence, even if disbelieved, could be turned into positive evidence that they had been induced. In an elegantly fair examination of the evidence as to payment of the workmen's travel expenses home Lord Gifford indicates that as there was nothing illegal in the employers paying the men to come and fill the places of the locked-out local workmen, there was nothing illegal in paying their expenses home.[20] The Lord Justice-Clerk, however, agreed with the findings below and had some harsh things to say about the defender. In *Lumley v. Gye*,[21] in which Johanna Wagner was enticed by the defender while under contract to the plaintiff, the defendant was found liable. *Lumley* was founded on in *Couper* but it was argued in the Inner House that *Lumley* was not accepted by the profession in England.[22] However, that did not find favour with the division, the Lord Justice-Clerk's dissent being only on the interpretation of the facts to which the law had to be applied. In *Findlay v. Blaycock*[23] a 23-year-old woman sued the father of a man, whom at one time she was engaged to marry, for damages, alleging against him that he wrongfully induced his son, then a minor, to break off his engagement with her. A date had been fixed for the marriage. The father wrote to the pursuer's father saying that he was annoyed that the proposal that a marriage should take place had been put forward without his permission or consent, or even without it being brought to his notice by the proper people concerned. Lord President Normand said:

"It is no doubt true that, if a person knowing that another person has a contractual relation with a third party, induces that person to break that contractual relation, he may be liable to the third party whose contract in consequence of his action is thereby breached. There are illustrations of that both in Scotland and England."[24]

The action failed for the lack of a "particular averment from which any obliquity of motive can be inferred." In other words the conduct of the

---

[19] *ibid* at 694.
[20] *ibid*. at 696.
[21] (1853) 2E. & B. 216.
[22] *Couper v. Macfarlane*, at 688.
[23] 1937 S.C. 21.
[24] *ibid*. at 25.

defender was not actionable as being for a lawful purpose. In *British Motor Trade Association v. Gray*[25] Gray was a motor dealer. The market in cars at the time, after the war, was difficult. There were few new cars. There was thus a poor second hand market as well. New cars attracted a premium. Cars were sold under a covenant that they would not be resold to others within a year. Gray being well aware of this scheme bought cars from a person who had purchased "covenanted" vehicles. This case makes it clear that the contract protected must be a valid legal contract. It was argued unsuccessfully that it was in restraint of trade. If it had been then there could be no delictual liability. It was held that this could be a delict and that there was a wider rule protecting all contracts not just those of workmen (the rule established in the older authorities). The following passage illustrates the expansion of the rule:

"I am prepared to affirm expressly that it is only by accident that the Scottish illustrations have centred around the contract of service and the wrong of "harbouring servants" that these are only instances of the wider rule, and that on principle the wider rule as more fully developed in England, must be considered as part of the law of Scotland. It remains to consider the precise form and limitations of the wider rule, for even our own decision of *Findlay v Blaylock* shows that in some situations a third party may lawfully induce the breach of a contract between two other persons."[26]

In *Square Grip Reinforcement v. MacDonald*[27] the doctrine was considered **7-30** in the context of industrial relations. The pursuers, manufacturers and suppliers of steel reinforcements, dispensed with collective bargaining through the trade unions and bargained directly. Some of their workers joined a union and called a strike. Thereafter certain officials and members of the union attended at building sites where contractors known to be customers of the company were operating and induced workers there to refuse to offload lorries carrying the materials supplied by the company, and to threaten that if the lorries were offloaded all the workers on the site who were members of the union would cease work. Customers were forced to refuse to take delivery of the pursuers' materials, and so to break their contracts with the pursuers. Lord Milligan had to deal with trade union immunities with which this chapter is not concerned but he did find that there had been an inducement to breach:

"In my opinion it is necessary and relevant in considering whether a person has induced another person to do something or to refrain from doing something to have in mind the relative positions of the persons involved. It is also relevant to have in mind any evidence there may be tending to show whether the person who is alleged to have done the inducing is anxious that the other person should act or refrain from acting in a certain way. If it is shown that he is desperately anxious that

---

[25] 1951 S.L.T. 247.
[26] *ibid., per* Lord President Cooper at 254.
[27] 1968 S.L.T. 65.

something should happen then it is not unlikely that he will try to bring pressure on the other person, whereas if it appears that he is not really interested in whether any action is taken or not a remark which might in the former case have been construed as an inducement would fall to be treated as of relatively minor importance. As Lord Radcliffe pointed out in *J. F. Stratford & Co. Ltd v. Lindley*[28] very little may swing the balance . . . In my opinion it has been established that all the respondents at one time or another and in one way or another induced the men concerned not to offload the petitioners' materials and that as a result the petitioners' customers were in breach of their contracts with the petitioners. It is, I think, highly significant that in the case of all the sites, except possibly Crudens, the blacking of the material followed very closely upon a visit from one or more of the respondents. There was throughout the case an underlying suggestion by the respondents that the fact that the petitioners' lorries were not offloaded was in some instances at least due to a decision of the men themselves or to the decision of the steel fixers taken in the beginning of March. If this had in fact been the position it is somewhat surprising that the respondents did not lead evidence (other than that of Mr Cairns) from the men who ought to have done the offloading."[29]

In *Rossleigh v. Leader Cars*,[30] Lord Mayfield, accepted that *BMTA* was the leading authority on the topic. He did not accept the view of Lord Denning[31] that "turning a blind eye" to the existence of the contract might be sufficient unless the actings "are tantamount to enable the court to conclude that such actings were in effect intentional."[32] It is accordingly prudent in appropriate cases to intimate the existence of the contract in question to any party thought likely to attempt to procure a breach.[33] In *Secretary of State for Scotland v. Scottish Prison Officers' Association*[34] the Secretary of State sought interdict on the basis that this action, coming more than four weeks after the date of a strike ballot, was not protected by the provisions of section 10 of the Trade Union Act 1984. The letter had instructed the holding of meetings of members on December 18, 1990 without having asked for permission but first having informed the governor that meetings would be held. The intention had been that the members would have been acting in such a way as would interfere with the performance of their contracts of employment.

"I was not referred to any decision as to the meaning of the definition of 'relevant act' in s. 10(5). I was referred to the Employment Act 1988

---

[28] [1964] 3 All E.R. 102.

[29] *ibid.* at 73–74.

[30] 1987 S.L.T. 355.

[31] In *Daily Mirror Newspapers Ltd v. Gardner* [1968] 2 Q.B. 762.

[32] In the earlier case of *Square Grip Reinforcement v. MacDonald*, it was held the union members knew enough: " they all knew that the firms referred to on record were customers of the petitioners and that the materials were being sent to the customers in furtherance of contracts between the petitioners and their customers . . . although they did not know the terms of the contracts between the petitioners and their customers they all realised, or, in any event, must have realised that blacking would injure the petitioners and would cause a breach of contract between the customers and the petitioners."

[33] See *e.g. Merkur Island v. Laughton* [1983] 2 A.C. 570.

[34] 1991 S.L.T. (O.H.) 658.

where the phrase, 'members of the union are likely to be, or have been, induced' is used several times. In my view, if a union official goes to a factory and makes a speech or shouts an order that every union member is to stop work, that could be an act of inducing persons to break their contract of employment whether the union members accepted the union official's advice or instructions or ignored it totally."[35]

In *Akram v. Commission for Racial Equality*[36] a proof before answer was allowed where it was alleged that the pursuer had been told to resign or be dismissed as a result of a proposal agreed between the defenders, the pursuer's employer and the regional and district councils. Distinguishing *Findlay v. Blaylock*,[37] it was considered that the defenders had to aver and prove justification. Strictly speaking this appears to be interference in a contract as the parties were not inducing the employer to break the contract. This is the kind of case which could raise other questions of economic delict.

English authority is often consulted. One of the most important is *D.C.* **7–31** *Thomson & Co. v. Deakin*. In that case it was said that there are three forms of committing the tort: (1) direct persuasion; (2) direct intervention; and (3) indirect intervention.[38] It was also established in *D.C. Thomson* that in cases of intervention rather than persuasion there must be the use of some independently unlawful means. The Scots lawyer should note that these English cases are not universally accepted. Weir is the most trenchant:

"How did we [English lawyers] get into our present pickle? In a way the source of the greatest harm has been *Thomson v. Deakin* . . . Difficult on its facts, it is another of these cases where obiter dicta have been taken as gospel, for although judgment was correctly given for the defendant, its effect has been to extend liability in favour of plaintiffs."[39]

A further extension took place in *Torquay Hotel Co. Ltd v. Cousins*,[40] in **7–32** which (at least according to Lord Denning) there was technically no breach of contract because the parties had provided an exclusion in the contract to cover the situation where delivery was prevented as a result of circumstances outside their control. It was held to be enough that the defender prevented or hindered performance of the contract. These cases have been adopted and approved since in *Lonrho v. Fayed*.[41] This "interference with

---

[35] *ibid., per* Lord Morton of Shuna at 659.
[36] 1994 G.W.D. 22–1372.
[37] 1937 S.C. 21.
[38] See *Merkur Island Shipping Co.* [1983] 2 A.C. 570, where the interference was some three steps removed from the contract. Weir is critical: "Unfortunate consequences therefore follow on extending the tort of inducing breach of contract so as to embrace prevention of performance, even when there is no breach; first, that liability may be imposed on a defendant who has used no wrongful means, which is a gross restriction on liberty, and secondly, that the defendant may be held liable to those he had no intention to harm, entailing a large increase in the number of possible plaintiffs, something we normally try to avoid." T. Weir, *Economic Torts* (Oxford, 1998), p. 38.
[39] T. Weir, *Economic Torts* (Oxford, 1998), p. 38.
[40] [1969] 2 Ch. 106.
[41] [1991] 3 W.L.R. 188.

contract" is robustly critiqued by Weir: "The law should address the wrong of a defender having another person wrong the pursuer rather than asking if the pursuer's right to contractual services has been interfered with."[42] He quotes Lord Bingham dealing with the same distinction pithily: "In concentrating on the right . . . the judge did take his eye off the wrong."[43] Weir considers *Torquay* as wrongly decided submitting there was liability for causing harm through unlawful means—the procuring of breach by the drivers.[44]

An interesting case as it deals with the interests in business in conflict with other freedoms, namely that of free speech and protest is *Middlebrook Mushrooms Ltd v. Transport and General Workers Union*.[45] It was held that handing out leaflets urging potential customers not to buy the plaintiffs' mushrooms was not tortious. It was not direct interference because the leaflets were addressed to the customers not to the supermarket managers. It would require unlawful means to make the conduct actionable.

Conspiracy

7-33 The great case and the great Scottish case, indeed the only Scottish case, is *Crofter Hand Woven Harris Tweed Co. v. Veitch*.[46] The appellants were producers of tweed cloth in the island of Lewis in the Outer Hebrides. Their business was to purchase yarn which was sent to the crofters for weaving in their own homes. The appellants would then sell the tweed. Mr Veitch was the Scottish Area Secretary of the Transport and General Workers Union. The other respondent was Mr Mackenzie, the Stornoway Branch Secretary of the Union. The case was not for damages but for interdict against the two respondents in order to stop an "embargo" on all yarn arriving for the appellants at the port of Stornoway, connected by a service of steamers with the mainland, and upon certain tweeds despatched by the appellants from that port. Again, as in passing-off, it was not suggested that there was any material difference between the Scottish law of delict and the English law of tort. The basis of this case was the deal between the Union and the Harris Tweed Producers' Association to keep out other producers such as the petitioners. Both bodies benefited, the employers restricted competition and the workers ensured that their employers were secure and able to pay wages. There are a number of important dicta which essentially lay down the limits within which business is conducted within the law:

"the tort of conspiracy is constituted only if the agreed combination is carried into effect in a greater or less degree, and damage to the plaintiff is thereby produced. It must be so, for, regarded as a civil wrong, conspiracy is one of these wrongs (like fraud or negligence) which sound in damage, and a mere agreement to injure, if it was never acted upon at

---

[42] T. Weir, *Economic Torts*, p.29.
[43] *ibid.* at p.30, citing *Law Debenture Trust Corp. v. Ural Caspian Oil Corp.* [1995] 1 All E.R. 157.
[44] *ibid.* at p.37.
[45] [1993] T.L.R. 11. Weir agrees with this decision: *Economic Torts*, p.42.
[46] 1942 S.C.(H.L.) 1.

all and never led to any result affecting the party complaining, could not produce damage to him."[47]

The requirements in this case were said to be (a) agreement between the two respondents; (b) to effect an unlawful purpose; and (c) resulting in damage to the appellants. (a) and (c) were held to be established. The main question then was what is an unlawful purpose? In explaining this idea a number of other propositions are stated which are clear markers in the law.

"(1) if A is damaged by the action of B, A nevertheless has no remedy against B, if B's act is lawful in itself and is carried out without employing unlawful means. In such a case A has to endure *damnum absque injuria*. (2) It makes no difference to the above proposition that B in so acting had the purpose of damaging A. A bad motive does not *per se* turn an individual's otherwise lawful act into an unlawful one. (3) If C has an existing contract with A and B is aware of it, and if B persuades or induces C to break the contract with resulting damage to A, this is, generally speaking, a tortious act for which B will be liable to A for the injury he has done him. In some cases, however, B may be able to justify his procuring of the breach of contract . . . But if the act which damages A is not that of a single individual, but is due to a combination of two or more persons, then it is no longer possible to say that motive or purpose is immaterial."[48]

This raises the curious point noted as long ago as the *Mogul* case, that it was strange that something may be unlawful if done by several which is not unlawful if done by one. It is now no longer necessary to examine this curious rule as it has been approved again by the House of Lords.[49] So far as the matter of purpose is concerned:

"The test is not what is the natural result to the plaintiffs of such combined action, or what is the resulting damage which the defendants realise or should realise will follow, but what is in truth the object in the minds of the combiners when they acted as they did. It is not consequence that matters but purpose."[50]

Even then there may be cases where the combination has more than one "object" or "purpose." The analysis of human impulses soon leads us into the quagmire of mixed motives, and even if we avoid the word "motive" there may be more than a single "purpose" or "object." It is enough to say that, if there is more than one purpose actuating a combination, liability must depend on ascertaining the predominant purpose. If that predominant purpose is to damage another person and damage results, that is tortious conspiracy. If the predominant purpose is the lawful protection or promotion of any lawful interest of the combiners (no illegal means being

---

[47] *ibid.*, *per* Lord Chancellor Simon at 5.
[48] *ibid.*, *per* Lord Chancellor Simon at 8.
[49] *Lonrho plc. v. Al-Fayed* [1991] 3 WLR 188.
[50] *Crofter Hand Woven Harris Tweed Co. v. Veitch*, *per* Lord Chancellor Simon at 10.

employed), it is not a tortious conspiracy, even though it causes damage to another person."[51]

It was upon this ground that the case fell. The result aimed at was to create a better basis for collective bargaining, and to improve wage prospects. This was held not to be unlawful because the object was the legitimate promotion of the interests of the combiners. After a number of cases in England it was made clear by the House of Lords in *Lonrho plc v. Al-Fayed*[52] that it is not an essential ingredient of the tort of conspiracy to injure that there was a predominant purpose to injure if the means were themselves unlawful.

INTIMIDATION

7-34 The leading case is the English case of *Rookes v. Barnard*.[53] Barnard and others conspired to threaten strike action by members of the union of which they were officials. This induced Rookes's employers, British Overseas Airways Corporation (BOAC) to dismiss him. No breach of contract was committed by BOAC against Rookes, who however, alleged that Barnard and the other defendants had intimidated BOAC by the threat of strike action. Because there was a "no strike" agreement the threat to withdraw their labour was a threat by the employees to breach their contracts with BOAC This intimidation by causing BOAC to terminate his employment had caused damage to Rookes. He was successful.[54] In *Hewitt v. Edinburgh and District Lathsplitters Association*,[55] the pursuer, who was a lathsplitter, took action for reparation against the defenders and the officials and members of the said Association. The pursuer had been a founding member and office bearer of the association. He had withheld his subscription and had been expelled. His fellow workmen had him dismissed from his job and then had him dismissed from his next job. The issues allowed all related to wrongful procurement of breach. The conduct was by way of threats of strikes. In a short opinion which appears to have followed on argument on the leading cases Lord Salvesen stated the law as follows:

> "These averments, in my opinion, disclose an actionable wrong. It was contended by the defenders that, as the pursuer did not allege that he had any contract of employment for a given period with any of the firms who ceased to employ him at the defenders' instance, the case was ruled by the decision in *Allen v. Flood* (1898) App. Cas. 1. That case, however, is quite distinguishable from the present, on the ground that there was no combination, but that the actings of the defender amounted to no more than an intimation of what would happen if the employer continued the plaintiff in his employment. The case, accordingly, does

---

[51] *ibid.*
[52] [1991] T.L.R. 320.
[53] [1964] 1 All E.R. 367. For a note see J.T. Cameron, "Intimidation and the Right to Strike", 1964 S.L.T. (News) 81.
[54] The decision has to be read against the background of the trade union immunities. See generally Clerk & Lindsell, *Law of Torts*, para. 23–91 *et seq.*
[55] (1906) 14 S.L.T. 489.

not conflict in the slightest with the later cases of *Quinn v. Leathem*
(1901) App. Cas. 495, and *Giblan* [1903] 2 K.B. 600. These two cases
appear to me to be absolutely in point; and as the decisions proceeded
upon principles which are equally applicable to Scotland as to England, I
have no difficulty in following them . . . The defenders further argued
that malice should be put into the issues. In my opinion that is not
necessary. If what was done is a legal wrong, it is of no consequence with
what motive it was done; just as if the Act in itself had been lawful, it
would not have been actionable because prompted by malice."[56]

There is authority of a sort in Stair[57]: "Extortion signifies the act of force, **7–35**
or other means of fear, whereby a person is compelled to do that which of
his proper inclination he would not have done. It doth also imply the
obligation of the injurer to the injured, to repair his loss and damage by
such act." Professor Walker approved the principle, basing it upon the
Roman *actio quod metus causa* and J.T. Cameron thought it consonant with
Scottish principle.[58] Developments of the principle will be found in the
English books but the following is a summary of the position there which
can be assumed to be likely to be followed here. Intimidation as a tort
following *Rookes* depends upon a three party situation: A strikes at C by
intimidating B to harm C. If the party intimidated ignores the threat then
there is no harm done and no action.[59] However, two party intimidation is
also recognised in both Scotland[60] and England.[61] The threats must be to
commit an illegal act.[62] This must be taken in Scotland to be subject to the
doctrine of *aemulationem vicini* albeit *quantum valeat*.

An extended discussion took place in *Micosta S.A. v. Shetland Islands* **7–36**
Council.[63] It was alleged that a public body, the harbour authority,
wrongfully threatened terminal operators to cancel a charterparty, which
threat worked and caused loss. As this is the only extended discussion of
the topic in a Scots case the critical passage is quoted in full:

"Realising that his references to a 'tort of intimidation' depended upon
English authority, counsel for the pursuers drew my attention to Walker,
Delict (2nd ed.), pp. 932–934: 'A person has a right of action if harm is
caused him by actings on the part of himself or of another, prompted by
threats on the part of a third party or by fear of what the third party may
do. The basis is the Roman actio *quod metus causa*. There is no action,
however, if the actings threatened are wholly legal' (p. 932). 'Intimidation or threats takes two forms. The first is by threats causing the
complainer himself to act to his detriment. This is not actionable if the
conduct threatened is lawful . . . but is actionable if the conduct

---

[56] *ibid.* at 491.
[57] Stair I,ix,8.
[58] J.T. Cameron, "Intimidation and Right to Strike", *op. cit.*
[59] *Morgan v. Fry* [1968] 2 Q.B. 710 at 724.
[60] See Stair, n.57 above.
[61] *Allen v. Flood* [1898] A.C.1; *News Group Newspapers v. SOGAT 1982* [1987] I.C.R. 180 at
204; *D & C Builders v. Rees* [1966] 2 Q.B. 617.
[62] *Allen v. Flood, ibid.*
[63] 1986 S.L.T. 193.

threatened is criminal or delictual' (p. 933). 'There is, moreover, clearly a wrong if the defender has threatened to commit a wrongful act, *e.g.* assault, or, *a fortiori*, a crime' (p. 934).

Counsel for the defenders contended that, if the pursuers could not succeed on their first ground, they could not succeed on the alternative ground. He maintained that there was no authority to suggest that a public body was liable for intimidation in respect that that body had intimated that, in certain events, there would be a purported exercise of power which was ex hypothesi invalid. Accordingly, in his submission, if there is a remedy here, it must lie under the first head.

If the foregoing proposition for the defenders were not well founded, counsel for the defenders accepted that this is a difficult area of the law. He submitted that an examination of the authorities showed that an action based on threats could not be brought against the instigator of the threats unless there was conspiracy.

According to counsel for the defenders, unless the thing threatened was itself something that would sound in damages (*i.e.* was tortious or delictual), the threat was not actionable. In other words, unless the act is actionable if done, threatening to do it is not actionable. In my opinion, the submission by counsel for the defenders is well founded. As Professor Walker says to be actionable, what is threatened must be delictual. This coincides with the views expressed in Winfield and Jolowicz at p. 492: 'In the ordinary simple situation in which A's act operates directly to cause injury to B, then, even if the injury was intended, B may recover damages from A only if A's conduct amounts to a tort or breach of contract as against him and it makes no difference that A's conduct is in some extrinsic sense unlawful.'"[64]

BREACH OF CONFIDENCE

7-37 This is a much more difficult obligation to identify. In the usual run of things confidential information, that which is sought to be retained as private, is not imparted unless the imparter trusts the primary confidant. People will tell their wife, their secretary, their doctor or their clergyman; they might not tell their bar-man. In one set of circumstances there is an expectation that the information will not travel further. Often there will be an implied contract but in many cases this is not so easy. Even the obvious example of the doctor is not clearly encompassed within this scheme now that many doctors are employed in the National Health Service within hospitals and the patient does not contract with the board. The priest and penitent is an even better example there being no contract in these circumstances. If information is revealed the confider is both affronted by the release of the information and may also suffer patrimonial damage. A number of Scottish cases have dealt with the problem in the past.[65]

---

[64] *ibid.* at 199–200.
[65] Among the most often considered are *Brown's Trs v. Hay* (1898) 25 R. 1112; *Levin v. Caledonian Produce (Holdings) Ltd*, 1975 S.L.T. (Notes) 69.

Professor Walker expressed interesting views and the Law Commission prepared a paper. Professor Carey Miller has provided us with an interesting comparative examination of the applicability of civilian principle.[66] *Roxburgh v. Seven Seas Engineering Ltd*[67] is an example of a common approach before developments in the late 1980's. Lord Robertson in rejecting a petition took a very strict view of the need for a pre-existing consensual relationship:

> "In order to state a relevant case based upon breach of confidentiality a pursuer or petitioner must aver primarily an agreement to treat the material as confidential and a relationship giving rise to the duty. Here there is no such relationship and no basis for any such agreement. The respondents have no relationship with the petitioner giving rise to any such duty. Whatever may be thought of the propriety or morals of the respondents' action they have in my opinion committed no wrong in law against the petitioner."[68]

The whole issue was re-examined in the cases arising out of the publication **7–38** of the book "Spycatcher".[69] In *Attorney-General v. The Observer Ltd*; *Attorney-General v. Times Newspapers*,[70] the press were publishing extracts from a book written by a former government security service officer said to be detrimental to national security. Lord Keith's approach was that the emphasis is not upon wrongdoing and thus must lead to suspicion that the basis of the obligation may not be delictual: "The obligation may be imposed by an express or implied term in a contract but it may also exist independently of any contract on the basis of an equitable principle of confidence."[71] Even although we regularly associate the idea of a duty of care with negligence or with liability for unintentional harm, this is a wider notion. Thus, the following passage is not conclusive of the proposition that the obligation of confidence is delictual:

> "It is a general rule of law that a third party who comes into possession of confidential information which he knows to be such, may come under a duty not to pass it to anyone else."[72]

One of the difficulties that might have arisen had the obligation been expressly made out to be delictual is that the loss necessary to sustain an aquilian action would be missing, although it would still be arguable that the revelation of the information should sound in damages on the basis of the *actio injuriarum*. Not a problem with this equitable obligation:

> "As a general rule it is in the public interest that confidences should be respected and the encouragement of such respect may in itself constitute

---

[66] D.L. Carey Miller, "Privacy: Interception of communications" 1980 S.L.T. (News) 209.
[67] 1980 S.L.T. (Notes) 49.
[68] *ibid*. at 50.
[69] Although the whole law had been reviewed by the Scottish Law Commission. They concluded that statutory intervention might be required to supplement the existing law. See Scot. Law Com. No. 90, Cmnd. 9385 (1984).
[70] [1988] 3 W.L.R. 776.
[71] *ibid*. at 781.
[72] *ibid*. at 786.

a sufficient ground for recognising and enforcing the obligation of confidence even where the confider can point to no specific detriment to himself."[73]

7-39 In *Lord Advocate v. The Scotsman Publications Ltd*[74] some of the issues which had been canvassed in England were canvassed through the Scottish courts. *Scotsman Publications* did not involve prejudice to the Crown in that the information was eventually admitted to be non-prejudicial. However, Lord Keith took the opportunity to agree that the law in Scotland was the same as the law in England:

> "The judges of the Second Division, having considered such authorities upon the law of confidentiality as existed in the Scottish Corpus Juris, came to the conclusion that Scots law in this field was the same as that of England, in particular as respects the circumstances under which a person coming into possession of confidential information knowing it to be such, but not having received it directly from the original confider, himself comes under an obligation of confidence. That conclusion was, in my opinion, undoubtedly correct. While the juridical basis may differ to some extent in the two jurisdictions, the substance of the law in both of them is the same."[75]

Of the older cases, *A.B. v. C.D.*[76] is thought provoking. The pursuer had separated from her husband and consulted the defender, who was a medical practitioner, when pregnant. Two years later the defender was consulted by the husband and gave evidence for him in an action for separation at the instance of the wife. The evidence was based on the knowledge obtained when she had been examined by the doctor before on the instructions of her own lawyers, that the pursuer had perhaps wanted to abort her child. While the headnote refers to contract, contract does not feature to any degree in the argument or the opinions. The doctor was engaged by the pursuer's lawyer and it is not entirely certain that they would be agents for the purpose of establishing a contract between her and the doctor. The Inner House would not allow the issue that the Lord Ordinary had on confidentiality but on the facts alleged—that they were too general. As Lord Trayner said: "sometimes it would be a 'breach of confidence' to even mention the consultation at all. In other cases, where the patient had a cold it might be permissible."[77] That has to be doubted now and must have been doubtful then, if it were compared with priest and penitent, would it be in order to tell the grocer that the butcher had confessed to a venial as opposed to a mortal sin?
Cases are not common.[78]

---

[73] [1988] 3 W.L.R. 776 at 782, per Lord Keith of Kinkel.
[74] 1989 S.L.T. 705.
[75] *ibid.* at 708.
[76] (1904) 7 F. 72.
[77] *ibid.*
[78] See *Waste Systems International Inc v. Eurocare Environmental Services Ltd*, 1999 S.L.T. 198.

WRONGFUL REFUSAL TO CONTRACT

This wrong is included here because it can be committed by a business, but **7–40** it is not necessarily the case that it is a wrong against a business interest. Its theoretical significance is enormous and its practical significance virtually non-existent. Only the common law is described here. Practitioners will be aware that a business refusing to contract with another, say a supplier refusing to sell to a retailer, may be in breach of either domestic or European Union competition law and may thereby be liable for a penalty or in certain circumstances, damages. Normally a person is under no obligation to contract with another. In two sets of circumstances the law is different: (i) the defender was a common carrier and so was obliged to take the goods; and (ii) where the defender was an innkeeper who refused to allow the pursuer board and lodgings. The Scots law is set out solely in *Rothfield v. North British Railway Company*,[79] although the opinions depend upon earlier *obiter dicta*. As will be seen from the analysis of this theoretically significant case, the authority actually relied on was English. That said, ancient statutory provision was identified to support the idea.[80] While this discussion appears in the business interests chapter it does seem that the head of liability, which is of course clearly non-contractual, is based on the danger to the safety of the person. Henry Rothfield was a money lending Jewish German. These facts were pled.[81] It was alleged that he associated with other money-lenders and borrowers or applicants for loans. His business methods had been adversely commented on in the public press. The hoteliers said that his presence and business were not suited to the hotel and made him objectionable as a guest in the hotel, both to other guests, specifically military and naval officers who had formed a large proportion of guests since the start of the first world war. He stayed in the hotel for a large part of the year. The action was something of a set piece with the defenders making it clear he was not welcome and the pursuer making

---

[79] 1920 2 S.L.T. 269.

[80] By the Lord Ordinary (Anderson): "Thus the Act 1424, cap. 25, 'ordainyt that in all burowis townyss of the realme and thruthfaris, quhar common passagis are, that thar be ordanyt hostilaris and resetteris, haifande stabillis and chawmeris to ridaris and gangaris, fynde with thame brede and aile, and all uther fuyde, alsueill to horse as men, for resonable price efter as the chapis of the cuntre standis.' This was followed by the Act 1425, cap. 11, which provided that no traveller on horse or on foot should lodge in any other place than these hostelries, excepting those who travelled with a large retinue, who were allowed to lodge with their friends, if they sent their horses and followers to the hostelry. Burgesses were forbidden, under penalty of a fine, to receive such travellers. By the Act 1427, cap. 3, the King ordained all his burgesses in the realm 'quod faciant fieri hostellaria seu hospicia publica in burgis honesta et competencia more aliorum regnorum ad recipiendum omnes et singulos hospites tam pedestres quam equestres per regnum laborantes sub pena.' By the Act 1535, cap. 23, the former Acts were approved, and further provision was made for securing that proper accommodation should be made for travellers, to be sold 'apoun ane competent price ande as siclike stuff is saulde commonlie in the cuntre about quhare sik ostillaris duellis.' "

[81] The 1920 volume of Session Cases shows an action of suspension against one Henry Rothfield under the Money Lenders Act 1900 (which was unsuccessful): *Inglis v. Rothfield*, 1920 S.C. 650. It shows another, *Munro v. Rothfield*, 1920 S.C. 118, in which the defender was a creditor in what looked like a money lending transaction and the defender was designed at the same address as the defender in the *North British Railway* case. Rothfield was successful in this case too.

sure that he set himself up as being a traveller in writing so that it could inevitably be refused. Other key facts were that he had been insulted in the press through his association with a money-lender called Cohen. There appears to have been a real worry at the time about soldiers and sailors borrowing money.

It was accepted that the origin and development of the law in Scotland and England was different but that the result had come to be the same.[82] Lord Dundas, relying on English cases and previous Scots cases, stated the law as being that while innkeepers or hotel-keepers may not refuse guests capriciously or maliciously, every hotel-keeper must have a certain power of selecting his guests, or perhaps, to speak more precisely, of rejecting certain guests. A hotel-keeper may, in his discretion, reject persons "because their manners and habits are not suitable to the class of people whom he receives." He is not only entitled but bound to have due regard to the status and reputation of his hotel, and to the proper interests of those he receives in it.[83] The decision in the case came to be based on the defender's conduct, not on simple facts that he was a money lending Jewish German. On these points, which we would today describe as discriminatory, Lord Dundas said: "The pursuer is a Jew; he is also a money-lender. These facts by themselves, either separately or in conjunction, would not be of any significance in the case."[84] The Lord Justice-Clerk (Scott Dickson) said: "I agree also, to a certain extent, with his views as to the objection that the pursuer is a money-lender. That objection could never, in my opinion, be taken as in itself sufficient to justify his exclusion." The decision in the case to reverse the Lord Ordinary's finding was based on the impression given by the pursuer and what others said about him. Lord Dundas said:

> "It is not proved either that the pursuer actually conducted his money-lending business in the hotel, or that the allegations against him in Truth (the press) are wholly true in fact. But the defenders' case needs no such proof. They have enough, if the circumstances justified them, as I think they did, in coming honestly to the resolution that, having due regard to the decency, order, and repute of their hotel, and to the legitimate interests of those whom they received in it, the conduct and manners of the pursuer rendered him unsuitable to the class of people whom they took into their hotel. They were, in my judgment, entitled to reject the pursuer, in the bona fide exercise of their discretion."[85]

This could be called a reasonable subjective view or, if an objective test then it is defender objectivity rather than fly-on-the-wall objectivity. It is clear that it is not possible to exclude a potential guest on the basis that the landlord does not like the look of him.

---

[82] *Rothfield v. North British Railway Company*, at 276.
[83] *ibid.* at 279.
[84] *ibid.* at 279.
[85] *ibid.* at 280.

MALICIOUS FALSEHOOD

It is a wrong in certain circumstances to say things detrimental to a **7–41** business.[86] Malicious falsehood has most right to be in this chapter on its own because as shall be seen its scope is mainly in relation to business matters.[87] However, as the mode of commission is by word it is treated together with defamation and other verbal injuries in Chapter 8.

---

[86] Defamation may in this respect protect a business interest.
[87] Indeed in one case it was argued alongside passing-off: *Argyllshire Weavers Ltd v. A. Macaulay (Tweeds) Ltd*, 1965 S.L.T. 21.

CHAPTER 8

INSULT, HONOUR, FAME, REPUTATION AND PRIVACY

Introduction

There are many ways of wronging by words. Many are reparable, some are **8–1**
not. *Hedley Byrne* liability,[1] fraud[2] and passing-off[3] are examples dealt with
elsewhere in this book. This chapter looks at certain forms of wronging by
words where the nature of the harm relates to certain identifiable interests
as well as related cases of insulting words and the delict of malicious
falsehood which is more difficult to classify.[4] Unusually in the modern law
of delict there is no complete consensus as to the organisation of the law
nor its naming. Professor Norrie has made a number of points bearing on
terminology and analysis.[5] He differs from Professor Walker on a number
of points.[6] There is little in the law reports of the second-half of the
twentieth century which assists in clarifying the basis of recovery in this
country. Naming is not without consequence. In one case an action which
might have founded a case of verbal injury was dismissed because it did not
satisfy the test of defamation which was the only basis upon which the claim
was made.[7] Walker has a genus of verbal injury which comprises defamation (including libel and slander), *convicium* and malicious falsehood.[8]
Norrie argues that there are only two types of cases—defamation and
verbal injury cases (which includes malicious falsehood).[9] In this book the
division is into verbal injury (in a narrow sense), *convicium* (*quantum
valeat*), malicious falsehood (because although very similar to verbal injury
it is not directed at the person of the pursuer) and defamation. It would
accordingly be appropriate to treat malicious falsehood from a pursuer's
point of view as being in the chapter relating to economic interests as did
Professor Walker. For convenience and reflecting the defender's point of
view it can be treated here. Cases are not all that common possibly because
legal aid is generally not available for pursuers and many defenders will not

---

[1] *Hedley Byrne v. Heller and Partners* [1964] A.C. 465. See Chap. 10.
[2] See para. 7–7 *et seq.*
[3] See para. 7–10 *et seq.*
[4] Insult can form part of an assault claim. See *Rutherford v. Chief Constable for Strathclyde
Police*,1981 S.L.T. (Notes) 119, in which such a claim was on the facts refused.
[5] K. Norrie, "Hurts to Character, Honour and Reputation: A reappraisal", 1985 J.R. 163; K.
Norrie, *Defamation and Related Actions in Scots Law* (Butterworths, 1995).
[6] Professor Walker's treatment in *Delict* (1966), Vol. 2 extends to some 118 pages.
[7] *Thomson v. News Group Newspapers Ltd*, 1993 G.W.D. 14–825.
[8] Walker, *Delict* (2nd ed., 1981), pp. 729–847.
[9] Norrie, *Defamation and Related Actions in Scots Law*, Chap. 3.

carry insurance against such liability meaning that it is normally necessary to have both a well-off pursuer and defender.[10]

8–2   The roots of liability in Scotland are in the jurisdiction of the Roman Catholic Church which of course had jurisdiction over certain matters in Scotland before the reformation and before establishment of the Court of Session.[11] There is a record even very early in the history of the Court of Session of it taking cognisance of a slander case.[12] However, Balfour's Practicks reveals no civil action but that is hardly surprising when we read what attitude the law took to the use of words:

> "It is statute and ordanit, that na manner of man mak, write, or imprent any billis, writingis, balladis, famous or slanderous to ony persoun, spiritual or temporal, under pane of death, and confiscation of all his movabill gudis."

"Lease making" or verbal sedition was also a crime subject to the death penalty. There is an historical review in the Lord Justice-Clerk's opinion in *McKellar v. Duke of Sutherland*[13] which explains that it was only with *Auchinleck v. Gordon* that the Court took jurisdiction.[14] Stair considered fame reputation and honour to be among the interests which the law protects and described them as being "in some way reparable."[15] Reparable by damages where by hurt of fame the pursuer's "gain ceaseth". The basis

---

[10] In *Joyce v. Sengupta* [1993] 1 All E.R. the English courts held that malicious falsehood cases did not fall within the prohibition on legal aid and so there was no bar against a person framing their case in that way. In some respects it seems that things were better in the 16th. century before the Court of Session and the Commissaries took over from the Church courts. It seems that people much poorer than those who can litigate today could either complete an action or at least start one leading to a settlement. The other side of the coin was that instead of there being ludicrous gold-digging actions arising from some inattention or anger modest fines would be imposed.

[11] The Consistory Court or the Court of the Official had jurisdiction in defamation. Walker, *History*, Vol. II, p.405. The English history appears to be similar: Watson, *Society and Legal Change* (Scottish Academic Press, 1977), pp. 62–63. Ollivant offers two reasons why there was a smooth transition from the Church Court of the Official to the secular courts: (i) the consistory court was a direct substitute; (ii) the people who ran the courts tended to be the same, "Sir James Balfour, the last official of Lothian, became the chief commissary of the new court in Edinburgh, while in the local commissariats also many of the old ecclesiastical judges slipped smoothly into their new roles as servants of the state": *The Court of the Official in Pre-Reformation Scotland* (1982, Stair Society), Vol. 34, pp. 163–165. Walker charts some early history including references to the Leges Quatuor Burgorum and the Acta Dominorum Concilii (1479–95): Walker, *History*, II, p. 621.

[12] (1542) Legal History, Stair Society (1958) Vol. 20 at p. 268.

[13] (1859) 21 D. 222.

[14] (1755) M. 7348.

[15] Stair, I,ix,4. Stair does not explain what is meant by honour and reputation. His view may have been similar to that of Pufendorf: "Reputation in general is the value of persons in common life by which they may be measured against others or compared with them and either preferred or put after them": *De officio hominis et civis juxta legem naturalem* (1673) (Tully ed., Silverthorne trans., C.U.P. 1991). Pufendorf distinguishes between simple and intensive reputation. The first an assumption of general fitness. Intensive reputation is honour — a judgment and recognition of the superiority of another. The same theme can be seen in Hume: "special regard must be had to the character and station of the person, of whom they (the words) are spoken, because imputations may be very injurious and prejudicial, when made against one person, which are harmless or at least are of far less consequence, if applied to others." 138–139.

is that victims are "disenabled for their affairs."[16] The practice of demanding a written apology or palinode was long ago disapproved.[17]

One of the things that is rather lost sight of in modern discussions is what **8–3** it is this chapter of the law is really about. Professor Norrie says that "as a society, we (rightly) pay less heed today to notions of honour than we used to . . . In today's society we might well be unsympathetic to claims for damages based solely on insult to honour."[18] There is no evidence though that what Norrie says is the case. What can be said is that there is no access to justice for ordinary people defamed and it might be solicitors reading this book will be able to speak to the pent-up demand that there is for such actions albeit the repute of a poor insignificant person is unlikely to be such that cases would exceed the summary jurisdiction. Many cases of defamation and dishonour are dealt with *brevi manu* by the victim and are reported in the breach of the peace section of the criminal reports. It is submitted that among the poor, honour and reputation are among the most highly prized assets.

VERBAL INJURY

Guthrie Smith writing in 1889 recognised a head of non-defamatory verbal **8–4** injury: "When the words, although not slanderous in themselves, have been spoken falsely with a view to prejudice, and did actually prejudice the pursuer in some particular way, an action lies."[19] His only Scots authority is *Torrance v. Weddel.*[20] The allegation in the case was that the defender stated to a member of the council that was to award a cleaning contract by competitive tender that the pursuer had offered the defender money not to put in an offer. The Lord President decided the case as slander.[21] Lord

---

[16] Stair's examples are: (1) The merchant called a bankrupt who loses both because no one wants to deal with him and because his creditors fall upon him; (2) The man about to be married who is said to have a disease or be impotent who the loses his match and tocher. Then Stair makes the positive statement "such actions upon injurious words, as they may relate to damage in means, are frequent and curious among the English; but with us there is little of it accustomed to be pursued, though we own the same grounds, and would proceed to the same effects with them if questioned." This does rather support the view that there was little Scots legal authority available at the time Stair was writing. He records *Deans v. Bothwell*, Feb. 5, 1669 where the court approved an order of the Commissaries at Edinburgh on an action for slander and defamation ordaining the slanderer to make acknowledgment of the injury before the congregation and to pay one hundred pounds Scots to the victim and as much to the poor.

[17] *Chalmers v. Douglas*, Feb. 19, 1790. In *McLean & Co v. Blair* (1801) Hume's Decisions 609, the defender was the proprietor of a tan works. Her tenant left her premises and became a partner in a new firm in the same line of business. She reproached the new firm and its partners and publicly doubted its credit. The imputations did not affect the business materially. The pursuers were the firm who brought an action before the Commissary of Dunkeld with concurrence of the fiscal concluding for palinode and damages and a fine to the fiscal. The Commissaries awarded damages and imposed a fine. On a bill of advocation by the defender, the case was remitted with a reduced award. A reclaiming motion to Inner House was refused without answers.

[18] *Defamation and Related Actions in Scots Law*, p.1.

[19] Guthrie-Smith, *The Law of Damages*, p. 240.

[20] (1868) 7 M. 243.

[21] Guthrie-Smith, *The Law Of Damages*, p. 245. But see the discussion of *Waddell* which follows showing that at this time "slander" and defamation appear to have had a wider connotation.

Deas considered that it was either slander or a case of a false statement causing damage.[22] Thus the case is not a direct authority for non-slanderous verbal injury. The leading case on this head, at least in recent times, is *Paterson v. Welch*.[23] The pursuer was a governor of college A. The defender was a governor of college A but also a chairman of the school board of B. The defender made the statements complained of at a meeting of the School B and at another meeting. Here it was alleged that a false report was made of the pursuer's comments at a meeting of the governors of college A. So the complaint is that the pursuer says that the defender said that the pursuer said the pupils from the board schools would contaminate the genteel children attending College A. The defamatory claim (slander) was held not to apply on the facts. Lord President (Robertson) said:

> "But assuming, as I now do, that the words sued on do not found a claim of damages on the head of slander, it by no means follows that they are not actionable. The true case of the pursuer is this—he says to the defender, 'You publicly asserted that I said certain things; your assertion was false; it was made with design to injure me, and I have been injured.' In my opinion that is a good claim in damages. In judging of the relevancy of such a claim, it is of course necessary that the words ascribed to the pursuer should be such as reasonably support the essential averments, that the attributing of them to him was done with an intention to injure, and with the result of injuring. But subject to this observation, it seems to me that when speech is ascribed to A by B, A will have an action if: (1) the statement of B is false; (2) the statement was made with design to injure; and (3) injury has resulted. The pursuer's case complies with these conditions. He begins by saying that he never used the words ascribed to him. These words are invidious words, to utter which may well be supposed to bring down on him, who was alleged to have used them, the hatred of his neighbours. The pursuer goes on to say that the defender ascribed these words to him, because the defender calculated their effect, and desired to inflict that injury on him. He ends by saying that the falsehood did its work; that he has become an object of public hatred; that the people have tried to burn him in effigy at his own door; that his personal comfort and public influence have been impaired; and all this through the falsehood of the defender."[24]

The case involves a false statement, an ascription of an unpopular view and public hatred. Shortly after *Paterson*, *Waddell v. Roxburgh*[25] was decided. Here the pursuer sued the defender who was publisher and printer of the following: "This contract was secured by the lowest offerer in a mean and contemptible manner. We attach no blame to any of the burgh officials, but to the unfair advantage taken by the successful offerer to secure the contract." In the Inner House an issue of slander was allowed to go to the

---

[22] *ibid.*, p. 246.
[23] (1893) 20 R. 744. See also *Cunningham v. Phillips* (1868) 6 M. 926.
[24] *ibid.* at 749.
[25] (1894) 21 R. 883.

jury on the basis of the innuendo of dishonesty. A second issue was unsuccessfully argued on the basis of *Paterson*: "Whether the said statement [concerned] the pursuer, and whether the said statement was false, and was made and published by the defender with design of injuring the pursuer, to his loss, injury and damage?" This was not allowed and the following comments were made about the scope of *Paterson*. Lord Kinnear said:

"It appears to me that the case of *Paterson v. Welch* has been somewhat misunderstood. It was not intended by the court in that case to lay down that whenever the words of which a pursuer complains are not in themselves slanderous, he may have an issue whether they exposed him to public hatred and contempt. I understand that the opinion of the Lord President . . . proceeded on this, that the words which the pursuer in that sanction was said to have used of a class of persons were not slanderous of that class, but that, nevertheless, to impute to the pursuer that he had used those words was an actionable wrong, because he undertook to show that they had been ascribed to him by the defender with the design of injuring him, and that he had in fact thereby been exposed to the public hatred and contempt. There were specific allegations of the special damage which had arisen to the pursuer from the words in question having been ascribed to him. I have no doubt that the form of issue adopted in that case was better calculated to bring the question fairly before the jury than the ordinary form of issue. Therefore I see no reason for dissenting from the judgment. It may be that to confine the use of the word slander to cases where the language complained of is obviously and on the face of it defamatory and injurious would be convenient, but I should rather have thought that all actionable words which are either injurious to the character or credit of the person of whom they are spoken, or which expose the person with reference to whom they are uttered to public hatred and contempt, are defamatory or slanderous words. However that may be, I am of the opinion that if the language of which the pursuer complains is calculated to expose him to public hatred and contempt, that is slanderous language. If it is not calculated to expose him to public hatred or contempt, or to do him any injury,—if, when properly constructed, it does not assail his character or credit,—then it is not slanderous or actionable at all . . . the pursuer must have an issue of slander in ordinary form or no issue at all."[26]

Lord McLean agreed, as did Lord Adam who was one of the judges in *Paterson*. *Waugh v. Ayrshire Post Ltd*[27] is perhaps also in this line. Two alternative issues were sought, one for slander and one following *Paterson*. The pursuer complained that the defenders had published a letter bearing to be from the pursuer but which in fact he had not written. He was an Orangeman and the letter was full of suggestions of bloodletting towards Catholics. The Lord President was able to avoid considering the *Paterson* form of issue by taking view that the allegations were of slander.[28] *Obiter*,

---

[26] (1894) 21 R. 883 at 886.
[27] (1894) 21 R. 326.
[28] *ibid.* at 329.

Lord Adam agreed that it was a case of slander but that it could be shown that publication had been made "with a view to do the pursuer injury, and done him injury".[29] Again it might be noted that this is an "attribution" case.[30]

8–5 The last major, but incomplete, discussion can be found in *Steele v. Scottish Daily Record and Sunday Mail Ltd,*[31] A motor dealer sued a newspaper as it had portrayed him as hard-hearted in enforcing his legal rights under a legal contract, the following passage reflecting the tone of the article complained of: "You're in the big time, Mr Steele, probably you didn't know the tough times Mr McLeod was coming through. Come on . . . let's show us that the big time has a big heart too." The case was argued in various ways at various stages as can be seen by Lord Wheatley's comment:

> "The learned sheriff dealt with the case as one of convicium although there appears to have been at that stage a certain amount of inter-play between convicium and verbal injury. This is perhaps not surprising in view of the mixed opinions which have been expressed about the constituents of these two types of actions and of defamation down through the years."[32]

In the Inner House counsel accepted the case was one of verbal injury and it was accordingly so treated. This restricts the extent to which the case can generally be relied. By verbal injury however it is clear that the court understood, as did counsel, a case of *Paterson v. Welch* verbal injury—the discussion taking place around the three conditions in Lord Robertson's opinion. Lord Wheatley said:

> "As I see the position, it is this, If the words used are slanderous or can be innuendoed as slanderous, the proper form of action is one of slander. In that situation the courts have refused to allow an issue of verbal injury to stand alongside an issue of slander arising out of the same species facti."[33]

From this it can be said that verbal injury is a residual category, available only where the remarks are not defamatory. Another development in the *Steele* case is that it is probably necessary to aver and prove particular injury rather than some general injury. This meant that for example there had to be intention to injure in the sense of incurring solatium and a separate case made in relation to harm to the business of the motor trader.

---

[29] (1894) 21 R. 326.

[30] A more recent expression of the same idea is that of Lord Strachan in *Moffat v. London Express Newspapers Ltd*, 1950 S.L.T. (Notes) 46. Lord Strachan in holding that the pursuers' averments on verbal injury were irrelevant said under reference to *Outram v. Reid* (1852) 14 D. 577; *Paterson v. Welch* (1893) 20 R. 744; *Waddell v. Roxburgh* (1894) 21 R. 883; *Andrew v. Macara*, 1917 S.C. 247; and *Balden v. Shorter* [1933] 1 Ch. 427: "It may, in my opinion, be taken as settled that an action for verbal injury arises only if the following three circumstances occur, *viz.* (1) that the statements founded on are false; (2) that there was a deliberate design to injure; and (3) that special damage is proved."

[31] 1970 S.L.T. 53.

[32] *ibid.* at 60.

[33] *ibid.* at 61.

In cases of verbal injury the words must be injurious and that was **8–6** interpreted as meaning that while not slanderous they should bring the pursuer in to public hatred and contempt. This was explained by Lord Wheatley as follows:

"In this very unusual type of action, namely verbal injury . . . the words complained of must produce something more than public disapproval, adverse comment or criticism. I do not consider, however, that people would have to "hate" the complainer in the full sense of that word . . .. something of the order of condemn or despise is the proper test. This I would regard as something stronger than the test laid down in England by Lord Atkin in *Sim v. Stretch* (1936) 52 T.L.R. 669, namely 'tending to lower the plaintiff in the estimation of right thinking members of society.'"[34]

It was held that the article did not meet the test even though it was accepted that the article was irresponsible, biased and inaccurate. It was accepted that the article would probably give offence and it may well have had an effect on his business.[35]

Mention must be made of *Trapp v. Mackie*,[36] for in that case the plea was that the pursuer suffered loss, injury and damage by maliciously false evidence given at an inquiry to the effect that Dr Trapp had altered building plans. Lord Fraser said in the House of Lords "The action is apparently not based on defamation but on some other form of verbal injury, either convicium or malicious falsehood. There may be room for doubt about the exact meaning of these words—see Report of the Committee on Defamation, Cmnd. 5909 (1975) paras 595–598, and about whether either of them would apply to this action."[37] However, as he took the view that the occasion was absolutely privileged he considered it was not necessary to investigate the matter.

CONVICIUM: HARMFUL RIDICULE BY TRUE STATEMENTS.

Guthrie Smith describes this as a species of verbal injury: **8–7**

"a specially aggravated kind—the loud and public denunciation of an individual by different persons, one or more, acting in concert. To be hooted and insulted in this way on the public street is evidently a worse wrong than any form of private scandal. It, may, moreover, often lead to public disturbance; and hence, while the truth of the libel is a good plea in all other cases, in this case the maxim applies *veritas convicii non excusat*".[38]

---

[34] 1970 S.L.T. 61 at 62.

[35] *ibid*. Lord Milligan, at 64, agreeing put the matter thus: "'Public hatred and contempt' are strong words and mean more than causing the person referred to be looked on with disapproval or even disgust. They cannot connote, in my opinion, something akin to popular revulsion."

[36] 1979 S.C. 38.

[37] *ibid*. at 51.

[38] Guthrie-Smith, *The Law of Damages*, p. 241.

His authorities are in the Digest.[39] There is a line of relevant cases, the foundation case being *Sheriff v. Wilson*.[40] A series of articles were published vilifying the pursuer. The Lord Justice-Clerk considered that a man could be driven to a state of almost desperation by such conduct.[41] It was thus actionable. The basis was that it would have been punished under the old law and there was authority in Erskine.[42] Glegg goes to considerable trouble to demonstrate the existence of this type of liability. He produces a report of the case *McLaren v. Ritchie* from reports in *The Scotsman* newspaper in 1856. The report forms an appendix to the first edition of the book. He records that an issue was allowed of "holding up to public hatred, contempt and ridicule" without the need for malice. The complaint was against a series of eleven articles likening the pursuer's character to that of a snake. The charge is reproduced by Glegg because that is where the essence of the law has to be transmitted. Lord Justice-Clerk Hope said that it was suggested that the pursuer was a man who traduced his friends for this own malignities. On the other hand it should also be appreciated that the defender pled that simply proving the statements false would not be sufficient; the language was figurative—they argued that the pursuer had to show the language was used for the purpose of holding the pursuer up to public contempt and ridicule. He also records an earlier argument of the Dean of the Faculty (Inglis):[43]

> "The true description of a case of this kind was, not that it was a combination or collection of actionable statements or epithets, but on the contrary that it was a combination or collection of statements or epithets not actionable, or not necessarily actionable, but the provoking repetition of which constituted that which was described in the issue as holding the pursuer up to public hatred, contempt and ridicule . . . it was a charge of having by repeated articles, and by the use of contemptuous epithets, so injured the feelings of the pursuer as to entitle him to damages . . . the complaint was not that they were false, but that they were scurrilous, and abusive, and offensive."

8–8   It should be appreciated, as Norrie points out, that it was not always the case that it was assumed that truth should be a defence to defamation cases.[44]

8–9   One point perhaps not often enough made is that even if it is the case that *veritas* is not a defence to a *convicium* case, it may well be substantially mitigatory of damages. In an old case when *veritas* was not a clear defence to defamation, *Chalmers v. Douglas*[45] the defence of *veritas convicii* was pleaded and held to be irrelevant by Commissioners. A Bill of Advocation was brought to the Court for review. The general opinion of the Court seemed to be that in a civil action the proof of *veritas* may be admitted in order to alleviate the award of damages.

---

[39] (1) D.47.10.15.4; (2) D.47.10.11.12.
[40] (1855) 17 D. 528.
[41] *ibid.* at 531.
[42] Ersk., 4,iv,80.
[43] at p103 fn.2.
[44] This was conclusively decided in *McKellar v. Duke of Sutherland* (1859) 21 D. 222.
[45] (1785) M. 13939.

The status of Convicium

Convicium as a separate head is rejected by many writers.[46] It is described **8–10** as a myth in the Stair Encyclopaedia.[47] Walker's treatment and that of Norrie together say all that can be said. It is the case that verbal injury traditionally was the name of the genus. That has now been lost and there is a history of treatment of non-defamatory cases as verbal injury. There is no disagreement that there is such a category of cases. If on the basis that they do generally involve cases of public ridicule and hatred they were taken into a category called for the want of a better name (making it clear this was a species rather than a genus) *convicium*, then that in itself would not really matter all that much. To that extent Professor Walker's taxonomy has much to commend it. On the other hand, it is the case that the particular name *"convicium"* is seldom used outside its other use as the Latin term for defamation. The substance of the dispute or enquiry must be in relation to actual facts. The critical case is the ridicule of the hunchback. If public hatred and ridicule cases are all taken into narrow verbal injury, then falsity is on the authorities necessary. It must be asked what is the law in relation to the ridiculed hunchback? It is submitted that the law is as stated by Professor Walker and then on the basis mainly of the authority he cites. The Stair Memorial Encyclopaedia is overly optimistic when it suggests that malicious publication about a physical deformity would be dealt with under defamation—the truth of the statement would doom such an action from the start. It is clear from the cases relied upon by Glegg and Professor Walker, some of which are discussed above, that Scottish courts, whether influenced by the Digest or the Church tradition have considered it wrong to hound a person maliciously for no good purpose.[48] It is not the case that the law encourages the telling of the truth as a jural postulate. The requirement for malice means that a free press acting properly has nothing to fear.

Malicious Falsehood

Malicious falsehood is very like verbal injury. This category of case has no **8–11** doubt come in from England[49] but is quite consonant with Scots theory. It is precisely the same as what has come to be known as verbal injury (or a branch of *convicium*) whereby the wrong is the malicious communication to third parties false statements causing loss about the pursuers title, heritage, goods or business.[50] If it may be assumed, as seems reasonable, that

---

[46] McKain, Bonnington and Watt, *Scots Law for Journalists* (6th. ed., 1995), p. 20, goes so far as to say that journalists should proceed on the basis that it is no longer part of Scots Law. See Norrie, *The Law of Defamation and Related Actions in Scots Law*, pp. 35–38.

[47] *Stair Memorial Encyclopaedia*, Vol. 15, para. 558, "The non-existence of convicium".

[48] See, *e.g. Cunningham v. Phillips* (1868) 6 M 926 at 928.

[49] See Clerk & Lindsell, *Law of Torts*, Chap. 22.

[50] *Hamilton v. Arbuthnot* (1750) Mor. 13923; *Philp v. Morton* (1816) Hume 865; *Buchan v. Walch* (1857) 20 D. 222; *Yeo v. Wallace* (1867) 5 S.L.R. 253; *Broomfield v. Greig* (1868) 6 M. 563; *Parlane v. Templeton* (1896) 4 S.L.T. 153; *Harpers Ltd. v. Greenwood and Batley* (1896) 4 S.L.T. 116; *Bruce v. Smith* (1898) 1 F. 327; *Argyllshire Weavers Ltd v. A Macaulay (Tweeds) Ltd*, 1965 S.L.T. 21; *Craig v. Inveresk Paper Merchants Ltd*, 1970 S.L.T. (Notes) 50.

malicious falsehood is encompassed within the term "verbal injury" in section 3 of the Defamation Act 1952, then it is not necessary for the pursuer to aver and prove special damage if the words on which the action is founded are calculated to cause pecuniary damage to the pursuer. Cases are not common because often the effect of the words is to affect the pursuer directly in which case defamation or verbal injury will meet the case.

Some clear examples are *Bruce v. Smith Ltd*,[51] in which it was said the pursuer's building had been run up and might not stand long, with an obvious effect on its market value. The pursuer had found it difficult to let and assumed it could only be sold at a very reduced price. The pursuer's first plea was that the statements were false, calumnious and malicious and that reparation should follow. The action was held by the Lord Ordinary to be relevant on a review of earlier authorities.[52] He was not swayed by the apparently negative *Broomfield v. Grieg*,[53] on the basis that in that case, where an action was not allowed, the statements were made about goods put before the public for sale and thus open to criticism. Thus if that reasoning was correct it would have been permissible for the defenders in *Bruce* to have awaited the first sale or let and then publish the story. When an issue was proposed there was no malice nor innuendo and this was allowed. Against that the defenders reclaimed and were unsuccessful. The Lord Justice-Clerk (MacDonald) and Lord Young concurring agreed with the Lord Ordinary.[54] Lord Trayner was not sure but could see nothing wrong.[55] Lord Moncrieff also agreed but adding that this was also a case of ordinary slander of the pursuer as affecting his reputation in his trade as a developer. This, it is submitted, is sufficient authority to admit of this head of injury. The only difficulty is whether in fact it is not simply a form of verbal injury. In *Philip v. Morton*,[56] it was said the pursuer did not own goods he was selling.

Craig v. Inveresk Paper Merchants Ltd,[57] is the kind of case which the delict meets well and which is encountered in practice. It was alleged that the defenders were saying the pursuers would be going out of business.[58]

DEFAMATION

What is defamatory

8–12 A Scottish answer to the question "what is defamatory?" is that set out by Lord McLaren in the case of *MacFarlane v. Black & Co*.[59]:

"it is not necessary, in order that the statement should be calumnious, that it should impute a crime; a statement may amount to a libel if it

---

[51] (1898) 1 F. 327.
[52] *Hamilton* (1750) Mor. 13923; *Macrae v. Wicks* (1886) 13 R. 732; *McLean v. Adam* (1888) 16 R. 175.
[53] (1868) 6 M. 563.
[54] *Broomfield v. Grieg*, at 332.
[55] *ibid.*
[56] (1816) Hume 865.
[57] 1970 S.L.T. (Notes) 50.
[58] The case failed only on vicarious liability.
[59] (1887) 14 R. 870 at 873.

accuses a person of what is universally considered to be an immoral act, or it imputes conduct which is contrary to the generally accepted standard of honour or propriety amongst gentlemen—amongst the class of persons to which the individual aggreviated belongs".

In *Cuthbert v. Linklater*[60] the *MacFarlane* test was applied with the substitution of women for gentlemen, to render objectionable the suggestion that the pursuer had placed a flag in a gents urinal. The second part of the last sentence quoted from *MacFarlane* is not as happy as that offered in the English case of *Sim v. Strech*[61] which is generally accepted: "tending to lower the plaintiff in the estimation of right thinking members of society." That must be taken with another alternative aspect—shunning. The example of the informer is a good example. On the face of it right-thinking people might think an informer a good person, one who helps with the administration of justice. On the other hand it is an unpleasant way of earning a living involving deception. It has been held that to call a person an informer is defamatory. In *Kennedy v. Allan*[62] the Inner House held an allegation relevant that the defender circulated a letter from the stamp office penalising him for having granted an unstamped receipt to the pursuer and his colleagues on the stock exchange. Members of the stock exchange dealt in unstamped documents. In *Graham v. Roy*[63] the allegation was that the defender had informed on the pursuer to the exciseman. It was expressly argued that this could not be defamatory, an informer being a legal officer, and it could not be defamatory to say that a person gave information to repress an illegal act like smuggling. Lord Fullerton said: "It may be legitimate to give information, but an informer is by no means a popular character."[64] The Lord President focused on what is perhaps a more important point—the pursuer alleged that the defender had suggested the informing was done for reward.[65] In *Wim v. Quillan*[66] it was held that to call a man an informer was derogatory where the sting was that the pursuer, an Irishman, had given evidence to the Crown. These cases raise the tension between right-thinking and shunning. In an Irish case an allegation that a man had denounced the Fenian Conspirators was held not to be defamatory.[67]

It must be emphasised, especially because different views have been **8–13** expressed, that the test is not that of the reasonable *Guardian* reader in the senior common room.[68] The court does not determine whether members of society ought to regard a particular allegation as defamatory but rather whether the person's fame or honour would be lowered by the remark. Nor is there any vouching in authority for Professor Norrie's view that a right thinking man is like a reasonable man and that a reasonable person is not

---

[60] 1935 S.L.T. 94.
[61] (1936) 52 T.L.R. 669.
[62] (1848) 10 D. 1293.
[63] (1851) 13 D. 634.
[64] *ibid.* at 636.
[65] *ibid.*
[66] (1899) 2 F. 322.
[67] *Mawe v. Piggott* (1869) Ir. Rep. 4 Cl. 54. See also *Berry v. Irish Times* [1973] I.R. 368; *Byrned v. Dean* [1937] 1 K.B. 818.
[68] See, *e.g.* Norrie, *Defamation and Related Actions in Scots Law*, p.10.

prejudiced because prejudice is, by definition, irrational.[69] Rather the comparison can be made with passing-off where the test is the idiot on the hoof. Society is as it is and right-thinking people may well be prejudiced or bigoted. It is not so much that different writers or different judges have different views of what is dishonourable or infamous conduct (which is likely), it is that the test the law applies is not so open to divergence of personal views as Professor Norrie argues. His leading example is homosexuality with another being the allegation that a person is HIV positive. Neither allegation on his view of the law is defamatory. It is submitted that both of those appellations would be such as to entitle the pursuer to an issue.[70] Nor, it should be emphasised, does it matter that some conduct such as homosexuality is less criminal than once it was, or that it has been recognised instead of ignored by some aspects of the legal system.[71] On the other hand, over a period of time if a large proportion of literally famous people adopt a certain mode of conduct *de facto* the position can be arrived at where once disapproved conduct is now no longer possibly defamatory.[72] Another of Norrie's examples raises an interesting point. He believes that to say that someone physically chastises their children within the law would now be considered defamatory.[73] There are actually statistics available on this point.[74] Some of Professor Norrie's results might be caused by the use of the wrong test, or an erroneous application of the correct test. Professor Norrie says the right-thinking person is "a contemporary person who moves with the times and who does not maintain attitudes of 20 or even 10 years ago." That conclusion mentioned is unsupported by authority and, it is submitted, wrong. A jury will contain persons of various ages whose right-thinking may or may not be rooted in their own experience. Right-thinking people may well still adhere to the values of 50 years ago or indeed those of approximately 2000 years ago regardless of their age and fashion. Lord Anderson in *Cuthbert v. Linklater*,[75] was in a Norrie-like position of being very doubtful in his own mind whether there was a defamatory imputation but he recognised that the matter was one for the jury.

---

[69] *ibid.* at p.20.

[70] For an English view see Clerk & Lindsell, *The Law of Tort*, paras 21–21 and 21–30.

[71] See, *e.g.* the remarks of Lord McLean in *H.M. Advocate v. McKean*, 1996 S.L.T. 1383: "In these somewhat more enlightened days of sexual equality I can see no reason why the law should not extend uniformly to a man and a woman. In other words, a wife or female companion should have the benefit of the mitigating plea of provocation equally with the husband or male partner. I also see no reason why, in the modern context, the plea should not also be available to homosexual couples who live together and are regarded in the community as partners bound together by ties of love, affection and faithfulness—although I have to say that, until this case, the law has not so far been extended to them." That is still not to say that to call a woman a lesbian is not defamatory, it is to say that where the issue is *dole*, a lesbian need not be jailed for life when a heterosexual woman would not.

[72] Norrie's example of "living in sin" is perhaps correct or at least an example of the revolution in morals necessary to make the once defamatory clearly not defamatory, *Defamation and Related Actions in Scots Law*, p.20. It must be admitted that in one recent Outer House case, without any reference to Professor Norrie's work, it was held that to call a person a homosexual was not defamatory: *Quilty v. Windsor*, 1999 S.L.T. 346.

[73] Norrie, *Defamation and Related Actions on Scots Law*, p.21.

[74] Report on *Family Law* (Scot. Law Com. No. 135, 1992).

[75] 1935 S.L.T. 94; see para. 8–18 for the facts.

Finally, while the test is that of the right-thinking man, in determining **8–14** whether a statement is defamatory, in judging whether something is capable of bearing a defamatory meaning the test to be applied is what would be understood and inferred by the ordinary reader.[76] *The Grand Theatre and Opera House (Glasgow) Ltd v. George Outram and Co. Ltd*[77] is in many respects a typical case. The theatre company sued the newspaper company for a paragraph heading: "Glasgow Theatre Surprise. 'Grand' to Be Wound Up. Petition in Court." It was held that the paragraph did not have a defamatory imputation. Lord McLaren said:

> "Without imputing to the ordinary reader a knowledge that might only be possessed by a lawyer, these paragraphs are to be read by people with the ordinary knowledge educated members of the public might be supposed to have regarding the proceedings. I think any reasonable reader when he came to the words 'Petition in Court' would at once see that this was a question still undecided, because if it had been decreed that the theatre was to be wound up, then the liquidation proceedings would be out of court, and there would be an end to it. I think the words 'Petition in Court' clearly limit the meaning of what came before to this extent, that there was a proceeding in court which might result in the Grand Theatre being wound up. The paragraph which follows just says the same thing in much greater detail and in more explicit language."[78]

Defamatory statements are often collected in categories. At one time life **8–15** may have been sufficiently simple that the categories would have some considerable force but now they should treated as being merely convenient—useful for pedagogical purposes.[79] There now follows the usual catalogue of previous cases which all agree are only really illustrative and do indeed have to be read against the mores of the times. Indeed it can fairly be said that as the test of defamation is very similar in England and the society is for the present virtually identical, guidance on what is thought to be defamatory can as well or better be obtained from a contemporary English case as opposed to a Scots case from the last century.

Criminality

The first of these old heads are imputations of criminality. Pleaders may **8–16** find examples among the noted cases.[80] The simple use of the word criminal is not of itself necessarily defamatory. but the word "criminal" may have been used, as it sometimes is, only in the sense of "highly reprehensible."[81]

---

[76] *Duncan v. Associated Scottish Newspapers*, 1929 S.C. 14, *per* Lord Anderson at 20; *Lewis v. Daily Telegraph Ltd* [1964] A.C. 234, *per* Lord Reid at 258.

[77] 1909 2 S.L.T. 75.

[78] *ibid.* at 77.

[79] This view is also held by Norrie, *Defamation and Related Actions in Scots Law*, p. 18.

[80] *Paterson v. Shaw* (1830) 8 S. 573 (cheating at cards that being then an offence); *Lawrie v. Campbell v. Manzies* (1855) 17 D. 1132 (saying that a criminal warrant issued); *McTernan v. Bennett* (1898) 1 F. 333 (assault); *Dundas v. Livingston & Co* (1900) 3 F. 37 (embezzlement); *McGilvary v. Bernfield* (1901) 8 S.L.T. 300 (breach of the peace); *Young v. Young* (1903) 10 S.L.T. 367 (murder); *Buchanan v. Glasgow Corp.* (1905) 13 S.L.T. 99 (spitting); *Davidson v. Anderson* (1905) 12 S.L.T. 350 (indecent exposure); *Watson v. McEwan* (1905) 7 F. (H.L.) 109 (attempted abortion); *Dowgray v. Gilmour* (1906) 4 S.L.T. 51 (perjury); *Kufner v. Berstecher*, 1907 S.C. 797 (embezzlement); *Wragg v. D.C. Thomson*, 1909 2 S.L.T. 315 (murder); *Smith v.*

Insolvency

8–17 Many ordinary people today live their lives in a state of either practical insolvency, absolute insolvency or both so it is not always the case that such an allegation will be defamatory. Accusations of insolvency about a person in a trade or profession are likely to be considered *ex facie* defamatory.[82] Allegations of bankruptcy are likely to be defamatory.[83] Blacklist cases are a good illustration of the principle. In *Russell v. Stubbs Ltd*,[84] the defenders published the pursuer's name in a "black list" of persons who had decree taken against them. It was held in the House of Lords that this did not support an innuendo of inability to pay debts. In *Mazure v. Stubbs Limited*.[85] the defender published an entry saying that a decree in absence had passed. The pursuer innuendoed the publication as meaning that the pursuer was given to or had begun to refuse or delay to make payment of his debts and that he was not a person to whom credit should be given. The pursuer was successful after proof. On appeal to the House of Lords it was held that this was an acceptable innuendo although of a lesser libel than had been tried and failed in *Russell*. It was said:

> "I am, therefore, of opinion that the decision in Russell v. Stubbs has not the effect contended for by the appellants, and indeed a careful examination of the judgments shews that they are rather against than in favour of the appellants in the present case. It is one thing to impute insolvency; it is another thing altogether to say, as is said here, that the pursuer was given to or had begun to refuse or to delay to make payment of his debts, and the statement in the note as to insolvency not being imputed by the publication of the entry does not rebut the possibility that the entry might be understood as importing a slighter degree of embarrassment, an imputation which might nevertheless prejudicially affect the trader. For these reasons, I am of opinion that this appeal should be dismissed with costs."[86]

Walker, 1912 S.C. 224 (fraud); *Mills v. Kelvin & James White Ltd*, 1913 1 S.L.T. 153 (theft); *Smith v. Paton*, 1913 S.C. 1203 (theft); *Adams v. Templeton & Co.*, 1913 2 S.L.T. 241 (theft); *McLeod v. AR Ure & Young*, 1915 1 S.L.T. 151 (fraud); *AB v. XY*, 1917 S.C. 15 (sodomy); *West v. MacKenzie*, 1917 S.C. 513 (fraud); *Mandelston v. North British Railway Co.*, 1917 S.C. 442 (fraud); *Mitchell v. Smith*, 1919 2 S.L.T. 115 (fraud); *Jardine v. North British Railway Co.*, 1923 S.L.T. 55 (fraud); *Rae v. SSPCC*, 1924 S.C. 102; *Harkness v. Daily Record*, 1924 S.L.T. 759 (murder); *Dunnet v. Nelson*, 1926 S.C. 764 (theft); *Hines v. Davidson*, 1935 S.C. 30 (attempt to pervert the course of justice); *MacDonald v. Martin*, 1935 S.C. 621(embezzlement); *Harper v. Provincial Newspapers*, 1937 S.L.T. 462 (theft); *Woods v. Moir* (1938) 54 Sh. Ct Rep. 272 (fraud); *Rodgers v. Orr*, 1939 S.C. 121 (theft); *Borland v. Denholm* (1942) 58 Sh. Ct Rep. 182 (theft); *Neville v. C. & A. Modes*, 1945 S.L.T. 189 (theft); *Andrew v. Penney*, 1964 S.L.T. (Notes) 24 (theft); *Turnbull v. Frame*, 1966 S.L.T. 24 (fraud); *Waddell v. BBC*, 1973 S.L.T. 246 (murder); *Smith v. Graham*, 1981 S.L.T. (Notes) 19 (assault); *McCluskie v. Summers*, 1988 S.L.T. 55 (perjury); *Sutherland v. B.T.*, 1989 S.L.T. 531 (theft); *Gecas v. STV*, 1992 G.W.D. 30–1786 (war crimes).

[81] *Per* Lord Dundas in *Couper v. Lord Balfour of Burleigh*, 1913 1 S.L.T. 122.

[82] *McVean & Co. v. Blair* (1801) Hume 609; *AB v. CD* (1904) 7 F. 22.

[83] *Louthers v. Rae*, Hume 592; *McVean & Co v. Blair* (1801) Hume 609; *Couseland v. Cuthil* (1829) 5 Mur. 148; *Outram v. Reid* (1852) 14 D. 577. See also *McPherson v. McPherson*, Hume 644 (formerly bankrupt); *Anderson v. Hunter* (1891) 18 R. 467 (soon to be bankrupt).

[84] 1913 S.C.(H.L.) 14.

[85] 1919 2 S.L.T. 160.

[86] *ibid.* at 162–163.

Immorality, Dishonesty and lying

Cuthbert v. Linklater[87] is probably the best example on this topic now **8–18** considered to be difficult.[88] The pursuer was known as Wendy Wood and was a political activist. The defender's novel "Magnus Meriman" mentioned a political activist called Beaty Bracken and the character had removed a Union Jack from Edinburgh Castle and placed it in a public urinal. The pursuer had in fact removed a flag from Stirling Castle but had folded it up. The Lord Justice-Clerk (Aitchison) held that to be defamatory without an innuendo as being an imputation of indelicacy of a gross kind against a woman.[89] The less well-defined a society's moral code, the more politically plural it is and the more multi-cultural it is, the more difficult it will be win a case on this head and thus the less likely it will be that such cases will be brought as for example where a person is called an "adulterous scoundrel"[90]. Dishonesty is another example.[91] It is not always criminal and so cannot be treated as such, yet to be dishonest is under some codes an offence. It can arise as an aspect of professional competence or conduct for most professions consider honesty to be important. Yet it is not the case that "liar" is considered always to be defamatory.[92] A more obvious and recent example is *May v. Teague Homes*,[93] an action for defamation by a former director of the company against the company and others. It is an unusual mode of alleged defamation consisting of an entry in the annual company accounts "defalcation by director". In *McCann v. Scottish Media Newspapers Ltd*[94] an attempt to have a defamation case struck out at debate failed. The allegations related to statements in the press that the chairman of a football club had made misleading statements in the company accounts in order to boost the value of his own shares.

Fitness for Profession or Occupation

Obviously aspersions in this area are most likely to have financial effects. **8–19** Examples include accusing a solicitor of conducting cases for his own benefit rather than that of his clients,[95] that a merchant would cheat on the

---

[87] 1935 S.L.T. 94.

[88] See also *Richardson v. Walker* (1804) Hume 623; *A.B. v. Blackwood & Sons* (1902) 5 F. 25; Ersk. 4,iv,80; *Finbury v. Moss Empires*, 1908 S.C. 929.

[89] Some, hopefully illuminating, background material relating to this case including the "admonition" published at the start of the novel can be found in Stewart, *Casebook on Delict*, (2nd ed., W. Green, 1997), pp. 393–394.

[90] *Cleland v. Mack* (1829) 5 Mur. 70.

[91] *Ross v. Ronald* (1834) 12 S. 936.

[92] *Fleming v. Craig*, 1939 S.L.T. (Sh Ct) 24; *Carroll v. BBC*, 1997 S.L.T. (Sh. Ct) 23.

[93] 1996 Rep. L.R. 123.

[94] 1999 S.C.L.R. 636.

[95] *McRostie v. Ironside* (1849)12 D. 74. See also *Bayne v. Macgregor* (1862) 24 D. 1126; *Manson v. Macara* (1839) 2 D. 208; *Grant v. Ramsay*, Hume 611. It was held not ex facie defamatory of a solicitor that he be called a liar: *Carroll v. BBC*, 1997 S.L.T. (Sh. Ct) 23.

fish market,[96] that a doctor had neglected his patients,[97] that a chemist prescribed cheaper medicines,[98] or that a matron was unfit for her post,[99] that a gardener has allowed too many weeds and inadequately tilled land under his care.[1] There are many other cases.[2] The context is very important. In *Vallance v. Ford*[3] the pursuer worked for Durrant, a ladies' tailor in Edinburgh in pre-*prêt-a-porter* days. The defender ordered skirts and the pursuer was cutting and fitting them. The pursuer alleged that the defender had complained to her employer Durrant that the pursuer "was grossly unfit for her duties, and that her services should be dispensed with." At the same time, for the purpose of injuring the pursuer, she stated to the said manager, "Redfern has got a splendid skirt-fitter; why don't you try and get her to come here?" On another occasion it was alleged the defender said "She cannot cut a skirt; she does not even know how to begin to fit a skirt. She does not know her business at all," or used words of like import and effect. The pursuer innuendoed these words to mean that the pursuer was unfit to hold the post of a skirt cutter and fitter. The Lord Ordinary (Low) dismissed the action as irrelevant:

> "It would have been a different matter if the defender had gone to a third party and volunteered the statement that the pursuer was not fit for the position of skirt cutter and fitter. But the remarks were made with reference to the particular skirt when an attempt was being made to fit it, and they were addressed to the tradesman who had undertaken to supply the skirt, in presence of his servant whose duty it was to cut and fit it. In these circumstances I do not think that the words alleged can be read as amounting to more than an expression of opinion on the defender's part that the skirt was so badly cut as to show that the pursuer could not cut a skirt, and was therefore unfit for the post of skirt cutter to a ladies' tailor. Therefore, although I think that the alleged words (assuming them to have been used) were unnecessary, and in bad taste, and suggest that the person who used them had lost her temper, I am unable to hold that in the circumstances they are actionable."[4]

Disease

8–20 In some cases the fact that a person suffers from a disease is simply a misfortune. But some diseases at some times in some places can cause the person to be shunned. Only saints want to have dinner with lepers. There

---

[96] *Landles v. Gray* (1816) 1 Mur. 70.

[97] *Simmers v. Morton* (1900) 8 S.L.T. 285. See also *Marshall v. Renwicks* (1834) 13 S. 1127; *Bruce v. Ross & Co.* (1901) 4 F. 171; *Balfour v. Wallace* (1853) 15 D. 913.

[98] *Gall v. Slessor*, 1907 S.C. 708.

[99] *Couper v. Lord Balfour of Burleigh*, 1913 1 S.L.T. 122.

[1] *Cadzow v. The Distress Committee of the City of Edinburgh.*, 1914 1 S.L.T. 493. See also other farming cases: *Dun v. Bain* (1877) 4 R. 317; *McKeand v. Maxwell* (1895) 3 S.L.T. 295 at 321.

[2] *Richardson v. Wilson* (1879) 7 R. 237 (sheriff officer); *Keay v. Wilson*, (1843) 5 D. 407, *McIver v. McNeil* (1873) 11 M. 777; *Carmichael v. Cowan* (1862) 1 M. 204 (hotels and inn keeper); *McKerchar v. Cameron* (1892) 19 R. 383; *Leitch v. Lyll* (1903) 11 S.L.T. 394; *Auld v. Shair*, (1875) 2 R. 191 940; *McBride v. Williams* (1869) 7 M. 427; *Bryson v. Inglis* (1844) 6 D. 363; *Jardine v. Creech* (1776) Mor. 3438 (teachers).

[3] (1902) 10 S.L.T. 555.

[4] *ibid.* at 556.

was no dispute in *Farrell v. Boyd*,[5] that to say of a person to his employer that he suffered from gonorrhoeal rheumatism was defamatory.[6]

Miscellaneous cases

It is important to have such a category even if only for presenting cases for illustration or for pedagogic reasons so that new categories of defamation can be collected and odd cases are not forced into other categories. Cases that fail are usefully collected too—an example is *Thomson v. News Group Newspapers Ltd.*[7] The alleged false statement was that a footballer had concealed an injury. On the face of it that might just suggest he was robust but was said to imply that was unfit, a deceiver of his employers and his teammates and was endangering his future. It was held that none of the various complaints constituted defamation, in particular the deception was read by the judge as being only as against the public, his employers and teammates. In *Peat v. Newsgroup Newspapers Ltd*[8] a number of allegations of defamation "of doubtful relevancy" were permitted to go to proof before answer. The pursuer's allegations were that statements in the sports pages suggested that the pursuer, an accountant and chairman of a football club treated players like dirt, was ignorant in his treatment of them, made a string of broken promises, was parsimonious in paying star players small wages and refused to see a player inferring poor man-management skills. "Collusion" implied trickery or deceit and in context could be defamatory.[9] *Jameson v. Bonthrone*[10] seems astonishing to modern eyes until it is realised the pursuer was a lawyer in a huff. The pursuer was a procurator fiscal, holder, he said, of an "honourable and exalted" office who had been called a damned puppy by the defender. Lord Deas did not consider this actionable: **8–21**

> "A 'pup' or 'puppy' is not always an offensive animal, and, on the contrary, it is sometimes an object of affection. The word becomes offensive only in consequence of certain conventional but varying meanings attached to it when applied to a man. Sometimes it means 'a fop'; sometimes an attention to dress short of a fop; very often it simply means the person is presumptuous. In short it is not a word which is necessarily slanderous. Everything depends upon the circumstances."[11]

Innuendo

An apparently innocent statement can have a defamatory meaning. That defamatory meaning is the innuendo (following an English term of pleading). It must be an alternative meaning which the words can reason- **8–22**

---

[5] 1907 15 S.L.T. 327.
[6] See also *Friend v. Skelton* (1855) 17 D. 548 (habitual drunkenness). *Mackintoch v. Weir* (1875) 2 R. 877, sometimes cited, is of no real value on the allegation of insanity.
[7] 1992 G.W.D. 14–825.
[8] Unreported, March 8, 1996.
[9] *Waverley Housing Management Ltd v. BBC*, 1993 G.W.D. 17–1117.
[10] (1873) 11 M. 703.
[11] *ibid.* at 704. "Blackguard" has been held to be actionable but is no longer so often used as a grave insult: *Brownlie v. Thomson* (1859) 21 D. 480.

ably bear. As Lord Shaw put it: "the innuendo must represent what is reasonable, natural or necessary inference from the words used, regard being had to the occasion and circumstances of their publication."[12] Lord Kinnear said:

> "The law is perfectly well settled. Before a question of libel or slander is submitted to a jury the Court must be satisfied that the words complained of are capable of the defamatory meaning ascribed to them. That is a matter of law for the Court. If they are so, and also of a harmless meaning, it is a question of fact for a jury which meaning they did convey in the particular case."

The defender cannot deny a reasonable innuendo by saying that he did not mean it. As Lord Glenlee said "That would be like pulling a man by the nose, and telling him you did not mean to insult him."[13] In the House of Lords in *Langlands v. Leng*,[14] the facts arose out of a meeting of a school board. Comment was made that the estimates for a building, had turned out to amount to much more than the architect had originally estimated. There was comment on the system under which the architect had a regular engagement with the board, by which he was to be the architect and paid the usual *ad valorem* commission on all alterations or enlargements of existing buildings, whereas in the case of new buildings there was to be competition for the position of architect. The chairman gave notice after some discussion that he intended to bring up the consideration of the situation at a subsequent meeting, and to propose the termination, or ask the meeting to consider the termination of the agreement with the architect. The architect had a private practice and so could compete with other architects for the work of new buildings, but he benefited from the arrangement by having a monopoly of any work which could be brought under the heading of enlargements. Two cases had caused worry because the enlargement costs were so high. The newspaper published a report of the meeting and a leading article. It incorporated the following passage:

> "For a considerable time past the 'enlargements' have been much bigger jobs than the erection of new structures, *e.g.* the enlargement of Morgan Academy costing about £20,000, and the projected enlargement of the Harris Academy, which would cost about £32,000. The rule, as interpreted, is an absurdity . . . and it puts a premium upon a certain kind of advice."

This was innuendoed to the effect that he used his position corruptly for his personal benefit. Viscount Haldane explained the exercise:

> "The question which we have to deal with we have to decide as judges of law. It is whether it is possible, if the language used is read in its ordinary sense, to say that it is such as can reasonably and naturally

---

[12] *Russel v. Stubbs*, 1913 1 S.L.T. 428 at 432.
[13] *Black v. Brown* (1826) 5 S. 508 at 514.
[14] 1916 S.C. (H.L.) 102.

support the innuendo. It is not enough for the pursuer to say: 'The language is ambiguous; it is capable of one of two meanings—either is equally probable, and it is for the jury to choose which it will put on it.' The pursuer must make out his case, and the pursuer must therefore, if he wishes to succeed, when he puts forward his innuendo, put it forward either on the footing that the language taken by itself supports the innuendo, or that there is extrinsic evidence, extrinsic to the libel itself, which shews that that was the sense in which the words were intended to be construed . . . In Scotland there has always been the very useful procedure under which at an early stage of the action the issues are settled by the Court, and on the question whether an issue should be submitted to the jury has arisen the power of the Court to decide at that early stage upon the question of libel or no libel, without prejudicing the pursuer . . . That being so, what we have to do is as judges of law to answer the question whether the words in controversy in this appeal can be said to be libellous. It is for us to say whether they support the innuendo. It is not to the point that some judges have taken a view as if on a question of fact in the Court below. It is in reality a question of law which it is our duty sitting here to decide; and we can only take into account the fact that other judges have thought that the words might be so construed to the extent of treating their opinion with respect. But the question is one of law pure and simple."[15]

In *Fairbairn v. SNP*[16] Lord Ross adopted an observation of Madden J. in an English case saying that the question is really one of common sense and depended on the answer to the inquiry: "What meaning would be attributed to the document by the persons to whom it is addressed?"[17] He went on to accept that a statement that an M.P. failed to collect his mail could mean that he was not attending to his constituents' business.[18] In *Kennedy v. Baillie*[19] the defender was the law agent of the proprietor of an estate. He wrote to the pursuer that he, the pursuer had done one thing (approached his landlord direct for a new lease) contrary to an assurance that he had not done it. This was alleged to be an innuendo of wilful falsehood. It was held that it was not but it must be said that this was partly because the addressee of the statement was well aware of the context.[20] In *Boal v. Scottish Catholic Ptg. Co.*,[21] the pursuer, a journalist and lecturer brought an action against the defenders for alleged defamation in their newspaper. A report of a charitable home being founded in which the pursuer was involved asked "what guarantee is there that the money subscribed does not go to the private profit of . . . the scribbling Boal." It was held that this supported an innuendo of dishonesty. In *Godfrey v. W &*

---

[15] *ibid.* at 106. The Scots Law Lords Kinnear and Shaw of Dunfermline accepted that and both agreed that in the circumstances the innuendo was not made out.
[16] 1980 S.L.T. 149.
[17] *ibid.* at 152.
[18] *ibid.*
[19] (1855) 18 D. 138.
[20] The case did have to go before both divisions as on the first hearing the court was divided 2–2.
[21] 1908 S.C. 667.

D.C. Thomson[22] it was argued that leaving without an address was capable of innuendo. Worse, it was suggested that the pursuer had pretended to be a bona fide traveller. An innuendo that the pursuer had combined with a socialist to get a bigger audience and was thus a man who had his principles was rejected; the Lord President wisely considered they were just appreciating that their own audience of extremists would be slight. They wanted to have a "logomachy" or "flyting" or, in English, a debate.

It is possible to plead a number of innuendos from the one statement as in *Shanks v. BBC*[23] where nine were pled. However, objection is likely to be taken if the innuendos are inconsistent.[24] In *Caldwell v. Monro*[25] it seemed to be accepted that it was possible to use an innuendo to show that a statement not defamatory actually is so when the surrounding circumstances make it clear that the statement actually has a target instead of being a general charge. In this case the allegation that a person had forged a letter. In *Campbell v. Ritchie & Co*[26] the pursuers brought an action for damages for slander against the publishers of the *Edinburgh Evening Dispatch* which had published an article reporting that they had been convicted under new regulations against catching birds by bird-liming. The report was admitted to be accurate in relating to the convictions. It also described the methods of bird-liming accurately but it referred to the pursuers as thieves. The Lord Ordinary (Mackenzie) approved an issue that statements bore the innuendo that the pursuers were guilty of theft. The defenders reclaimed successfully and the action was dismissed. The catching of wild birds was not theft. The language used was intemperate, but could not bear the innuendo sought to be put upon it.[27]

In *Ellis v. National Free Labour Association*[28] the defenders published a leaflet stating that the pursuer had been dismissed for "withholding monies belonging to [the defenders] contrary to its bye laws." The Inner House reversed allowance of issues on an innuendo of dishonesty. On the law of dishonest appropriation then applying the bye-law merely required money to be paid to chief office on the day it was received. In *Lloyd v. Hickley*[29] the statement at a shooting estate meeting that the pursuer had over-shot was sufficient to support an innuendo that the pursuer was unscrupulous and dishonest but not that he did not keep to his contracts, because his lease limited him to shooting so many stags a season. In *Archer v. Ritchie & Co*[30] the pursuer was Grand Worthy Chief Templar of the Independent Order of Good Templars in Scotland. The defenders published an account of the re-election of the pursuer. They said he indicated he would not stand and would support another candidate but then he had not done so. The innuendo was that the pursuer was guilty of deceitful and dishonourable conduct and habitually indulged in such conduct. There was a reference to

---

[22] (1890) 17 R. 1108.
[23] 1993 S.L.T. 326.
[24] *Carrol v. BBC*, 1997 S.L.T. (Sh. Ct) 23.
[25] (1872) 10 M. 717.
[26] 1907 S.C. 1097.
[27] *ibid., per* Lord Ardwall at 1102. The case fell within the principle in *Wardlaw v. Drysdale* (1898) 25 R. 879.
[28] (1905) 7 F. 629.
[29] 1967 S.L.T. 225.
[30] (1891) 18 R. 719.

"crooked ways". It was held that the publication did not bear the innuendo proposed and at most the article reported discourteous conduct. In *N.G. Napier Ltd v. Port Glasgow Courier*[31] a newspaper published an article stating that a hire-purchase firm's activities were being investigated by the Board of Trade; that they were selling up the effects of two families under decrees; that one of the families had been in arrears with payments because of ill-health; that the firm had refused to accept reduced instalments or to take back the articles hired; that they had arrested wages over the festive season; and that they adopted "get paid quickly" methods. The pursuers suggested that this meant that they were untrustworthy, dishonest, in the conduct of their business and acted oppressively. It was held that the words were not defamatory nor capable of supporting the innuendo.

Publication, Communication and Intention

It is sufficient that the statement has been communicated to the pursuer **8–23** alone. *Ramsay v. MacLay*[32] marks the end of any question about the point as it was not vigorously opposed.[33] The Lord Justice-Clerk (MacDonald) said "it is settled law that in this country the aggrieved party is entitled to sue for damages in respect of the injury done to his feelings."[34] *Gall v. Slessar*[35] was a straightforward case of a letter being written by one man to another which was held actionable. The damages, £30 in those times, were intended not to be a large sum but not a nominal sum either.[36] The modes of communication are various and in Scotland it is often said that there is no difference between libel and slander. This means that the mode of communication has not been a source of difficulty. Imputations against the chastity of a married woman were held actionable even although not made in words, nor in writing but by means of certain gestures and the exhibition of pictures or effigies.[37] In *McKay v. McCankie*[38] the rule that there was no need for communication of a written statement was applied to an oral statement. On the other hand it might still be appropriate to take a freer view of speech, while accepting no technical legal distinction. Hume makes the point:

"many things are actionable when reduced to this from which would not be so if spoken only, because, when committed to writing, and, still more if printed, the scandal is more widely disseminated, and lasts longer, and makes a deeper and more serious impression. It has therefore been held, that compositions even of a looser kind than any of those yet

---

[31] 1959 S.L.T. (Sh. Ct) 54.
[32] (1890) 18 R. 130.
[33] *ibid.* at 132. The defenders argued: "There was no dispute that a letter addressed to a person might found an action of damages at his instance, but to found an action for damages in respect of slander there must be an averment that the charges were false."
[34] *ibid.* at 133. See also *McKay v. McCankie* (1883) 10 R. 537.
[35] 1907 S.C. 708.
[36] *ibid., per* Lord Low at 715.
[37] *White v. Smith*, March 3, 1798, cited Hume III, 137 (Hume Session Papers, Vol. lxvii, No. 41).
[38] (1883) 10 R. 537.

mentioned—papers which did not contain any specific or precise charge, reducible under any of the above mentioned heads, but which tended in a general way, to vilify or depreciate, and hold out to ridicule or contempt, are actionable."[39]

It is unlikely that communication of a message to functionaries like secretaries or telephonists would be sufficient to constitute communication but the case often cited in this connection did not rule out a possible case where it is averred and proved that the secretary understood the communication and the defender was defamed.[40] In England this does constitute publication but many other interesting issues arise.[41] In one case the allegation was that the slander was by non-verbal communication. In *Drysdale v. Earl of Rosebery*[42] the pursuer had been the factor of the defender's estates. He raised an action for damages for slander based on the actions of the defender's law agent, on the defender's instructions, whereby he attended at the pursuer's office and caused a substantial number of papers to be removed after a search. The Lord Ordinary (Salvesen) held the action irrelevant. On appeal Lord President (Dunedin) agreed that the innuendo sought to be put on the actings could not reasonably be put on them. He agreed that there may be an actionable wrong of the nature of slander by actions alone. But in this case the pursuer wished to put the innuendo that the defender had represented that he had been unfaithful in the discharge of his duty. A person was entitled to investigate his agent's accounts without thereby charging him with dishonesty.

8-24   From the point of view of a person called a "thieving liar" it is irrelevant whether or not the maker intended to make the statement because the damage is done. From the point of view of the maker there is a considerable difference: there are very strict controls over liability for negligently caused harm and especially so over negligently caused economic loss. The difficult case is defamation where malice is presumed. The law in Scotland is that defamation can be committed accidentally; that is without meaning to injure the pursuer. There is old authority in support of that.[43] The recent authority is equally clear and was directly influenced by the leading English case. In *Wragg v. D.C.Thomson & Co. Ltd*[44] the Lord President said that in view of the then recent decision of the House of

---

[39] Hume III, 140.

[40] *Evans & Sons v. Stein & Co.* (1904) 7 F. 65. See the statutory defence discussed at the end of this section.

[41] *Bryanston Finances v. de Vries* [1975] Q.B. 703.

[42] (1902) 2 S.L.T. 2.

[43] *Findlay v. Ruddiman* (1763) Mor 3436.

[44] 1909 2 S.L.T. 315 and 409. See also *McLean v. Bernstein and Others* (1900) 8 S.L.T. 42 concerning an action of slander against the first defender who caused an advertisement to be published in the *Daily Record*. The proprietors were also called as additional defenders and they argued at debate that the action was irrelevant as laid against them. They argued that they could only be liable if the advertisement was plainly libellous or such as to put a publisher on his guard. The pursuer was not mentioned by name in it. It was held that the action was relevant against them although the Lord Ordinary (Stormonth Darling) made it clear that when the matter went to the jury the case would be considered differently in relation to each defender.

Lords in the English case of *Jones v. Hulton & Co.*,[45] the Court was not prepared to withhold an issue. Dealing first with the Scots case, *Wragg*, the facts were that the defender newspaper proprietors published a report "George Reeves shoots wife twice then ends his own life". That the report did not refer to the pursuer is vouched for the fact that he raised the action for slander against the paper. Mr. Wragg was a music hall artiste and comedian, known professionally as George Reeves. The article was "lifted" from an American paper and the defence was that it was clear it did not apply and that there was no intention to refer to the pursuer. The Lord Ordinary in allowing the issue to proceed without need for proof of intention said:

> "Taking it then, on that hypothesis I have come to the conclusion, although with hesitation, that the defenders' conduct might reasonably be held to involve slander of the pursuer, and that might reasonably be held that such slander was due in law to the defender's fault . . . Whether the notice was of and concerning the pursuer would be for the jury to say. On the question of whether it is necessary to aver and prove that the defenders actually intended to refer the pursuer, or whether it is not enough that they acted so as to lead people reasonably to believe that they referred to the pursuer, I concur with the majority of the Court of King's Bench in *Jones v. Hulton & Co.* [1909] 2 K. B. 471) presently under appeal to the House of Lords. No doubt, if it was clear that no one could reasonably conclude that the paragraph referred to the pursuer, then the case ought not to be allowed to proceed. The defenders argued that there was sufficient in the article, even cursorily read to show that the occurrence could not have happened in Great Britain. There is force in the defenders' criticisms, but I am bound to say that when I read the article for the first time these points escaped me, although I noticed them when I read the article carefully a second time with a view of seeing whether such points were not in the article. The defenders also maintained that, even if the article did not obviously exclude the pursuer, there was nothing to identify him with the George Reeves mentioned in the article except the name . . . The London Directory for 1909 only contains two instances and there are none in either the Edinburgh or Glasgow Directories."[46]

Hulton as indicated was confirmed in the House of Lords and was followed in the Inner House. *Hulton* was a case where the defendants published a humorous article about one Artemus Jones saying he was accompanied by a woman who was not his wife. The plaintiff was a barrister named Artemus Jones. The rule in the case is mitigated by the proviso that the plaintiff must show any facts necessary to allow a reasonable person to believe the article referred to the plaintiff. The principle has gone further in England, for example in *Newstead v. London Express Newspapers*,[47] the Court of Appeal extended the rule to the case where a statement was true as stated

---

[45] [1909] 2 K.B. 444, aff. (H.L.) December 6,1909.
[46] *Wragg v. D.C. Thomson & Co.*, at 316–317.
[47] [1940] 1 K.B. 377.

of an actual person but defamatory of another unintentionally. The story ran, "Harold Newstead, a 30–year-old Camberwell man, who was jailed for nine months liked having two wives at once." This was true concerning a Camberwell barman but not of the plaintiff who was a hairdresser in Camberwell of almost the same age. A finding of liability was upheld on appeal. The plaintiff won one farthing in damages but of course expenses generally follow success. It is not the case however, that *Wragg* represents an English imposition. There are at least two Scottish cases where the same approach was taken.[48]

8–25   The above discussed questions of responsibility for publication and intention are affected by the 1996 Defamation Act. In defamation proceedings a person has a defence if he shows that: (a) he was not the author, editor or publisher of the statement complained of; (b) he took reasonable care in relation to its publication; and (c) he did not know, and had no reason to believe, that what he did caused or contributed to the publication of a defamatory statement.[49] The "author" is the originator of the statement, but does not include a person who did not intend that his statement be published at all; "editor" means a person having editorial or equivalent responsibility for the content of the statement or the decision to publish it; and "publisher" means a commercial publisher whose business is issuing material to the public, or a section of the public, who issues material containing the statement in the course of that business.[50] A person is not to be considered the author, editor or publisher of a statement if he is only involved:

(a) in printing, producing, distributing or selling printed material containing the statement;

(b) in processing, making copies of, distributing, exhibiting or selling a film or sound recording[51] containing the statement;

(c) in processing, making copies of, distributing or selling any electronic medium in or on which the statement is recorded, or in operating or providing any equipment, system or service by means of which the statement is retrieved, copied, distributed or made available in electronic form;

(d) as the broadcaster of a live programme containing the statement in circumstances in which he has no effective control over the maker of the statement; and

(e) as the operator of or provider of access to a communications system by means of which the statement is transmitted, or made available, by a person over whom he has no effective control.

---

[48] In *Reid v. Outram* (1852) 14 D. 577 a publication referred to "John Reid, wine and spirit merchant, Glasgow," but missed out the address which had been published in the *Gazette*. The defenders were held liable to another in the same business with a similar name but in a different street. In *Paterson v. Shaw* (1830) 5 Mur. 281 it was held incompetent to prove that an incident took place in another house in the same town to a man of the same name. On the other hand in 1872 and under reference to *Reid*, counsel argued to rebut a plea of "innocence of intention": *Caldwell v. Monro* (1872) 10 M. 717 at 721.

[49] s. 1(1).

[50] s. 1(2).

[51] As defined in Part I of the Copyright, Designs and Patents Act 1988.

In a case not within paragraphs (a) to (e) the court can have regard to **8–26** those provisions by way of analogy in deciding whether a person is to be considered the author, editor or publisher of a statement.[52] Employees or agents of an author, editor or publisher are in the same position as their employer or principal to the extent that they are responsible for the content of the statement or the decision to publish it.[53] In determining for the purposes of this section whether a person took reasonable care, or had reason to believe that what he did caused or contributed to the publication of a defamatory statement, regard shall be had to—(a) the extent of his responsibility for the content of the statement or the decision to publish it; (b) the nature or circumstances of the publication; and (c) the previous conduct or character of the author, editor or publisher.[54]

In *Godfrey v. Demon Internet*[55] it was held that the defenders, an internet **8–27** service provider, were not commercial publishers of an item on a news server and so were not publishers for the purposes of defamation. However, they were liable because they failed to show that they met the requirements of subs. (1)(b) and (1)(c) of the Act. Essentially it seems that they did not act quickly enough when made aware of the possibly defamatory quality of the news posting.

A related point is whether defamation exhausts the legal system's **8–28** response to negligently used words damaging the reputation. It has been decided in England that that is not the case in *Spring v. Guardian Assurance plc*.[56] The House of Lords decided that the *Hedley Byrne* principle applied to an employer's reference notwithstanding that if the case had been brought in defamation a defence of qualified privilege would have been met. It was thought that most employers give careful references anyway and if they do not and deliver, as in this case, "the kiss of death" they should compensate the victim. It has been followed in Scotland.[57]

Of and concerning

The cases noted above make it clear that it is essential that the defamatory **8–29** statement is of and concerning the pursuer. This is in opposition to humanity in general and a group of individuals in particular. In *Browne v. D.C. Thomson & Co Ltd*[58] an action for slander by the Roman Catholic Bishop of Cloyne, Ireland and other individuals against publishers of the *Dundee Courier* in relation to an article which stated that "the Roman Catholic religious authorities" in Queenstown, County Cork, had instructed that all Protestant shop assistants were to be dismissed and further that any Roman Catholic shopkeeper who refused to comply had been ruined. *Hulton v. Jones*[59] was followed, the Lord President (Dunedin) deciding that

---

[52] s. 1(3).

[53] s. 1(4).

[54] s. 1(5). This section does not apply to any cause of action which arose before the section came into force: s. 1(6).

[55] [1999] 4 All E.R. 342.

[56] [1994] T.L.R. 381. See K. Norrie, "Defamation, Negligence and Employers References" 1994 J.L.S. 418.

[57] *Donlon v. Colonial Mutual Group*, 1997 S.C.L.R. 1088. See Chap. 10.

[58] 1912 1 S.L.T. 123.

[59] [1910] A.C.20; see above.

it was for the jury to decide whether the pursuers were the persons understood to be referred to as "the Roman Catholic religious authorities". That is that it had to be shown that these pursuers were themselves damnified by these words not merely as members of a group itself damnified. A fine distinction. In *Caldwell v. Monro*[60] the defender had not identified any particular person with the alleged defamatory remark; he said a letter was a forgery. It took some tortuous averments to make that allegation appear by a process of deduction to be that to the audience in question only the pursuer could be the target. He tried to do this by way of innuendo which seems to have been accepted as a legitimate way to proceed albeit this is not the usual role of innuendo which shows the meaning of a statement rather than the target. It is a matter for the jury to decide.

Repetition

8–30 The repetition of the same libel after an action is raised can be admitted to prove the *animus* of the original libel.[61] In more relaxed times the repetition of the mere gossip was held not actionable: a woman mentioned in her own house a current report in the town that the minister had got intoxicated, fought with a companion and thrown bottles and she stated that she believed it to be true. This was held insufficient through a lack of *animus injurandi*.[62] Again there was no liability where a person repeated a current Glasgow rumour concerning the solvency of a druggist, saying that he had failed in business. There was no *animus malus* and the defender had named the author of the report.[63] Repetition is relevant to suggest malice when that is required but it is equally consonant with good faith that an allegation be repeated.[64]

Anonymous Publication

8–31 Imputing authorship of anonymous letters was held to be defamatory as suggesting dishonourable conduct.[65] Damages were awarded where it could be shown a person wrote and published anonymous letters.[66] In *Mactaggart v. MacKillop*[67] the Second Division confirmed an order for the production of a typewriter to help identify an anonymous defamer.

Defences[67a]

Disclaimer

8–32 In meaning to do no harm a writer might well try to disclaim any intention of defaming another. This is unlikely to meet with any success. Lord Shaw commented on the strategy in the black-list case *Mazure v. Stubbs*,[68]

---

[60] (1872) 10 M. 717.
[61] *Edwards v. MacIntosh*, 1823 3 Mur. 379.
[62] *Rose v. Robertson* (1803) Hume 614.
[63] *Gardner v. Marshall* (1803) Hume 620.
[64] *Couper v. Burleigh*, 1913 1 S.L.T. 122.
[65] *Menzies v. Goodlef* (1835) 3 S. 1136; *Home v. Sandie* (1832) 10 S. 508.
[66] *Melville v. Crichton*, 1820 2 Mur. 277.
[67] 1939 S.L.T. 203.
[67a] For unintentional defamation see paras 8–25 to 8–28 above.
[68] 1935 S.L.T. 94.

"A conditioned or specialised slander of that kind is not known to the law; the results of a calumnious falsehood arise from the impression which it—all of it, including reservations, cautions and all the rest—makes upon the minds of the readers, an impression which may be quite apart from any artificial restriction which the author of the falsehood sought to impose. It is for those results that the author or promulgator of the libel is responsible. The law itself is not inconsiderate of all the legitimate excuses for error in such publications, but it cannot accept the will of the author of a wrong as the measure of the consequence of that wrong."[69]

That was a case of a black-list. Another common example is in artistic works where it is often said that "Any reference to any person living or dead is purely coincidental". On the basis of *Cuthbert v. Linklater*,[70] discussed above[71], that the longer the disclaimer the more it looks like a smoking gun.

Apology

Palinode or public withdrawal and admission of falsity was the essential **8–33** remedy in the early days of defamation.[72] A horse dealer who had insulted others when informed of what he had said, having himself forgotten, immediately offered to apologise in any terms sought by the others. Sensibly there was held to be no ground for an action of defamation.[73] It is likely that where there has been no publication beyond the recipient this will still be the case. An early apology which reaches all those who hear or read a statement should mitigate damages.

Offer of Amends

The Defamation Act 1996 repealed section 4 of the Defamation Act 1952.[74] **8–34** A person who has published a statement alleged to be defamatory may offer to make amends in relation to the statement generally or in relation to a specific defamatory meaning which the person making the offer accepts that the statement conveys (to be called a qualified offer).[75] The offer must be in writing, expressed to be an offer in terms of the Act and if it is a qualified offer it must state the defamatory meaning concerned.[76] The offer must be to make a suitable correction and a sufficient apology, to publish the correction and apology in a reasonable manner practicable in the circumstances and to pay the victim compensation and costs.[77] An offer cannot be made after serving a defence.[78] An offer can be withdrawn before

---

[69] *ibid.* at 165.
[70] *Cuthbert v. Linklater*, 1935 S.L.T. 94.
[71] See para. 8–18 above.
[72] For an example see Walker, *History*, V, p. 240 n. 285.
[73] *Ewart v. Mason* (1806) Hume 633.
[74] "Never really taken seriously in practice because no one can remember it ever having been successful." Gillian Wade, "The Defamation Bill 1996" (1996) Rep B. 9–2.
[75] Defamation Act 1996 s. 2(1) and (2). These provisions replace the defence of unintentional defamation provided by s. 4 of the Defamation Act 1952.
[76] 1996 Act, s. 2(3).
[77] 1996 Act, s. 2(4).
[78] 1996 Act, s. .2(5).

acceptance and a renewal is treated as a fresh offer.[79] Once accepted the victim cannot bring or continue proceedings. If the details are not agreed the court can make the necessary orders and can settle the damages on the common law basis.[80] Unless it can be shown that the offeror knew or had reason to believe that the statement related to the victim and was both false and defamatory, the offer is a defence if the publisher wants to use it but if he does he may not use any other defence.[81] The offer may be relied on in mitigation of damages whether or not relied on as a defence.[82]

In rixa

8–35 Remarks made in anger and known so to be do not affect a person's reputation although they may be insulting. In *Fleming v. Craig*[83] the defender in the presence and hearing of all the persons present called the pursuer a "damned liar". Minutes later the pursuer in the presence and hearing of the others asked the defender to withdraw the statement he had made. The defender, it was averred, deliberately stated in the hearing of the others that he would not withdraw his statement but would repeat it. And he did. The pursuer then said that he would do something to vindicate his reputation. The defender said "Go on and summons me and I shall answer it when I get it." So the pursuer did. In court the defender argued that the words complained of were spoken *in rixa*.

> "They were not intended to convey any charge of untruthfulness. They were merely a denial, expressed it may be in strong terms, of a statement which had been made by the pursuer. It was important to note that the words were used with reference to a particular statement. The language complained of was that of a man who admittedly had lost his temper, and there was no attack on the pursuer's character. From the pursuer's own statement of the circumstances it appeared that the words used were not calumnious, and there was therefore no question which could be sent to trial . . . it appears that mere words of abuse which were not intended to convey a defamatory imputation, and were not so understood by those who heard them, are not slanderous. As Lord Dunedin said in the case of *Agnew*, if slang is used it must be taken according to its ordinary meaning. It may, I think, be said that usually to call a man a liar, or even a damned liar, is not intended as an attack upon his general veracity. Sometimes the words are used playfully, sometimes they are intended as mere abuse, and very commonly, I think it may be said, they are not taken seriously . . . In Cooper on *Defamation* (2nd ed. p. 93) it is pointed out that the defence of rixa involves three elements: (1) that the words were used in the heat of a squabble; (2) that they were not intended to convey, and (3) that they did not in fact convey, the imputation which the words in their natural meaning would import. As regards (1), it was pointed out by Lord M'Laren in *Christie v. Robertson* above cited that it is not a sufficient

---

[79] 1996 Act, s. 2(6).
[80] 1996 Act, s. 3.
[81] 1996 Act, s. 4.
[82] 1996 Act, s. 4(5).
[83] 1939 S.L.T. (Sh Ct) 24.

defence in law to say that the words complained of were spoken in heat. It is necessary to find out the real sense in which the words were used. As regards items (2) and (3), the questions there referred to are essentially questions of fact. No doubt there must be a relevant condescendence of circumstances from which it might reasonably be inferred that the words were used in a sense which was defamatory. As regards that matter, the pursuer, after narrating the circumstances, says that the words were used maliciously, and that, having regard to the persons in whose presence they were uttered, they were liable to damage his prospects of retaining his employment."[84]

A proof before answer was allowed and after proof the defender was successful.[85]

Vulgar abuse

Reference to the section above provides sufficient authority for the proposition that mere vulgar abuse is not defamatory and the same reasons apply. It is because those hearing the slander disregard it. Various derogatory slang works would be defamatory if treated as a statement of fact, but may now be common parlance, and would not be actionable if used simply as vulagar abuse.[85a] **8–35a**

Fair retort

The essence of this defence is that readers or eye-witnesses should be aware that the defender has been wounded and is fighting back. In *National Union of Bank Employees v. Murray*[85b] Lord Birnam said "I am further of opinion that in stating that the pursuers' misrepresentations were deliberate, the defenders honestly believed, and had good reason to believe, that this was so and that they did not issue the leaflet maliciously but in good faith and by way of fair retort to the pursuers' attack." Like the other defences some immediacy is suggested, and time to reflect will make the defence ever more difficult. **8–35b**

---

[84] *ibid.* at 26.

[85] *ibid.* at 27, the sheriff said: "The law does not give redress for mere rudeness, and while I have no doubt that the pursuer was much hurt in his feelings, I am unable on the evidence to hold it proved that the statement complained of was intended as an attack upon his character. The pursuer's reputation is well known to the persons in whose hearing the remark was made. While they may have regarded the defender's language as intemperate, I do not think they can have regarded the words used as more than a far too strong and a very rude denial of a statement which the pursuer had made. I sympathise with the pursuer in his anxiety to vindicate his reputation, but I am unable to hold that in the circumstances the language used was such as to render the defender in law liable in damages." On appeal the sheriff upheld that decision: "The use of somewhat coarse language in denying a particular statement of fact as to which parties were at variance does not appear to amount to a slander." Many authorities of long standing to similar effect are collected in Hume, III, 142–143.

[85a] See the US rapper Ice Cube, quoted in R. Abel. *Speech and Respect,* 44th Hamlyn Lectures (Sweet & Maxwell). In older times "whore" was not actionable in a quarrel: *Reid v. Scott* (1825) 4 S. 5.

[85b] 1949 S.L.T. (Notes) 25.

Fair Comment

8–35c If an article or statement in a newspaper is an expression of opinion upon a matter of public interest which involves no mis-statement of fact and no attack upon private character, then it is not actionable.[85c] In the early days it is not entirely clear what attitude the court took to comment.[85d] The matter is only tangentially dealt with in *Godfrey v. W & DC Thomson.*[85e] Lord McLaren commented at 1114 that " expression of an opinion as to state of facts truly set forth is not actionable, even when that opinion is couched in vituperative or contumelious language." In one of the most important Scottish cases, *Crotty v. McFarlane,*[85f] the imporant issue was said to be whether criticism expressed honest opinions however unjust, or was couched in reckless and exaggerated language that no reasonable man would have used. It was held that the language in the case was acceptable even though it was hostile or even if it was grossly unjust. In *Shanks v. BBC*[85g] it was averred that the pursuer had given the defenders an explanation about certain matters which was not reflected in a subsequent television broadcast. Lord Osborne held that he was unable to exclude this averment as irrelevant because it might relate to the defence of fair comment. It has been held more recently that calling a sports administrator a "dictator" might fall within the defence, as the phrase no longer had the connotation of murder associated with Hitler or Stalin.[85h] "Malicious misuse of public money" said of a councillor was fair comment.[85i] "Fair" suggests some relevant connection with the facts. In *Moffatt v. London Express Newspapers Ltd*[85j] officebearers of the National Union of Mineworkers, Scottish Area, sued for slander or alternatively for verbal injury. An article headed "what makes a man spit at his country?" said that at the opening of the International Miners Conference at Amsterdam the Scottish delegation "ostentatiously remained seated" during the playing of the British National Anthem. In the fourth paragraph the article asked: "What turned Mr Moffatt [the first pursuer], son of God-fearing Scottish parents, into a man who will now apparently honour every country but his own?" The pursuers averred that the headline, the reference to "ostentatiously" remaining seated, and the question in the fourth paragraph were defamatory of the first pursuer. The Lord Ordinary (Strachan) held that none of the statements was actionable without innuendo. So far as the first pursuer was concerned he sustained the action on the ground that the headline and statements quoted were capable of bearing the innuendo suggested. The defenders pleaded *inter alia* "fair comment". The pursuers argued that such a defence could be maintained only if it was shown that the comment was warranted by the facts stated in the article.[85k] His

---

[85c] *Archer v. Ritchie & Co.* (1891) R. 719 at 727; *Boal v. Scottish Catholic Printing Co.,* 1907 S.C. 1120.

[85d] See *Muller v. Robertson* (1853) 15 D. 661.

[85e] (1890) 17 R. 1108.

[85f] Jan. 27, 1891; *Casebook* Ext. 86.

[85g] 1993 S.L.T. 326.

[85h] *Farry v. News Group Newspapers Ltd,* 1996 G.W.D. 2-109.

[85i] *Brooks v. Lind,* 1997 Rep.L.R. 83.

[85j] 1950 S.L.T. (Notes) 46.

[85k] Under reference to *Wheatley v. Anderson,* 1927 S.L.T. 127.

Lordship refused to withdraw the defence of fair comment from the jury. He said: "I have with some hesitation allowed the first innuendo to go to the jury and I think that the defence of fair comment must go with it". The nature of the averments necessary to rebut fair comment have been considered.[86] There are many examples in the reports.[87]

Veritas

In defamation, because it is established by a type of statement which is **8–36** assumed to be false, the defender must establish the truth. Truth is therefore truly a defence.[88] It is now of course accepted that *veritas* is a defence. The reasons for *veritas* being a defence rather than a non-constitutive factor are obvious; it is to make those who make certain kind of statement responsible and therefore very careful. It also makes the victim's task easier. Frequently a motion for a defender to lead at the proof will be made and successful. In *Fairbairn v. SNP*[89] the law was accepted as being that "to establish a defence of *veritas*, the respondents would have to prove the truth of all the material statements in the defamatory matter complained of, justifying everything in the defamatory statement which is injurious to the pursuer."[90] The precise terms of section 5 of the Defamation Act 1952 should be kept in view along with this statement of principle: "Where there are two or more charges the defence is not to fail if the truth of every charge is not proved, if the words not proved to be true do not materially injure the pursuer's reputation having regard to the truth of the remaining charges."[91] At an interim interdict stage, prima facie evidence of a defence of *veritas* may prevent interdict being granted or continued.[92] The defence must meet the defamatory allegation. In *Beattie v. Mather*[93] an action by an inspector for the poor related to defamatory statements to the effect that he had starved the poor and robbed them of

---

[86] *Waverley Housing Management Ltd v. BBC*, 1993 G.W.D. 17–1117.

[87] e.g. *Gray v. SSPCA* (1890) 17 R. 1185; *Bruce v. Ross & Co.* (1901) 4 F. 171; *Wheatley v. Anderson & Miller*, 1927 S.C. 133, this latter is important for the allowing that the facts can be in a sense submerged and need not be set out in exhaustive detail. There may be no dogmatic point here. It may always be a matter of circumstance; the more obscure in time or place the facts relied on, the more difficult it may be to substantiate the defence.

[88] As Norrie reminds us truth was only conclusively decided to be a defence in *McKellar v. Duke of Sutherland* (1859) 21 D. 222. Prior to that the matter was open. In *Dyce v. Kerr, Ewan & Booth*, July 9, 1816, F.C. the pursuer was the physician of Aberdeen lunatic asylum. The first defender was one of the managers of the asylum. He had been dissatisfied by the pursuer's conduct in the treatment of patients and called a general meeting of managers who approved the pursuer's conduct. The pursuer sued for damages for defamation of character in relation to the publication of a letter about him in the press. He also called the recipient of the letter and the publisher. The Lord Ordinary (Pitmilly) found that in the circumstances the defenders ought not to be allowed proof of *veritas convicii*. On a reclaiming petition to the Second Division the court was equally divided. The Lord Justice-Clerk and Lord Robertson thought proof should be allowed. Lord Bannatyne and Glenlee thought not. The case was held over for the opinion of Lord Pitmilly, who stuck to the view he had taken in the Outer House. The reclaiming petition was refused. Proof would be allowed only in mitigation of quantum of damages not in justification.

[89] 1980 S.L.T. 149.

[90] *ibid.* at 153, relying on Walker, *Delict* (1966) at p.800.

[91] For a good example see *Gecas v. Scottish Television Plc.*, 1992 G.W.D. 30–1786.

[92] *Fairbairn v. SNP*, 1980 S.L.T. 149.

[93] (1860) 22 D. 952.

their rights. The defenders sought to prove that there were instances of the poor being starved and relief refused. All seven counter issues proposed by the defenders were refused. The words complained of were of a general nature. The proposed counter issues did not meet it. Some related to the management of the poor house which was the duty of others, the rest were matters of judgement. The essence of the defence is to meet the sting.[94] In *Sarwar v. News Group*[95] the pursuer reasonably complained that the defenders were not offering to prove the truth of everything they said. The learned temporary judge noted that *Andrew* was not cited in *Fairbairn*. While not disagreeing with *Fairbairn* he concentrated on the word "material" in the quotation cited above to explicate the problem in terms of a sting approach.

A frank pursuer can in fact destroy his own case. In *Carson v. White*[96] the pursuers sued a solicitor. The solicitor called up a bond and advertised the pursuers' house for sale. The alleged defamation was uttered in a letter in the course of a correspondence between the defender and a firm of solicitors who were acting on behalf of one of the pursuers, and who proposed to the defender to withdraw the sale:

> "If, then, it appears, at this stage, that the statements complained of are true, and that the counter-issue of *veritas* would inevitably and necessarily be affirmed if the case were sent to a jury, the defender 's counsel contended, and I agree with the contention, that the duty of the court is to determine the action now . . . Now, it seems to me that the decrees referred to by the defender in his tenth statement of facts, being unchallenged as to their authenticity and legal effect by the pursuers, are, in conformity with what was laid down in *Addie* (*supra*) in the same position as if they had been produced by the pursuers in substantiation of their averments. So treating these productions, and having examined them, I hold that they 'completely disestablish the pursuers' case.' I shall, therefore, on the whole matter, sustain the defender's first plea in law and dismiss the action."[97]

The court may disallow an issue if it does not in fact kill the sting.[98] The defender may not be allowed to overjustify by saying much more than necessary to kill the sting.[99]

A very full contemporary consideration of the defence in a dramatic case is *Gecas v. Scottish Television Plc.*[1] In that case the broadcasters pled

---

[94] *Andrew v. Penny*, 1964 S.L.T. (Notes) 24.
[95] 1999 S.L.T. 327.
[96] 1919 2 S.L.T. 215.
[97] At 216.
[98] *British Workman's and General Assurance Co v. Stewart* (1897) 24 R. 624. See also *Hunter v. McNaughten* (1894) 21 R. 850 in which allegations of addiction to alcohol of a minister were allowed and proof of particular episodes allowed to go to *veritas*, it being for the jury to decide if this had been intoxication or merely "instances of this gentleman being overtaken." *per* Lord President Robertson at 853.
[99] *H v. P.* (1905) 8 F. 232 is a good example, the defender not being allowed to prove against a woman various other episodes of adultery (although the decision is useful for the careful treatment of what evidence might yet be led in such a case).
[1] 1992 G.W.D. 30–1786.

justification against a defamation case based on nine particular allegations of involvement in war crimes. An allegation of "finishing off" still living executed prisoners was not successfully defended. However, four were held not to have in fact been made by the broadcast. But the defence succeeded on allegations of war crimes against Soviet citizens, that he was a mass murderer and he belonged to a batallion that did nothing other than murder civilians. In *Baigent v. BBC*[2] the pursuers sought damages in respect of allegations made about their nursing home. There was a secret film shown. The BBC failed in their defence of *veritas*. They were held liable in substantial damages.

So far as pleading is concerned a dictum of Lord President Inglis in *Craig* **8–37** *v. Jex-Blake*[3] settled the position:

"The rule of our practice is that if the defender undertakes to prove the truth of words, spoken or written, complained of in an action of slander, he must undertake that in the record in distinct and positive terms. And not only so, but he must take a counter issue, putting to the jury the question, whether what is complained of is true in whole or in part; if it be in part, then specifying distinctly what part. And if such an issue is not taken it is not competent to prove the truth of the words spoken either in whole or in part, either for express and direct purpose of showing the truth, or for the other purpose suggested of mitigating the damages. All that is so well settled that it is quite unnecessary to cite cases in support of it."[4]

Convictions

Section 12 of the Law Reform (Miscellaneous Provisions) (Scotland) Act **8–38** 1968 provides for the conclusiveness of convictions for purposes of defamation actions. The *Digest* says, "It is not right or just to condemn anyone for bringing a wrongdoer into disrepute, for it is necessary and proper for the offences of wrongdoers to be known."[5] The purpose of the 1974 Act is that certain offenders be treated as if they had not been charged or convicted of a spent offence.[6] However, the policy of the Act is limited. A defender is not prevented from using the defence of *veritas*.[7] The section prevents the malicious publication of a spent conviction. Malicious in this sense means "some spiteful, irrelevant or improper motive."[8] The fact of the spent conviction can also be used in support of a defence of fair comment or privilege or to rebut an allegation of malice contradicting a defence of qualified privilege.

Section 12(2) of the Defamation Act 1996 corrects the problem that arose when the criminal conviction sought to be relied upon was not that of

---

[2] 1999 S.C.L.R. 787.
[3] (1871) 9 M. 973.
[4] *ibid.* at 979.
[5] D.47.10.18.
[6] s. 4(1), s. 8.
[7] s.8(3).
[8] For an English case on the topic see *Herbage v. Pressdram Ltd* [1984] 1 W.L.R. 1160.

the other party to the action. The defender could not plead *veritas* if the actual criminal had not had the conviction set aside. That can now be done.

Absolute Privilege

8–39 If there is absolute privilege there is no claim. This is a matter of public policy to support free speech. The categories are as follows.

Statements in Parliament

8–40 The Bill of Rights 1688, Art. 9[9] provides that "freedom of speech and debates or proceedings in Parliament ought not to be impeached or questioned in any court or place out of Parliament." That of course predates the Union. M.P.s decided that they wanted to be able to sue for defamation and the law was changed accordingly in the Defamation Act 1996. Where the conduct of a person in or in relation to proceedings in Parliament is in issue in defamation proceedings, he can waive for the purposes of those proceedings, so far as concerns him, the protection of any enactment or rule of law which prevents proceedings in Parliament being impeached or questioned in any court or place out of Parliament.[10] Where a person waives that protection: (a) any such enactment or rule of law shall not apply to prevent evidence being given, questions being asked or statements, submissions, comments or findings being made about his conduct, and (b) none of those things shall be regarded as infringing the privilege of either House of Parliament.[11] The waiver by one person of that protection does not affect its operation in relation to another person who has not waived it.[12] The M.P.s retain their protections and immunities because nothing in the section affects any enactment or rule of law so far as it protects a person (including a person who has waived the protection) from legal liability for words spoken or things done in the course of, or for the purposes of or incidental to, any proceedings in Parliament,[13] in particular: (a) the giving of evidence before either House or a committee; (b) the presentation or submission of a document to either House or a committee; (c) the preparation of a document for the purposes of or incidental to the transacting of any such business; (d) the formulation, making or publication of a document, including a report, by or pursuant to an order of either House or a committee; and (e) any communication with the Parliamentary Commissioner for Standards or any person having functions in connection with the registration of members' interests.[14]

Parliamentary Papers

8–41 The Parliamentary Papers Act 1840 concluded the struggle between the Commons and the Courts by establishing absolute privilege for parliamentary papers.

---

[9] having statutory effect by 2 W & M c.1.
[10] s. 13(1).
[11] s. 13(2).
[12] s. 13(3).
[13] s. 13(4).
[14] s. 13(5). In this subsection "a committee" means a committee of either House or a joint committee of both Houses of Parliament.

Court proceedings

There is absolute privilege for statements made in court extending to the **8–42** judge, counsel and witnesses.[15]

Fair and accurate reports of judicial proceedings

It was arguable that fair and accurate reports of judicial proceedings were **8–43** absolutely privileged at common law.[16] The matter has been put beyond doubt by the Defamation Act 1966. A fair and accurate report of proceedings in public before a court to which the Act applies[17], if published contemporaneously with the proceedings, is absolutely privileged.[18]

Qualified Privilege

A statement is protected if honestly made by a person in the discharge of a **8–44** public or private duty of some kind or in his own affairs in a matter where his interest is concerned.[19] The critical issue becomes that of malice—if the occasion is protected by qualified privilege, the protection is only lost if the pursuer can prove malice.[20] It is not necessary, as in wrongful diligence cases to absent malice and want of probable cause.[21] Want of probable cause may however assist in drawing an inference of malice.[22] That is now examined as it applies to all cases of qualified privilege. In *Farrell v. Boyd*,[23] where a doctor stated to a person's employer that the employee suffered from gonorrhoeal rheumatism it was held that the mere fact that a medical man makes a wrong diagnosis on an insufficient examination, and adheres to it when it is brought to his knowledge that other medical men take a different view, does not necessarily imply malice. To establish malice in

---

[15] *Cunningham v. The Scotsman Publications Ltd*, 1987 S.L.T. 698.

[16] See *Richardson v. Wilson* (1879) 7 R. 237, *per* Lord President Inglis at 241; Lord Deas at 242 and Lord Mure at 243. See *Wright & Greig v. Outram & Co.* (1890) 17 R. 596 for a consideration of what is "fair and accurate". In this case the report was not protected because it omitted to report parts of the proceedings which would have shown that the representation contained in the report as published was not true. In *Cunningham v. The Scotsman Publications Ltd*, 1987 S.L.T. 698 Lord Clyde said that the Scottish cases disclosed the general principle that a fair and accurate report of what takes place in court may be protected by *qualified privilege*.

[17] Namely: (a) any court in the United Kingdom; (b) the European Court of Justice or any court attached to that court; (c) the European Court of Human Rights; and (d) any international criminal tribunal established by the Security Council of the United Nations or by an international agreement to which the United Kingdom is a party. "Court" includes any tribunal or body exercising the judicial power of the State: s.14(3).

[18] s. 14(1). A report of proceedings which by an order of the court, or as a consequence of any statutory provision, is required to be postponed shall be treated as published contemporaneously if it is published as soon as practicable after publication is permitted: s. 14(2).

[19] *Dunnet v. Nelson*, 1926 S.C. 764. For a case where damages were awarded where it was not proved that the statement was made in discharge of a duty see *Laird v. Aitken* (1823) 2 S. 507.

[20] It is not necessary, as in wrongful diligence cases, to absent want of probable cause: *Tytler v. Mackintosh* (1823) 3 Mur 236; *Webster v. Paterson & Son*, 1910 S.C. 459; *Notman v. Commercial Bank of Scotland Ltd*, 1938 S.L.T. 428. It can however be proved to show malice: *Notman*.

[21] *ibid.*

[22] *Notman v. Commercial Bank of Scotland.*

[23] (1907) 15 S.L.T. 327.

such a privileged occasion there had to be proof of malice either from something extrinsic to the report or from the exaggerated terms in which his opinion was given. Repeating the remarks too widely can be argued as displaying malice. In *Cadzow v. The Distress Committee of the City of Edinburgh*[24] the essence of the claim for loss of privilege was that the Committee received the report and had it printed. It was held that:

"There are thirty-five members of the Distress Committee. Thirty-five copies were thus required for circulation. It was, in my opinion, a reasonable proceeding to have the copies printed for circulation. I am unable to hold that the fact of the Distress Committee having the report so printed represents such a degree of recklessness on their part as infers malice. It was, in my opinion, a reasonable incident in the ordinary course of their business as a public body."

In *Couper v. Burleigh*[25] it was argued that the following factors showed malice, namely: (1) the unnecessary strength of the defender's language; (2) his refusal to disclose the source of his information; (3) his failure to enquire into the truth of the charge before communicating it; (4) his reiteration of the charge after it had been disproved by two enquiries; and (5) his refusal to retract and apologise when the third enquiry exonerated the pursuer. Unjustifiable repetition of a charge might shew malice.[26] In *The National Union of Bank Employees v. Murray and Others*[27] the argument was again that the language used could infer malice. Lord Birnam commented that "to subject language used on privileged occasions to a strict scrutiny and to hold all excess beyond the actual exigencies of the occasion to be evidence of express malice would greatly limit, if not altogether defeat, the protection which the law gives to statements so made".[28] *Macaskill v. Silver*[29] was another case where it was sought to treat the language used as inherently malicious. It was said:

"In the present case, if it had been possible to corroborate in detail Chief Inspector Johnston's account of the defender's conversation with him, I would have held that malice might have been inferred from the language used. The more extreme allegations which the inspector said were made were, however, without corroboration."[30]

In *Hamill v. Lord Advocate*[31] the evidence was that the intention was to bring a state of affairs to the notice of the pursuer's employers and not to injure the pursuer. A plea of qualified privilege was upheld in relation to an admittedly defamatory letter. To lose the defence something more than negligence was required.[32] Motive was crucial.[33] Remarks on the law of

---

[24] 1914 1 S.L.T. 493.
[25] 1913 1 S.L.T. 122.
[26] *Douglas v. Main* (1893) 20 R. 793. See also *Simmers v. Morton* (1900) 8 S.L.T. 285.
[27] 1949 S.L.T. (Notes) 25.
[28] Under reference, *inter alia*, to *Lyal v. Henderson*, 1916 2 S.L.T. 2.
[29] 1948 S.L.T. (Notes) 63.
[30] *ibid.* at 63–64. Corroboration is however no longer required: Civil Evidence Act 1988.
[31] 1994 G.W.D. 33–1960.
[32] *Hayford v. Forrester Paton*, 1927 S.L.T. 507.
[33] *Fraser v. Mirza*, 1993 S.L.T. 527.

privilege, necessary for the decision, in *Pearson v. EIS Ltd*,[34] perhaps go too far. This was an application to have an address revealed under the Administration of Justice (Scotland) Act 1972. It was said that in raising an action for defamation which suggests a defence of absolute or (obiter) qualified privilege the pursuer must at the outset address that defence. This is doubtful in principle and result. The pursuer is entitled to state a relevant case and wait for the defence. The action may be undefended.

The categories of privilege are never closed and depend on the circumstances of the occasion.[35] The main recognised categories are now summarised.

Discharge of a duty

The free exchange of views in a democracy requires a certain degree of **8–45** latitude in making statements where the statement is made not through caprice but because a person has assumed or is under a moral or social duty to speak. So, for example, it is in order to make a complaint to a chief constable about the conduct of a sergeant.[36] Statements made to candidates in elections are controlled by statute.[37] A recent examination of the defence appears in *Hamill v. Lord Advocate*.[38] A plea of qualified privilege was upheld in relation to an admittedly defamatory letter. It was said that to lose the defence something more than negligence was required.[39] Motive was crucial.[40] The evidence was that the intention was to bring a state of affairs to the notice of the pursuers' employers and not to injure the pursuer. The occasion had not been misused. *Rogers v. Orr*[41] was a case of alleged charges of theft against a student by the Dean of a medical school, made both in the presence of other students and by a notice affixed on a board open to public inspection. The case is significant for the important observation that when facts inferring malice are relevantly averred their improbable character in relation to the alleged slander is not a reason for refusing an issue.

Interests of another

A classic example of this is the character reference about another individual **8–46** to the extent that the reply deals with relevant matter.[42] In the English negligence case of *Spring v. Guardian Assurance*[43] it was held that there was no such defence against a negligence claim. The defenders tried to use that fact as a reason why negligence liability should not be imposed.

Between persons having a common interest

A communication is privileged where made between parties, one who has **8–47** an interest in making it and the other having an interest to receive it so long as they are in good faith and the statement is not published more

---

[34] 1997 S.C.L.R. 933.
[35] *James v. Baird*, 1916 S.C. (H.L.) 158, *per* Earl Loreburn at 163–164.
[36] *Cassidy v. Connachie*, 1907 S.C. 1112.
[37] *Bruce v. Leisk* (1892) 19 R. 482. 1952 Act, s. 10.
[38] 1994 G.W.D. 33–1960.
[39] Under reference to *Hayford v. Forrestor Paton*.
[40] *Fraser v. Mirza*.
[41] 1939 S.L.T. 43.
[42] *Dundas v. Livingstone* (1900) 3 F. 37.
[43] [1995] 2 A.C. 296.

widely than necessary. The most influential case is the decision of the Privy Council in *Macintosh v. Dun*.[44] The defendants carried on an extensive business as a trade protective society, under the name of "The Mercantile Agency," which consisted in obtaining information with reference to the commercial standing and position of persons in New South Wales and elsewhere, and in communicating such information confidentially to subscribers to the agency in response to specific and confidential enquiry on their part. They issued forms for requests for information. The defendants were sued for damages for libel in respect of certain statements made by them about the plaintiff in response to a request for information by a subscriber. The High Court of Australia gave judgment for the defendants. The Privy Council reversed that decision. The only question raised by the appeal was whether or not the occasion on which the libels (as they were admitted to be) were published was a privileged occasion. Lord Macnaghten's opinion was in the negative. He first pointed out that the defendants were to be regarded as volunteers in supplying the information, and that their motive in so doing was not a sense of duty, but a matter of business.

> "Their motive is self-interest. They carry on their trade just as other traders do, in the hope and expectation of making a profit."[45] His Lordship then considered whether it is in the interest of the community and the welfare of society that "the protection which the law throws around communications made in legitimate self-defence, or from a bona fide sense of duty, should be extended to communications made from motives of self-interest by persons who trade for profit in the characters of other people," and gives answer in the negative, because "it is only right that those who engage in such a business, touching so closely very dangerous ground, should take the consequences if they overstep the law."[46]

In *Barr v. The Musselburgh Merchants' Association*,[47] *Dun* was considered on similar but different facts.

> "It seems to me that the present defenders' position places them on the safe or favoured side of the line thus drawn by Lord Macnaghten. The information complained of was circulated by them among their members 'in legitimate self-defence'; they are not 'persons who trade for profit in the characters of other people.' I think *Macintosh v. Dun* affords a clear and authoritative rule for the decision of questions like this . . . I see no reason to doubt that the principles of law laid down or approved in *Macintosh v. Dun* are applicable in Scotland as well as in England; and I think it may be deduced from these that the law does, in the general interests of society, extend the protection of privilege to communications made in bona fide (though erroneously) about a third person, where the

---

[44] [1908] A.C. 390.
[45] *ibid*. at 400.
[26] *ibid*.
[47] 1911 2 S.L.T. 402.

parties making and receiving it have a legitimate business interest in the communication ... Accordingly, it appears to me that, when this Association circulated the leaflet complained of among its members, the communication was privileged, because every one of the members had a legitimate interest in its contents; and that they were entitled to obtain and share these, so long as the matter was gone about honestly and without malice."[48]

A contemporary case is *Chapman v. Barber*.[49] The case was between two directors of a company. Chapman sent Barber draft minutes of a board meeting. Barber thought the minutes suggested that he (Barber) had been conducting himself improperly and responded by accusing Chapman of acting against company policy and misleading the board with a malicious and inaccurate minute. Chapman pointed out that Barber's version had been seen by non-directorial staff. The case raises two points: (i) the scope of the defence; and (ii) how it can be lost by unnecessarily wide circulation.[50] The court held that the statements were covered by qualified privilege and the fact of others seeing the document which had after all been marked "private and confidential" and sent in the usual way did not result in the privilege being lost.[51] In *Lloyd v. Hickley*[52] the occasion was a meeting between the representatives of the owner of that estate and of a neighbouring estate; the defender, who was the factor of the neighbouring estate, stated that the pursuer had overshot during the 1963 season. The pursuer raised an action for damages in that he had suffered injury to his feelings "as an honourable man and a sportsman". The meeting had been to try to settle certain litigations between the two estates. As the existence of privilege depended on the circumstances a proof before answer was allowed.

Protection of one's own interests

A person relying on published attacks has qualified privilege so long as **8–48** pertinent.[53] However, if the defender goes beyond the attack there is no qualified privilege as was held in *Milne v. Walker*,[54] in which the pursuer was a school governor and had accused the defender of dishonestly attempting to palm off substandard goods on his school. The defender replied with a broad attack on the pursuer alleging that he had told consummate and deliberate lies about the defender and others.[55]

Reports and The Defamation Act 1996

As discussed above, fair and accurate reports of court proceedings have **8–49** absolute privilege. The Act expressly provides for the qualified privilege of certain reports. The nature of the protection varies as to whether the

---

[48] at 405.
[49] 1989 S.L.T. 830.
[50] The court considered the English case *Edmondson v. Birch & Co* [1907] 1 K.B. 371 on this point.
[51] See also *Shaw v. Morgan* (1888) 15 R. 865; *Leitch v. Lyal* (1903) 11 S.L.T. 394.
[52] 1967 S.L.T. 225.
[53] *Gray v. SSPCA* (1890) 7 R. 1185.
[54] (1893) 1 S.L.T. 157.
[55] Upheld on reclaiming (1893) 1 S.L.T. 332.

matter is a Schedule I, Part 1 case or a Schedule I, Part 2 case. The publication of any report or other statement mentioned in Schedule 1[56] to this Act is privileged unless the publication is shown to be made with malice, subject as follows.[57] In defamation proceedings in respect of the publication of a report or other statement mentioned in Part II of that Schedule,[58] there is no defence under this section if the plaintiff shows that the defendant—(a) was requested by him to publish in a suitable manner[59] a reasonable letter or statement by way of explanation or contradiction, and (b) refused or neglected to do so.[60] Whether a Schedule I or II matter the protection does not apply to the publication to the public, or a section of the public, of matter which is not of public concern and the publication of which is not for the public benefit.[61] The Act is not intended to protect the publication of matter the publication of which is prohibited by law, or as limiting or abridging any privilege subsisting apart from the Act.[62]

A "public figure" defence?

8–50 One special point might be mentioned here and that it has been argued that there ought to be a "public figure" defence in defamation. Bonnington states that there is such a defence in continental systems and in America.[63] He argues that the absence of such a defence is contrary to the European Convention on Human Rights and that in due course the position may have to change.[64] He suggests that Scots law is not so set against such a defence as English law on the authority of *Langlands v. Leng*,[65] the facts of which are discussed above in a different context. In the course of his speech Viscount Haldane did advert to what may be at least a different approach to such cases:

> "The first thing that I wish to say is that in dealing with a newspaper article written about a public functionary, considerable latitude is

---

[56] (1) A fair and accurate report of proceedings in public of a legislature anywhere in the world; (2) a fair and accurate report of proceedings in public before a court anywhere in the world; (3) a fair and accurate report of proceedings in public of a person appointed to hold a public inquiry by a government or legislature anywhere in the world; (4) a fair and accurate report of proceedings in public anywhere in the world of an international organisation or an international conference; (5) a fair and accurate copy of or extract from any register or other document required by law to be open to public inspection; (6) a notice or advertisement published by or on the authority of a court, or of a judge or officer of a court, anywhere in the world; (7) a fair and accurate copy of or extract from matter published by or on the authority of a government or legislature anywhere in the world; and (8) a fair and accurate copy of or extract from matter published anywhere in the world by an international organisation or an international conference.

[57] s. 15(1).

[58] See the Defamation Act 1966, Sched. 1, Pt II, paras 9–15.

[59] "In a suitable manner" means in the same manner as the publication complained of or in a manner that is adequate and reasonable in the circumstances.

[60] s. 15(2).

[61] s. 15(3).

[62] s. 15(4).

[63] A.J. Bonnington, "U.K. Defamation Practice and the Defamation Act 1996" (1997) S.L.P.Q. Vol 2(3) 202, citing *Sullivan v. New York Times* (1964) 376 U.S. 254, a case depending upon constitutional free speech.

[64] *ibid.* at 212.

[65] 1916 S.C. (H.L.) 102.

allowed by the law. Any gentleman who takes the position of architect under the school board of Dundee is filling a capacity as a public official, and he must expect criticism, such criticism as the law might not recognise as justified in the case of a merely private person, but readily admits when it is in the public interest that criticism should be brought to bear upon the conduct of public officials. When a person is in a public capacity he may be criticised by the newspapers in the public interest; and that rebuts the presumption of malice in law which the Court might otherwise make, and leaves malice in fact to be proved, and malice in fact to be found, either in the special language of the article or in circumstances proved which point to some motive of enmity to the particular individual. Now, what strikes me very strongly, applying that principle to the documents before us, is, that on reading them there is a criticism, and a pretty severe criticism, upon the position of an official who is under such a system as I have already described, in the relation of architect to the school board of Dundee, and an intimation that what exists cannot be a good system and must have a tendency to lead to extravagant advice. That is a severe comment upon the system itself, but so far as it is a comment upon the system, it comes within the privilege and justification of which I have spoken. Therefore the real question is, not whether there is criticism upon Mr Langlands, but whether there is criticism upon Mr Langlands in his capacity of a public servant. Now I myself find nothing which goes beyond the limits of what I have said. Of course it is disagreeable to everybody to be criticised, particularly disagreeable to a person in Mr Langland's position who has a private practice as an architect, and I wish very emphatically to say that while Mr Langlands must bear the disagreeableness of that comment, the basis upon which I proceed in the opinion I am expressing and the advice I am offering to your Lordships is this: that I read this report and article as containing nothing in derogation of Mr Langland's professional conduct as a private individual. What is there is directed purely to his public capacity and the system under which he is officially employed. Now this is the very basis of my opinion, because while it is in the public interest that the press should exercise freely its right of criticism in regard to public affairs, it is equally important that the right of a private individual to have his character respected should be maintained, and that people should not as private persons be exposed to unjustifiable and arbitrary comment. Therefore, in submitting to your Lordships that what the Court of Session did was wrong, and that the judges there ought to have held that there was nothing in the language which could support the innuendo, I am not in any way suggesting to your Lordships that if I thought for a moment that the 'Dundee Advertiser' had without justification attacked Mr Langland's private reputation and capacity, I should have been giving your Lordships the advice which I am tendering at this moment. It is because I think the case stands on a very different footing of which I have already spoken, that I have come to the conclusion now expressed."[66]

That passage looks very much like a qualified privilege point but on the other hand it does refer rather to the person than the occasion. However,

---

[66] At 106–107.

the Scots law Lord, Lord Shaw of Dunfermline did not seem to think there was any special defence, indeed as he points out in the following passage there was no question of a qualified privilege defence. So if this case is some support for a public figure defence it must be different and presumably stronger than a defence of qualified privilege, although it might be suggested that if there were such a defence it could usefully operate in precisely the same way as qualified privilege. Here is the critical passage:

"According to the Scottish practice, when the words are in themselves false and calumnious and are put in issue, general malice is assumed from the fact of their being false and calumnious, and that being so, there is no necessity upon either party to refer specifically to malice. But the necessity to insert specific reference to malice arises in this way: that although a slander or libel may be false and calumnious in its terms, nevertheless it may have been used on an occasion which was privileged in the sense that the person who uttered it had the right erroneously and even falsely to make his statement. In such circumstances malice enters a Scottish record by way of a suggestion by the pursuer that the privilege which the defender pleads disappears in consequence of the special malice which is averred; and it has been the practice for many years, and I presume is still the practice, that if the record is in that state, namely, that the defender pleads privilege and the pursuer counters it by a special plea of specific malice, the case approaches the jury in this situation: that if in the course of the enquiry before them it does appear that the occasion was privileged, then the pursuer is entitled to prove as matter of fact circumstances going to the malice which would rebut the privilege. That is the state of procedure in Scotland. There is no requirement in this case for anything in the nature of an averment of special malice, and I think the learned counsel on both sides did well not to deal with or handle that topic in their pleadings. In the present case all that there is, is a record without any averment of supplementary or elucidatory facts and circumstances; there is a certain printed matter referred to, and it is said that that printed matter has the defamatory construction or inference to which I have alluded. I do not think it has, and I do not think that so far as Mr Langlands is concerned it is a reasonable view to take of what was said with regard to him. A newspaper has the right, and no greater or higher right, to make comment upon a public officer or person occupying a public situation than an ordinary citizen would have; and when an ordinary citizen of Dundee would remark to his neighbour that the system referred to at that meeting was an absurd system because it produced a possible conflict between interest and duty, that citizen was exercising a just and proper right of criticism; and so far as I can see, this newspaper went not one step beyond that point."[67]

On the basis of the case cited it appears all that Scots law offers the defamer of a public figure is (1) that the person may be speaking on a

---

[67] At 109–110.

privileged occasion and absence of malice will allow free expression[68]; and (2) a statement on true facts can easily fall within the defence of fair comment on a matter of public interest.[69] If such a defence is needed then it is submitted Scots law will require legislation or perhaps as Bonnington suggests some dramatic judicial response to European human rights law.[70]

Jury Trial

There is certainly a perception in England that juries make unnecessarily **8–51** large awards of damages.[71] In Scotland this is not necessarily the case but it is possible that a jury would award more than a judge sitting alone. Thus this is the very kind of case where the pursuer might seek a jury and the defence try to avoid one. To do so it is necessary to show special cause in terms of the Court of Session Act 1988, ss. 9(b) and 11. The point was taken and argued fully in *Shanks v. BBC*.[72] The main point made was that the pleadings disclosed a large number of financial transactions including mention of 27 companies. As the allegations related to the professional behaviour of both a chartered accountant and an advocate, the obligations of such professions would have to examined in detail. It was held that defamation cases were no different from others but that the circumstances constituting special cause would differ from case to case. It was held that in this case there was special cause shown. This was on the basis if the volume of educative necessary to paint the background, because the damages would involve difficult calculations; there was a risk of confusion because of the number of issues; some averments were of doubtful relevancy; there were difficult issues of fact and law in relation to the obligations of the professionals. A proof before answer was the consequent order.[73] In so doing a passage in Cooper was rejected:

> "Counsel for the pursuer sought to persuade me that, in assessing whether 'special cause' existed, it was appropriate to adopt a different standard in relation to 'an action for libel or defamation' as compared

---

[68] In *McLaughlan v. Orr, Pollock & Co.* (1894) 22 R. 38, *per* Lord McLaren at 42: "It is hardly necessary to point out that the constitution of this country tolerates the utmost freedom in the discussion of the conduct and motives of those who take part in its public business, whether in the higher plane of statesmanship or in the conduct of local affairs . . . It is only when private character is attacked, or when the criticism of public conduct is combined with the suggestion of base or indirect motives that redress can be claimed."

[69] In *Mutch v. Robertson*, 1981 S.L.T. 217, a letter was sent to the Secretary of State for Scotland by the secretary of the Labour group of a regional council, on behalf of the members of the Labour group. It was held, *inter alia*, that in deciding whether criticism of a person holding public office was capable of bearing a defamatory meaning, the test to be applied was whether the ordinary man could reasonably infer from the criticism that the office-holder was dishonest or was guilty of dishonourable behaviour, or if his public conduct was combined with the suggestion of base or indirect motives.

[70] A starting point may be found in *Lingens v. Austria* (1986) 8 E.H.R.R. 407; *Castells v. Spain* (1992) 14 E.H.R.R. 445; *Oberschlick v. Austria* (1995) 19 E.H.R.R. 389 and *Thorgeirson v. Iceland* (1992) 14 E.H.R.R. 843.

[71] See *e.g. Rantzen v. MGN Ltd* [1994] Q.B. 670; *John v. MGN Ltd* [1996] 2 All E.R. 35.

[72] 1993 S.L.T. 326.

[73] It was also held that in considering the issue of "special cause" in terms of s. 9 of the Court of Session Act 1988, it was appropriate to look at the authorities decided under s. 4 of the Evidence (Scotland) Act 1866.

with the other actions enumerated in s. 11 of the Act of 1988. He contended that in a case such as the present there was 'an almost irresistible presumption in favour of allowing issues'. In this connection he referred to the passage, already mentioned, to be found at p. 265 of Cooper on *Defamation and Verbal Injury* (2nd ed.). I have come to the conclusion that this contention is unsound, although, of course, I recognise that it is likely that in actions for defamation the factors which may be thought to amount to special cause will be different from those which may be similarly viewed in, for example, an action for damages for personal injuries, since 'special cause' must relate to the circumstances of the particular case under consideration. In the provisions of the Act of 1988, which I have already quoted, I note that no distinction is drawn between 'an action for libel or defamation' and any of the other enumerated actions. In the work mentioned, Cooper at p. 265 says: 'it is extremely doubtful whether the court would order proof before a judge instead of a jury trial if either party—and particularly if the pursuer—objected to its being so dealt with', in an action for defamation. In support of this proposition the learned author cited the case of *Rhind v. Kemp & Co.* (1893) 1 SLT 367. That case was, so far as appears from the very brief report, an action of damages based upon the taking of decree in absence for a debt previously paid. In a reclaiming motion it was held that the Lord Ordinary had erred in holding that 'special cause' existed in the circumstances of that case. As it was presented in the reclaiming motion, the case was not an action of defamation. In my opinion, this authority does not support the proposition contained in the passage from the work which I have already quoted, which in my view is incorrect."

There are few cases where this point has been considered in such detail in this context. The only thing that might be added by way of comment is that it is considered perfectly acceptable to try accountants and lawyers in the criminal courts where the subject's very liberty is at stake—the issues are just as complex.

Damages

8–52 Success in a defamation action requires at least an award of solatium for hurt feelings and lowered self-esteem.[74] By way of example where the defamation was a false complaint against a policeman Lord McDonald said:

"During this period of four months he was no doubt subjected to a degree of worry as to his future and some embarrassment. There is, however, no question of damage to his career or prospects in the police force. This is a unique case and I received no help from the decided cases on damages cited to me. What is clear is that the sum sued for (£10,000) is utterly ridiculous . . . I consider that an appropriate award of damages to the pursuer is £200 ."[75]

---

[74] *Anderson v. Palombo*,1986 S.L.T. 46 approving Walker, *Delict*, (2nd ed.), p. 785.
[75] *ibid.* at 49.

An extra Division of the Inner House has given some guidance on the computation of damages in this area. In *Winter v. News Scotland Ltd*,[76] the victim of defamatory remarks claimed that publication by newspapers had subjected her to lengthy disciplinary proceedings, caused her to suffer depression and meant she found it difficult to leave the house. A jury awarded her £50,000. A motion to review the award was rejected.[77] The court would only review an award if it indicated gross injustice.[78] In particular it was stated: (1) to be inappropriate to relate defamation cases to personal injury cases; and (2) English cases were of no assistance proceeding on very different principles. The factors to be considered were damage to health, reputation and feelings. The worse the allegations the worse the injury. This case has reasonably been applied as giving a general idea of the maximum level of an award. In *McCluskie v. Summers*,[79] damages were mitigated by the limited circulation of the defamation—it had been limited to Aberdeen trade union circles and at the parliamentary office of the leader of the Labour party. The victim had managed to be elected to the office of general secretary of a union shortly afterwards and so his reputation had perhaps not been that badly harmed. The defenders' character is irrelevant to aggravate or mitigate damages.[80] Where the earning capacity of a pursuer is affected the damages can be very high indeed, reflecting the financial loss.[81] Contrary to the normal compensation principle, aggravated damages may be awarded. This is a matter to be decided after proof.[82] Taking a plea of *veritas* which later fails may result in aggravation.[83]

PRIVACY

While it might be the case, as Professor Norrie suggests, that people are **8–53** less interested in honour and reputation than they were in the last century, they may be more interested in their privacy. There are signs of this to see all around—people prefer cars to buses and trains; they prefer private rooms rather than wards in hospital, the boom in public housing replaced the situation where several families would share the one tenement building, entertainment is found on the television in the living room rather than the theatre, the carry-out meal rivals communal dining and slowly work is being

---

[76] 1991 S.L.T. 828.

[77] In England the Court of Appeal can now substitute its own view: Clerk & Lindsell, *Law of Torts*, para. 21–02.

[78] Following *Landell v. Landell* (1841) 3 D. 819.

[79] 1988 S.L.T. 55.

[80] *Cooper v. MacIntosh* (1823) 3 Mur 359; *Scott v. McGavin* (1821) 2 Mur. 493. Evidence as to the pursuer's character may be led but if so the defender may attack it: *Hislop v. Staig* (1816) 1 Mur. 21. But see *Cleland v. Mack* (1829) 5 Mur. 72 and *Bryson v. Inglis* (1844) 6 D. 363.

[81] *Capital Life Assurance Society Ltd v. Scottish Daily Record and Sunday Mail*, cited by B. McKain in his Defamation Update Course, February 1997; Norrie, *Defamation and Related Actions in Scots Law*, p.165.

[82] See *James v. Baird*, 1916 S.C. 520; *Stein v. Beaverbrook*, 1968 S.C. 272; *Sarwar v. News Group*, May 29, 1998.

[83] *Sarwar v. News Group Newspapers*, 1999 S.L.T. 327, approving Walker, *Delict* (2nd ed.), p. 791.

carried out in small units or at home instead of in huge factories and offices. The technology of intrusion has expanded. Longer lenses, electronic surveillance and satellite technology mean that it is easier for privacy to be invaded. This issue raises again the response of the law to interests as opposed to conduct. Many cases can be met by protecting other interests involved or using existing remedies, such as nuisance, trespass or confidentiality.[84]

The idea that a legal right to privacy existed emerged most notably in an article in an American journal: Warren & Brandeis, "The Right of Privacy".[85] The claim was based on English common law[86] but obviously the U.S. constitution has been influential. The demand has been more recent in Scotland and the United Kingdom; mainly in the last few decades.[87] Scandals, many relating to the Royal Family, television personalities or politicians resulted in calls for action. These calls were met by reports which have been followed by inaction.[88] There has been useful comment in the Scottish legal journals.[89] Recommendations for a tort or delict of infringement of privacy are thus stalled. If this demand continues it may well be that in time there will be an increased recognition by the courts that conduct not otherwise wrongful is so if it infringes the privacy of another. The progress of the law on this pure question can be charted as having moved from that of Lord Justice-Clerk (Thomson) in 1957: "I know of no authority to the effect that mere invasion of privacy however hurtful and whatever its purpose and however repugnant to good taste is itself actionable"[90] to that of Lord Jauncey in *Henderson v. Fife Police*,[91] in which the order to a woman prisoner to remove her bra was held to be an infringement of liberty. The Court can, it is submitted, take this step at any time especially now that Article 8 of the European Convention on Human Rights has been enacted as effective in domestic law.[92]

---

[84] See the review in M. Hogg, "The Very Private Life of the Right to Privacy" in Hume, *Papers on Public Policy*, Vol. 2 No. 3 1994.

[85] (1890) Harv. L.R. 193.

[86] *Prince Albert v. Strange* (1849) 2 De G. & Sm. 293.

[87] Blom-Cooper, "The right to be let alone" (1989) J.L.S. 402.

[88] First Calcutt Report: Report of the Committee on Privacy and Related Matters, Cm. 1102 (June 1990); Second Calcutt Report: Review of Press Self-regulation, Cm. 2135 (Jan 1993); Lord Chancellor and Scottish Office: *Infringement of Privacy* (July 1993).

[89] A.J. Bonnington, "Privacy: letting the Right Alone" 1992 S.L.T. (News) 289; M.A. Hogg, "Privacy: A Valuable and Protected Interest in Scots Law" 1992 S.L.T. (News) 349; D. Carey-Miller, and H. Lardy, "Callcutt II: Comments from a Scots Perspective" 1993 S.L.T. (News) 199; G.T. Laurie, "Privacy, Paucity and the Press" 1993 S.L.T. (News) 285.

[90] Unrep. June 18, 1957. Cited by M. Hogg "The Very Private Life of the Right to Privacy", *op. cit.*

[91] 1981 S.L.T. 361.

[92] Human Rights Act 1998.

CHAPTER 9

LEGAL PROCESS

INTRODUCTION

General

This chapter considers wrongs done in connection with legal proceedings. **9–1** In a way there would appear to be no real reason for having a separate chapter of the law. However, in many political systems (our own included) access to the machinery of justice is considered an important aspect of the machinery of government. Access to justice imports a freedom to bring matters to a court for determination of grievances. Some checks have to be placed on the freedom to use the machinery of justice for its efficient functioning. In general in Scotland, the courts are open to all and there are limited instances of restraint. Some restraints are properly considered in books on the adjective law: thus this book does not deal with procedural devices such as the sisting of mandataries and the need for certain parties to find caution and other similar procedural devices.[1] In the same way that the Ritz Hotel is open to all, there are aspects of the legal aid scheme that bear upon the broader question of access to justice. Older books deal with wrongs in the legal process in considerable detail. This is probably because in earlier centuries much of the administration of justice was in private hands. For most of the twentieth century justice came more and more to be under the control of government administration. In the latter years of the century that trend became subject to scrutiny and in some cases, reversed. Accordingly the aim of this chapter has been to set out the principles with illustrations but not to chart the details of the application of the law to situations unlikely to be encountered again. This chapter does not deal with verbal injuries but there is an overlap as where judges use their position to insult persons in court or persons use pleadings to defame others.[2] In a sense the issue is the same because abuse of process and verbal injury have as a common ancestor the Roman *actio injuriarum*, but that ancestor is so distant that it is dangerous to treat the two lines of authority as easily interchangeable—especially so far as privilege and the requirement of probable cause is concerned. Some aspects of the legal process or wrongful use of it do not involve any special delict. So the wrongful arrest of an individual falls to be considered under wrongs to the person.[3]

---

[1] See MacPhail, *Sheriff Court Practice* (2nd ed., W. Green, 1998).
[2] See Chap. 8.
[3] See Chap. 4.

Perjury is a crime and it might be thought that on general principle a civil
action should succeed where harm has been done by perjury—it can hardly
be complained that the true cause was the failure to unmask it before the
fact finder. Negligent testimony would now generally be a matter of the law
of negligence.[4]

Many cases in this area of activity may raise human rights issues in the
future and some of the existing authorities may require review in that light.

Negligence

9–2 Carelessness in raising a civil action has been held not to be a source of
liability.[5] Policy dictates that persons are encouraged to take their disputes
to the court. The granting of a negligence action by the House of Lords in
an English case (followed in Scotland) in a situation previously thought to
be governed by the law of defamation would also suggest that negligence
can overcome the rules of a known head of liability.[6] One day that issue will
be directly addressed in this compartment of the law. For the moment it
must be assumed that the law reflects the proper balance between the
citizen's freedom to litigate and the citizen's freedom from litigation and
that the careless raising of litigation is something which must be tolerated.
It is in circumstances like this that the lesser wrong of carelessness must be
taken to be included within the greater wrong of intentional action. Many
actions would in any event be for economic loss in which case it might not
be fair just nor reasonable to impose a duty. Even then public policy
grounds may operate to exclude.

Expenses

9–3 The normal penalty for raising an ill-founded action is expenses against
unsuccessful litigants. That is no compensation to the winner for it usually
hardly even approaches the legal expenses of defending the case. A solicitor
who is not a party to an action can be made liable for the wasted expenses
of litigation. While very common in England, there is no direct authority in
Scots law although there are many cases where this is ordered or accepted.
Bankton says "If, during the dependence of a cause, an advocate discovers
that it is unjust or calumnious, he ought to desert it, in consequence of his
oath at his admission, and in point of conscience and justice to his
character"[7] In *Stewart v. Stewart*[8] a solicitor delayed an action negligently
being unaware of the merits of the defence. He was held liable by the
sheriff after an examination of the English cases:

> "It has long been recognised that for certain breaches of duty, such as
> failing to attend court, a solicitor may be found personally liable in

---

[4] In *Stanton v. Callaghan* [1998] T.L.R. 468, it was held in the Court of Appeal that an
expert witness is immune on grounds of public policy from an action in negligence as his
freedom to change his mind is an essential part of the judicial process. The logic of this is as
vulnerable as that supporting the barrister's immunity. See Chap. 12. The fear of liability in
negligence encourages risk management and care; immunity encourages arrogance.

[5] See *Ormiston v. Redpath Brown* (1866) 4 M. 488.

[6] *Spring v. Guardian Assurance Co.* [1995] A.C. 296; *Donlon v. Colonial Mutual Group*, 1997
S.C.L.R. 1088.

[7] IV,iii, 13.

[8] 1984 S.L.T. (Sh. Ct) 58.

expenses. In my opinion it is equally a breach of duty if a solicitor improperly uses the procedure of the court to delay the achievement of a result to which a litigant is entitled. When a pursuer asserts a claim by serving a summons or initial writ, he is entitled to the remedy he seeks unless his opponent can show some ground in fact or law why this should not be granted. If no appearance is entered, the pursuer is entitled to decree in absence. If appearance is entered and defences are lodged, the pleadings have to be adjusted and the law debated and the facts ascertained, and it may be months or years before the remedy is achieved. But this delay is not something to which a defender is entitled in order that he may postpone the discharge of his obligations. It arises solely because the time is required to ascertain the truth if there is a genuine dispute about the facts or the law. It seems to me to follow that if a defender who has no defence either in fact or in law uses the procedures not to establish his right but to delay the enforcement of a right which is undeniable, he is guilty of an abuse of process and, if he is a solicitor, ought to pay what his conduct has cost the other party to the litigation . . . I do not intend to suggest that a solicitor acts improperly in all cases by entering appearance and stating a defence which may turn out to be unsubstantial. It may be perfectly proper, if there is initially doubt about the facts or the law, to put in skeleton defences to preserve the position while investigations are made. But as soon as the facts and the law are elucidated, and it appears that there is no defence to the action, the defence should be withdrawn and decree allowed to pass. It is in my opinion improper to allow the defence to stand until the action reaches the head of the queue of cases awaiting disposal, and then to consent to decree. That is to use the intervening time not for the necessary purpose of determining disputed issues of fact or law, but for the improper purpose of delaying the enforcement of a right about which there is no longer any dispute . . . There were moreover at least three occasions when he ought particularly to have considered whether he should persist in the defence, first when legal aid was refused for want of probable cause, secondly at the hearing of the motion to find caution, when the defence was reiterated, and thirdly at the start of proceedings on the day of the proof, when it was intimated that the defence was maintained."[9]

Malice, Wrongful and Probable Cause

Professor Gretton with some justification says that "the test of 'maliciously **9–4** and without probable cause' is not a wholly clear one" and that the authorities are not very helpful.[10] In this chapter, the word malice is often used. In the context of diligence its meaning is perhaps clear from the exchange in the House of Lords between the Lord Chancellor (Haldane) and Lord Dunedin in the case of *Shields v. Shearer*,[11] the Lord Chancellor said:

---

[9] *ibid.* at 60–61.
[10] G.L. Gretton, *Inhibitions and Adjudications* (2nd. ed., 1996), p. 70.
[11] 1914 1 S.L.T. 360.

"Between malice in fact and in law there is a broad distinction, which is not peculiar to any particular system of jurisprudence. A person who inflicts an injury upon another person in contravention of the law is not allowed to say that he did so with an innocent mind; he is taken to know the law, and he can only act within the law. He may therefore be guilty of malice in law, although, so far as the state of his mind is concerned, he acts ignorantly, and in that sense innocently. Malice in fact is quite a different thing; it means an actual malicious intention on the part of the person who has done the wrongful act, and it may be, in proceedings based on wrongs independent of contract, a very material ingredient in the question of whether a valid cause of action can be stated."[12]

Lord Dunedin said:

"I think, perhaps, I had better add to what he has said that I think my noble and learned friend has used terms which are not perfectly familiar terms in Scotland—I mean 'malice in law' and 'Malice in fact'—but which are exactly represented, in the cases which have turned upon these matters, by the distinction between cases where malice may properly be inferred from the mere wrongful act that is done, and cases where it is necessary in the Scottish phraseology to aver facts and circumstances out of which malice may be inferred—such a case, for instance, as the case of *Beaton v. Ivory* (1887 14 R. 1057)."

That case itself decided that "maliciously" added nothing when the complaint was that a person was arrested without reasonable grounds of suspicion.

"Wrongful" appears in issues where malice in law type cases are considered. It does not mean wrongful in the sense of a breach of duty. It merely means not according to the applicable rules of law applying to the conduct complained of.

In *Strachan v. Stoddart*,[13] Lord Pitmilly said that "want of probable cause" was an English expression but not a technical one and thought that the court could not object to it, certainly because it was in the legislation for the protection of magistrates but also because the same concept was clear in Scots cases. The rest of the court concurred enthusiastically.

Public Officer

9–5 In earlier times much law focused on whether a person was a public officer. This concept is still very important,[14] but it is now probably seen within a wider concept of public policy so that it is no longer really necessary for a person to be employed publicly nor to be an officer for the special rules, if any there be to apply. The basic rule, which applies where the matter is governed by precedent, is that although a public officer may have com-

---

[12] *ibid.* Graham Stewart uses this terminology: *A Treatise on the Law of Diligence* (1898, reprinted 1985), p. 773.

[13] (1828) 7 S. 4.

[14] See the police arrest cases in Chap. 3.

mitted an error in the discharge of his duty, he cannot be made responsible without an allegation of malice and want of probable cause, especially when the error was not that of the officer but that of his superiors.[15] Public officers in the discharge of their duties are similarly protected. The protection is not absolute. "The law does not allow a public officer to run riot."[16] They are entitled to the protection of probable cause:

> "It is for the benefit of the public and for the interests of justice and good government that public officers acting in the execution of their duty should be surrounded by very considerable protection".[17]

The other point which should be made is that the need for the immunity is that there is probably liability on public officers for abuse of powers. There are few cases now, most issues under this head being dealt with under negligence. However, the dictum quoted above shows that the principle is alive and well.[18]

Judicial immunity

Superior court judges are immune to actions for damages.[19] In *McCreadie v. Thomson*[20] the pursuer complained that a magistrate was convicted and sentenced for breach of the peace under a statute which allowed for imprisonment instead of under one which did not. The complaint was framed on the basis of the statute. The magistrate's legal assessor pointed out the error but the magistrate persisted. It was accepted that this was an error and outside the jurisdiction of the magistrate. Lord Justice Clerk McDonald stated the general principle; **9–6**

> "Upon the question of immunity of the judges of the Supreme Court there can be no doubt. The principle is clear, and the decisions are emphatic. The principle is that such judges are the king's judges directly, bound to administer the law between his subjects, and even between his subjects and himself. To make them amenable to actions of damages for things done in their judicial capacity, to be dealt with by judges only their equals in authority and by juries, would be to make them not responsible to the king, but subject to other considerations than their duty to him in giving their decisions, and to expose them to be dealt with as servants, not of him, but of the public."[21]

The same rule is said to apply to sheriffs, often on the basis of *Harvey v. Dyce*[22] but that is a case of verbal injury, the report is very brief and the

---

[15] *Pyper v. Ingram* (1901) 3 F. 514.
[16] Lord Kinloch in *Urquhart v. Dick* (1865) 3 M. 932.
[17] *per* Lord President Inglis in *Beaton v. Ivory* (1887) 14 R. 1057 at 1062. See also *Robertson v. Keith*, 1936 S.C. 29.
[18] See also C.T. Reid, "Damages for Deliberate Abuse of Power" 1988 S.L.T. (News) 121.
[19] A. Olowofoyeku, "The Crumbling Citadel: Absolute Judicial Immunity De-rationalised" [1990] L.S. 271.
[20] (1907) 15 S.L.T. 216.
[21] *ibid.* at 216–217. See also Stair, IV,1,5; Ersk., I,ii,32; *Haggart's Trs v. Hope* (1824), 2 Sh. App. 125; *Harvey v. Dyce* (1876) 4 R. 265; *Primrose v. Waterston* (1902) 4 F. 783; *Pollock* (1829) 8 S. 1.
[22] (1876) 4 R. 265.

pursuer was a party litigant.[23] An earlier case in the House of Lords suggests that the protection might be limited to cases absent malice and want of probable cause certainly in cases of arrest. In *Watt v. Thomson*[24] the pursuer was a lawyer who took a process away from an interim interdict hearing despite being asked for it. He was arrested on a process caption granted by the sheriff, which itself was held to be a protected judicial proceeding. There were insufficient averments from which actual malice could be inferred merely that the judge was annoyed (rightly it was held) that the pursuer had not returned the process. Surprisingly the issue was raised in the recent case of *Russell v. Dickson*.[25] A sheriff seemed to entertain doubts about the conduct of an accused person's solicitor. As a result when the accused pled guilty the sheriff remanded the accused (not his solicitor) in custody so that inquiries could be made into the conduct of the case. On quashing the convictions the High Court held that the decision to remand was in excess of this powers. The proceedings were incompetent and the decision not to allow bail was described as excessive and unreasonable. In the subsequent damages action the temporary judge held that the sheriff was entitled to absolute immunity:

> "No doubt the sheriff could lose his immunity in certain situations, even in certain situations which might arise in the course of his sitting on the bench. Where, as here, he is dealing with a complaint and with the accused person who is before him it cannot be said that he is not acting as a judge."[26]

This decision must be doubted.[27] The simple fact that there is a complaint being dealt with does not mean the judge is actually carrying out his judicial function. It seems that being unable to do much about the solicitor in the case the judge was much harsher on the accused than was proper.[28]

So far as magistrates are concerned at common law, *McCreadie v. Thomson*[29] sets out the position. They cannot be made amenable for words used, however severely they may comment on the conduct of individuals, provided such words are uttered when acting in the exercise of their magisterial functions. It is accepted that the judge must be able to express himself freely in dealing with matters before him and

> "must not be hampered by apprehension that he may be sued in a civil court and subjected to damages, as if what he said had been uttered by him as an ordinary citizen, not acting in a public judicial capacity, it being uttered for what presumably at the time seemed to him to be good

---

[23] The Lord President relied on *Scott v. Stansfield* [1868] L.R. 3 Ex. 22 which had been cited in argument

[24] (1870) 8 M. (H.L.) 77.

[25] 1998 S.L.T. 96.

[26] *ibid*. at 101E. He considered himself bound by dicta in *Harvey v. Dyce* (1876) 4 R. 265.

[27] *ibid*. at 101. The temporary judge reached his conclusion reluctantly and thought the result at best anachronistic.

[28] *ibid*. The learned temporary judge considered the *Stair Memorial Encyclopedia*, Vol. 15, "Obligations", para. 518 and D.L. Carey-Miller, "Defamation by a Judge" 1980 J.R. 88. Both contributions are in respect of defamation rather than imprisonment.

[29] (1907) 15 S.L.T. 216.

and just cause. But while this is so, it is a totally different question whether a magistrate who does official acts when sitting as such which he has no power to do under a statute in accordance with which he is bound to act, and which judicial acts have the effect of restraining the liberty of the subject, and subjecting him to penalty in his person, is immune from civil consequences for the wrong he has done. I do not think that this has ever been held, and the opposite has been held in many cases. Where a magistrate, professing to sit as such, and dealing with a case which he has no jurisdiction to deal with at all, commits what is an undoubted wrong upon a citizen, both by principle and practice he is held liable for the wrong done."[30]

The court then dealt with the distinction, still discussed, between acts outside the jurisdiction and cases of excess of jurisdiction:

"The wrong is as great in the latter as in the former. For as well might he have no jurisdiction at all as step outside the jurisdiction which he does possess, to do something which he could not do if he held himself within the limits prescribed to him by the law under which he was called to exercise his jurisdiction."[31]

It was held that where there is no jurisdiction the error is so gross that it is equal to *dole* and there is no need to establish malice. In the later case of *MacPhee v. Macfarlane's Executor*[32] the pursuer was imprisoned on a warrant granted under statutory powers. The Inner House held no error had been made. Lord Clyde stated the law had there been an error. There were no averments of malice and the pursuer relied on *McCreadie*. A statutory defence available to magistrates requiring proof of malice and want of probable cause was also pled. Lord Clyde appeared to support the point that at common law there was no need to show malice in an *ultra vires* case and indeed that even the statute would offer no protection:

"Even if I had thought that the magistrate erred in thinking that section 24 warranted the continuations granted by him, I should still have thought him protected by section 59. The pursuer's case is wholly apart from any malice on the part of the magistrate, or any want of probable cause for the course he took. It appears from the Sheriff-Substitute's note that the practice, not only in Glasgow, but throughout Scotland, ever since the Act of 1908 came into force, supports the action of the magistrate. How could he be made answerable in damages for an error in the interpretation of the statute which he made in common with practically all other Scottish magistrates? The answer to this, which is made on behalf of the pursuer, is that section 59 will only protect a magistrate so long as he does not act *ultra vires*. Now that is a perfectly sound proposition, for if a magistrate acts in a way in which it is outwith his duty as a magistrate to act, his robe falls from his shoulders and

---

[30] *ibid.* at 1183.
[31] *ibid.* at 1184.
[32] 1933 S.L.T. 148.

section 59 ceases to apply. But a magistrate does not necessarily act outside his powers as a magistrate because he makes an honest mistake in applying the law. Prior to the passing of the Summary Jurisdiction (Scotland) Act, 1908, there are cases—of which *McCreadie v. Thomson* (1907 S.C. 1176) is the last—which support the doctrine that a mistake (in a matter which affects personal liberty)—even an honest mistake in interpreting the statutes which regulate the discharge of a magistrate's jurisdiction—may form the ground of an action of reparation, apart altogether from malice. Even in the cases referred to it was recognised that the mistake had to be a glaring one, or the irregularity gross, before liability could be incurred. But the doubts and difficulties to which the doctrine illustrated by these cases were exposed are removed by section 59 of the 1908 Act, which requires, *inter alia*, that malice and want of probable cause shall be alleged."[33]

It was held in *Watt v. Thomson*[34] that sheriffs' clerks have no special protection like that of the sheriff.

Statutory Immunity

9–7 The present immunity by statute is provided by section 170 of the Criminal Procedure (Scotland) Act 1995. That Act provides that no judge, clerk of court or prosecutor in the public interest may be found liable for or in respect of any proceedings taken, any act done or any judgment, decree or sentence pronounced in summary proceedings under the 1995 Act unless the person has been imprisoned, the sentence has been quashed and malice and want of probable cause are averred.[35] It is a defence to show that the person suing was guilty of the offence concerned and that he had undergone no greater punishment than was assigned by law to such offence.[36] There is a two month limitation period unless a shorter period is fixed.[37] Importantly it has been held in relation to similar legislation that

---

[33] *ibid.* at 154. Lord Sands expressly agreed but reserved his opinion on the precise scope of *McCreadie*: "I am not disposed to quarrel in any way with the doctrine that where a magistrate acts completely ultra vires he may be made answerable for what he does. Whether a mistake in the construction of an Act of Parliament, coupled with a certain view of the common law such as occurred in the case of *McCreadie*, amounts to *ultra vires* is a question on which it is difficult to arrive at the same conclusion as in the case of *McCreadie*. Of course the case of *McCreadie* must be regarded, unless reviewed, as binding upon us. But it was a somewhat special case, and I shall not regard it as binding unless the circumstances are that the magistrate before whom the accused is brought charged with a statutory offence takes it upon him to sentence the accused as if it had been a common law offence. If these were the particular circumstances we should probably be bound to follow *McCreadie*. I should reconsider the matter in any other circumstances. In *Russell v. Dickson*, 1998 S.L.T. 96 at 100 the temporary judge, it is submitted correctly, stated that any distinguishing as is suggested in the rubric of *MacPhee* was *obiter*."

[34] (1870) 8 M. (H.L.) 77.

[35] s. 170(1).

[36] s. 170(2).

[37] There are many authorities under legislation to a similar effect in previous criminal procedure and cognate Acts: *Rae v. Strathern*, 1924 S.C. 147; *Graham v. Strathern*, 1924 S.C. 699. Cases on computation under previous legislation include *Hill v. Dymock* (1857) 19 D. 955; *Ashley v. Magistrates of Rothesay* (1873) 11 M. 708, this latter holding that a summons served (not signetted) on the June 15 was timeous in respect of a wrong committed on April 15. The roots of this provisions it has been pointed out were derived from English law: *Strachan v. Stoddart* (1828) 7 S. 4, *per* Lord Pitmilly at 6.

the act which is sought to be protected must be essentially within the scope of the judicial function.[38]

CIVIL LITIGATION

General

The only penalty for failure in an action is generally an award of expenses **9-8** as taxed.[39] Generally a party having title and interest to oppose can oppose any proceedings he wishes subject only to an award of expenses being made against him.[40] Normally this is a sufficient deterent. In civil cases two early cases suggest that clear evidence of malice and want of probable cause is required.[41] Using process moderately and in good faith results in no liability and there must be an averment of malice and want of probable cause.[42] The basic rule applies

> "Where a person acts in the exercise of a legal right and in the ordinary use of legal forms of procedure, and where it is said that he has abused that right, the law holds that malice or an intention to injure must be proved, and also that it must be shewn that he had no probable cause for what he did"[43]

When an action in court has been settled but agents continue to take decree, this attracts liability but on the basis that such conduct infers the necessary malice and lack of probable cause.[44] Where statute provided for arbitration and the parties sought a ruling on the interpretation of the legislation instead of arbitration, the judge in the Outer House considered that this could be an abuse of process, compelling the court to grant an order when it was clear the statute had provided another course. This was held not to be the case in the Inner House—the judge being obliged to resolve the question put by the litigants.[45]

Wrongful Diligence

The law is well settled as a result of many decisions in previous centuries **9-9** when it appears that law agents and messengers at arms were perhaps less well organised, educated and regulated as today they are. Nonetheless, mistakes are still made and there is always the possibility of the creditor making mistakes or misinforming agents and messengers. The creditor is

---

[38] *McCrone v. Sawers* (1835) 13 S. 443; *Fergusson v. McNab* (1885) 12 R. 1083.

[39] *Kennedy v. Police Commissioners of Fort William* (1877) 5 R. 302 *per* Lord Gifford at 307: "The costs of suit are the damages for bringing a groundless claim."

[40] *Gordon v. Royal Bank* (1826) 5 S. 164; (1846) *Walker v. Gemmill* 8 D. 838.

[41] *Somerville v. Thomson*, May 19, 1815, F.C.; 6 Pat. App. 393; *Cleland v. Lawrie* (1848) 10 D. 1372.

[42] *per* Lord President Inglis in *Kinnes v. Adam* (1882) 9 R. 698 at 702. This claim was founded on a sequestration which had been recalled on purely technical grounds.

[43] *Henning v. Hewetson* (1852) 14 D. 487, *per* Lord Justice-Clerk Hope at 488.

[44] *Davies v. Brown* (1867) 5 M 842.

[45] *Strathclyde Regional Council v. Glasgow District Council,* 1992 S.L.T. 51.

always liable even although he has employed independent contractors.[46] It is accepted that there is a distinction to be made between diligence done as of right, in which malice and want of probable cause must be shown and other cases, such as interdict where the creditor requires to make a representation to the court to obtain the order. Such a statement must be true, and if it was not and but for it the court would not have granted the order then there is in effect strict liability.[47] However, that statement must be qualified. First "as of right" is a rather fluid concept as is apparent from *MacRobbie v. McLellan's Trustees*,[48] in which the defenders were agents who obtained decree for expenses in an action of maills and duties irregularly and then charged in respect of that decree. The pursuer had the charge suspended. It was held unnecessary to aver and prove malice and want of probable cause. This it appears is because the decree having been taken very wrongly the diligence following it which would normally be thought of as being carried out as of right, in this case was not.[49] Graham Stewart accepts that in cases of interdict there may be no liability if the case is one where the status quo has not been inverted. The classic statement in *Wolthekker* says it does not matter that the statement was in good faith or not that it must be "unjustifiable" for liability to attach. Whether that word is important or not is not clear.[50] The thought that "unjustifiable" allows the creditor to comment on the grounds for the mis-statement—perhaps to show that as well as being in good faith he took at least reasonable care—is rather negatived by *Fife v. Orr*.[51] In that case interim interdict was applied to stop the sale of certain goods. Unfortunately some of the goods were never really at issue. The defender was right so far as nine out of 266 articles were concerned. His condescendence accepted he did not own all the goods but "this was not brought forward by him in such a prominent way as to attract the attention of the Sheriff, and in particular, the complainer did not directly inform the sheriff that he did not desire interdict to the full extent."[52] The Lord President (Robertson) said:

> "It seems perfectly clear that the contention of Mr Campbell that liability for damages is to be determined by the fairness and reasonableness of the person who applies for interdict is not borne out by the authorities. If any person asks interdict on statements of fact made by him to the Judge he does so at his own peril, and the mere circumstance that he may have been misled, or sanguine, will not justify him in a question with the person whom he has injured."[53]

Graham Stewart[54] made the distinction, accepted by Maher and Cusine,[55] between orders obtained on a warrant and those on *ex parte* statements.

---

[46] *Anderson v. Ormiston and Lorain* (1750) Mor. 13949.

[47] *Wolthekker v. Northern Agricultural Co.* (1862) 1 M. 211.

[48] (1891) 18 R. 470.

[49] *ibid., per* Lord McLaren at 475.

[50] It is not reproduced in Scott Robinson, *The Law of Interdict*, (2nd. ed., Butterworths, 1994).

[51] (1895) 23 R. 8.

[52] *ibid., per* Lord McLaren at 11.

[53] *ibid.* at 10.

[54] *A Treatise on the Law of Diligence* (1898, reprinted 1985).

[55] *The Law and Practice of Diligence* (Butterworths, 1990), para. 12.1.

The general rule is that action taken on *ex parte* statements is *periculo petentis*. But Graham Stewart says that it is a matter of circumstance—there may be interdict cases where the status quo is not inverted and these may have to be dealt with differently. Interim interdict which is obtained *periculo petentis* does not require proof of malice and want of probable cause.[56] This is not an inflexible rule and is not applied where the interdict protects established possession on a habile title until some dispute is settled.[57] However, in the most cases where *ex parte* statements are made and diligence follows the diligence is wrongful if the statements are not correct. It has even been decided that this applies even if there is information withheld. In *Fife v. Orr*[58] owners of property interdicted a sale. However, they knew and said as much in the condescendence that they were aware that the sale comprised other property. It turned out only a small amount of property was theirs. It was held that they had not been frank enough with the court. No one is liable for enforcing an *ex facie* regular decree.[59] An incompetent warrant does not protect the creditor.[60]

It is wrongful to do diligence when it has been agreed to delay such.[61] If the creditor has exaggerated the sum, he and neither the agent nor the messenger is liable.[62] Arrestment on the dependence, although it can cause considerable loss is not actionable without proof of malice and want of probable cause.[63] The same is true of arrestment generally. Subject to malice and lack of probable cause wrongful arrestment will found an action.[64] If however, the proceedings themselves are inept then there is no need to show malice and want of probable cause. *Brodie v. Young*[65] was a case concerning allegedly nimious arrestments, the defender having dropped his case. The court held that malice and want of probable cause had to be averred.[66] In *Houlden v. Couper*[67] the pursuer raised an action of damages against the trustee of his bankrupt sons for having caused the pursuer's house to be entered by an auctioneer and an inventory of the furniture and effects there made. The pursuer was successful after trial and damages of £90 were awarded. The defender had claimed that the actings of the pursuer and his sons had given him good grounds for suspicion but the trial judge had refused to give the jury such a direction. Before the Inner House on a bill of exceptions Lord President (Inglis) said that the judge was correct to charge the jury that if the house belonged to the

---

[56] *Miller v. Hunter* (1865) 3 M. 740; *Kennedy v. Police Commissioners of Fort William* (1877) 5 R. 302.

[57] *Moir v. Hunter* (1832) 11 S. 30; *Kennedy v. Police Commissioners of Fort William* (1877) 5 R. 302.

[58] (1895) 23 R. 8.

[59] *Aitken v. Finlay* (1837) 15 S. 683.

[60] *Bell v. Gunn* (1859) 21 D. 1008; *Ormiston v. Redpath Brown & Co.* (1866) 4 M. 488.

[61] *Cameron v. Mortimer* (1872) 10 M. 817.

[62] *Henderson v. Rollo* (1871) 10 M. 104.

[63] *Wolthekker v. Northern Agricultural Co.* (1862) 1 M 211; *Kennedy v. Police Commissioners of Fort William, ibid.*

[64] *Wolthekker, ibid.*; *Henning v. Hewetson* (1852) 14 D. 487; *Lord Duffus v. Davidson* (1828) 4 Mur. 558; *Hallam v. Gye* (1835) 14 S. 199.

[65] (1851) 13 D. 737.

[66] *Henning v. Hewetson, ibid.*; *Mantle v. Miller* (1856) 18 D 398; *Ford v. Muirhead* (1858) 20 D. 951.

[67] (1871) 9 S.L.R. 169.

pursuer and the furniture in it was the pursuer's, then they should find for him. The defender's belief was irrelevant and the actings of the pursuer and his sons had not featured in the evidence.[68] *In Dramgate Ltd v. Tyne Dock Engineering,*[69] arrestment on the dependence was carried out on a ship but without jurisdiction so to do because there had been a failure to arrest the ship to found jurisdiction. It was held that as in this case the arrestment was wholly unjustifiable, then the defenders could not have the protection of malice and want of probable cause. In so ruling Lord Penrose commented that the malice and want of probable cause protection was no longer treated as an absolute as it had in the past.[70]

CRIMINAL PROSECUTION

Criminal Proceedings

9–10 It has long been settled that a public prosecutor can only be liable on proof of malice and want of probable cause. It is a pre-requisite that the pursuer has been acquitted of the charge or the charge has been abandoned against him. In *Hill v. Campbell*[71] the pursuer admitted he had been convicted and that was fatal. It was also emphasised in that case that facts must be averred from which malice may legitimately be inferred.[72] It is not sufficient that there has been a mistaken view of the law taken to establish want of probable cause. In *Craig* v. *Peebles,*[73] the pursuer was able to show his conviction in the Justices Court had been suspended by the Court of Justiciary. The following passage of the Lord Justice-Clerk admirably sets out the law:

> "I am very far from saying that in ordinary circumstances, where an allegation of want of probable cause is necessary, a general allegation to that effect is not sufficient. Although it rests upon the pursuer of such an action to prove want of probable cause, it may be partly proved by the defender's inability to shew probable cause. But it would be of the worst example to allow mere words to become the foundation for a trial."[74]

Turning to the case before him the Lord Justice-Clerk explained that the record showed the issue was one of fact and law and legal inference from facts upon which people might reasonably differ. Indeed he had sat on the Justiciary suspension and was "far from thinking the question one free from doubt."[75] Nor is it sufficient that the charge is irrelevant.[76] Both malice and probable cause are required:

---

[68] *ibid.* at 170.
[69] 1999 S.C.L.R. 1.
[70] In cases such as the leading case of *Wolthekkar, ibid.*
[71] (1905) 8 F. 220.
[72] *ibid.* at 224, on the authority of *Beaton v. Ivory* (1887) 14 R. 1057.
[73] (1876) 3 R. 441.
[74] *ibid.* at 445.
[75] *ibid.* at 446.
[76] *Mains v. MacLullich* (1861) 23 D. 1258.

"if a man's malice is as foul and black as it can be represented, yet if he has probable cause for the complaint he cannot be liable to any action for a malicious prosecution; and, on the other hand, if it has been found that he has no probable cause for the complaint, but his mind was devoid of malice, neither can an action be maintained."[77]

There is no need to aver malice and want of probable cause where there is execution of an illegal warrant.[78] The law has remained the same through the twentieth century.[79] The practical effect of this branch of the law is limited. The Lord Advocate is, and has been for some time, immune from action in respect of solemn matters.[80] In relation to solemn proceedings the Criminal Procedure (Scotland) Act 1887 brought the fiscal under the authority of the Lord Advocate in solemn matters and allowed him the same immunity.[81] In summary matters the Procurators Fiscal and deputes acting under his authority have always been liable to damages under various statutes.[82] If there is a conviction which stands no action is possible on the doctrine of *res judicata* let alone the statute.[83] It is not possible by seeking reparation to review a decision of the High Court of Justiciary.[84]

Wrongful prosecution

The protection given to criminal prosecutors has been extended to others **9–11** who have made accusations to the accused or others.[85] Thus there is still the need to show malice and want of probable cause which is to say that he must have a genuine belief in the truth or probable truth of the accusation or the information conveyed based on reasonable grounds. The policy of the law requires that men should be protected who bring forward accusations founded upon probable cause.[86] A private prosecutor has no immunity nor the benefit of the statutory defence but as is well known private prosecutions are rare. Cases by education authorities for poor school attendances are very numerous in the district courts and run in the name of the authority. In *MacAuley v. School Board of North Uist,*[87] the action complained of was an action by a school board official. It was clear they had used the wrong procedure which resulted in the present pursuer serving a

---

[77] *Young v. Leven* (1822) 1 Sh. App. 179. See *Urquat v. Dick* (1865) 3 M. 932. A wide scope is given to prosecutors because *animus injurandi* is not wrong in a procurator fiscal who is "one whose duty it is to be a terror to evil doers": *per* Lord Neaves *Craig v. Peebles* (1876) 3 R. 441 at 447.

[78] *Bell v. Black & Morrison* (1865) 3 M. 1026.

[79] *Hill v. Campbell* (1905) 8 F. 220; *Mills v. Kelvin & White,* 1913 S.C. 521; *Notman v. Commercial Bank of Scotland,* 1938 S.C. 522.

[80] *Henderson v. Robertson* (1853) 15 D. 292; *Hester v. McDonald,* 1961 S.C. 370.

[81] *Hester, ibid.*

[82] *Summary Procedure (Scotland) Act 1864.*

[83] *Gilchrist v. Anderson* (1838) 1 D. 37; *Mclellan v. Miller* (1832) 11 S. 187; *Kennedy v. Wise* (1890) 17 R. 1036.

[84] *Moore v. Secretary of State for Scotland,* 1985 S.L.T. 38.

[85] *Ferguson v. Colquhoun* (1862) 24 D. 1428; *Lightbody v. Gordon* (1882) 9 R. 934; *Hassan v. Paterson* (1885) 12 R. 1164; *Cassidy v. Connochie,* 1907 S.C. 1112; *West v. Mackenzie,* 1917 S.C. 513; *Croucher v. Inglis* (1889) 16 R. 77.

[86] *Lightbody v. Gordon* (1882) 9 R. 934.

[87] (1887) 15 R. 99.

term of imprisonment. However, it was held that as they were acting in the public interest and under a public duty it was necessary to aver and prove malice and want of probable cause. In the case of complainers malice and want of probable cause is required.[88] Recklessness in making the complaint may infer malice and want of probable cause.[89] The complaint must be made regularly and not repeated after it has been made.[90] A complainer who discovers facts which negate the charge should not allow the prosecution to continue.[91]

---

[88] *Rae v. Linton* (1875) 2 R. 669; *Green v. Chalmers* (1888) 6 R. 318; *Dallas v. Mann* (1853) 15 D. 746; *Thomson v. Adam* (1865) 4 M. 29.
[89] *Denholm v. Thomson* (1880) 8 R. 31.
[90] *Henderson v. Henderson* (1855) 17 D. 348; *Walker v. Cumming* (1868) 6 M. 318.
[91] *Richmond v. Thomson* (1838) 16 S. 995.

CHAPTER 10

NEGLIGENCE

Negligence simply means lack of care. The law is called into play by **10–1** pursuers who are usually unhappy at a *result*. The claim is opposed by a defender who will certainly dispute the legal effect of the result but who can be expected to raise the matter of his *conduct*. Scots law, which is adversarial and founded on ideas of corrective justice, is also shaped by its own curious history. The Roman law tradition derived from the *lex aquilia* established liability for loss "wrongfully" caused. Later civilian developments allowed "wrongfully" to be interpreted as culpably. Lack of care is one form of *culpa*. Thus in the civilian tradition the way was open for some cases of lack of care to have the legal consequence of damages. It is to be noted, however, in that tradition there was a view which required that the damage (result) was to a legally recognised interest before the pursuer could get off the ground. Indigenous Scots remedies, such as assythment, charted in Stair were initially remedial and result orientated. The contemporary legal response in Scotland to lack of care is centred around the legal concept of a duty of care. While the concept of "duty" is recognised by natural lawyers like Stair, it did not in itself form a focus for decision in Stair's law. By the end of the nineteenth century actions for death from personal injury and actions for personal injury conflate and there are numerous instances of liability for lack of care, derived partly from the assythment tradition and perhaps borrowed from the civilian tradition. As shall be seen, Scots law in the early twentieth century came together with English legal thinking to adopt a duty of care model as the primary legal tool for deciding which cases of lack of care would or would not be actionable.[1]

(A) THE DUTY OF CARE

The universally accepted but yet debated analysis is to look for a loss **10–2** caused by a breach of a duty of care. The duty is determined by the law (in the context of the factual matrix) and is the most difficult element of the factors which make up a negligence case to advise upon—this is because

---

[1] Black, in a full historical analysis of the law, accepted that the duty of care concept is part of the law of Scotland: R. Black, "A historical survey of delictual liability in Scotland for personal injuries and death." [1975] C.I.L.J.S.A. 46,189,316; [1976] 9 C.I.L.J.S.A. 57. Interestingly an English academic has recently argued that the stage has now been reached such that the duty concept should be abandoned and replaced by a fault principle: B. Hepple, "Negligence: the Search for Coherence" [1998] C.L.P. 69 at 93. Note that he proposes that compensation for personal injury and death would be removed from the tort system.

causation is meant to be a common sense matter and breach is determined by the evidence of those who know about the activity. Duty has a positive practical value. If it has been held before that there is a duty then there is no need for sophisticated legal arguments. If there is a duty in precedent organisations can take practical decisions as to precautions or insurance. It gives this branch of the law of obligations the same kind of predictive value as the law of contract. The difficulties appear when there is no precedent and it has to be asked whether there is or is not a duty. It is the duty element which is the responsibility of the lawyer to investigate and, if challenged, to argue.

10–3   At the time of writing there are three main principles, guides or tests as to the existence of a duty, and one shadow or ghost principle which infuses many of the cases, even from the last ten years. How each relates to the other is not yet clear. Nor can it be said that the principles themselves are secure. They are noted in this paragraph imperfectly and briefly to allow for further discussion only. These are:

(1) the neighbour principle where there is a duty if it is reasonably foreseeable that the defender's contemplated conduct will harm the pursuer, a principle probably restricted to physical injury and perhaps applicable to property damage;

(2) the reliance or *Hedley Byrne* principle[2] whereby loss (including economic loss) is recoverable if the pursuer relied on the defender and it was reasonable that he should so rely, or alternatively put: the defender assumed responsibility towards the pursuer;

(3) the incremental/pragmatic principle whereby it is asked whether it is fair, just and reasonable to impose a duty where none has been imposed before. Due regard must be had to extending the law only by analogy with previous cases.

There is a fourth, temporarily partially rejected, principle based on (1) and (2) which held sway for some time. It pulls together these ideas and emphasises a concept of proximity. It was expressed by Lord Wilberforce in *Anns v. Merton*[3]:

"Through the trilogy of cases in this House *Donoghue v. Stevenson*, *Hedley Byrne & Co. Ltd v. Heller & Partners Ltd* and *Home Office v. Dorset Yacht Co. Ltd*, the position has now been reached that in order to establish that a duty of care arises in a particular situation it is not necessary to bring the facts of that situation within those of previous situations in which the duty of care has been held to exist. Rather the question has to be approached in two stages. First one has to ask whether, as between the alleged wrongdoer and the person who has suffered damage there is a sufficient relationship of proximity or neighbourhood such that, in the reasonable contemplation of the former, carelessness on his part may be likely to cause damage to the latter, in

---

[2] From *Hedley Byrne & Co. Ltd v. Heller & Partners Ltd* [1964] A.C. 465.
[3] [1978] A.C. 728.

which case a prima facie duty of care arises. Secondly, if the first question is answered affirmatively, it is necessary to consider whether there are any considerations which ought to negative, or to reduce or limit the scope of the duty or the class of person to whom it is owed or the damages to which a breach of it may give rise."[4]

Anns also brought the idea of proximity into greater focus as it could be argued to be a requirement of the *Anns* formulation. On one view proximity simply restates reasonable foreseeability or it can be another expression of remoteness of injury. As time went by proximity began to take on a more symbolic meaning and eventually became a rhetorical focus for deciding that there might not be liability. Later developments, particularly the pragmatic/incremental approach favouring defenders have made it less regularly discussed.[5] The last quarter of a century has seen an oscillation in approach between these principles and other ideas unparalleled in legal history. The House of Lords has changed its mind completely once and now regularly lays down important decisions by majorities of 3–2. In the nineteenth century there were only a small number of academic lawyers to help but now there are a huge number. Judges sometimes take account of that work. The diversity found among the judges is often multiplied in the universities and so it remains the case that clear simple principles are not to be found. Indeed there is an approach, which will be noted in this chapter, which relies heavily on incrementalism in the detection of new duties which is a partial retreat from principle.[6]

Against that background, this chapter is written within legal practice on the assumption that there can be right answers in hard cases and that it is necessary to examine very carefully the cases which determine the result in later cases.[7]

Established Duties

Where the law has already ruled that in certain typical factual circum- **10–4** stances there is in law a duty, then the benefit of a system of precedent and *stare decisis* is that the law is settled. Well before the start of the twentieth century negligence could found an action for damage to property and for injury to a person or for the death of a relative.[8] The wheel need not be reinvented and the leading cases need not be canvassed anew in what are essentially variations of well known cases. So it is not, as some seem to

---

[4] *Anns v. Merton* at 751.

[5] Lord Oliver said in *Alcock v. Chief Constable of South Yorkshire Police* [1992] 1 A.C. 310: "And in the end it has to be accepted that the concept of "proximity" is an artificial one which depends more upon the court's perception of what is the reasonable area for the imposition of liability than upon any logical process of analogical deduction . . . in deciding [the question of proximity] the court has reference to no defined criteria and the decision necessarily reflects to some extent the court's concept of what policy—or perhaps common sense—requires."

[6] Unless of course one adopts as a principle, pragmatism. See, *e.g.* Brint and Weaver (eds) *Pragmatism in Law & Society* (Westview Press, Boulder, 1991). See especially the chapter by Dworkin, "Pragmatism, Right Answers, and True Banality", p. 359.

[7] See Dworkin, *op. cit.* for the (correct) argument that this is a weak and commonsensical claim and not some attempt to reveal a metaphysical truth.

[8] See Chap. 1.

think, a new duty if a person is run down by a snowmobile or a jet ski rather than a motor car.[9] The only difference is that it will be harder to say that the duty was breached—what particular things should have been done by the jet-skier. It may be possible for a new principle to subsume an older one and for the paradigm to shift. The movement of negligence itself into activities formerly controlled by other delicts is an example. However, care must be taken not to take it for granted that this has happened, especially if the older theory of liability is easier to aver and prove.[10]

The Neighbour Principle

10–5 Until the enunciation of the neighbour principle there was no universal rule that carelessness meant liability. Indeed there were, and still are, important decisions, especially in economic loss in the opposite direction.[11] It is against that background that the next case should be seen. It did not invent liability for negligence. It has not been the last word and it was not the first. It did lay down a general principle from which it could be said in new types of cases that there was a legal duty. Most significantly of all it was the case in which the duty of care method of regulating negligence was established.

10–6 In *Donoghue v. Stevenson*[12] the facts were never established as the case proceeded on averments assumed to be true as is still the procedure in Scotland. Thus what follows refers to what was alleged for the purposes of the legal arguments. The pursuer was in a cafe with a friend. The friend ordered for the pursuer—ice cream and ginger beer (a soft drink) suitable to be used with ice cream as an iced drink. Her friend was supplied by the said cafe proprietor with a bottle of ginger beer manufactured by the defender for sale to members of the public. The bottle was made of dark opaque glass. The cafe proprietor poured some of the ginger beer from the bottle into a tumbler containing the ice cream. The pursuer then drank some of the contents of the tumbler. Her friend then lifted the ginger beer bottle and was pouring out the remainder of the contents into the pursuer's tumbler when a decomposed snail, which had been, unknown to the pursuer, her friend, or the cafe owner, in the bottle, floated out of the bottle.[13] Mrs Donoghue sued for pain and suffering as a result of realising

---

[9] In a case of direct physical injury the law is governed by the neighbour principle and there is no need for a duty enquiry. In particular it is not necessary to ask whether it is fair, just and reasonable to impose a duty.

[10] In *Reitze v. Strathclyde Regional Council*, 1999 G.W.D. 17–810, the pursuer complained that the defenders had negligently allowed himself and his stepdaughter to be taken whitewater rafting by insufficiently trained instructors. It was held and supported on appeal that these averments were suitable for inquiry. The case seems to have been pled on the basis of assumption of responsibility and negligent misrepresentation. Theoretically that is possible but, with respect, in many cases that would be to peril the case unnecessarily—the case being one of physical injury foreseeability would be sufficient. Certainly it would be an argument of some elegance to enhance a basic neighbour case with an argument that the tougher reliance model could be satisfied. In a case, perhaps like this one, it might be that on the facts the easiest thing to prove was that the defenders assumed responsibility for the safety of the pursuer and with that confidence the case was pled accordingly.

[11] See paras 10–16 *et seq*.

[12] 1932 S.C. (H.L.) 31. See generally J.C. Smith and P. Burns "*Donoghue v. Stevenson*—The Not-So-Golden Anniversary" (1983) 46 M.L.R. 147.

[13] See Lord Rodger's reconstruction of the facts of the case and his attempt to sketch a life of Mrs Donoghue at [1988] C.L.P. 1.

that she had ingested the polluted brew. She was successful in the Outer House, unsuccessful in the Inner House by a 3–1 majority but the House of Lords allowed the case to proceed to proof before answer by a 3–2 majority. The case settled thereafter. It was never judicially established that the snail was actually in the bottle.

The case is important for two main reasons: **10–7**

(1) it held a manufacturer to be liable to a consumer who had no contract with the manufacturer, who himself had a contract with the retailer and argued that his obligations should be limited to the contracting party. This is the "manufacturer" ratio of the case which is discussed in more detail in the chapter on product liability[14]; and

(2) in establishing liability where there had been none before, the House of Lords had to explain the basis of that liability. In so doing as a matter of logic it was possible that the same principle would explain existing cases of liability for negligence and provide a principle from which liability could be deduced in other cases. This is the "neighbour" principle.

As a preliminary point it should be said that while *Donoghue* is a decision of the House of Lords in a Scottish appeal, Scots law was not argued nor discussed in it in any detail. As Lord Atkin put it:

"The case has to be determined in accordance with Scots law, but it has been a matter of agreement between the experienced counsel who argued this case, and it appears to be the basis of the judgment of the learned judges of the Court of Session, that, for the purposes of determining this problem, the laws of Scotland and of England are the same. I speak with little authority on this point, but my own research, such as it is, satisfies me that the principles of the law of Scotland on such a question as the present are identical with these of English law, and I discuss the issue on that footing. The law of both countries appears to be that, in order to support an action for damages for negligence, the complainant has to show that he has been injured by he breach of a duty owed to him in the circumstances by the defendant to take reasonable care to avoid such injury."

The same view was taken in the of Lord Macmillan's speech[15]:

"At your Lordship's bar counsel for both parties to the present appeal, accepting, as I do also, the view that there is no distinction between the law of Scotland and the law of England in the legal principles applicable to the case, confined their arguments to the English authorities."

This has led many to wonder whether or not this was an English imposition or innovation. The first point is that both the Lord Ordinary and one

---

[14] See Chap. 15.
[15] The published version. See A. Rodger, "Lord Macmillan's Speech" (1992) 108 L.Q.R. 236.

dissenting member of the Inner House had already found for Mrs. Donoghue. The other is that, as indicated above, the language of duty was not unknown in Scotland. The most interesting contribution to this inquiry is the revelation of the text of a "Scottish" draft of Lord Macmillan's speech.[16] In any event the position now is that there is no disputing the law is the same in both jurisdictions—even if it changes regularly![17]

Lord Atkin's dictum

10-8   "But acts or omissions which any moral code would censure cannot, in a practical world, be treated so as to give a right to every person injured by them to demand relief. In this way rules of law arise which limit the range of complaints, and the extent of their remedy. The rule that you are to love your neighbour becomes in law, you must not injure your neighbour; and the lawyer's question, who is my neighbour? receives a restricted reply. You must take reasonable care to avoid acts or omissions which you can reasonably foresee would be likely to injure your neighbour. Who, then, in law, is my neighbour? The answer seems to be—persons who are so closely and directly affected by my act that I ought reasonably to have them in contemplation as being so affected when I am directing my mind to the acts or omissions which are called in question."[18]

This dictum, constituting or expressing the wider ratio of the case was stated against the caveat:

"To seek a complete logical definition of the general principle is probably to go beyond the function of the judge, for the more general the definition the more likely it is to omit essentials or to introduce non-essentials. The attempt was made by Brett, M.R. in *Heaven v. Pender* (1883) 11 Q.B.D. 503 in a definition to which I will later refer. As framed, it was demonstrably too wide, although it appears to me, if properly limited, to be capable of affording a valuable practical guide."[19]

It was also stated against the recognition that English law recognised many heads of liability for negligence.

"the Courts have been engaged upon an elaborate classification of duties as they exist in respect of property, whether real or personal, with further divisions as to ownership, occupation, or control, and distinctions based on the particular relations of the one side or the other, whether manufacturer, salesman or landlord, customer, tenant, stranger, and so on."[20]

---

[16] (1992) 108 L.Q.R. 236.

[17] Although it is accepted that different societies, and thus different legal systems, accepting the same theory may come to different results based on the factual background: *Invercargill City Council v. Hamilton* [1996] A.C. 624. There is also the possibility of a neo-civilian revisionism directing attention to legally protected interests rather than broader issues of fairness justice and reasonableness.

[18] *Donoghue v. Stevenson*, 1932 S.C.(H.L.) 31 at 44.

[19] *ibid.*

[20] *ibid.*

Scots law was not all that different in this regard, the first 1927 edition of Gloag & Henderson treating of a number of factual situations although prefaced by general statements.

Lord Macmillan's Speech

The speech has an equally powerful expression of general principle making **10–9** it equally clear that people may be careless with impunity in many cases, the notion of duty being necessary to create liability. The speech is also regularly relied on today for its famous floodgate opening words in the middle of the following extract, "The categories of negligence are never closed":

> "The law takes no cognizance of carelessness in the abstract. It concerns itself with carelessness only where there is a duty to take care and where failure in that duty has caused damage. In such circumstances carelessness assumes the legal quality of negligence, and entails the consequences in law of negligence. What then are the circumstances which give rise to this duty to take care? In the daily contacts of social and business life, human beings are thrown into, or place themselves in, an infinite variety of relations with their fellows; and the law can refer only to the standards of the reasonable man in order to determine whether any particular relation gives rise to a duty to take care as between those who stand in that relation to each other. The grounds of action may be as various and manifold as human errancy; and the conception of legal responsibility may develop in adaptation to altering social conditions and the changing circumstances of life. The categories of negligence are never closed. The cardinal principle of liability is that the party complained of should owe to the party complaining a duty to take care, and that the party complaining should be able to prove that he has suffered damage in consequence of a breach of that duty. Where there is room for diversity of view, it is in determining what circumstances will establish such a relationship between the parties as to give rise, on the one side, to duty to take care, and, on the other side, to a right to have care taken."[21]

Development of the principle

At first the case was significant because of its narrower product liability **10–10** ratio. It has been said that "no practitioner seems to have based an argument on the neighbour principle until (perhaps) the East Suffolk case in 1940".[22] However, in the line of product liability cases it was increasingly

---

[21] *Donoghue v. Stevenson*, 1932 S.C.(H.L.) 31 at 258.

[22] Heuston, "Overview of the Law of Negligence", Paisley Papers 69 citing *East Suffolk Rovers Catchment Board v. Kent* [1941] A.C. 74. The same article traces the academic neglect of the principle in Oxford and Cambridge universities. B. Hepple, "Negligence: The Search for Coherence" [1997] C.L.P. 69 at 77, records that Lord Atkin's principle was not followed in *Farr v. Butters & Co.* [1932] 1 K.B. 146 at 168 and the leading textbook denied a general principle in the 1939 edition.

employed.[23] So far as Scotland is concerned the case was certainly cited[24] prior to its next reconsiderations in the major Scottish House of Lords appeals *Lockhart v. Barr*[25] and *Bourhill v. Young.*[26] In *Bourhill* a motorcyclist overtook, and passed on the near side, a stopped tramway car. A motor car, coming along the main road from the opposite direction, turned to its right and crossed in front of the tramway car in order to enter a side road which joined the main road some 40 or 50 feet away from the stopping place and from the front of the stationary tramway car. The motor cyclist, driving too fast, ran into the motor car just as it was about to enter the side road. The pursuer was a fishwife. She had been a passenger on the tramway car and had gone round the front of the tramway car to the off side of the driver's platform to get her creel. At the moment of the collision she was standing on the road with her back to the tramway car getting the creel on to her back. She did not see and could not have seen, the collision. She proved that the noise of the collision had produced in her a fright or terror which resulted in nervous shock. However, in the pleadings it had been admitted that "the pursuer's terror did not involve any element of reasonable fear of immediate bodily injury to herself." Lord Macmillan's speech makes it clear that this was a case involving consideration of duty. It also offers a further consideration of the principles upon which the existence of duty is or can be predicated:

> "The late John Young [the motorcyclist] was under no duty to the appellant to foresee that his negligence in driving at an excessive speed and consequently colliding with a motor car might result in injury to her; for such a result could not reasonably and probably be anticipated. He was therefore, not guilty of negligence in a question with the appellant."[27]

10–11 This proposition was derived from a statement of wider principle which has been often cited since:

> "The duty to take care is the duty to avoid doing or omitting to do anything the doing or omitting to do which may have as its reasonable and probable consequence injury to others, and the duty is owed to those to whom injury may reasonably and probably be anticipated if the duty is not observed. There is no absolute standard of what is reasonable and probable it must depend on circumstances and must always be a question of degree."[28]

---

[23] See *Grant v. Australian Knitting Mills* [1936] A.C. 85. The importance of *res ipsa loquitur* was appreciated in an anonymous note in the S.L.T. when *Donoghue* was decided: "Liabilities of Food Manufacturers to Consumers" 1932 S.L.T. (News) 129. And see also *Lockhart v. Barr*, 1943 S.L.T. 266 in which it was held that although *res ipsa loquitur* did not apply the pursuer did not have to prove how phenol got into a translucent bottle.

[24] *Pollock v. Glasgow Corporation*, 1936 S.L.T. 277; *Buchanan & Carswell v. Eugene Ltd*, 1936 S.L.T. 93; *Carlin v. Clan Line Steamers Ltd*, 1937 S.L.T. 190; *Eccles v. Cross and McIilwham*, 1938 S.L.T. 502; *Degan v. Magistrates of Dundee*, 1940 S.L.T. 375; *Lambie v. Western SMT*, 1945 S.L.T. 62.

[25] 1943 S.C. (H.L.) 1.

[26] 1942 S.C. (H.L.) 78.

[27] *ibid.* at 88.

[28] *ibid.*

On the question of culpability Lord Wright put the matter thus:

"What is now being considered is the question of liability, and this, I think, in a question whether there is duty owing to members of the public who come within the ambit of the act, must generally depend on a normal standard of susceptibility . . . It is here, as elsewhere, a question of what the hypothetical reasonable man, viewing the position, I suppose *ex post facto*, would say it was proper to foresee . . . The lawyer likes to draw fixed and definite lines and is apt to ask where the thing is to stop. I should reply it should stop where in the particular case the good sense of the jury or of the judge decides . . . I may add that the issue of duty or no duty is, indeed, a question for the court, but it depends on the view taken of the facts."[29]

It must be remembered that *Donoghue* was decided on the basis of forseeable physical injury. Further consideration of how the neighbour principle has developed can only take place by comparison and contrast with the different principles discussed below in various different contexts.

Foreseeability

Foreseeability is at the heart of the neighbour model of liability. The **10–12** foreseeability enquiry itself is essentially a jury question and it is harm of the kind which has taken place which is the object of enquiry.[30] Lord Keith of Avonholm said in *Miller v. South of Scotland Electricity Board*,[31]

"It has been pointed out in other cases that it is not necessary to foresee the precise accident that happened; and similarly it is not necessary, in my opinion, to postulate foreseeability of the precise chain of circumstances leading up to an accident. There does not seem to be anything fantastic or highly improbable in the series of happenings that are alleged to have led to the accident here. If it is reasonably probable that an accident may happen from some act of neglect or commission that may be enough to discharge the initial onus on the pursuer though it would remain, of course, to show that the pursuer was within the class of persons to whom a duty was owed. The question is: was what happened so remote that it could not be reasonably foreseeable?"[32]

In *Hughes v. Lord Advocate*[33] the matter was extensively canvassed in the **10–13** House of Lords. Post Office workmen were working on telephone cables. Access was by a ladder in a manhole about nine feet deep which had been opened for the purpose. A hut was put over the manhole and four red warning paraffin lamps were placed at the site. The workmen went for a tea-break leaving the site unattended and the manhole open. A tarpaulin had been thrown over the shelter tent for additional protection. The ladder

---

[29] *Bourhill v. Young*, 1942 (H.L.) 78 at 92.
[30] See generally, F. Bates "What must be foreseen?" 1970 S.L.T. (News) 97.
[31] 1958 S.L.T. 229.
[32] *ibid.* at 236.
[33] 1963 S.L.T. 150.

was removed from the manhole and laid on the ground nearby. Two boys, aged eight and ten years began to play with the equipment. They went into the manhole swinging one of the lighted lamps on a rope. The younger boy tripped and knocked the lamp into the manhole. A violent explosion occurred as a result of which he fell into the hole and sustained severe burns. The Lord Ordinary found that the explosion was caused by paraffin escaping when the lamp was knocked into the hole and forming vapour which was ignited by the flame, and that such an occurrence was rare and could not have been foreseen.[34] Now we are dealing with the concept of foreseeability as creating a duty of care. *Hughes* whilst an examination of foreseeability can be said to be concerned more with breach of duty than the existence of duty. However, what is clear is that despite the unusual sequence of the accident, duty was clear. At first instance in rejecting liability the Lord Ordinary (Wheatley) considered there was sufficient foreseeability for duty:

> "I am satisfied on the evidence that the pursuer was a "neighbour" within the meaning of Lord Atkin's dictum in regard to whose safety the Post Office workmen had a duty to take reasonable care, and that it was reasonably foreseeable that he might be injured by failure to exercise such reasonable care. As I have already pointed out, this was a public street along which children like the pursuer, *inter alios*, were entitled to travel. The Post Office workmen knew this, as children were in the habit of using this street, *inter alia*, to get to and from the local school during week-days, and I reject entirely their somewhat feeble contention that they did not anticipate that children would be using the street because it was a Saturday afternoon. Certainly no reasonable man would have ignored the very live possibility of children using that street and passing close to the manhole on any day of the week."[35]

The House of Lords confirmed that there was liability as well as duty.

10–14   Many of the cases considered below show the development of the idea of foreseeability, especially the cases discussed in third party intervention.[36] A few other cases will serve as examples of the practical issues which the enquiry involves, albeit it results in a legal conclusion. In *Holland v. British Steel Corporation*,[37] a plumber collapsed as result of exposure to excessive heat and had a heart attack. It was held this was within the scope of foreseeability. In *Brash v. East of Scotland Water Authority*[38] it was held that operators of a JCB knew, or ought to have known, that if they started their digger it would startle the nearby horses causing them to injure themselves. In *Fraser v. Glasgow Corporation*[39] the council had power to remove a car which had become a wreck and a plaything for children. A child put a lighted rag into the petrol tank which still had petrol in it resulting in burning. They were told there was an abandoned car but they were told

---

[34] The First Division, Lord Carmont dissenting, agreed.
[35] 1962 S.L.T. 90 at 95.
[36] See paras 10–56 *et seq.*
[37] 1974 S.L.T. (Notes) 72.
[38] Unrep, Edinburgh Sheriff Court, October 27, 1998.
[39] 1972 S.L.T. 177.

nothing of its condition so the case had to fail on the lack of this factual basis.[40] However, in the Division, the Lord Justice-Clerk (Grant) made a helpful observation on the issue of foreseeability which reflects the fact that it always involves an ex post facto hypothetical exercise of foresight:

"Quite apart from that, however, it seems to me that the pursuer fails to clear the hurdle of foreseeability. Even if the defenders had known of the dilapidated condition of the car and that it was an allurement to children, I am unable to hold that it was reasonably foreseeable that 'such children playing on or about the said car might apply a lighted match to the said car, and in particular the area of the said petrol tank, and thereby cause an explosion sufficient to endanger other children such as the pursuer'. Although I speak as one without the attributes of even a minor prophet, I would have regarded the chances of such an accident as being most unlikely. It may well be that, if an abandoned car becomes a playground for children, there may be some risk of falling off, cutting fingers on broken glass and so on. But that is a very different thing from saying that the defenders, even armed with all the knowledge which the pursuer would impute to them here, should reasonably have foreseen an accident of the type and nature which occurred in the present case. For these reasons I would uphold the interlocutor of the Lord Ordinary subject to a minor technical amendment. As proof has been taken and decree of absolvitor is being granted it is, I think, inappropriate to deal at this stage with the defenders' first plea-in-law to the relevancy and I would delete the reference thereto."[41]

As a matter of practice pursuers will be expected to set out facts and circumstances from which foreseeability can be expected to be established.[42]

Fragmentation

The next stage of the law, which is the one current at the time of writing, is **10–15** that the attempt to state the law as being based on reasonable foreseeability with policy exceptions has been largely abandoned. The law is now seen as being broken into areas of duty, no duty and arguable new duties. New duties develop incrementally. It must be fair, just and reasonable to impose a new duty.[43] While this is practical it does give the law an air of arbitrariness. The fact that some of the divisions relate to the nature of the harm or the status or nature of the defender suggest that utilisation of the policy exemption from *Anns* and the *injuria* requirement of the civilian law are still of some fundamental value. The divisions are not logical, they are practical—derived from practice. They are:

---

[40] There was no argument as there might well be today that the regulation 6 of the Removal of Vehicles (Scotland) Regulations 1961 (S.I. No. 1473), was not such as to allow for a civil action. It was not founded on as part of a breach of statutory duty.

[41] *Fraser v. Glasgow Corporation*, 1972 S.L.T. 177, *per* Lord Justice-Clerk (Grant) at 181.

[42] See generally *Robb v. Dundee District Council*, 1980 S.L.T. (Notes) 91. If there is a proof, the circumstances established must be such as to establish reasonable foreseeability, *e.g.* *Campbell v. John McNee*, 1972 S.L.T. (Notes) 65.

[43] *Caparo Industries plc v. Dickman* [1990] W.L.R. 605, *per* Lord Bridge at 617–618.

(1) economic loss;

(2) indirect physical loss and indirect property damage;

(3) public law cases;

(4) third party cases; and

(5) nervous shock cases.

To an extent the divisions are a result of history and development. The economic loss cases concentrate on the pursuer's loss and the extent of the defender's potential liability. The public law cases can, and do involve the economic loss questions but raise, independently questions about the range of the law of negligence, rather than being about the granting of judicial immunity, which the cases sometimes resemble. Third party cases ask how far the defender must control other people to protect the pursuer. Nervous shock cases resemble economic loss cases as raising questions about the pursuers loss and the extent of the defender's potential liability. It is always of interest to look for analogies and themes across the cases.

(1) Economic Loss

10–16 Although economics, *inter alia*, is to do with money and money is a kind of universal solvent, the loss of money is not what lawyers now mean when they talk about economic loss cases. There is an enormous amount of literature.[44] The first stage of analysis is to distinguish: (i) direct injury to the person of the pursuer or direct damage to his property and its consequences; (ii) financial losses unaccompanied by injury to the person, or damage to the property, of the actual pursuer; and (iii) other financial claims including, *inter alia*, cases of indirect harm to the pursuer's person or property. Cases in the first category are not economic loss cases at all so far as present legal theory is concerned. At the worst they fall into the category of cases of remoteness of damage where the defender, being liable for some legally recognisable harm, disputes the scope of the consequential losses. It must be appreciated that economist or those who follow law and economics might not agree with that view. The second category of cases can also be distinguished into two further distinct categories: (a) primary cases where the phenomena generating the litigation do not involve injury to person or damage to property at all; the appellation "pure" economic loss could reasonably be applied to this kind of case; and (b) secondary cases where the reason that the pursuer suffers an economic loss is because of personal injury or property damage to another party.[45] The third category is a residual one. Recovery of economic loss in the lawyers sense was made widely possible only by developments after *Donoghue v. Stevenson*[46] which

---

[44] See *e.g.* P. Cane, P. "Economic loss in tort: is the pendulum out of control?" (1989) 52 M.L.R. 200; P. Clifford and C. Sharp, "Negligence , Duty , Economic Loss and Policy" (Note) [1995] Tort L. Rev 169.

[45] See for this analysis A.B. Wilkinson and A. Forte, 1985 J.R. 1 at p. 8. This obviously antedates the language of primary and secondary victims in the nervous shock cases discussed below in Chap. 10.

[46] 1932 S.C. (H.L.) 32. See Chap. 10.

was itself not immediately treated as warranting an expansion of liability.[47] While the judicial landmark in the United Kingdom may well have been the dissent of Lord Denning in *Candler v. Crane, Christmas & Co.*,[48] the authoritative ruling came in *Hedley Byrne v. Heller and Partners*[49] albeit the plaintiffs did not actually recover damages. The plaintiffs were advertising consultants. They booked advertising for clients on the basis that they (Hedley Byrne) themselves would be contractually liable to the advertiser. Accordingly, it was important for them to make inquiries into the credit worthiness of their customers. In this case they did so by contacting their own bankers who in turn contacted the defenders who were the bankers of the client company, Easipower. In reply the defendants said Easipower were believed to be "respectably constituted and considered good for its normal business engagements" and that it "would not undertake any commitments they were unable to fulfil." A later enquiry obtained a similar response by letter with a statement that the letter was "without responsibility." It was, however, quickly held in Scotland that although *Hedley Byrne* may have opened up recovery for certain economic losses it did not allow all such losses to be recovered, in particular secondary economic loss.[50] So there is no general principle of recovery of economic loss on the basis of reasonable foreseeability, nor does the *Hedley Byrne* reliance formulae provide a solution for every problem.

Primary Cases

Advice and Misstatements

Hedley Byrne in Scotland

Hedley Byrne[51] is the start of a long line of cases where economic losses **10–17** have been held recoverable, although the plaintiffs were not successful in *Hedley Byrne* itself.[52] The economic losses are primary losses and the bulk of the cases concern advice or misstatements. The principle is developed in England and abroad. First though it is worth noting the applicability of the principle in Scotland. That *Hedley Byrne* was not fully understood nor fully adopted in Scotland for a while is clear from Lord Stotts comments in *Edie v. McKinnon's Transport Ltd*[53] in which a man was injured as a result of allegedly negligent advice given by another workman. It was in fact the defenders who raised *Hedley Byrne*. They argued that there were not sufficient averments of reliance to support the case. The pursuer disavowed any reliance upon *Hedley Byrne*. Lord Stott commented correctly that the case was not binding on him. He considered the argument opened up questions as to the applicability of the doctrine to Scots law, in particular whether it extended beyond the case of advisers carrying on a business or profession. Lord Stott preferred the analysis that this case could fall within

---

[47] *Donoghue v. Stevenson*, 1932 S.C. (H.L.) 32.
[48] [1951] 2 K.B. 164.
[49] [1964] A.C. 465.
[50] See paras 10–27 *et seq.*
[51] *Hedley Byrne v. Heller and Partners* [1964] A.C. 465.
[52] *Anns v. Merton LBC* [1978] A.C. 728 was another important landmark.
[53] 1973 S.L.T. 31.

Donoghue. However, he conceded: "it is not an argument that should be carried too far; otherwise a passer-by who in all innocence gives wrong directions to a stranger on the street who asks him the way could be held responsible for any mishap that may befall the stranger in consequence of following his well intentioned advice."[54]

One of the first cases in which both *Hedley Byrne* and *Anns*[55] were considered in Scotland was *Twomax Ltd v. Dickson McFarlane & Robinson*.[56] In that case the issue was the liability of accountants and auditors in respect of accounts relied upon by a non-contracting party. Lord Stewart in the Outer House cited the Wilberforce trilogy dictum[57] with approval and decided in favour of the pursuers on the basis of a duty arising on the basis of proximity, reasonable foreseeability of loss and the pursuers' reliance, reasonably to be expected by the defenders.[58] This decision itself would now have to be considered against the much stricter view of accountants' liability in *Caparo v. Dickman*.[59]

10–18   The *Hedley Byrne* principle was most clearly adopted in the Inner House decision in *Martin v. Bell Ingram*.[60] The pursuers were potential purchasers of a house. Their building society requested the defenders to produce a survey report. The report noted a ceiling crack which was not considered serious but made no reference to any sagging or other structural instability in the roof. The subjects were valued at £35,000. On receipt of the report, the building society passed on the terms of the report to the pursuers who bought the house for £33,500. About 18 months later the defenders carried out a further inspection in connection with a further advance which the pursuers were obtaining. Nothing was said regarding any defect in the roof. Six months later the pursuers advertised the house at £48,500. One potential purchaser surveyed the house and told the sellers that the survey had found a serious roof sag. Thereafter the pursuers had remedial works carried out but they had difficulty in selling the house which was eventually sold for £39,000. The pursuers had no contract with the defenders. The defenders were contracted to the building society. The loss was economic as the house they bought did not hold up as well in the market as could reasonably have been expected. It was admitted that a surveyor acting properly would have noticed the defects and that the defects were such as materially affected the value. The defenders were found to be liable. Other Scottish cases have followed.[61]

10–19   In *Bank of Scotland v. 3i Plc*[62] the pursuers were allowed a proof before answer on the basis of *Hedley Byrne*. The claim was that the pursuers had only increased the overdraft of a now insolvent company because of assurances from one of the defenders' employees who was also a director of

---

[54] *Edie v. Mckinnon's Transport Ltd*, 1973 S.L.T. 31 at 33.

[55] *Anns v. Merton LBC*. See para. 10–3 above.

[56] 1983 S.L.T. 98.

[57] *Donoghue, Hedley* and *Dorset Yacht*—see Chap. 10.

[58] He found assistance in, *inter alia*, the English case of *J.E.B.Fastners Ltd v. Marks, Bloom & Co.* [1981] 3 All E.R. 289.

[59] *Caparo Industries plc v. Dickman* [1990] 1 AC 605. See Chaps 10 and 12.

[60] 1986 S.L.T. 575.

[61] Many are collected below in Chap. 12 on professional liability now that the principle of liability is well accepted and recognised.

[62] 1990 S.C. 215.

the now insolvent company. However, after proof absolvitor was granted. On the evidence available and on consideration of the leading post-*Hedley Byrne* English cases[63] it was held that there was insufficient proximity, nor would it be fair, just or reasonable to impose one. That is the language of these more recent English cases, but it is submitted that it would have been enough to say that there was insufficient evidence to show that reliance had reasonably been induced.[64] An important application of the principle in Scotland can be found in *Smith v. Carter*[65] in which a surveyor carried out a survey for a friend, a Ms Aitchison, who was contemplating purchasing a house. He agreed to report to the building society funding the purchase. Unknown to the surveyor the pursuer was to be a co-purchaser. The Lord Ordinary held that the case was not irrelevant. Although there might be many pursuers (usually only a few) the liability was the same and would simply be divided among the pursuers. The case deals with two important aspects of *Hedley Byrne*—the absence of the need for there to be remuneration for the advice; and the need for it to be established that it was reasonable for the defender to consider that the pursuer would rely on the statement. The case is correctly decided but comes close to the kind of cases which judges have repeatedly wanted excluded—friendly advice; and, statements made to all and sundry as in magazine article. In *VAG Finance Ltd v. Specialised Security (Scotland) Ltd*[66] a proof before answer was allowed. It was alleged that a trade purchaser of a car let under a leasing agreement having been advised that the balance outstanding was £11,981, sold the car to an innocent third party and sent £9,600 to the company. There was insuffient to support fraud but it was held a negligence case could proceed notwithstanding *Murphy*,[67] the court finding support in *Scott Lithgow Ltd v. GEC Electrical Projects*.[68] In *Donlon v. Colonial Mutual Group (U.K. Holdings) Ltd*,[69] Scots law has followed the most recent English development of *Hedley Byrne*, namely *Spring v. Guardian Assurance plc*[70] and held that a careless reference is actionable by a former employee against his employer.[71] It was held in *Macdonald v. FIFA and SFA*[72] that the two organisations did not owe a duty to a spectator for the costs he

---

[63] *Caparo Industries plc. v. Dickman* [1990] 2 A.C. 605; *James McNaughten Paper Group Ltd v. Hicks Anderson & Co.* [1991] 2 W.L.R. 641.

[64] A proof before answer was allowed under reference to the same to English cases where it was alleged a local authority had assured builders that they would obtain improvement grants. *Margrie Holdings Ltd v. City of Edinburgh District Council*, 1992 G.W.D. 17–994, but this decision was reversed by the First Division in that there were insufficient averments to support the delictual claim: 1994 S.L.T. 971; 1993 S.C.L.R. 570.

[65] 1995 S.L.T. 295.

[66] 1994 G.W.D. 29–1762.

[67] *Murphy v. Brentwood D.C.* [1990] 3 W.L.R. 414. See Chaps 9 and 10.

[68] 1992 S.L.T. 244. See J. Convery, "Subcontractors and the Contractual Matrix", 1996 Rep. B. 9–10.

[69] 1997 S.C.L.R. 1088.

[70] [1995] 2 A.C. 296.

[71] Taking account of the fact that the critical misstatement was based on an interpretation of the remuneration aspects of the pursuers' contract and that the sheriff and Sheriff Principal in the event were held to have got that wrong, the finding that the defenders were careless looks high. However, as the employer and a party to the contract they were in the best position to make sure matters were clear.

[72] 1999 S.C.L.R. 59.

incurred due to the late cancellation of an international football match to which the pursuer had travelled. It was not fair just and reasonable to impose a duty.

English Cases

10–20 There are an enormous number of cases on this point in England. Only those which have influenced the theoretical approach in both jurisdictions, or which are of obvious practical value are considered here. It was always clear from *Hedley Byrne* that the misstater had to be held to have reasonably foreseen that the statement would be relied upon by a person such as the actual pursuer harmed. This was considered in detail by the House of Lords in *Caparo Industries plc. v. Dickman*.[73] The defenders, who were accountants, were auditors to a company. Such an audit is carried out in terms of statutory requirements. The plaintiffs alleged that on the basis of the accounts they bought more shares and took over the company. The accounts, it was alleged, were negligently prepared and so the plaintiffs suffered loss on the transaction. The House of Lords held there was no duty of care between the accountants and potential purchasers of shares. The accountants owed a duty to the shareholders as members of the company to prepare the accounts properly to the extent that the share-holders could utilise the accounts to judge the health of their company. They did not owe a duty to potential purchasers of shares. This is a fine distinction and becomes more difficult to sustain when the example of the shareholder who sells his shares as a result of wrongly prepared accounts is concerned. Lord Bridge distinguished the two types of investment decision in such a way that although not decided the case of sale might be decided differently.[74] *Caparo* has come to be seen as part of the "retreat from *Anns*", but in focusing on the issues of assumption of responsibility it is really only a gloss upon the *Hedley Byrne* principle. It has not stopped cases which are cases of reasonable reliance by the plaintiff where the defendant knew or reasonably ought to have known that the statements would be relied upon. If specific representations are made to a potential acquirer with the intent to induce reliance then a case is stateable on the basis of this proximity, the potential pursuer being identifiable.[75] The question of identity is a difficult one. It could never be a necessity that the plaintiff ought to be known by individual name.[76] Thus, it must be the case that the plaintiff need only fall into a category of persons. However, the investing population of the world is such a category and on that would raise the problem of indeterminate liability. The English Court of Appeal has laid down some guidelines the courts should consider in such cases:

(1) The purpose for which the statement was made;

---

[73] [1990] 1 All E.R. 568.

[74] See the discussion and application of the case in *Al-Nakib Investments v. Longcroft* [1990] 3 All E.R. 321.

[75] *Morgan Crucible Co. plc. v. Hill Samuel* [1991] 1 All E.R. 148.

[76] If, however, the name of the pursuer is known as a class of one that raises the possibility of liability based on that foreseeability and proximity, perhaps on a paracontractual basis.

(2) The purpose for which it was communicated;

(3) the relationship between the parties;

(4) the size of any class to which the person receiving the advice belonged;

(5) the state of knowledge of the adviser; and

(6) reliance by the person in receipt of the advice.[77]

The Court of Appeal in *BCCI (In Liquidation) v. Price Waterhouse and Ernst & Whinney*,[78] recognising developments in other economic loss cases such as *White v. Jones*[79] refused to allow a case to be struck out on pleadings, even although it was against audit accountants. More dramatically, the accountants were auditors of a different company to the one who audited the plaintiffs' accounts. The liquidators of a failed bank (BCCI) sued their own auditors (Price Waterhouse) and the auditors of another group member (Ernst & Whinney). The special facts alleged in this case were that there was in fact a very close identity between the two companies and that accordingly the auditors of the other group member were effectively in the driving seat so far as the audit was concerned. Absent that sort of relationship, the *Caparo* arguments would usually succeed. The actual or presumed knowledge of the adviser in the circumstances was the focus of enquiry.[80]

The House of Lords applied the reliance principle in a more subtle case in *Williams v. Natural Life Health Foods*.[81] The plaintiff signed up for a franchise with Natural Life. He alleged he had been induced into the transaction by materials from the company but also from one of the directors. His franchise did not do anything like as well as predicted by the company and collapsed in 18 months. Then the franchise vendor company went into liquidation. The case continued against the director who was mentioned in the literature as having the ability to make the venture successful. It was held that the case must fail because it was necessary that the plaintiff could be said to have reasonably relied on an assumption of responsibility. Cases might arise in the future where the director sued was more active in assuming some responsibility or engendering reliance reasonably. In *Williams* the case looked very weak, there had been no personal dealings between the parties and no exchanges or conduct on his part other than to allow the company to utilise his name and experience to sell the franchises. Looking at the whole circumstances the plaintiff could reasonably be said to be relying only on the company.

The power of the principle in doctrine is emphasised by the decision of **10–21** the House of Lords in *Spring v. Guardian Assurance plc*[82] in which a 4–1 majority held that the *Hedley Byrne* principle applied to an employment

---

[77] *James McNaughton Paper Group Ltd v. Hicks Anderson & Co.* [1991] 1 All E.R. 134. See also *Grampian Regional Council v. Cowan & Linn*, 1989 S.L.T. 787.

[78] [1998] T.L.R. 125.

[79] [1995] 2 A.C. 207 discussed in Chap.12.

[80] See the sequel on the quantification of damages at [1998] T.L.R. 210 when the case came back to Chancery.

[81] [1998] T.L.R. 271.

[82] [1995] 2 A.C. 296.

reference, notwithstanding that if the case had been brought in defamation a defence of qualified privilege could have been run successfully. Abbreviating the facts the plaintiff was unsuccessful in gaining employment because of a bad reference. It was not true and had been given as a result of an inadequate investigation into the material in the reference. The economic loss caused was reasonably foreseeable and thus *Donoghue* and *Hedley Byrne* were applicable. However, for a long time it has been accepted that a defamatory statement made in this context is protected by qualified privilege. Thus it was argued that to allow recovery based on negligence would circumvent the policy of the law in allowing unimpeded expression. Not only that it might result in "defensive" rather than frank, references. This was not considered sufficient to leave the victim uncompensated. *Hedley Byrne* meant that there could be liability for a reference which was too good—why should there not be liability for one that hurt through being too bad. The public benefit in references is enhanced by accurate and careful references.[83] The reasoning was obviously applicable to Scots law and it is possible it sits better in that there may still be an aquilian root to our law of defamation which should not be hindered by the requirement, if there is one, that privilege negating *animus injuriandum* need not affect the aquilian claim. In due course it was followed in Scotland.[84] An attempt to apply the rule to a doctor's report failed. In *Kapfunde v. Abbey National plc*[85] a doctor was employed to assess medical questionnaires of job applicants. It was alleged that he had been careless in reporting that the job applicant was likely to have a higher than average absence record. The case appears to have been argued against the background of the fair, just and reasonableness test, but with respect to the majority in the Court of Appeal it does not seem that the principle involved was any different from *Spring*. It is submitted that this case might best have been left to have been decided as it was below on the finding that taking into account the task the doctor was undertaking there was no breach of duty.[86]

10–22   In *Henderson v. Merret Syndicates Ltd*[87] the action was between Lloyds names and those whom they said had negligently caused them to lose on their Lloyds investment.[88] Superficially the scheme operates by the "name" agreeing to be responsible to an unlimited amount, being worth a certain sum and depositing a fraction of it. Normally this was easy money and becoming a Lloyds name carried a cachet. Bad weather in the U.S. and large damages claims, ironically probably based on tort, brought about enormous losses. The names case at its most honourable was that they did not mind losing but the way their involvement was handled by their agents and sub-agents was negligent lacking all care for their interests. Liability was established unanimously in the House of Lords on the basis of *Hedley*

---

[83] *Spring v. Guardian Assurance plc* [1995] 2 A.C. 296, *per* Lord Goff at 324 and Lord Lowry at 326. Lord Woolf at 352 explains how the practice of open appraisal in institutional employment has not inhibited free and frank criticism.

[84] *Donlon v. Colonial Mutual Group (U.K. Holdings) Ltd*, 1997 S.C.L.R. 1088.

[85] [1998] T.L.R. 222.

[86] The same approach had been taken in *Baker v. Kaye* [1996] T.L.R. 724.

[87] [1995] 2 A.C. 145.

[88] The background is very complex and there have been exponential developments: See P. Cane, "Contract Tort and the Lloyds' Debacle" in *Consensus ad Idem* (Rose ed., Sweet & Maxwell, 1996), p. 5.

Byrne but at least on one view[89] by going a step further by accepting that liability extended to careless or dilatory omissions as well as to careless acts. It is, of course, impossible to do justice to the complicated facts of the case in summary form, but the essential facts raising the legal points can be shortly stated. The plaintiffs were "names" in the Lloyds insurance market. A name pledged his credit to underwriters that they might sell insurance knowing that if the risk materialised there were sufficient assets from which claims could be met. Insurance is always a gamble with the insurer offering the odds. To make money he must ensure the premiums cover the claims. Risks can be so great that there is reinsurance with other underwriters taking part of the risk. It was considered both a mark of status and a privilege to be a name. There were contractual arrangements in place between the names and what for now can be called Lloyds. The cases before the House involved different types of contractual arrangement. The name needed an agent, unless himself an agent. A "members agent" advised names on which syndicates to join and signed the names up to these syndicates. "Managing agents" ran syndicates. They also reinsured contracts and paid out the claims. There was a third category of agent, a hybrid known as a combined agent—managing syndicates and placing names and thus placing the advised name in their own syndicates. The names might or might not know anything about the insurance market. It was a form of investment and like the man in the street who puts some money into a unit trust not knowing what the fund manager does with it, the name may have been given rather simple choices. In the event there were catastrophes mainly in the U.S. which required Lloyds to pay out. At the time in question there was a further complexity. The agreements entered into differed depending on whether the name was a direct or an indirect name. The direct name came into a more direct relationship with a normally more remote managing agent when the managing agent was a combined agent, that is also the names members agent. In such a case the members agent aspect of the deal between the parties came to govern also the relationship between the name and the syndicate. If however, the name entered into a syndicate which was not managed by his combined or members agent his agent had to enter into a sub-agency agreement appointing the managing agent the sub-agent of the name.

In the *Merrett* appeals the agents were combined agents but eventually split, one company being a members agent and one a managing agent. The related *Feltrim* appeals involved an underwriting company which acted as managing agents and an unrelated group of members agents who found together as a result of having placed their names in Feltrim syndicates. The three types of *Merrett* actions were based on complaints of negligent reinsurance and a single complaint to the actual writing of insurance. In the *Feltrim* actions the managing agents were sued for their negligent underwriting in the London market "excess of loss" business. They covered too much and reinsured too little. The members agents were sued as being contractually liable for the fault of the managing agents: the sub-contractors of the indirect names. These claims raised some contractual matters, matters relating to fiduciary duties and tortious matters. Only the delictual

---

[89] Lord Mustill (dissenting) in *White v. Jones* [1995] 2 W.L.R. 187.

matters are treated here. So far as direct names suing the managing agents was concerned it would seem simple to sue on the contract. But in English law at least the contractual claim faced limitation. No doubt it was also sought to have another defendant, especially the one who allegedly made the mistakes. Lord Goff considered that the solution lay in *Hedley Byrne*.[90] He re-examined that case and pointedly supported the view that the ratio is based on relationship and that relationship can arise from an assumption of responsibility. Once a case falls under that principle, even if it is for economic loss, then there is no need to embark upon the fair, just and reasonable test as the defendant has by definition assumed that respon- sibility. Applying this to the case (and leaving aside the contractual matrix) there was a duty in this case. The names held themselves out as having special expertise. They knew that the names would rely on their expertise and performance. Lord Goff then moved onto the big issue: "All systems of law which recognise a law of contract (or delict) have to solve the problem of the possibility of concurrent claims arising form breach of duty under two rubrics of the law."[91] He noted that in the civilian tradition France has adopted an anti-cumulative view whereas German law permits it.[92] Lord Goff thought the answer was to expand *Hedley Byrne* to cover cases not only of gratuitous services but those rendered under a contract.[93] It is possible to assume responsibility to more than one party in respect of the same activity. He then, however, went to pains to try to suggest that the case before him was rather special. The *Hedley Byrne* principle he thought would not be applicable to defective workmanship cases.[94] The idea of *Henderson* as extending *Hedley Byrne* to any assumption of responsibility, not just misstatements has since been accepted in the Court of Appeal, although on the facts the necessary reasonable reliance was not made out.[95]

Disclaimers

10–23 *Hedley Byrne* itself was a disclaimer case which was why there was no liability.[96] But why? The obvious answer is that the plaintiffs were told not to rely on the statement and if reliance was the basis of liability then QED,

---

[90] *Henderson v. Merret Syndicates Ltd* [1995] 2 A.C. 145 at 178–181.

[91] *ibid.* at 184. See generally J.G. Fleming, "Tort in a Contractual Matrix" (1995) 3 Tort L Rev 12.

[92] His speech features an erudite examination of the progress of English law. It transpires that *Esso Petroleum v. Mardon* [1976] Q.B. 801 was another landmark with the Court of Appeal accepting concurrent liability—expressly by Denning M.R. and, according to Goff, implicitly by Ormrod and Shaw L.JJ. A review of commonwealth cases showed a willingness to recognise concurrent liability, but not where it was a way of escaping a contractual limitation or exclusion, *per* Le Dain J. in *Central Trust Co. v. Rafuse* (1986) 31 D.L.R. (4th.) 481, or unless the terms of the contract preclude the tortious liability. Thomsas J. in *Rowlands v. Callow* [1992] 1 N.Z.L.R. 178.

[93] See generally B.S Markesenis, "An Expanding Tort Law—the Price of a Rigid Contract Law" (1987) 103 L.Q.R. 354; F.M.B. Reynolds, "Tort Actions in Contractual Situations" (1985) 11 N.Z.L.R. 215; K.M. Stanton, "Insurance: The Hedley Byrne Principle and Concurrent Liability" (1995) Tort L. Rev 85; S. Whittaker, "The Application of the 'Broad Principle of Hedley Byrne' as between Parties to a Contract" 1997 L.S. 169.

[94] To this extent favouring the decision in *Simaan General Contracting Co. v. Pilkington Glass Ltd* [1988] Q.B. 758. The decision in *Junior Books* which, however, did not require to be reconsidered.

[95] *Williams v. Natural Life Health Foods* [1998] T.L.R. 271.

[96] See generally A.D.M. Forte, "Disclaiming Liability for Negligent Property Surveys" 1986 S.L.T. (News) 293.

no liability. The engendering of expectations and their protection is the business of contract. Even in contract it has been considered in modern times[97] that some contracting parties are entitled to be protected from their bargains. Inequality of bargaining power may be the political or economic concept underlying the modern law embodied in the Unfair Contract Terms Act and perhaps its European analogues.[98] The law of delict already looked sceptically on attempts by wrongdoers to escape liability by steps taken prior to the harm or materialisation of a risk.[99] This particular topic is treated under defences. But, in relation to cases of engendered reliance it is not necessarily a defence but a non-constitutive factor. It can be argued that the disclaimer does not say "I am liable but this lets me off". Instead it says "I am not liable at all because if you read this and understand it then you will not rely upon it, I shall not have engendered reliance and thus there is no liability." The second view is undoubtedly correct so far as the *Hedley Byrne* disclaimer is concerned. If the disclaimer comes after the reliance has engendered a liability then it comes too late.[1] It was thought, with some reason that the Act as originally enacted did not cover non-contractual disclaimers in Scotland.[2] It did apply in England.[3] However, in one Inner House case it was held that the unamended Act could apply to terms in a contract to which the party complaining was a party, but the party complained of was not where the party complained of was the beneficiary of the exclusion. In a jurisdiction which recognises *ius quaesitum tertio* this may not be as curious as it seems. The Act was amended in Scotland by the Law Reform (Miscellaneous Provisions) (Scotland) Act 1990 putting the matter beyond doubt in practice but the theoretical issues will remain. Persons who assume responsibility are best advised to protect themselves in two ways—by defining their obligations carefully and meeting them and by contracting out of them so far as the law permits. Parties relying on others should not rely upon the law of delict to protect them but should contract either with potential defenders or with insurance companies.

Defective products

This is, of necessity, a very narrow category of cases. The reasons for this **10–24** will be seen as the exposition develops. The rhetoric and decisions focus around a paradigm case. The paradigm is that of the ordinary manufactured product: a brick, a bolt, a hammer or a spanner. In whatever way it is expressed, it is an intuitive point that a manufacturer of a product should owe no duty to an ultimate consumer (as opposed to the immediate contractual purchaser) in respect of a *defective* product, as opposed to the case of a *dangerous* product. Analysis of this category of cases is best centred around the Scottish case in the House of Lords of *Junior Books v. The Veitchi Company*.[4] The problem in that case was concisely put by Lord Fraser:

---

[97] And early times! See generally Atiyah, P.S., *The Rise and Fall of the Freedom of Contract* (Oxford, 1979).

[98] Directive 93/13 O.J. L95/29; Unfair Terms in Consumer Contracts Regulations 1994 S.I. 1994 No. 3159 (July 1, 1995).

[99] Different things.

[1] *Martin v. Bell Ingram*, 1986 S.L.T. 575.

[2] *Robbie v. Graham & Sibbald*, 1989 S.L.T. 870.

[3] *Harris v. Wyre Forrest D.C.* [1989] 2 W.L.R. 790. *Smith v. Eric S Bush* [1989] 2 All E.R. 514.

[4] 1982 S.L.T. 492. See J.G. Logie, "The Final Demise of Junior Books?" [1989] J.R. 5 and I.S. Stephenson, "Goodbye Junior Books" (1988) 138 N.L.J. 483.

"The appeal raises an important question on the law of delict or, strictly speaking, quasi delict, which is not precisely covered by authority. The question is whether the appellants having (as must at this stage be assumed) negligently laid a floor which is defective, but which has not caused danger to the health or safety of any person nor risk of damage to any other property belonging to the owner of the floor, may in the circumstances averred by the respondents be liable for the economic loss caused to them by having to replace the floor."[5]

There were three main parties involved in this work: the employer, Junior Books; the main contractor, Ogilvie; and the nominated sub-contractor, the Veitchi Company. Ogilvie did not appear in the process. for as is now known (but was not known to the House) they were insolvent. This explains why the more obvious contractual route was not taken. The decision of the House by a majority of 4–1 was that the employer could recover direct from the contractor. This provoked a considerable furore both academic[6] and judicial.[7] The important thing to do, now that the fuss has died down, is to determine what law the case lays down. Lord Brandon's dissent has been cited often and indeed it should be noted that the majority did not, in any real sense, dissent from the sense of it. The following passage is important as stating law that is the foundation of non-recovery which any argument to sustain liability must distinguish:

"In the case of a manufacturer or distributor of goods, the position would be that he warranted to the ultimate user or consumer of such goods that they were as well designed, as merchantable and as fit for their contemplated purpose as the exercise of reasonable care could make them. In the case of sub-contractors such as those concerned in the present case, the position would be that they warranted to the building owner that the flooring, when laid, would be as well designed, as free from defects of any kind and as fit for its contemplated purpose as the exercise of reasonable care could make it. In my view, the imposition of warranties of this kind on one person in favour of another, when there is no contractual relationship between them, is contrary to any sound policy requirement."[8]

This view was supported very strongly by Lord Keith in the majority:

"They supplied them with a defective floor. Such an act can, in accordance with the views I have expressed above give rise to liability in negligence in certain circumstances. But it does not do so merely

---

[5] Stephenson (1988) 138 N.L.J. 483 at 494.
[6] See Logie, *op. cit.*; B.S. Markesenis, "An Expanding Tort Law—The Price of a Rigid Contract Law" (1987) 103 L.Q.R. 354 and Stephenson, *op. cit.*
[7] *Tate & Lyle Foods and Distribution Ltd v. Greater London Council* [1983] 2 A.C. 509; *Muirhead v. Industrial Tank Specialities* [1986] Q.B. 507; *Maloco v. Littlewoods Organisation Ltd*, 1987 S.L.T. 425; *Simaan Construction Co. v. Pilkington Glass Ltd (No. 2)* [1988] 2 W.L.R. 761 and see also *Greater Nottingham Co-operative Society Ltd v. Cementation Piling and Foundations Ltd* [1988] 3 W.L.R. 396; *D. & F. Estates Ltd v. Church Commissioners for England* [1988] 3 W.L.R. 368.
[8] *Junior Books v. The Veitchi Company*, 1982 S.L.T. 492 at 504.

because the flooring is defective or valueless or useless and requires to be replaced. So to hold would raise very difficult and delicate issues of principle having a wide potential application. I think it would necessarily follow that any manufacturer of products would become liable to the ultimate purchaser if the product, owing to negligence in manufacture was, without being harmful in any way, useless or worthless or defective in quality so that the purchaser wasted the money he spent on it . . . To introduce a general liability convering such situations would be disruptive of commercial practice, under which manufacturers of products commonly provide the ultimate purchaser with limited guarantees usually undertaking only to replace parts exhibiting defective workmanship and excluding any consequential loss. There being no contractual relationship between manufacturer and ultimate consumer, no room would exist, if the suggested principle were accepted, for limiting the manufacturer's liability. The policy considerations which would be involved in introducing such a state of affairs appear to me to be such as a court of law cannot assess, and the question whether or not it would be in the interests of commerce and the public generally is, in my view much better left for the legislature."[9]

What the above passage does not do is distinguish between some features which may regularly occur in production of goods, which do not regularly occur in production of buildings. The important factor is the range of potential pursuers. Goods normally issue forth to all and sundry whereas houses and buildings are limited to a normally smaller number.[10] The answer cannot be to simply distinguish between goods and heritage. The majority decided upon a notion of proximity. Proximity allows some cases to come in and some to be excluded without drawing an arbitrary line between heritage and goods. Thus Lords Fraser and Roskill were able to accommodate the paradigm case within the doctrine of proximity:

"I would decide this appeal strictly on its own facts. I rely particularly on the very close proximity between the parties which in my view distinguishes this case from the case of producers of goods to be offered for sale to the public."[11]

As we have seen Lord Keith had also agreed that the paradigm case should be excluded, although not articulated so clearly in terms of proximity. It is a dictum of Lord Roskill's which, it is submitted, accurately reflects the extent to which, at its highest, *Junior Books* is authority for a legal rule for recovery of a certain type of economic loss:

"I therefore ask first whether there was the requisite degree of proximity so as to give rise to the relevant duty of care relied on by the respondents. I regard the following facts as a crucial importance in

---

[9] *Junior Books v. The Veitchi Company*, 1982 S.L.T. 492 at 496.
[10] Although clearly multi-occupancy, tower blocks with different land-holding interests overlapping are not uncommon and indeed are, in view of the sums involved likely to reach the courts.
[11] *Junior Books v. The Veitchi Company*, 1982 S.L.T. 492 at 494.

requiring an affirmative answer to that question. (1) The appellants were nominated subcontractors. (2) The appellants were specialists in flooring. (3) The appellants knew what products were required by the respondents and their main contractors and specialised in the production of those products. (4) The appellants alone were responsible for the composition and construction of the flooring. (5) The respondents relied upon the appellants' skill and experience. (6) The appellants as nominated sub contractors must have known that the respondents relied upon their skill and experience. (7) The relationship between the parties was a close as it could be short of actual privity of contract. (8) The appellants must be taken to have known that if they did the work negligently (as it must be assumed that they did) the resulting defects would at some time require remedying by the respondents expending money upon the remedial measures as a consequence of which the respondents would suffer financial or economic loss."[12]

To any practitioner used to arguing closely and at length on the basis of precedent, this judgment could cause no great difficulty. The leading speech expressly declares itself to be doing no more than applying the law as already set out in *Hedley Byrne*. Further, it specifies in considerable detail what factors allowed the necessary finding of relationship, proximity or assumption of responsibility. It is only the fear of extension to other cases, properly raised in academic writing, and supported by speculative argument by the profession, that made this statement of the law a problem.[13]

10–25   There is another factor which has not been emphasised sufficiently in discussions of the case. *Junior Books* was, like *Donoghue*, argued on the basis of a plea to the relevancy. The defenders were unlikely to give credence to the claim against them by arguing on the basis of their contract with the main contractor. Lord Fraser and Lord Roskill could not have done more to emphasise that this was indeed an important consideration. In short, in other cases, these are the very factors that can be used in defence.[14] The best example is from Lord Fraser and it is a model for an argument against a *Junior Books* type case:

"a duty not to produce a defective article sets a standard which is less easily ascertained because it has to be judged largely by reference to the contract. . . . A Building constructed in fulfilment of a contract for a price of £100,000 might justly be regarded as defective, although the same building constructed in fulfilment of a contract for a price of £50,000 might not. Where a building is erected under a contract with a purchaser, then provided the building, or part of it, is not dangerous to persons or to other property and subject to the law against misrepresentation, I see no reason why the builder should not be free to make with

[12] *ibid*. at 501.

[13] Obviously in the absence of the necessary proximity or assumption of responsibility there is no duty and that was held to be the case in *Hamble Fisheries Ltd v. L Gardner and Son* [1999] T.L.R. 7. The plaintiffs sued for damages for a defective engine. The defendants were the purchasers of the manufacturers of the engine.

[14] *British Telecommunications plc v. James Thomson & Sons (Engineers) Ltd*, 1997 S.L.T. 767.

the purchaser whatever contractual arrangements about the quality of the product the purchaser wishes. However jerry-built the product, the purchaser would not be entitled to damages from the builder if it came up to the contractual standard. I do not think a subsequent owner could be in any better position, but in most cases he would not know the details of the contractual arrangements and, without such knowledge, he might well be unable to judge whether the product was defective or not. But in this case the respondents, although not a party to the contract with the appellants, had full knowledge of the appellants contractual duties , and this difficulty does not arise. What the position might have been if the action had been brought by a subsequent owner is a matter which does not have to be decided now."[15]

This point was too perplexing for Lord Brandon. He asked, "by what standard or standards of quality would the question of defectiveness fall to be decided?" Using the paradigm case as the position of greatest weakness for the majority he put the matter in this way:

"In the case of goods bought from a retailer, it could hardly be the standard prescribed by the contract between the retailer and the wholesaler, or between the wholesaler and the distributor, or between the distributor and the manufacturer, for the terms of such contracts would not even be known to the ultimate buyer."[16]

It is submitted that this is not the correct view and that instead Lord Fraser was correct to leave the matter open. In *Junior Books* the contracts were not before the court. If they had been it is difficult to think of a case which could not have been justly resolved. In that *Junior Books* is a species of *Hedley Byrne* liability, the contractual documents could show whether or not and to what extent, the defender assumed responsibility for the work done.

The position in Scotland is that *Junior Books* has been considered and **10–26** applied a number of times, quite correctly, as an instance of reliance based liability which will only occur in certain, usually uncommon, situations.[17] It will continue to be so used, especially as any doubts as to its validity must have been removed by its treatment in *Murphy*[18] wherein it was treated properly as a reliance case. In the sheriff court a proof before answer was allowed[19] where an upstairs proprietor sued builders working on the downstairs property. Claims for redecoration and loss of rental were also allowed to proceed to proof before answer.[20] On the other hand, an argument that Scotland had steered a different course and that *Junior Books* was binding in a case of allegedly defective design instructed by a third party but known to be intended for use by the tenant did not carry

---

[15] *Junior Books v. The Veitchi Company*, 1982 S.L.T. 492 at 495.

[16] *ibid.* at 504.

[17] *Norwich Union Life Insurance Society v. Covell Matthews Partnership*, 1987 S.L.T. 452; *Grampian Regional Council v. Cowan & Linn*, 1989 S.L.T. 787.

[18] *Murphy v. Brentwood DC* [1990] 3 W.L.R. 414. See Chaps 6, 10 and 19.

[19] Even after *D. & F. Estates*: *D & F Estates v. Church Commissioners* [1988] 3 W.L.R. 368.

[20] *Watson v. C. & D. Builders*, 1989 G.W.D. 28–1286.

favour in *Strathford East Kilbride Ltd v. HLM Design Ltd.*[21] Strathford were affiliated to the Ford Motor Co. Ford engaged HLM to design a new dealership. Strathford leased the dealership from Ford. It needed expensive repairs causing economic losses. It was held not to be the same contractual chain as *Junior Books* (which is true but not necessarily determinative). Clearly too the pursuers did not own the premises whereas *Junior Books* owned the floor. There were interesting contractual and *ius quaesitum tertio* cases.[22]

Secondary cases

The non-recovery rule

10–27 The general position here is that the overall concern over recovery for economic loss remains and the *Hedley Byrne* head of liability is generally speaking of no assistance. The non-recovery position is vouched by many cases of high authority both in Scotland and in England. It was held in the mid-nineteenth century that an employer could not recover for the loss of his employee's services when the employee had been injured by the defender.[23] This was followed in slightly different circumstance is an early twentieth century case.[24] In a case dealing with secondary harm deriving from property damage rather than personal injury, the House of Lords refused to allow recovery where a person suffered loss as a result of damage to property but where the pursuer did not own that property.[25]

10–28 While it might have been thought that *Hedley Byrne* meant the rule might no longer apply that was revealed not to be the case in *Dynamco Ltd v. Holland and Hannen and Cubitts (Scotland) Ltd.*[26] That case was at the instance of occupiers of a factory against contractors who were working nearby. The contractors cut the electricity cable leading to the factory. The claim was one for a purely economic loss on the ground that the plant was unable to operate for over 15 hours. The cable it should be noted belonged to the South of Scotland Electricity Board.[27] The same decision was arrived at after another 20 years of jurisprudence, albeit the issues canvassed were much wider, perhaps unnecessarily so.[28] In *Blackburn v. Sinclair,*[29] the driver of a taxi was slightly injured. He sued for damage to the taxi. He was buying it on hire-purchase. He was held not entitled to sue on the bright-line rule. It was of course accepted that he might have a claim for loss of use or hire of another vehicle. To the extent that the case says that the hirer may sue for the damage to his interest it is correct and indeed it is correct on the application of the bright-line rule.

---

[21] 1999 S.L.T. 121; 1997 S.C.L.R. 877; 1997 Rep. L.R. 112.
[22] A case by occupiers against sub-contractors was dismissed in *Charcuterie Continental v. Lintec Laminations Ltd*, 1998 G.W.D. 10–484. See generally J.M. Arnott, "Defects in Building and Pure Economic Loss" (1989) 34 J.L.S. 183.
[23] *Allan v. Barclay* (1864) 2 M. 873.
[24] *Reavis v. Clan Line Steamers*,1925 S.L.T. 538.
[25] *Simpson & Co. v. Thomson* (1877) 5 R. (H.L.) 40.
[26] 1972 S.L.T. 38.
[27] See the later English case for similar issues: *Spartan Steel & Alloys Ltd v. Martin & Co (Contractors) Ltd* [1973] Q.B. 27.
[28] *Coleridge v. Miller*, 1997 S.L.T. 487.
[29] 1984 S.L.T. 368.

Another branch of secondary cases are those where goods are damaged **10–29** while they are not the property of the buyer. The buyer having taken the risk of damage cannot sue the seller but seeks to sue the person whose lack of care caused the loss. Old cases made it clear this was an economic loss and thus subject to the non-recovery rule. However, *Hedley Byrne* forced a reconsideration. That reconsideration was not successful.[30] *Anns* did however appear to widen the *Hedley Byrne* principle and there followed two successful challenges at first instance.[31] However, the House of Lords took the opportunity of forcefully emphasising the non recovery rule in *Leigh and Sillivan Ltd v. Aliakmon Shipping Co. Ltd.*[32] The plaintiffs argued that *Hedley Byrne*, *Anns* and *Junior Books* had so changed the law that the old cases should be ignored. The grounds were that *Junior Books* was not in point. The policy of the law had been to refuse such claims and this generated certainty in the law which is of value to commerce. Cases where this problem arose were unusual.

Where the pursuers do not have property in the goods but certain **10–30** contractual rights in respect of them, the exclusionary rule applies. In *East Lothian Angling Association v. Haddington Town Council*,[33] the pursuers who held permissions to fish in the Tyne were unable to sue the Burgh for polluting the river and causing damage to the fish they actually fished and economic loss by the loss of permits to fish. Their property right was insufficient. Interestingly, it was thought that the claim would in any event have been too remote for the riparian proprietors. The Inner House followed the bright line non-recovery in *Nacap Ltd v. Moffat Plant Ltd*[34] in which damage was done to a pipe, owned by a third party, upon which the pursuers were working, and for which the pursuers were contractually responsible.

Exceptions to the non-recovery rule in secondary cases

There is one principal exception to (or perhaps a proviso within) the **10–31** rule. That was expressed by Lord Penzance in an *obiter* comment in one of the leading cases.[35] The pursuer can succeed where he has a title to the property like lien or hypothec. It is submitted that by this was meant a contractual right which brought about a right in respect of the property which was good against the owner. The Scottish case *United Technologies Corp. Inc. v. North Scottish Helicopters Ltd*[36] it is submitted goes too far if it is to find support under this dictum.

---

[30] *Margarine Union GmbH v. Cambay Prince Steamship Co.* [1969] 1 Q.B. 219 ("The Wear Breeze").

[31] *Schiffart & Kohlen GmbH v. Chelsea Maritime Ltd ("The Irene's Success")* [1982] Q.B. 481 (now overruled); *The Nea Tyhi* [1982] 1 Lloyd's Rep. 606 (*obiter*), now disapproved.

[32] [1986] W.L.R. 902. See J. Adams and R. Brownsword, "The Aliakmon and the Hague Rules" [1990] J.B.L. 23.

[33] 1980 S.L.T. 213.

[34] 1987 S.L.T. 221 and see also *Mull Shellfish Ltd v. Golden Sea Produce Ltd*, 1992 S.L.T. 703. See *Black v. Braer Corp.* 1999 S.L.T. 1401; *Eunson v. Braer Corporation*, 1999 S.L.T. 1405 which, while considering the interpretation of the Merchant Shipping (Oil Pollution) Act 1971, discusses similar common law issues. See also S.L. Stuart, "Title to Sue in Respect of Damage to Property" 1986 S.L.T. (News) 257; W.J. Stewart, "Economic Loss from Damage to Others' Property", 1987 S.L.T. (News) 145.

[35] *Simpson & Co. v. Thomson* (1877) 5 R. (H.L.) 40.

[36] 1988 S.L.T. 77.

10-32   There is an exception in substance but not in form created by statute: the Administration of Justice Act 1982, ss. 7–10. As will be seen below[37] the Act provides for a defender to pay money to a pursuer which represents either money that the pursuer has to pay to others or another party, but it should be noted that the procedure and provisions are carefully ordered to prevent one of the dangers sought to be avoided by the non-recovery rule. The defender is faced with a single quantifiable claim. The person who has been injured by the wrong is protected by a trust, that most suspect of doctrines in Scotland.[38]

10-33   There is a potential exception, presently not open on the basis of authority. Its leading judicial exposition is that of Goff, L.J. (as he then was) in the Court of Appeal decision in *Leigh and Sillivan Ltd v. Aliakmon Shipping Co. Ltd*.[39] It is as follows:

> "There is a recognisable principle underlying the imposition of liability, which can be called the principle of transferred loss. Furthermore, that principle can be formulated. For the purposes of the present case, I would formulate it in the following deliberately narrow terms, while recognising that it may require modification in the light of experience. Where A owes a duty of care in tort not to cause physical damage to B's property, and commits a breach of that duty in circumstances in which the loss of or physical damage to the property will ordinarily fall on B but (as is reasonably foreseeable by A) such loss or damage, by reason of a contractual relationship between B and C, falls upon C, then C will be entitled, subject to the terms of any contract restricting A's liability to B, to bring an action in tort against A in respect of such loss or damage to the extent that it falls on him C."[40]

This is not yet Scots law nor is it English law, having been rejected by the House of Lords. A reader with a case worth a very large sum of money may well try to have the House "do a *Murphy*".[41] In *White v. Jones*[42] Lord Goff again discussed the principle of transferred loss.[43] He tried to vindicate his position in *Aliakmon*[44] by reference to the fact that the Law Commission[45] introduced the Carriage of Goods by Sea Act 1992. He did accept that *White* was not a case of transferred loss but thought there were parallels.[46] There is no doubt that the bright line rule becomes much less attractive in situations like this one. There is only the one loss and so there are no problems with the floodgates fear. From there the argument is that in cases where there is a very small class of injured individuals then these victims or one of their number is within the scope of reasonable foreseeability. That

---

[37] See para. 18–35.
[38] A. Reed, "Carer's Recompense Held on Trust" [1994] J.P.I.L. 215.
[39] [1986] W.L.R. 902 (HL). The Court of Appeal report is [1985] Q.B. 350.
[40] *ibid.* at 917.
[41] It should be noted that the actual result in some of the carriage of goods cases has been reformed in favour of the pursuer by legislation: Carriage of Goods Act 1992.
[42] *White v. Jones* [1995] 2 A.C. 207. See Chap. 12.
[43] *ibid.* at 264.
[44] *Leigh and Sillivan Ltd v. Aliakmon Shipping Co. Ltd* [1986] A.C. 785.
[45] Both Commissions, Scottish and English, did.
[46] *White v. Jones* [1995] 2 A.C. 207 at 265.

argument was disposed of trenchantly by Lord Fraser in the case of a damaged vessel under charter in the *"Mineral Transporter"*.[47] His view was that it was not possible to draw a line at any particular class—like a class in a school there could always be more people in it or it could be described as a subset of a larger class. While this may benefit from a certain logic, it does not accord with common-sense which is often prayed in aid today in duty questions. If A drops a bomb on a school he knows within reasonable bounds the sort of damage that will be caused. It is true on the other hand that if negotiating a premium on an insurance policy the insurers would point out there are some very large comprehensives and some very small village schools. But the range of damage and the range of premiums could be adjusted. The difference between logic and common sense is that the whole world will not actually ever be in the same school. Thus in the Commonwealth there have been decisions in favour of liability where in fact the range of potential plaintiffs was to the reasonable foreseeability of the actual defendant, very small.[48] While the objection to this at the time the *Mineral Transporter* was decided, that such an approach means that each case has to be taken individually, the English law has now committed itself to doing that by use of the fair, just and reasonable test.

Diverted Assets

This section discusses a clutch of cases which are distinguishable from **10–34** others involving financial loss. Here the pursuer should have had an inheritance but through neglect it goes somewhere else. Because it is the *testator* who relies on the solicitor preparing the will and not the beneficiary, the *Hedley Byrne* reliance principle cannot be used to establish liability. The foundation case is *Ross v. Caunters*[49] which although a decision of a single judge in Chancery, carried considerable weight. A solicitor failed to warn a testator that under the applicable English law a legacy to an intended beneficiary would not be valid if signed by the spouse of the intended beneficiary.[50] In a later case a solicitor who failed to incorporate a clients instructions in favour of a third party in an enforceable deed was held, following *Caparo*, not to owe a duty to the third party who was disappointed because the living client had changed his mind.[51] The key factor in the judges' opinion was that in this case it was possible for the client to reinstate the provision, he was not dead as in *Ross v. Caunters*.[52] Accordingly, it was not being said that there could not be a duty in the case of *inter vivos* deeds, the example being given where an employee lost because of the employer's (client) instructions being carelessly implemented by a solicitor in respect of some tax efficiency scheme.

The law has been settled in England by the House of Lords decision **10–35** *White v. Jones*.[53] It was held that a solicitor owes a duty of care to a disappointed beneficiary where the solicitor negligently carries out the

---

[47] *Candlewood Navigation Corp. Ltd v. Mitsui Lines* [1986] A.C. 1.
[48] *Norsk Pacific Steamship Co. Ltd v. Canadian National Railway Co.* (1992) 91 D.L.R. (4th) 289; *Caltex Oil v. The Dredge Willemstad*, (1976/77) 136 C.L.R. 529.
[49] [1980] 1 Ch. 297.
[50] See *Clarke v. Bruce Lane* [1988] 1 All E.R. 364.
[51] *Hemmes v. Wilson Brown* [1993] T.L.R. 365.
[52] [1980] 1 Ch. 297.
[53] [1995] 2 A.C. 207.

client testator's instructions, in this case to prepare a fresh will benefiting the plaintiffs. The main difficulty, which nearly had Lord Nolan voting in the other direction, is the asymmetry of the case: the beneficiaries under the old will took the estate. Although not unlike the well-known *Ross v. Caunters*, *White* is different because in *Ross* a solicitor was sued for a failure in the production of an effective will whereas in *White* the defect had been one of execution in that the will had not been produced at all. These cases are especially difficult in that the value is transferred to someone—just the wrong someone. The person who does not get the estate does not suffer a loss to their patrimony but fails to make an anticipated gain. This was yet another 3-2 House of Lords negligence decision.[54] This decision bears to be an extension of *Hedley Byrne* but obviously (due to the nature of the loss) it is quite different. It does not fit into the reliance aspects of that case so well for the beneficiaries do not rely on a particular solicitor but the step taken was to extend the *assumption of responsibility* interpretation of *Hedley Byrne* to protect the intended beneficiaries.[55] Lord Goff concluded that a tort remedy as suggested in *Ross* could not apply. Not only that he did not think that *Hedley Byrne* itself applied—it had to be extended. Lord Browne-Wilkinson explained that assumption of responsibility goes back as far as *Nocton v. Lord Ashburton*.[56] He took reassurance from the fact that in *Merrett* assumption of responsibility extended to negligent acts as much as negligent statements.[57] It was also important in making it clear that the fact a contract existed did not mean that the tortious duty was excluded in this particular case—the contract between the testator and the solicitor would not stand in the way.[58]

10-36   The effect of the case from an economic point of view is not the usual one of making a defender pay for a loss of the plaintiff. In this case the loss is of an expectation, something normally protected by contract. The original beneficiaries take the testators money and the plaintiffs take the solicitors insurers money.[59] Thus there is no restoration of the *status quo ante* because those who benefited from the negligence keep their gain. Thus the reservations must remain about this head of liability.[60] There are two main

---

[54] Lord Keith among the dissenters.

[55] *White* also dealt with the last remaining vestige of "privity" in tort, the rule laid down in the Scottish House of Lords appeal of *Robertson v. Fleming* (1861) 23 D. (H.L.) 8, discussed in Chap. 12, in the context of the liability of solicitors, the only defenders to which it still arguably applies. It was not over-ruled.

[56] [1914] A.C. 932.

[57] *White v. Jones* [1995] 2 A.C. 207 at 274.

[58] Although based on *Merrett* it could if it were the case that there were something in that contract that protected the doctor.

[59] Unless there are "conveyancing" provisions which would allow the will to be rectified as appears to be the case in England. There is authority that in some cases, that has to be sought. In *Walker v. Geo. H. Mendicott & Son* [1998] T.L.R. 734 it was held in the Court of Appeal that *White v. Jones* would not apply if there were another remedy available. In *Walker* the allegation was that the solicitor did not correctly understand his instructions and make the appropriate provision in favour of the plaintiff. However, under English law, section 20 of the Administration of Justice Act 1982 it is possible for a person such as the plaintiff to petition for rectification of the will. That should have been tried first. This provision has the valuable effect of properly directing the benefit. Later in *Horsfall v. Haywards* [1999] T.L.R. 173 the Court of Appeal while upholding the general approach in *Walker* held that the facts before them were not such that an application for rectification had been required of the plaintiff.

[60] However, it is refreshing to see that reasonable foreseeability came into Lord Goff's justification for what could be said to be an extension of *Hedley Byrne*.

features which support liability: (1) that there is a loss (albeit a curious one) caused by neglect; and (2) there is a public interest in solicitors preparing wills and where they fail the victims should be compensated. Lords Mustill and Keith dissenting could not see anything sufficiently special in the relationship which would not extend liability in an uncontrolled way. Perhaps Lord Nolan in the majority reached the true ground by saying that a professional man or artisan who undertakes to exercise skill which may cause loss assumes a liability. This is a very old principle and could be seen as one which is similar to *Hedley Byrne*, which helped form *Hedley Byrne* but which is independent thereof. So long as liability is limited to the professional or the artisan then the potential defenders are identified. They know to insure. Their insurer then wants to know how much to charge by way of premium and must thus know the extent of liability. Providing the solicitor enquires as to the value of the estate there would be no trouble. Before these cases he need not have asked as there was no claim. Now as there might be, it is essential to make sure that the value of the estate which might be the measure of a claim against him is covered by the limit of his indemnity insurance. A letter of instruction from the testator could determine this matter and help limit the amount of the assumption of responsibility. Many artisans, however, do not have indemnity insurance. Neither is it likely that intended beneficiaries could contract with the solicitor.

The decision in *White* has already been extended having been held to **10–37** apply to a major plc offering a will-making service.[61]

(2) INDIRECT PHYSICAL INJURY AND INDIRECT PROPERTY DAMAGE

The distinction between primary and secondary economic loss serves very **10–38** well as an organising structure both for exposition and for prediction. A recent phenomena has been to over-plead *Murphy*, to say that in every new set of facts the duty must be fair, just and reasonable. That seems both unnecessary and potentially dangerous to the structure of the law and to reaching the correct result. *Murphy* did not require such a step and the rhetorical convenience of fair, just and reasonable may have led to its adoption. It is also favourable to defenders and so may be used perhaps rather cynically as another string to the bow. However, full "Murphyisation" received support in *Marc Rich & Co. AG v. Bishop Rock Marine Co. Ltd.*[62] It has been perceived as justifying the use of the fair, just and reasonable test in all new cases and so requires careful examination. A tanker developed a crack in its hull carrying a cargo incorporating the Hague Visby rules. It was inspected by a surveyor acting for the vessels classification society. The surveyor recommended permanent repairs in dry-dock there and then in Puerto Rico but the surveyor was persuaded to change his mind, allowed temporary repairs and the vessel to sail. The *Nicholas H* sank as a result of the temporary welding failing. After sundry claims the cargo owners were still carrying a loss and sued the classification

---

[61] *Esterhuizen v. Allied Dunbar Assurance plc.* [1998] T.L.R. 369.
[62] [1995] 3 All E.R. 307.

society. For the purposes of the legal argument on duty the parties accepted that the plaintiffs had title to sue, it was foreseeable that lack of care was likely to expose the cargo to physical damage, that the damage suffered was physical damage and that the damage was as a result of the carelessness of the surveyor. At first instance the plaintiffs were successful. The Court of Appeal allowed an appeal on the basis that the cargo having been sent under the Hague Visby rules meant that the shipowner and not the defendants was under a duty. The House of Lords decided by a 4–1 majority to agree with the Court of Appeal and refused the appeal. Lord Steyn gave the speech in which the majority concurred. The factual and legal background is certainly essential to an understanding of the case. Owners to insure must have their ships classified by societies such as the third defendants Nippon Kaiji Kyokai (NKK). Charterers will not hire unclassified or uninsurable ships. Therefore the role of the classifiers is of enormous commercial importance. NKK were a non-profit organisation and a non-governmental organisation set up to promote safety of life and ships at sea.[63] The survey was carried out because the owners were obliged to seek it. The plaintiff appellants argued strongly that as this was a case of foreseeable physical property damage to a party with admitted title to sue the case should not be thwarted by reference to decisions in other more difficult areas such as economic loss and nervous shock. The requirements for proximity and the need to meet a fair, just and reasonableness test were not applicable. But Lord Steyn relied on a dictum of Saville L.J. in the Court of Appeal to say that whatever the nature of the harm these matters were to be considered.[64] This case was too special on its own facts to be decided by analogy with *Donoghue*, or indeed any later cases.[65] All the relevant facts were considered and weighed including the suggestion that the surveyor was actually dealing with the ship which held the plaintiffs' cargo—he was physically proximate.[66] This approach if documented in the same way as was done by Lord Steyn would certainly allow first instance decisions to be subject to scrutiny. Very importantly lest it be thought this case over-ruled *Donoghue*, Lord Steyn made it clear that he did not agree, as was argued by the plaintiffs that this was a case of *direct* physical loss. The shipowner was directly responsible for the cargo. Certainly *Minchella* could not be said to have taken responsibility for the safety of the drink and so there is a valid distinction. And it is easier in a case such as that posited by Lord Steyn where there would probably have been liability if the surveyor had dropped a lighted match into the hold full of combustable material.[67] Reliance was argued but was not sufficient to establish liability. Lord Steyn considered the reliance of the owners was on the carriers. It must be assumed therefore that there was insufficient pleading to argue that they would rely on a shipowner assisted by classification societies—that they would only send their goods by a shipowner or charterer whose ship was registered and complied with the registration society's requirements. The major factor against the imposition seems to have been the effect on

---

[63] *March Rich & Co. AG v. Bishop Rock Marine Co. Ltd* [1995] 3 All E.R. 307 at 324.
[64] *ibid.* at 327.
[65] *ibid.* at 327.
[66] *ibid.* at 327.
[67] *ibid.* at 328.

the operation of international trade including the effect of insurance.[68] The fact that the classification societies act for the collective welfare was thought to justify a more careful imposition of duties of care where direct physical damage was not the issue.[69] There was a fear that they might take a more defensive position. At the end of his review of the various arguments Lord Steyn was willing to assume without deciding that there was sufficient proximity but that it was not fair, just and reasonable to impose such a duty. The decision is a unfortunate. It dubiously utilises the fair, just and reasonableness test in a case of property damage. It is the duty of courts applying justice between litigants to do so without considering the insurance market. If liability had been established for what would, if true, have been an atrocious piece of work, risking life as well as cargo, the market would adjust. If the likes of NKK are there to preserve life and property on the seas then they must not be encouraged to yield to pressure and allow dangerous ships to sail. A wolf in sheep's clothing is more dangerous than the obvious wolf. The argument that the societies would face expensive insurance costs is of course one that depends entirely upon the risk involved. Clearly there would be a premium but there is a market in insurance and if the NKK surveyors normally do a better job than this one did then the premium will be low. If normally they had done as this surveyor did at the outset—which was to insist on permanent repairs in dry dock then claims will be few. If they did decide to act unprofessionally—to force ships to undergo unnecessary repairs at cost to all parties then the result would at least be safety. However, as there appears to be a market in classification societies the unprofessionally over-cautious would soon no longer be consulted. Assume too that although these are "non profit organisations" they are large organisations which charge for their services and employ many and are no doubt administered by highly paid officials. If they cannot do the right thing then the ship-owners, insurers or government could put something else in place. The essence of the case seems to be the need for an independent expert on the ground. That in itself does not demand one of these societies.

Marc Rich has been taken in Scotland as allowing theoretical issues from **10–39** primary economic loss cases to be brought to bear in a property damages case. In *British Telecom v. Thomson*[70] a subcontractor's work caused property *damage* (unlike in this respect *Junior Books*). Yet the case was argued as if it were an economic loss case. The claim was not allowed and that finding upheld on appeal by a 2–1 majority in the Inner House.[71] That finding was reversed in the House of Lords but strictly on interpretation of the contract which was part of the contractual matrix founded upon.[72] It can

---

[68] *ibid.* at 330. Reference is made there to two academic articles: P.F. Cane, "The Liability of Classification Societies" [1994] L.M.C.L.Q. 363; M. Clarke, "Misdelivery and Time Bars" [1990] L.M.C.L.Q. 314.

[69] *ibid.* at 321.

[70] [1997] Rep. L.R. 23.

[71] See generally J. Convery, "Contractual Structures and Duty of Care: *British Telecommunications plc v. James Thomson & Sons Ltd*", 1997 S.L.T. (News) 113; J. Convery, "Contractual Settings and Duty of Care: A Re-appraisal" (1999) Rep. B. 27–4.

[72] However, it should be noted that according to Lord Mackay who gave the only reasoned speech, the position in argument before the House of Lords was somewhat different from that presented in the Court of Session.

tentatively be suggested that it can be taken from that House of Lords Appeal that *Marc Rich* should not be treated as being of wide general significance. In *Coleridge v. Miller*[73] there was another case of simple property damage which is burdened by a consideration of what it is thought *Murphy* did to the law. Once the defender has damaged the pursuer's property in a reasonably foreseeable way causing harm of the kind which was envisaged only remoteness of damage can save the wrongdoer.

10-40   The law may be coming back on course with a Court of Appeal decision which forced a reconsideration of *Marc Rich*. In *Perrett v. Collins*[74] the plaintiff claimed damages for injuries sustained when the plane in which he was a passenger crashed. He sued, *inter alios*, the inspector who inspected it for a certificate of airworthiness and the certifying authority. It was accepted that the harm was reasonably foreseeable and there had been carelessness. The defendants understandably founded on *Marc Rich*. They argued the fair, just and reasonableness test applied. Hobhouse, L.J. said that *Marc Rich* was of no assistance as it was an economic loss case and not a personal injury case. This is with respect, dodging the issue, which has been discussed above. It is submitted that although indeed it was like an economic loss case it was a property damage case and as such could and probably should have been dealt with under the neighbour principle. In short, it is submitted that the defenders were right to submit the *Marc Rich* rule was applicable. Then it is possible to say with Hobhouse, L.J. that a further balkinisation could be carried out by saying that *Perrett* is about indirect physical injury and that the rule for indirect physical injury is different to the rule for indirect property damage. That would be the logical exposition. The difficulty would then be whether it is right to have different rules. Because the Court of Appeal did not confront the issue directly the position is presently unclear. It is submitted that while there can be two opposite rules some justification would have to be forthcoming other than that personal injury is sometimes sadder than property damage. Sometimes it is, but not if one compares the broken finger with the wrecked core business asset.

(3) Public Law

10-41   In traditional analytical jurisprudence, delict is analysed as part of the private law, distinct from public law. For ease of exposition and on practical grounds this division can be supported. The theoretical literature is vast and often helpful.[75] Courts in the United Kingdom are reluctant to intervene

---

[73] 1997 S.L.T. 487.
[74] [1998] T.L.R. 393.
[75] See *e.g.* D. Brodie, "Public Authorities and the Duty of Care" [1996] J.R. 127; S.H. Bailey and M.J. Bowman, "The Policy/Operational Dichotomy—a Cuckoo in the Nest" [1986] C.L.J. 430; J.J. Doyle, "The Liability of Public Authorities" (1994) 1 Tort L. Rev 189; A.M. Dugdale, "Public Authority Liability: To what Standard? (1994) 1 Tort L. Rev 143; I.N. Duncan Wallace, "Negligence and Defective Buildings: Confusion Confounded?" (1989) 105 L.Q.R. 46; I.N. Duncan Wallace, "No Somersault after Murphy: New Zealand follows Canada" (1995) 111 L.Q.R. 285; B. Feldthusen, "Failure to Confer Discretionary Public Benefits: The Case for Complete Negligence Immunity" [1997] Tort L.R. 17; Justice J. Sopinka, "The Liability of Public Authorities: Drawing the Line" (1993) 1 Tort L. Rev 123; S. Todd, "Negligence Liability of Public Authorities: Divergence in the Common Law" (1986) 102 L.Q.R. 370; S. Todd, "Defective Property: The Turn of the Privy Council" (1996) Tort L. Rev. 91.

where the true arbiter should be a ballot box. The making of an allegation of lack of care for which the government is liable is not the place for arguing that the incident happened because the government did the wrong thing so far as the pursuer is concerned; there may be many other citizens who would agree with it and they cannot all be called. It should also be remembered that it is possible for justice to be achieved in cases not involving large political issues through a system of administrative law; a system which has built into it the legitimate public interest At this extreme the courts cannot and, it might be said under the present constitution, should not interfere. So there are cases which have the effect of protecting some defenders from what would otherwise be instances of liability. These can also be seen as cases where reasonable foreseeability and proximity do not overcome what can in some cases be called public policy, but in some others might reasonably be called jural policy—the separation of analytical legal categories.

Statutory duty

Many public authorities operate under statutory provisions. Sometimes they **10–42** confer powers, sometimes they impose duties and sometimes both. This should be seen as the background against which the decision to impose a duty is taken. Cases of statutory duty proper[76] are different. In such cases it is being argued that as a matter of construction a certain legal person is liable under a statute. Cases where the authority is the occupier of premises, employer of workers or the keeper of an animal do not present difficulties because in such cases the authority is not in any sense acting as a creature of public law nor is it being sought to be made liable through its powers. In these cases the authority is liable just like an individual.

The Great English Cases

The landmark case was *Dorset Yacht v. Home Office*.[77] The Home Office **10–43** claimed they were immune from liability in respect of damage caused by escaping borstal boys to the plaintiffs' property when they had been allowed to escape through the inattention of borstal officers. The defendant was unsuccessful. After that *Anns v. Merton LBC*[78] held a local authority liable for not having spotted the contravention of house-building regulations. In that case Lord Wilberforce adopted the distinction between operational matters which are likely to attract liability and policy matters which would not. That distinction was criticised by academics.[79] It was specifically considered by Lord Keith in *Rowling v. Takaro Properties Ltd*.[80] He said the

---

[76] Described in Chap. 11.

[77] [1970] A.C. 1004.

[78] [1978] A.C. 728.

[79] S.H. Bailey and M.J. Bowman, "The Policy/Operational Dichotomy—A Cuckoo in the Nest" [1986] C.L.J. 430 and see for a more up to date consideration B. Feldthusen, "Failure to Confer Discretionary Public Benefits: The Case for Complete Negligence Immunity" [1997] Tort L.R. 17; Justice J. Sopinka, "The Liability of Public Authorities: Drawing the Line" (1993) 1 Tort L. Rev 123.

[80] [1988] A.C. 473.

House was aware that the distinction was not a touchstone of liability but that it helped express the idea that the courts wanted to treat some issues such as the allocation of scarce resources as non-justiciable. Nor is that formulation always anti-liability.[81] In the mid-1990s a Home Secretary refused to resign over a matter which he considered to be operational, saying that he would only resign if a matter were one of policy—while he was responsible for the prison service he was not for every decision. If that view were shared by constitutional lawyers then the operational/policy distinction could indeed become a touchstone. If the politician will not resign over an operational matter then it is sufficiently unimportant, in a constitutional sense, for it to be justiciable before the courts. Other factors affect the liability of public authorities. As it is now considered that it ought to be fair, just and reasonable to impose a new duty, the problems of an authority can be taken account of under that formulation. The existence of alternative remedies (like judicial review) is an important, albeit not decisive, factor.[82]

10–44   In some cases it is clear that policy in the sense of public policy rather than policy/operation can be the ground of decision. The leading modern case is *Hill v. Chief Constable of West Yorkshire*,[83] in which it was held the police were immune from a tort action in respect of having carelessly released a serial killer. Lord Keith considered that the police should not be diverted by court action, they should not have to practice defensively and a court was not the best place to judge police activity. The decision has been followed many times so much so that some earlier cases are harder to reconcile with the more recent.[84] It has been held that the Crown Prosecution Service did not owe a duty to a defendant; in this case one who was arrested for rape and detained for 22 days until released when the prosecution was abandoned. The Court of Appeal applied *Caparo Industries Plc v. Dickman* to reject a duty.[85] The application to the fire brigade has been equally interesting as decisions are not entirely consistent and all sorts of tests are brought to bear.

10–45   In England the fire brigade featured in a number of cases which eventually went to the Court of Appeal.[86] In the Queen's Bench case *Church of Jesus Christ of Latter-Day Saints v. Yorkshire Fire and Civil Defence Authority*[87] it was alleged the brigade had allowed a fire which

---

[81] *Lonrho plc v. Tebbit* [1991] 4 All E.R. 973.

[82] *Rowling v. Takaro Properties Ltd* [1988] A.C. 473; *Curran v. N.I. Co-ownership Housing Association* [1987] A.C. 718; *Murphy v. Brentwood D.C.* [1991] 3 A.C. 398.

[83] [1989] A.C. 53.

[84] Compare *Knightly v. Johns* [1982] 1 W.L.R. 349 and *Rigby v. Chief Constable of Northamptonshire* [1985] 1 W.L.R. 1242 with *Osman v. Fergusson* [1993] 3 All E.R. 345 and *Ancell v. McDermott* [1993] 4 All E.R. 355. The European Court of Human Rights ruled in *Osman* that the decision in *Hill* deprived plaintiffs of the right to a proper hearing. In *Costello v. Chief Constable* [1998] T.L.R. 803 an inspector did not come to the aid of a wpc being attacked by a prisoner. While the Court of Appeal strongly affirmed the non-liability rule protecting the police from liability for failing to protect the public, because there was a "police duty" (from the rules under which officers operate) to protect a fellow officer, there could be a legal duty as well. Since *Osman* the police have been held to owe a duty to an informant not to disclose his identity: *Swinney v. Chief Constable (Northumbria) (No. 2)* [1999] T.L.R. 402 (although it was held in this case that there was no breach of the duty).

[85] *Elguzouli-Daf v. Commissioner of Police for the Metropolis* [1994] T.L.R. 598.

[86] See generally J. Convery, "Suing the Fire Brigade" (1996) Rep.B. 10–2.

[87] [1996] T.L.R. 238.

should have been easily contained to burn down a much more extensive area of the plaintiffs' property. There were seven fire hydrants around the church and it was alleged that four did not work and three were not found. It was held not to be fair, just or reasonable to impose a duty despite the damage being foreseeable and there being a proximate relationship. It was for the individual to insure against fire not for the community to do so. The insurance question is debatable and the level and nature of the conduct complained of does not seem to be very high. In *Capital and Counties plc v. Hampshire County Council*[88] a public policy immunity was not allowed. The fire officer at the scene of a fire ordered that the sprinkler system be turned off by mistake. Potential fire fighting was unlikely to be affected by considerations of liability, as opposed to Lord Keith's fear of defensive policing. These were operational decisions not depending on the allocation of resources. The brigade also had exclusive control of what it was doing. In another Queens Bench decision *John Munroe (Acrylics) Ltd v. London Fire and Civil Defence Authority*[89] no duty was accepted The brigade were called to a place where several fires had been started but had gone out. They did not inspect the unoccupied premises of the plaintiffs which had been affected and burnt. Even although the damage was physical this was considered a novel category. The plaintiffs argued that when called out and attending a fire the brigade had a duty to take care.[90] However, it was considered that the brigade caused no more damage than the original event. This might be a causation case. The fires were started by the second and third defenders. There is a presumption that the first cause continues and the brigade could be exculpated not on a lack of duty to do their job properly but because their fault did not eclipse that of the second and third defenders. But it certainly shows a reluctance to hold this particular authority liable.

All three cases were appealed to the Court of Appeal.[91] All the appeals were refused. It was held that a fire brigade was not under a common law duty to answer a call but could be liable for a danger it created as in the *Capital and Counties* case, the station officer's mistake costing £16m.[92] In *Kent v. Griffiths*,[93] by analogy with the fire brigade cases, it was sought to have a claim against the ambulance service struck out. The Court of Appeal allowed the case to proceed. While there was no duty in general to respond to a 999 call, once it had been the call has been accepted there could be a duty. The main practical reason for allowing the case to proceed was that acceptance of the call precludes those with the patient looking for alternative means of delivering the patient.

In *X (Minors) v. Bedfordshire County Council*[94] the House of Lords in a **10–46** series of related appeals provided extensive protection to public authorities. The cases are of value in relation to the two areas of council activity with

---

[88] [1996] 1 W.L.R. 1553.
[89] [1996] 3 W.L.R. 988.
[90] Taking the same line as the Scots case *Duff v. Highland and Islands Fire Board*, 1995 S.L.T. 1362.
[91] [1997] T.L.R. 141. Requiring the talents of nine Q.C.s.
[92] See generally A. Bartlett and J. Waite, "Searching for Duties of Care: the Fire Brigade Cases" [1997] J.P.I.L. 147.
[93] [1998] T.L.R. 818.
[94] [1995] All E.R. 353.

which they expressly deal and impact on general principle. They are now regularly cited. There were said to be two categories of cases in the appeals: "abuse cases" where the complaint was that children had been harmed because the council failed to take care of them while having various statutory powers to protect children[95]; and the "education cases" where the complaint was that the council had powers to help in the education of children with special needs and had failed so to do. The leading speech was that of Lord Browne-Wilkinson. Some of the propositions stated were essentially lacking in any novelty. "The breach of a public law right by itself gives no claim for damages".[96] In any event his Lordship was at pains to say that he was not attempting any general statement of the applicable law but was seeking to give logical structure to the various arguments canvassed before him.[97] He accepted the well-known cases of breach of statutory duty in which it is accepted that a private law duty arises from a particular statutory duty.[98] He noted these tended to be specific and limited duties and did not involve "general administrative functions imposed on public bodies and involving the exercise of administrative discretion."[99]

A re-analysis of *Dorset Yacht* resulted in it being stated that the case was not authority for the proposition that there is liability for the careless exercise of a statutory duty—only for the imposition of a general duty of care.[1] On the key question of the existence of an ordinary duty of care his Lordship again declined to lay down a general theory or principle.[2] On this core issue the following propositions were laid down, confirmed or can be taken[3]:

(1) A common law duty may arise in the performance of statutory functions.[4]

(2) There is a distinction to be made between taking care in exercising a statutory discretion whether or not to do an act, as, for example, closing a school; and, having decided to do an act taking care in the manner of doing it, as for example looking after the physical condition of pupils in a school.[5]

(3) An authority cannot be liable in damages for doing that which Parliament has authorised.[6]

(4) If the decision is so unreasonable that it falls outside the statutory discretion there may be room for a private law duty.

(5) In considering the "unreasonable" issue under (4) above the test is not the *ultra vires* rule.

---

[95] One of these cases was in fact a case where the council did exercise their powers and took a child into care only to discover later that they had acted on the wrong information.

[96] *ibid.* at 363.

[97] *ibid.* at 364.

[98] See Chap. 11.

[99] *X (Minors) v. Bedfordshire County Council* [1995] 3 All E.R. 353 at 365.

[1] *ibid.* at 367.

[2] *ibid.* at 368.

[3] The numbering here does not follow that of Lord Browne-Wilkinson.

[4] *X (Minors) v. Bedfordshire County Council, op. cit.* at 368.

[5] *ibid.* at 368.

[6] *ibid.* at 368.

(6) In considering (4) above policy matters may arise and they are not matters for the court.

(7) If the courts are not excluded under (6) then the ordinary rules of negligence apply.

(8) An authority may also be liable vicariously or directly, in that through an employee they are purporting to comply with their own direct duty.[7]

It must be said that this particular exposition is, as his Lordship admitted, not necessarily of considerable general assistance. He narrowed the case that will attract liability to a core case over which there might not be much dispute—carelessness in the practical manner in which an act has been performed. That is not much more help than the policy/operational dichotomy.

The decisions in the cases based on these propositions were that in the **10–47** "education cases" there were no "standard" breach of statutory duty cases. On the common law arguments in the "abuse cases" it was considered not to be appropriate to strike the cases out on the "non-justiciable" point as evidence would probably be necessary. However, the ordinary principles of negligence applied and, in a case such as this where a new duty was in contemplation, the fair, just and reasonable test would be applied. These cases would fail that test as liability would interfere with the statutory system. Child care is a sensitive matter, local authorities might act defensively in respect of children and delay taking important decisions being afraid, there are statutory controls of maladministration; and finally, there were no previous analogous cases.

In the education cases the issues were justiciable. At the next stage of considering whether to impose a duty Lord Browne-Wilkinson had not found the matter easy and had changed his views from time to time.[8] He also appreciated that not to find liability might be to allow a grossly negligent authority to escape the consequences of its failure. There was, it was held, no duty: While successful cases would be few there might be many vexatious cases; there were no analogous cases. However, the authority could come under a direct "personal" common law duty in relation to the psychological services it offered:

"Once the decision is taken to offer such a service, a statutory body is in general in the same position as any private individual or organisation holding itself out as offering such a service. By opening its doors to others to take advantage of the service offered, it comes under a duty of care to those using the service to exercise care in its conduct."[9]

The leading example where a duty has been found in the current era is *Welton v. Essex*,[10] discussed below[11] in the context of the overlap with *Hedley Byrne*.

---

[7] *ibid.* at 372.
[8] *ibid.* at 391.
[9] *ibid.* at 392.
[10] [1995] A.C. 633.
[11] See paras 10–55 *et seq.*

X v. Bedfordshire has been discussed and applied many times. One example is *Harris v. Evans*.[12] An HSE inspector decided that the entrepreneurial plaintiffs bungee-jumping operation was contrary to HSE policy. In due course three local authorities shut down the plaintiffs' businesses. The Secretary of State, as a result of the intervention of an M.P., confirmed that the HSE had no policy against using cranes for bungee-jumping. So the local authorities themselves did make a mistake and could be said to be entitled to follow the information they received—there was also an appeal mechanism against their orders. The plaintiff tried to argue from *Welton* but failed. The inspector was not in a sufficiently independent professional role as, for example, a council doctor. An attempt to argue from the dicta in *X v. Bedfordshire* in favour of liability in cases of failure to treat dyslexia by a school authority failed at first instance and in the Court of Appeal.[13]

The influence of European human rights law resulted in the House of Lords accepting that cases such as *X v. Bedfordshire* should not be dealt with by way of striking out without hearing the facts and arguments as to the actual case.[14]

10–48   *Stovin v. Wise*[15] is yet another House of Lords decision on this same general topic, this time dealing with a different kind of case. Stovin on his motor bike collided with Mrs Wise who was not keeping a good lookout. She settled with him but called the council as third parties due to the state of the crossroads where the accident took place. There had been three previous accidents. The council's surveyor examined the site and agreed it was dangerous and that work should be done. This was approved by the council providing the owners of the land would agree to the work being done. Nothing was achieved but, if the council had not delayed, the works could have been done because the owners would have agreed to the work without the need for the council to exercise its statutory powers. By a 3–2 majority[16] the House of Lords denied recovery. Lord Hoffman gave the majority speech. For the majority this was a case involving omissions and thus *Donoghue* could offer only limited help.[17] There is an important distinction between acts and omissions which can be explained on the basis of the political need to impose action on others. Morally there is the "why pick on me?" argument. Anyone could have tried to fix the junction. It was recognised that there are many exceptions—occupiers' liability, and cases of reliance such as lighthouses. It was appreciated the Court of Appeal, which had imposed liability, had noted the omission point and had taken the view that by starting to act this was no longer an omission case[18] and it is common sense principles of causation which determine what is an act or an omission.[19] The failure to conclude the negotiations to adjust the junction did not cause the injury. Lord Hoffman accepted that in this case the "why

---

12 [1998] T.L.R. 284.
13 *Phelps v. Hillington LBC* [1997] T.L.R. 502; [1998] T.L.R. 691; See G. Junor, *"Phelps—Not Necessarily Mission Impossible"* (1999) Rep.B. 26–1.
14 *Barrett v. Enfield LBC* [1999] 3 W.L.R. 79.
15 [1996] A.C. 923.
16 Although a total of six judges seised of the case found for the plaintiff, the defendant just won over the most important three.
17 *Stovin v. Wise*, at 943.
18 *ibid.* at 945.
19 *ibid.*

pick on me?" point did not apply; only the council had the power to solve the problem.[20] *Anns v. Merton*[21] was reviewed, not for its over-ruled finding in relation to economic loss but for its finding that the authority could be liable in respect of a failure to exercise its powers. The two stage *Anns* test was described as being really the same as the more recent formulations but, simply put, the other way around.[22] Lord Hoffmann left open the question whether *Anns* was wrong in ruling that the courts could impose common law duties. It was, however, clear that the policy/operational distinction was inadequate to be a guide to liability.[23] He did not think the lighthouse type of case caused a problem as it was based on representation and reliance and not on the public nature of the authority. Canadian cases where *Anns* had been used along with the policy/operational distinction to impose duties were not thought to be helpful.[24] *Stovin* on its facts was not a compelling case however viewed. Despite the decision having been taken that the work ought to be done, there was no time scale for it. It could have been done in one, two or three years. That would put it in a different budgetary cycle. The cost had not been ascertained. The judge at first instance did not make a finding that the decision was irrational. There was a computer system which identified black spots. This was not such a black spot.[25] There was nothing which suggested that even if this power could raise a duty to act, that a failure so to do would sound in civil liability.[26]

The reasoned dissenting speech was that of Lord Nicholls. He started by **10–49** saying that but for the failure to exercise power the accident would not have happened.[27] That suggests at least causation in fact. Causation was an important aspect for the majority in deciding whether conduct was an act or omission. While accepting that the authority did not create the danger, they did not view the distinction between acts and omissions as being free from controversy and clear cut.[28] Nonetheless, the minority accepted that the distinction was sound in this particular area of law. There has to be a "special justification" for imposing an obligation.[29] The categories of special cases is not closed. Occupiers' liability, as accepted by the majority, is a clear example. In this case where a combination of features were present which would make action desirable, it was still necessary to do more as the case could still fall into the paradigm case of the young child drowning in the shallow pool in respect of whom, of course, there is no duty to act. For Lord Nicholls the council were not mere bystanders, they had a power to

---

[20] *ibid.* at 946.
[21] [1978] A.C. 728.
[22] *Stovin v. Wise* [1996] A.C. 923 at 949.
[23] *ibid.* at 951.
[24] *Barratt v. North Vancouver* (1980) 114 D.L.R. (3d) 577; *Just v. British Columbia* (1989) 64 D.L.R. (4th) 689; *Brown v. British Columbia* (1994) 112 D.L.R. (4th) 1. See generally S.M. Waddams, "Further Reflections on Economic Loss: A Canadian Perspective" (1994) 1 Tort L. Rev. 116.
[25] *Stovin v. Wise, op. cit.* at 956. Although there had been accidents in 1976, 1982 and one some nine months before Mr. Stovin's.
[26] Even in England a breach of a positive statutory duty will impute liability regardless of any *Stovin* issues: *Goodes v. East Sussex County Council* [1999] T.L.R. 13.
[27] *Stovin v. Wise*, at 929.
[28] *ibid.* at 930.
[29] *ibid.*

change things. The decision in *Anns* was not merely left without comment but was praised. It liberated the law from the unacceptable yoke of the rigid rule against liability in English law.[30] It was accepted that *Anns* liability had to be kept under control.[31] Although he went on to accept that the pithy fair, just and reasonable test has advantages. It was accepted that this was a case of a pure omission. However, in the public sphere this is not the same problem—the omission can be a breach of a public law duty. Then the question is that, also considered by the majority, whether and to what extent the omission should be met by damages. It was noted that sometimes by special dealing a council can come under an obligation, for example, where it had said it would carry out a demolition.[32] This case was not like that. The council's failure was the same for everyone.[33] For Lord Nicholls, despite the reference to a lack of finding of irrationality, considered that there was evidence of a failure to meet the public law duty as the council had not acted like a sensible authority with a proper appreciation of its responsibilities.[34] Even with all of these factors it is still necessary to find something special to impose a liability in damages because Parliament in statutory cases could have done that. It turned out that this could only be answered by reviewing the cases. In the common law jurisdiction this is an entirely proper way of proceeding. As the years have gone by, taking into account the many decisions in the commonwealth there is sufficient material available for marks and notes to be posted. Thus, authorities omitted, one may consider the following:

(i) the subject matter of the statute;

(ii) its intended purpose;

(iii) whether a concurrent common law duty might inhibit the proper and expeditious discharge of the statutory functions;

(iv) the nature of the loss;

(v) the ability of the plaintiff to protect himself;

(vi) the adequacy of the public law remedies; and

(vii) the presence or absence of a particular reason why the plaintiff was relying or dependent on the authority.[35]

Reliance was important for the minority because it can be actual or general. Reasonable reliance can arise out of general dependence.[36] A power to remove dangers can fall into this sphere—air traffic control is a good example.[37] It was accepted that in some cases a bright line exclusionary rule

---

[30] *ibid.* at 931.

[31] *ibid.* at 932. There is an interesting near digression on the *Caparo* tripartite test—to the effect that it is wrong to make proximity a third condition.

[32] Under reference to *Parramatta City Council v. Lutz* (1988) 12 N.S.W.L.R. 293. And since *Stovin*, see *Welton*.

[33] Except perhaps those who regularly use the road and realise that it is a bad junction?

[34] Under reference to *Secretary of State for Education and Science v. Tameside MBC* [1977] A.C. 1014.

[35] *Stovin v. Wise* [1996] A.C. 923 at 937.

[36] *ibid.* at 937.

[37] *Swanson Estate v. Canada* (1991) 80 D.L.R. (4th) 741.

had been adopted but Lord Nicholls preferred that a more flexible approach be taken to concurrent cases. He did notice the point that unfamiliar road users were at risk of death. In cases like *Stovin* road users unfamiliar with dangerous junctions depend on the authorities. Lord Nicholls felt that failing to rectify this known serious risk was similar to the authorities not carrying out roadworks properly. Even although highway authorities do not occupy the highway the situation is similar enough for the imposition of liability not to be too novel. Imposition of liability would have the salutary effect of tightening administrative procedures and avoiding needless road tragedies. Local authorities being responsible they would not indulge in artifice to avoid liability.[38]

It is submitted that between them their Lordships did canvass every issue **10–50** that has been raised since *Anns*. On the facts of the actual case the majority make strong points. The junction was not actually a blackspot. The decision was not to act right away; not indeed to act at any defined time. People die on the roads every day. Unlike a hole in the pavement which is rather unexpected, bad road junctions are common. Those unfamiliar with an area should normally expect the worst. Many junctions have existed for centuries. So far as a statement of the law is concerned the minority view is the more impressive. The payment of damages for carelessness is salutary. Except in a time when government and the taxpayer would pick up the cost without question, common law duties would improve the safety of individuals. But Parliament now knows about *Anns* and there is a view that the law having been so declared Parliament if it wanted to keep authorities free from liability when imposing duties upon them could easily do so.

Scottish cases

There is no modern distinctive Scottish approach. The relative absence of **10–51** litigation is curious. In *Hallett v. Nicholson*[39] Lord Dunpark set out three propositions taken from the authorities then on the books:

"(1) Acts or omissions committed by a statutory authority in the proper exercise of its statutory authority in the proper exercise of its statutory duties or powers do not found a cause of civil action . . . (2) Acts or omissions which are committed by a statutory authority in the course of an improper exercise of its statutory duties or powers and which infringe the rights of third parties may be actionable at civil law. (3) For such an exercise to be improper it must be either (a) not authorised by statue or (b) not made bona fide in the interest of the public within the limits of any statutory discretion."

In *Bonthrone v. Secretary of State for Scotland*[40] the court examined the **10–52** effect in Scotland of the leading English cases at that time and developed the exposition of Lord Dunpark in *Hallet*. The pursuer's complaint against the Secretary of State was that in the exercise of certain powers, he failed to

---

[38] *Stovin v. Wise*, at 941.
[39] 1979 S.C. 1.
[40] 1987 S.L.T. 34.

warn members of the public of the risks inherent in the triple vaccination designed to immunise children against diphtheria, tetanus and whooping cough, and by so doing, failed to exercise the degree of care which it was incumbent upon him to exercise. Lord Grieve added the following to Lord Dunpark's exposition:

> "Where the exercise of a statutory power confers a discretion on the authority entitled to exercise it as to the manner in which, or the means by which it is to be exercised, then if the discretion is exercised within the ambit of the power, and in bona fide, albeit the exercise of it can be shown to display an error of judgment, a person who suffers loss as a result of the exercise of the power will not have an action of damages against the authority which exercised it. In my opinion the taking of reasonable care in connection with the exercise of a statutory power such as is conferred on the Secretary of State by section 10 of the 1972 Act, does not arise until the discretionary stage of its exercise has ceased and the executive stage has begun."[41]

10–53   Other cases have considered the same issues but have not advanced the law beyond that set out above.[42] Accordingly it is still the law that a body carrying out public law duties can be brought before a court under the private law but only in the special circumstances outlined above. Reasonable foreseeability is not enough. The conduct complained of must have (in some way) escaped from the legitimate operation of political or administrative discretion. If a public law remedy or other statutory regime applies, it will be more difficult to bring the case before the court.

Scotland followed the English lead in relation to public policy: *Ward v. Chief Constable*[43] followed the immunity given in England.

10–54   *Anns* has been treated as authoritative here and *Stovin* keeps *Anns* under some restraint. Scots law has never been so fussy about the distinction between acts and omissions.[44] Nor has the public/private distinction been adopted wholeheartedly, at least in the field of judicial review.[45] An example of the contemporary approach of the courts might be seen in *Duff v. Highland and Islands Fire Board*.[46] The fire brigade were called to a fire and left thinking that they had extinguished the fire. It broke out again and burnt the house and the neighbouring house down. The brigade were

---

[41] *ibid.* at 41.

[42] See *Johnstone v. Traffic Commissioner*, 1990 S.L.T. 409, a case against the traffic commissioner for failing to instruct a fuller specialist medical report and instead revoking a driver's PSV licence on the basis of a hospital discharge summary; and *Ross v. Secretary of State for Scotland*, 1990 S.L.T. 13, a case involving smallpox vaccination. Where it was held, after a consideration of *Bonthrone* that the duties alleged were within the area of discretion and in the absence of averments of bad faith, the averments were refused probation; *Wilson v. McCaffrey*, 1989 S.C.L.R. 250 where in dismissing a case against a local authority for their failure to exercise a power under the Building (Scotland) Act 1959, s. 13(1)(a), by requiring people to leave premises while compulsory building demolition was in progress, *Bonthrone* was cited. It was held that the power was a discretionary one.

[43] 1991 S.L.T. 292.

[44] See Lord McKay's speech in *Maloco v. Littlewoods Organisation Ltd*, 1987 S.L.T. 425, discussed in Chap. 10.

[45] *West v. Secretary of State for Scotland*, 1992 S.L.T. 636.

[46] 1995 S.L.T. 1362.

assoilzied on the evidence. Factors that might have helped establish liability like the existence of smoke in the bedroom were not proved and *Ward* was distinguished. Lord McFadyen considered that as the brigade had actually gone into action no such questions arose.[47] At the time of writing the most exhaustive treatment of the topic in a Scottish case is *Forbes v. Dundee District Council*.[48] The pursuer lost her footing and fell when descending a staircase. She alleged that this was because of the irregularity of the steps which varied from step to step and from left to right. The case was raised against the council—not the designers, builders, owners or occupiers. The basis was that the stairs failed to meet building regulations and the council had the power to approve the plans and inspect the works to ensure compliance with the regulations. There was an exhaustive review of the great English cases, *X v. Bedfordshire*[49] being particularly influential. Lord Nimmo-Smith thought it essential to have regard to the fair, just and reasonable test. He decided there ought to be no duty in this case. The statutory framework in *Forbes* is a system for protecting the public. The case was one of practical failure as the plans were examined but carelessly, and it was not a non-justiciable issue as where the council had to redeploy its staff away from building regulation examinations to other work. While it is true that *Stovin v. Wise* involved personal injury to the plaintiff, the framework of protection of the public was not the same. On balance *Forbes* is the kind of case in which liability can be, and perhaps should have been, imposed.[50]

Overlap with Hedley Byrne

While the *Hedley Byrne* principle applies independently of the identity of **10–55** the defender, the issues which make authorities immune can negate it. On the other hand the giving of advice directly in response to an enquiry may be seen to be a relatively operational decision.[51] In *Tidman v. Reading Borough Council*[52] a local authority was not held to be liable for informal guidance given to an enquirer. Buxton J. went so far as to say that in the case of a formal approach on an important matter, a duty of care could conceivably arise. In *Welsh v. Chief Constable of Merseyside Police*[53] it was accepted that an assumption of responsibility could arise by conduct. The most important case in this line is *Welton v. Essex County Council*.[54]

---

[47] In *Gibson v. Chief Constable of Strathclyde*, 1999 S.C. 420; 1999 S.C.L.R. 661; 1999 Rep. L.R. 78, it was held that taking into account developments such as *Osman* the idea of a blanket immunity for the police required reconsideration. It did not apply in this case which was one of performance of an operational task concerned with human safety—the failure to block off the south end of dangerous collapsed bridge.

[48] 1997 S.C.L.R. 682. See also D. Brodie, "The Boundaries of Murphy—Part II", 1997 Rep.B. 16–3; G. Robertson, "Duty of Care and the Negligent Fireraiser", 1980 S.L.T. (News) 13.

[49] *X v. Bedfordshire County Council* [1995] 3 All E.R. 353 and see Chap. 10; *Barrett v. Enfield LBC* [1999] 3 W.L.R. 79.

[50] *Stovin v. Wise* [1996] A.C. 923 was held not to be in point in the Scots case *Mcknight v. Clydeside Buses Ltd*, 1999 S.L.T. 1167, where the failure was to mark a low bridge. There had been accidents before.

[51] See generally, D. Brodie, "Hedley Byrne and Public Authorities" (1997) Rep.B. 18–2.

[52] [1994] T.L.R. 572.

[53] [1993] 1 All E.R. 692.

[54] [1998] T.L.R. 235.

Decided by the Court of Appeal after the *X v. Bedfordshire*[55] decision in the House of Lords, it was a case raised against the council and one of their social workers by a family arising out of the fact that they were foster parents and the council placed a 15-year-old known sexual abuser with them. They alleged that they specifically asked about this and were told that there was no problem in this regard but that the truth was the 15-year-old had in fact been warned for indecently assaulting his sister. The court had refused to strike out negligence claims for the children. By a majority the Court of Appeal held that the claims against the authority and the social worker should not be struck out.[56]

(4) THIRD PARTY INTERVENTION

10–56 This is simply a descriptive name for a number of cases similar each to the other where the key issue is whether and to what extent the fact that the loss injury or damage was caused by a person other than the defender destroys the pursuer's case. There are cases of such liability before *Donoghue v. Stevenson*, decided mainly on the idea of remoteness.[57] While many cases can be treated as duty cases, the nature of the intervention of the third party can constitute a causal factor becoming a *nova causa interveniens* and releasing the defender. The cases raise the idea of the difference between acts and omissions and the idea of the scope and range of the duty. The focus now in all such cases is the House of Lords decision in the Scottish appeal *Maloco v. Littlewoods Organisation Ltd*,[58] in which important prior cases were considered. That said it should be noted that Lord Brandon for one did not consider that this case laid down anything:

> "It is axiomatic that the question whether there has been negligence in any given case must depend on the particular circumstances of that case. That being so, I do not think that these appeals can in the end be determined by reference to other reported cases in which the particular circumstances were different, even though some degree of analogy between such other cases and the present one can legitimately be drawn. Nor do I think that it is possible, however helpful it might otherwise be, to lay down any general principle designed to apply to all cases in which the negligence alleged against a person involves the unauthorised acts of independent third parties on premises owned or occupied by that person."[59]

That having been said, the speeches show that issues of principle are involved and the case is at least guidance for this difficult practical problem. The speeches in the House reveal a divergence of approach between two of

---

[55] [1995] A.C. 633—the anti-liability decision in the House of Lords.

[56] *Welton* was relied on unsuccessfully in *Harris v. Evans* [1998] T.L.R. 284.

[57] J.G. Logie, "Special Relationships, Reasonable Foreseeability and Distinct Possibilities" [1988] J.R. 77. See also S. Stuart, "Bad Neighbours", 1984 S.L.T. (News) 45.

[58] *Maloco v. Littlewoods Organisation Ltd*, 1987 S.L.T. 425.

[59] *ibid.* at 427.

their Lordships. As that divergence has not been reconciled counsel are entitled to emphasise whichever is most favourable although in many cases both would produce the same result. In view of the speeches which all agree that a great deal depends upon the facts of a case, it is necessary to set out the facts of this case in some detail. Littlewoods purchased the cinema from its previous owners with entry on May 31, 1976 with the intention to demolish it within a short time and replace it with a supermarket. On July 5, 1976 a fire broke out in the cinema damaging both the Cafe Maloco and St. Paul's Church. The cinema was a substantial building, a brick-built auditorium with a flat timber and felt-covered roof on a steel frame. Legal entry was given on May 31, 1976. The keys were not handed over to Littlewoods until mid-June. During that time the previous owners employed contractors to remove fittings and equipment from the cinema which were worth taking away. From about the end of the third week in June 1976 the cinema remained empty and unattended by anyone connected with Littlewoods. Children had began to break into the cinema during the four days that Littlewoods contractors were doing preliminary work towards the end of the third week in June 1976. The contractors locked and secured the premises when they finished work each night. They discovered on their return clear signs that the premises had been forcibly entered. Fire doors had been forced open from inside. The contractors then secured these doors. When they finished they left the premises as secure as they could. Thereafter children began to come to the cinema to play making a mess and breaking things. More importantly during the time that the Littlewoods contractors were working inside the main building one of the contactors' employees saw lengths of old cinema film lying just outside and noticed signs of someone having attempted to set fire to them. The type of film used in the cinema was non-flammable and no fire had occurred. The beadle of St. Paul's Church saw signs of someone having tried to light a fire inside the building. He discovered that the carpet, where oil has been spilled on it, was burning. He put it out and told the session clerk of St. Paul's about it. No one informed the police or Littlewoods about any of these matters. It was accepted by the pursuers that the only precaution that was likely to be effective in preventing the entry of vandals was to arrange for a twenty-four hour watch. The importance of some of these facts will become clear from the treatment that follows of the two main speeches but perhaps the most important to bear in mind is the finding that the film was not specially non-flammable. Many people assume that it is and if it had been then the case might have been easier to decide.

Needle of Probability

Lord Mackay was aware from the First Division decision that there had **10–57** been an earlier difference of opinion between the two divisions, it being thought that there were two possible tests: (i) whether the intervention was likely; or (ii) whether the intervention was "very likely". This may have set the tone and approach of his speech. Consideration was given to the previous decisions considering these issues.[60] *Hughes v. Lord Advocate*[61] was

---

[60] *Evans v. Glasgow District Council*, 1978 S.L.T. 17; *Carrick Furniture House Ltd v. Paterson*, 1978 S.L.T. (Notes) 48; *Graham (Thomas) & Co. Ltd v. Church of Scotland General Trustees*, 1982 S.L.T. (Sh. Ct) 26.
[61] 1963 S.C. (H.L.) 31.

cited as showing the courts' acceptance of the unpredictability of children's behaviour. Another case cited *Squires v. Perth and Kinross District Council*,[62] will be discussed later in this section. The kernel of Lord Mackay's position so far as deciding the actual case is concerned can be seen in the following passage:

> "In my opinion, the question whether, in all the circumstances described in evidence, a reasonable person in the position of Littlewoods was bound to anticipate as probable, if he took no action to keep these premises lockfast, that, in a comparatively short time before the premises were demolished, they would be set on fire with consequent risk to the neighbouring properties is a matter for the judges of fact to determine."[63]

Even that has within it an implied test—that of a "probable" intervention. The crucial facts were the absence of intimation to Littlewoods and the absence of facts inferring a duty to inspect. In discussing the legal principles applicable Lord Mackay turned to a passage of Lord Reid in *Dorset Yacht*, itself cited in many third party intervention cases:

> "where human actions forms one of the links between the original wrongdoing of the defendant and the loss suffered by the plaintiff, that action must at least have been something very likely to happen if it is not to be regarded as *novus actus interveniens* breaking the chain of causation. I do not think that a mere foreseeable possibility is or should be sufficient, for then the intervening human action can more properly be regarded as a new cause than as a consequence of the original wrongdoing. But if the intervening action was likely to happen I do not think that it can matter whether that action was innocent or tortious or criminal. Unfortunately, tortious or criminal action by a third party is often the "very kind of thing" which is likely to happen as a result of the wrongful or careless act of the defendant. And in the present case, on the facts which we must assume at this stage, I think that the taking of a boat by the escaping trainees and their unskillful navigation leading to damage another vessel were the very kind of thing that these borstal officers ought to have seen to be likely."[64]

Then Lord Mackay provides an explanation of the paragraph which reconciles (or at least makes otiose the drawing of any distinction) the divergent views of the First and Second Divisions:

> "It was accordingly not critical whether the test was foreseeability of that damage as likely or very likely. At the state at which Lord Reid used the phrase 'very likely' . . . he was giving his view on what the two cases he had cited showed . . . When Lord Reid turns to state his own position,

---

[62] 1986 S.L.T. 30.
[63] *Maloco v. Littlewoods Organisation Ltd*, at 431.
[64] *Dorset Yacht Co. v. Home Office* [1970] A.C. 1004 at 1030, quoted by Lord MacKay in *Maloco* at 432.

he does so on the basis that the intervening action was likely to happen."[65]

Rounding up these dicta (and many others) Lord Mackay arrives at the "needle of probability" dictum which merits repetition as stated, although it is not a definition, nor a principle, merely guidance:

"The more unpredictable the conduct in question, the less easy to affirm that any particular result from it is probable and in many circumstances the only way in which a judge could properly be persuaded to come to the conclusion that the result was not only possible but reasonably foreseeable as probable would be to convince him that, in the circumstance, it was highly likely. In this type of case a finding that the reasonable man should have anticipated the consequence of human action as just probable may not be a very frequent option. Unless the judge can be satisfied that the result of the human action is highly probable or very likely, he may have to conclude that all the reasonable man could say was that it was a mere possibility. Unless the needle that measures the probability of a particular result flowing from the conduct of a human agent is near the top of the scale, it may be hard to conclude that it has risen sufficiently from the bottom, to create the duty reasonably to foresee it."[66]

This case is certainly consonant with previous authority, being a reasonable gloss on Lord Reid's dictum. Where this guideline arguably falls down is in failing to state how far along the scale the needle has to go to trigger liability. Since we are not told what the scale is measured in it does not have very much predictive value in allowing people to decide whether or not to pay for the 24 hour security or whether to take out insurance in respect of certain possible or quite possible third party interventions. Its flexibility leaves the judge of first instance considerable scope. Nonetheless the argument that property owners should know the scope of their liabilities is entitled to weight. As can be seen Lord Goff of Chieveley's treatment gave full weight to these considerations.

Deaf gardeners, asthmatics and old ladies

Lord Goff thought this kind of case one where liability should be **10–58** exceptional. He began from the principle that there should not be liability at all. He explains why in the following passage:

"Why does the law not recognise a general duty of care to prevent others from suffering loss or damage caused by the deliberate wrongdoing of third parties? The fundamental reason is that the common law does not impose liability for what are called pure omissions . . . one thing is clear, and that is that liability in negligence for harm caused by the deliberate wrongdoing of others cannot be founded simply upon foreseeability that

---

[65] *Maloco v. Littlewoods Organisation Ltd*, at 432.
[66] *ibid.* at 433.

the pursuer will suffer loss or damage by reason of such wrongdoing. There is no such general principle."[67]

Lord Goff then considers the exceptions based mainly on authority:

(1) A duty of care may arise from a relationship between the parties, which gives rise to an imposition or assumption of responsibility upon or by the defender.

(2) The defender may be vicariously liable for the third party's act.

(3) He may be held liable as an occupier to a visitor on his land.

(4) A duty may arise from a special relationship between the defender and the third party, by virtue of which the defender is responsible for controlling the third party.[68]

(5) In a case between adjoining occupiers of land, there may be liability in nuisance if one occupier causes or permits persons to gather on his land, and they impair his neighbour's enjoyment of his land and even if such persons come on to his land as trespassers, the occupiers may, if they constitute a nuisance, be under an affirmative duty to abate the nuisance.

(6) There may well be other cases.

(7) When the defender negligently causes or permits to be created a source of danger, and it is reasonably foreseeable that third parties may interfere with it and, sparking off the danger, thereby cause damage to persons in the position of the pursuer. The classic example for Lord Goff was *Haynes v. Harwood*,[69] in which the defendant's carter left a hand-drawn van unattended in a crowded street, and the horses bolted when a boy threw a stone at them. A police officer who suffered injury in stopping the horses before they injured a woman and children was held to be entitled to recover damages from the defendant.

(8) Lord Goff put the hypothetical case of a person deputed to buy a substantial quantity of fireworks for a village fireworks display on Guy Fawkes night. He stores them, as usual, in an unlocked garden shed abutting onto a neighbouring house. It is well known that he does this. Mischievous boys from the village enter as trespassers and, playing with the fireworks, cause a serious fire which spreads to and burns down the neighbouring house. Liability might well be imposed in such a case; for, having regard to the dangerous and tempting nature of fireworks, interference by naughty children was the very thing which, in the circumstances, the purchaser of the fireworks ought to have guarded against. But liability, he said, should only be imposed under this principle in cases where the defender has negligently caused or permitted the creation of a source of danger

---

[67] *ibid.* at 438.
[68] Lord Goff gave the example of *Dorset Yacht Co. Ltd v. Home Office* [1970] A.C. 1004.
[69] [1935] 1 K.B. 146.

on his land, and where it is foreseeable that third parties may trespass on his land and spark it off, thereby damaging the pursuer or his property.

(9) Where the defender has knowledge or means of knowledge that a third party has created or is creating a risk of fire, or indeed has started a fire, on his premises, and then fails to take such steps as are reasonably open to him

There is a negative formulation as well. Lord Goff in a number of illustrations from life points out why liability must be constrained:

"(1) In ordinary households in this country, there are nowadays many things which might be described as possible sources of fire if interfered with by third parties ranging from matches and firelighters to electric irons and gas cookers and even oil-fired central hearing systems. These are commonplaces of modern life; and it would be quite wrong if householders were to be held liable in negligence for acting in a socially acceptable manner.

(2) Where an old lady goes out to spend the day with her married daughter and leaves a ground floor window open for her cat.

(3) Where a stone deaf asthmatic habitually sleeps with his bedroom window wide open at night.

(4) Where an elderly gentleman leaves his french window open when he is weeding at the bottom of the garden, so that he can hear the telephone."[70]

Lord Goff thought that liability could not be imposed on an occupier of property in negligence simply because it can be said that it is reasonably foreseeable, or even (having regard, for example, to some particular temptation to thieves in adjacent premises) that is a highly likely, that, if he fails to keep his property lockfast, a thief may gain access to his property and thence to the adjacent premises. He took the view that to do that would presuppose that the occupier of property is under a general duty to prevent thieves from entering his property to gain access to neighbouring property, where there is a sufficient degree of foresight that this may occur:

"But there is no general duty to prevent third parties from causing damage to others, even though there is a high degree of foresight that they may do so. The practical effect is that everybody has to take such steps as he thinks fit to protect his own property, whether house or flat or shop, against thieves . . . He has to form his own judgment as to the precautions which he should take, having regard to all the circumstances of the case, including (if it be the case) the fact that his premises are a jeweller's shop which offers a special temptation to thieves."[71]

---

[70] *Maloco v. Littlewoods Organisation Ltd*, 1987 S.L.T. 425 at 441.
[71] *ibid.* at 441.

Lord Goff considered that accordingly *Squires v. Perth and Kinross District Council* was wrongly decided.[72] Reasonable foreseeability is not the correct approach, he considered:

> "It is very tempting to try to solve all problems of negligence by reference to an all-embracing criterion of foreseeability, thereby effectively reducing all decisions in this field to questions of fact. But this comfortable solution is, alas, not open to us. The law has to accommodate all the untidy complexity of life and there are circumstances where considerations of practical justice impel us to reject a general imposition of liability for foreseeable damage."[73]

Post-*Maloco* decisions

10–59 A significant Scottish application is *Fry's Metals Ltd v. Durastic Ltd.*[74] A company entered into a lease with another company of factory and office premises for the six month period to March 23, 1984. Two separate alarm systems protected the premises; a conventional bell system mounted on an exterior wall manually set by a key, and a private system installed by a security company at the request of the tenants, connected to the offices of the security company by landline. The tenants notified the security company that cover would not be required after 30 March. On April 2 the tenants sought to hand over the keys to the landlords. The keys were refused because electricity and gas meters required to be read before the handover was complete. This took place on April 9. On April 7, the premises were broken into and vandalised. Both alarm systems failed to operate. The landlords sued the tenants for loss caused by the failure of the private alarm system. It was argued on the basis of Lord MacKay's speech that there was a duty in delict to take care in respect of the occupation of premises to prevent damage by the action of a third party arises if, but only if, the injury or damage by third parties arising from the act or omission of the person against whom the duty of care is alleged is highly probable. Lord Dervaird held that test had been met. In the English case of *Cunningham v. Reading Football Club Ltd*[75] the plaintiffs were injured at a football match by bits of terracing thrown at the police. Four months earlier concrete had been thrown. The club knew it was a local derby and knew that trouble might arise. This is reminiscent of the earlier Scottish case *Hosie v. Arbroath F.C.*[76] in which the club were held liable for gates felled by supporters. More recently in Scotland in *Gillon v. Chief Constable*[77] a police officer who was told to stand with her back to the ground was "run-down" by a footballer. She sued her employer and lost on the basis of *Bolton v. Stone*[78]

---

[72] N.B. the dictum of Lord Wylie in *Evans v. Glasgow District Council*, 1978 S.L.T. 17 at 19, namely that there is "a general duty on owners or occupiers of property . . . to take reasonable care to see that it (is) proof against the kind of vandalism which was calculated to affect adjoining property" was criticised by Lord Goff as being too wide.

[73] *Maloco v. Littlewoods Organisation Ltd*, at 442.

[74] 1991 S.L.T. 689.

[75] [1991] T.L.R. 153.

[76] 1978 S.L.T. 122.

[77] 1996 Rep. L.R. 165.

[78] [1951] A.C. 850. See para. 10–80 below.

unlikeliness. But it is an example of the fact that although there was another human being in the chain of events a case could be made out.[79]

(5) NERVOUS SHOCK

This section considers claims for non-physical injury not following on **10–60** ordinary physical injury. It raises the question of the scope of the duty of care in the sense of the class of potential pursuers. It is not clear when the term "nervous shock" came into legal, let alone psychiatric literature.[80] A consultant psychiatrist has recently described it in such a way that it is clearly considered as a legal label:

> "This I take to mean a response outside the normal range of emotional reaction or grief. In practice nervous shock seems to equate to a psychiatric diagnosis, a decision that the victim has become "ill" and is not showing a variant of the normal response."[81]

So the term can very usefully be used as a legal technical term to signify the legally troublesome area where the pursuer has become mentally ill as a result of the negligence of the defender.[82] It may be assumed that there was a time when the medical and legal issues converged. Doctors recognised nervous shock and thus so did the lawyers. O'Brien very helpfully points out that much of the early scientific work was carried out during and after the First World War in relation to shell shock. Shell shock was caused it was thought by a commotion of the brain. Soon it was realised that it was not related to a near-miss—the derivation of the "shock". It is well-known the attitude of the military legal system at the time was to consider many cases as cowardice rather than what we would now call illness.

Lawyers and psychiatrists now share some common ground with some- **10–61** thing called PTSD (post-traumatic stress disorder),[83] thought by the ordinary lawyer to be the new name for nervous shock. Taking account of the view expressed above that nervous shock is and must remain a term of art, PTSD may or may not be nervous shock and some nervous shock may not be PTSD. PTSD is a convention for doctors. They do this not to help lawyers but to help patients. By classifying like cases there is the possibility that like treatments can be found. So for a doctor to say that someone suffers from PTSD is not like a doctor saying another person has a broken

---

[79] In *Leslie v. Secretary of State for Scotland*, 1999 Rep. L.R. 39, it was accepted that the prison authorities have a duty to take care for those in their custody including a duty to protect prisoners from attacks by other prisoners. In this case the convict was unsuccessful because it was not foreseeable that the particular incident would have come about. The perpetrator had been recommended for downgrading and plastic cutlery was in use along with body searching. How he got the knife was a mystery.

[80] Lord Lloyd of Berwick used the term in inverted commas in *Page v. Smith* [1996] A.C. 155.

[81] L.S. O'Brien, "The Validity of the Diagnosis of Post-Traumatic Stress Disorder" [1994] J.P.I.L. 257.

[82] A use urged by Brennan, J. in *Jaensch v. Coffey* (1984) 54 A.L.R. 417 at 425.

[83] G.J. Turnbull, "Post-Traumatic Stress Disorder—a Psychiatrist's Guide" [1997] J.P.I.L. 234.

leg. It is to say that the patient says that he has experienced certain things and exhibits certain symptoms. That it is a subjective and arbitrary diagnosis is shown by the fact that it changes over time. That said, what must be noted from O'Brien's study is that a mixture of tests, including biological tests can create a fairly certain diagnosis—it is not all subjective and it does not all depend upon what the patient says: "psychophysiological responses probably constitute a reliable adjunctive diagnostic test which can be rendered robust to dissimulation . . . biological markers for PTSD are not yet perfected, but that the most likely candidate at this stage is urinary noradrenaline:cortisol ratio." The diagnostic criteria current at the time of writing include potentially delictual events as the very kind of things which may found in persons who are diagnosed as having PTSD. By the time this is read it will possibly be out of date. There are two issues: what do medical men consider to be illness as opposed to malingering, cowardice or lachrymosity?; and what does the reasonable man in the twenty-first century consider could be harmful in light of his knowledge?[84] Tommy Atkins in the Great War might, with the judges, have said a man was a coward if he ran from the bombs. Now if one engages with popular culture, it is not too difficult to discover that in this regard people are what Tommy Atkins would call "softer". Television has brought to the knowledge of generations the idea that trauma can cause mental illness. Thus the judges may simply be reflecting, not just new diagnoses, but a newer, deep and sustained awareness of causes and effects of mental illness.

Any duty must be owed to the pursuer. This rule which is now part of our overall theoretical structure emerged from a nervous shock case—*Bourhill v. Young*.[85] From that case it was accepted that shock such as caused a miscarriage was actionable but there was no duty if the particular pursuer was not foreseeable.[86] In this case a woman bystander who saw the aftermath of an accident was too remote in law to be allowed to claim.[87] That idea remains central to the law of negligence generally and to nervous shock. An unforeseen pursuer cannot claim at all. The most recent analysis (considered below) of primary and secondary victims fits within this framework.

---

[84] "Courts of law must act on the best medical insight of the day. Nowadays courts accept that there is no rigid distinction between body and mind. Courts accept that a recognizable psychiatric illness results from an impact on the central nervous system. In this sense therefore there is no qualitative difference between physical harm and psychiatric harm . . . and psychiatric harm may be far more debilitating than physical harm. It would, however, be an altogether different proposition to say that no distinction is made or ought to be made between principles governing the recovery of damages in tort for physical injury and psychiatric harm . . . But nowadays we must accept the medical reality that psychiatric harm may be more serious than physical harm", *per* Lord Steyn in *White v. Chief Constable* [1999] 2 A.C. 455 at 492–493.

[85] 1942 S.C. (H.L.) 78.

[86] There is an early case where without much argument or consideration it seems to have been accepted that anxiety for a daughter's wrongfully caused illness was actionable. In *Soutar v. Mulhern* (1907) 14 S.L.T. 862, the pursuer sought damages for anxiety caused to him by his daughter suffering diphtheria because of the state of the premises. Prior to the hearing in the Inner House the pursuer produced a statement showing losses amounting to £58 being (1) illness of daughter: £22; (2) illnesses of 3 members of family: £13; and (3) expense of removal: £22. The first claim was allowed to go to proof before answer and the other two were excluded.

[87] Although in fact she was physically close at the time of the accident.

Fright

A mere fright is not enough; the quality of the shock must reach a certain **10–62** level: "It is not enough . . . for the pursuers in each case to show simply that they got a fright and suffered an emotional reaction, if no visible disability or provable illness or injury followed."[88] But if the fright produces nervous shock that is and has been for a very long time good enough. In *Wallace v. Kennedy*[89] the pursuer was walking in a street carrying an infant. The defender's motor van, being driven by an employee, was laden with a clothes basket which projected over the side. The basket hit a lamppost which crashed to the ground. The pursuer had to jump aside to avoid physical injury but she suffered fright to the extent that nervous shock produced bodily illness. The Lord Ordinary (Johnston) agreed with defenders that damages were not due for mere fright, but said:

"it does not follow that you may not recover for the consequences of mere fright. To found a claim for damages there must be physical injury of some kind. But actual impact is not necessary to produce physical injury. It may be equally produced by nervous shock producing bodily illness."[90]

In *Gilligan v. Robb*[91] the pursuer sought damages for nervous shock caused by the defender's cow entering her house in Glasgow as it was being driven from the cattle market. The sheriff allowed a proof before answer and so the pursuer appealed for jury trial. The defender argued the action was irrelevant. The court allowed issues without giving any opinions and without calling on counsel for the pursuer. On averments it was said that the pursuer was "hysterical for a considerable time, and had to be put to bed, her pulse being high, and her heart was slightly affected. She had to remain in bed for several weeks thereafter, being constantly attended by her medical man and in point of fact she is still in her doctor's hands. She has not yet recovered from the effects of the fright, and it is believed and averred that the effects will be permanent."[92] So the courts were not all that nervous about nervous shock and the ability, even of a jury, to spot a malingerer. Nervous shock is as stated above an antique term for actionable injury. At the time of writing the most likely diagnosis to be actionable is post-traumatic stress disorder, discussed generally above. However, other non-physical, non-economic loss ought to be and can be recovered. The traumatic events which get a case of PTSD going are also events which trigger more obvious illnesses; especially where there is a pre-disposition:

"There is a very long established body of psychiatric research showing that life events can cause, precipitate, or 'bring forward' psychiatric

---

[88] *Simpson v. ICI*, 1983 S.L.T. 601. A recent clear statement in the House of Lords is that of Lord Steyn in *White v. Chief Constable* [1999] 2 A.C. 455 at 491–500.

[89] (1908) 16 S.L.T. 485.

[90] *ibid.* at 485–6. At the time of that decision it was stated that the the nervous shock had to be occasioned by immediate and personal bodily injury—not apprehension for another following *Dulieu v. White & Sons* [1901] 2 K.B. 669.

[91] 1910 2 S.L.T. 77.

[92] *ibid.* at 78.

illness. For example, specific phobic anxiety states such as fear of driving can be caused by traumatic accidents; depression and other illnesses for which the victim had a propensity but from which they had not suffered may be precipitated by life events; and patients who are well but suffer from illnesses such as bipolar disorder may have their next episode of illness brought forward by months or years by a life event or trauma."[93]

It might be wondered how many lawyers or reasonable men would consider someone with schizophrenia to be well. A very bad fright could be argued one day to be nervous shock despite present scepticism. Although O'Brien has grave reservations about the diagnosis DSM IV 308.3 acute stress disorder has a minimum duration of two days and a maximum of 42 days. ICD-10 acute stress reaction resolves in two or three days. Finally a non-actionable fright may or may not become actionable as a result of consequent physical injury depending upon the general foreseeability principles.[94] The policy reasons expressed in the most recent House of Lords 3–2 majority expression of the law are against the recognition of even a medical diagnosis of fright.[95]

Phlegm and Reasonable Fortitude

10–63 Generally people are assumed to have the customary phlegm in they can take the rough and smooth of life. This basic rule requires clarification. The phlegm approach is old and appears early in the cases. In the Outer House case of *Cooper v. Caledonian Railway Co.*[96] the Lord Ordinary (Stormonth Darling) discusses the idea in the context of remoteness of injury by reference to an American case of 1897 in which it was said "Not only the transportation of passengers and the running of trains, but the general conduct of business and of the ordinary affairs of life, must be done on the assumption that persons who are liable to be affected thereby are not peculiarly sensitive and are of ordinary physical and mental strength."[97]

---

[93] O'Brien, *op cit.* at p. 272.

[94] Compare and contrast *Slattery v. BRB* (1966) 1 KIR 336; *Brook v. Cook* (1961) 105 S.J. 684.

[95] "At any rate, the courts have developed sufficient confidence in medical expertise to be willing to award damages for mental disturbances which manifest themselves in bodily symptoms (such as a miscarriage) or in a 'recognised psychiatric illness.' The latter is distinguished from shock, fear, anxiety or grief which are regarded as a normal consequence of a distressing event and for which damages are not awarded. Current medical opinion suggests that this may be a somewhat arbitrary distinction; the limits of normal reaction to stressful events are wide and debatable, while feelings of terror and grief may have as devastating an effect upon people's lives as the 'pain and suffering' consequent upon physical injury, for which damages are regularly awarded." *per* Lord Hoffmann in *White v. Chief Constable* [1999] 2 A.C. 455 at 501. Note however, that while there are cases of extreme grief which are not compensated: *Hinz v. Berry* [1970] 2 Q.B. 40; but might be if it results in a pathological grief disorder *Vernon v. Bosley* [1997] 1 All E.R. 577 at 610.

[96] (1902) 4 F. 880.

[97] *ibid.* at 882 citing a Massachusetts judge in *Spade v. Lynn and Boston Railroad* (1897) 60 Amer. St. Rep. 393. He thought that the lady in his own case who had to go to bed for a few weeks with vomiting and giddiness could not have been robust enough. The Inner House gave her proof. In view of this decision a proof before answer was reluctantly allowed in *Fowler v. North British Railway Company*, 1914 2 S.L.T. 95 (I.H.), another case of a railway carriage door swinging open and causing nervous shock. If it had not been for *Cooper*, the court would have thought the case irrelevant but they allowed enquiry, although by proof only because of the delicacy of the questions of fact and law involved.

This focus by the courts on the character of the victim might not be as natural as it might be thought. O'Brien indicates that after the First World War, the leading psychiatrists of the time were essentially Freudian: "They tended to believe that the weak and those who had failed to resolve the conflicts of childhood were those at risk of shell shock." Against that background the old judges would have been right to ask if the pursuer was a wimp for that by the standards of medicine at the time was required for the nervous shock diagnosis. Now it is different. O'Brien recounts a study which showed that 17 per cent of Vietnam veterans in a sample of 15,000 at sometime fitted the diagnostic criteria for PTSD. Now when it is accepted that the sample of persons consists entirely of fighting men, healthy in body and ready in spirit, it might be thought (PTSD being recognised as a form of nervous shock) that the ordinary pursuer can suffer PTSD without having had to encounter a hugely horrific incident so long as meeting the PTSD requirements. PTSD requires a "traumatic event".[98] The most recent cases suggest an important exception. In *Page v. Smith* it was held that the phlegm requirement only applied to what has come to be known as a secondary victim.[99] In the case of persons like *Page* who are directly harmed as participants the wrongdoer must take his victim as he finds him.

Reasonable Foreseeability and Proximity: Primary and Secondary Victims

"Nervous shock" cases have to be dealt with within the prevailing theories **10–64** of liability.[1] There will be a duty if there is already a duty to keep harmless from harm of the type which has occurred or under the neighbour principle. The neighbour principle it will be remembered is founded on reasonable foreseeability but within a notion of proximity—the duty being owed to those closely and directly affected. This is the starting point for a case of nervous shock even in cases where the event giving rise to the shock is injury to another person. So in principle persons who witnessed others being injured at a disaster at a football stadium could recover.[2]

The law can now only be stated by reference to binding authority with the inconsistencies and illogicallities that implies. First there are well established "control mechanisms" The leading case on the main controls is still *McLoughlin v. O'Brian*,[3] an obvious attempt to restate the law. In its

---

[98] "The decision of the House of Lords in *Bourhill v. Young* [1943] A.C. 92, appeared to many to combine what was in theory a simple foreseeability test with a robust wartime view of the ability of the ordinary person to suffer horror and bereavement without ill effect." *per* Lord Hoffmann in *White v. Chief Constable* [1999] 2 A.C. 455 at 501.

[99] Discussed further below.

[1] H. Teff, "Liability for Negligently Inflicted Nervous Shock" (1983) 99 L.Q.R. 100. Lord Hoffmann sums up the problems just now and after his own efforts as follows in *White v. Chief Constable* at 503: " My Lords, this story of the ebb and flow of tort liability for psychiatric injury has often been told and I have recounted it again at some length only because I think it must be borne in mind when we come to deal with the authorities. In order to give due weight to the earlier decisions, particularly at first instance, it is necessary to have regard to their historical context. They cannot simply be laid out flat and pieced together to form a timeless mosaic of legal rules. Some contained the embryonic forms of later developments; others are based on theories of liability which had respectable support at the time but have since been left stranded by the shifting tides."

[2] *per* Lord Keith in *Alcock v. Chief Constable* [1992] 1 A.C. 310.

[3] [1983] A.C. 410. For earlier attempts see *Boardman v. Sanderson* [1964] 1 W.L.R. 1317; *Hambrook v. Stokes Bros* [1925] 1 K.B. 141, *King v. Phillips* [1953] 1 All E.R. 617, *Bain v. Kings & Co. Ltd*, 1973 S.L.T. (Notes) 8.

own holding it was generous so far as allowing a claim based on the aftermath, the plaintiff only appreciated the horror some time after the accident had happened and some distance away.[4] So far as guidance is concerned Lord Wilberforce dismissed the fear that there might arise "an industry of lawyers and psychiatrists who will formulate a claim for nervous shock" on the basis that courts should be able to deal with unmeritorious claims in this sphere as in any other. Foreseeability was the starting point[5] subject to three possible control mechanisms:

(1) Claims might not be successful if an injury is to some stranger as opposed to a member of a person's family.

(2) Pursuers generally should be close in time and space to the accident.

(3) The media by which the shock is caused may be relevant to restrict liability—it should normally be direct.[6]

Alcock v. Chief Constable, South Yorkshire[7] tested these guidelines. The decision of the House of Lords had involved some 16 actions raised by people who were not at the actual incident: some were in the stadium, some saw it on television and one actually saw it on television but on a bus just outside the ground.[8] The issue was said to be proximity with reasonable foreseeability as the guide. It was held that the category of plaintiff was not limited to husband and wife and parent and child. The closeness of tie has to be proved by the plaintiff although it can be assumed in many cases. Thus it was held that in the case of brothers and brothers in law there was no special tie of affection. A parent and a fiancé were within the close ties.

10–65   Lord Keith set out an analysis of the subject: "In the ordinary case of direct physical injury suffered in an accident at work or elsewhere, reasonable foreseeability of the risk is indeed the only test that need be applied to determine liability."[9] He described it as a "secondary sort of injury brought about by the infliction of physical injury, or the risk of physical injury, upon another person."[10] There needs to be proximity as well as foreseeability. He accepts that a series of categories of plaintiff is not appropriate.[11] The ties of love and affection can be investigated although it will be harder to prove in cases outside the nuclear family and very hard in cases of bystanders although a particularly horrific incident may conceivably mean that unrelated persons might be affected.[12] Proximity includes proximity in time and space and the "aftermath" doctrine was approved. Communication through third parties was not thought by Lord Keith to be

---

[4] In Scotland a proof before answer had been allowed in *Bain v. Kings & Co. Ltd, ibid.* where a mother saw her child with injuries after an explosion.

[5] *Brice v. Brown* [1984] 1 All E.R. 997.

[6] See generally N.J. Mullany, "Recovery for Psychiatric Injury by Report: Another Small Step Forward" (1996) Tort L. Rev. 96.

[7] [1992] 1 A.C. 310.

[8] The 16 were test cases for some 150 similar claims; only 10 went on appeal to the House.

[9] *Alcock v. Chief Constable, South Yorkshire*, at 396.

[10] *ibid.* at 396. See generally D. Brodie, "Primary and Secondary Nervous Shock" (1995) Rep.B. 5–2.

[11] *ibid.* at 397.

[12] *ibid* at 397.

sufficient and cases which suggested it was were seriously doubted.[13] "Mere mental suffering" with no physical injury is not recoverable but is compensated to an extent by the bereavement claim in the Fatal Accidents Act 1976. Lord Ackner agreed with an earlier example of Lord Robertson[14] that the estate of a negligent window cleaner falling to a gruesome death would be liable to a pregnant passer by. Lord Ackner defined shock as a sudden[15] appreciation which violently agitates the mind and not more gradual assaults on the nervous system.[16] Lord Ackner followed the Wilberforce line and essentially agreed with Lord Keith on the love and affection point.[17] He would not as a matter of principle rule out simultaneous transmission as where a balloon full of children catches fire—the impact of the television pictures could be worse than the actual scene.[18] Lord Oliver took a different approach to the fundamentals than Lord Keith in thinking that compensatable injury can be caused by direct assault on the mind—this being a result of the growing appreciation and understanding of modern medical science.[19] Such a victim is in fact a "primary victim".[20] The label "liability for nervous shock" can be misleading.[21] Other primary victims would be rescuers and those who are led to believe they have been the cause of another's death.[22] Putting a person into the position of being an unwilling participant is enough.[23] He noted the "no grief" rule but could see the logic in it.[24] He considered the case of persons uninvolved who can be called secondary victims but that terms should not obscure the fact that he still has to be owed a duty himself.[25] Lord Oliver accepted both points about TV, that is that in this case it was not enough but in others it might be.[26] Lord Jauncey reserved his position on bystanders.[27] He followed *McLoughlin* closely. He disagreed with TV liability because defendants would know the rule is not to show gruesome things.[28] He made no comment on the

---

[13] As did Lord Ackner, *ibid.* at 401. In *Ravenscroft v. Rederiaktiebologet Transatlantic* [1991] 3 All E.R. 73 the plaintiff was injured by a fork lift. His mother did not see the incident nor was she present at his later death nor did she see the body. She suffered "a prolonged grief reaction as defined in the International Classification of Grief Code 309.1, namely a prolonged depressive reaction which was not specifiable as manic depression but which might be psychotic or neurotic and might be long lasting." The court upheld her claim primarily based upon foreseeability but also adopting the new phraseology of the general law, saying it was fair, just and reasonable to make the link between plaintiff and defendant. See also *Hevican v. Ruane* [1991] 3 All E.R. 65.

[14] The Lord Ordinary in *Bourhill*, 1941 S.C. 395 at 399.

[15] H. Teff, "The Requirement Of Sudden Shock In Liability For Negligently Inflicted Psychiatric Damage" [1996] Tort L. Rev. 44.

[16] *Alcock v. Chief Constable, South Yourkshire* [1992] A.C. 310 at 401.

[17] *ibid.* at 403.

[18] *ibid.* at 406.

[19] *ibid.* at 407.

[20] *ibid.* at 407.

[21] *ibid.* at 407.

[22] He gave the example of *Dooley v. Cammell Laird & Co. Ltd* [1951] 1 Lloyd's Rep. 271. See generally, D. Brodie, "Nervous Shock and Professional Rescuers" (1997) Rep. B. 13–2.

[23] *Alcock*, at 408.

[24] *ibid.* at 410.

[25] *ibid.* at 411.

[26] *ibid.* at 417.

[27] *ibid.* at 422.

[28] *Alcock v. Chief Constable, South Yorkshire* [1992] A.C. 310 at 423.

"burning children in the balloon" hypothetical discussed in the case. There need indeed be no primary victim.[29]

10–66 The Inner House had an interesting point to consider in *Robertson v. Forth Road Bridge Joint Board*.[30] Three men went to remove a sheet of metal from a bridge. One was blown over. The other two sued for nervous shock and PTSD. Both saw the body fall off the side of the bridge and one had known the deceased for a good many years. A failure to have a safe system of work was admitted. Following *McLoughlin* the court held that the workmen were not within the group of persons who could recover. Ties of love and affection like those of a close family were required—the closest emotional ties. It was accepted that personal involvement in the incident or a completely horrific occurrence could overcome this hurdle, but the evidence was not sufficiently gruesome in this case. The Lord President considered the men to be simply bystanders and nothing could be taken from the fact that they were fellow workmen. The employment relationship had nearly convinced Lord Cowie that there was a duty but he was persuaded by the Lord President's opinion that this was not the case. Nor was this the kind of case where it could be said that the shock was caused by the employer allowing the pursuer to become "the involuntary cause of another's death or injury".[31]

10–67 Another issue, not clearly anticipated in the earlier cases, arose in *Page v. Smith*.[32] A teacher who had for some years suffered from a condition at the time of the case called ME was in a collision of moderate severity[33] with the defender. The plaintiff was not physically injured but within about three hours his condition returned in a virulent way preventing him from working. At first instance there had been controversy about the disease but it was found that ME was in fact a medical condition despite scepticism on the part of some doctors and perhaps members of the public.[34] It was also held at first instance that the plaintiff was not malingering.[35] Nonetheless, it should be borne in mind that these were points which could be made and were made in this case. The Appeal Courts have to put out of their mind the possibility that they as judges of first instance would have found differently. The leading speech is that of Lord Lloyd of Berwick in whose speech the 3–2 majority concurred. He accepted a factual distinction between primary and secondary victims and that this distinction should have legal consequences.[36] The primary victim is directly involved but others who suffer through what they see or hear are secondary victims. Lord Lloyd followed the judge at first instance and tried to treat the case simply. It is recognised that drivers owe a duty to other road users and that the defender was in breach of that duty in the sense that he drove carelessly. Had he so much as bruised the plaintiff he would have been

---

[29] *ibid*. at 412.

[30] 1994 S.L.T. 568, and see the earlier hearing on relevancy at 566. See also below at 10–68.

[31] The result is the same as was reached in the English decision *McFarlane v. EE Caledonia Ltd* [1994] 2 All E.R 1. See J. Blaikie, "Nervous Shock: Traumatised Fellow Workers and Bystanders", 1994 S.L.T. (News) 297.

[32] [1996] 1 A.C. 155.

[33] *ibid*. at 185.

[34] *ibid*.

[35] *ibid*.

[36] Following Lord Oliver in *Alcock v. Chief Constable, South Yorkshire*, at 410–411.

liable for some damages and there would have been no question of reopening the question of duty. It thus goes against common sense (which is often mentioned as a touchstone of proximity or duty) that just because, luckily, he was not physically injured he could not recover. It is of course the case that it was noted that medical science progresses.[37] However, be that as it may the important point, perhaps a little lost sight of, is whether and to what extent that expansion of science filters through to the community at large. Thus the decision is clearly correct if rationalised on the basis of accepting that medicine recognises trauma can cause mental problems without the need for the body to be broken and that drivers in general have a broad awareness that this is the case. So far as this latter point is concerned the accident took place in 1987 and one must wonder when the public at large became aware that such consequences can follow. When contemplating whether to drive carelessly or not the defendant might have thought that he could cause physical injury resulting in paraplegia or if directing his mind to a moderate collision (which seems unrealistic) he might have thought he would cause inexpensive minor injuries. He might of course, it must be remembered, have foreseen that his victim might have been a very important employee whose few days off work might cost his employer dear. Reviewing these factors he would realise that the economic loss was irrecoverable and could budget for the costs should he actually be careless which he would try not to be. He would however be insured for the accident and so would only be contemplating the loss of his insurance policy (except the no claims bonus and excess) but that fact must be read subject to what is essentially a fiction that having contracted with his insurers *uberrimae fidei* he would still contemplate very hard in their interests. The chances are that the victim is not a key man in his company and the chances are that he will not have a pre-existing mental condition which is rather easily exacerbated. Only if it can be said that the mental injury is equivalent to physical injury can he justly be held liable.

Even then there is one more critical point dividing the House. That is the question of reasonable fortitude or the customary phlegm. For Lord Keith, who accepted that there was foreseeability of physical injury and proximity, the key point was that shock was not foreseeable to a normal person. With respect that view is not correct if proximity exists. The victim must be taken as found. A haemophiliac in the car would have been compensated if a minor collision had caused him to bleed to death. That is bad luck for the defendant that he did not collide with a tougher man as it is that he did not collide with someone of the customary phlegm rather than Simon Page. It must always be remembered that duties among road users were established well before *Donoghue v. Stevenson*.[38] The only difference in this case from cases decided in the nineteenth century is the recognition of the injury. A final point in favour of the dissent is that the majority view bears a worrying resemblance to the *Anns/Dutton* hearsay that economic loss could be treated as property damage even although his property did not actually fall down and hurt anyone. That logic was clearly persuasive at the time and for some time. Is the majority in *Page* guilty of the same logical error? Not if it

---

[37] *Page v. Smith, op. cit.* at 187.
[38] 1932 S.C. (H.L.) 31. For road traffic cases see Chap. 16.

can be accepted that the interest in one's mental health is equivalent to the security of one's body parts. That is easier today than it would have been once—not just because of medical science but because of the lack of faith generally held in the community of the mind/body dichotomy. Lord Ackner added that if it had been necessary to deal with a man of normal fortitude then the event was still foreseeable as such a one could in his view have suffered PTSD.[39] Thus, it is submitted this case is sound and perfectly consonant with Scots law if it is read as saying that the neighbour principle applies in cases of direct harm to the person and that certain mental illnesses are considered within the idea of direct harm to the person.[40] Causation of the condition must of course be established.[41]

10–68   The decision in *Page* would not affect the Scots decision in *Robertson v. Forth Bridge Joint Board*.[42] The workmen in that case were not primary victims. Thus the secondary rules applied. On the other hand it could be argued, as it was, that the pre-existing recognised duty of care owed encompassed nervous shock caused ultimately by the employers' fault. The Lord President thought it wrong that an ordinary bystander could not recover but one who was an employee could. There is force to that and maybe the point in this case is that the other workmen were not exactly bystanders—they were on the same mission. At this stage it is appropriate to note that in the context of employers' liability it has been held that the employer owes a duty to the employee to protect him from foreseeable mental illness as in *Walker v. Northumberland Council*.[43] This gives some considerable support to the new primary/secondary theory.

10–69   The latest attempt by the House of Lords to state the law was in *White v. Chief Constable of South Yorkshire*,[44] the appeal against the decision known under the name *Frost v. Chief Constable of South Yorkshire* in the Court of Appeal. A 2–1 majority in the Court of Appeal applied the decision in *Page* to allow the claim of a policeman who suffered shock in the Hillsborough disaster. Lord Justice Rose in the majority in the Court of Appeal saw the policeman as a primary participant. This was because they were employees in the course of their employment and because they were rescuers. The House of Lords by a 3–2 majority reversed the Court of Appeal and disallowed the claim. Lord Steyn while accepting the contemporary approach to mental illness as being as serious or worse than ordinary physical injury held that the law was still entitled to deal with problems of indeterminate liability and policy. He attempted to specify the policy grounds. His first ground, the need for psychiatric evidence, with respect seems unconvincing where the same evidence is need in consequential cases. The second point he made was that the ability to claim compensation unconsciously makes people at least think they have PTSD or something like it. His only evidence for this was that people injured at work often have mental consequences and those injured at sport just get on with it. With

---

[39] Lord Browne-Wilkinson found support in Scottish cases: *Currie v. Wardrop*, 1927 S.C. 538 and *Brown v. Glasgow Corporation*, 1922 S.C. 527.

[40] See *contra*, J.M. Thomson, "Page v. Smith—A Scottish Footnote" (1996) 112 L.Q.R. 383.

[41] *Giblett v. P. & N.E. Murray Ltd* [1999] T.L.R. 401.

[42] 1996 S.L.T. 263. See para. 10–66 above.

[43] [1995] 1 All E.R. 737. See the next case, *White v. Chief Constable*, for the scope of *Walker*.

[44] [1999] 2 A.C. 455.

respect that seems unsupported by any evidence whatsoever. The third, again offered without any quantitative analysis is that there would be many more claims. Fourthly, he points out that the consequences for a tortfeasor might be disproportionate. Yet again this is not strong especially in England where there is a remoteness rule of reasonable foreseeability.

It was held by the majority that *Walker* could not be relied upon because that was a case of primary liability as the worker had been injured by the employers' conduct. It was, the majority pointed out, an error to assume that employment by itself exempted the plaintiff from the control mechanisms of secondary cases. After a review of the history he decided that the plaintiff could not succeed on the basis of being a primary victim because the duty of the employer to the employee had not actually been extended to cover psychiatric injury.[45] Lord Hoffmann put this point:

"If one starts from the employer's liability in respect of physical injury, it seems an easy step, even rather forward-looking, to extend liability on the same grounds to psychiatric injury. It makes the law seem more attuned to advanced medical thinking by eliminating (or not introducing) a distinction which rests upon uneasy empirical foundations. It is important, however to have regard, not only to how the proposed extension of liability can be aligned with cases in which liability exists, but also to the situations in which damages are not recoverable. If one then steps back and looks at the rules of liability for psychiatric injury as a whole, in their relationship with each other, the smoothing of the fabric at one point has produced an ugly ruck at another. In their application to other secondary victims, the *Alcock* control mechanisms stand obstinately in the way of rationalisation and the effect is to produce striking anomalies."[45a]

With respect, on the assumption that the law has fragmented in a pragmatic way in relation to nervous shock, then to start a growth of categories of primary victim based on existing relationships does seem to be an appopriate way of going about things in an era of incrementalism.

In *White*, the category of rescuer was reviewed around the only case **10–70** actually in point—the first instance case of *Chadwick v. British Railways Board*[46] and it was said that the rescuer "must at least satisfy the threshold requirement that he objectively exposed himself to danger or reasonably believed that he was doing so." This, it was said, left a practical law but one which if it needed rationalising had to be undertaken by Parliament. One particularly weak point was that the solution of allowing all claims was to be rejected for unstated policy reasons and because precedent was against it.

There are some other cases of note. In *Schofield v. Chief Constable of* **10–71** *West Yorkshire*[47] a policeman and policewoman went to collect some guns from a house. On finding them the policeman shot one of the guns into a folded mattress. This was, in terms of police rules, unlawful. The police-

---

[45] Lord Steyn referred to Hilson, "Nervous Shock and Categorization of Victims" [1998] Tort L.R. 37 at p. 42.
[45a] [1999] 2 A.C. 455 at 506.
[46] [1967] 1 Q.B. 912.
[47] [1998] T.L.R. 319.

woman as a result of this was found at trial to have suffered PTSD. In view
of the way in which the law had been laid down the only issue was whether
the plaintiff was a participant and it was held that she was, therefore the
customary phlegm inquiry was ruled out. It should be noted that there was
some reference to the WPC being at risk of physical injury although what it
was is not clear. In *Haggerty v. EE Caledonia*,[48] the Court of Appeal had to
revisit the issue in the case of an off-duty worker on a supply ship who
witnessed the Piper Alpha disaster. It seems he was some 500m away and a
fireball fizzled out some 50m in front of him. It was held that the decision
that he was not a primary victim was correct as his fear of his own life was
not a rational one.[49] In *Hunter v. British Coal Corporation*[50] a workman who
was not present at the scene of an accident but for which he believed
himself to be responsible was not owed a duty by his employers. The
majority of the Court of Appeal considered that he was too distant in space
and time to proximate. It was commented that as the English Law
Commission were working on the topic it would not be right to expand the
law.[51] A woman who suffered shock on hearing that her daughter had been
abducted and assumed the worst, which in fact materialised, was not
sufficiently proximate and seeing her daughter's severely mutilated body
three days later did not bring her within *McLoughlin* proximity.[52] In *Burke
v. Royal Infirmary of Edinburgh*[53] Lord Eassie applied the "take your victim
as you find him" rule to agree that had liability been established a man
could recover for "abnormal pain disorder" which had no physical cause
but which did result from a fall. That is consistent with *Page*. In *Campbell v.
North Lanarkshire Council*[54] a proof before answer was allowed so that it
could be determined whether the pursuer was a primary or a secondary
victim and this will often be the case.

10–72　　So intractable appears the mission of providing a common law bright line
that attempts have been made to resolve the matter by statute. The English
Law Commission issued a consultation paper.[55] That has recently been
followed by a report which may well be influential in this area.[56] The
Commission accept that foreseeability cannot be the only test in all cases—
the floodgates fear is alive and well. The Commission proposes to abolish
the need for victims to be close in space and time. The distinction is not
strictly between primary and secondary victims but between immediate
victims and others. To mirror the present state of the law an *Anns*-like
policy defence is proposed in a new post-*Murphy* form whereby the court
can dissapply the duty if it is found to be just and reasonable not to apply a
duty. They recommend the abolition of the requirement for shock which

---

[48] [1997] T.L.R. 69.
[49] Another plaintiff, McFarlane, had lost his case earlier in the Court of Appeal [1993]
T.L.R. 476 and was suing his barrister in the joined case.
[50] [1998] T.L.R. 111.
[51] See generally K. Wheat, "Nervous Shock: Proposals for Reform" [1994] J.P.I.L. 207.
[52] *Palmer v. Tees Health Authority* [1998] T.L.R. 351.
[53] [1998] T.L.R. 365.
[54] Unreported, June 30, 1999.
[55] No. 137. For comment in Scotland see M. O'Carroll, "Nervous Shock: Proposals for
Reform" (1995) 40 J.L.S. 231; for a practitioner-orientated comment see K. Wheat, "Nervous
Shock: Proposals for Reform" [1994] J.P.I.L. 207.
[56] *Liability for Psychiatric Illness* (Law Com. No. 249, 1998).

although apparently shocking is not so if taken with the introductory section of this part of this chapter. The Royal College of Psychiatrists Mental Health Law Group said that the idea of shock-induced illness had no scientific or clinical merit.[57] In place of an open-ended test of a tie of love and affection the Commission proposes to fix a list of guaranteed claimants[58] with others having to show their entitlement.

(B) BREACH OF THE DUTY OF CARE

The Basic Test: The Reasonable Man

This is the practical question. The basic test is simply that a person must **10–73** take reasonable care. This has been said to be an impersonal test. The test of the reasonable man set against the care a person ordinarily takes in their own affairs was established in England in the eighteenth century.[59] The civilian doctrine of *culpa* depended upon the conduct of the *bonus paterfamilias*.[60] All the main themes involved in the investigation into breach are apparent from the following quotation from the speech of Lord Macmillan in *Muir v. Glasgow Corporation*[61]:

"The degree of care of the safety of others which the law requires human beings to observe in the conduct of their affairs varies according to the circumstances. There is no absolute standard, but it may be said generally that the degree of care required varies directly with the risk involved. Those who engage in operations inherently dangerous must take precautions which are not required to persons engaged in the ordinary routine of daily life. It is, no doubt, true that in every act which an individual performs there is present a potentiality of injury to others. All things are possible, and, indeed, it has become proverbial that the unexpected always happens, but, while the precept *alterum non laedere* requires us to abstain from intentionally injuring others, it does not impose liability for every injury which our conduct may occasion. In Scotland, at any rate, it has never been a maxim of the law that a man acts at his peril. Legal liability is limited to those consequences of our acts which a reasonable man of ordinary intelligence and experience so acting would have in contemplation . . . The standard of foresight of the reasonable man is, in one sense, an impersonal test. It eliminates the personal equation and is independent the idiosyncrasies of the particular person whose conduct is in question. Some persons are by nature unduly

---

[57] *ibid.*, para. 5.29(2).

[58] Spouse, parent, child, sibling, co-habitant of two years or more including homosexual co-habitants. In Scotland it would probably be better to adopt the categories already fixed in the Damages (Scotland) Act 1976, which of course does not have the two-year time limit and does not sanction homosexual relationships.

[59] *Vaughan v. Menlove* 3 Bing N.C. 468.

[60] G. MacCormack, *Daube Noster*, p. 202 especially nn. 6, 7 and 8. It should not be thought that it is necessarily accepted that the *bonus paterfamilias* view depended always upon reasonable foreseeability. See Zimmerman, *The Law of Obligations*, pp. 1008–1009, n. 69 for the folksy definitions of the modern *bonus paterfamilias* in South Africa.

[61] 1932 S.C. (H.L.) 3.

timorous and imagine every path beset with lions. Others, of more robust temperament, fail to foresee or nonchalantly disregard even the most obvious dangers. The reasonable man is presumed to be free both from over-apprehension and from over-confidence, but there is a sense in which the standard of care of the reasonable man involves in its application a subjective element. It is still left to the judge to decide what, in the circumstances of the particular case, the reasonable man would have had in contemplation, and what, accordingly, the party sought to be made liable ought to have foreseen. Here there is room for diversity of view."

These themes can be said to be (1) a test, objective, but from the point of view of the defender and not from that of the pursuer or a fly-on-the-wall observer; and (2) the precise standard is set as a jury question but often decided by judges acting as juries. *Hughes*[62] is another example of the principle:

"So we have (first) a duty owed by the workmen, (secondly) the fact that if they had done as they ought to have done there would have been no accident, and (thirdly) the fact that the injuries suffered by the appellant, though perhaps different in degree, did not differ in kind from injuries which might have resulted from an accident of a foreseeable nature. The ground on which this case has been decided against the appellant is that the accident was of an unforeseeable type. Of course, the pursuer has to prove that the defender's fault caused the accident and there could be a case where the intrusion of a new and unexpected factor could be regarded as the cause of the accident rather than the fault of the defender. But that is not this case. The cause of this accident was a known source of danger, the lamp; but it behaved in an unpredictable way . . . The explanation of the accident which has been accepted, and which I would not seek to question, is that, when the lamp fell down the manhole and was broken, some paraffin escaped, and enough was vaporised to create an explosive mixture which was detonated by the naked light of the lamp. The experts agree that no one would have expected that to happen; it was so unlikely as to be unforeseeable. The explosion caused the boy to fall into the manhole: whether his injuries were directly caused by the explosion, or aggravated by fires which started in the manhole, is not at all clear. The essential step in the respondent's argument is that the explosion was the real cause of the injuries, and that the explosion was unforeseeable."[63]

Usual Practice

10–74 Experience shows that many people under a duty of care try to do what everyone else does. This is as much the case with individuals as businesses but it is very likely to be found in business where almost every aspect of a company will be dictated by the line of work in which they are engaged.

---

[62] *Hughes v. Lord Advocate*, 1963 S.L.T. 150.
[63] *ibid.*, *per* Lord Reid at 151.

Thus the precautions which are taken are likely to be modelled on competitors and perhaps in practice by firms where managers formerly worked. A reasonable employer will at least do what others have successfully done to prevent accidents; failure to do this should require some explanation. Earlier in the century this factual situation came to be treated as a matter of law rather than a common inference of fact under the name of the Dunedin formula taken from the speech of Lord Dunedin in *Morton v. William Dixon Ltd*[64]:

"Where the negligence of the employer consists of what I may call a fault of omission, I think it is absolutely necessary that the proof of that fault of omission should be one of two kinds, either to shew that the thing which he did not do was a thing which was commonly done by other persons in like circumstances, or to shew that it was a thing that was so obviously wanted that it would be folly in anyone to neglect to provide it."[65]

This was well established. So much so that in the Division Lord MacKay said "One may fairly say with a considerable experience of charging juries that in similar circumstances this illuminating statement must have been used as a proper direction in scores of cases."[66] It was dealt a serious blow in the House of Lords when it was said in *Paris v. Stepney Borough Council*[67]:

"the rule is stated with all the Lord President's trenchant lucidity. It contains an emphatic warning against a facile finding that a precaution is necessary when there is no proof that it is one taken by other persons in like circumstances. But it does not detract from the test of the conduct and judgment of the reasonable and prudent man. If there is proof that a precaution is usually observed by other persons a reasonable and prudent man will follow the usual practice in the like circumstances. Failing such proof the test is whether the precaution is one which the reasonable and prudent man would think so obvious that it was folly to omit it."[68]

A dictum of Lord Reid suggests that after that the common practice point is one in favour of the workman:

"Apart from cases where he may be able to rely on an existing practice, it is the duty of an employer, in considering whether some precaution should be taken against a foreseeable risk, to weigh, on the one hand, the magnitude of the risk, the likelihood of an accident happening, and the possible seriousness of the consequences if an accident does happen, and, on the other hand, the difficulty and expense and any other disadvantage of taking the precaution. Here the likelihood of an accident

---

[64] 1909 S.C. 80.
[65] *ibid*. at 89.
[66] *Carroll v. Andrew Barclay & Sons Ltd*, 1947 S.L.T. 223 at 228.
[67] [1951] A.C. 367.
[68] *ibid*. at 382.

may have been small, but at least it was sufficient to prevent the respondents from maintaining that the accident could not have happened without the appellant being negligent. And the consequences of any accident were almost certain to be serious. On the other hand, there was very little difficulty, no expenses and no other disadvantage in taking an effective precaution. Once it is established that danger was foreseeable and, therefore, that the matter should have been considered before the accident, it appears to me that a reasonable man weighing these matters would have said that the precaution clearly ought to be taken."[69]

In *Brown v. Rolls Royce Ltd*[70] the pursuer failed to gain the apparent benefit of the dictum and this was held to be equally valid in that the dictum was a mere statement of sense. It was found in fact that the provision of barrier cream was a common practice. The pursuer sought to argue that this created an onus which the defender had failed to rebut. However, it was made clear that this was only one fact which had to be considered with others and other inferences by the court of first instance.

10–75   Yet the rule was applied with full force in the division upholding a refusal of a workman's claim in *Riddick v. Weir Housing Corporation Ltd*[71]:

"The measure of the employer's liability, however, is not what a dermatologist believes even if at the end of the day his view comes to be generally accepted, but what is accepted in the trade at the time of the onset. The rule of *Morton v. William Dixon Ltd*, 1909 S.C. 807, at p. 809; 1909 1 S.L.T. 346, applies to this case."[72]

It was influential for Lord Wier in *Gibson v. Strathclyde Regional Council*[73]:

"The relevancy of the pursuer's averments in that case, as well as in this case, should be tested by reference to the well known line of authority

---

[69] *Morris v. West Hartlepool Steam Navigation Co. Ltd* [1956] A.C. 552 at 574.

[70] 1960 S.L.T. 119.

[71] 1971 S.L.T. 24.

[72] *ibid.*, *per* Lord Migdale at 28. Lord President Clyde was not impressed by the drift away from the rule. He called the reversal of the rule in *Stepney* by Lord Normand "a small modification on the latter part of the rule." It was cited and used to sufficient effect to have a sheriff reverse a finding of liability below in *Gilfillan v. National Coal Board*, 1972 S.L.T. (Sh. Ct) 39 at 44: "The fact that a workman, such as the pursuer, is entitled to take the defenders' system as he finds it and to do his daily work in accordance with that system, does not mean that his advisers, when an action is contemplated, are relieved from the responsibility of themselves considering, with the aid of expert advice if necessary, what precautions the defenders ought to have taken. Having formed their own opinion on these matters, it is then their duty in a case such as this to give to the defenders in the pleadings fair notice of the case which it is proposed to make against them." Ironically in *Morton* itself expert witnesses (but for the employers) were castigated by Lord President Dunedin: "I am bound to add, and I do this for the benefit of employers, that the only difficulty I have had in the matter has been caused by the absurd attitude taken up by their expert witnesses. When the matter was put to them, instead of taking the frank line and saying that it is no use, that it is not in any view necessary, and that they did not think it would be any good, they started absurd theories as to its interfering with the ventilation and so on, which really are a disgrace to their idea of the intelligence of anyone who was listening to them. I should like expert witnesses to know the impression they make on my mind when they give that sort of evidence. On the whole matter I am of opinion that there ought to be a new trial."

[73] 1993 S.L.T. 1243.

commencing with *Morton v. William Dixon Ltd* and ending with *Brown v. Rolls Royce Ltd*. In this case, the pursuer's case is based on a duty on the part of the defenders to carry out a daily inspection of drains in busy city streets such as the one where the pursuer is said to have met with her accident. Their failure to do so is said to have been the cause of her accident. There are no averments that such a system was commonly operated by other local authorities in their city streets. For the pursuer's case to pass the test of relevancy in the absence of averments of practice, in my opinion, there must be averments which make it absolutely clear that the fulfilment of the duty of reasonable care required a system of daily inspection."[74]

The formula was cited to Lord Thomson in *Macdonald v. Scottish Stamping And Engineering Co. Ltd*[75] in a case where the workman failed to show desiderated precautions were common practice:

"I fully appreciate that the incorporation of such devices would lead to a drop in the rate of production and I fully appreciate also that such a drop in production might be unpalatable on economic grounds not only to the defenders but also to their employees for they are paid piece work rates. Nonetheless, where as here a machine has been proved to be dangerous the employer must, in my opinion, take such steps as are reasonably practicable to reduce the danger in the interests of the safety of his employees."[76]

The case and the doctrine continued to be and are yet cited. Now it should **10–76** only be for the proposition of good sense which can be used for pursuer or defender that something which is usually done suggests that reasonable care has been taken, but equally other facts which suggest it is not an exercise of reasonable care are shown then the court can find there is liability. The pursuer does not have to desiderate a system for the whole area of activity. The pursuer should aver at least the bare bones of an alternative which would have obviated the risk and which it would have been folly to ignore.

Emasculating the reasonable man

Examples of "what is it I must do to meet the standard of the reasonable **10–77** man" appear throughout this book. The chapters on occupiers, producers, employers, keepers of animals and roads provide manifold examples some of which by virtue of statute are matters of law and others illustrations of the conduct of the reasonable man—who of course finds himself in a dress when the defender is a woman. The time will come when A.P. Herbert's essay "The Reasonable Woman" will be found not to be amusing at all. At the time of writing to mention it is to be considered politically incorrect or question-beggingly, inappropriate. Citation of Herbert's title serves as a useful reminder that the use of the reasonable man might now lead to error

---

[74] *ibid.* at 1247.
[75] 1972 S.L.T. (Notes) 73.
[76] *ibid.* at 74. The doctrine was applied but in favour of the workman on the "folly" point in *Stewart v. Colvilles Ltd*, 1963 S.L.T. (Sh. Ct) 15.

because of the very active role women play in society. Of course if men and women are the same instead of equal under the law then there will be no difference at all. If there is a distinct female view of conduct it ought to become part of the breach inquiry; which it would do more easily if juries decided cases instead of mainly male judges. Use of the reasonable man as a test shows that the position of women in law is still marginalised. In some of the examples in this book the paragon is neutered as the reasonable "occupier" or the reasonable "keeper" or "producer"—often as a result of statute which has for some time tried to be gender neutral. It is possible to say that the cases upon which this text book is founded depend upon a masculine ethic of anti-social, self-interested, wealth based, dehumanising utilitarian calculations.[77] An alternative standard might be proposed of a feminine ethic of care and concern for needs and welfare. A standard of conscious care and concern of a responsible neighbour or social acquaintance might be better formulated. Wright argues this could, however, ordain less care than some versions of the so called masculine standard.[78] The issue of standard need not be taken for granted, need not be what the last judge said it was, need not be what the senior partner says it is, not what the Q.C. says it is—it is supposed to be a matter of fact and a change in what must be done can be effected by averment and proof of what it is that the reasonable man would have done had she been there.

A Utility Test: Learned Hand

10–78　A desire to predict or to classify has perhaps led to more structured attempts at stating what should or should not be done. In truth the inspiration for some of these approaches may owe something to the jurisprudential movement of law and economics centred in the U.S.[79] Whatever the history of the matter it is possible to find cases where some particular feature has come to the attention of the court and a category of case can be said to exist. It is also possible that economics may be an important factor in the court's approach to care but the law has not adopted economics as the sole basis upon which the issue of breach is determined. If applied rigorously it can effect a redistribution of wealth which is not the underlying philosophy of this branch of the legal system which is essentially corrective.

10–79　　An economic approach to breach was memorably expressed by Judge Learned Hand.[80] $B<PL$ suggests negligence where B is the burden or cost of avoiding accidental loss, P is the increase in probability of loss if B is not undertaken and L is the probable magnitude or cost of such loss. While supporting a utilitarian point of view and an economic point of view that approach can be brought into other approaches. It is often criticised

---

[77] L. Bender, "A Lawyer's Primer on Feminist Theory and Tort" (1988) 38 J. Legal Educ. 3. I am indebted to Wright, "Standards of Care in Negligence Law" in *Philosophical Foundations of Tort Law* (Owen, ed., 1996) for this trail.

[78] Wright, *ibid.* at p. 255.

[79] W.M. Landes and R.A. Posner, *The Economic Structure of Tort Law* (1987); G. Calibresi "Some Thoughts on Risk Distribution and the Law of Torts" (1961) 70 Yale LJ 499. P. Cane (ed.) *Atiyah's Accidents, Compensation and the Law* (4th. ed., 1987), Chap. 24.

[80] In *U.S. v. Carroll Towing Co.* 159 F 2d 169 (2d Cir 1947). An early formulation appears in H.T. Terry, "Negligence" (1915) 29 Harv. L. Rev. 40.

although the various components can be seen in cases.[81] The Hand approach may have been given some currency in Scotland by an article and the teaching of Professor Wilson.[82] Nonetheless it is essential to caution against thinking that to follow these elements as marks or guides is to adopt the Hand formula for to do so is to commit to a philosophy of law which has extensive implications.[83]

Probability

The care that must be taken depends upon the circumstances. Rifle **10–80** shooting in a proper range is different from rifle shooting in Sauchiehall Street. This aspect of liability appears clearly stated in the *Digest*:

"if a pruner threw down a branch from a tree and killed a slave passing underneath (the same applies to a man working on a scaffold), he is liable only if it falls down on a public place and he failed to shout a warning so that the accident could be avoided. But Mucius says that even if the accident occurred in a private place an action can be brought if his conduct is blameworthy—and he thinks there is fault when what could have been seen by a diligent man was not foreseen, or when a warning was shouted too late for the danger to be avoided. Following the same reasoning it does not matter much whether the deceased was making his way through a public or a private place, as the general public often make their way across private places. But if there is no path, the defendant should be liable only for positive wrongdoing, so he should not throw anything at someone he sees passing by; but on the other hand he is not deemed blameworthy when he could not have guessed that someone was about to pass through that place."[84]

In *Bolton v. Stone*[85] a woman was struck by a ball hit for six out of a cricket ground. She was walking on a quiet road adjacent to the park. The ball went over a 17 foot fence which was about 80yds from the batsman. The woman was about 100yds from the batsman, the accident would have been prevented by a very large fence or the cessation of playing cricket. Taking into account the fact that the road was seldom used and that such powerful strokes had been played only six times in thirty years, it was held that the risk was such a small one that a reasonable man would be entitled to ignore it.[86] Thus a reasonable man foreseeing harm to others can, in some circumstances, take no steps at all to prevent that harm.[87]

---

[81] See Wright, "The Standards of Care in Negligence Law", *op. cit.*

[82] W.A. Wilson, "The Analysis of Negligence", 1961 S.L.T. (News) 1.

[83] A more thematic approach is given by Professor Atiyah: "First, the degree of probability that damage will be done by the conduct which is challenged; secondly, the magnitude of the harm which is likely to be done if the risk unfortunately materializes; thirdly, the value or utility of the object to be achieved by the conduct in question; and fourthly, the burden in terms of cost time and trouble, of taking precautions against the risk of damage."

[84] D.9.2.31; Inst. 4.3.5.

[85] [1951] A.C. 850.

[86] A change in the facts can bring about a different result: see the other cricket case of *Miller v. Jackson* [1977] Q.B. 966.

[87] *Bolton v. Stone, per* Lord Radcliffe at 869. And see *Titchiner v. BRB*, 1984 S.L.T. 192.

10-81   The same issues had been canvassed in Scottish cases notably by a court of seven judges in *McLeod v. Magistrates of St. Andrews*.[88] In that case a proof before answer was allowed to a woman struck on the face by a golf ball when crossing the old course by a public footpath. *Bolton* was considered in Scotland in *Lamond v. Glasgow Corporation*.[89] In this case a pedestrian on a path alongside a golf course was struck by a ball. At proof it was established that about 6,000 shots went out of bounds each year although no one had previously been struck. It was held that the injury was foreseeable. Although the path was never busy there were various pedestrians using it between 9 a.m. and 5 p.m. Lord Thomson held there to be a real risk of injury. The cost/benefit analysis was accepted.[90] It was held that either a fence could have been built or the course re-designed.[91] *Bolton* may have been applied in *Hill v. Lovett*,[92] in which it was asked whether the risks of dogs biting a person entering premises were such as to be sufficiently probable to require precautions and the question answered in the affirmative. *Lewis v. Buckpool Golf Club*[93] was an action by a golfer who was injured by a mis-hit golf ball against the golf club and the player who struck the ball. On appeal the sheriff's decision after proof that the second defender (the player) was liable for the lack of care in failing to wait until the pursuer had got out of the way was upheld. The sheriff had assoilzied the club. After a consideration of, *inter alia*, *Bolton* it was accepted by the sheriff principal that there was a real risk, as distinct from a mere possibility that a player driving off from the fifth tee might strike a player who was putting at the fourth, especially if the player was of limited ability. In *Gillon v. Chief Constable*,[94] the pursuer was a police officer who was injured when a footballer came off the field and knocked her over to her injury. She had been under orders to face away from the pitch. The case was essentially one of employers' liability but it was held after a consideration of *Bolton* and relevant evidence that the happening was unforeseeable on he basis that there were no reported happenings. With respect this is a more simple case where it seems obvious that if you make people stand with their backs to an obvious and foreseeable hazard such as players coming off the pitch, which they do in every game, an accident is inevitable. This is reminiscent of the famous case in the *Digest* of the barber who shaves a person next to a place where people are playing ball.[95] In the circumstances where the facts place the effectively blindfolded policewoman in the obvious ambit of danger there ought to be liability. In *Pearson v. Lightning*[96] the Court of Appeal upheld a finding of liability in another golfing case. It was a fine case because the ball which hit the plaintiff hit off a tree. Normally that might be thought to be plain bad luck. However, in this case it was held that the shot was such a tricky one that the risk although small was foreseeable and the

---

[88] 1924 S.C. 960.
[89] 1968 S.L.T. 291.
[90] *ibid.* at 293.
[91] See *Whitefield v. Barton*, 1987 S.C.L.R. 259 for another consideration in the sheriff court, this time for damage to a car by a golf ball.
[92] 1992 S.L.T. 994.
[93] 1993 S.L.T. (Sh. Ct) 43.
[94] 1997 S.L.T. 1218.
[95] D.9.2.11. Pr.
[96] [1998] T.L.R. 270.

stroke took place on the plaintiff's side of the rough. Harking back to the *Digest* quotation, the player did shout fore.

Magnitude of harm

If *Bolton v. Stone* had been about escaping table tennis balls then the issue **10–82** would have been even easier. A ping-pong ball can seldom do any injury of any significance and so the reasonable man can do pretty much as he pleases with a ping-pong ball. At the other end of the spectrum if the harm which will result is likely to be serious the reasonable man takes more care. This was made clear in a case where it was held that the reasonable employer would provide a one-eyed man with goggles where he might not supply them to a two eyed man as the possibility of blindness necessitating the greater care.[97]

Utility

This is an altogether more difficult focus on the reasonable man. Society **10–83** may permit more danger where it can be seen that the activity is socially beneficial. This idea can be seen in the English case *Daborn v. Bath Tramways Motor Co.*[98] It was held that it was not careless to drive an ambulance with a defective signalling system because in wartime there was a need for every possible vehicle to be used. The task of the court was to, "balance the risk against the consequences of not assuming that risk and in the present case that calculation seems to me to work out in favour of the plaintiff." This involves allowing the reasonable man quite a wide ranging review of what is proper in society as opposed to the particular issue confronting him. Scots courts are not populated by Utilitarian philosophers and its not known how many Kantians populate the bench. The touchstone is still the reasonable man. In some cases utility may attract most reasonable men; in others many reasonable men would not follow the course of crude utility.

Cost

This is an issue which does appear in the cases. *Bolton* and the other cases **10–84** mentioned in the context of usual practice[99] clearly show the cost of fencing featuring in the reasonable man's deliberations.[1] But the difficulty is in assigning value particularly in reparation where it can cost more to falsely call a famous person a thief than it does if a pauper's leg is broken. The absence of exemplary or penal damages means that a company can take a decision which means that inevitably persons will be injured where it considers the damages are affordable. Courts in Scotland will have been influenced by Professor Wilson's adoption of Lord Reid's rather economic approach, but in personal injury cases at least the ethical refusal to set a real purchase value on live human beings makes a cost benefit analysis

---

[97] *Paris v. Stepney B.C.* [1951] A.C. 850. See also *McKinley v. British Steel Corporation*, 1988 S.L.T. 810.

[98] [1946] 2 All E.R. 333.

[99] See para. 10–74.

[1] See also *Reid v. Greater Glasgow Health Board*, 1976 S.L.T. (Notes) 33.

entirely academic or at best a model.[2] It is not possible to buy the right to injure a person's hand and so an economic analysis cannot be the answer although it can as in this case be a useful approach to formulating the question.[3]

Hindsight

10–85 Cases are investigated and heard after the want of care—often quite some time after. In that time steps may well be taken to prevent similar accidents, either locally by fencing some danger or nationally or internationally by altering some design or regulation. However, while the investigation of breach involves looking back into the past, this must be done without taking into account the knowledge and effect of the accident itself. This was identified as a danger in Scotland as long ago as 1861 when Lord Justice Clerk Inglis said:

> "It is not sufficient to subject a party to liability for the consequences of an accident when people after the accident see how it might have been prevented, and say that he was bound to have seen that before the accident. There are many precautions adopted on the teaching of accidents such as this, and yet the omission of such precautions may not amount to that want of due precaution or that neglect for which an employer is responsible."[4]

More famous today is Lord Denning's expression of the same idea: "We must not look at the 1947 accident with 1954 spectacles."[5]

A Lower Standard

10–86 It might be asked whether children, the infirm or the uneducated need live up to a standard which is actually unattainable for them. The defender objectivity test would suggest that a child should be judged by the standard of the reasonable man in the position of a child, or if the defender is blind then the reasonable man unable to see. With certain activities, especially if there is compulsory insurance, the temptation is to find the child or the blind man who, driving a lorry, runs down the pursuer. With the blind man it is possible to find liability based on the antecedent negligence in driving

---

[2] An example of a case where it is submitted the cost/benefit approach was taken too far is *McErlean v. J & B Scotland Ltd*, 1997 S.L.T. 1326 in which a woman was injured while trying to clear a production line. The case raises some of the other points considered above which are broadly within the economic/Learned Hand approach and so it is worth examination in some detail. It was upheld on appeal. The following point was made in support of acquitting the defenders of negligence: "Accordingly the proper approach to this case is, I think, simply to ask whether the employers did, in all the circumstances, fail to take reasonable care. In considering that question, the circumstances to be taken into account include the magnitude of the risk, the seriousness of any injury which may result, and the difficulty and practicability of any measures required to eliminate it. In this case, there was a known risk, but it was a risk of minor injury." At 1330.

[3] Compare this case with *Macdonald v. Scottish Stamping and Engineering Co. Ltd*, 1972 S.L.T. (Notes) 73. See also Chap. 10 which also appreciates the economics or at least the cost.

[4] *Finningham v. Peters* (1861) 23 D. 260 at 264.

[5] *Roe v. Minister of Health* [1954] 2 Q.B. 66.

at all. So too with an ill person who becomes more ill whilst driving. With the child or the adult incapax it would be best to exculpate but find the person charged with the care of the person liable.[6] Alternatively some of the cases can be seen as exceptions. In the often cited case of *Nettleship v. Weston*[7] the Court of Appeal held a learner driver to owe the skill and care of the ordinary driver to the passenger who sat in with her but by a majority allowed a deduction of 50 per cent contribution because of his awareness of the risks. The correct approach, it is submitted, is that the standard should be lower—the reasonable man who cannot drive, being asked to drive like a good driver. It is possible on the principle *ars spondet artiam* to heighten the duty when a specially skillful task is considered. Driving is such a task as is vouched by the need to pass a test.

A Higher Standard

The reasonable man cannot, with any hope of success carry out brain **10–87** surgery. As the reasonable man test is an objective test, to apply this test to cases of skilled persons would be to allow them to escape liability in all but the most gross cases where the conduct was such that no care could reasonably be exercised—as in the case of a drunken surgeon. So the law applies a higher standard based on that of the ordinary practitioner practising in the profession. This matter is discussed at length in the context in which it normally occurs—that of professional negligence.[8]

Impractical and Immoral Standards

Sometimes a standard cannot be set for lack of evidence. It may also be the **10–88** case that a standard cannot be set on grounds of policy. The court will not set the standard of the reasonable burglar for the reasonable man does not burgle and the court would not want to hear such evidence. Such cases are normally considered under the *ex turpi* defence.

Multi-layered Standards

The days of the guild are nearly gone. Professions share each others' **10–89** functions. Nurses do what doctors did. Estate agents do what lawyers did. Professions are encouraged to be multi-disciplinary and persons to be multi-skilled. Demarcation in the workplace has gone. The one-stop shop is everywhere. Banks sell insurance. Insurers sell financial services. Against that background an early contract case based on negligence against a company for dentistry work is helpful. The defenders argued that they were only expert in supplying and fitting false teeth not in removing the teeth in relation to which they only had to do their poor untrained non-qualified best as their operatives were not qualified dentists.[9] It was held *spondet peritiam artis*, the practitioner holding himself out to do dentistry had to meet the standard of a dentist.

---

[6] Or the person in charge of the vehicle on a third party intervention case if careless or jointly if he permitted the use on the basis of he does who causeth do.

[7] [1971] 2 Q.B. 691.

[8] Chap. 12.

[9] *Dickson v. Hygenic Institute* 1910 1 S.L.T. 111.

10–90   Done well, the one-stop shop can be very beneficial. There is the potential for confusion of responsibilities or a gap in responsibility. This arose in *G. Percy Trentham Ltd v. Beattie Watkinson and Partners*[10] The pursuers were building contractors and the defenders were the civil engineers under the contract. A wall collapsed during the building work and the pursuers had to reinstate it. They sued the defenders as having failed to exercise the care of a reasonably competent engineer. They had failed to investigate the soil and ground conditions, failed to identify problem soil and failed to direct shoring thus rendered necessary. In a careful analysis Lord Jauncey thought there was potentially the proximity for a duty. He had the benefit of the revision of the law undertaken by Lord Keith in *Peabody*[11] and the fair, just and reasonableness requirement. He considered that there was proximity but that the scope of any duty depended upon reliance and in this case the contractor had the necessary skills to resolve the problem encountered and did not have to rely upon the defenders. On the facts of the case there was no duty. Obviously the practical answer to avoid these difficulties is either contractual provisions or statements defining obligations but they will continue to arise so long as multi-disciplinary operations continue.

10–91   Within a profession the same principle applies. The less experienced member of the profession who holds himself out as a specialist or the trainee who does the qualified person's work is judged by the higher standard, not his own level of competence.[12]

(C) CAUSATION

10–92   It is first necessary to show that in a practical way the mistake that was made actually brought about the result complained. This is sometimes called causation in fact (as opposed to causation in law) but the Scots courts do not take any such rigid analysis. Causation is a concept.[13] To say that something is a cause of some event is apparently descriptive of phenomena but always incorporates an approach to responsibility. Nor even can much refuge be taken in science. History shows us that the perfect cutting edge of scientific knowledge is always wrong and never true— Newton improves upon Galileo, Einstein upon Newton and ever onward. For the courts there are no certainties, nor need there be for the law operates on the basis of probabilities. And the law allocates responsibilities. This is all that the word "cause" can really signify in delict—that the phenomenon A was probably responsible for phenomenon B. Scientists and philosophers have concepts of causation but they are not necessarily those of the lawyer.[14] As a test of responsibility causation is therefore useless as it has to be known in what cases there is responsibility. On the other hand as marking out one part of the enquiry into responsibility it serves a practical

---

[10] 1987 S.L.T. 449.
[11] *Peabody Donation Fund (Governors) v. Sir Lindsay Parkinson & Co. Ltd* [1985] A.C. 210.
[12] *Wilsher v. Essex Area Health Authority* [1988] A.C. 174.
[13] The problems are universal in western legal thinking: S.M. Waddams, "Causation in Canada and Australia" (1993) 1 Tort L. Rev. 75.
[14] H. Reece, "Loss of Chances in the Law" [1996] M.L.R. 188.

purpose. When the idea of probability is factored in to the enquiry it can be understood why some cases are considered under the heading of this word. What is being looked at is the way in which the conduct of the defender brought about the pursuers' loss injury or damage and when it is said that the defender did not cause it, it is being said that he is not responsible because his conduct would probably not normally (naturally) result in the harm. Sometimes the role of causation can be stated in terms of policy:

"Perhaps Glanville Williams was right in saying: "When the lawyer uses the conception of causation, he is not bound to use it in the same way as a philosopher, or a scientist, or an ordinary man. The concept can be moulded by considerations of policy [see [1961] CL.J. 62 at 75]."[15]

Further, causation is a useful way of identifying a dispute which focuses not so much upon what the defender did or did not do (because this is assumed or proved), but upon what others (including the defender) did or did not do. Thus it is submitted that while the use of the term "cause" and the use of causation within the law of delict is tautologous it can nonetheless be seen as useful in focusing one of the important issues of responsibility and helping to answer the question, notwithstanding that the defender did something stupid, should he still be responsible because of other phenomena.[16]

Causation as a concept applies not only in delict but also in other areas of the law of obligation such as contract and unjust enrichment[17] and across the law, criminal law being perhaps another area where analogies can properly be made.[18] It can also function differently in strict liability as opposed to cases of fault and may differ again in intentional harm cases. In many cases causation is not difficult as where the driver runs over the pedestrian on the zebra crossing. More difficult is where scientific or medical issues arise and here the pursuer needs to explain that in fact, although it is not intuitively decernable, the conduct brought about the result. The rhetorical strategy is to ask if "but for" the error the result complained of would have come to pass. In *Barnett v. Chelsea and Kensington Hospital Management Committee*[19] a doctor failed to treat a patient who later died. However, the patient had been well poisoned and there was nothing that the doctor could have done to save him. In *Kay's Tutor v. Ayrshire Health Board*[20] although it was admitted that there had been a careless overdose it was not clear on the basis of the scientific and medical evidence that the overdose rather than disease caused the harm complained of. The claim could not succeed. *Hughes*,[21] discussed above,

---

[15] *per* Lord Edmund-Davies, in *Jobling v. Associated Dairies Ltd* [1981] 2 All E.R. 752 at 759.

[16] See Hart and Honore, *Causation in the Law* and P. Cane (ed.), *Atiyah's Accidents, Compensation and the Law*, Chap. 4; an up to date discussion can be found in J. Stapleton, "The Gist of Negligence" (1988) 104 L.Q.R. 213 and 389.

[17] See W.J. Stewart, *Restitution in Scotland* (W. Green, 1992), para. 5.27 and articles and cases cited therein.

[18] See for example Jones and Christie, *Criminal Law* (2nd ed., W. Green, 1996), Chap. 5. But care must be taken because the objects of the two branches of the law are different the ascription of responsibility can be quite different.

[19] [1969] 1 Q.B. 428.

[20] 1987 S.L.T. 577.

[21] *Hughes v. Lord Advocate*, 1963 S.L.T. 150.

also raises this issue because it was suggested that the harm was caused by an unexplained explosion rather than the explained paraffin lamps. If the responsibility issue is broken into two questions then if there is a factual cause it is a matter for the law to say whether in law it is a legal cause and in this it utilises simple common sense.[22] So even this so called legal cause is a jury question.

Common Sense

10–93 The appeal to common sense is frequently encountered in the courts.[23] It is especially often met in relation to causation. This can be explained by a desire to keep very technical and scientific evidence as a matter of fact for a jury or a judge and not as a final determinant of liability. A very useful study has been published surveying other disciplines which indicates that there may not be much of a core to the notion of common sense and it should be required reading for anyone who makes appeal to that idea.[24] However, that does not mean that common sense is of no value in this area of the law. First, it should be noted how the common sense test is introduced:

> "The choice of the real or efficient cause from out of the whole complex of the facts must be made by applying common sense standards. Causation is to be understood as the man in the street, and not as either the scientist or the metaphysician would understand it."[25]

The question of the appropriateness of conduct is judged by the standard of the reasonable man, the question of duty mediated by reference to the reasonable man and so the question of ascription of responsibility to phenomena can equally be a matter for decision by a jury (and correctable if patently ludicrous). What should also be appreciated about scientific evidence is that science can be treated as what is known and by definition everything else is not. Thus, while scientific evidence may be able to establish causation, science is more likely to be silent upon it. The courts in the United Kingdom do not subscribe to the idea of trial by experts and in simple cases expert evidence as to causation and responsibility will be the exception.[26] The Second Division recently considered the common sense of causation in *Clements v. Shell U.K. Ltd.*[27] The tenant of a salmon netting station alleged that Shell whilst laying a pipeline had allowed the channel to be blocked and silted up. The court, however, considered that the silt which blocked the river was produced by a natural mixing of salt water and fresh water. So while the concurrence of the silting and the laying of the pipe

---

[22] Which is neither all that sensible nor all that common.

[23] The common sense of judges will permit the dissection of an event into stages so that it was held that even although a workplace was unsafe the pursuer could not succeed where he lost his footing just after climbing over the unsafe part of his workplace: *McLean v. Caledonian Macbrayne*, 1999 G.W.D. 5–269: see now 1999 G.W.D. 35–1713, IH.

[24] Mullany, "Common Sense Causation — An Australian view" (1992) 12 O.J.L.S. 431.

[25] *Yorkshire Dale S.S. Co. v. M.O.W.T.* [1942] A.C. 691 at 706.

[26] *Liddell v. Middleton* (1996) 5 P.I.Q.R. 36.

[27] 1991 G.W.D. 35–2153.

happened about the same time they were coincidental and not linked in any way. Common suspicion that they might be was displaced by expert testimony which was accepted of a natural cause. The continuing force of the common sense approach and its practical effect can best be seen in the recent decision of Lord Osborne in *P.'s Curator Bonis v. CICB*.[28] A child was born as a result, it was alleged, of incestuous rape. One point that had been made below was that the injuries were caused by the incestuous genetic element rather than the act of violence. Lord Osborne said:

"I do not think it is disputed that the court ought to adopt the common sense approach to causation referred to in a number of decisions . . . The message which emerges from these cases is that causation is not to be examined in any metaphysical or scientific sense, but in the wider and more liberal sense in which the matter would be understood by the man in the street applying commonsense standards . . . the respondents draw a distinction between the birth of the child, which they accept was directly attributable to an act of rape, and the "injuries". It appears to me that a jury or the ordinary man would not draw such a distinction. I consider that they would accept that the birth of the child and its disabilities were both directly attributable to the same criminal act, namely the acknowledged act of rape."[29]

Anyone can hold a perfectly unreasonable (illegitimate) view of causation. There are people (millions) who read their horoscope to see what will happen to them in the course of the next few days, based only on the time of their birth and the location of the planets, but the courts are entitled to reject that view.

But For

It has to be established that a given breach is at least a cause in the sense **10–94** that but for the act or omission that causes the breach the accident would have taken place. One Scottish appeal has considered the issue virtually in isolation. In *Porter v. Strathclyde Regional Council*[30] a nursery assistant slipped on some spilled food. Accepting that there had been a breach of duty the question before the court was whether there had been the necessary causation. The answer was that the following test was wrong:

"the pursuer does not have to establish that the precautions desiderated would necessarily have avoided the accident. It is sufficient if she establishes, on a balance of probabilities, that the taking of the desiderated precautions would have materially diminished the risk of the accidents happening."[31]

This was held to be the wrong approach, instead the correct approach enunciated for the court by Lord Justice-Clerk Ross was:

---

[28] 1997 S.L.T. 1180. The facts are discussed in context in Chap. 2.
[29] *ibid*. at 1200.
[30] 1991 S.L.T. 446.
[31] *ibid*. at 448.

"The normal and proper test of causation to apply in a case of this kind is whether the pursuer has established that the system desiderated by the Lord Ordinary would probably have prevented this accident."[32]

This is to say that in most ordinary cases "all or nothing" "but for" probable causation is required. However, as this is a mere expression of common sense the issue has to be approached in a common sense fashion as can be seen in the contrasting decision of an Extra Division in *Muir v. Cumbernauld and Kilsyth District Council*.[33] In this case a binman was injured picking up a sack either by a glancing blow from a sharp object in the sack or from something piercing the sack and his supplied pvc gloves. The evidence showed that latex gloves would have prevented a glancing but not a piercing injury. The sheriff's finding was that the cause of the injury was the failure to provide the appropriate gloves. It was said that *Porter* "in no way derogates from the accepted test which is that a pursuer must prove on balance of probabilities that the breach of duty caused or materially contributed to his injury."[34] The complaint in this case by the reclaimers was an impressive one. They said that as the sheriff had not found which kind of blow it was, then as one type of blow would have been prevented by the precautions actually taken the failure to provide another type could not be a cause. However, the court treated one non-needle like wound like another—a glance and a cut were all much the same. Latex gloves would have prevented cutting injuries and the failure to provide them caused the injury. Nothing could better summarise the court's view of the facts necessary for causation than the finding in fact they inserted: "The wearing of [latex gloves] would have materially lessened the risk of the pursuer sustaining an injury of the type he in fact sustained and would probably have prevented said accident."[35]

It is submitted this is correct. The court simply took the view that the distinction taken in argument, and no doubt in evidence, between a piercing injury and a glancing injury was a false, or at least unimportant, distinction. It was a case of the expected sort of wounding when tough gloves are not worn. It is also best seen as an example of all or nothing causation as there was a chance and perhaps a significant chance that the injury was due to a factual situation which would not have attracted liability as it would not have penetrated the weaker pvc gloves.

10–95   The "but for" test is not so useful in cases of coincident sufficient causes, that is where two things could have caused the incident as a matter of fact but both actually did. Accordingly theorists have developed other ideas, one involving INUS conditions (Insufficient Necessary part of an Unnecessary but Sufficient condition).[36] This leads to a form of alternative theory, the NESS test (Necessary Element of Sufficient Set).[37] It is put thus: "a

---

[32] *ibid.*

[33] 1993 S.L.T. 287.

[34] *ibid.* at 289.

[35] *ibid.* at 290.

[36] Developed by J.L. Makie, *The Cement of the Universe: A Study of Causation* (1974), pp. 59–63, cited in Honoré, "Necessary and Sufficient Conditions" in *Philosophical Foundations of Tort Law* (Owen ed., Oxford, 1996), pp. 364–366

[37] R. Wright, "Causation in Tort Law" (1985) 73 Cal. L. Rev. 1735 cited in Hart and Honoré, *ibid.*

particular condition was a cause of (contributed to) a specific result if and only if it was a necessary element of a set of antecedent actual conditions that was sufficient for the occurrence of the result".[38] Hart and Honoré would largely agree with this save that their view requires one of the antecedent conditions to persist until the result occurs.[39] Both the "but for" test and the NESS test are difficult because they require the assumption of a counter-factual position—that what did happen did not happen.[40]

There is another difficulty with cases of successive sufficient causes. The **10–96** English courts have attempted solutions. In *Baker v. Willoughby*[41] the defendant injured the plaintiff's left leg. Before trial he was shot by robbers and the leg was amputated. The defendant argued this meant that there was no loss to compensate. By treating the wrong as causing the loss of the ability to lead a full life instead of the stiffening of a leg, the House held the original defendant liable for the stiffening of the leg. In *Jobling v. Associated Dairies*[42] the House returned to the issue in a case where a worker had been injured but before the trial had succumbed to an illness which made him incapable of work. In this case it was held that the employers were liable for loss of earnings up to the disability through disease. Lord Wilberforce in this case said: "no general, logical or universally fair rules can be stated which will cover, in a manner consistent with justice, cases of supervening events, whether due to tortious, partially tortious, non-culpable or wholly accidental events."[43] That statement reflects the difficulties in reconciling these two cases. The most tempting is that the robbery was criminal whereas the disease was natural. When awarding damages for future loss the court discounts for the vicissitudes of life. Where in a case like *Jobling* they have actually materialised, then it seems foolish not to reflect that. *Jobling* does seem to be correct on this basis. Honoré argues that where the second incident is sufficient to cause all the loss there is a causal solution— that the first actor causes a kind of loss of a chance—the loss of a tort remedy.

A relevant Scots case is *Glendinning v. PJ Waddell*[44] in which a worker **10–97** had one accident and then another two years later. He sued for his condition after the second but alleged fault only in respect of the first. The defenders claimed that the pursuer had not to specify to what extent his incapacity was attributable to the earlier accident and what his condition would have been if the second accident had not taken place. It was held that it was necessary to canvass all the evidence and a proof before answer was allowed. The decision of the First Division in *MacKenzie v. Middleton Ross & Arnott*[45] is another important case. Its potency is affected by the fact that the point at issue is the valuation of the lost chance of litigation, but it is clear that the approach of Scots law to causation was fully canvassed and considered. The position, altered to assume it was the primary case not

---

[38] *ibid.*
[39] Hart and Honoré, *op. cit.* at 366.
[40] *ibid.* at 373.
[41] [1970] A.C. 467.
[42] [1981] 2 All E.R. 752.
[43] *ibid.* at 755.
[44] 1988 S.L.T. 401.
[45] 1983 S.L.T. 286.

litigated, is that the pursuer's husband is run down by the first defender and then, when lying down on the road was run down by another car driven by a learner driver.[46] The Lord Ordinary found that the first driver was not negligent. He found that the deceased's serious head injuries sustained in that accident were not fatal. On appeal it was conceded that the Lord Ordinary had to be wrong because he made an assumption rather than finding a fact.

10–98 Finally, Honoré points out that "but for" is not much help in advice cases because where people are "acting for a reason their conduct cannot be determined. People make decisions for many reasons, however, 'but for' reasons are often not reasons *for* making a decision or acting on it, but are reasons against not making it".[47] At this level something very like common sense seems to be required: sufficiency in the sense of what a person would regard as an adequate ground upon which to act and decide. This theoretical point is rather supported by the cases now that representations engendering reliance are actionable. An example is *Spring v. Guardian Assurance Plc*[48] in which the victim of a bad reference did *not* have to prove that but for the negligent reference he would have got the job.[49] Here the NESS test helps answer the causation point swiftly and easily.

The first cause operates until overwhelmed (*novus actus interveniens*)

10–99 Causation is usually discussed where there are competing causes. The law is more attracted to diachronicity than synchronicity. From multiple causes, the later event is more likely to be thought the cause than the first event. The law is not always happy with that arrangement especially if it is remembered that the delict may be an intentional one where someone for example shoots the pursuer and the attending doctor is careless in his treatment. The judicial answer to such a case can be seen in the following passage:

> "There are certain propositions that I think are well established and beyond question in connection with this class of case. One is that human action does not *per se* sever the connected sequence of acts ... The question is not whether there was new negligence but whether there was a new cause ... It must always be shown that there is something which I will call ultroneous, something unwarrantable, a new cause coming in disturbing the sequence of events, something that can be described as either unreasonable or extraneous or extrinsic. I doubt very much whether the law can be stated more precisely than that."[50]

Nonetheless an attempt can be made to formulate matters more precisely. One attempt was the last opportunity rule associated with *Davies v. Mann*[51]

---

[46] To prove that the truth is at least as complicated as the law lecturers' examination questions, it was said that the victim had been very drunk and contributory negligence was raised.

[47] *MacKenzie v. Middleton Ross & Arnott*, at 383.

[48] [1994] 3 W.L.R. 354.

[49] *ibid.*, per Lord Lowry, 375–376.

[50] *The Oropesa* [1943] P. 32.

[51] (1842) 10 M. & W. 546.

which ascribed causality to the actor who had the last opportunity to avoid an accident is only of use as a guide, if at all, to cases where one of the participants is stationary. In later cases it has been held that the rule is of no value.[52]

A most interesting Scots case is *Gray v. North British Railway.*[53] A dog **10–100** was entrusted to the railway company. It was not thought at all dangerous. It escaped from the custody of the company at Waverley Station. On the facts it was accepted that there was no fault on the part of the staff at Waverley. They had tied it up in the luggage room instead of putting it in the kennels but it was not thought at all dangerous. It escaped and ran over a mile to the Botanic gardens where the Professor, who was the curator, told three gardeners to get rid of it. They secured it and two of them went to get the police and one remained with the dog, got bitten and became the pursuer. The railway company were not at fault. According to the Lord President the fault may have been at the gardens.[54] Lord Adam considered the conduct of the gardeners to be the proximate cause.[55] Lord McLaren thought the injury too remote and not a direct and immediate consequence.[56] In *McDonald v. Smellie*[57] the pursuer's child was bitten by the defender's dog and died of meningitis. On appeal it was argued that the death could not have been caused by the initial bite of the defender's dog. The only medical evidence was to the effect that if the child had not suffered from the bite he would not have died.[58] Lord Young said that it was clear death was attributable at least in part to the bite.[59] In *Sabri-Tabrizi v. Lothian Health Board*[60] the pursuer claimed damages for a failed sterilisation but admitted that she consented to having sex after being aware that the operation had not been a success. The subsequent *copula* was held not to be a *novus actus interveniens.*

Where the duty includes prevention or avoidance of another causal factor

If the duty to take care includes the obligation to take steps that other **10–101** persons' actions will not bring about the risk, then the fact that others have factually caused the loss does not exculpate. This is clear from the third party intervention cases.[61] So where there was a duty not to leave scaffolding in such a position that it would be an allurement to thieves, the fact that the loss was caused by a burglar who did not use the scaffolding, did not prevent the conduct of those leaving the scaffolding being the legal cause.[62] Many common law workmen's cases are an example of the same

---

[52] *The Boy Andrew v. The St Rognvald*, 1947 S.C. (H.L.) 70; *Rouse v. Squires* [1973] Q.B. 889.
[53] (1890) 18 R. 76.
[54] *ibid.* at 78.
[55] *ibid.* at 79.
[56] *ibid.* at 79.
[57] (1908) 5 F. 953.
[58] *ibid.* at 956.
[59] *ibid.* at 958. There is talk in the case of a predisposition to meningitis, which was discounted, but the foundation for which is not apparent in the report. In any event perhaps this is a case where the bite was a necessary element of sufficient set.
[60] 1998 Rep. L.R. 37.
[61] See paras 10–56 *et seq.*
[62] *Squires v. Perth & Kinross District Council*, 1986 S.L.T. 30.

principle. Although the pursuer may have been injured because of his fellow employee's act, the legal cause is the employer's conduct because the duty encompasses prevention of this risk.

10–102   Another practical manifestation of the different results which can be obtained by analyzing a problem through the duty and causation inquiries is apparent in the *Banque Bruxelles Lambert* litigations.[63] In the House of Lords the plaintiffs claim to "big" damages resulting from potential negligence due to a falling market were resolved on the basis of the "duty" inquiry; in the Court of Appeal causation was an important focus. Professor Stapleton suggests that neither approach is the best and that the necessary line-drawing is best dealt with by a remoteness of damage inquiry.[64] In all difficult cases all the "windows" should be looked through.

10–103   A breach of duty which actually and materially increases the risk of harm can be held to be the cause of that harm. This is the rule taken from *McGhee v. N.C.B.*[65] The word "actual" is designed to show that the case has since been interpreted as requiring a "factual" foundation. There must be shown a probability that the breach makes the actual harm complained of happen and then it must be material. This is clearly seen in Lord Mackay's speech in *Kay's Tutor v. Ayrshire and Arran Health Board*[66] dealing with the applicability of *McGhee*. The following passage shows how Lord Mackay (correctly) showed the *McGhee* rule to be inapplicable:

> "In my opinion, it is not right to ask whether it materially increased the risk of neurological damage when the evidence available distinguishes between different kinds of neurological damage. As I have said, the evidence upon which this part of counsel's submission depends is the record of the cases of overdose to which I have referred. In none of those who survived an overdose, and the number of cases is very small was the particular type of neurological damage which results in deafness found in these cases that an overdose of penicillin materially increases the risk of a different type of neurological damage, namely that which causes deafness, when no such deafness has been shown to have resulted from such overdose. Apart from Mr. Williams' evidence that, in his opinion, deafness was caused in Andrew by direct effect of penicillin on the auditory nerve, which opinion the Lord Ordinary felt unable to accept as establishing the appellant's case in the light of the other evidence, there was no evidence, accepted by the Lord Ordinary that penicillin in overdose or otherwise had caused or contributed to deafness. It is not necessary to consider in this case whether, if the appellant had a sufficient factual basis for the argument which he advanced, based upon the decision of this House in *McGhee's* case, his submission was correct since, in my opinion, the essential factual foundation for the submission is missing."

---

[63] Named after *Banque Bruxelles Lambert Sa v. Eagle Star Insurance* which was in fact not taken to the House of Lords but the decision in that case was disapproved in *South Australia Asset Management Corp. v. York Montague Ltd* [1996] 3 All E.R. 365. See Chap. 18.

[64] J. Stapleton, "The Normal Expectancies Measure in Tort Damages" (1997) 113 L.Q.R. 257.

[65] 1973 S.C. (H.L.) 37.

[66] 1987 S.L.T. 577.

A similar result was reached in another case also involving medical evidence. A workman had been exposed to asbestos and suffered lung cancer—he had not however suffered from asbestosis. While it appears to have been accepted that lung cancer can follow from asbestosis which follows from asbestos exposure, there was no medical evidence showing that exposure to asbestos which does not result in asbestosis ever caused lung cancer. *McGhee* was founded on. It was held that the necessary factual link was not there and the case was not proved.[67] In a case where the pursuers averred that death was 'inter alia' due to lead poisoning a proof before answer was allowed.[68] Lord Cameron said:

"I ... agree with the general proposition that in order to establish liability it is necessary to show that the negligence of which complaint is made must in a substantial sense cause or contribute to the injury sustained. As the issue of contribution must in many, if not in most cases be one of degree it is one which can only be accurately and satisfactorily determined once the facts have been ascertained, and is not readily to be decided by a scrutiny or analysis of the particular language in which a pleader may have chosen to frame his record ... Now had the pleader used the adjective 'material' or 'substantial' in describing the extent or quality of the lead poisoning . . .. the defenders would . . . have had little to say ... the words used 'inter alia' are in a sense indicative of some measure of materiality."[69]

It is not to be presumed that among possible causes that which results from a breach of duty is the operative cause.

In *Wilsher v. Essex Area Health Authority*[70] the House of Lords made it **10–104** clear that the argument that conduct which has created a risk which materialises must be a cause is to be rejected. This states the obvious.

The all or nothing rule

A breach of duty either is or is not a cause. If, on balance of probabilities, a **10–105** phenomenon is held to cause the harm then the all or nothing rule will favour the pursuer even although there may well be other causes—the defender bears the whole responsibility:

"I think that the position can be shortly stated in this way. It may be that, of the noxious dust in the general atmosphere of the shop, more came from the pneumatic hammers than from the swing grinders, but I think it is sufficiently proved that the dust from the grinders made a substantial contribution. The respondent, however, did not only inhale general atmosphere of the shop: when he was working his hammer, his face was directly over it and it must often have happened that dust from

---

[67] *Vize v. Scott Lithgow Ltd (No. 2)*, 1991 G.W.D. 9–549. See also *Porter v. Strathclyde Regional Council*, 1991 S.L.T. 446; *Muir v. Cumbernauld and Kilsyth District Council*, 1993 S.L.T. 287.

[68] *Bruce v. Stephen & Sons Ltd*, 1957 S.L.T. 78.

[69] *ibid.* at 80.

[70] [1988] 2 W.L.R. 557.

his hammer substantially increased the concentration of noxious dust in the air which he inhaled. It is therefore probable that much the greater proportion of the noxious dust which he inhaled over the whole period came from the hammers. But on the other hand some certainly came from the swing grinders, and I cannot avoid the conclusion that the proportion which came from the swing grinders was not negligible. He was inhaling the general atmosphere all the time, and there is no evidence to show that his hammer gave off noxious dust so frequently, or that the concentration of noxious dust above it when it was producing dust was so much greater than the concentration in the general atmosphere, that special concentration of dust could be said to be substantially the sole cause of his disease . . . In my opinion, it is proved not only that the swing grinders may well have contributed but that they did in fact contribute a quota of silica dust which was not negligible to the pursuer's lungs and therefore did help to produce the disease."[71]

The issue was freshly considered in *Hotson v. East Berkshire Health Authority*[72] but the idea of allocating damages on the basis of the proportion of causation was rejected. After trial and in the Court of Appeal the plaintiff had been entitled to 25 per cent of full damages where it was shown that a condition arose as a result of a failed diagnosis but where there was a 75 per cent chance of this arising anyway. The House of Lords held that this finding was effectively that the cause of the condition was more likely to be natural than as a result of the failure of diagnosis and so the case failed completely. This issue is now discussed under the rubric "loss of a chance". It has causal aspects. However, while it could be partially discussed here and partially under the heading of damages, in this book the topic of the loss of a chance is discussed in the context in which it has most often arisen, that of professional liability.[73] The present rule is at least clear and is as stated.

Contributing causes

10–106 Where there are two operative causes, one of which does not eclipse the other, then the solution is to apportion. In a situation where there is a pursuer and two defenders, the liability of the defenders can be apportioned between them although the pursuer is entitled to recover from each on the all or nothing rule and because they are joint wrongdoers. If the pursuer has caused the accident, other than having been solely at fault then the matter is one of contributory negligence.

Balance of probabilities

10–107 There is no need to show certainty. It is still all or nothing causation which is required and so once there are 51 chances to 49 that the conduct caused the loss, causation is established as it is if there are 51 chances that it materially contributed to the loss.[74]

---

[71] *per* Lord Reid in *Wardlaw v. Bonnington Castings,* 1956 S.C. (H.L.) 26.
[72] [1987] A.C. 750.
[73] See Chap. 12.
[74] See generally *Muir v. Cumbernauld and Kilsyth District Council,* 1993 S.L.T. 287.

No cause

The pursuer must always establish the cause of the incident.[75] In **10–108** *McWilliams v. Sir William Arrol & Co.*,[76] a Factories Act case the workman fell from a steel tower to his death. It had been held in the courts below that the employers were under a duty to provide safety belts with ropes attached and it was not denied that if the worker had worn one he would not have died. The case could hardly be a clearer one where causation alone is the issue. The House held that as there was evidence that this particular worker would not have worn a belt the failure to provide one was not the cause of the fatal injuries. That must be correct. If a more simple duty to provide food is imagined, there should not be fault if the pursuer has declared he is to fast to death. The pursuer in such cases may be held in to be the author of his own misfortune.[77] However, it is a matter for assessing the probabilities in each case and it will be seldom that a defender will escape liability where he fails to prevent the risk envisaged by the duty he has breached.

(D) REMOTENESS OF DAMAGE

Once there is a loss caused by a breach of duty, justice still demands mercy **10–109** for the wrongdoer just as it does in other areas of the law. Just as damages in contract are restricted by the well-known principle now symbolised even in Scotland, where it was developed, by *Hadley v. Baxendale*[78] so too are the damages payable by the wrongdoer. In principle the same rules apply regardless of whether the wrong was intentional or accidental. In Scotland the rule is not clear but the following passage satisfies most of the judges most of the time:

> "The grand rule on the subject of damages is, that none can be claimed except such as arise naturally and directly out of the wrong done; and such therefore, as may reasonably be supposed to have been in view of the wrongdoer."[79]

Of course liability and mercy are easily and perhaps legitimately confused. In contract the argument has been raging for most of the last century that the remoteness rule is part of the liability issue.[80] So from time to time it is perfectly natural that that idea is explored in delict. However, it ought to be done consciously. The liability issue is not so relatively clear that the damages issue ought to be left until the end of the analysis even in actual

---

[75] See para. 10–92.

[76] [1962] 1 W.L.R. 295.

[77] In *Ferguson v. Stringfellow*, 1999 G.W.D. 9–436 it was held that the pursuer must have released a safety device on a fairground attraction himself and so was the cause of his own misfortune.

[78] (1854) 9 Ex. 341.

[79] *Allan v. Barclay* (1864) 2 M. 873. See Chap. 10.

[80] G. Gilmore, *Death of Contract* (Ohio State University Press, 1974); Fuller & Perdue (1936) 46 Yale LJ 52, at p. 373.

cases. But the Scottish system of pleading means that the defender can seek a ruling on any failure in the pursuer's case.

10–110   Remoteness of injury is part of the duty inquiry—should the defender have foreseen this kind of risk? Remoteness of damage is the inquiry which follows liability where mercy is to be shown to some wrongdoers as in many other areas of the law. There are two great English cases which are not discussed here because the Scottish courts refuse so to do.[81] Cases where there is not already actionable damage are more likely to be causation cases and the exercise is to see whether the supposed causal chain has broken before the remote damage is reached.

The Grand Rule

10–111   In *Allan v. Barclay*[82] an engine belonging to the defender had broken down on the public road and was left in an oblique position across the road. It could have been moved easily to a safe position. At night one of the pursuer's workmen came upon it and his horse was frightened by the light attached to it. The pursuer's claim was in respect of the services he lost as a result of the workman being injured: "The services of the said William Hill were of the utmost importance to the pursuer, as being acquainted with the pursuer's business, and with his customers, he was instrumental, to a very great extent, both in maintaining and in extending it." Lord Kinloch refused the claim. Before uttering the grand rule he said:

"Nor is it easy to say where the claim of reparation will stop. The person injured may be a worker in a manufactory, where the loss of his services causes a cessation of the labours of half a dozen others; the want of the services of these may impede those of hundreds; the work may be entirely stopped; an order, involving thousands of pounds, may be prevented from being executed. Many other illustrations may be figured."[83]

Then comes the rule:

"The grand rule on the subject of damages is, that none can be claimed except such as naturally and directly arise out of the wrong done; and such, therefore, as may reasonably be supposed to have been in the view of the wrongdoer. Tried by this test, the present claim appears to fail. The personal injuries of the individual himself will be properly held to have been in the contemplation of the wrongdoer. But he cannot be held bound to have surmised the secondary injuries done to all holding relations with the individual, whether that of a master, or any other."[84]

---

[81] *Re Polemis and Furness, Withy and Co. Ltd* (known as "Polemis") [1921] 3 K.B 560; *Overseas Tankship (UK) Ltd v. Morts Dock* (known as "the Wagon Mound No. 1") [1961] A.C. 388. The reason for the difficulty in reconciling or understanding these two cases can be found in M. Davies, "The Road from Morocco: *Polemis, Donoghue*, No Fault" (1982) 45 M.L.R. 534. See also R. Kidner, "Remoteness of Damage: the Duty Interest Theory and the Re-interpretation of the Wagon Mound" [1989] L.S. 1.

[82] (1864) 2 M. 873.

[83] *ibid*. at 874.

[84] *ibid*.

The rule is *obiter* because the case failed because of the lack of the sufficient averments about the existence of the contract. However, it has been cited with approval time and time again.

Thin Skull Cases

These are cases where the kind of harm is of a kind which is encompassed **10–112** by the duty but very much more extreme. This is the logical position at which the idea of remoteness should apply to assist the defender. However, this species of claim involves personal injury to a predisposed pursuer and the idea that a wrongdoer should take their victim as they find them is a strong one. The leading Scottish case is *McKillen v. Barclay Curle & Co. Ltd.*[85] The pursuer was injured at work and among other things fractured a rib. The pursuer had dormant tuberculosis. When he was examined after his accident it was discovered that he had active tuberculosis. The necessary causal link was not established in fact. However on the issue of remoteness Lord Clyde said:

"It has never been the law of Scotland that a man guilty of negligence towards another is only liable for the damage in respect of physical injuries which a reasonable man would foresee as likely to follow from it. On the contrary it has always been the law of Scotland as I understand it that once a man is negligent and injures another by his negligence he is liable for all the damage to the injured man which naturally and directly arises out of the negligence. He must take his victim as he finds him, and if his victim has a weak heart and dies as a result of the injury the negligent man is liable in damages for his death, even although a normal man might only in the same circumstances have sustained a relatively trivial injury. The principle of Scots law was laid down as long ago as 1864 by Lord Kinloch in *Allan v. Barclay* (1863) 2 M. 873, at 874, and his statement of the law has never since been controverted. The doctrine of reasonable foreseeability with all its subtle ramifications may be applied in determining questions of liability (see *Bourhill v. Young*, 1942 S.C. (H.L.) 78, 1943, S.L.T. 105; *Muir v. Glasgow Corporation*, 1943 S.C. (H.L.) 3, 1944 S.L.T. 60). It has no relevance once liability is established and the measure of damage is being determined."[86]

That is to say that reasonable foreseeability is not the test. The test is direct and natural consequences and that the fact that some people are predisposed to more serious injury is a direct and natural consequence. It is direct as it follows immediately and it is natural in that it is a perfectly natural state. For Lord Guthrie too the matter was settled by the grand rule. There is in his opinion however the idea that the foreseeability of the reasonable man is an issue:

"This particular pursuer has a weak chest, and his weak chest was injured by the defender's negligence. There is no ground for holding that

---

[85] 1967 S.L.T. 41.
[86] *ibid.* at 42.

a reasonable man would have assumed that the pursuer had a sound pair of lungs, and no justification for limiting an award in his favour to the amount which would have been due to another person with a stronger constitution. I think that it is well settled in our law, that, if negligence is established, the wrongdoer must take his victim as he finds him."[87]

The thin skull rule is approved but the rationale is less than entirely clear. For Lord Migdale there was no need to examine the two leading English cases. There were sufficient Scottish authorities:

"I will content myself with saying that there is a formidable body of opinion to support the view that the rule laid down in *Re Polemis* . . . was not and is not the law of Scotland. I would refer to what was said by Lord Russell of Kilowen and by Lord MacMillan in *Bourhill v. Young* at 85 and 89 and by Lord Justice Clerk Cooper in *Steel v Glasgow Iron and Steel Co.*, 1944 S.C. 237 at 248 (1944 S.L.T. 70) where he says that 'the rule of the reasonable and probable consequence is the key which opens several locks . . . Maybe whether the damages claimed are too remote'. On the other hand I know of no case of personal injury where damages have been refused where they flowed directly from the injury but could not be reasonably foreseen. It may be that the doctrine of reasonable foreseeability gives way in the class of personal injuries to the other rule that a wrongdoer must take his victim as he find him . . . But I prefer the view that the doctrine of reasonable foreseeability does extend to the measure of damages and can be invoked by a defender if the damages are too remote but not in a case of personal injuries. In such a case the wrongdoer is liable in reparation for the loss, injury and damage, which flow naturally and directly from his wrongful act, because he ought to have had in contemplation that his victim might be a sickly person whose health was such that a fall would start off complications which would not be likely to afflict a person in normal health. That is what Lord Kinloch said in the case of *Allan v. Barclay* (supra) at 874 [his Lordship quoted the grand rule]. This statement of the law has stood unchallenged for over a hundred years and is still sound. The wrongdoer must pay for the injuries suffered by his victim provided they arise naturally and directly from the wrongful act, because he ought to have contemplated that he might be an unusually frail person or one afflicted with a latent trouble liable to be reactivated."[88]

So that is another version of the position one based on reasonable contemplation. So far as trying to express Scots law in terms of the debates in English law perhaps Lord Cameron usefully states a good practical position:

"I do not think it is necessary or even helpful to support a conclusion on this matter by reference to English authorities. It may be that in this matter the law of England has reached the same conclusion as the law of

---

[87] *ibid.* at 43–44.
[88] *ibid.* at 45.

Scotland, but I do not find it helpful in determining what is the law of Scotland to endeavour first to discover what is the law of England, when Scottish authority is plain and of long and undoubted standing."[89]

The Grand Rule Today

We are left then with the grand rule. It is not too bad. The courts, even **10–113** after years of debate in England, seem satisfied with this test. In *Runciman v. Borders Regional Council*[90] the grand rule was applied to allow a proof before answer in a case of financial loss. The pursuer claimed among other things interest charges in respect of having to borrow to buy property it being alleged that a sale fell through due to the defenders' negligence. The need to borrow and incur interest could be a matter arising directly and naturally out of a failed sale. In *Lafferty v. Alex Snowie*[91] the grand rule did not find favour with the parties. It was agreed that the test of remoteness in tort set out in *Koufos v. Czarnikow*[92] should apply. The case involved damages for failure to obtain a liquor licence. On this test the claims for increased overdraft interest and a lower sale price for the business were recoverable but a lowering in the pursuer's credit rating and a loss on having to sell his domestic property were on the averments made not supported. In *Margrie Holdings Ltd v. City of Edinburgh District Council*[93] the pursuers sought to recover the cost of borrowing incurred by them whilst the defenders failed to pay out instalments of a grant. An earlier action to enforce payment of the grant had been successfully pursued and settled extra-judicially. The defenders argued that they were entitled to assume that the pursuers would be able to fund the short-fall themselves and that their impecuniosity should not be brought home to them. It was held there were insufficient averments of foreseeability. That might be just another way of saying that there was no liability but it had been argued the loss was a direct consequence which is the language of remoteness. English cases were considered and the reference to remoteness may have been unconscious. It is submitted that the role of foreseeability in negligence liability having settled in such away that the defender already is protected from remote liabilities, fairness to the pursuer suggests that the direct consequences rule is the better.

---

[89] *ibid.* at 46.
[90] 1987 S.C. 241.
[91] 1987 G.W.D. 19–743.
[92] [1969] 1 A.C. 350 at 385.
[93] 1994 S.L.T. 871.

CHAPTER 11

STATUTORY LIABILITY, EUROREP AND HUMAN RIGHTS

STATUTORY LIABILITY

There is no completely authoritative expression of the basis of liability **11–1** where a person is made to pay damages because they have infringed some statutory rule where the statute does not make provision for such a payment.[1] Two extreme cases can be ignored as presenting little difficulty. A statute may provide that a person will be liable to pay civil damages. Alternatively a statute may expressly state that it is not to be enforced by way of a civil action. This chapter considers cases where the statute is silent. The mere fact that a duty has been created by a statute will not entitle a person injured by the breach of that statutory duty to claim damages from the person upon whom the duty is imposed. The solution in each case must depend upon what the intention of Parliament was in enacting the obligation in question, and what persons consequently have a right to enforce it or to found upon it as a basis for a claim of damages.[2]

Theory

An enforcement theory

One view of the nature of this liability is that it is the statute that imposes **11–2** the obligation, parliament simply assuming that the mechanisms of the courts will deal with enforcement. As the action will usually be for damages for a loss caused, the process will resemble a delictual action. "Eurorep", discussed in this chapter very obviously fits into this theory and perhaps suggests that it is the best theory.

A special duty theory

If liability in delict is explained as being based upon breach of duty, then **11–3** statutory liability is simply yet another breach of duty, the statute indicating what the duty is.

Sui generis liability

It is submitted that this liability is better considered not as *sui generis* but by **11–4** its nature much akin to delict and suitably treated along with it. The courts have no place in "double-guessing" the statutory provision:

---

[1] See generally, R. Buckley, "Liability in Tort for Breach of Statutory Duty" (1984) 100 L.Q.R. 204.

[2] Lord President Clyde in *Pullar v. Window Clean*, 1956 S.L.T. 18 at 21.

"All that it is necessary to show is duty to take care to avoid injuring; and if, the particular care to be taken is prescribed by statute, and the duty to the injured person to take the care is likewise imposed by statute, and the breach is proved, all the essentials of negligence are present. I cannot think that the true position is, as appears to be suggested, that in such cases negligence only exists where the tribunal of fact agrees with the legislature that the precaution is one that ought to be taken. The very object of the legislation is to put that particular precaution beyond controversy."[3]

Certain factors can be seen to be relevant in deciding whether or not an obligation to pay damages arises from a statutory provision and it is appropriate to consider each in turn referring to other cases illustrative or declaratory of the principle.

Intention to protect pursuer

11-5 The provision relied on must be shown to have been intended to protect the pursuer as where it was shown in a case where the statutory provisions relied upon appeared in a section entitled "Provisions as to Safety."[4] In *Poliskie v. Lane*[5] the question arose as to whether scaffolding on which pursuer was working under "control" of the defender if the pursuer was an independent contractor alone on site requiring a consideration of the Construction (Working Places) Regulations,[6] reg. 3(1). It was held (*obiter*) that the pursuer was not owed a duty under the regulations. In the leading case of *Pullar v. Window Clean*[7] the idea of a class of persons protected of which the pursuer must be a member was explained by Lord President Clyde:

"If the class of persons for whose protection it is alleged that the duty was imposed is indefinite and difficult to define, this would tend to exclude the construction of the section which would give a right to civil damages for breach . . . and would favour the view that the legislature intended the sanction of prosecution for a penalty as appropriate and sufficient for the obligation imposed by the section. . . But where the predominant purpose of the statute is manifestly the protection of a particular class of workmen by imposing on their employers for instance the duty of taking special measures to secure their safety then the inference is readily drawn that the legislature intended to confer on these workmen a right to sue for damages where the duty is not fulfilled . . . Accordingly, before a right to civil damages can arise out of the statutory duty imposed there must be a manifest or clear intention to

---

[3] *McMullan v. Lochgelly Iron and Coal Co.*, 1933 S.C. (H.L.) 64 at 67, *per* Lord Atkin.

[4] *ibid.* at 66, *per* Lord Atkin. In another case it was argued that a duty was not owed to a person who was carrying out maintenance to actually implement the defender's duty under the Mines and Quarries Act 1954, s. 48(1) and (2) but this was rejected: *Weir v. N.C.B.*, 1982 S.L.T. 529 rejecting *Walsh v. N.C.B.* [1956] 1 Q.B. 511.

[5] 1981 S.L.T. 282.

[6] S.I. 1966 No. 94.

[7] 1956 S.L.T. 18.

confer such a right and a definite class of persons upon whom the right is so conferred."[8]

In *Pullar* the pursuer could not establish a sufficiently clear class of persons. The applicable Dean of Guild legislation although it provided for measures which would provide safety for some window cleaners in some buildings, it was not "designed to constitute a charter for window-cleaners."[9]

Intention to bind defender

In a case under the Construction (Lifting Operations) Regulations 1961,[10] **11–6** reg. 3(1), the question was whether the defender as the person owning a crane on hire was under the duty owed to the pursuer. It was held that the owner was liable. This required it to be held that it was "using" the crane to let it out on hire.[11] In *Watt v. Fairfield Shipbuilding*[12] the point argued was whether the pursuer was protected by the Asbestos Industry Regulations 1931. He worked as an electrician on ships which were being built. He had to work alongside other tradesmen who stirred up much asbestos and he had to work on it himself. The point taken by the second defenders was that the regulations applied to the asbestos industry not to subsequent users—general protection was not effected until the Asbestos Regulations 1969. It was held that the regulations applied to an industry rather than types of workplaces.

Intention for Civil enforcement

This is a matter for interpretation. An early Scots case is *Morris v. Boase* **11–7** *Spinning Co. Ltd*[13] concerning an action by the father of a deceased girl aged 13 who was killed when working in a spinning work. She had deliberately removed a guard from a piece of dangerous machinery and climbed into it, whereupon she was caught by her hair. The jury found for the pursuer. However, the Inner House allowed a new trial but there was no evidence to support the verdict. There was a breach of the Factories and Workshops Act 1878 by employing a girl who was under the required age in full-time work but that was a matter of a penalty and it was not thought that the full-time working contributed to the accident by way of fatigue. English decisions in this regard are helpful. In *Pullar v. Window Clean*[14] the Lord President (Clyde) accepted and adopted many English cases:

"If for instance the legislature has provided no machinery by way of penalty or otherwise for enforcing compliance with the duty there is a presumption that a civil right of action accrues to the person damnified

---

[8] *ibid.* at 22.
[9] *Pullar, ibid.* at 17.
[10] S.I. 1961 No. 1581.
[11] *Teague v. William Baxter & Son Ltd*, 1982 S.L.T. (Sh. Ct) 28.
[12] Unreported, November 3, 1998.
[13] (1895) 22 R. 336.
[14] 1956 S.L.T. 18.

by the breach. Otherwise the duty might never be performed (*Cutler v. Wandsworth Stadium Ltd* [1949] A.C. 398, *per* Lord Simonds at 407 and Lord Normand at 413). On the other hand however, where machinery is incorporated into the statute for enforcing compliance with the statutory obligation the position is different. The presence of such machinery does not necessarily deprive the injured person of a civil remedy based on the breach of statute (*Groves v. Lord Wimbourne* [1898] 2 Q.B. 402), but, as Lord Tenterden, C.J., said in *Doe v. Bridges* (1831) 1 B. and Ad. 847 at 859: 'where the Act creates an obligation and enforces the performance in a specified manner, we take it to be a general rule that performance cannot be enforced in any other manner'. This passage has frequently been adopted and quoted with approval in the House of Lords, (*e.g. Pasmore v. Oswaldtwistle Urban District Council* [1898] A.C. 387 *per* Lord Halsbury, L.C., at 394; *Cutler v. Wandsworth Stadium Ltd* (*supra*) *per* Lord Simonds at 407). The Courts however, have deprecated laying down any hard and fast rules on the matter. As Lord Simonds said in *Cutler* at 407: 'The only rule which in all circumstances is valid is that the answer must depend on a consideration of the whole Act, and the circumstances including the pre-existing law in which it was enacted'. The issue was similarly expressed in the same case by Lord Normand at 413 when he said: 'If there is a penalty clause the right to a civil action must be established by a consideration of the scope and purpose of the statute as a whole'".[15]

In *Pullar* itself, a reading which considered the entire act rather than the applicable section was preferred. In *Houston v. Buchanan*,[16] a Glasgow solicitor bought a car for his brother and took out an insurance in his brother's name, which covered its use both for private and business purposes. When the car was no longer serviceable, Buchanan replaced it with a Ford van and this time he took out an insurance policy in his own name which covered the use of the van for business purposes only. But he never said anything to his brother about how the van was to be used, nor did he tell him about the restriction in the policy. The certificate of insurance, which showed that the use of the van was restricted to business purposes, was sent on to Buchanan's brother, who did not read it but just put it into his driving licence. An accident occurred through the fault of the brother, while he was driving the van for private purposes, and the House of Lords held, reversing the judgment of the First Division of the Court of Session, that by giving his brother the unrestricted control of the van Buchanan had permitted him, in contravention of section 35 of the Road Traffic Act, 1930, to use it without the requisite policy of insurance in respect of third party risks, and that an accident having occurred, Buchanan was liable in damages to the representative of the person who had been

---

[15] See para. 21–22.
[16] 1940 S.C. (H.L.) 17, 1940 S.L.T. 232.

killed.[17] The House of Lords took the view that "the appellant's right to recover damages depended on the answer to the question did the respondent use or cause or permit James Buchanan to use the van?":

"It is not in dispute that there was no policy of insurance in force covering the use of the Ford van for private purposes. Did the respondent in these circumstances permit his brother to use the Ford van for private purposes? I think the right answer to this question was given by Lord Carmont, who was of opinion that the handing over of the complete control of the vehicle to James Buchanan was unambiguous and had the effect of sanctioning general use. The respondent never at any time suggested that he had the intention to restrict the user of either of the cars, and as to the first car he knew that in fact it was used without restriction. On these undisputed facts I have come to the conclusion that the respondent permitted the use of the Ford van by his brother for purposes not covered by any insurance. Accordingly, I move that this appeal be allowed."[18]

In *Fleming v.McGillivray*[19] a pedestrian who had been run into and injured by a motor-van sued (i) the owner of the van; and (ii) a police constable who was driving it at the time of the accident. The court held that the action was incompetent, before it had been established (i) that the driver of the van as the person primarily responsible was unable to pay the damages claimed; (ii) that he had no employers who could be made to pay; and (iii) that the policy of insurance did not cover the particular risk in question. On appeal this decision was affirmed by the First Division. The decision had to be applied in the similar later case of *Draper v. Gilchrist*,[20] even although it was unlikely the driver could pay and despite dicta in the English case of *Monk v. Warbey*[21] indicating that there was no need to raise a separate action.

In terms of the Employers' Liability (Compulsory Insurance) Act 1969, **11–8** employers are obliged to insure themselves for claims by their workmen. The Court of Appeal held in *Richardson v. Pitt-Stanley*[22] that a director was under no civil liability for a failure to effect insurance for the company. However, it is submitted the better view prevailed in the Scottish case *Quinn v. McGinty*.[23] The pursuer sued a director of his employer company for the directors' failure to comply with the statutory obligation to insure in

---

[17] Actually the pursuer brought no less than three actions. In the first, against the brother, the jury awarded her £750 damages for the death of her son and £299 of expenses. But the brother had no money and when charged could not pay. She then brought an action, under section 10 of the Road Traffic Act, 1934, against the insurance company with whom Buchanan had insured the van, for the damages and expenses she had been awarded in the previous action. The company pleaded that it was not liable, because the van was insured for business purposes only; this plea was sustained and the action dismissed. She then brought a third action against Buchanan himself.

[18] *Houston v.Buchanan, ibid., per* the Lord Chancellor (Caldecote) at 37.

[19] 1945 S.L.T. 301.

[20] 1952 S.L.T. (Sh. Ct) 34.

[21] [1935] 1 K.B. 75.

[22] [1995] 2 W.L.R. 26.

[23] 1999 S.L.T. (Sh. Ct) 27.

terms of the Employers' Liability (Compulsory Insurance) Act 1969. The sheriff found against him but the sheriff principal, following the dissent in *Richardson*, allowed the action applying *Monk v. Warbey* and *Houston v. Buchanan*.[24]

Breach of Duty

11–9 Before there can be a breach of duty it must be determined what the standard imposed by the duty was. This question is logically separate from the question as to whether there is a duty at all. This idea is clear from *Nimmo v. Alexander Cowan Ltd*[25] Lord Upjohn said:

> "one must approach its true construction bearing in mind the object of the Act itself . . . It is not in doubt that the whole object of the Factories Act is to reinforce the common law obligation of the employer to take care for the safety of his workmen . . . I cannot believe that Parliament intended to impose upon the injured workman or, if dead, his widow or other personal representative the obligation to aver with the necessary particularity the manner in which the employer should have employed reasonably practicable means to make and keep the place safe for him, although the pursuer can nowadays consult experts he is at a great disadvantage compared to the employer. He may have little recollection of the accident, or of course he may have been killed, and his widow be in an even worse state . . . [The employer] must know and be able to give the reasons why he considered it was impracticable for him to make the place safe. If he cannot explain that it can only be because he failed to give it proper consideration, in breach of his bounden duty to the safety of his workmen . . . In my opinion Parliament intended to impose upon the occupier the obligation of averring and proving at the trial that it was not reasonably practicable to make and keep the place of work safe, so that the pursuer's averments cannot be dismissed as irrelevant."[26]

An example is *Craigie v. North of Scotland Hydro Electricity Board*[27] interpreting the Electricity Supply Regulations 1937, reg. 9(1)(ii). The regulations imposed a duty on the defenders that their installations "shall . . . be efficiently protected by fencing . . . or other means so as to prevent access to electric lines and apparatus therein by any unauthorised person." The equipment had been inspected 17 days before the accident. It was held there had been no breach of duty as the required standard was not absolute but was met by fencing of an appropriate height and efficient enough to prevent access at the time it was built. Often it is simply a matter of fact and circumstances.[28]

---

[24] *ibid.*
[25] 1967 S.L.T. 277.
[26] *ibid.* at 282.
[27] 1987 S.L.T. 178.
[28] See *e.g.* the approach to lifting cases in *Watson v. Foster Menswear Ltd*, 1982 S.L.T. 448 a case under the Offices, Shops and Railway Premises Act 1963, s. 23 where lifting an 80lb load was a breach of the duty. See also *Hamilton v. Western S.M.T. Co. Ltd*, 1977 S.L.T. (Notes) 66.

Causation

A statute can make proof of causation unnecessary.[29]   **11–10**

Defences

The general defences apply in principle although the terms of the particular **11–11**
statute must be examined. Contributory negligence is generally available to
defenders. An example is *Anderson v. Thames Case Ltd*[30] in which an
experienced employee put his hand in a machine to take out a rag without
stopping the machine or slowing it down. He was 50 per cent to blame for
the accident. *Volenti non fit injuria* is generally not available because if
liability is predicated upon the will of Parliament then there ought not to be
an escape from liability contrary to the duty created.

Damage

There seems to be no clear direct authority on remoteness of damage in **11–12**
statutory liability cases. Probably the same approach would be taken as in
the general law. Some suggestions that the same rule does apply can be
found in *Drew v. Western SMT*.[31] A boy was killed as a result of a breach of
a statutory regulation as to the lighting of vehicles. Lord McKay in the
Second Division said:

> "So much explained, then, it is enough to say by preliminary that I
> cannot find any grounds whatever in fact or in law for giving the benefit
> of "remoteness" whether that be treated as remoteness in time, or
> remoteness in logic, to the maintenance, contrary to a safety statute, of
> an unlit obstacle in the full and public path likely to be taken by
> approaching traffic from behind."[32]

In the Outer House in the well-known *McKew v. Holland & Hannen &
Cubitts (Scotland) Ltd*[33] Lord Robertson applied traditional remoteness of
damage doctrine to what was both a common law and statutory claim.

In *Rose v. Bouchet*, 1999 S.C.L.R. 1004 where the sheriff principal upheld granting of
absolvitor in a case brought under the Disability Discrimination Act 1995, s.12. The pursuer
was a blind man who got about with aid of his dog. He phoned the defender who had a guest
house looking for accommodation. He pointed out that he did not have any accommodation
in his guest house but that he had a self-contained flat. The pursuer then said that he was
blind and he asked if there was any objection to the dog staying too. The defender then said
that he thought that access to the flat (which was being worked upon) would be dangerous for
a blind person. The pursuer sued. It was held that there was an obvious case of discrimination
in terms of the Act on the basis of the pursuer's disability. However, it was held that the
defender would not be liable where he held the opinion that his behaviour was necessary not
to endanger the pursuer's safety, providing that in addition to such a genuinely held belief it
was reasonable in all the circumstances to hold that belief.
[29] *Wardlaw v. Bonnington Castings*, 1956 S.C. (H.L.) 26.
[30] 1987 S.L.T. 564.
[31] 1947 S.L.T. 92.
[32] *ibid.* at 95.
[33] 1968 S.L.T. 12.

Eurorep

11–13 Similar to the cases set out above is the idea of enforcing European Union law through the national courts by way of reparation for violation of the European Union law. The similarity is that there may be no express provision for damages and it is the national system of law, particularly that dealing with compensation in the civil courts, that gives effect to the right of damages on breach. The difference is that the actual test set out above of statutory liability, in particular the intention of Parliament test, does not apply. It started with an English case in which it was suggested that a breach of European competition law might be actionable in the United Kingdom's courts for damages.[34] The next development was more spectacular and came from the fact that some directives allow the Member State some considerable discretion in fashioning local law to meet European Union objectives. If they do not act there is a gap in the community enforcement mechanism.[35] In a pair of related cases the European Court of Justice provided a national right of damages.[36] In *Francovich* workers who were uncompensated sought damages against the state for payment of wages as provided by the directive or alternatively for compensation for the loss as a result of the failure of the state to implement the directive. On a preliminary ruling it was held that the directive just failed to meet the twin criteria for direct effect as the State had a considerable discretion. But the court allowed the compensation claim:

> "The full effectiveness of rules of Community law would be undermined and the protection of the rights which they create weakened if individuals were unable to obtain reparation when their rights were infringed as a result of Member States' violation of community law."[37]

There are three conditions for such a case: (1) the result prescribed by the directive must involve the attribution of rights to individuals; (2) the content of those rights must be identifiable from the provisions of the directive; (3) a causal link must exist between the violation of the Member State's obligation and the damage suffered by the injured persons.[38] *Francovich* dealt with a directive and so it was arguable that it applied only to directives and not to other European Union legislation. It was also a case of a failure to legislate.

---

[34] *Garden Cottage Foods v. Milk Marketing Board* [1984] A.C. 130. See also *Bourgoin v. Ministry of Agriculture* [1986] Q.B. 716 which crucially in this context did not apply *Garden Cottage Foods* to public bodies.

[35] G.H. Downie, "New Right to Damages in Community Law", (1992) 37 J.L.S. 424. See also C. Boch, and R. Lane, "A New Remedy in Scots Law: Damages from the Crown for Breach of Community Law", 1992 S.L.T. (News) 145.

[36] C–6/90 *Andrea Francovich v. Italian Republic*; C–9/90 *Danila Bonifaci & Others v. Italian Republic* [1992] I.R.L.R. 84. Directive 80/987 was intended to provide workers with a minimum level of protection in the event of the insolvency of their employers. The Italian Government failed to implement the directive by the deadline for implementation of October 23, 1983 and so was sued by the Commission. A ruling was made against Italy. *Commission v. Italian Republic* [1989] E.C.R. 143. Nothing had been done by May 1991.

[37] para. 34.

[38] para. 40.

The European Court of Justice took the law a stage further in two joined **11–14** cases.[39] In *R. v. Secretary of State for Transport, ex p. Factortame Ltd*,[40] companies owned and operated by Spanish citizens sought judicial review complaining of the illegality of a U.K. statute and related regulations. A first ECJ reference declared that any national rules precluding remedies enforcing community law were inapplicable and so injunctions could be brought against the Crown and national courts could declare U.K. legislation inapplicable. In the second reference the U.K. legislation was ruled to have been contrary to European Union law. It was changed by the U.K. Parliament as a result. The plaintiffs then sought the damages they had claimed in the original judicial review as they had been precluded, they said, from fishing by what had been declared to be illegal legislation. It was held that such a right to damages did arise. In *Brasserie du Pecheur SA v. Germany*[41] French brewers complained that the German law on beer duty was contrary to European Union law and they had sustained a loss as a result. They too were entitled to damages. The ECJ based its rules for establishing liability on its existing rules on non-contractual liability of the Community. Community law confers a right to reparation where three conditions are met: (i) the rule of law infringed must be intended to confer rights on individuals; (ii) the breach must be sufficiently serious; (iii) there must be a direct causal link between the breach of the obligation resting on the state and the damage sustained by the injured parties.

In deciding whether the matter was sufficiently serious the decisive test is whether the Member State has manifestly and gravely disregarded the limits on its discretion. Certain factors can be taken into account (as can others not listed by the court) in approaching that question:

(a) the clarity and precision of the rule breached;

(b) the measure of discretion left to the Member State;

(c) whether the infringement and any damage caused were intentional or voluntary;

(d) whether any error of law was excusable;

(e) the contribution, if any, a Community institution might have made;

(f) the adoption or retention of national measures.

Where there has been (1) a judgment finding an infringement established; (2) a preliminary ruling or (3) an established body of ECJ jurisprudence then the breach is sufficiently serious.

A number of practical points were also laid down in the joint cases. The **11–15** obligation to make reparation did not depend on a condition based on any concept of fault (intentional or negligent) beyond that of a serious breach

---

[39] For a detailed analysis see M. Upton, "Crown Liability in Damages under Community Law Parts 1 & 2", 1996 S.L.T. (News) 175 and 211; P.P. Craig, "Once More into the Breach: The Community, the State and Damages Liability" (1997) 113 L.Q.R. 67.

[40] [1990] 2 A.C. 85 (H.L.); [1991] 1 A.C. 603, ECJ (C–48/93).

[41] C–46/93 [1996] 2 W.L.R. 506; P. Spink, "British Beer and Brussels" (1996) 41 J.L.S. 395; P. Spink, "*Brasserie du Pecheur*: Defining the boundaries of State Liability for Breach of Community Law" (1996) 41 J.L.S. 355.

of community law. The extent of reparation must be commensurate. The local system may set the criteria but they must not be less favourable than those applying to similar claims based on domestic law and must not be such as in practice make it impossible or excessively difficult to obtain reparation. Damages for loss of profit could not be ruled out as many cases involve commerce. Exemplary damages where they apply nationally could not be ruled out either. The date from which damages would be payable was not cut off at the date of a decision—there was no temporal limitation. An early application of this new regime appeared in *R. v. H.M. Treasury, ex parte British Telecommunications plc*.[42] BT sought annulment of certain United Kingdom regulations which purported to give effect to a council directive on procurement. It was held that the United Kingdom had erroneously given effect to the directive. However, this conduct did not meet the "sufficiently serious" criterion and there was no liability to make reparation. In this case the rule concerned was not clear enough and there was no case law applicable and no guidance from the Commission when the rules were adopted. There have been no Scots actions at the time of writing but guidance may be sought from Mr.Upton's work as to how best to frame such an action—judicial review seems the safest course.[43] Guidance on this new type of claim for a new type of wrong may be sought in cases from other jurisdictions.

11–16　　In *R v. Ministry of Agriculture and Fisheries, ex parte Hedley Lomas (Ireland) Ltd*[44] the Community had laid down rules for stunning animals before slaughter. The United Kingdom thought it had sufficient evidence that the Spanish were not properly applying the legislation. So they stopped giving export licences to the detriment of Hedley Lomas. The *Brasserie* conditions were met in this case. Article 34 prevents the imposition of quantitative restrictions and measures having equivalent effect. It had long ago been decided that this gave individuals rights.[45] So far as the "sufficiently serious" question was concerned, in this case there was only a narrow (or no) discretion at issue and the mere breach of community law was sufficient. Causation was a matter for the national court to determine. The picture was made complete when in *R v. Secretary of State (Factortame Ltd No. 5)*[46] the Court of Appeal followed the ECJ ruling to hold the United Kingdom liable in damages to the Spanish fishermen for such a grave and manifest breach of the Treaty that it was sufficiently serious within the ECJ's jurisprudence without investigation of intention or negligence. A case more like those that might be expected to concern the ordinary practitioner in the future is *Dillenkofer v. Germany*[47]. The plaintiffs lost money when their holiday companies went bust. They sued the State for failure to have implemented the directive on package travel swiftly enough to have covered their cases. The Court referred to the *Brasserie* criteria and the *Francovich* criteria. The Court explained that although

---

[42] [1996] 3 W.L.R. 203.
[43] M. Upton, "Crown Liability in Damages under Community Law. Part 2", 1996 S.L.T. (News) 211.
[44] [1996] T.L.R. 353.
[45] *Pigs Marketing Board v. Redmond* [1978] E.C.R. 2347.
[46] [1998] T.L.R. 261.
[47] [1996] T.L.R. 564.

Francovich, another non-transposition case, did not expressly mention the need for serious breach, it was implied within it. Thus failure to transpose European law into domestic law within the set time limit is *per se* a serious breach. In this case the rights conferred and the persons on whom they were conferred was clear.[48] The *Dillenkofer* approach was commended in *R. v. Secretary of State, ex parte Sutton*,[49] to allow interest on social security benefit arrears to be claimed as reparation for a failure to properly transpose European Union law.[50] To know that there is a remedy for a client depends upon a knowledge that there is an applicable European Union rule which meets the client's case, not just the Scots law of reparation.[51]

HUMAN RIGHTS

This is not a statement of all of the human rights law which might be **11–17** relevant to Scots law because the influence of human rights law will enter into many other branches of the law. European human rights law in the local courts is so new that it still requires to be treated in a separate section such as this, if for no other reason than that its interpretation is governed by special rules requiring it to be interpreted in a conventionist way.[52] There are a few cross references elsewhere in this book to this section to flag up possible cases but over time there will be many more and this area will expand to the extent that human rights are protected in Scotland by an award of reparation. So this section only deals with the effect of the Human Rights Act 1998 on the availability of reparation.[53] The Act provides additional remedies to those already provided by the law.[54] The practitioner will, however, have to consider less direct approaches particularly in cases of legislation where it is possible to argue of a human rights interpretation and to seek a declaration of incompatibility of legislation.

If it is the case that the Scots law of reparation can operate by virtue of the recognition of an interest by the courts then these rights and freedoms are the very things—now part of the law in a formal sense—which can be used directly or in combination to forge new reparable interests. While that is a general approach to these newly articulated rights there is an express mechanism for cases involving a public authority. It is unlawful for a public

---

[48] The U.K. joined the case to argue that late transposition should not be a matter of *per se* liability and that it would have to be shown that it was a manifest and grave breach. The directive was implemented by the U.K. in the Package Travel, Package Holiday and Package Tours Regulations 1992 (S.I. 1992 No. 3288).

[49] [1997] T.L.R. 218.

[50] Social Security Council Directive 79/7 [1979] O.J. L6/24.

[51] See *e.g.* A. O'Neil, "Francovich Damages and the Working Time Directive", 1996 S.L.T. (News) 381. Another example of a potential case relates to the MIB, see *Mighell v. Reading* [1998] T.L.R. 605 where the Court of Appeal held that applicants under the scheme could not rely on the Second Council Directive 84/5 [1984] O.J. L8/17. No opinion was expressed on whether the MIB was an emanation of the state for the purposes of Euro-rep.

[52] See Arts 2(1) and (2) of the European Convention on Human Rights. See also the internal rules of construction in Arts 17 and 18.

[53] At the time of writing the Act was not in force although it had effect in Scotland while the book was in MS by virtue of the Scotland Act 1998.

[54] Art. 11 of E.C.H.R.

authority to act in a way which is incompatible with a convention right.[55] A person who is a victim of the unlawful act[56] can bring proceedings against the authority under the Act[57] or rely on the convention rights in any legal proceedings[58]—perhaps to substantiate a new view of an existing wrong. It should be noted that Articles 1 and 13 are not treated because it is argued that the Act itself achieves the aims of these articles.

Convention Rights and Fundamental Freedoms

Right To Life

11–18 Everyone's right to life must be protected by law. No one should be deprived of his life intentionally save in the execution of a sentence of a court following his conviction of a crime for which this penalty is provided by law.[59]

Prohibition Of Torture etc

11–19 No one should be subjected to torture or to inhuman or degrading treatment or punishment.[60] In *A. v. United Kingdom*[61] the applicant had been caned by his step-father sufficient to cause bruising. The step-father was acquitted on the defence of reasonable chastisement by a jury. It was held that the chastisement was excessive by European standards. It was further held that the United Kingdom was liable for not having taken steps to protect persons such as the applicant. The United Kingdom was held liable for damages of £10,000 and £20,000 costs.

Prohibition Of Slavery And Forced Labour

11–20 No one can be held in slavery or servitude.[62] No one shall be required to perform forced or compulsory labour.[63]

---

[55] Section 6(1). Subject to the detailed provisions of subs 6(2)–(6), mainly permitting action in respect of judicial acts but exempting Parliament.

[56] If proceedings are brought by way of judicial review then a person is only to have title and interest to sue if he is a victim: s. 7(4). Victim of an unlawful act is specially defined: s. 7(7).

[57] s. 7(1)(a). This envisages a special procedure and rules. It envisages a one year prescription with an equitable override: s. 7(5).

[58] s. 7(1)(b).

[59] Art. 2(1). Deprivation of life shall not be regarded as inflicted in contravention of this Article when it results from the use of force which is no more than absolutely necessary: (a) in defence of any person from unlawful violence; (b) in order to effect a lawful arrest or to prevent the escape of a person lawfully detained; (c) in action lawfully taken for the purpose of quelling a riot or insurrection: Art. 2(2). See *McCann v. UK* (1996) E.H.R.R. 97; *X v. UK* (1980) 19 D.R. 244.

[60] Art. 3. See also *Ireland v. United Kingdom* (1979–80) 2 E.H.R.R. 25; *Ribitsch v. Austria* (1995) 21 E.H.R.R. 573 (assault in police custody).

[61] [1998] T.L.R. 578. See also *Tyrer v. UK* (1978) 2 E.H.R.R. 1; *Costello-Roberts v. UK* (1993) 19 E.H.R.R. 112; *Campbell and Cosans v. UK* (1982) 13 E.H.R.R. 441.

[62] Art. 4(1).

[63] Art. 4. "For the purpose of this Article the term 'forced or compulsory labour' shall not include: (a) any work required to be done in the ordinary course of detention imposed according to the provisions of Article 5 of this Convention or during conditional release from such detention; (b) any service of a military character or, in case of conscientious objectors in countries where they are recognised, service exacted instead of compulsory military service; (c) any service exacted in case of an emergency or calamity threatening the life or well-being of the community; (d) any work or service which forms part of normal civic obligations": Art. 4(3). See *Van der Mussele v. Belgium* (1984) 6 E.H.R.R. 163.

Right To Liberty And Security

Everyone has the right to liberty and security of person. No one can be **11–21**
deprived of his liberty save in the following cases and in accordance with a
procedure prescribed by law:

(a) the lawful detention of a person after conviction by a competent
court;

(b) the lawful arrest or detention of a person for non-compliance with
the lawful order of a court or in order to secure the fulfilment of any
obligation prescribed by law;

(c) the lawful arrest or detention of a person effected for the purpose of
bringing him before the competent legal authority on reasonable
suspicion of having committed an offence or when it is reasonably
considered necessary to prevent his committing an offence or fleeing
after having done so;

(d) the detention of a minor by lawful order for the purpose of
educational supervision or his lawful detention for the purpose of
bringing him before the competent legal authority;

(e) the lawful detention of persons for the prevention of the spreading
of infectious diseases, of persons of unsound mind, alcoholics or
drug addicts or vagrants;

(f) the lawful arrest or detention of a person to prevent his effecting an
unauthorised entry into the country or of a person against whom
action is being taken with a view to deportation or extradition.[64]

Everyone who is arrested shall be informed promptly, in a language which
he understands, of the reasons for his arrest and of any charge against
him.[65] Everyone arrested or detained in accordance with the provisions of
paragraph 1(c) of this Article must be brought promptly before a judge or
other officer authorised by law to exercise judicial power and is entitled to
trial within a reasonable time or to release pending trial. Release may be
conditioned by guarantees to appear for trial.[66] Everyone who is deprived of
his liberty by arrest or detention is entitled to take proceedings by which
the lawfulness of his detention must be decided speedily by a court and his
release ordered if the detention is not lawful.[67] Then there is a clear
reparation provision: "Everyone who has been the victim of arrest or
detention in contravention of the provisions of this Article shall have an
enforceable right to compensation."[68] That is not to say either that this is

---

[64] Art. 5(1). For Art. 5(1)(f) see *Chahal v. UK* (1997) 23 E.H.R.R. 413.

[65] Art. 5(2).

[66] Art. 5(3). There are extensive derogations mainly applicable to this Article in respect of
the civil insurrection in Northern Ireland which is regulated internally by successive
Prevention of Terrorism Acts. See Schedule 3 to the Human Rights Act 1998 (c. 46). See
Lawless v. Ireland (1961) E.H.R.R. 1; *Fox Campbell and Hartley v. UK* (1991) 13 E.H.R.R. 157;
Brogan v. UK (1989) 11 E.H.R.R. 1; *Murray v. UK* (1994) 19 E.H.R.R. 193.

[67] Art. 5(4). See, *e.g. Ashingdane v. UK* (1985) E.H.R.R. 528; *Thynne, Wilson and Gunnell v.
UK* (1991) E.H.R.R. 666.

[68] Art. 5(5).

the only provision which will result in reparation merely that this is a clear instance.

In *Steel v. United Kingdom*[69] the European Court of Human Rights considered a breach of Article 5(1) by the United Kingdom in respect, *inter alia*, of the arrest of three persons for breach of the peace for handing out leaflets and holding up banners at an arms sale. It was held that Article 10(2) was also breached. However, it was held that the United Kingdom had not breached Article 5(5) which gives an enforceable right to reparation because the applicants could bring civil actions against the police in the national courts. The demonstrators were however awarded £500 each for non-pecuniary damages and expenses of £20,000.

Right To A Fair Trial

11–22 In the determination of his civil rights and obligations or of any criminal charge against him, everyone is entitled to a fair and public hearing within a reasonable time by an independent and impartial tribunal established by law. Judgment must be pronounced publicly but the press and public may be excluded from all or part of the trial in the interest of morals, public order or national security in a democratic society, where the interests of juveniles or the protection of the private life of the parties so require, or to the extent strictly necessary in the opinion of the court in special circumstances where publicity would prejudice the interests of justice.[70]

This article has already had a dramatic impact on the ordinary law of reparation. *Osman v. United Kingdom*[71] is one of the most remarkable decisions affecting delict from the European Court of Human Rights and is a good example of the sort of cases that can be expected. The applicants complained that the police had been negligent in their investigation of a teacher who eventually shot and killed a pupil's father, shot and injured a pupil, shot and injured the headmaster and shot and killed the headmaster's son. They lost their damages action before the English Court of Appeal on the authority of the exclusionary rule in *Hill v. Chief Constable of West Yorkshire*.[72] The European Court of Human Rights held that the automatic application of *Hill* was contrary to Article 6(1) of the Convention. The fact that they could have sued the killer or the psychiatrists was not to the point, the applicant had not had the chance to have a determination on the conduct of the police. The applicants were awarded £10,000 for the loss of the chance to have sued the police. As a result the House of Lords appear to have accepted that the practice of striking-out is not convention friendly in relation to negligence cases where the court has the task of weighing up interests.[73] This must have implications for the Scottish procedure of dismissing cases at debate. It might just have to stop except in the most obvious cases. The law has already the reached the stage where personal injury reparation cases are not supposed to be dismissed on

---

[69] [1998] T.L.R. 575.

[70] Art. 6 (1).

[71] [1998] T.L.R. 68. See also *Golder v. UK* (1979–80) 1 E.H.R.R. 524 (entitlement of prisoner to consult a lawyer to raise civil proceedings).

[72] [1989] A.C. 53.

[73] *Barrett v. Enfield L.B.C.* [1999] 3 W.L.R. 79.

relevancy but still they are and the dispensation for relevancy does not apply to specification. Legal aid for civil proceedings is another human right.[73a]

Everyone charged with a criminal offence shall be presumed innocent until proved guilty according to law.[74] Everyone charged with a criminal offence has the following minimum rights:

(a) to be informed promptly, in a language which he understands and in detail, of the nature and cause of the accusation against him;

(b) to have adequate time and facilities for the preparation of his defence;

(c) to defend himself in person or through legal assistance of his own choosing or, if he has not sufficient means to pay for legal assistance, to be given it free when the interests of justice so require;

(d) to examine or have examined witnesses against him and to obtain the attendance and examination of witnesses on his behalf under the same conditions as witnesses against him;

(e) to have the free assistance of an interpreter if he cannot understand or speak the language used in court.[75]

No Punishment Without Law

No one can be held guilty of any criminal offence on account of any act or **11–23** omission which did not constitute a criminal offence under national or international law at the time when it was committed. Nor shall a heavier penalty be imposed than the one that was applicable at the time the criminal offence was committed.[76]

Right To Respect For Private And Family Life

Everyone has the right to respect for his private and family life, his home **11–24** and his correspondence.[77] There must be no interference by a public authority with the exercise of this right except such as is in accordance with the law and is necessary in a democratic society in the interests of national security, public safety or the economic well-being of the country, for the prevention of disorder or crime, for the protection of health or morals, or for the protection of the rights and freedoms of others.[78] English law has been held not to be vigorous enough in regulating police telephone tapping.[78a]

[73a] *Airey v. Ireland* (1979–80) 2 E.H.R.R. 305.

[74] Art. 6(2).

[75] Art. 6(3).

[76] Art. 7(1). This Article does not prejudice the trial and punishment of any person for any act or omission which, at the time when it was committed, was criminal according to the general principles of law recognised by civilised nations: Art. 7(2). See, *e.g. Welch v. UK* (1995) 20 E.H.R.R. 247; *SW v. UK* (1996) E.H.R.R. 363.

[77] Art. 8(1). See, *e.g. Rees v. UK* (1997) 9 E.H.R.R. 56; *Cossey v. UK* (1991) 13 E.H.R.R. 622.

[78] Art. 8(2). See, *e.g. Gaskin v. UK* (1990) 12 E.H.R.R. 547; *Chappell v. UK* (1990) 12 E.H.R.R. 1; *Silver v. UK* (1983) 5 E.H.R.R. 347; *Campbell v. UK* (1993) 15 E.H.R.R. 137; *Halford v. UK* (1997) 24 E.H.R.R. 523.

[78a] *Malone v. UK* (1985) 7 E.H.R.R. 14.

Freedom Of Thought, Conscience And Religion

11-25 Everyone has the right to freedom of thought, conscience and religion; this right includes freedom to change his religion or belief and freedom, either alone or in community with others and in public or private, to manifest his religion or belief, in worship, teaching, practice and observance.[79] Freedom to manifest one's religion or beliefs is subject only to such limitations as are prescribed by law and are necessary in a democratic society in the interests of public safety, for the protection of public order, health or morals, or for the protection of the rights and freedoms of others.[80]

Freedom Of Expression

11-26 Everyone has the right to freedom of expression.[80a] This right includes freedom to hold opinions and to receive and impart information and ideas without interference by public authority and regardless of frontiers. This Article shall not prevent States from requiring the licensing of broadcasting, television or cinema enterprises.[81] The exercise of these freedoms, since it carries with it duties and responsibilities, may be subject to such formalities, conditions, restrictions or penalties as are prescribed by law and are necessary in a democratic society, in the interests of national security, territorial integrity or public safety, for the prevention of disorder or crime, for the protection of health or morals, for the protection of the reputation or rights of others, for preventing the disclosure of information received in confidence, or for maintaining the authority and impartiality of the judiciary.[82]

Freedom Of Assembly And Association

11-27 Everyone has the right to freedom of peaceful assembly and to freedom of association with others, including the right to form and to join trade unions for the protection of his interests.[83] No restrictions shall be placed on the exercise of these rights other than such as are prescribed by law and are necessary in a democratic society in the interests of national security or public safety, for the prevention of disorder or crime, for the protection of health or morals or for the protection of the rights and freedoms of others. This Article does not prevent the imposition of lawful restrictions on the exercise of these rights by members of the armed forces, of the police or of the administration of the State.[84]

Right To Marry

11-28 Men and women of marriageable age have the right to marry and to found a family, according to the national laws governing the exercise of this right.[85]

---

[79] Art. 9(1).

[80] Art. 9(2).

[80a] See, *e.g. Handyside v. UK* (1976) 1 E.H.R.R. 737; *Goodwin v. UK* (1996) 22 E.H.R.R. 123; *Sunday Times v. UK* (1992) 14 E.H.R.R. 229; *Tolstoy v. UK* (1995) 20 E.H.R.R. 442.

[81] Art. 10(1).

[82] Art. 10(2). Nothing in this Article may be regarded as preventing the States from imposing restrictions on the political activity of aliens: Art. 11.

[83] Art. 11(1). See, *e.g. Young, James and Webster v. UK* (1982) 4 E.H.R.R. 38.

[84] Art. 11(2). Nothing in this Article may be regarded as preventing the States from imposing restrictions on the political activity of aliens: Art. 11.

[85] Art. 12. See, *e.g. Rees v. UK* (1987) 9 E.H.R.R. 66.

Prohibition Of Discrimination

The enjoyment of the rights and freedoms set forth in the Convention must **11–29** be secured without discrimination on any ground such as sex, race, colour, language, religion, political or other opinion, national or social origin, association with a national minority, property, birth or other status.[86]

Protection Of Property

Every natural or legal person is entitled to the peaceful enjoyment of his **11–30** possessions. No one may be deprived of his possessions except in the public interest and subject to the conditions provided for by law and by the general principles of international law. The preceding provisions do not, however, in any way impair the right of a State to enforce such laws as it deems necessary to control the use of property in accordance with the general interest or to secure the payment of taxes or other contributions or penalties.[87]

Right To Education

No person can be denied the right to education. In the exercise of any **11–31** functions which it assumes in relation to education and to teaching, the State shall respect the right of parents to ensure such education and teaching in conformity with their own religious and philosophical convictions.[88]

Right To Free Elections

The High Contracting Parties undertake to hold free elections at reason- **11–32** able intervals by secret ballot, under conditions which will ensure the free expression of the opinion of the people in the choice of the legislature.[89]

The Death Penalty

The death penalty is abolished. No one may be condemned to such penalty **11–33** or be executed.[90]

---

[86] Art. 14. Nothing in this Article may be regarded as preventing the States from imposing restrictions on the political activity of aliens: Art. 11.

[87] First Protocol Art. 1.

[88] First Protocol Art. 2.

[89] First Protocol Art. 3.

[90] Sixth Protocol Art. 1. A State may make provision in its law for the death penalty in respect of acts committed in time of war or of imminent threat of war; such penalty shall be applied only in the instances laid down in the law and in accordance with its provisions. The State shall communicate to the Secretary General of the Council of Europe the relevant provisions of that law: Sixth Protocol Art. 2.

CHAPTER 12

SKILLED AND PROFESSIONAL PERSONS

The questions, "who is skilled" and "what is a profession" are not easily **12–1** answered. This is not the place to try to answer them. The two terms have a core of certainty and a penumbra of uncertainty and there is many a dodgy operator languishing in that shade. Changing political, economic and social factors make it impossible to try to lay down the duties of certain potential defenders. A doctor should still not amputate the wrong leg and a solicitor should not sue the wrong defender. Who is to say with certainty what a modern accountant does in his "firm" which spans continents and apart from adding up, provides consultancy for business? Indeed how many Scottish lawyers reading this book could comment on the conduct of one of the multi-national law firms who number governments and space-agencies among their clients?

The basis of liability

Where a professional person causes physical injury normally the neighbour **12–2** principle applies.[1] Where the loss is financial, liability is now more often based on the idea of reliance discussed above,[2] in particular the liability established in *Hedley Byrne* based on mutually reasonable reliance or assumption of responsibility. That broader principle is enough to subsume earlier cases of liability. Indeed it is enough to doubt older cases more favourable to professionals. New cases are examined on the basis of the *Hedley Byrne* principle as it has been developed or, as some might say, restricted, by later developments. So although solicitors and accountants have been held liable for their mistakes before, if a new type of defender arises the court will look at the matter afresh. One of the main cases restricting *Hedley Byrne* did on its facts involve accountants. In *Caparo Industries plc v. Dickman*[3] Fidelity plc bought some shares in Caparo. When they saw the statutory accounts produced by the defendants' solicitors they bought more, indeed they in due course bought all the rest. It turned out Caparo was not a good buy and the plaintiffs lost £400,000 instead of making about £1.3m. It was held in the House of Lords that as auditors there was no duty owed by the defendants. Lord Bridge based this partly on the ground of *Hedley* itself—the defender has to know that the pursuer will

---

[1] See *Kelly v. Edinburgh D.C.*, 1983 S.L.T. 593 for a case against architects by a person injured by going through a pane of glass. The standard of care is however still the professional one. See also the less apposite *Edie v. McKinnon's Transport*, 1973 S.L.T. 31 in which the advisor was experienced rather than skilled.

[2] See Chap. 10.

[3] [1990] 1 A.C. 605.

reasonably rely. He thought that in this case the accounts were put into general circulation and thus could be argued to be relied on by strangers as opposed to the directors for whom they are prepared. Lord Bridge in the familiar way of legal rhetoric justified this by positing a different case—if this action were allowed then lenders or merchants dealing with the company should be able to sue. Such a hypothetical raised the floodgates fear. It might have been thought that the claim was stronger based on the fact that *Caparo* had already bought shares and were in a closer relationship to the accounts, this after all is the way in which shareholders monitor the performance of their company. This was to no avail either. The special factual situation alleged that the accountants should have realised that this particular company at this particular time was vulnerable to a take-over did not help either. More about accountants appears below[4] and more about economic loss above.[5]

12–3   Policy was a major feature of the decision in *White v. Jones*,[6] a case of an intended beneficiary suing a solicitor, discussed in detail above.[7] The fair just and reasonable policy approach was taken, this time resulting in a finding of liability. The case was difficult because the professional error was not based on advice but on a failure to act. The failure did not cause a loss as in *Hedley Byrne* but in a failure to obtain a gain. Lord Goff of Chieveley explicitly decided the case on the basis of doing practical justice, solicitors play an important role in society and preparing wills is one of the things the public expects to be done right, especially those of modest means.

12–4   *Henderson v. Merrett Syndicates Ltd*[8] is important. It established that the existence of a contract between the parties did not exclude a delictual duty. *Hedley Byrne* was revived as the general foundation; the new situation in that case was capable of creating a duty; most significantly the House of Lords acknowledged (perhaps for the first time) the possibility that liability might attach to careless or dilatory omissions as well as to careless acts.

12–5   A feature of the law since liability has become prevalent is the attempt to avoid it. Because the essence of liability is reliance, statements which discourage that reliance can prevent liability arising.[9] Thus, in the context of professional liability it must always be asked to what extent reliance was engendered and what steps if any were taken to restrict that. This often involves examining any written documentation supplied.

The Standard of Care

12–6 Before the leading Scots case *Hunter v. Hanley*[10] the law appears to have been that indeed skilled persons were not liable save for gross negligence. In *Hunter* the defender obtained a verdict in a jury trial. The basis of the decision is therefore centred on the charge. The case resulted from the breaking of a hypodermic needle when the defender was giving the pursuer

---

[4] See para. 12–44 below.
[5] See paras 10–16 *et seq.* above.
[6] [1995] 1 All E.R. 691.
[7] See para. 12–22 below.
[8] [1994] 3 All E.R. 506.
[9] Subject to statutory controls. See the discussion at para. 10–23 above.
[10] 1955 S.C. 200.

the twelfth of a series of injections of penicillin. It was alleged that the type of needle employed on the occasion in question was not strong enough, and that "any doctor possessing a fair and average knowledge of his profession would have known this". In his charge to the jury Lord Patrick directed as follows:

"There must be such a departure from the normal and usual practice of general practitioners as can reasonably be described as gross negligence. I could use from cases of high authority in the House of Lords, Scots cases, much stronger adjectives than that, but all that I will say to you in conclusion on the general topic is that there must be a serious departure from a normal practice, if that normal practice has been proved, and the serious departure must involve a substantial and serious fault".[11]

In considering the justification for this direction Lord President Clyde remarked that the reference to "gross negligence" may have come from the fact that it appeared in the pleadings of the case. He went on to consider what the law actually was. It was accepted that the degree of want of care which constitutes negligence must vary with the circumstances.[12] The following passage is often considered when the *Hunter* test is in issue:

"where the conduct of a doctor, or indeed any professional man, is concerned the circumstances are not so precise and clear cut as in the normal case. In the realm of diagnosis and treatment there is ample scope for genuine difference of opinion and one man clearly is not negligent merely because his conclusion differs from that of other professional men, nor because he has displayed less skill or knowledge than others would have shown. The true test for establishing negligence in diagnosis or treatment on the part of a doctor is whether he has been proved to be guilty of such failure as no doctor of ordinary skill would be guilty of it acting with ordinary care—Glegg, *Reparation* (3rd ed.), p. 509. The standard seems to be the same in England: Salmond, *Law of Torts* (11th ed.), p. 511."[13]

The Lord President went on to deal with the significance of gross negligence which he admitted did in fact appear in the authorities:

"In relation however, to professional negligence, I regard the phrase "gross negligence" only as indicating so marked a departure from the normal standard of conduct of a professional man as to infer a lack of the ordinary care which a man of ordinary skill would display. So interpreted, the words partly describe what I consider the sound criterion in the matter, although, strictly viewed, they might give the impression that there are degrees of negligence".[14]

He then formulated a test designed to establish liability cases of deviation from normal practise in the context of the actual case:

---

[11] *ibid.* at 202.
[12] Under reference to *Caswell v. Powell Duffryn Associated Collieries* [1940] A.C. 152, *per* Lord Wright at 175–176.
[13] *Hunter*, at 204.
[14] *ibid.* at 206.

"It follows from what I have said that in regard to allegations of deviation from ordinary professional practice—and this is the matter with which the present note is concerned—such a deviation is not necessarily evidence of negligence. Indeed it would be disastrous if this were so, for all inducement to progress in medical science would then be destroyed. Even a substantive deviation from normal practice may be warranted by the particular circumstances. To establish liability by the doctor where deviation from normal practice is alleged, three facts require to be established. First of all it must be proved that there is a usual and normal practice; secondly it must be proved that the defender has not adopted that practice; and thirdly (and this is of crucial importance) it must be established that the course the doctor adopted is one which no professional man of ordinary skill would have taken if he had been acting with ordinary care. There is clearly a heavy onus upon a pursuer to establish these three facts, and without all three his case will fail. If this is the test, then it matters nothing how far or how little he deviates from the ordinary practice. For the extent of deviation is not the test. The deviation must be of a kind which satisfies the third of the requirements just stated."

12–7 This test has been applied and considered many times. *Hunter* was accepted by both sides as laying down the proper test in a case involving architects.[15] The test is generally accepted but its precise scope is debated.[16] The Second Division in *Stephen v. Scottish Boatowners Mutual Insurance Association*[17] refused to apply *Hunter* as the test applicable in an inquiry as to whether a ship's captain had exercised "all reasonable endeavours" to save his ship in terms of a policy of insurance. This was perfectly acceptable as the task for the court was one of interpretation of a document. The test is not applied to every case involving persons with skills. It was not applied to a liquidator in *MacRae v. Henderson*[18]:

"It was further submitted by counsel for the defender that the standard of care to be applied was to be related to the standard of the ordinary liquidator. That was a submission based on *Hunter v. Hanley*. That was a case concerning an allegation of deviation from normal practice of a doctor. It was held that it had first to be proved that there was a usual and normal practice; that the defender had not adopted that practice; that it had to be established that the course adopted was one which no professional man of ordinary skill would have taken if he had been acting with ordinary care. In my view, however, the circumstances of this case do not put the liquidator in the same category as the professional man in Hunter. In the circumstances of this case the liquidator had to exercise reasonable care to protect interests by ingathering debts in the

---

[15] *Kelly v. Edinburgh D.C.*, 1983 S.L.T. 593.
[16] *ibid.* See also Contributed, "Medical Negligence: *Hunter v. Hanley*, 35 Years On" 1990 S.L.T. 325. D.K. Feenan, "Medical Negligence (*Hunter v. Hanley* 35 Years On : A Reply" 1991 S.L.T. 321; L. Sutherland, "A Single Standard of Care" (1995) Rep.B. 6–11; K. Norrie, "Common Practice and the Standard of Care in Medical Negligence" (1985) J.R. 145.
[17] 1989 S.L.T. 52.
[18] 1989 S.L.T. 523.

particular circumstances of the present liquidation. The circumstances of the present case are not such that the pursuers were bound to rely on the practice or standard of the ordinary liquidator."[19]

The test was not applied to exculpate architects in *Wagner Associates v. Joseph Dunn (Bottlers) Ltd.*[20] The architects (pursuers, but defenders in the counterclaim for professional negligence) used one brick coping which was not as well respected as concrete coping. However, because there was skilled evidence that it would be proper to give a warning and information if the brick coping were used there was no room for the test. An attempt to use the *Hunter* test to exculpate builders failed in *Morisons Associated Companies Ltd v. James Rome & Son Ltd.*[21] Lord Cameron said:

"Counsel argued for the defenders that the position of a builder was the same as a doctor, and that it would, therefore be necessary to show that the defenders had acted in a way which no builder of reasonable skill exercising reasonable care would have acted in the circumstances. I do not think this is so. The practise of medicine is only permitted to those who have attained a fixed standard of professional qualifications. Further, the practise of medicine is not an exact science and methods of practice and treatment vary with the movement of professional opinion and the expansion of the horizon of scientific knowledge. The standard of qualification of a builder is not recognised and defined in the same way. An old established craft of the builder is not subjected to the same divisions and movements in professional opinion or fluctuations in diagnosis and prescription . . . A builder or any other skilled tradesman is only required to possess a reasonable degree of competence and to display it in his work . . . What is the measure of the standard in each case must be judged against the practice ruling in the particular trade at the particular time. I think also that where different opinions as to method may reasonably be held by persons equally skilled in the particular trade or craft, selection of one which has in fact led to certain injurious consequences in preference to another which might have led to a different result is not necessarily proof of negligence . . . unless these consequences were within the realm of the reasonably foreseeable as certain or likely to ensue. On the other hand error of judgement however honestly arrived at, does not necessarily exculpate from liability."

He went on to examine the issue of practice and found that it had not been criticised by any practical builder. If it had that would make a difference for a builder but not for a doctor.[22]

The same idea appears in England,[23] the *Hunter* case having been **12–8** influential. MacNair J. stated the test in slightly different terms:

---

[19] *ibid.* at 526.
[20] 1986 S.L.T. 267.
[21] 1962 S.L.T. (Notes) 75.
[22] The defenders were held liable in contract but not in delict.
[23] See A.C. Malcolm (The Hon David K), "The High Court and Informed Consent: The *Bolam* Principle Abandoned" (1994) 1 Tort L. Rev. 81.

"I myself would prefer to put it this way, that he is not guilty of negligence if he has acted in accordance with a practice accepted as proper by a responsible body of medical men skilled in that particular art. I do not think there is much difference in sense. It is just a different way of expressing the same thought. Putting it the other way round, a man is not negligent, if he is acting in accordance with such a practice, merely because there is a body of opinion who would take a contrary view."[24]

An important case is *Gold v. Haringey Health Authority*.[25] The Court of Appeal held that the *Bolam* test applied to a doctor giving contraceptive advice.[26] Following an earlier House of Lords decision, *Sidaway v. Bethlem Royal Hospital*,[27] it was held that a doctor's duty was not to be dissected into parts. The test was whether the advice would have been given in the way that it was by a responsible body of medical opinion. The view has been expressed that the test in Scotland and in England are the same[28] and also that they are radically different.[29] The position is, it is submitted, that neither of these tests should be treated as statutory definitions. The use of the phrase "no professional man" cannot it is submitted be intended to mean that the case is lost if a single doctor says he too would have followed the course complained of. However, the responsible body can be rather small as in *Defreitas v. O'Brien*.[30] In this case it was argued that the practice of a small body of practitioners could not be the basis of judging a defendant's conduct—there had to be a substantial body of opinion. It was held that so long as the there was a responsible body of opinion there was no need to have a head count. It was perfectly acceptable to judge conduct by a small band of specialists.

12–9   In higher standard cases it is essential to a call an expert witness for the test cannot be applied without it. If it is not available a standard cannot be set.[31] It has been held that where an expert witness testified that the act or omission of a professional person which was alleged was something which another professional person of ordinary skill and competence would do or omit to do, then for the pursuer to succeed the evidence of the expert would have to be rejected.[32] In a case where evidence went both ways it was held the doctor's treatment had been sound and correct.[33] One matter which arises frequently is the precise application of the *Hunter* test to rank and specialisms within a profession. The medical profession is much more rigidly structured than many others such as for example solicitors. Thus the

[24] *Bolam v. Friern Hospital Management Committee* [1957] 1 W.L.R. 582 at 587.
[25] [1987] 3 W.L.R. 649.
[26] See generally A. Grubb, "Contraceptive Advice and Doctors—A Law unto Themselves?" (1988) C.L.J. 12.
[27] [1985] A.C. 871.
[28] *ibid., per* Lord Scarman.
[29] Contributed article "Medical Negligence: *Hunter v. Hanley* 35 Years On", 1990 S.L.T. 325. See also D.K. Feenan, "Medical Negligence (*Hunter v. Hanley* 35 Years On: A Reply)", 1991 S.L.T. 321.
[30] [1995] T.L.R. 86.
[31] *Muir v. Stewart*, 1938 S.L.T. 437 and compare *King v. Pollock* (1874) 2 R 42.
[32] *Philips v. Grampian Health Board (No. 2)*, 1992 S.L.T. 659; 1991 S.C.L.R. 817.
[33] *Doherty v. British Telecommunications Plc*, 1993 G.W.D. 322069.

test of the ordinary practitioner requires some refinement or else a person who intentionally consulted a very highly skilled practitioner would find it hard to succeed if that doctor met the standard of the ordinary doctor but not the standard of that segment of the profession of which he held himself out as being a member. So far as specialism is concerned a gynaecologist is expected to know more about female health than a paediatrician who in turn should know more about the health of children than the anaesthetist who should know more about anaesthesia and its effects. That vertical division is subject to a broad horizontal layering of houseman, registrar, senior registrar, consultant. Against this background the legal approach is to reflect the background in setting the standard. In *Hunter v. Magistrates of Glasgow*[34] the issue is not fully addressed but a case against a registrar was dismissed as irrelevant because a breach of the *Hunter* test had not been properly averred. There is a fuller consideration in the English case *Wilsher v. Essex Area Health Authority*.[35] It was held there that the appropriate horizontal standard was that of the office held in the hospital even if the defendant was new to the post and still training. The duty may be discharged by referring the matter to a senior colleague who adopts it.[36] One very important practical issue is how is a conflict of evidence to be dealt with. Obviously there is no conflict if one expert is not accepted as an expert or is not credible (unlikely) or is not reliable (not at all impossible). The situation arises where there is one properly qualified credible and reliable witness on each side. Normally it is a matter for the judge to decide which body of evidence is to be preferred. The matter was considered in the Outer House in *Gordon v. Wilson*[37] which was a case where it was alleged that there had been a failure to diagnose a condition as early as it should have been diagnosed. It was held that both witnesses (on opposite sides giving opposing testimony) were credible and reliable.[38] Lord Penrose decided not so much that the conflict destroyed the pursuer's case but that the existence of evidence that the defender acted in accord with the standards of the profession meant he simply could not be liable. This decision was arrived at after a consideration of leading English cases.[39] In particular the following passage from Lord Scarman's speech in *Maynard* was considered and applied:

"I have to say that a judges 'preference' for one body of distinguished professional opinion to another also professionally distinguished is not sufficient to establish negligence on a practitioner whose actions have received the seal of approval of those whose opinions, truthfully expressed, honestly held, were not preferred. If this was the real reason for the judge's finding, he erred in law even though elsewhere in his judgment he stated the law correctly."[40]

---

[34] 1969 S.L.T. (Notes) 35.
[35] [1987] Q.B. 730.
[36] *Maynard v. West Midlands Health Authority* [1984] 1 W.L.R. 634.
[37] 1992 S.L.T. 849.
[38] *ibid.* at 852.
[39] *inter alia*, Bolam, *Maynard v. West Midlands Regional Health Authority* [1985] 1 All E.R. 635 and *Sidaway v. Governors of Bethlem Royal Hospital* [1985] A.C. 871.
[40] *Maynard*, at 639, quoted by Lord Penrose in *Gordon, op cit.* at 853.

Certainly in a sense this has to be right. If *Hunter* was a relaxation or reformulation of gross negligence then a professional who acts in accord with a responsible body of opinion has not been grossly negligent. In another sense great care must be taken in excluding the judge or jury as a matter of law from considering the conduct in question. On the theory which sees the professional standard as an application of the reasonable man standard then the reasonable man can still have his say having been fully informed from the witness box as to the professional matters. If it is a distinct standard then professional evidence is, in theory, the end of the matter. However, it has long since been appreciated that the entire law of negligence is a matter of the judicial application of community standards. On that analysis it is essential that the courts, and the people through their presence on civil juries, retain the right to categorise certain conduct as negligent. It may be that what is being suggested here is no more than saying that on a factual matter which does not raise technical issues of the profession basic common sense can be brought into play. It is not impossible to conceive of a situation where a profession disappears into its own theorems and can produce bodies of responsible acknowledged experts who in truth are talking nonsense—the history of ideas is littered with examples. The only protection for the citizen is some locus to interfere on the margins. The rhetorical focus for such arguments could be through the word "responsible". It tends to be under utilised, indeed displaced, referring it seems in many of the cases to the witnesses, who inevitably will be responsible and eminent. That word does, it is submitted, allow for another debate as to whether the honestly held, credible and reliable testimony ought to be admitted.

12–10   There are authorities which allow some scope to the argument that the courts have the ability to over-rule the professions.[41] Perhaps the most helpful Scottish case is a decision of Lord Caplan in *Peach v. Chalmers & Co*[42] where there was a conflict of expert opinion in a case of surveyor's negligence. *Maynard* was cited by senior counsel as clinching the point.[43] Lord Caplan considered that it was possible to reject a strand of expert opinion if grounds existed for doing so.[44] By this it becomes clear he does not mean the kind of overarching right canvassed above but by reference to issues justiciable by the ordinary juryman or judge. The answer to the enquiry before him was not, however, simply a matter of expert opinion; the opinions as to retrospective value were purportedly based on certain facts. It is submitted all that Lord Caplan did is what any judge is entitled to do with expert evidence—that is to scrutinise it for reliability. Incidentally, the case also raises another issue on this often critical point; Lord Caplan thought it "perhaps unfortunate" that none of the calculation experts produced much documentary evidence to support views expressed.[45] This is of course a matter of balance. The whole purpose of having an

---

[41] See *G & K Ladenbrau (U.K.) Ltd v. Crawley and de Reya* [1978] 1 All E.R. 682; *Midland Bank Trust Co. Ltd v. Hett Stubbs & Kemp* [1979] Ch. 384.
[42] 1992 S.C.L.R. 423.
[43] As were *Skirt 'n' Slack Centre of London Ltd v. Brydon*, Unreported, March 14, 1986; *Phillips v. Grampian Health Board*, 1991 S.C.L.R. 817.
[44] *Peach*, at 427C.
[45] *ibid*. at 427A.

expert witness is for him to explain the matters which cannot be understood by the ordinary juryman. There is a danger that if the experts go too closely into the foundations of their opinions the judge may come up with an untutored and erroneous theory of his own.[46] It should finally be appreciated that this case is reported on quantum. The true "professional" question was whether the house had been correctly surveyed and it was not disputed that the surveyor had bungled; he had misunderstood and incorrectly described the construction of the house.[47] So while expert evidence is necessary in a professional case not all evidence in a professional case goes to liability.

In *Bolitho v. City and Hackney Health Authority*,[48] decided in the House **12–11** of Lords, despite a senior nurse conveying on a number of occasions her serious concerns about a child's treatment, no doctors came. One doctor explained this by saying that she had flat batteries in her bleeper. Eventually the child's respiratory system collapsed and during revival he suffered serious brain damage. Breach of duty was established on the failure of the senior doctor, called regularly by the nurse, to have the boy treated. It was common ground that intubation so as to provide an airway would have ensured that the respiratory failure which occurred did not lead to cardiac arrest. The judge had evidence from eight medical experts, all of them distinguished. Five of them were called for the plaintiff and they were all of the view that, at least after the second episode, any competent doctor would have intubated. On the other side, the defendants called three experts all of whom said that, on the symptoms presented by Patrick as recounted by a sister and a nurse, intubation would not have been appropriate. The judge at first instance found that one of the defenders' witnesses was very impressive although he did have a gut feeling that the plaintiff's position was right or that the defenders' position was not: "Mr Brennan also advanced a powerful argument—which I have to say, as a layman, appealed to me—to the effect that the views of the defendants' experts simply were not logical or sensible." It was held that:

> "the court is not bound to hold that a defendant doctor escapes liability for negligent treatment or diagnosis just because he leads evidence from a number of medical experts who are genuinely of opinion that the defendant's treatment or diagnosis accorded with sound medical practice . . . The use of [the following adjectives all used in important cases] responsible, reasonable and respectable all show that the court has to be satisfied that the exponents of the body of opinion relied upon can demonstrate that such opinion has a logical basis. In particular in cases involving, as they so often do, the weighing of risks against benefits, the judge before accepting a body of opinion as being responsible, reasonable or respectable, will need to be satisfied that, in forming their views, the experts have directed their minds to the question of comparative risks and benefits and have reached a defensible conclusion on the matter."[49]

---

[46] See *Kay's Tutor v. Ayrshire and Arran Health Board*, 1987 S.L.T. 577.
[47] *Peach*, at 424C.
[48] [1997] 3 W.L.R. 1151.
[49] *ibid.* at 1158–1159.

The conclusion was that "if, in a rare case, it can be demonstrated that the professional opinion is not capable of withstanding logical analysis, the judge is entitled to hold that the body of opinion is not reasonable or responsible." It may be hoped the word "defensible" in *Bolitho* is taken and expanded beyond the apparent intention of its author. It ought to be within the power of the courts in cases where they understand the essence of the conflict of expert evidence to take a position that one body however reputable is unacceptable.[50]

Finally, the pursuer must always prove the essential facts and failure to do so is fatal.[51]

Special losses

Public expectations

12–12 Economic loss is not a speciality of professional liability cases although many now require such losses to be considered. As has been discussed above, and will be further discussed later in this chapter, a case involving solicitors resulted in a plaintiff recovering a sum the plaintiff had not actually lost but which failed to accrue to him.[52] Part of the rationale of that decision was that the need for the public to have confidence in this particular skill of will production demanded compensation. This thinking could easily extend to other professions.

Lost Chances

12–13 The beneficiaries in the will cases are able to show not only that they had a chance of getting a windfall, they also show that it was inevitable that they would have done so if the testator has died. Other cases raise the issue in a less black and white fashion. The skilled person raises the expectation and perhaps engenders the reliance of others that there is a chance a certain result might follow. The doctor treating a wound does not normally do so if there is no hope at all and the solicitor should not raise an action if it is known that there is absolutely no hope of success. The architect really ought to be designing something which should not fall down. Thus most skilled persons can, by failing to exercise the appropriate degree of skill, lose a pursuer the chance of a better outcome. Similar issues arise in ordinary cases where a driver runs down a pedestrian who, had his leg not been removed, might have been in with a chance of playing football for Glasgow Rangers. This kind of case has always been valued and awarded. Thus it does not provide a problem of mensuration. It is more difficult where it is not a consequence of recognised loss wrongfully caused but is instead alleged to be the loss itself. Scots law has taken to a distinction

---

[50] Important decisions helping the Court keep some degree of control cited in support by Lord Browne-Wilkinson in *Bolitho* were: *Hucks v. Cole* [1993] 4 Med. L.R. 393 and *Edward Wong Finance Co. Ltd v. Johnson Stokes & Master* [1984] 1 A.C. 296.

[51] *Bradnock v. Liston*, 1993 S.L.T. 554: it was not shown that the damage alleged by an over forceful forceps delivery had actually happened; *Crowe v. Lothian Health Board*, 1993 G.W.D. 1171; *Morrison v. Forsyth*, 1995 S.L.T. 539, where an allegation that a call had been made and not responded to failed because there was no record of it in the practice call book.

[52] *White v. Jones* [1995] 2 A.C. 207.

between legal right cases and others. It is a workable one for core cases and intuitively satisfactory but cannot be the logical answer.[53]

Kyle v. P & J Stormonth Darling W.S.[54] is the leading modern case. It was **12–14** held by an Extra Division that even the loss of the chance to press a legal right, if it had an ascertainable value, was actionable. It was not necessary to show that the action, which it was alleged had not been raised, would have been successful. The actual blunder in this case was the failure to lodge appeal papers in a case the pursuer had lost before the sheriff and the sheriff principal. The actual appeal had been marked and legal aid granted. This case involved a consideration of two important cases on the general topic of loss of a chance, namely *Kenyon v. Bell*[55] and *Yeoman v. Ferries*.[56] The former was distinguished and the latter followed.[57] *Kenyon* was not a "legal right" case. The father of a little girl aged two-and-a-half years brought an action of reparation against a medical practitioner on the ground that he was negligent in treating an injury to the eye of the child. The pursuer averred that, on March 15, 1951 the child, then aged sixteen months, was found lying on the kitchen floor, her head resting on a broken cup with the lower lid of her left eye cut and bleeding profusely. She was taken to the casualty ward of the local hospital where she was seen by the defender who was the resident medical officer. He instructed a nurse to put drops in the child's eye and to apply powder. No further treatment was ordered and the defender stated that it was unnecessary to consult the family doctor or to return to the hospital. At the end of June 1951 the child's eye began to water and it was found that there was severe internal haemorrhage in the left eye which had a detached retina and a bulged iris. The eye was removed on July 10, 1951. The pursuer further averred that the defender failed to exercise reasonable care and ordinary professional skill when he examined the child's eye on March 15, 1951, and that as a result of the defender's negligence the child lost her eye or, alternatively lost a material chance that her eye would be saved. Lord Guthrie did allow that proof of a material loss of a chance might be enough:

"In the present case the pursuer does not require to prove with 'absolute certainty' or 'beyond reasonable doubt' that the loss of the eye was caused by the defender's failure to exercise proper care and skill. He is entitled to succeed if that is the natural and reasonable inference from the evidence. Now, the pursuer has repeatedly used the word 'material' to qualify the chance of saving the eye by proper treatment. The significance of that word can only be assessed upon a consideration of expert evidence after proof. It may be that the chance of saving the eye by proper treatment was so material that the natural and reasonable inference is that its loss was due to the absence of such treatment. In that event the pursuer would succeed. On the other hand, the evidence may show that the child's misfortune cannot be properly attributed to

---

[53] See n. 65 below.
[54] 1994 S.L.T. 4.
[55] 1953 S.C. 125.
[56] 1967 S.L.T. 332.
[57] See also *Eldin v. Campbell Middleton Burness & Dickson*, 1989 S.L.T. 122 in the Inner House.

fault on the part of the defender. As it is a matter of degree, I think that the proper course is to allow an inquiry into the averments."[58]

Yeoman, the decision of Lord Avonside followed in *Kyle*, was one where an action was time barred. It was agreed that £3000 was the maximum which would have been received and £1000 would have been a moderate award. Lord Avonside awarded that sum. This was on the basis that reasonable defenders at the time of a proper claim would have settled at this sum. In this particular case it was possible to show the case probably would not have been successful, however, at the time the defenders would not know this.[59] There has to be some measurable prospect of success in a case where it is said that a failure to appeal has lost a settlement.[60]

12-15   There is something unsatisfactory about the distinction. What is so special about a legal right? One thing is that it is not fact dependent. It does not mean that chance has to be heaped upon probability. But that might only mean that such cases are on one end of a spectrum. *Hotson*[61] is a good focus because of the 1 in 4 chance that the breach did not prevent the loss. *Hotson* was not the last word on the topic. It was not universally welcomed: "The House of Lords decision is a decision of striking analytical poverty and legal cowardice. It is remarkable for what it did *not* decide."[62] On one view it was not a loss of a chance case at all. The starting point has to be that causation can be established on balance of probabilities based on a but-for starting point. *McGhee*[63] allows for a cause to be established on the basis of the increase of risk. Another factor which in its own right is not disputed is that the courts do assess chances in two relevant situations: (1) they will award an expectancy chance[64]; (2) the chances of a person already legally recognised as injured getting better or worse will be assessed as they are, routinely, in many personal injury cases. It is when all these things are lumped together that the result can be unintended. One of the best attempts at analysis is that of Reece.[65] Phenomena are "deterministic when their past uniquely determines their future". Phenomena are "indeterministic when they have a random component".[66] She accepts this is easier to

---

[58] *ibid.* at 129. The case failed on the facts, it being found that the child would have lost her eye anyway as a result of the accident: unreported, April 9, 1954. Cited by R.H. Dickson, *Medical and Dental Negligence* (T. & T. Clark, 1997), p. 16.

[59] See also *Robertson v. Bannigan*, 1965 S.C. 20.

[60] *Haggarty v. Ross Harper & Murphy*, 1991 G.W.D. 30–1826: a decision of the Second Division but one argued by a party litigant.

[61] See para. 10–105.

[62] C. Foster, "A Plea for a Lost Chance: *Hotson* Reconsidered." (1995) N.L.J. 228, citing Lord Mackay at [1987] A.C. 750 at 786, 789 and Lord Bridge at 782–783.

[63] See para. 10–103.

[64] *Chaplin v. Hicks* [1911] 2 K.B. 786. A Scottish equivalent, being a contract case, is *Stewart v. Wright Johnston and McKenzie*, 1994 G.W.D. 22–1331 in which the solicitor failed to attend an auction as instructed; the client lost the chance to buy a property which was specially important to him. The defenders' attempt to have the case dismissed failed and proof before answer was allowed. The case later settled with a substantial payment of damages.

[65] H. Reece, "Losses of Chances in the Law" (1996) M.L.R. 188. Other academic studies of value to practitioners are J.G. Fleming, "Probabalistic Causation in Tort Law" (1989) 68 Can. Bar Rev. 661; J.G. Fleming, "Probabilistic Causation in Tort Law: A Postscript" (1991) 70 Can. Bar Rev. 136; M. Lunney, "What Price Chance?" (1995) L.S. 2.

[66] Reece, "Losses of Chances in the Law", *ibid.* at 194.

state than apply. To deal with this in a workable way she utilises the idea of a quasi-indeterministic event and a quasi-objective chance to describe non-indeterministic events which are so because of the state of human knowledge. *Barnett v. Chelsea and Kensington Hospital Management Committee*,[67] in which the plaintiff was poisoned by arsenic so effectively that the failure to treat had no effect, is a determined case. The case of a negligently lost lottery ticket is indeterministic. Reece takes the view that *Hotson* was a deterministic case, although the child was not examined it was humanly possible to have come to a decision as to whether with treatment he would have got better or not. Deterministic cases are appropriate for an all or nothing approach based on a "but-for" approach but quasi-deterministic cases are appropriate for the Court of Appeal approach of awarding the loss of the chance. Indeed Reece goes on to argue that it is questionable whether the legal system's traditional approaches are appropriate for indeterministic cases.[68] It transpires that the "chance" analysis is a response to trying to use causal concepts in indeterministic cases—"the chance of the effect is determined by prior circumstances, so that it is the chance of the event which is caused. For example, tossing a coin does not cause the coin to land heads, but it does cause the chance that the coin will land heads".[69]

The consequences of adopting this analysis is that many medical cases, which, unlike *Hotson*, are indeterministic, can and ought to be resolved by a loss of a chance approach. The legal right cases fit into the same category as misrepresentation cases. Reece cites Lord Lowry in *Spring v. Guardian Assurance Plc.*,[70]: "Once the duty of care is held to exist and the defendants negligence is proved, the plaintiff only has to show that by reason of that negligence he has lost a reasonable chance of employment . . . he does not have to prove that but-for the negligent reference, Scottish Amicable would have employed him."[71] *Kyle* has perhaps unnecessarily committed Scots law to the "but-for" test in other cases worthy of a loss of a chance approach in its desire to respect earlier authority. It does reveal the relaxed attitude that would be expected on Reece's analysis to causation in such cases:

> "If the same analysis is made of the present type of case where, as a result of his solicitor's negligence in failing to take a peremptory step timeously, a litigant or would be litigant loses the right to advance in court against a third party a claim that he would otherwise have been able to advance, the same three elements are present. The negligent act consists of the agent's neglect to take the peremptory step timeously. The loss consists of the inability to pursue the claim thereafter. The causal link between the act and the loss presents little problem in such a case."[72]

One good thing about *Yeoman* approved in *Kyle*[73] is that it allows the **12–16** pursuer to run a case for the full sum subject to a discount if it becomes treated as a loss of a chance:

---

[67] [1969] 1 Q.B. 428.
[68] Reece, *op. cit.*, at p. 205.
[69] *ibid.* at p. 206.
[70] [1994] 3 W.L.R. 354.
[71] *ibid.* at 375–376. Quoted in Reece, *op. cit.*, at p. 203.
[72] Reece, *op. cit.*, p. 206.
[73] *ibid.* at 193.

"I have also come to the view that the averments of damage, which are not expressed in terms of a valuation of lost opportunity, but appear to assume loss of an appeal which would have succeeded, are nonetheless sufficient to justify going to proof, even although a substantial discount might be appropriate if the only real prospect of success were held to lie in some not particularly favourable settlement."[74]

12–17 The next major Scots case will no doubt review authority from England. Among these *Stovold v. Barlows*[75] decided in the Court of Appeal will be of special interest. The plaintiff bought a house on bridging. He had to sell quickly. His solicitors, the defendants, sent the critical documents to the wrong firm by DX. The correct firm were not in the DX and so they did not get the papers in time. The purchaser withdrew. The house was sold for a lower price. While at first instance he was awarded the whole difference, on appeal, he was given half on the basis that the potential purchaser might not have purchased.[76] The decision of the First Division in *MacKenzie v. Middleton Ross & Arnot*[77] shows a very careful examination of the actual valuation of a lost chance of action where again an action became time barred. It is unusual that the evidence required is supplied by the judges, having themselves obviously been counsel in such cases in times gone by. That position, although efficient and cheap, is unsatisfactory. The evidence must be on record in the transcript so that a fair hearing can be held on appeal. In this case the opinion of the whole court was given by only one of their Lordships and so it cannot be known what the range of opinion was. It is notable too that they did not agree with either side's own views. Neither are all claims settled by advocates. An experienced defender's solicitor will have perhaps more experience of settling claims. Balancing that, the judges are not keen to hear arguments that their assessment of success is invalid:

"I consider that a judge in a case of this kind, having heard the evidence available to him, is entitled to draw on his own experience in a field in which the probabilities are open to decision and practice with knowledge. The purported application of narrow limits of legalistic rectitude to preserve a solicitor from the consequences of his admitted negligence is at once distasteful in suggestion and unjust in result."[78]

LEGAL PRACTICE

Solicitors

12–18 It should perhaps first be appreciated that the modern solicitor is a creature of statute highly trained and highly regulated. Lawyers in Scotland's past have been regulated and trained in many different ways at different times. Cases should be read in that context. Even as this is written the role of the

---

[74] *ibid.* at 268.
[75] [1995] N.L.J. 1649.
[76] See also *First Interstate Bank of California v. Cohen Arnold & Co.* [1995] T.L.R. 664.
[77] 1983 S.L.T. 286.
[78] *Yeoman v. Ferries*, 1967 S.C. 255 at 264, *per* Lord Avonside.

solicitor, the expectations of their clients and the harms they might cause are changing. Nothing below should be seen as fixing a particular duty—that will always depend of the facts and circumstances of the particular case and the care taken by practitioners at the time of the breach (and, it must now be added, the legitimate expectations of clients at the time of the breach).

Duty

The basis of liability is that set out in *Hedley Byrne*. There are dicta in **12–19** *Robertson v. Fleming*[79] that suggest a solicitor cannot be liable to a person who is not his client. It can be said, with justification, to be obiter because in the case the solicitor was held liable but on the basis of *ius quaesitum tertio*—that was the *ratio decidendi*. Another and, it is submitted correct, view is that there was only reference to *ius quaesitum tertio* because it was considered that the law was that a solicitor could not be liable to a person other than his client in delict. Certainly the Inner House of the Court of Session read the case in this way. In *Tully v. Ingram*[80] Lord President Robertson said:

"The liability sought to be established is the liability of a law-agent, and that liability must arise out of a contract of employment. Now, the first question is, who is the person who employed the law-agent, and from whom did the law-agent accept the employment?"[81]

In *Tully* the Lord Ordinary (Kyllachy) had allowed the action, elegantly subject to a reduction for the solicitor's charges had they done what was required. Lord McLaren said:

"The criterion of liability as laid down by, I think, all the noble Lords who took part in the decision of *Robertson v. Fleming* was this, that in order that a person taking a benefit should have a right of action founded on professional negligence he must be able to show that the agent was employed by him or with his authority. In order to make an agent responsible, it is not enough that as between the donor and the donee there should be an assent to employment. It is necessary to show that he was actually employed on the authority of the donee".[82]

The important questions just now are: (1) whether the solicitor-protecting rule in *Robertson* exists; (2) whether it applies until it is inevitably overruled at the first opportunity; or (3) it stands at least in Scots law.

The recent authority is as follows. In *Midland Bank Plc v. Cameron Thom* **12–20** *Peterkin and Duncans*[83] it was said that to establish liability:

"(1) the solicitor must have assumed responsibility for the advice or information given to the third party; (2) the solicitor, expressly or

---

[79] (1861) 4 Macq. 167.
[80] (1981) 19 R. 65.
[81] *ibid*. at 71.
[82] *ibid*. at 76–77. See also *Auchinloss v. Duncan* (1864) 21 R. 1091.
[83] 1988 S.L.T. 611.

impliedly, must have let the third party know he claimed, by reason of his skill or profession, the requisite skill or knowledge to have given the advice or information; (3) the third party must have relied on the advice or information as a matter for which the solicitor had assumed personal responsibility; and (4) the solicitor must have been aware that the third party was likely to rely on that advice or information".[84]

This is an application of *Hedley Byrne*. That would be to treat any *Robertson* rule as not applicable. However, it is to be noted that *Robertson* is not cited nor discussed and it was a matter of concession that "situations can arise in which a solicitor owes a duty not only to his client but to a third party who relies upon what that solicitor tells him".[85] *Midland Bank* was relied on for that proposition in a rare case in which a claim of professional negligence against an advocate was not struck out.[86] However, the *Hedley Byrne* line did have to contend with the older authority and in *Weir v. J.M. Hodge*[87] it was held, in obedience to *Robertson* that a solicitor who makes a mistake drawing a will depriving beneficiaries of money, owed no duty to the beneficiaries.[88] In *Bolton v. Jameson & MacKay*[89] it was accepted that a solicitor can, if there are sufficient averments, be liable to a third party like a wife providing a close and direct relationship of proximity can be established.

12–21   A 3–2 decision of the House of Lords in *White v. Jones*[90] established for England that a solicitor owes a duty of care to a disappointed beneficiary where the solicitor negligently carries out the client testator's instructions, to prepare a fresh will benefiting the plaintiff. The main difficulty, which nearly had Lord Nolan voting in the other direction, is the asymmetry of the case: the beneficiaries took under the old will, the effect of the case economically is not the usual one of making a defendant pay for a loss of the plaintiff. In this case the loss is of an expectation, something normally protected by contract. The original beneficiaries take the testator's money and the plaintiffs take the solicitor's insurers' money. Thus there is no restoration of the status quo ante because those who benefited from the negligence keep their gain. Lord Mustill was nearly tempted by the facts of the case to allow recovery, but as the case had been argued on general duties he did not. There had been a meeting convened by the testator when he told the soon to be plaintiffs of his intentions and told one to phone the solicitor to make the change and so solicitor and client both knew that the contract for legal services was to benefit third parties. Mustill's argument that the principle would apply outside wills seems very strong, the only ground for distinction being the unconvincing one that it is in the public interest that solicitors prepare wills.[91]

---

[84] *ibid.* at 612.
[85] *ibid.* at 616.
[86] *Connolly-Martin v. D.* [1998] T.L.R. 507. See 12–30 below.
[87] 1990 S.L.T. 266.
[88] The same view was taken by Lord Cameron in *MacDougall v. Clydesdale Bank Trustees*, 1993 S.C.L.R. 832, following *Robertson*.
[89] 1989 S.L.T. 222.
[90] [1995] 2 A.C. 207.
[91] *White v. Jones* [1995] 2 A.C. 207.

Breach

In the first instance and in many cases the question of what ought to have **12–22** been done is answered by the law of contract express or implied. While there may be many cases where it hardly matters whether the case is founded on contract or delict it may well be much easier in common contracts to imply obligations of care, perhaps much higher than would be set by the law of delict.[92] Solatium, usually associated with delictual claims can be recovered in contractual cases, although strictly that ought to be on the basis that the contract involves some degree of peace of mind being given.[93] The standard a solicitor must reach under the law of delict will, as in any other case, be a matter of evidence from those who know what this is—presumably experienced solicitors in the appropriate area of activity. This will vary from time to time depending on the ability of the general body of lawyers and the expectations engendered by them.[94] It was possible for Guthrie Smith once to say:

> "A solicitor consulted by a client does not guarantee that the opinion which he may give, either on point of law or as regards the proper mode of procedure, shall turn out correct, he is only bound to advise to the best of his judgement; and if he go astray, the fact does not infer negligence, unless the advice tendered, or the course followed, was so grossly erroneous, as to be altogether inexcusable in any ordinary well-informed member of the profession."[95]

This statement and the cases upon which it is based predates the *Hunter v. Hanley* disregard of gross negligence and the abandonment of general practice as a defence. But old cases like *Rowland v. Stevenson*,[96] would be decided in the same way in that the issue is deviation from general practice coupled with an inability to show that any other practitioner of ordinary skill exercising ordinary care would proceed in the same way. Until recently, unlike medicine, all solicitors really held themselves out as being of ordinary skill or being the ordinary practitioner, although there would always be some individuals and some firms with a specialist reputation, to which the registrar/consultant arguments from medicine would apply. Now solicitors are allowed to apply for and advertise specialities and if they do they will have to reach a higher standard and be judged by the standards of others in the speciality.

Interpretation of the Law

Frame v. Campbell[97] laid down an important point. A solicitor was **12–23** instructed to take out a private prosecution. He raised it under the wrong section of an Act. The magistrate did not notice nor did the sheriff-

---

[92] A collection and discussion of the facts establishing contractual cases can be found in Rennie, *Solicitors Negligence* (Butterworths, 1997). Some examples can be seen in *Hopkinson v. Williams*, 1993 S.L.T. 907; *Glasper v. Rodger*, 1996 S.L.T. 44; *McLennan v. Warner*, 1996 S.L.T. 1349.

[93] *McAllister Hall v. Anderson Shaw & Gilbert*, 1995 G.W.D. 25–1334.

[94] For a then current review of cases and a statement of the practitioner author's own views on many issues see R. Rennie, *Solicitor's Negligence* (Butterworths, 1997).

[95] *ibid.* at p. 46.

[96] (1827) 5 S. 838 (affirmed 4 W. & S. 177).

[97] (1836) 14 S. 914.

substitute. The accused were ultimately acquitted and sued the solicitor's
employer for damages for wrongful imprisonment. The employers claimed
relief from the lawyers. They were successful. It is a case by a client direct
and did not raise *Robertson* problems. The Lord Justice Clerk (Boyle) held
that a solicitor had to exercise ordinary skill when carrying out an ordinary
matter. It might have been different if the point had been a nice or a fine
one. Lord Meadowbank thought the monopoly right of appearance important and the protection of the lieges from want of skill.[98] He did however
express himself in terms of the gross negligence test abandoned in *Hunter*
but which does rather express the difference between this kind of case and
the "nice" point type of case. Applying that test Lord Meadowbank found
himself in a 3–1 minority by considering that notwithstanding the monopoly
the matter was not that obvious having fooled not only the judges but the
defence as well! Obviously standards of education have increased but so too
has the complexity of the law and the pressure of business. The *Hunter* test
now serves the lawyer and the law is still that an error of judgement in
relation to a legal point upon which there can be a difference of view will
not found liability.

Litigation and Contentious Work

12–24 *Batchelor v. Pattison and Mackersy*[99] is authority for saying that in the
conduct of a litigation where counsel is instructed, the other solicitor
cannot be liable for following counsel's conduct, the power to handle the
case in bona fide falling into the hands of counsel.

It also seems to be generally accepted that the advocate or barrister's
immunity should extend to solicitors carrying out advocacy. So a solicitor
may be immune for not asking a witness a question, but not immune for
failing to precognosce a witness. The lost chance cases discussed above are
good examples of these cases.[1] There can be a duty owed to the opposition
in rare cases.[2]

In Chambers

12–25 Different practical points arise in relation to chambers practice like
conveyancing and security work. Where a person is buying (as is normally
the case) a good and marketable title, the solicitor is under an obligation to
check that is what has been paid for. This seems to have been established at
a proof before answer in the sheriff court in *Haberstitch v. McCormick and
Nicholson*.[3] In the same way when investing money any title involved must
be properly searched against; it is not enough when instructed to draw
necessary papers to simply prepare the necessary deeds.[4] When arranging a
security the basic duty is simply to do the appropriate conveyancing and not
to value the security.[5] On the other hand it may be the case that the

---

[98] A theme apparent in *White v. Jones* [1995] 2 A.C. 207.

[99] (1876) 3 R. 914.

[1] See para. 12–13 above.

[2] See 12–20 above.

[3] 1975 S.L.T. 181. (The report of the Inner House decision on damages).

[4] *Graham v. Hunter's Trs* (1831) 9 S. 543; *Campbell v. Clason* (1838) 1 D. 270. Both cases
offer interesting discussions of the quantification of damages.

[5] *Midland Bank v. Cameron Thom Peterkins and Duncans*, 1988 S.C.L.R. 209; *Ronaldson v.
Drummond & Reid* (1881) 8 R. 956; *Stewart v. McClure Naismith, Brodie & MacFarlane* (1886)
13 R. 1062; (1887) 15 R. (H.L.) 1.

solicitor, in his "man of business guise" goes further.[6] *Stirling v. Mackenzie, Gardner & Alexander*[7] is clear authority that where instructions are received to invest money in a heritable security, then the duty is indeed to take care that the security is financially as well as legally sufficient. However, such was the respect for law-agents at that time that Lord Young and the Lord Justice Clerk (Moncreiff) could not, despite serious reservations, find the agents liable without the matter being very clear and so concurred with Lord Rutherford-Clark who set out in detail why in particular circumstances the security, although lent to another client, was sufficient. Many cases are essentially contract cases where what is in issue is the proper interpretation of the instructions given.[8] In *Brady v. Neilsons*[9] a proof before answer was allowed in a case where the solicitor allegedly acted for both parties in a loan transaction. The facts had to be heard to decide whether the inference could be made that the solicitor was actually acting for both parties. In *Summit Financial Group Ltd. v. Slaughter & May*[10] it was held that where an agreement is prepared by two different departments someone should have an overview to take care that the document achieves its purpose. In *Watson v. Bogue (No.2)*[11] the pursuer failed comprehensively on the facts but Sheriff Macphail was of the opinion that the case would have failed for lack of proof of instructions which would have obliged the solicitors.[12]

The failure to prepare a will could easily never come to court, the client **12–26** being beyond the reach of courts. The testator may of course have threatened his relatives with disinheritance and so there will be some hearsay evidence of the possible existence of a will. In England solicitors have been held liable where they had heard the essence of a will from a person who was an intended testator and they might reasonably have been aware that there was a degree of urgency as a result of health.[13] Two beneficiaries deprived of their expectancies under the wills were able to recover. The basis of liability in such cases is probably an expansion of the well-known *Hedley Byrne* liability.[14]

---

[6] Detailed professional rules promulgated in recent years mean that the facts of a case like *Oastler v. Dill, Smillie & Wilson* (1886) 14 R. 12 are unlikely to be seen again. Money given in for investment was placed as a second charge instead of a first charge at a poor return and lent to the solicitor's relative for whom he also acted.

[7] (1886) 14 R. 170.

[8] In *Bank of East Asia Ltd v. Shepherd & Wedderburn*, 1995 S.C. 255; 1995 S.L.T. 1074; 1995 S.C.L.R. 598. On the basis that it could not be said that the pursuers would necessarily fail at proof, an Extra Division upheld an allowance of proof before answer in a case of alleged negligence. The core of the case was that the pursuers alleged that they should have been advised that certain sums would have been obtained in full and not under deduction of retentions and that the instructions given were such that advice was required.

[9] 1999 G.W.D. 4–209.

[10] [1999] T.L.R. 273.

[11] 1998 G.W.D. 1827.

[12] See also *Leeds & Holbeck Building Society v. Alex Morison & Co.*, 1999 G.W.D. 9–434.

[13] *Smith v. Claremont Haynes & Co.* [1991] T.L.R. 409.

[14] See the discussion at para. 12–19 above. See generally, J. Blaikie, "The Dilatory Solicitor and the Disappointed Legatee" 1993 S.L.T. (News) 329; J. Blaikie, "Professional Negligence: The Dilatory Solicitor and the Disappointed Legatee (1996) S.L.P.Q. 245; J. Blaikie, "Negligent Solicitors and Disappointed Beneficiaries" 1989 S.L.T. (News) 317.

12–27   Conflicts of interest are now so closely regulated by professional rules that losses caused by such action are unlikely to found litigations, but in the absence of professional disciplinary measures such action may in certain circumstances constitute negligence.[15]

12–28   *Bolton v. Jameson & MacKay*[16] dealt with an important point which has arisen in other jurisdictions about the extent to which a person's solicitor owes a duty to some other person. Solicitors acting for a husband drew up a minute of agreement under which the husband promised not to sell the matrimonial home without his wife's consent and undertook to pay her half the proceeds. He later, after divorce, sold the house and vanished with the proceeds. The case based on negligence failed for lack of sufficient averment in the Inner House. There was insufficient proximity it was said in a brief opinion of the court written at the defender's request because the Outer House decision had been reported and an article had appeared on it in the *Scots Law Times*. The particular knowledge of these solicitors might have been sufficient to support a duty of care case differently pled. There would of course be no duty on a different firm of solicitors to have detected the previous minute. The court made the important point that even if there had been a breach of duty it might have been impossible to establish "but-for" causation as the husband would probably have managed to carry out his unethical plot by going to another firm. While lawyers have professional duties to their profession colleagues, in England it has been held that there is no duty owed by one side of solicitors to another in a conveyancing transaction. There had been an erroneous declaration but that had been on the client's behalf.[17] The answer was "not to the seller's knowledge". The fact that the representation was on behalf of another was not enough in itself to negative a duty of care.[18] It was not however, fair, just and reasonable to impose a duty in the context of conveyancing. Duties to other third parties have been discussed above.[19] The loss of a chance issue[20] can arise in conveyancing.[21] In *National Home Loans v. Giffen Couch & Archer*[22] the Court of Appeal held that solicitors who acted for a borrower and the plaintiff lenders were not liable for not disclosing that the borrower had arrears on his existing mortgage. The case turned as most must on the terms of the instructions given by the lenders.[23] In *The Mortgage Corporation v. Mitchells Roberton & Franchi Wright*[24] the pursuers lent money to a borrower who spent it all and from whom it could not be recovered. They

---

[15] *Stewart v. McClure, Naismith, Brodie & MacFarlane* (1886) 13 R. 1062; (1887) 15 R. (H.L.) 1; *Ronaldson v. Drummond & Reid* (1881) 8 R. 956; *Wernham v. McLean Baird & Nelson*, 1925 S.L.T. 266. It does not do so automatically: *Oastler v. Dill, Smille & Wilson* (1886) 14 R. 12.

[16] 1989 S.L.T. 222.

[17] *Gran Gelato Ltd v. Richcliff (Group) Ltd* [1991] T.L.R. 594.

[18] *ibid.*, under reference to *Smith v. Eric S. Bush* [1990] 1 A.C. 831.

[19] See paras 12–22, 12–32.

[20] See para. 12–13 above.

[21] See *e.g.* H. Wilkinson, "The Loss of a Chance in Conveyancing Transactions" (1996) 146 N.L.J. 88.

[22] [1997] T.L.R. 498.

[23] This case was not like *Mortgage Express v. Bowerman* [1996] 2 All E.R. 836, where the problem with the debtor turned up in the course of the transaction. See generally R. Rennie, "Negligence and the Duty to Disclose—A Turning of the Tide?" (1997) J.L.S. 405; R. Rennie, "Negligence Instructions and the Lender's need to Know", (1994) J.L.S. 135.

[24] 1997 S.L.T. 1305.

sued the first defenders who had been instructed by them to advance the money only on receipt of a first ranked security, *inter alia*, for negligence. They agreed the case could go to proof before answer. The second defenders argued they owed no duty of care. It was held that in the facts and circumstances the borrowers' agents, knowing the basis on which the money was advanced, were brought within proximity; and proof before answer was allowed.[25]

Evidence

It is probably essential that evidence of practice be led on the basis of a **12–29** record averring practice. Where a recognised specialism exists the evidence would best come from a solicitor registered in that speciality. However, that evidence must in all the circumstances be relevant and not unnecessary because of the nature of the case.[26] It must also be appreciated that in some areas of work the client's reliance on the solicitor comes very close to insurance, *i.e.* where an action is to be raised on time or a title prepared.

Advocates

If the function and tasks of the solicitor have changed considerably over the **12–30** century, the Bar has changed hardly at all. Thus old authorities hardly need to be reviewed for changing conditions. There is a tradition in the United Kingdom that members of the bar cannot be liable for their negligence. So far as England is concerned that matter is now clearly settled and easily understood, whatever view one may take of the position. In *Rondel v. Worsley*[27] it was established beyond doubt that a barrister is not liable in respect of advocacy. The justifications are various. Public policy demands that cases should not be reheard—something that would often be required to show what would have happened "but for" the neglect of the case. Barristers ought to be able to carry out their duties fearlessly without worrying about themselves. Because barristers are compelled to take clients it is unfair that they can be sued by them afterwards. It is submitted only the first has any significant merit. All good and able professional men work better if they are free from suit as it makes taking difficult decisions solely on the merits easier. However, the legal system has been through all of this with doctors. The *Hunter* test,[28] which would apply to barristers if they were liable, allows a very considerable scope for the exercise of judgement and essentially prevents an error of judgement creating liability providing some other responsible advocates would have done the same thing.[29] The rationale of *Rondel* was reinforced in the later case of *Saif Ali v. Sydney Mitchell & Co.*,[30] where it was held that a barrister could be liable for work outside of court, in this case by letting time-limits go past and leaving the

---

[25] See also *Cheltenham & Gloucester Building Society v. Mackin*, 1997 G.W.D. 32–1645.
[26] *Central Govan Housing Association Ltd v. R. Maguire Cook & Co.*, 1988 S.L.T. 386.
[27] [1969] 1 A.C. 191.
[28] See para. 12–8 above.
[29] Thus the commonly encountered difficult decision of deciding not to call the accused would not attract liability unless the Crown case were based on some statutory presumption requiring the leading of no evidence.
[30] [1978] 3 All E.R. 1033.

plaintiff with no one to sue. There was no intimate connection with the court work itself and thus the three grounds for the immunity did not apply.[31] The barrister's immunity was yet again confirmed in *Kelley v. Corston*.[32] In this case the plaintiff complained of a settlement in court. The judge started from the position that generally settlement of litigation was not covered by the immunity but it was in cases where the settlement needed active participation by the judge to approve it. Door of the court settlements were also held to be within the immunity. In *Atwell v. Perry & Co.*[33] it was held that counsel's ignorance of authority which precluded him from taking an unanswerable defence and calling witnesses was protected by the barrister's immunity. A decision not to appeal would not be so protected. In the more curious and unusual case of *Connolly-Martin v. D.*[34] it was held that the barrister's immunity did not extend to a case where a barrister gave an undertaking he was not instructed to give and then inexplicably told a party that they were no longer bound by it.

12–31   *Batchelor v. Pattison and Mackersy*[35] was a claim by the pursuer that he sustained through the wilfulness, maliciousness, gross negligence, systematic disregard of instructions, and ill-guided recklessness, or one or other of them, on the part of the defender, Mackersy as agent, and the other defender employed by him as counsel, or one or other of them, in their management or conduct of an action in the Court of Session.[36] Lord President Inglis set out the principles applicable. The case could not be one of contract because an advocate acts by vocation.[37] He also must normally accept instructions.[38] Counsel has full power to do as he wishes with the case unless fired and so long as he acts in bona fide.[39] Although it was noted that even in the nineteenth century this power was not often exercised through "considerations of propriety and expediency".[40]

12–32   The Bar now provide services to others with the right to instruct. Those persons not being solicitors trained in the law the full responsibility for every aspect of the case must fall on counsel as opposed to the instructing surveyor (or other authorised instructing professional). A professional rule that the basis of instruction between the solicitor and advocate should be in writing would be of assistance to everyone. No doubt in due course the Bar's indemnity insurers will speak to the Law Society's indemnity insurers to insist upon this as a matter of risk management. Developments in the criminal law at the time of writing have opened to some extent the issue of the responsibility of the Bar. It has been held that defective representation of an accused person can be a mode of establishing a miscarriage of justice.[41] These rules bring about the result that those conducting a case will

---

[31] The two Scottish Law Lords dissented on this point, preferring that there be a blanket immunity for all.

[32] [1997] T.L.R. 466.

[33] [1998] T.L.R. 479.

[34] [1998] T.L.R. 507.

[35] (1876) 3 R. 914.

[36] *ibid.* at 914.

[37] This means nothing at the time of writing. We are all workers now.

[38] This is still the case in theory.

[39] *Batchelor, ibid.* at 918.

[40] *ibid.*

[41] *Anderson v. H.M. Advocate*, 1996 S.L.T. 155.

look over their shoulder to "play safe" to avoid an appeal. If they are so doing then one of the policy reasons for the immunity is lost. The criminal appeal also has to retry the case to a considerable extent and so another justification is lost. It may not be too long until all proceedings are recorded on sound or sound and vision. When that happens it is much easier to review the conduct of a case. The advocates' immunity, it is submitted, cannot last much longer. The present position whereby a solicitor who in the middle of a multi-million pound MBO, in the middle of the night, wrongly deletes a critical warranty is liable but an advocate who fails to call a critical witness in a £5000 reparation proof, after years of preparation, is not, is untenable.

Solicitor Advocates

Members of the Law Society of Scotland: solicitors who have satisfied the **12–33** requirements of the legislation may appear in courts where heretofore advocates have had exclusive rights of audience. Solicitor advocates remain solicitors and are not members of the Faculty of Advocates. On the basic principles outlined at the start of this chapter they will be liable, when exercising rights of audience, to the standard of the advocate in that court. It is in any event the only applicable standard because if solicitors cannot appear there can be no standard of solicitor-appearing-in the Inner House. The interesting point would be if it were sought to hold the solicitor advocate to higher standard in a sheriff court case. However, it seems to be generally accepted that solicitors acting as advocates have the advocates' immunity and so these issues will not often arise.

Licensed Conveyancers and Paralegals

For business reasons it has been thought useful to have a cadre of staff who **12–34** are trained and knowledgable in the law; these are paralegals. For economic and political reasons it has been thought appropriate to have a cadre of individuals who are sufficiently trained and knowledgable in the law to do conveyancing; these are licensed conveyancers. The paralegals in this jurisdiction at the time of writing do not display sufficient indiciae of professionalism to be involved in *Hunter*-like liability although obviously their employer will be liable to the extent the paralegal has been held out.

MEDICAL PRACTICE[42]

This ancient and learned profession has developed over the years from a **12–35** time when it could barely offer any foreseeable outcome. Since it has been able to offer reliably repeatable outcomes, expectations have risen as has disappointment.[43] There is a complication with medical cases because

---

[42] See generally Lord Justice Otton, "Damages for Medical Negligence and Personal Injury: An Overview" [1998] J.P.I.L. 99, J. Peysner, "Health Care Litigation: Examination, Diagnosis and Prognosis" [1995] J.P.I.L. 91.

[43] Claims rose fourfold between 1987–1995: R.H. Dickson, *Medical and Dental Negligence* (T & T Clark, 1997), p. 5 citing defence society records.

doctors often treat by way of physical interference with the person. This raises the possibility of a delictual claim for assault[44] rather than upon negligence with which this chapter is principally concerned. The attempt to use the need for consent to be informed as a way of controlling medical practice without the law of negligence has not succeeded in the United Kingdom.[45] In a case of assault the taking of reasonable care or appropriate care is strictly irrelevant as a defence. Contractual arrangements can of course impose a higher duty as where a private clinic chooses to guarantee a sterilisation operation. The absence of a contract is of course irrelevant and interestingly so it was held even before *Donoghue*.[46]

Warning of Risks

12–36 A doctor has a duty in appropriate circumstances to warn of risks.[47] In *Goorkani v. Tayside Health Board*,[48] the pursuer became infertile through a course of drug treatment. The drug treatment was to save the sight of the pursuer's one remaining effective eye. It was successful, however, the pursuer claimed he should have been warned of the risk or the availability of sperm banking. It was held that there was no fault in not offering sperm banking as that was not officially available at the hospital but the patient should have been told of the risk. This was a case not of normal practice but of the exercise of knowledge that the doctor did in fact possess.[49] However, the court found that the pursuer if he had been warned would have accepted the risk to save his sight.[50] Thus damages were awarded for the distress in discovering by surprise the infertility. In another case a girl had elective cosmetic surgery involving serious procedures with a 10 per cent risk of death. The result was she said considerable mental distress and much pain and suffering. It was held that the warnings given to her parents were sufficient on the evidence and no fuller advice would have made any difference.[51] In another cosmetic plastic surgery case a woman complained that she had not been told properly of the risks of failure of the various operations. It was held that the risks of matters not turning out to be as expected had been advised and a consent form signed.[52] *Cameron v. Greater Glasgow Health Board*[53] is a case where the pursuer became pregnant after a sterilisation operation.[54] The case would have failed on causation but it is interesting to note that the negligence approach to such cases allowed the Lord Ordinary to say that it was for the pursuer to prove that she had not been warned. That seems very harsh as it requires proof of a negative. On the other hand that statement is against the background that the three

---

[44] See Chap. 4.
[45] See Chap. 4 and see generally K. Norrie, "Informed Consent and Duty of Care", 1985 S.L.T. (News) 289.
[46] *Edgar v. Lamont*, 1914 S.C. 277.
[47] See *Moyes v. Lothian Health Board*, 1990 S.L.T. 444, discussed in Chap. 4.
[48] 1991 S.L.T. 94.
[49] *ibid.* at 95F.
[50] *ibid.* at 95.
[51] *Comber v. Greater Glasgow Health Board (No. 2)*, 1992 S.L.T. 22; 1991 S.C.L.R. 904.
[52] *Hsuing v. Webster*, 1992 S.L.T. 1071. This case also proceeded on breach of contact.
[53] 1993 G.W.D. 6–433.
[54] See generally on sterilisation cases, L. Sutherland, "Failed Sterilisation" (1995) Rep.B. 3–5.

doctors who gave evidence spoke to a usual practice they had at the time of giving a warning—against that it might be acceptable to make such a finding. Further support for the actual decision comes from the finding that the pursuer herself had a hazy recollection and was therefore probably unable to expressly deny that she had been warned in which case the onus may have shifted back.

Failure to Diagnose or to Treat or Treat Properly

A failure to diagnose or treat properly can be fault subject to the *Hunter* **12–37** test.[55] *Fisher v. McKenzie*[56] represents one of the relatively rare cases in the courts where a doctor has been held to have failed the *Hunter* test. The doctor failed to diagnose serious dehydration. The child patient died. The cause of the illness was rare but the symptoms together with the history of vomiting were sufficient to suggest treatment had been necessary. Another case of liability is *McDonald v. Lothian Health Board*[57] in which a doctor was held to have failed to meet the standard in relation to a biopsy on a maxillary sinus. In another case a man was diagnosed by a hospital as suffering from sub-arachnoid haemorrhage and sent to a neurosurgeon at a different hospital who discharged him. The man died. This looks like a very strong case, but it was held that medicine was not exact and on the evidence other surgeons would have taken the same steps and no others. A test which would have revealed the condition was not in use at the time. And, following ordinary principles the fact that the doctor later wrote to the G.P. that he regretted the error of judgement was discounted as self-flagellation.[58] Where a woman had her uterus torn during an abortion it was accepted that in this case it was understandable that the doctor had not known precisely where the uterus was and an earlier examination would not have necessarily revealed this potential problem.[59] Many cases fail on the facts.[60]

Causation

Causation is often difficult in negligence cases.[61] Thus where a women **12–38** suffered a non-haemorrhagic stroke a week after being prescribed a low dose contraceptive pill, it was held on evidence mainly from medical

---

[55] Apparently dull matters can attract liability, see generally W.S. Scott, *"Rhodes v. Spokes and Farbridge*: G.P. Referral Letters and the Negligent Omission of Information" [1997] J.P.I.L. 274.

[56] 1994 G.W.D. 30–1823.

[57] 1995 S.L.T. 1033; 1995 S.C.L.R. 412.

[58] *Stuart v. Grampian Health Board*, 1993 G.W.D. 11–773.

[59] *Fulton v. Lothian Health Board*, 1993 G.W.D. 6–432.

[60] See, *e.g. Farrer v. Lothian Health Board*, 1999 G.W.D. 14–653 where the pursuer failed on a conflict of medical expert testimony and in any event it was held that even if the correct diagnosis had been made it was not established that it could have been successfully repaired; *Johnston v. Ayrshire and Arran Health Board*, 1998 G.W.D. 40–2078, where a case complaining of negligent conduct of an operation failed.

[61] See Chap. 10. See also J.G. Logie, "Proof of Causation in Medical Negligence Cases", 1988 S.L.T. (News) 25; A.F. Phillips, "Further Reflections on Medical Causation", 1988 S.L.T. (News) 325; A.F. Phillips, "Medical Negligence and No-Fault Compensation", 1989 J.L.S. 239; E. Russell, "Establishing Medical Negligence—A Herculean Task", 1998 S.L.T. (News) 17. Matters are not helped by the problems faced by poor pursuers, see generally D. Sandison, "Medical Negligence Claims: The Paucity of Funding", 1995 J.L.S. 309. The new private legal insurers charge higher premiums for medical negligence cases.

journals that the cause was cryptogenic.[62] Equally difficult are cases where the breach of duty has cause the patient to lose the chance of a cure or to recover.

Defences

12–39 The general defences apply and limitation will often be a problem for pursuers who may experience a minor problem and not seek treatment which then becomes more serious. The present formulation of the law seems to allow plenty of scope to allow persons who attend their doctor when symptoms appear to maintain their actions.[63] Stoical persons who do not want to trouble their doctor may fare less well. The difficulty with medical negligence cases as opposed to building cases is that the relationship is based on trust and it may seem unpleasant for a patient to complain to his own doctor about the doctor himself.

Civil Jury Trial

12–40 While civil jury trial remains, medical cases often generate argument as to whether trial or proof is the appropriate mode of enquiry. In a consumer oriented, anti-professional, complaining culture, defenders may well prefer the dispassionate logic of a judge but many of the issues raised in medical cases are no more difficult than many others—the *Hunter* test was developed in the context of the appropriate charge to a jury. Many potential jurors will still have a high opinion of their own doctor and perhaps doctors in general. They may still feel that the doctor for all his modern appearance as a kind of scientist is yet a kind of benign magician. Issues can usually be easily framed. It is where inferences may have to be made that the jury becomes less suitable.[64]

SURVEYORS

12–41 Surveyors have been around for a long time and liability on their part is known as long ago as Grotius.[65] Modern liability based on *Hedley Byrne* was placed upon a surveyor who had in the usual way been instructed by the lender and not the potential purchaser in the Scottish courts.[66] Surveyors' liability is notable among the others considered in this chapter in that there

---

[62] *Ingram v. Ritchie*, 1989 G.W.D. 27–1217.

[63] See, *e.g. Philips v. Grampian Health Board (No. 2)*, 1992 S.L.T. 659; 1991 S.C.L.R. 817.

[64] *Miller v. Lanarkshire Health Board*, 1993 S.L.T. 453.

[65] Cited Wilkinson and Forte at p. 5. However, it was only recently that property owners found themselves having to pay for the services of surveyors albeit not having any contractual relationship with them. The building societies were compelled (and the banks preferred) to have some assurance that the money advanced was indeed secured by realisable heritage. They thus engaged surveyors but charged their potential lenders for this outlay. Thus the last quarter of the 20th century has seen a number of cases in Scotland and even more in the U.K. The most notable is *Martin v. Bell Ingram*, 1986 S.L.T. 575.

[66] *Martin, ibid.* English law reached this conclusion earlier in *Yianni v. Edwin Evans & Sons* [1982] Q.B 438. See generally for the background at that time: C. Slater, "House Valuations and Surveys", 1988 J.L.S. 89.

is a serious attempt to control liability not by the blunderbuss of potentially ineffective disclaimers[67] but by the clear and fair way of specifying the liability which is being assumed and thus the reliance that should be made—the delictual obligation itself is shaped. Thus most surveyors now specify different levels of survey and undertake to do an amount of work depending on the level. This setting out of the obligation intended to be assumed has already been the subject of decision in England.[68] The essence of these cases is respect for the task undertaken—the evidence in the cases indicates that level 1 survey take about half an hour, every avenue does not have to be investigated unless to the practised eye it would show the risk of trouble. If there are reasons to spend more time then that is just the surveyor's bad luck if he is on a fixed fee.[69] Surveyors, held to the higher standard of care benefit too from the *Hunter* exception for difference in diagnosis—different surveyors can take different approaches when weighing up the various factors involved.[70]

The delictual duty may be owed more widely that to the potential **12–42** purchaser alone.[71] This problem is often addressed by stating on the survey that it is provided only for the addressee.[72] Damages may well be due for inconvenience and worry caused by owning a property worth less than the valuation.[73] It has been accepted in one case that a valuation should be within 10 per cent of the true valuation in valuing a domestic house.[74] The quantification of damages in negligent survey cases raise difficult questions which have been litigated to the full.[75]

An engineer was held liable where the pursuers' architect and chartered **12–43** surveyors recommended a report from an engineer.[76] Although the survey was based only on a visual inspection the pursuers managed to prove sufficient features which ought to have been noticed and which a competent surveyor would have recognised as requiring further instructions for a more detailed examination.

---

[67] See the English case of *Smith v. Eric S. Bush* [1990] 1 A.C. 831, discussed 12–30. In *Martin, ibid.*, there was a disclaimer that came too late—the damage had been done.

[68] *Whallye v. Roberts* [1990] 6 E.G. 104; *Lloyd v. Butler* [1990] 47 E.G. 56; *Roberts v. J. Hampson* [1990] 1 W.L.R. 94.

[69] Distilled from the above noted three cases.

[70] *Peach v. Chalmers & Co.*, 1992 S.C.L.R. 423, which was, however, a decision on quantum rather than liability so the existence of two strands of expert evidence did not rule out the claim.

[71] *Smith v. Carter*, 1995 S.L.T. 295.

[72] In *Stewart v. Ryden Residential Ltd*, 1999 G.W.D. 12–576, the defender surveyors took the argument that reliance on their report was not reasonable as the instructions came in a different name. However, there was enough to show that the allegation that the survey was carried out under contractual duties. The related averments based on delict were reluctantly allowed to proof before answer as well.

[73] *Fraser v. D.M. Hall*, (1996) Rep.L.R. 148.

[74] *Peach, ibid.*

[75] See Chap. 23. P. Wade, "High Valuations v. Bad Lending", (1995) Rep.B. 4–2. For the calculation of the contributory negligence reduction see *Platform Home Loans Ltd v. Oyston Shipways Ltd* [1999] T.L.R. 123.

[76] *Reid Furniture Co. Ltd v. Nicholson & Jacobsen Ltd*, 1990 G.W.D. 31–1782.

MISCELLANEOUS PROFESSIONS

Accountants

12–44 All of the general comments set out above apply to accountants.[77] It will have been noted that some of the great cases involve accountants, particularly *Caparo v. Dickman*. That non-liability decision was followed in *James McNaughton Paper Group v. Hicks Anderson & Co.*,[78] which while containing a useful attempt to state the law held that no duty was owed to a predator company who had seen the draft accounts prepared for the chairman of the target company. In Scotland before these cases, in *Twomax Ltd v. Dickson, McFarlane & Robinson*,[79] accountants had been held to have a duty to potential investors in a situation where when prepared the company was not for sale but they ought to have foreseen that it might be.[80] Although *Twomax* was reclaimed and the case raised by one pursuer was settled it was accepted that a duty was owed as set out by the Lord Ordinary. The case is certainly still of interest in relation to its examination of what an accountant should do in auditing and preparing accounts. In *Maddison v. Muir*,[81] the pursuer sued an accountant for a loss made on an investment. The action was dismissed in the sheriff court because the pursuer did not aver a departure from professional practice nor was the standard of care averred. The sheriff principal allowed the appeal and a proof before answer. It was said that the *Hunter* test only applied where there was an allegation of failure to follow a usual practice. The only issue was whether the defender exercised the skill and care of a reasonably competent member of the profession. That did not need to be averred being a matter of law. In another case it was held that accountants who were the auditors of a family company owed a duty of care in valuing the shares when they were being sold by a member of the family—there was a conflict of interest.[82] However, it had not been shown that the value the pursuer put upon the shares was indeed the true value and so the case failed on proof. Where an accountant acted as a financial accountant he was held liable to the partners in a business which collapsed in part due to his failure to make inquiry of the stocktakers since this would have revealed that the company was in a much worse position than it seemed. The finding that he was also a highly paid consultant seems to have enlarged his duty from that of an accountant and may have done so materially. In another case a failure to claim stock relief for a company was professionally negligent.[83] In one more recent case it was held that in principle auditors could be liable to the company for a failure to detect that the company was

---

[77] See generally J.G Logie, "Liability in Negligence of Company Accountants and Auditors", 1991 S.L.T. (News) 169.

[78] [1991] 2 Q.B. 113.

[79] 1983 S.L.T. 98; 1984 S.L.T. 424.

[80] The decision was arrived at after with support from *Ross v. Caunters* [1980] 1 Ch. 297 (which although it was in a sense followed in *White v. Jones* [1995] 2 A.C. 207 its rationale was not) and upon the now discredited two-stage *Anns* test. Lord Stewart also found support in *JEB Fastners Ltd v. Marks Bloom & Co.* [1981] 3 All E.R. 289.

[81] 1991 G.W.D. 40–2489.

[82] *Anderson v. Pringle & Watt*, 1991 G.W.D. 19–1167.

[83] *Herd & Mackenzie (Buckie) Ltd v. Mackenzie*, 1987 G.W.D. 32–1170.

insolvent prior to it paying a dividend which it would of course not have paid had it known.[84]

Architects

Architects will be liable on the developed *Hedley Byrne* principle. Because **12–45** they are involved with the built physical environment they may be liable on the neighbour principle if they build a house which falls down or otherwise foreseeably affects safety.[85] In a case relying strongly on *Junior Books*, architects were held to be capable of owing a duty to the owners of a building whose roof leaked causing them repairing losses and loss of rental income.[86] A purchaser of a house from a builder who finds that the garage will not take his car meaning that he has to pay for a lock-up will encounter the rule in *Department of Environment v. Bates*[87] which prevents a claim for economic loss by a subsequent purchaser against the original negligent builder (at least in England). The contractual matrix in which an architect is often found may well ground a defence to the delict case.[88]

Architects are placed in a kind of judicial function by many of the standard form contracts and sometimes are thought to be so even where the standard forms are not in place. They can be held liable for careless certification.[89] They do not have a judicial nor statutory immunity from such actions. In *Scotstown Building Co Ltd v. Kerr*,[90] the architect was employed by the pursuers who designed a house for another company who sold it to a purchaser. The purchaser only paid the price on the receipt of a completion certificate prepared by the defender and addressed "to whom it may concern." The pursuers paid the purchaser damages when it was found that the subjects were not complete. They sought to recover this from the architect who it seems had made a mistake. The case clearly suffers from the difficulty surrounding the law of relief but it was also held that the case based solely on negligent misrepresentation failed through want of averments of reasonable foreseeability of loss and proximity between the purchaser and the architect. Perhaps if the case had been pled differently a case could have been made out; a certificate often indicates an assumption of responsibility and to address it to whom it may concern is to invite a wide range of engendered reliance. In another case, Lord Coulsfied allowed a proof before answer against architects who, it was alleged, along with structural engineers and quantity surveyors had caused the pursuer housing association some considerable loss.[91] The case is complicated, although no more so than most building cases. The original error was by the structural engineers who it was said had not followed professional practice and seems to have been compounded by the quantity surveyors failing to include

---

[84] *Sasea Finance Ltd (In Liquidation) v. KPMG* [1998] T.L.R. 527.

[85] See *Kelly v. Edinburgh District Council*, 1983 S.L.T. 593.

[86] *Norwich Union Life Insurance v. Covell Mathews Partnership*, 1987 S.L.T. 452. If such a case arose today a very much more careful review of the authorities would be required.

[87] [1990] 3 W.L.R. 457.

[88] See *British Telecommunications plc v. James Thomson & Sons (Engineers) Ltd*, 1997 S.L.T. 767.

[89] *Sutcliffe v. Thackrah* [1974] A.C. 727.

[90] 1990 G.W.D. 4–222.

[91] *Castlehill Housing Association Ltd v. Ramsay & Chalmers*, 1995 G.W.D. 25–1321.

certain works in the tender documents. A whole series of problems arose
and the pursuers alleged that the architects wrongly authorised the main
contractor to carry out more expensive works. The pursuers also alleged
that the architects were blameworthy with the quantity surveyors who had
advised the association that it was in breach of its contract with the
contractors and should terminate one contract, pay damages and enter
another more expensive one. *Rowallan Creamery Ltd v. Henry Dawes &
Sons*[92] is also typical of many cases encountered in practice. The pursuers
claimed for defective building work. They claimed that the architects had
failed to supervise the contract properly. They also adopted averments
made by the defender builders that there were design defects. Lord Prosser
treated the pleadings in a way much more generous than many a local
sheriff. The averment "supervise properly" could be read as meaning "in
accordance with the standards which would have been shown by a
reasonably competent architect." There was no need to plead any particular
form or frequency of supervision. It was in this case not necessary to make
a *Hunter* type deviation averment where the pleadings as a whole disclosed
a failure to exercise reasonable care. A very similar decision was given by
Lord Marnoch in relation to frequency scope and manner of architectural
supervision in *Dundee District Council v. James Parr and Partners*.[93] He
considered that a general introductory averment of a duty to exercise
reasonable care and skill of reasonably competent architects was sufficient
to distinguish the case from the earlier case of *J. Dykes Ltd v. Littlewoods
Mail Order Stores*.[94] In *J. Dykes Ltd* the second defenders, with whom the
report is concerned, were consulting engineers to the first defenders who
were being sued by the pursuers' adjoining proprietors whose buildings had
been damaged by building works. The case was dismissed, *inter alia*, for
want of fair notice as to the professional standard of the time.[95] The line is
a fine one. It may be that all that is required is for the pleader to make it
clear whether the case is based on deviation from normal practice or is one
of breach of the duty to take professional care.

In *Aberdeen District Council v. Alexander Hall & Son (Builders) Ltd*[96] an
architect sued by a building employer called as a third party those who
marketed a special roofing system which had been installed by other
defenders, the subcontractors. The architect averred he had relied on their
brochure and a visit by the roofing company to the site. The roofing system
providers argued they were merely sellers of materials. The architect's case
was dismissed. There was nothing to show that there was anything wrong
with the roofing system. Even if the brochure had gone so far as to imply
that there was a duty to advice, there were no averments about what advice
would have made a difference.

The basic *Hunter* test applies so that there is no prima facie case against
an architect where a code of practice has not been followed.[97] The same test
has been used in a case based on contract between the contracting parties.[98]

---

[92] 1988 S.L.T. 95.
[93] 1991 G.W.D. 36–2174.
[94] 1982 S.L.T. 50.
[95] The critical passage in Lord Stewart's opinion is midway through p. 52.
[96] 1988 G.W.D. 19–847.
[97] *Kelly v. Edinburgh District Council*, 1983 S.L.T. 593.
[98] *Wagner Associates v. Joseph Dunn (Bottlers) Ltd*, 1986 S.L.T. 267.

Bankers

Most dealings of banks are regulated by contract express or implied. In **12–46** *Weir v. National Westminster Bank plc*[99] it was held that a bank did not owe a duty of care to an agent of a disclosed principal. While a banker owes a duty to his customer to pay a cheque the bank does not owe a duty to the payee to take care in honouring the customer's cheque.[1] These are both justifiable on the *Hedley Byrne* assumption of responsibility principle.

Financial Services

In *P. Boyes (Contracts) Ltd v. Mardun Investment Co. Ltd*[2] the pursuers set **12–47** up a pension scheme for their directors—they were its founders but not the trustees. The pursuers claimed that form of scheme was less beneficial than an alternative and they sued, alleging negligent advice, for a sum which, if invested in the existing scheme would have provided benefits comparable to those under the alternative. The defenders argued that loss would fall on directors or trustees not the company.[3] This part of the case failed. The pursuers claimed a loss but the proceeds would never be directly available to the company but only as trustee for the benefit of the directors. It was also thought, following *Esso Petroleum v. Hall Russell & Co. Ltd*[4] that the company had no relevant loss it could claim. Any payment by the pursuers would be made voluntarily and they did not even undertake to use any sums recovered in this way.

Others

Insurance is organised by contract. As we have seen from *Merritt*[5] the long **12–48** accepted point that delictual duties can arise in the absence of contract is now widely accepted even in complex matters involving economic losses. Some of the arrangements developed over the centuries in relation to insurance mean that some contractual provisions are unstated and some contractual provisions have very special meanings. Nonetheless as *Merritt* shows questions can arise around the relationships. The deregulation of the financial sector of the economy has led to many persons dealing in insurance and traditional arrangements breaking down. The same can easily be said of stock-broking. It has been held in England that an insurers broker did not owe a duty to the insured as to the adequacy of the insurance cover.[6] It has also been held that the insurance brokers of a company do not owe a duty to the directors.[7]

---

[99] 1993 S.C. 515; 1994 S.L.T. 1251.
[1] *National Westminster Bank v. Barclays Bank* [1975] Q.B. 654.
[2] 1994 S.L.T. 1298.
[3] Under reference to *Allan v. Barclay* and *Caparo Industries v. Dickman*.
[4] 1988 S.L.T. 33; 874.
[5] *Henderson v. Merrit Syndicates* [1995] 2 A.C. 145 discussed at para. 10–20.
[6] *Stevenson MacMillan v. A.W. Knott Becker Scott* [1990] 1 Lloyd's Rep. 98. A proof before answer has been allowed in Scotland in a case against brokers in relation to their arrangement of the policy: *Luss Estates Co. v. G.B. Garman & Co.*, 1999 G.W.D. 23–1117.
[7] *Verderame v. Commercial Union* [1992] T.L.R. 164.

12–49   It has been held that joint liquidators who carried out acts after seeking and obtaining the approval of the court could not be liable in delict.[8] In that case though senior counsel for the pursuers conceded that the court had been appraised of all the relevant facts. If that had not been the case perhaps the position would have been different.[9]

12–50   Cases often arise about the liability of sports instructors. In *Rieley v. Kingslaw Riding School*[10] a girl was badly injured when on a pony lesson with the defenders. They were assoilzed but there is no report on this aspect of the decision.

12–51   In *Pozzolanic Lytag Ltd v. Bryson Hobson Associates*[11] it was held that a project manager was obliged to ensure that proper insurance arrangements were in place for the liability of contractors. He had to ensure the adequacy if necessary by taking professional advice from lawyers and insurance brokers and could not simply act as a postbox sending evidence of proposed arrangements to the client without comment.

12–52   Teachers, while clearly members of a profession were not in the past sued for anything other than over zealous chastisement and sometimes lack of care in supervision.[12] Recent years have seen teachers and other instructors being held sued in relation to a range of activities.[13]

---

[8] *Highland Engineering Ltd v. Anderson*, 1979 S.L.T. 122.

[9] *ibid.* at 125.

[10] 1975 S.L.T. (Notes) 10. Taken to a seven judge court on another point 1975 S.L.T. 61.

[11] [1998] T.L.R. 760.

[12] *Avery v. New Park School*, 1949 S.L.T. (Notes) 7; *Hutchison v. Dumfries County Council*, 1949 S.L.T. (Notes) 10; *Henderson v. Edinburgh Corporation*, 1950 S.L.T. (Notes) 63; *Sutherland v. Glasgow Corporation*, 1959 S.L.T. (Notes) 51; *Skinner v. Glasgow Corporation*, 1961 S.L.T. 130; *Colquhoun v. Renfrew County Council*, 1973 S.L.T. (Sh. Ct) 50.

[13] See generally, A. Bowen, "Teachers as Professionals: *Hunter v. Hanley* Rides Again", 1999 S.L.T. (News) 11.

CHAPTER 13

PREMISES AND OCCUPIER'S LIABILITY

This chapter should be read against the background that another party may **13–1** be liable on another basis. Thus it may be that a negligence case would be raised on the basis that the defender allowed others to use his property causing loss to others,[1] or that the defender's practices in the use of his premises caused them to be dangerous and damage the pursuer's adjoining premises.[2] It may also be that a person who has not entered onto premises but is injured by material coming from the premises would be able to sue on the basis of negligence.[3] Alternatively, a claim in nuisance might be possible although generally that should be where there is a continuing incident and the defender would still have to be at fault.[4] There may be concurrent liability with other statutes and if they provide a higher standard the pursuer will at most sue under occupier's liability in the alternative. Accidents caused by premises to tenants might be pursued against the landlord but the possibility of taking action against contractors should not be over-looked.[5] In *Banna v. Delicato*,[6] it was held that a shopper who tripped in a shop was entitled to sue under regulation 12(3) of the Workplace (Health Safety and Welfare Regulations) 1992 which had been assumed to be only for the protection of workers. The regulation imposes a higher standard of duty.

The Occupier's Liability (Scotland) Act 1960

So far as occupiers are concerned the law is in the Occupier's liability **13–2** (Scotland) Act 1960. The Act was passed to remove from Scots law the influence and rules of the law of England, applied by the House of Lords in *Dumbreck v. Addie & Sons*[7] which, shortly put, perilled the pursuer's case on the capacity in which he entered the premises. The Scots law before that case had been based upon the simple notion of reasonable care.[8] Some

---

[1] *Squires v. Perth & Kinross District Council*, 1984 S.L.T. (Sh. Ct) 52; *Maloco Smith v. Littlewoods Organisation*, 1987 S.L.T. 452.

[2] *H & A Scott Ltd v. J Mackenzie Stewart and Co. Ltd*, 1972 S.L.T. (Notes) 69.

[3] See cases like *McLeod v. Magistrates of St. Andrews*, 1924 S.C. 960; *Bolton v. Stone* [1951] A.C. 850.

[4] *R.H.M. Bakeries v. Strathclyde Regional Council*, 1985 S.L.T. 214. See the golf and cricket cases discussed in Chaps 6 and 10.

[5] See *Murphy v. Brentwood District Council* [1990] 3 W.L.R. 414. There is no Scottish equivalent of the Defective Premises Act 1972.

[6] 1999 S.L.T. (Sh. Ct) 84, followed in *O'Brien v. Duke of Argyll's Trs*, 1999 S.L.T. (Sh. Ct) 88.

[7] 1929 S.C. (H.L.) 51.

[8] *e.g.* *Pollock v. Cassidy* (1870) 8 M. 615; *Stark v. McLaren* (1871) 10 M. 31; *McMartin v. Hannay* (1872) 10 M. 411; *Beveridge v. Kinnear* (1883) 11 R. 387; *Daily v. Allan* (1885) 12 R. 841; *Murphy v. Smith* (1886) 13 R. 985; *Cormack v. School Board of Wick* (1889) 16 R. 812.

cases from that era are still helpful in considering what ought to be done. Between *Dumbreck* and the Act, Scots law had to make the English distinction between invitee, licensee or trespasser.[9] Cases prior to the Act should thus be read subject to this point.[10] It is the case that the statute and common law are often pled as alternatives and indeed found to be cumulative grounds after proof.[11] It is submitted that this only appears illogical[12] because the system of pleading duties is itself illogical. The facts once narrated may be proffered to support both pleas in law and might on given facts support one or the other or both. In such a situation, where the facts pled are ex facie within the statute a proof before answer will be needed. The matter is one of alternative legal analyses not alternative inconsistent facts. The main point of substance is that in a case under the Act the enquiry into foreseeability of harm of the kind arising is excluded by the act and averments thereanent cannot properly be desiderated by the defender.[13] That also explains why the Act did not simply restore the common law. There is no need for the pursuer to negate remoteness of injury. If an alternative common law case is taken that benefit is lost but any technical argument as to the applicability of the Act is elided. If the occupier took reasonable care in the circumstances then there is no liability in either case.

The nature of the liability

13–3 The Act lays down the standard of care and the circumstances covered by this standard:

> "The care which an occupier of premises is required, by reason of his occupation or control of the premises, to show towards a person entering thereon in respect of dangers which are due to the state of the premises or to anything done or omitted to be done on them and for which the occupier is in law responsible shall, except in so far as he is entitled to and does extend, restrict, modify or exclude by agreement his obligations towards that person, be such care as in all the circumstances of the case is reasonable to see that that person will not suffer injury or damage by reason of any such danger."[14]

---

[9] The law in England has changed since but is not identical to the Scots Law: see Occupier's Liability Act 1957; Occupier's Liability Act 1984; Clerk & Lindsell, *Law of Torts*, Chap. 10.

[10] The state of the law just prior to the Act can be seen in *Murdoch v. A. & R. Scott*, 1957 S.L.T. 11 in the Inner House. A schoolgirl, aged 11, was seriously injured when her arm was caught in a motor driven cement mixer in a building site. It was held that the doctrine of invitee, licence and trespasser applied. The Sheriff after proof had found the girl to be a trespasser. One argument was that the doctrine of categories did not apply because the occupiers were neither owners or tenants. Another argument was that the accident did not arise from static condition of the site. Both were rejected. Lord Patrick (at 16) makes clear that this was an attempt to apply *Donoghue v. Stevenson* to the law of occupiers' liability where the defender was neither owner or tenant. This was rejected because of *Dumbreck v. Addie*. See the note by W.A.W. at 1957 S.L.T. (News) 65 which reveals the intellectual and practical difficulties.

[11] See *e.g. Beggs v. Motherwell Bridge Fabricators Ltd*, 1998 S.L.T. 1215; *Hill v. Lovatt*, 1992 S.L.T. 944.

[12] See the very helpful discussion in *Stair Memorial Encyclopedia*, Vol. 15, at pp. 316–319.

[13] The question of reasonable care by the occupier is a legitimate question but a different one.

[14] s. 2(1).

Who can sue?

General

The pursuer must be a person entering on the premises. A person who has **13–4**
not entered must sue in the general law of negligence or in nuisance or
perhaps for breach of some statutory duty as where suffering from the
effects of pollution emitted from the premises. A person who has at some
stage entered the premises and is injured outside the premises may be
protected by the Act on the basis that the occupier has an unsafe exit on
the premises.[15] Firemen and others who enter unexpectedly are also
entitled to protection having entered on the premises. The issue in such
cases is usually what precise precautions should be taken as few people
actively consider what firemen are likely to do. The issue was examined in
Bermingham v. Sher Brothers.[16] While it was accepted that some duty was
owed which might extend to warning of known dangers,[17] it did not extend
to providing a firescreen which would have prevented the injuries.[18] In
McGrory v. One Plus[19] the defenders unsuccessfully reclaimed a finding that
they were liable to the pursuer who was a fireman. He was injured by a
pane of glass when he was inspecting the premises after a fire. It was
accepted there had been a crack in the glass. Expert evidence was given and
accepted. The facts gave rise to an inference of negligence in respect of a
failure to maintain external paintwork.[20] A police officer was allowed a
proof before answer when he fell through a garden slab into an outhouse
while executing a warrant.[21] A school child can sue those who run the
school.[22] A football fan waiting to get through a turnstile was within the Act
presumably because the ground surrounding the stadium was also the
defenders' premises.[23]

Trespassers

It was the English law that legally categorised plaintiffs. The 1960 Act **13–5**
intended to do away with categories of pursuers. It did. There are no
special provisions relating to trespassers as there still are in England. The
care to be taken varies in the circumstances and so in some, perhaps many
circumstances, less care need be taken for a trespasser. This was made clear
by Lord Reid in the House of Lords decision in *McGlone v. British Railways
Board*,[24] in which the defenders had taken reasonable care even although a
boy had been able to overcome the fencing they provided around their
electricity transformer. The defenders succeeded, not because the boy was a

---

[15] *Duff v. East Dunbartonshire Council*, 1999 G.W.D. 22–1072.
[16] 1980 S.L.T. 122.
[17] *ibid.*, *per* Lord Fraser at 125.
[18] See also *Flannigan v. British Dyewood Co. Ltd*, 1970 S.L.T. 285 in which a fireman was not
allowed to utilise the Factories Acts to establish a duty for him to be working in a safe place.
[19] 1994 G.W.D. 5–282.
[20] Under reference to the English case *Henderson v. Henry E. Jenkins & Son* [1970] A.C. 282.
[21] *Perry v. Hoggan*, 1993 G.W.D. 22–1390.
[22] *Cormack v. Wick and Pulteneytown School Board* (1889) 16 R. 812; See also *Davis v.
Kilbirnie School Board*, 1911 2 S.L.T. 371; *McCluskey v. Lord Advocate*, 1994 S.L.T. 452.
[23] *Hosie v. Arbroath Football Club Ltd*, 1978 S.L.T. 122.
[24] 1966 S.L.T. 2.

trespasser but because they had done enough to take care of him by fencing and posting a notice.[25] A person who comes on to another's unfenced land—just because it is unfenced—is not necessarily considered a trespasser in any event.[26] In *Dawson v. Scottish Power*[27] the pursuers' 11–year-old son was injured when he went to retrieve his football which landed on the defenders' substation. He tried to climb over and impaled his finger on a spike at the top of the fence. The fence was six feet high but had reduced effectively to four feet as a result of the build up of rubble. It was as a matter of common sense and the evidence of a health and safety expert reasonably foreseeable that a boy would try to go over a fence for his ball and six feet or two metres was the safe height.

Who can be sued?

Occupiers

13–6 The defender is principally the occupier of premises. The Act defines this party as "a person occupying or having control of land or other premises."[28] To determine the issue of control the common law must be referred to.[29] The test is possession and control and will be a matter of fact in each case. In *Telfer v. Glasgow District Council*[30] the second defenders, the Co-operative Society were in the course of selling property to the Glasgow District Council. Both the Council and the Society were sued. As the Society had the keys and the *de facto* power to exclude others, the Society, and not the District Council, were held to be occupiers.[31] Ownership is not necessary nor indeed is any form of title however limited as can be seen in *Poliskie v. Lane*,[32] where an independent contractor was held to be liable. Nor is ownership sufficient as was made clear in *Pollock v. Stead & Simpson Ltd*[33] in which a case against one of the defenders based solely on infeftment was dismissed. In *Murray v. Edinburgh District Council*[34] the pursuer was a home help and was injured when a wooden panel containing a ventilator fell onto her wrist when she was working in a council house tenanted by an individual. The case under section 2(1) failed as it was not averred that the defenders were in occupation and control. *Todd v. British Railways Board*[35] raises a modern problem of occupation and control. The pursuer alleged that he slipped on a pavement in Waverley station while employed as a conductor. The issue arose because it was not clear whether British Railways Board or Railtrack were responsible partly due to the allocation of functions set up under the Railways Act 1993. While that Act

---

[25] See *Galloway v. King* (1872) 10 M. 788 for a similar decision long ago.
[26] *Hamilton v. Hermand Oil Co.* (1893) 20 R. 995.
[27] 1999 S.L.T. 672.
[28] s. 1(1). This was the law before the Act: *Kennedy v. Shotts Iron Co.*, 1913 2 S.L.T. 121.
[29] s. 1. For pre-Act authority see *Laurie v. Magsistrates of Aberdeen*, 1911 2 S.L.T. 231; *Baillie v. Shearers J.F.* (1894) 21 R. 498.
[30] 1974 S.L.T. (Notes) 51.
[31] The same approach was taken in *Feely v. Co-operative Wholesale Society*, 1990 G.W.D. 221; and see also *Miller v. Glasgow District Council*, 1989 G.W.D. 1347.
[32] 1981 S.L.T. 28.
[33] 1980 S.L.T. (Notes) 76.
[34] 1981 S.L.T. 253.
[35] Unreported, February 24, 1998.

transferred ownership, Lord Penrose correctly thought that irrelevant. So far as the 1960 Act is concerned it was complained that there were insufficient averments to set up occupation or control. Lord Penrose held that specification was not required of the factual basis of occupation and control. A bald averment was sufficient. The case was relevant under the Act on the basis that it was said that the premises were a train station. A landlord was not in occupation and control of let premises.[36] The Crown is bound by the Act.[37] Joint owners are jointly and severally liable.[38]

Landlords

Where premises are occupied or used by virtue of a tenancy under which **13–7** the landlord is responsible for the maintenance or repair of the premises, it is the duty of the landlord to show towards any persons who or whose property may from time to time be on the premises the same care in respect of dangers arising from any failure on his part in carrying out his responsibility aforesaid as is required to be shown by an occupier of premises towards persons entering on them.[39] This makes the landlord an occupier even although he is not physically in occupation. So in respect of urban subjects governed by legislation which provides for forms of "habitability",[40] the landlord will be the proper defendant. A tenant's wife had an epileptic fit and fell on a fire which had been improperly secured by a previous tenant and so spilled coals on to her. The previous work, if properly inspected prior to the new tenancy would have shown the possibility of danger. It was held the authority as landlords were obliged to carry out an inspection of the premises prior to entry by the new tenant and his "delictual" family prior to the new let. They failed properly so to do and were held liable.[41] Allowing a house to become damp such that it affected a child's asthma has fallen within the Act.[42] This, despite the argument extensively discussed and argued in that case that older authority meant that privity precluded non-tenants from suing.[43] However, it is necessary for the use of this section that the landlord does indeed have the obligation to take the desiderated care of the premises. The case of *Murray v. Edinburgh District Council*,[44] a case under section 3(1), failed. It was irrelevant as the defenders' responsibility for maintenance of panel was not averred, nor was there any averment that the defenders had cause to know of defect. The landlords' obligation did not include inspection, or dealing with matters not brought to his attention.[45]

---

[36] *Murray, ibid.* at 255. The case against the landlord based on s. 3 also failed.
[37] s. 4.
[38] *Gillon v. Chalmers* (1900) 8 S.L.T. 75.
[39] s. 3(1).
[40] See generally, P. Robson and S. Halliday, *Residential Tenancies* (2nd ed., W. Green 1998).
[41] *Lamb v. Glasgow District Council*, 1978 S.L.T. (Notes) 64.
[42] *Guy v. Strathkelvin District Council*, 1997 S.C.L.R. 405. The common law rule was in *Cameron v. Young*, 1908 S.C.(H.L.) 7.
[43] For *volenti* and the landlord's claim see Sheriff Gordon's decision in *Hughes*, noted at 13–27.
[44] 1981 S.L.T. 253.
[45] *ibid.* at 255–256.

Land and Premises

Generally

13–8 The Act applies to land and premises. It has been held to be applicable to a piece of open land in a holiday camp[46] and was mentioned in *McCluskey v. Lord Advocate*[47] where the forestry commission were held not to be liable to a woman who slipped off a footpath and fell on to a rock. The path was not one of the forestry commission's paths. The idea that there exists a right of way over land otherwise in possession and control was rejected in a sheriff court case reviewing the authorities and referring to a still unreported Inner House case.[48] "Premises" are not defined in the Act and is a matter to be determined in each case. The Act also imposes liability for certain areas which (as they have been separately described) are not premises and may be described as notional premises.[49] So the following are covered by the Act: fixed or moveable structures, including any vessel, vehicle or aircraft.[50] The common law covered things like public hoists.[51] It covers a workshop on a caravan site.[52]

Public roads and streets

13–9 It is a matter of debate as to whether these are now covered by the Act. Gloag and Henderson state: "The Occupiers' Liability Act does not apply to public roads, streets or footpaths which at common law or by public or private Acts are the responsibility of public bodies."[53] The passage has been approved in a recent case.[54] Rights of way raise infrequent but interesting problems[55] and the law in this area has rather grown along its own lines. There is a possibility that in addition to the common law the Occupier's Liability (Scotland) Act 1960 applies.[56] This topic is treated in Chapter 16 on transportation.

---

[46] *Cairns v. Butlins*, 1987 G.W.D. 14–533.

[47] 1994 S.L.T. 452. There is a full discussion of this general topic and some very interesting comparative material in D. Mckenzie et al., "Civil Liability for Injury and Damage Arising from Access to the Scottish Countryside" (1997) 2 S.L.P.Q. 214.

[48] *Johnstone v. Sweeney*, 1985 S.L.T. (Sh. Ct) 2. The unreported case is *McQueen v. Vale of Leven District Council*, January 24, 1973.

[49] s. 1(3).

[50] For a bus see *Andrew v. Scottish Omnibuses Ltd*, 1972 S.L.T. (Notes) 72. Liability in transport cases can be based on ordinary principles of negligence applying to the activity as where a bus driver drives off too quickly; indeed in such a case the act may be inapplicable as it is more difficult to describe such activity as something done or omitted to be done: *Turnbull v. Lothian Regional Transport*, 1995 G.W.D. 29–1542.

[51] *Mulholland v. Glasgow Harbour Tunnel Co.* 1903 5 F. 637.

[52] *Morley v. Campbell*, 1998 S.L.T. 325.

[53] *The Law of Scotland* (10th ed., W. Green, 1995), p. 533.

[54] *Lamont v. Monklands District Council*, 1992 G.W.D. 4–200.

[55] See J. Blackie, "Liability as Occupier to User of a Right of Way" 1994 S.L.T. (News) 349, considering the English case of *McGeown v. Northern Ireland Housing Executive* [1994] 3 All E.R. 53.

[56] For a consideration of possession and control, a phrase incorporated into the Act, see *McLement v. Magistrates of Kirkintilloch*, 1962 S.L.T. (Notes) 91.

The Acts or Omissions: "State of the Premises or to anything done or omitted to be done on them"

These words should be given their plain and ordinary meaning. Examples **13–10** decided to date include: poor lighting[57]; leaving things lying about over which people can trip[58]; the failure to find a hole during regular inspections of land,[59] leaving a surface slippery because wet.[60] A failure to mark unexpected steps can incur liability as where a salesman fell and the steps were not marked by either a notice or a warning strip.[61] Liability extends to a failure to take into account the actings of other parties. In *Hosie v. Arbroath Football Club Ltd*,[62] the club were liable when fans forced down a door by their sustained pressure injuring the pursuer. There were safety devices available and in use which would have prevented the door being lifted off. Another case based on the act, that the club should have had more turnstiles and all of them manned, was on the facts alleged, unsuccessful.[63] In *Galbraith's Curator ad Litem v. Stewart*[64] a building contractor was held liable for injuries to a child playing with building materials. It was held the site was an allurement to children, that there was no need to fence it and have it patrolled if it had been kept safe by pipes being wedged, and that the defender was liable on the foreseeability principle in *Hughes*. The eight-year-old child was not held to have been contributorily negligent. In the case of a landlord an example is leaving a toilet bowl damaged.[65] *Sinclair v. Falkirk District Council*[66] was a case where a child fell from a chute on a children's playground. She sustained head injuries landing as she did on the tarmac surface. The case was based on the failure to cover the surface in bark, rubber or other soft material. On "expert" evidence including reference to BS 5696 Part 3 1979, it was accepted that there was a risk of injury but that it was thought not to be one likely to materialise. Lord Marnoch applied a cost benefit analysis in the context of the risk to hold that the cost of resurfacing need not have been incurred in exercise of reasonable care.

Particularly significant is *Bygate v. Edinburgh Corporation*.[67] In that case a **13–11** proof before answer was allowed where the pursuer made clear averments of something omitted to be done rather than simply complaining of lack of maintenance. For example: "to provide a stop on the floor of the roping pen to prevent the roping pen gate from opening inwards to more than an angle of about 45 degrees from its shut position, or alternatively, to provide for said roping pen gate opening outwards."[68] Where a ramp would be

---

[57] *Millar v. Fife Regional Council*, 1990 S.L.T. 651; although it is perfectly possible to descend a stair in the dark and it may only be where the absence of light is unexpected that there may be liability: *Teacher's Trs. v. Calder* (1900) 2 F. 372.

[58] *McMillan v. Lord Advocate*, 1991 S.L.T. 150.

[59] *Cairns v. Butlins*, 1989 G.W.D. 40–1879.

[60] *Todd v. British Railways Board*, 1998 G.W.D. 11–568.

[61] *Cole v. Weir Pumps Ltd*, 1995 S.L.T. 12; 1994 S.C.L.R. 580.

[62] 1978 S.L.T. 122.

[63] *ibid*. at 124–125.

[64] 1998 S.L.T. 1305; 1998 Rep. L.R. 64.

[65] *Hughes' Tutrix v. Glasgow District Council*, 1982 S.L.T. (Sh. Ct) 70.

[66] 1997 S.L.T. 757.

[67] 1967 S.L.T. (Notes) 65.

[68] *ibid*. at 66, *per* Lord Leechman.

dangerous if icy, steps to make it safe involve a regular and careful inspection to determine whether gritting is appropriate.[69] Whether or not safe common stairs should be lit is a matter of fact and degree.[70] An occupier does not normally have to provide specially for the fact that those entering on the premises may be intoxicated.[71] In *Hay v. City of Edinburgh*[72] the pursuer went to the toilet after his Christmas lunch. He slipped and fell. It was alleged he was drunk. The pursuer was successful (subject to contributory negligence). The toilets it was noted were frequently used by drunk persons meaning that the reasonable occupier of such premises must take account of his regular users.

13–12 A case complaining of the height of a banister being too low was unsuccessful where there was no evidence of current careful practice, although evidence of non-applicable current building regulations desiderating an extra 8.5 inches was treated as irrelevant.[73] A man succeeded when he fell down stairs leaving premises he had visited as a salesman. It was held that the steps were dangerous because of the lack of a warning, either by notice or by a coloured warning strip.[74] Although the facts of *Hazard v. Glasgow Pavilion*[75] are unusual, different facts can raise similar issues and the allowance of a proof before answer is significant. A person fell from a stage after being hypnotised by a performer. The true basis of this case may be general negligence rather than the statute—knowing people were to be hypnotised, precautions were not taken to prevent foreseeable mishaps.

13–13 It can still be said that the occupier will not be liable for latent defects so long as appropriate inspection has taken place for the manifestation of any such defects.[76] That inspection is of the essence can be seen in the case of the lady who fell through the floor of a shop.[77] In this case the defender, a yearly attendent could not reasonably have seen the defect, it being latent but he could have seen it if he had gone into the disused cellar. The case is clearly a narrow one it being clear that no more was desiderated than a walk round inspection of the premises taken on lease.

13–14 Sometimes nothing need be done. In *Titchener v. British Railways Board*[78] a railway line was so obvious a risk that often nothing at all needed to be done by way of precautions. So a case based on a failure to repair fencing failed because there was no need to fence the railway in the first place. Although it was stated *obiter* by Lord Hailsham that the position might be different in relation to children and indeed there is old Scots authority to that effect.[79] Indeed, in *Neill v. West Lothian Council*,[80] the sheriff principal upheld a finding of liability on the council where a child died jumping over

---

[69] *Doherty v. Artagen Properties Ltd*, 1981 S.L.T. (Notes) 33 (pled to reflect the terms of the Act).
[70] *Davie v. Edinburgh Corporation*, 1977 S.L.T. (Notes) 5.
[71] *ibid*.
[72] 1998 G.W.D. 13–679.
[73] *Martin v. Greater Glasgow Health Board*, 1977 S.L.T. (Notes) 66.
[74] *Cole, ibid*.
[75] 1994 G.W.D. 13–850.
[76] *Paterson v. Kidd's Trs* (1896) 24 R. 99.
[77] *Dolan v. Burnet* (1896) 23 R. 550.
[78] 1984 S.L.T. 192.
[79] *Haughton v. North British Railway Co.* (1892) 20 R. 113.
[80] 1996 G.W.D. 14–1529.

their fence. It was in a state of disrepair and had it been in repair would have deterred the child. *Titchener* was considered. The Council had been warned and did not treat the repair as urgent. The child was younger than in other cases such as *Titchener*. The contributory negligence figure of 60 per cent was left undisturbed. In cases of occupation of open land subject to a right of way it has been held that the duty is not a positive one to maintain the way but to avoid himself creating dangers or perhaps failing to maintain safety devices put in place by his own act.[81]

Where people tripped over a weather bar from time to time and the **13–15** accident could have been avoided by a different kind of weather bar, liability was established.[82] A woman who fell when the sign post she was leaning on gave way did not succeed as it was not established that the defenders should have known of the defect.[83]

While cases involving dog bites or other injuries by animals are now **13–16** likely to be dealt with under the Animals (Scotland) Act 1987, in principle, the Occupiers Liability (Scotland) Act 1960 applies to an occupier's conduct in keeping animals on premises and it was so held in the Outer House in *Hill v. Lovett*.[84]

The 1960 Act does not relieve an occupier of any higher duty of care **13–17** incumbent upon him,[85] such as the employer's duty to provide for his employees under the Factories Act or other legislation.[86] This has been most remarkably demonstrated in the decision in *Banna v. Delicato*,[87] in which it was held that a shopper who tripped in a shop was entitled to sue under regulation 12(3) of the Workplace (Health Safety and Welfare Regulations) 1992 although the shopper was not a worker.

The action by a passenger injured in a collision raised against the driver **13–18** is probably not best considered as a matter of occupier's liability for the accident is hardly due to the state of the premises. However, where a door which opens unexpectedly or a handrail falls off the Act applies. In collision cases the passenger can sue both drivers and ought to succeed unless there has been an inevitable accident. Passengers can be injured without a collision and cases involving buses provide most examples such as where a driver accelerates sharply.[88]

Cases decided under the old common law are still of some value but **13–19** changes in conditions need to be taken into account for a common law case and the specialities of the statute in cases under the Act. So far as land is

---

[81] *Johnstone v. Sweeney*, 1985 S.L.T. (Sh. Ct) 2.

[82] *McMillan v. Lord Advocate*, 1991 S.L.T. 150.

[83] *Western v. Eastern Scottish Omnibuses Ltd*, 1989 G.W.D. 140.

[84] 1992 S.L.T. 994. It was also opined that there may well have been employer's liability upon one defender for failing to provide a safe place of work, *per* Lord Weir at 997.

[85] 1960 Act. s. 2(2).

[86] See *e.g. Todd v. British Railways Board*, 1998 G.W.D. 11–568, a case involving a railway station with interesting arguments about contractual responsibilities. The relevant statute here was the Offices Shops and Railway Premises Act 1963.

[87] 1999 S.L.T. (Sh. Ct) 84; 1999 Rep. L.R. 89. See also *O'Brien v. Duke of Argyll's Trs*, 1999 S.L.T. (Sh. Ct) 88.

[88] *Fleming v. Lothian Regional Transport*, 1995 G.W.D. 5–278. See also *McLaughlin v. Glasgow Corporation*, 1963 S.L.T. (Sh. Ct) 53; *Fraser v. W. Alexander & Sons (Northern) Ltd*, 1964 S.L.T. (Notes) 79; *Andrew v. Scottish Omnibuses Ltd*, 1972 S.L.T. (Notes) 72; *Wyngrove's Curator Bonis v. Scottish Buses Ltd*, 1966 S.L.T. 273, HL; *Clues v. Western S.M.T. Co. Ltd*, 1977 (Notes) 51.

concerned, dangerous pits should be fenced where they are beside the highway although the rule against liability from ownership alone would exclude more distant pits.[89] The absence of a baluster through which a child fell inferred fault, the defect having been there for some time.[90] A child fell through the railing of a common stair, a banister being missing. It had been missing for months and the property factor informed.[91] Leaving a trap door in a shop open is fault.[92] Doors ought to be marked clearly and there has been said to be liability where a person walked through a cellar door instead of a toilet.[93] Where the door is clearly marked there is no liability.[94] Allowing children to play among chemical soaked straw left on ground where children often played to the knowledge of the defenders can be fault.[95] A collapsing cricket grandstand suggests fault.[96] It was held actionable to open the outer gate of a lift for a guest and to let him walk to his death down the shaft.[97] There was no liability where a bridge was unfenced and unlit but used only by workmen who knew it well and there was no liability simply through ownership of the bridge which was not unduly narrow.[98] Normally natural or obvious features will not attract liability.[99]

Defences

Assumption of Risk

13–20 Section 2 of the 1960 Act specifically adopts a defence of assumption of risk:

> "(3) Nothing in the foregoing provisions of this Act shall be held to impose on an occupier any obligation to a person entering on his premises in respect of risks which that person has willingly accepted as his; and any question whether a risk was so accepted shall be decided on the same principles as in other cases which one person owes to another a duty to show care."

Although it has been said this is merely an English form of the maxim *volenti non fit injuria*,[1] the obscurity surrounding that maxim, is such that it is better to treat the defence in its own terms, although clearly the clause after the semi-colon refers to common law cases but does rather assume the

---

[89] *Black v. Cadell*, Feb. 9, 1804, F.C.; *Mack v. Allan & Simpson* (1832) 10 S. 349; *Hislop v. Durham* (1842) 4 D. 1168; *McFeat v. Rankin's Trs* (1879) 6 R. 1043.

[90] *Grant v. Fleming*, 1914 S.C. 228.

[91] *McMartin v. Hannay*, (1872) 10 M. 411.

[92] *Somerville v. Hardie*, (1896) 24 R. 58 and see *Brady v. Parker* (1887) 14 R. 783.

[93] *Cairns v. Boyd* (1879) 6 R. 1004.

[94] *Mackie v. Macmillan* (1898) 6 S.L.T. 222.

[95] *McCall v. Porter and Sons*, 1909 2 S.L.T. 407.

[96] *Mathew v. Perthshire Cricket Club*, (1904) 12 S.L.T. 635.

[97] *Greenlees v. Dundee Royal Hotel Ltd* (1905) 7 F. 382 and see also *Mathieson v. Aikman's Trs*, 1909 2 S.L.T. 353.

[98] *Robertson v. Adamson* (1862) 24 D. 1231.

[99] *Royan v. McLennans* (1889) 17 R. 103 (a pond); *Ross v. Keith* (1888) 16 R. 86 (a pond), *Allan v. Dunfermline District Council* (1908) 16 S.L.T. 410 (a sewage tank).

[1] See *McGlone v. British Railways Board*, 1966 S.L.T. 2; *Titchener v. British Railways Board*, 1984 S.L.T. 192.

principles are clear, which they are not. There was an extensive evaluation of the law in *Hughes' Tutrix v. Glasgow District Council*,[2] a landlords case in which a child injured her hand on a broken toilet bowl:

"Since the 1960 Act, the old law no longer exists, and this case is not raised in contract. The defence of volenti is specifically retained in the 1960 Act, by virtue of s. 2(3) . . . The landlord's obligation under s. 3 is the same as is required of an occupier in terms of s. 2, and so s. 2(3) would apply in this case. Professor Walker says of that section: 'The application of the maxim [*volenti non fit injuria*] to landlord and tenant cases is probably further limited by the effect of the Occupiers' Liability (Scotland) Act, 1960, s. 3, which imposes on a landlord towards his tenants and sub-tenants the duties of care owed by an occupier towards his visitors, so that only clear evidence of voluntary acceptance of specific known risks (s. 2 (3)) could be sufficient to make the maxim applicable' (Delict, p. 352). I accept that in this case there was a specific known risk, but I think that it is open to me to hold that the defenders have not shown that, in all the circumstances, the pursuer 'willingly' accepted the danger, far less that it can be inferred that she agreed to what would be tantamount to a variation of her contract (*c.f.* Rankine on Personal Bar, pp. 76–87) to the effect of relieving the defenders of their obligation to repair the bowl."[3]

Lord Johnston has recently decided, correctly, it is submitted, in the Outer House that s. 3 of the Act effectively overruled the effect of the existing common law rule which relied upon privity to deny the tenant's claim.[4]

Notices

The Act permits an occupier so far as otherwise entitled to do so, to extend, **13–21** restrict, modify or exclude his obligations by agreement. A notice may of course be a safety measure, *e.g.* "Danger Live Wires—Risk of Death." It may be an invitation to agreement: "Users by touching the wires agree that they will receive a potentially fatal electric shock" or it may be that it sets up a potential defence of *volenti non fit injuria*: "Touching these wires will result in a potentially fatal electric shock". Since the 1960 Act the legislature has provided further statutory control of agreements where premises are used as business premises.[5]

Proof

Despite the positive language of section 2, the Act does not impose an **13–22** evidential onus on the occupier.[6] This was decided in the Inner House where counsel for the pursuer indicated that the pleadings had been drafted

---

[2] 1982 S.L.T. (Sh. Ct) 70. See also *Dawson v. Scottish Power*, 1999 S.L.T. 672 in which the boy had been warned of the danger by his father and understood the risk. However, Lord MacLean commented section 2(3) was not pled. There was a finding of contributory negligence.

[3] *ibid., per* Sheriff Gordon at 73.

[4] *Guy v. Strathkelvin District Council*, 1997 S.C.LR 405. The common law rule was in *Cameron v. Young*, 1908 S.C.(H.L.) 7. Privity was of course the defence famously rejected in *Donoghue v. Stevenson*, 1932 S.C. (H.L.) 31.

[5] See section 16 of the Unfair Contract Terms Act 1977.

[6] *Wallace v. City of Glasgow District Council*, 1985 S.L.T. 23.

deliberately to enable the pursuer to do no more than aver that a danger existed on the premises over which the defenders had control and that as a result of that danger the accident had occurred. This was admittedly a result which was contrary to the common law position. Interestingly the pursuer argued by analogy from the interpretation in *Nimmo v. Alexander Cowan & Sons Ltd*[7] of the Factories Act 1961. The Inner House required that "the pursuer has to aver and prove that the danger was one of which the occupier knew or ought to have been aware, and why, and what steps were open to the occupier but not taken by him to remove the danger before the accident occurred." This regrettably often puts a practical burden on the pursuer of having to obtain evidence from people in the defender's own line of business to testify as to "steps open" which is understandably not always forthcoming. The burden of proof does not easily shift as was the case where a man fell into a hole, probably through a defect in a slab. He had not shown enough about the slab to allow any inference of fault to be shown.[8] The opinion has been expressed that evidence of a precognition officer taken with photographs of a stairway soon after a fall were sufficient to indicate that the steps were hazardous, that they had been for some time and that any reasonable system would have detected this.[9]

---

[7] 1967 S.L.T. 277, discussed in Chap. 14.
[8] *McQueen v. Ballater Golf Club*, 1975 S.L.T. 160.
[9] *Scott v. City of Glasgow District Council*, 1994 G.W.D. 28–1715.

CHAPTER 14

EMPLOYER'S LIABILITY

Introduction

The chapter is about the liability of employers in that capacity and not in **14–1** other capacities in which they may be liable, as for example occupiers[1] or keepers of animals[2]. Neither is it about employees' or workers' rights within their contract or under employment protection legislation[3]. These are now multifarious including rights not to be unfairly dismissed which attract compensation. Nor is it about the liability of an employer of a contractor. Still less is it about the liability of an agency who arrange employment for workmen.[4] It is about persons employed so far as the common law is concerned under a contract of service. Obviously the liability is that of an employer for an employee but, perhaps under pressure from employment legislation, people may find themselves liable for a wider range of workers than was the case in the past. *Gardiner v. Eurplas Ltd and Above Scaffolding*[5] is an example. This plaintiff was a sub-contractor and could work for others if he chose. He picked his own mate. However it was decided that long-term continuity, the defendant's close supervision of his work and the imposition of a corporate uniform and logo were enough to entitle him to the benefit of the duties of care to which an employee is entitled. However well meaning such flexibility might be, it does make it difficult for people to know precisely what insurance they ought to arrange.[6] This chapter does not attempt to set out all possible grounds of liability, in particular only selected statutory provisions are included. Nor does it attempt to deal with the many practical and factual issues which are at the heart of litigating cases for injured workers.[7]

---

[1] See Chap. 13.

[2] See Chap. 17.

[3] See Craig & Miller, *Employment Law in Scotland*, (2nd. ed., W. Green, 1996).

[4] See *Crombie v. McDermott Scotland Ltd*, 1996 S.L.T. 1238.

[5] Unreported, Queens Bench Division, February 14, 1997 noted [1997] J.P.I.L. (Digest) 189.

[6] See also *George v. George C Peebles & Son (No. 1)*, 1998 S.L.T. 685, a successful ladder case under the 1966 regs 31 and 32 where the pursuer was self-employed. The statutory background is however critical in this case. The same is true of *Mortimer v. Safeway Plc*, 1998 S.C. 520; 1998 S.L.T. 885; 1998 Rep. L.R. 84: a lorry driver sued a supermarket when he fell. His case was based on the Offices Shops and Railway Premises Act 1963, s. 8(1). He failed to prove the accident happened as averred but it was held that the Act did apply to people employed, albeit by contractors and was not restricted to the defenders' own employees, following *Wigley v. British Vinegars Ltd* [1964] A.C. 307 as opposed to *Reid v. Galbraith's Stores Ltd*, 1970 S.L.T. (Notes) 83.

[7] See generally works like McDonald et al., *Industrial Diseases Litigation* (Sweet & Maxwell, 1998); and articles like B. Langstaff, "Upper Limb Disorders: Work Related or Unrelated?"

COMMON LAW DUTIES

14–2 Most cases involve physical injury. Thus it ought to be possible to deal with injury to workmen on the basis of the general principle of foreseeable physical harm set out in *Donoghue*. However, the law before *Donoghue* already recognised a duty of care for workmen and so injured workmen cases tend to be considered as an independent line of authority, although subject to general principle. It must also be appreciated that employee cases can be rationalised or decided upon implied terms in the law of contract. As shall be seen, early on, cases were considered in certain practical categories and these categories still exert force today. On the other hand, as the liability at common law is for negligence, any cases not within the categories can be dealt with by the common law principles and any case within the categories which offends the general principle by denying liability requires to be scrutinised very carefully.

14–3 The doctrine of common employment (or "Collaborateur") needs to be mentioned because cases decided over the period when it was current are consciously or unconsciously affected by it.[8] The doctrine stated that a workman injured by a fellow workman could not sue his employer as being vicariously liable for the wrongdoing workman as a member of the public could.[9] This rule had the effect that the injured workman had to bring his case under the employer's primary duty to him. This may well have had the effect of expanding the primary duty. Now that the doctrine no longer operates, a vicarious liability case is possible. The primary duty has been around for a long time. It is clear in *Macdonald v. Andrew Wylie & Sons*[10] where it was contrasted with the case of the employment of an independent contractor. A workman was injured when scaffolding collapsed. The defenders were builders who had contracted with a firm of joiners for the erection of the scaffolding. One line of defence was "all parties not called". The jury were directed that if the defenders were not skilled in scaffold erection and engaged a tradesman of skill and experience in this work they would not be liable. The jury found for the defenders. A new was trial granted. Lord Young said:

> "According to the law of Scotland in the contract of master and servant . . . it is implied that the employer is responsible to his workmen for the condition of the scaffold which he has provided for them to work upon, and that without any reference to the mode employed by him to erect it."[11]

[1994] J.P.I.L. 14. M. Lazarowicz, "Health and Safety at Work" (1996) 41 J.L.S. 104, J.M. Parsons, "Asbestos Related Disease Claims—A Continuing Cause for Concern in the 1990s and Beyond" [1997] J.P.I.L. 5; S. Pheasant, "Repetitive Strain Injury—Towards a Clarification of the Points at Issue" [1994] J.P.I.L. 223, D. Stevenson, "Repetitive Strain Injury" (1994) 39 J.L.S. 49.

[8] Starting with *Reid v. Bartonshill Coal Co.* (1855) 17 D. 1017, it began to be reversed by statute starting with the Employers Liability Act 1880 but remained applicable until abolished by the Law Reform (Personal Injuries) Act 1948. See *Miller v. Glasgow Corporation*, 1947 S.C.(H.L.) 112; *Neilson v. Pantrini*, 1947 S.C. (H.L.) 64. See generally, T. Ingman, "Rise and Fall of the Doctrine of Common Employment" (1978) J.R. 106.

[9] Clearly expressed by Lord Ardmillan in *Sneddon v. Mossend Iron Co.* (1876) 3 R. 868, 873.

[10] (1898) 1 F. 339.

[11] *ibid*. at 344.

It was incumbent on the defenders to provide the scaffold in order that the work be done and the fact that they had employed a fit joiner did not discharge their liability to their workmen. Any liability of the scaffolder to the defenders was beside the point. Lord Trayner said:

"The rule that a person is not responsible for damage done through the neglect or fault of an independent contractor does not apply to a case like this. It applies where there is no relation between the person injured and the person who employs or engages the contractor"[12]

As explained above, well before *Donoghue* and the formulation of a general principle against negligent physical harm, Scottish courts had held employers responsible for injury to their workman. Thus there is a safe plant case to be found in 1849[13] a competent fellow employee case in 1871.[14] There is a safe place case in 1855.[15]

Safe Equipment and Plant

The duty is one of reasonable care and so inevitably it was found that where **14–4** the equipment supplied suffered from a latent defect, the worker could not recover.[16] The practical effect of that decision was attenuated by the Employer's Liability (Defective Equipment) Act 1969 which is discussed in detail below.[17] Many examples can be found both here and in England.[18] What follows is intended to be an illustrative collection of recent cases.

In *Boyle v. Lothian Regional Council*[19] plant was unsafe where a plate had **14–5** broken off and only a bar remained, the breakage having been reported by the injured person before the accident A fireman hit by a hose propelled by water pressure when it sheared from its connection recovered on the basis that the employers had failed in their duty to regularly inspect the equipment.[20] A man was successful in claiming his employers when a piece of wood he was cutting kicked up a guard and caused his thumb to be cut, this even although the employers' expert doubted that this could happen.[21] A dishwashing machine which leaked was not safe plant because a worker slipped on the puddle. It was known to be leaky. It would have been simple to disconnect it.[22] This one is trickier because the danger was really on the floor with the cause of the injury being a slippy floor but the injury was

---

[12] *ibid.* at 345.
[13] *Whitelaw v. Moffat* (1849) 12 D. 434 a worker was awarded damages by a jury when a chain snapped. On a motion for a new trial the court upheld the award even although there had been no positive proof of negligence. It seems to have been accepted that the happening of the accident indicated fault and the fact that there had previous accidents and no real inspection counted against the employers.
[14] *Stark v. McLaren* (1871) 10 M. 31.
[15] *Brydon v. Stewart* (1855) 2 Macq. (H.L.) 30.
[16] *Davie v. New Merton Mills Ltd* [1959] A.C. 604.
[17] See para. 14–21 below.
[18] See Munkman, *Employers Liability* (12th ed., Butterworths).
[19] 1991 G.W.D. 28–1691.
[20] *Matthews v. Lothian and Borders Fire Board*, 1992 S.L.T. 970; 1992 S.C.L.R. 575.
[21] *Ferguson v. Kingsmead Carpets Ltd*, 1994 S.L.T. 509; 1993 S.C.L.R. 823.
[22] *Cherry v. Strathclyde Regional Council*, 1993 G.W.D. 26–1639.

caused more by a defect in the machine rather than its dangerous condition. A worker succeeded on her own uncorroborated account of having been injured by a handle when a ratchet failed. There had been previous complaints.[23] Previous complaints are not essential but clearly help the court in considering whether the defender has behaved as a reasonable employer. Where a machine did have a history of danger it was not necessary for the pursuer to lead evidence that the simple precautions he desiderated were in use in similar factories.[24] A ladder, with wheels at its foot and no brake has been admitted to be in the circumstances unsafe.[25] At common law safe drinking water rather than polluted water ought to be supplied.[26] Where employers were aware of an employee's infirmity and could have supplied him with a wider barrow obviating the risk to him they were liable for not so doing despite the barrow they provided being of the sort used in the industry.[27] The duty extends to competent tradesmen who should themselves know what equipment to use as in *McIntyre v. Strathclyde Regional Council*[28] where the pursuer was an experienced joiner who was instructed to remove shuttering by his foreman who then left the site. The pursuer could not find the materials required to do the job safely and resorted to a less safe method of carrying it out. The shuttering fell on his foot and the defenders were held responsible for failing to supply suitable equipment.[29] Contributory negligence is not appropriate where there is no real choice but to use particularly poor equipment: in *Scott v. Kelvin Concrete Ltd*[30] safety features on the machine had either not been provided or had been disabled prior to the accident. Although the pursuer had failed to operate an isolator button through inadvertence the defenders' failures were so gross that there would be no contributory negligence.[31]

Safe Place

14-6 This heading does not always appear and is sometimes included with safe plant and equipment and is sometimes thought to be within the idea of a system of working. It may well have taken on a rubric of its own because various statutory provisions desiderated and continue to desiderate a safe place of work.[32]

An early safe place case may be *Bett v. Dalmenny Oil Co.*[33] Operations were carried out to the roof of a mine without proper support. There was a fall and nothing was done and eight days later the accident complained of occurred. The pursuers argued in terms of the common law and Lord

---

[23] *Tucker v. Gray Dunn*, 1994 G.W.D. 20–1235.

[24] *Macdonald v. Scottish Stamping and Engineering Co. Ltd*, 1972 S.L.T. (Notes) 73.

[25] *McCarvel v. Strathclyde Regional Council*, 1997 S.L.T. 1015; 1997 S.C.L.R. 573; 1997 Rep. L.R. (Quantum) 2.

[26] *Drummond v. Lord Advocate*, 1996 G.W.D. 1987.

[27] *McDonald v. Whiteford & Robertson*, 1980 S.L.T. (Notes) 2.

[28] 1994 S.L.T. 933.

[29] There was a finding of contributory negligence.

[30] 1993 S.L.T. 935.

[31] *ibid.*, *per* Lord Coulsfield at 936.

[32] See, *e.g.* a workplace should be properly lit to allow work to be carried out: *Lyons v. Babcock Energy Plc*, 1992 G.W.D. 566.

[33] (1905) 7 F. 787.

McLaren, in whose opinion the rest of the court concurred, described the case as laid on common law negligence and this was in the era of common employment. It was held there was fault and the only complicating factor was that reliance was placed upon the statutory duty, making it a criminal offence, by the Coal Mines Regulation Act 1887. It does seem clear that although this was influential this was not expressly a case of civil liability from statute.[34] Even then it is possible to describe the case as one of a safe system.

An uneven surface has been held to be sufficiently dangerous. The surface resulted from the infilling of a trench rather than wear and tear.[35] A woman succeeded when although she was sitting on a conveyor belt, she was struck on the head by articles from a higher conveyor belt.[36] In another case the British Railways Board were held not to be under a duty to keep the permanent way level[37] but they were liable for the failure of a fellow workman to secure an engine.

Place not that of the primary employer

A line of authority which does help bolster the idea of a safe place and **14–7** which is of great importance in its own right is that relating to workmen working on the premises of others. In *McQuilter v. Goulandris Bros*,[38] the deceased was working on a ship in dock and tripped and fell through an uncovered hatch to his death. This was because the place was poorly lit and there were protruding bolts on the floor. It was held that the fact that the work has to be carried out on the premises of a third party does not absolve an employer from his duty of exercising reasonable care for the safety of his workmen. The duty must still be fulfilled, although its scope is circumscribed by the fact that the work is being done on premises not within the possession and control of the employer. As the structure of the premises is outwith his control, and any defects beyond his power to rectify, his care for his workers can only be exercised within the limits imposed upon him by these circumstances. But he is still under the duty of exercising reasonable care to safeguarding them against dangers which he should anticipate and which he has power to avert.[39]

Competent fellow workmen

It has been clear for a long time that an employer has a primary duty to **14–8** provide properly qualified fellow workmen. In *Stark v. McLaren*,[40] an employer defender told his son to take down a dangerous part of the factory. He instructed the pursuer among others, who was injured during the operation. The defender was held liable as his son had no expertise in demolition (although he might also have been liable as proprietor). A

---

[34] *ibid.* at 790 for discussion of the statute.
[35] *Stewart v. North of Scotland College of Agriculture*, 1991 G.W.D. 14–877.
[36] *Neil v. John Walker & Sons Ltd*, 1993 S.C.L.R. 183.
[37] *Reilly v. British Railways Board*, 1992 G.W.D. 9–505.
[38] 1951 S.L.T. (Notes) 74.
[39] *ibid., per* Lord Guthrie at 75.
[40] (1871) 10 M. 31.

workman succeeded when his fellow workman failed to put on the brakes of a train which ran back down an incline and crushed him.[41] Another workman succeeded when he was run over by his fellow employee who was driving a fork lift truck.[42] Where an employer provided a workman with an incompetent fellow employee who engaged reverse instead of a forward gear, the workman succeeded.[43]

14-9   The duty is only of reasonable care, the employer does not guarantee the safety of his workmen at common law. Thus the unexpected practical joke attracts no liability as in *McLean v. Remploy Ltd*[44] where the pursuer was tripped up by a line of yarn tied across a passageway as a joke. The common law case failed because the pursuer failed to prove the employers were aware of the jokers.[45] If there is a notorious practical joker then liability might be brought home.[46] In *Gibson v. British Rail Maintenance Ltd*,[47] the pursuer won at first instance by coming to court offering to show that the employers were at fault in that their acting foreman had seen employees playing with a ball which hit the pursuer to his injury and had not stopped them but proving that there was a duty of constant supervision and that the acting foreman had been away. The defenders reclaimed on the basis that the case was not that on record. The defenders lost.

Safe System

14-10 As noted above the employer has long been required to provide a safe system. *Ramsay v. Wimpey & Co*[48] marks a kind of mid-point in safe system cases. A workman was trampled to death in a stampede of workers trying to get on buses to take them home. The Lord Ordinary and the Lord Justice-Clerk (Thomson) in the Inner House would have allowed a jury trial. Important to them was the fact that the employers provided the car park where the accident happened and arranged for the buses. There was a contractual obligation on the defenders, it was alleged, to provide transport. The case was rejected on a number of grounds but mainly that the worker was not actually in the conduct of the employers' business at the time. Even at the time of writing the notion of the safe system is subject to consideration as to its scope.

14-11 In *Forsyth v. Lothian Region*[49] the Inner House reconsidered the law on employers' duties in a case where a workman, with a known history of abdominal injury, sued in respect of a hernia sustained when lifting a heavy item while assisting another. The decision to assoilze the defenders was upheld. There was not a sufficient history of injury to demand a special system. A consultative document by the Health and Safety Eecutive was of no assistance as lifting was shared with another. *Paris v. Stepney*[50] was

---

[41] *Reilly, ibid.*
[42] *Mitchell v. Intercity Transport*, 1993 G.W.D. 29–1849.
[43] *Thomson v. Caberboard*, 1994 G.W.D. 27–1629.
[44] 1994 S.L.T. 687.
[45] Statutory cases under ss. 28(1) and 29(1) of the Factories Acts fell because it was not reasonably practicable for the employers to remove the yarn.
[46] *Smith v. Crossley Bros.* (1951) 95 Sol. Jo. 655.
[47] 1995 S.L.T. 953.
[48] 1952 S.L.T. 46.
[49] 1995 G.W.D. 204.
[50] *Paris v. Stepney Borough Council* [1951] A.C. 367. See para. 10–82 above.

distinguished as being a case about plant and equipment and not a safe system. The decision can be criticised on the basis that a safe system owed to a particular pursuer by a particular defender involves consideration of potential pursuers. If a defender knows about a susceptibility then the *Paris* logic should apply, but within the bounds of reasonableness: the system would not necessarily be more costly or difficult it could just say "people with abdominal problems should not be assigned to lifting work." The other argument is that the law would then insist on custom systems. There would not be a system of work in a given trade. The diversity of business and industry now is such that this might be no loss. In any event the modern criminal (and civil) statutory regulation demands tailoring to assessments of the workplace so again the common law imposes no additional considerable burden by including persons such as the actual pursuer with known physical propensities within the scope of the duty to potential pursuers.

Not infrequently it is found that the dangerous system is one of the employee's own devising, but this affords no escape for the defender as it is the employer's primary responsibility to establish and maintain the safe system.[51]

What follows is intended to illustrate the principle based on relatively **14–12** recent cases. It was not a safe system to leave a shop assistant to operate a forklift truck without instruction of supervision.[52] A workman succeeded when he was injured by a heavy weight falling on his head when a hook opened. The hook had stuck. The employer had no system of inspection and it was foreseeable that an accident might happen. There were no instructions to operators to report faults.[53] A man succeeded when he was injured trying to move his vehicle out of mud. He had been specifically instructed to take the van to the muddy track. There was no finding of contributory negligence. [54] In another case it was not a safe system to allow one employee to operate a basket washing machine where the baskets went in one end but had to be dealt with at the other. The greasy baskets fell to the floor making it slippy and causing the pursuer to slip.[55] A window cleaner who did not have his ladder footed on a sloping surface succeeded, albeit subject to contributory negligence, on the basis of the absence of a safe system. The employer had not issued detailed instructions about the footing of ladders nor devised a system for issuing instructions.[56] A bosun of a ferry succeeded when he was run down by a reversing lorry. The system was unsafe because the lorry drivers could not see what was behind them and some form of assistance should have been given.[57] A miner succeeded when he lost an eye. Splinters came flying back when he was using a coal cutting machine. He argued there should have been a system whereby he was told to wear goggles. The court agreed; the fact that the practice was to turn one's head away and that goggles were available if asked for was not good enough.[58] Although only a note, it is clear from *Jardine v. Protective*

---

[51] *Burns v. Harper Collins*, 1997 S.L.T. 607; 1996 S.C.L.R. 1135; 1996 Rep. L.R. 172.
[52] *Rooney v. Scottish Midland Co-operative Society*, 1989 G.W.D. 31–1436.
[53] *Sneddon v. Cameron Iron Works*, 1989 G.W.D. 17–745.
[54] *McQue v. British Railways Board*, 1989 G.W.D. 28–1287.
[55] *Docherty v. D.B. Marshall (Newbridge) Ltd*, 1991 G.W.D. 16–999.
[56] *Travers v. Muirhead*, 1992 S.L.T. 83.
[57] *Lee v. Ardrossan Harbour Board*, 1992 S.L.T. 340.
[58] *Copland v. National Coal Board*, 1991 G.W.D. 31–1869.

Services (Contracts) Ltd[59] that the system must take all reasonable care to prevent foreseeable harm. These employers did provide gloves and saw that they were worn. However, they did not warn of the dangers where the gauntlets had become damaged as they regularly were.

It was not a safe system to have only one quarter rope on a fishing net when two would have prevented the accident and it was obvious that one would be inadequate in the conditions faced by a trawler on the seas.[60] A nurse succeeded when she slipped on a small patch of oil as there was not a safe system for lubricating the machines from which the oil had come and it would have been possible for lubrication to have been done elsewhere.[61] A man succeeded when he fell off a tyre he was using as a mode of dismounting from a vehicle. The employers should have given him instructions on how to mount and dismount. This even although he was an experienced man. He had no experience of the machine in question.[62] In *King v. Smith*[63] the English Court of Appeal upheld a case against a window cleaner's employers for not providing him with a safe system. Millet L.J. said that in the years since *General Cleaning* was decided it was now appreciated that working on the sill was a dangerous practice and the most serious cause of accidents. He said that an employer should impose an embargo on his employees going on the window sill where the customer did not provide anchor points for a harness and the window was such as could be cleaned from the inside.

Allowing employees to lift unsafe weights might be a breach of the duty to have a safe system[64] but more often than not such a case fails and would now be better raised under the regulations. It has to be shown that the employer can reasonably foresee that an employee will lift too heavy a weight and this can be a difficult hurdle for the workman, one such failing even where he was trying to put out a fire.[65] In *Halliday v. Tayside Health Board*,[66] a nurse recovered damages for her back injury. However, she had had a back injury before. Her evidence that she advised her employers that her G.P. was unhappy about her working with heavy lifting was accepted. They knew of her history and sent her to a movement and handling course. However, the pursuer was the only one not to pass because she could not lift things at the course.[67] Where a person has to carry heavy loads he may have to be given a barrow.[68]

The conduct of other people has to be taken into account in devising a safe system and so a worker was allowed a proof when attacked by a disruptive pupil at a special needs school.[69]

---

[59] 1991 S.L.T. 641.
[60] *Duncan v. Scottish Marine Biological Association*, 1992 S.L.T. 554; 1992 S.C.L.R. 571.
[61] *Buchanan v. Lanarkshire Health Board*, 1993 S.L.T. 456.
[62] *Chisholm v. Lord Advocate*, 1992 G.W.D. 36–2144.
[63] [1995] P.I.Q.R. 48.
[64] *Watkinson v. British Telecom*, 1996 S.L.T. 72.
[65] *Crofts v. Roche Products Ltd*, 1995 G.W.D. 1416.
[66] 1996 S.C. 434.
[67] The "extra" facts are often necessary, thus absent the training argument, a porter injured lifting a corpse failed: *Milne v. Tayside Health Board*, 1995 G.W.D. 1–43.
[68] *Lindsay v. TNT*, 1996 G.W.D. 38–2231.
[69] *McLeod v. Aberdeen City Council*, 1999 G.W.D. 23–1115.

An excellent example of the need to take into account the willingness of **14–13** employees to do dangerous things to help out is *McGregor v. AAH Pharmaceuticals*.[70] An employee, instead of using stepladders, clambered up the lower shelves and unsurprisingly, fell. The employers had issued a booklet which had an instruction not to climb up the shelves and not to overreach. The employee won. There were no step ladders nearby despite complaints. The practice was still common place. Despite reprimands people were not subjected to disciplinary proceedings for ignoring the booklet. There was, standing the decision on liability, quite rightly no finding of contributory negligence.[71]

The idea of a safe system can be pushed too far. In the English case **14–14** *Pickford v. Imperial Chemical Industries Plc*[72] by a majority of the Court of Appeal a decision against liability for repetitive strain injury was reversed. In 1984 the Department of Health and Social Security included as a prescribed disease for the purpose of industrial injury benefit under the relevant legislation "PDA4: cramp of the hand or forearm due to repetitive movements." The plaintiff was a secretary. Her condition was caused she said by excessive typing for prolonged periods without proper breaks or rest pauses, which came about because the defendants did not give her the same instructions as they gave their typists working in the accounts department, who carried out typing for most of the day. While it was accepted that repetitive strain injury (although she sued it should be noted for PDA4) is potentially a form of actionable work-related upper limb disorder[73] this case was not actionable. It was considered that an intelligent secretary who has duties other than solid typing would use their common sense to take regular breaks without having to be told. The case would be different with someone obliged to input data all day without breaks.

The overall duty

It is well established that there is no need to bring a claim within one of the **14–15** recognised heads. An example is the English case *Petch v. Customs and Excise*.[74] In this case a claim was made on the basis that after having had one nervous breakdown the employers did not take more care of the employee to prevent the second nervous breakdown. It was admitted by the defenders that they owed a duty to ensure that duties allocated to the plaintiff did not damage his health. The concession was subject to the warning that the defenders would expect the issues of foreseeability and causation to be more difficult in cases of mental injury. Indeed the "nervous shock" case *Page v. Smith*[75] is relevant in this context because in that case it was held that a mental illness could be actionable in negligence even though there had been no physical injury. Taking both cases together it seems that in an appropriate case there is a duty to take care of a worker's mental health. In *Petch* the case failed as it had not been shown

---

[70] 1996 S.L.T. 1161.
[71] See also *Carney v. City of Glasgow*, 1976 S.L.T. (Notes) 20.
[72] [1998] 1 W.L.R. 1189.
[73] B. Langstaff, "Upper Limb Disorders: Work Related or Unrelated?" [1994] J.P.I.L. 14.
[74] [1993] I.C.R. 789.
[75] *Page v. Smith* [1996] 1 A.C. 155 discussed in Chap. 10.

that senior management were aware or ought to have been aware of the conditions under which the plaintiff was labouring. In a later case the necessary facts were established. In *Walker v. Northumberland County Council*[76] a local authority were held liable for failing to relieve the pressure of work on an employee who then had a nervous breakdown. However, he had already had one. So far as the first breakdown was concerned it had not been reasonably foreseeable. After that it was foreseeable. It should be said that it appears that an attempt was made to bring this case within the category of a safe system.[77] In *Ward v. Scotrail Railways Ltd*[78] a proof before answer was allowed in a case of "sexual harrassment" where it was alleged that the pursuer suffered psychiatric illness as a result of persistent unwanted attentions. Reference was made to the fact that non-molestation interdicts have been granted for some time. In *Rae v. Strathclyde Joint Police Board*[79] it was held that a proof before answer should be allowed in a case alleging that the employer should have protected the pursuer from passive smoking. In *Rorrison v. West Lothian College*[80] it was held that a case of psychiatric injury could not succeed because the foundation in earlier complaints was not made out and in any event the resulting psychiatric injury was difficult to pin down.

It has been held in relation to nervous shock that employment cases do not fall into a separate (and more liberal) category in the law of negligence.[81]

14–16   *Crombie v McDermott Scotland Ltd*[82] is another important case in this line of general cases. A worker was injured while using a defective walkway, his only means of access. He sued the occupiers, his allegedly *de facto* employers, the electrical contractors, and the agency whose payroll he was on at the time of the accident. The case is of special significance, it is submitted, for social, economic and cultural factors which cannot be fully vouched in this book and which were not of course discussed in the case. Just as it is possible to guess from *Morrison's Dictionary* that Scotland at that time was a land owning society, it is possible to say from cases straddling the nineteenth and twentieth centuries that the worker normally was part of a workforce of a manufactory. This case is empirical evidence for the sociologist that working patterns, for some at least, are different moving out of the twentieth century—the pursuer having been offered the job over the telephone.[83] While the decision to allow a proof before answer is not in itself determinative of the law,[84] it does decide that such a modern working relationship is not doomed to failure. Lord Hamilton first disputed that if the law could be so widely stated against liability as was the case in the textbooks, then before the court on the express basis that these were

---

[76] [1994] T.L.R. 603.

[77] A similar Scottish case was apparently settled for a substantial sum on similar grounds. See *Ballantyne v. Strathclyde Regional Council* discussed in A.W.D. McLean, "When Stress Fractures—Part 1" (1996) Rep.B. 12–3.

[78] 1999 S.C. 255.

[79] 1999 S.C.L.R. 793.

[80] 1999 Rep. L.R. 102.

[81] See *White v. Chief Constable*, discussed above at para. 10–69.

[82] 1996 S.L.T. 1238.

[83] He could today have found similar work by simply pointing and clicking on the internet.

[84] *Crombie, op. cit.*, particularly at 1242E.

perhaps too strongly founded on stevedore cases.[85] As this kind of case may come before the courts more often in the early twenty-first century,[86] the following passage is quoted at some length stating, it is submitted, the proper view, while at the same time noting the relevant contrary authorities:

"The test must be whether in all the circumstances the performance of his duty of reasonable care calls for steps to be taken by the employer to acquaint himself with the physical circumstances in which his employees are to work. Insofar as older authorities (such as *Taylor v. Sims & Sims* [1942] 2 All E.R. 375 and *Cilia v. H. M. James & Sons* [1954] 1 W.L.R. 721) tend to suggest that an employer has no duty to safeguard his workers against dangers arising from the state of the premises of third parties, they are not, in my view, consistent with the principles of the modern law. I see considerable force in the views subsequently expressed in the English courts about the approach adopted in those two cases. Counsel for the third defenders indeed made it clear that the third defenders did not maintain that an employer could never have a duty to inspect the premises of the third party. I also doubt whether the general formulations of responsibility found in some of the older Scottish cases (such as *Nelson v. Scott, Croall, & Sons* (1892) 199 425) accurately express those principles. In my view a variety of factors may be relevant to the issue whether or not a duty to inspect a third party's premises is incumbent on an employer sending men to work on those premises. Those factors may include the number of men being sent and the period for which they are sent (see *Cook v. Square D. Ltd, per* Farquharson L.J. at [1992] I.C.R. 262 at 271). In the present case it is averred that the pursuer was one of a number of men carrying out work at the first defenders' yard (the precise number is not specified) and that he and other workers started some three months before the accident. Also potentially relevant is the nature of the premises, including the character of the working conditions which the third defenders anticipated or could reasonably have anticipated their employees would experience there. It is true that it is not averred that these premises contained any particular hazard other than that which caused the accident but there may well be a difference between the potential risks of a construction site and of, say, domestic premises. It may also be important to know, as part of the general background, what grounds, if any, the third defenders had for supposing that others would put in hand and properly maintain safety arrangements at the site (a matter peculiarly within the third defenders' knowledge). In terms of the practicability of the third defenders taking

---

[85] "Notwithstanding the width of the statements in Glegg on *Reparation* (4th ed.), at p. 385, and in Walker on *Delict* (2nd ed.), at p. 575, I doubt whether any such general rule as that applied to stevedores can in modern circumstances properly be said to be applicable across all ranges of employment": *Crombie, ibid.* at 1242K. It is interesting that the case involving a stevedore, *Moriarty v. Forth Ports Authority*, 1972 S.L.T. (Notes) 85 was decided on the basis that the stevedores as primary employers were responsible when their worker was injured on another party's lorry.

[86] At the time of writing there are more people working in call centres than in mining, steel and car manufacturing combined.

any measures for the safety of their employees, the circumstance that the yard was in the order of 10 miles rather than 8,000 miles from their place of business may not be unimportant (*c.f. Cook v. Square D. Ltd*). *Johnson v. Coventry Churchill International Ltd* [1992] 3 All E.R. 14 demonstrates that an English company recruiting skilled men in the United Kingdom to work on a construction site in Germany may have a duty of care in relation to the safety of the arrangements at such a site. While I have reservations about some aspects of the judge's reasoning in that case, I am not persuaded that, in relation to the finding of negligence under English law (including a failure to arrange inspection), it was on its facts wrongly decided."[87]

This is a valuable recognition in a more fluid employment market of the existence of a primary liability on a primary employer. On the one hand there is the apparent nonsense that a company can be responsible for a floor it has never seen. The English case is even more perplexing on its face in that the primary employers are on a different island in a different country. On the other hand the prevalence the world over of quality standards means that it is possible for agencies to contract for safety to be delivered to their workmen—in some circumstances it might be that reasonable care by an agency type employer might be satisfied by checking that the destination employer is sufficiently certificated. Certainly such employers ought to take indemnities in relation to health and safety. A genuine agent is not an employer and it must be assumed that these cases arise because the agents put themselves for commercial reasons into the position of being employers. It is of course the case that even in cases where the employer owns and occupies the premises there is not always a general duty of inspection and so in distant cases the circumstances would have to be such that actual inspection would be required.[88]

14–17 An employer has been held liable in England for giving a bad reference in respect of a former employee.[89] However, this decision is based more on *Hedley Byrne* principle than employer's liability.

Unsuccessful cases at common law

14–18 Practical experience dictates that the principles stated above, together with the main examples of liability should not be encountered without there being many examples of the very many cases where workmen have not succeeded. Most cases turn on their own facts but without illustrations it is difficult to understand how the law actually applies to factual situations and the following cases are intended to show this. A cleaner who slipped on the floor she had just cleaned was the author of her own misfortune.[90] A man who tried to grab a hook from on board was struck by it, but failed in his case because the weather was not so bad that operations should have been suspended.[91] Where a man allegedly fell through a floorboard of a trailer he

---

[87] *Crombie, ibid.* at 1242–1243.
[88] *Shepherd v. Pearson Engineering Services (Dundee) Ltd*, 1981 S.L.T. 197.
[89] *Spring v. Guardian Assurance Plc* [1995] 2 A.C. 296. This was followed in Scotland in *Donlon v. Colonial Mutual Group*, 1997 S.C.L.R. 1088.
[90] *MacFarlane v. Greater Glasgow Health Board*, 1989 G.W.D. 34–1581.
[91] *Rowe v. Seaforth Maritime Ltd*, 1989 G.W.D. 29–1350.

failed since he did not show evidence of normal practice, nor did he aver and prove the defect nor what inspection would have revealed it.[92] A man who operated a tractor which he was not authorised to drive and injured himself by accidentally operating a lever was unsuccessful.[93] A workman who fell from a ladder when changing a light bulb tried to argue that it took two men to change a light bulb—in this case one to foot the ladder. It was held that this ground of fault was not made out.[94] A post office sorter failed in his claim for having had to drag a very heavy mail bag.[95] He said they failed to check the weight of the bags but there was no proved danger, nor a proven system that would have helped. The defenders said he should just have taken some letters out of the bag. When a man hurt his back lifting a heavy weight after having been told never to do so he was unsuccessful.[96] Even if the case had been put as a duty to police this prohibition it would have failed as able bodied assistance was available to him. A porter who was injured when a corpse fell when allegedly a fellow worker did not take her share of the weight, failed to recover damages. There was no evidence that three people should be employed for the task and there was an extrajudicial admission that the porter had been in a hurry and that it was his own fault.[97] It was held, *obiter* that where help was available a man who hurt himself lifting a weight had no case at common law nor at statute.[98] The simple fact that a workman slipped when carrying a load is not sufficient to demonstrate lack of care.[99]

In *Hopkins v. Cavity Sealed Unit Co Ltd*[1] the workman failed to establish **14–19** that he had fallen in a pothole as he got out of the cab of a lorry he had temporarily entered. There were discrepancies between his contemporary statements and his evidence and he did not succeed. He had, however, managed to establish that there were many potholes and indeed a large pothole and that there was no systematic inspection of the area. So although not an inherently safe place, the pursuer still fails if fault is not brought home to the employer.[2] A fireman on a training exercise was knocked from his ladder when his hose burst. The case put forward was failure to provide a safe place to work and a failure to inspect the area where the exercise took place (it was put forward that the hose had been cut by glass lying about). The temporary judge added that on the evidence a failure to inspect case or indeed a failure to provide a suitable hose case would have failed. In another case a man fell off a ladder but he did not establish that it was his employer's fault that he did so.[3] A nurse sued a doctor because he had not appreciated that the defibrillator wasn't fully

---

[92] *Cairney v. Alexander*, 1990 S.L.T. 568.
[93] *McCarthy v. Cunninghame District Council*, 1989 G.W.D. 29–1349.
[94] *Gripper v. British Railways Board*, 1991 S.L.T. 659.
[95] *Wilkinson v. Post Office*, 1992 G.W.D. 8–442.
[96] *Couper v. Remploy*, 1993 G.W.D. 27–1718.
[97] *Milne v. Tayside Health Board*, 1995 G.W.D. 1–43.
[98] *Dickson v. British Railways Board*, 1994 G.W.D. 26–1591.
[99] *O'Brien v. Monklands District Council*, 1989 G.W.D. 11–474.
[1] Unreported, January 4, 1996.
[2] In similar vein is *Gibson v. Strathclyde Regional Council*, unreported, January 5, 1996.
[3] *Park v. Thermal Transfer (Scotland) Ltd*, unreported, January 11, 1996. His own expert witness had never been asked to visit the locus and the pursuer's precise account had never been put to him. The defenders' expert was preferred.

charged. Because of that the nurse had to do hand massage. She fell and hurt her back which would not have happened but for the defibrillator being uncharged. It was held that there was no duty in this case because harm of this kind would not be foreseen.[4]

STATUTORY LIABILITY

Introduction

14-20 Statute has provided for the safety of workmen for some time. Civil actions were competent based upon the earliest of the mainly criminal statutes, the Employer's Liability Act 1880.[5] There is a huge body of decisions both in Scotland and in England on the two main statutes of the twentieth century, the Factories Acts 1937 and 1961. The main statutory provisions applying at the time of writing are considered in this next section. There are many other statutes which can result in an employer being liable and the practitioner is best advised to consult specialist texts.[6]

Employer's Liability (Defective Equipment) Act 1969

14-21 Still relevant is the Employer's Liability (Defective Equipment) Act 1969, a United Kingdom statute with a Scottish pedigree. As the basic law is that reasonable care is required, then a workman injured by equipment purchased from a responsible supplier would be forced to sue the supplier and not his employer.[7] The Act provides that the fault is that of the employer if an employee suffers personal injury in the course of his employment in consequence of a defect in equipment provided by his employer for the purposes of the employer's business and the defect is attributable wholly or partly to the fault of a third party (whether identifiable or not).[8] Contributory negligence is a defence and the employer has a right of indemnity against the supplier. "Equipment" includes any plant and machinery, vehicle, aircraft and clothing. The definition was very fully considered in the Scottish case of *Loch v. British Leyland U.K. Ltd.*[9] A pursuer was working on a production line. On this line axles were assembled to be subsequently fitted to lorries in the course of their assembly on another production line. The pursuer's duties involved or included the attachment to the axles of pieces of machinery called "actuators". These pieces of machinery formed part of the braking systems of the lorries. Two actuators were fitted to each

---

[4] *Park v. Lothian Health Board*, 1998 G.W.D. 19–990.
[5] *Flynn v. McGaw* (1891) 18 R. 554.
[6] Munkman, *Employers Liability* (12th ed., Butterworths); Hendy & Ford, *Redgrave's Health & Safety* (3rd ed., Butterworths); Watkins, *Health & Safety Handbook* (1997, Sweet & Maxwell). Some recent examples are *Bilton v. Fastnet Highlands Ltd*, 1998 S.L.T. 1323 and *Williams v. Farne Salmon & Trout Ltd*, 1998 S.L.T. 1329; 1998 Rep. L.R. 32 (occupational asthma considering the Control of Substances Hazardous to Health Regulations 1988); *Mortimer v. Safeway Plc*, 1998 S.C. 520; 1998 S.L.T. 885; 1998 Rep. L.R. 84 (Offices Shops and Railway Premises Act 1963, s. 8(1)).
[7] *Davie v. New Merton Board Mills Ltd* [1959] A.C. 604.
[8] s. 1(1).
[9] 1975 S.L.T. 67.

axle. A splinter of metal which came from a threaded metal rod forming part of one of the actuators got into his hand causing the injuries for which he sued for damages. It was established in evidence that prior to the accident the pursuer and other employees had frequently experienced roughness and skelps or threads of metal scratching their hands. They had complained to the foreman about this and the foreman did not deny that complaints might have been made by the workers. Counsel for the pursuer argued that the word had a wide meaning. Referring to a definition in the Shorter Oxford Dictionary he argued that "equip" means to provide what is required for action, that equipment in the context of the Act covered everything provided to the employee to equip for him what he had to do, that there was no reason why that should be confined to what one might call the tools for the job, but not the parts which were to be worked in the product which the employee was engaged on making. Lord Maxwell thought this was a wider meaning than was intended. Nonetheless the actuators were held not to be "equipment" within the meaning of the Act. However, "equipment" has been held to include a ship,[10] and soap.[11] In *Yuille v. Daks Simpson Ltd*[12] a ventilation system was held to fall within the definition. In order to be equipped for its purposes the factory needed a ventilation system and as it had to be supported, all of the system was equipment. The argument that the part which failed was part of the fabric failed.

A weakness in the Act is that it has been interpreted as there still being a **14–22** necessity to show something wrong with the article. Thus a man failed to recover damages when he was injured when a knife he was using broke. It was held that the most probable cause of the breakage was a previous fall and thus the provisions of the Employer's Liability (Defective Equipment) Act 1969 did not apply.[13]

A "defect" includes everything which renders the plant, etc. unfit for the **14–23** use for which it is intended when used in reasonable way and with reasonable care.[14] Thus soap, which was in itself not said to be in any way defective, was defective within the Act where it could be used safely with gloves but was not safe without. A ventilation system was defective where clips which provided the suspension link from roof trusses for the support of ducting and trunking were insufficient for their purpose.[15]

In the important decision of *Edwards v. Butlins*,[16] the Inner House **14–24** reversed the decision below to bring interpretation more into accord with the intent of the act. The case decides, it is submitted, that where the defenders pleadings can be read as accepting that the equipment was defective then the pursuer does not have to bring home liability to one of the two possible actual wrongdoers.

---

[10] *Coltman v. Bibby Tankers Ltd* [1988] A.C. 276.
[11] *Ralston v. Greater Glasgow Health Board*, 1987 S.L.T. 386.
[12] 1984 S.L.T. 115.
[13] *Marshall v. D.B. Marshall (Newbridge) Ltd*, 1991 G.W.D. 30–1807.
[14] *Yarmouth v. France* (1887) 19 Q.B.D. 647, *per* Lindley L.J. at 658 quoted with approval by Lord Kincraig in *Ralston v. Greater Glasgow Health Board*, 1987 S.L.T. (Notes) 386 at 387.
[15] *Yuill v. Daks Simpson Ltd*, 1984 S.L.T. 116.
[16] 1998 S.L.T. 500.

Statutory language in United Kingdom employers' legislation

14–25   As some familiar language has been used in the "new" legislation it might be useful to note that many of these phrases have been interpreted in the past and it is fair to say that it may be assumed that these interpretations are still valid unless there is something said to the contrary.[17] These regulations are meant to implement European Union legislation . As has been explained in Chapter 11, a "euro-rep" action is possible for defective transposition. The fact that the United Kingdom chose to retain many of its linguistic formulations opens the possibility of such challenge and indeed it has already been partially ventilated in a Scots case.[18] The phrase "practicable" was defined and its practical effect as effecting a reversal of the onus of proof was established in *Nimmo v. Alexander Cowan & Sons Ltd*,[19] a Scottish House of Lords decision. A workman sustained injury when unloading bales of pulp in a factory from a railway wagon. He claimed damages from his employers. He averred that he required to stand on certain bales in the course of his work, that the bales were insecure, and that while he was standing on one it tipped up "precipitating him to the floor" whereby he sustained serious injury. He further averred that the place at which he had to work was not made and kept safe for him working there, and so that the defenders' breach of their duty under section 29(1) caused the accident. The defenders contended that the pursuer's averments were irrelevant in as much as he had not averred that it was "reasonably practicable" for them to provide and maintain a safe means of access to his working place, while the pursuer maintained that the question of reasonable practicability was a matter of defend which, if it was to be raised, must be averred by the defenders. The court held that the pursuer's averments were relevant and stated:

> "In construing a statute and determining the incidence of the burden of proof the parties' respective means of knowledge and spheres of responsibility are important factors to be taken into account together with the form and content of the relevant statutory provisions. On a true construction of section 29(1) it is for the defenders to aver and prove by way of excuse for the unsafety of the working place that they had made it safe so far as reasonably practicable or that it was not reasonably practicable to make it any safer".[20]

14–26   That decision can be seen in application in *Robertson v. R.B. Cowe & Co.*[21] A workman was painting the stern of a fishing boat, which was on a slipway,

---

[17] See, *e.g. Kelly v. First Engineering Ltd*, 1999 S.C.L.R. 1025; 1999 Rep. L.R. 106.

[18] *McTighe v. East & Midlothian NHS Trust*, 1998 S.L.T. 969; 1998 S.C.L.R. 203; 1998 Rep. L.R. 21. The pursuer argued without objection (and without success) that regulation 5 of the Provision and Use of Work Equipment Regulations 1992 in allowing suitability to be judged by reference to reasonable foresight did not comply with the foundation European Directive allowing the pursuer to make a claim under the euro-rep head, the defenders being an emanation of the state.

[19] 1967 S.L.T. 277.

[20] See *Rae v. Strathclyde Joint Police Board*, 1999 S.C.L.R. 793 for s. 7 Offices Shops and Railway Premises Act 1963.

[21] 1970 S.L.T. 122.

from staging consisting of trestles and planks, which had been erected round the stern of the boat. The staging collapsed throwing the workman to the ground and causing him injuries. It was said:

> "Before the decision of the House of Lords in *Nimmo v. Alexander Cowan & Sons Ltd* I shared with your Lordships the view that in a case under s. 29(1) it was for the pursuer to aver and prove that it would have been 'reasonably practicable' for the employers to make and keep the working place safe but the House of Lords said that was not so. They decided it was for the employers to aver and prove by way of excuse for the unsafety of the working place that they had made it safe so far as was reasonably practicable to make it any safer. (Lord Guest at 281, Lord Upjohn at 282, and Lord Pearson at 285) . . . In this case, however the defender avers: 'There were no reasonably practicable steps to make and keep the said staging safe which the defenders did not take'. In evidence they contented themselves with showing that the materials and design were good and the erection was done by an experienced chargehand . . . In view of the decision in *Nimmo*, I think that all the pursuer has to do is to prove, as I think he has done, that the trestle fell over while he was working in a normal way. It is then for the defenders to show by way of excuse that it was not 'reasonably practicable' for them to have made and kept it safe. The defenders have not done that, and I think the pursuer is now entitled to succeed in his claim".[22]

Even cases prior to *Nimmo* will illustrate the idea of practicability. In *Fern v. Dundee Corporation*[23] an employee in a corporation bus depot sustained injury when he slipped on a patch of oil as he was guiding a single decker bus which was being driven in reverse. In an action at his instance against the Corporation on the ground that the defenders were, *inter alia*, in breach of their statutory duty it was held, after proof, that the pursuer slipped on a patch of oil which resulted in his injury. The defenders maintained that it was not "reasonably practicable" to keep the floor free from oil. The court held that on the facts, the defenders were liable in damages. There are other examples.[24]

There was a major revision of the approach to United Kingdom statutory **14–27** language in the mid-nineties. In *Mains v. Uniroyal Englebert Tyres Ltd*[25] it was held that it was proper to construe section 29(1) in a way more favourable to the pursuer than heretofore—that is by not glossing the statute by making "safe" depend upon reasonable foreseeability.[26]

---

[22] *ibid., per* Lord Migdale at 132.

[23] 1964 S.L.T. 294.

[24] *McWilliams v. Sir William Arrol & Co. Ltd*, 1961 S.L.T. 265; *Lynch v. Babcock Power Ltd*, 1988 S.L.T. 307; *Jenkins v. Allied Ironfounders Ltd*, 1970 S.L.T. 46; *Hall v. Fairfield Shipbuilding and Engineering Co. Ltd*, 1964 S.L.T. 97; *Sullivan v. Hall Russell & Co. Ltd*, 1964 S.L.T. 192; *Henderson v. Redpath Dorman Long Ltd*, 1975 S.L.T. (Sh. Ct) 27; *McGuire v. British Steel Corporation*, 1975 S.L.T. (Notes) 72; *Cillies v. Glynwed Foundries Ltd*, 1977 S.L.T. 97; *Brown v. Rowntree Mackintosh Ltd*, 1983 S.L.T. (Sh. Ct) 47; *Devine v. Costain Concrete Co. Ltd*, 1979 S.L.T. (Notes) 97; *McGuire v. British Steel Corporation*, 1975 S.L.T. (Notes) 72; *McCart v. Queen of Scots Knitwear Ltd*, 1987 S.L.T. (Sh. Ct) 57.

[25] 1995 S.L.T. 1115.

[26] Followed in *Beggs v. Motherwell Bridge Fabricators*, 1998 S.L.T. 1215; 1997 S.C.L.R. 1019; 1997 Rep. L.R. 87.

Statutory Provisions derived from European Union Legislation

Management of Health and Safety at Work Regulations 1992

14–28 By virtue of regulation 15, breach of a duty imposed by these regulations does not confer a right of action in any civil proceedings. The non-applicability is dissapplied in relation to any duty imposed by the regulation on an employer to the extent that it relates to work of a kind which could involve risk to the health and safety of a new or expectant mother[27] or her baby from any processes or working conditions, or physical, biological or chemical agents including those specified in the directive.[28] An attempt to base a case on regulation 3 failed.[29]

Workplace (Health Safety and Welfare) Regulations 1992

14–29 The regulations apply to a "new workplace" which is one used for the first time as a workplace after December 31, 1992. A "workplace" is defined in a complicated way and some applications of it require reference to the principal Act but the basic definition is "any premises or part of premises which are not domestic premises and are made available to any person as a place of work, and included (a) and place within the premises to which such person has access while at work; and (b) any room, lobby, corridor, staircase, road or other place used as a means of access to or egress from the workplace or where facilities are provided for use in connection with the workplace other than a public road.[30] Certain building operations are excluded[31] and things like mining and oil exploration rigs.[32]

14–30   The duty is placed on an employer to ensure that any workplace under his control complies with any applicable provisions of the regulations.[33] A person having control of a workplace in connection with the carrying on of a trade, business or other undertaking is likewise obliged.[34] Every person who is deemed to be the occupier of a factory under section 175(5) of the Factories Act 1961 has to ensure the premises comply with these rules.[35]

14–31   The workplace equipment, devices and systems must be maintained in an efficient state (from a health and safety point of view), in an efficient working order and in good repair. Cleaning must take place as appropriate.[36] Regulation 6 provides for ventilation. Regulation 7 provides for the temperature being reasonable but not by means of any injurious or offensive fumes. Sufficient thermometers must be produced. Regulation 8

---

[27] An employee who is pregnant; who has given birth within the previous six months; or who is breastfeeding: the Management of Health and Safety at Work (Amendment) Regulations 1994 (S.I. 1994 No. 2865).

[28] *ibid*.

[29] *Mitchell v. Campbeltown Shipyard Ltd*, 1998 G.W.D. 12–616.

[30] As defined in the Roads (Scotland) Act 1984, s. 151 (reg. 2(1)).

[31] As defined in the Factories Act 1961, s. 176 (reg. 3(1)(b)). Ships, as defined by reg. 2(1) of the Docks Regulations 1988, are also excluded (reg. 3(1)(a)).

[32] reg. 3(1)(c) and (d).

[33] reg. 4(1).

[34] reg. 4(2) and (3). Reg. 4(4) prevents this rule applying to a self-employed person or his/her partner.

[35] reg. 4(5).

[36] reg. 5.

provides for suitable and sufficient light which, so far as is reasonably practicable, shall be by natural light. Emergency lighting is required if there would otherwise be exposure to danger. Cleanliness and freedom from waste is required by Regulation 9 and extends to the floor wall and ceiling. So far as is reasonably practicable waste material must not be allowed to accumulate.[37] This is in addition to the provisions set out below in relation to slipping, tripping and falling. Regulation 10 on room dimensions and space requires free space to work and move about in with the Code of Practice setting this normally at 11 cubic metres. Regulation 11 provides for the worker to have a suitable work station with a suitable seat, suitable referring as much to the person actually using it as the task in hand.[38] In *Duncanson v. South Ayrshire Council*[39] the pursuer failed mainly on the facts of the case, failing to prove that a part of a cabinet was rough and jagged. It was held that in any event the arrangement of the cabinet trolley and table was suitable in terms of regulation 11 and that there was sufficient space in the room under regulation 10.

Regulation 12 states: **14–32**

"(1) Every floor in a workplace and the surface of every traffic route in a workplace shall be of a construction such that the floor or surface of the traffic routes is suitable for the purpose for which it is used. (2) Without prejudice to the generality of paragraph (1), the requirements in that paragraph shall include requirements that (a) the floor, or surface of the traffic route, shall have no hole or slope, or be uneven or slippery so as, in each case, to expose any person to a risk to his health or safety; (b) every such floor shall have effective means of drainage where necessary. (3) So far as is reasonably practicable, every floor in a workplace and the surface of every traffic route in a workplace shall be kept free from obstructions and from any article or substance which may cause a person to slip, trip or fall. (4) In considering whether for the purposes of paragraph (2)(a) a hole or slope exposes a person to a risk to his health or safety (a) no account shall be taken of a hole where adequate measures have been taken to prevent a person falling; (b) account shall be taken of any handrail provided in connection with any slope. (5) Suitable and sufficient handrails and, if appropriate, guards shall be provided on all traffic routes which are staircases except in circumstances in which a handrail cannot be provided without obstructing the traffic route."

Very detailed guidance is given in the Code of Practice which is required reading for the practitioner.[40] In *Banna v. Delicato*[41] it was held that a person who was not a worker could have the benefit of this regulation. In *O'Brien v. Duke of Argyll's Trustees*,[42] it was held following *Banna* that the

---

[37] reg. 9(3).
[38] In addition to the Code of Practice there is an HSE guidance publication called "Seating at Work": HAS(G) 57 (HMSO, 1991 ISBN 0118854313).
[39] 1999 S.L.T. 519; 1998 S.C.L.R. 1015; 1999 Rep. L.R. 35.
[40] See also HSE "Watch your step: Prevention of Slipping, Tripping and Falling Accidents at Work" (HMSO, 1985, ISBN 0118837826).
[41] 1999 Rep.B. 25–8.
[42] 1999 S.L.T. (Sh. Ct) 88.

pursuer's case was relevant where she alleged that when visiting an inn, she tripped over an allegedly rippled carpet.

14–33 Regulation 13 provides against falls or falling objects, which should normally be prevented other than by providing personal protective equipment such as hard hats and the like. So far as is practicable (note, not reasonably), every tank, pit or structure where there is a risk of a person in the workplace falling into a dangerous substance (as defined) in the tank, pit or structure, must be securely covered or fenced.[43]

Where necessary, for reasons of health and safety, windows or other translucent surfaces in a wall must be of safety material or protected against breakage of the material and be[44] marked to make it apparent. Windows, skylights and ventilators must be capable of being opened and closed[45] and cleaned safely.[46]

14–34 Another regulation likely to come before the practitioner frequently is Regulation 17. Every workplace must be organised in such a way that pedestrians and vehicles can circulate in a safe manner and the traffic routes[47] must be suitable, but the duty is only to the standard of reasonable practicability for a workplace which is not a new workplace, modification, extension or conversion. Sensibly motor vehicles and pedestrians are to be kept apart. There is a copious guidance.[48]

14–35 Doors and gates must be suitably constructed. Escalators and moving walkways must function safely and have an emergency stop button which is easily identifiable and readily accessible.[49] Suitable and safe sanitary conveniences must be provided at readily accessible places and they must be ventilated and lit, clean and orderly. Men and women must not share facilities.[50] Suitable and sufficient washing facilities must be available at readily accessible places. There must be showers if required by the nature of the work.[51] An adequate supply of wholesome drinking water must be provided which must be readily accessible at suitable places and provided with cups unless supplied in a convenient jet.[52] This explains the many "water-coolers" which have sprung up in offices all over the country.[53] Suitable and sufficient "accommodation" must be provided for clothing[54] and facilities for changing.[55] Suitable and sufficient rest facilities must be

---

[43] reg. 13(5).

[44] reg. 14.

[45] reg. 15. See also BS 8213 Part 1: 1991.

[46] reg. 16. Account may be taken of devices fitted to the building.

[47] By reg. 2 a "traffic route" is a route for pedestrian traffic, vehicles or both and includes any stairs, staircase, fixed ladder, doorway, gateway, loading bay or ramp.

[48] reg. 18.

[49] reg. 19. See also HSE "Ergonomic Aspects of Escalators used in Retail Organisations" CRR12/1989 (HMSO, 1989, ISBN 0118859382); BS 5656:1983 "Safety rules for the construction and installation of escalators and passenger conveyors".

[50] reg. 20.

[51] reg. 21. Perhaps had this been in place *McGhee* might never have happened. Detailed guidance is given in the Code of Practice right down to the number of "wash stations" per person which ought to be there.

[52] reg. 22.

[53] But only to the extent that it has given the vendors a reason to sell the product. It seems clear from the Code of Practice that a sink with cups which can be washed is fine.

[54] reg. 23.

[55] reg. 24.

provided and facilities to eat meals.[56] Rest rooms and rest areas must include suitable arrangements to protect non-smokers from discomfort caused by tobacco smoke.[57] Exemptions may be made from all the regulations in respect of the home forces or visiting forces.[58]

Provision and Use of Work Equipment Regulations 1992

There are three important preliminary definitions. "Use" in relation to **14–36** work equipment means any activity involving work equipment and includes starting, stopping, programming, setting, transporting, repairing, modifying, maintaining, servicing and cleaning, and related expressions shall be construed accordingly. "Work equipment" means any machinery, appliance, apparatus or tool and any assembly of components which in order to achieve a common end, are arranged and controlled so that they function as a whole.[59] "Suitable" means suitable in any respect which it is reasonably foreseeable will affect the health and safety of any person.[60] The regulations do not apply to or in relation to the master or crew of a sea-going ship.[61] They do apply to oil rigs and to self-employed persons.[62]

Every employer must ensure that work equipment is so constructed or **14–37** adapted as to be suitable for its purpose.[63] In selecting work equipment the employer must have regard to the working conditions and to the risks which exists including the risks posed by use of the equipment.[64] The employer must ensure that work equipment is used only for operations for which, and under conditions for which, it is suitable.[65]

There is a general duty to ensure work equipment is maintained in an **14–38** efficient state, in efficient working order and in good repair.[66] In *McMullan v. Glasgow Council*,[67] the pursuer was a 21–stone electrician who fell from a swing-back stepladder. He said one of the treads broke off. A common law case failed but a statutory case based on the absolute duty in the regulation succeeded. In *McTighe v. East & Midlothian NHS Trust*[68] a nurse in a lifting case failed in a case based on regulations 5 and 6. The equipment in question was the bed in which the patient was positioned, a part of which gave way. In *Duncanson v. South Ayrshire Council*[69] the pursuer failed mainly on the facts of the case, failing to prove that a part of a cabinet was rough and jagged which meant that it complied with regulations 5 and 6.[70]

---

[56] reg. 25.

[57] reg. 25(3). See also HSE "Passive smoking at work" IND(G) 63L (Rev) 1992.

[58] reg. 26. See also *Mulcahy v. Ministry of Defence* [1996] T.L.R. 39 for a general consideration of the army as employer.

[59] reg. 2.

[60] reg. 5.

[61] reg. 3.

[62] reg. 4.

[63] reg. 5(1).

[64] reg. 5(2).

[65] reg. 5(3). See the facts of *Smith v. Crossley Bros* (1951) 95 S.J. 655.

[66] reg. 6.

[67] 1998 G.W.D. 17–874.

[68] 1998 S.L.T. 969; 1998 S.C.L.R. 203; 1998 Rep. L.R. 21.

[69] 1999 S.L.T. 519; 1998 S.C.L.R. 1015; 1999 Rep. L.R. 35.

[70] See also *Martin v. Scottish Coal Co.*, 1998 G.W.D. 40–2077 in which the pursuer complained that his injury was due to a breach of regs 5 and 6. It was held that the case was not proved. The cause of the accident was the conduct of the pursuer in putting his hand in the wrong place.

Where the use of work equipment is likely to involve a specific risk to health or safety the employer must ensure that its use and repair is restricted to those designated.[71] Information, instruction and training must be given. Work equipment must conform to European Union standards.[72]

14–39   A new regulation replaces some of the familiar sections of the Factories Act:

> "11.—(1) Every employer shall ensure that measures are taken in accordance with paragraph (2) which are effective (a) to prevent access to any dangerous part of machinery or to any rotating stock-bar; or (b) to stop the movement of any dangerous part of machinery or rotating stock-bar before any part of a person enters a danger zone.[73] (2) The measures required by paragraph (1) shall consist of (a) the provision of fixed guards enclosing every dangerous part of rotating stock-bar[74] where and to the extent that it is practicable to do so, but where or to the extent that it is not, then (b) the provision of other guards or protection devices where and to the extent that it is practicable to do so, but where or to the extent that it is not, then (c) the provision of jigs, holders, push-sticks or similar protection appliances used in conjunction with the machinery where and to the extent that it is practicable to do so, but where or to the extent that it is not, then (d) the provision of information, instruction, training and supervision. (3) All guards and protection devices provided under sub-paragraphs (a) or (b) or paragraph (2) shall (a) be suitable for the purpose for which they are provided; (b) be of good construction, sound material and adequate strength: (c) be maintained in an efficient state, in efficient working order and in good repair; (d) not give rise to any increased risk to health or safety; (e) not be easily bypassed or disabled; (f) be situated at sufficient distance from the danger zone; (g) not unduly restrict the view of the operating cycle of the machinery, where such a view is necessary; (h) be so constructed or adapted that they allow operations necessary to fit or replace parts and for maintenance work, restricting access so that it is allowed only to the area where the work is to be carried out and, if possible, without having to dismantle the guard or protection device. (4) All protection appliances provided under sub-paragraph (c) of paragraph (2) shall comply with sub-paragraphs (a) to (d) and (g) of paragraph (3)".

14–40 Regulation 12 provides that special hazards must be prevented especially by using appropriate measures to minimise the effect of the hazards as well as to reduce the likelihood of it occurring, those hazards being parts falling or being ejected from the work equipment; rupture or disintegration of its parts; its catching fire or overheating; or its discharging gas or liquids which

---

[71] reg. 7.

[72] regs 8, 9 and 10.

[73] reg. 11(5) provides "Danger zone" means any zone in or around machinery in which a person is exposed to a risk to health or safety from contact with a dangerous part of machinery or a rotating stock-bar.

[74] reg. 11(5) provides "stock-bar" means any part of a stock-bar which projects beyond the head-stock of a lathe.

are used or stored in the equipment; the explosion of the equipment or article or substance produced, used or stored in it.[75] Employers must ensure protection from things at a very high or low temperature against burns scalding or searing.[76] Where appropriate equipment must have controls to start and vary equipment. It must only be possible to operate said control by deliberate action of the control unless part of the normal operating cycle of an automatic device.[77] A safe stop control must be provided where appropriate and one which operates in priority to other controls.[78] In some circumstances an emergency stop device needs to be fitted.[79] Other rules apply to controls.[80] Every employer must ensure that where appropriate work equipment is provided with suitable means to isolate it from all its sources of energy.[81] Every employer must ensure that work equipment or any part of it is stabilised by clamping or otherwise where necessary for purposes of health or safety.[82]

Suitable sufficient lighting must be provided.[83] So far as reasonably **14–41** practicable, maintenance must be possible when the machine is stopped.[84] Every employer must ensure that work equipment is marked in a clearly visible manner with any appropriate marking for reasons of health and safety.[85] Warnings unambiguous, easily perceived and easily understood must be displayed where appropriate.[86] The forces and visiting forces may be exempted.[87]

Personal Protective Equipment at Work Regulations 1992

Personal protective equipment (PPE) means all equipment (including **14–42** clothing affording protection against the weather) which is intended to be worn or held by a person at work and which protects him against one or more risks to his health or safety, and any accessory designed to meet that objective.[88] It has been held in the circumstances of one case that a bolt was not PPE.[89] The regulations took effect from January 1, 1993.[90] The regulations do not apply to ordinary working clothes which do not specifically protect health and safety; offensive weapons; portable devices for detecting and signalling risks and nuisances; PPE used for travelling on the road; where used during the playing of competitive sports or where there is other statutory provision as defined.[91]

---

[75] reg. 12(3) specifies the risks.
[76] reg. 13.
[77] reg. 14.
[78] reg. 15.
[79] reg. 16.
[80] regs 17 and 18.
[81] reg. 19.
[82] reg. 20.
[83] reg. 21.
[84] reg. 22.
[85] reg. 23.
[86] reg. 24.
[87] reg. 25.
[88] reg. 2. For a case under the common law considering the benefits and problems of PPE in the form of padded protective trousers for a chain saw operator see *Douglas v. Ladv*, 1996 G.W.D. 1981.
[89] *Kelly v. First Engineering Ltd*, 1999 S.C.L.R. 1025; 1999 Rep. L.R. 106.
[90] reg. 1.
[91] reg. 3.

14–43   Every employer must ensure that suitable PPE is provided to his employees who may be exposed to risk to their health or safety while at work, except where and to the extent that such risk has been adequately controlled by other means which are equally or more effective. PPE is not suitable unless it is appropriate for the risk involved, it takes account of ergonomic requirements and the state of health of the person who wears it, it fits, so far as reasonably practicable it is effective without itself increasing the overall risk, it complies with the law.[92] The PPE is to be compatible where more than one item is in use.[93] Before choosing the PPE the employer has to carry out an assessment which, in all but the most routine cases, ought to be recorded.[94] The PPE must be maintained in an efficient state, in efficient working order and in good repair which included replacement and cleaning.[95] Accommodation has to be provided for the PPE when not in use.[96] The employee is to be provided with such information, instructions and training as is adequate and appropriate to enable the employee to know the risks, the manner in which it is to be used and any action the employee is to take to make it work properly. The information must be "comprehensible to the persons to whom it is provided".[97]

14–44   The code indicates that the help is extensive including theoretical and practical training. Reasonable steps must be taken to ensure that the kit is properly used.[98] The employee is himself under a duty to use the kit and report its loss or defective condition.[99]

Again there is the possibility of exemption of the armed forces.[1]

14–45   An employer was found liable where a workman having to mow grass with a lawnmower on wet grass did not have suitable non-slippy shoes.[2]

Health and Safety (Display Screen Equipment) Regulations 1992

14–46 These regulations are new, not only like the other regulations in the sense of being newly expressed, but in the sense that there was barely any regulation at all in this field.[3] After the legislation a case at common law was successful before the Court of Appeal for a form of work-related upper limb disorder (not repetitive strain injury but PDA4) in connection with work like that covered by these regulations.[4] The key definitions are: "display screen equipment" means any alphanumeric or graphic display

---

[92] reg. 4.
[93] reg. 5.
[94] reg. 6.
[95] reg. 7.
[96] reg. 8.
[97] reg. 9.
[98] reg. 10.
[99] reg. 11.
[1] reg. 12.
[2] *Mitchell v. Inverclyde District Council*, 1998 S.L.T. 1157; 1998 S.C.L.R. 191; 1997 Rep. L.R. (Quantum) 29.
[3] These implement Directive 90/2701. See Lloyd and Simpson, "The Computer at Work", 1992 S.L.T. (News) 177.
[4] *Pickford v. Imperial Chemical Industries Plc.* Unreported, Court of Appeal, July 18, 1996; House of Lords [1998] T.L.R. 403. See generally B. Langstaff, "Upper Limb Disorders: Work Related or Unrelated?" [1994] J.P.I.L. 14.

screen, regardless of the display process involved (in what follows, such are called screen); "use" means use in or in connection with work; "user" means an employee who habitually uses display screen equipment as a significant part of his normal work; "workstation" means an assembly comprising (i) display screen equipment (whether provided with software determining the interface between the equipment and its operator or user, a keyboard or any other input device); (ii) any optional accessories to the display screen equipment; (iii) any disk drive, telephone, modem, printer, document holder, work chair, work desk, work surface or other item peripheral to the display screen equipment; and (iv) the immediate work environment around the display screen equipment.[5] The guidance indicates that an ordinary television screen is outside the rules but that microfiche readers are within the rules. The guidance also shows that there may be some difficulty in ascertaining who is a user. The guidance offers seven criteria which can be weighed up in making a decision. They are dependency, discretion, training, prolonged spells of over one hour, daily use, fast information transfer and criticality of errors. Drivers' cabs, screens on board a means of transport, portables (not in prolonged use), calculators and window typewriters are excluded from the regulations.[6] A suitable assessment must be carried out.[7] Very detailed provisions are made for workstations first put into service on or after January 1, 1993. Others had to be brought up to that standard by December 31, 1996.[8] Daily work on screens is to be planned to provide interruptions to reduce the workload.[9] In the guidance it is pointed out that short, frequent breaks are better than occasional, long breaks.[10] The employer must provide eye tests.[11] Adequate health and safety training in relation to the equipment used is to be given.[12] The users must be told about all aspects of health and safety relating to their workstations and the measures taken by the employer to comply.[13] The armed forces may be exempted.[14]

Manual Handling Operations Regulations 1992

This regulation, at the time of writing, has been the most commonly **14–47** litigated probably because such injuries are so frequent. Fatalities are rare but as at 1992 HSE information suggested that more than a quarter of all reported accidents were due to manual handling and about a third of three-day injuries. This regulation came into force on January 1, 1993.[15] "Manual handling operations" means any transporting or supporting of a load (including the lifting, putting down, pushing, pulling, carrying or moving thereof) by hand or by bodily force. "Load" includes any person and any

---

[5] reg. 1.
[6] reg. 1(4).
[7] reg. 2.
[8] reg. 3.
[9] reg. 4.
[10] This was thought to be common sense for secretaries with tasks other than typing in the House of Lords decision in *Pickford*, n. 4 above.
[11] reg. 5.
[12] reg. 6.
[13] reg. 7.
[14] reg. 8.
[15] reg. 1.

animal. Importantly, the word "injury" is subject to a restricted definition: "injury" does not include injury caused by any toxic or corrosive substance which (a) has leaked or spilled from a load; (b) is present on the surface of a load but has not leaked or spilled from it; or (c) is a constituent part of a load.[16] The regulations apply to a self-employed person,[17] but not to the master or crew of a sea going ship.[18]

14-48   Each employer must, so far as reasonably practicable, avoid the need for his employees to do any manual handling which involves a risk of their being injured.[19] If manual handling is necessary then the employer must assess the risk of their being injured according to the details in the schedule to the regulations.[20] Where it is not reasonably practicable to avoid the need for his employees to undertake any manual handling operations at work which involve a risk of their being injured the employer must take appropriate steps to reduce the risk of injury to the lowest level reasonably practicable[21] and must give general indications and, where possible, precise indications on the weight of each load and the heaviest side of any whose centre of gravity is not positioned centrally.[22] Employees have a duty to make use of any system laid down to comply with regulation 4(1)(b)(ii).[23] The armed forces may be exempted.[24]

14-49   This regulation repealed section 74 of the Factories Act which was held by the court not to create any civil liability. Section 72 had attracted liability.[25] More recently in *Watkinson v. British Telecom*[26] a workman succeeded in a case based on an injury to his back when he was moving heavy loads; liability was established both at common law and under statute. The workman had not been able to recall his precise movements at the time and this was thought not to be unreasonable. The inference could reasonably be made that his injury was caused by moving the heavy reels of paper. The employers were in breach of a common law duty to provide training in how to move the reels safely.[27]

14-50   In *Fraser v. Greater Glasgow Health Board*[28] a nursing auxiliary who hurt her back lifting a patient sued. She was assisting a staff nurse who had already trained her in lifting. The staff nurse instructed a certain mode of lifting. The defenders were held liable primarily because the lift had not been properly co-ordinated, the pursuer having one of her hands in the wrong place. While she was successful at common law the Manual Handling Regulations were held not to be applicable as they were said to apply to

---

[16] reg. 2.
[17] reg. 2(2).
[18] reg. 3.
[19] reg. 4(1)(a).
[20] reg. 4(1)(b)(i).
[21] reg. 4(1)(b)(ii).
[22] reg. 4(1)(b)(iii). Assessments of risk must be reviewed: reg. 4(2).
[23] reg. 5.
[24] reg. 6.
[25] See generally *Power v. Greater Glasgow Health Board*, 1987 S.L.T. 567 and *Fotheringham v. Dunfermline District Council*, 1991 S.L.T. 610. In each case reference was made to and reliance was placed upon the case of *Bailey v. Rolls Royce (1971) Ltd* [1984] I.C.R. 688. *Whitfield v. H & R Johnson (Tiles)* [1990] 3 All E.R. 426.
[26] 1996 S.L.T. 72.
[27] See too *Crofts v. Roche Products Ltd*, 1995 G.W.D. 26–1416.
[28] (1996) Rep.L.R. 62.

regular operations and not to an emergency. In *Cullen v. North Lanarkshire Council*[29] the workman was shifting loads from a truck to a skip. In doing so he lost his footing. There was no common law case and a case on the 1992 Manual Handling Regulations failed because they were said to be directed towards strain rather than loss of footing. That was not a convincing argument. The HSE guidance talks of "the transporting" of loads (p. 1) not just straining at lifting. At p. 6, para. 15 it seems clear that manual handling is accepted as involving moving, steadying or positioning in. "Manual handling also included the intentional dropping of a load and the throwing of a load whether into a receptacle or from one person to another". It was found that there was no risk of injury. Paragraph 62 states: "Additionally, because of the way in which pushing and pulling forces have to be transmitted from the handler's feet to the floor, the risk of slipping and consequent injury is much greater. For this reason pushing or pulling a load in circumstances where the grip between foot and floor is poor—whether through the conditions of the floor, footwear or both—is likely to increase significantly the risk of injury". This makes it clear that risk of injury is a wider concept than just strain and an assessment of the situation revealed in the report suggests that the regulations were not met. On appeal the Division, it is submitted correctly, reversed.[30] In *Anderson v. Lothian Health Board*,[31] Lord McFadyen took a mischief orientated approach. A workman strained his neck loading a laundry. The employers were held liable under both reg 4(1)(a) and 4(1)(b)(ii). They had not avoided the need for manual handling at all nor had they taken appropriate steps to lower the risk. They had already had a risk assessment carried out and the maximum weight to be lifted had been set at 40 kgs but no system was in place to prevent workers lifting that weight.

Lord Cameron also took a wider view more consonant with the mission **14-51** of the regulations in *Divit v. British Telecom*.[32] A workman was hurt while manipulating the flap on a kiosk door. The flap could be a load and the regulations were not confined to strain injuries. Both sides argued by reference to the Council directives and the schedule to the regulations which provides certain guidance. A proof before answer was allowed. In *Nicolls v. City of Glasgow*,[33] the pursuer had to shift bales of hay with a wheelbarrow. The bales restricted the worker's view. The injury due to a jolt on the uneven surface was a foreseeable possibility and thus within the regulations. However, cases where the employer has provided and instructed the use of proper equipment but this is ignored by the worker will still result in the employee failing even under these new regulations.[34] In *King v. Carron Phoenix Ltd*[35] it was held that had there been a causal

---

[29] (1996) Rep.L.R. 87.

[30] *Cullen v. North Lanarkshire Council*, 1998 S.C.L.R. 408, approving the approach in *Anderson v. Lothian Health Board* (1996) Rep. L.R. 88 next discussed. For a case taking a view rather different to *Cullen* subsequent to the Inner House decision see *Taylor v. City of Glasgow*, 1999 Rep.L.R. 124 (wardrobe lifting).

[31] (1996) Rep.L.R. 88.

[32] 1997 G.W.D. 12–530.

[33] Unreported, Glasgow Sheriff Court, December 23, 1996.

[34] *Urquhart v. Biwater Industries Ltd*, 1998 S.L.T. 576; 1998 S.C.L.R. 198: the pursuer did not use the crane provided but tried to lift concrete blocks himself.

[35] 1999 Rep.L.R. 51.

connection, there would have been no liability under regulation 4 where the task complained of was using a spanner to tighten bolts and the physical complaint was tennis elbow. In *Hall v. Edinburgh City Council*[36] the pursuer, a blacksmith, sued as a result of injury when he tried to move a 50kg. bag of cement with a colleague. The pursuer succeeded on the basis of his expert evidence and the HSE guidelines in establishing a breach of regulation 4(1)(a).

Other Regulations

14–52 Just as there are many statutes which may found a statutory case not dealt with in this book there are other important regulations. Most noteworthy are the Construction (Health, Safety & Welfare) Regulations 1996,[37] the detail of which is beyond the scope of this book. There is a very detailed definition of construction work.[38] It provides for "standard" protection such as safe places of work (so far as reasonably practicable) and other more practical and appropriate measures such as falling,[39] falling objects,[40] excavation,[41] cofferdams and caissons,[42] weather protection,[43] and lighting.[44] There are specific schedules specifying requirements for guard rails,[45] working platforms,[46] ladders,[47] and welfare facilities.[48]

---

[36] 1999 S.L.T. 744.
[37] S.I. 1996 No. 1592. In force September 1996.
[38] reg. 2.
[39] reg. 6.
[40] reg. 8.
[41] reg. 12.
[42] reg. 13.
[43] reg. 24.
[44] reg. 25.
[45] Sched. 1.
[46] Sched. 2.
[47] Sched. 5. Three metres is the new bright line.
[48] Sched. 6.

CHAPTER 15

PRODUCT LIABILITY

Introduction

Scots law did recognise delictual liability outwith contract in respect of **15–1** injuries caused by products in some circumstances. In one case the liability was upon the person who left a dangerous machine in a public place.[1] In another case the owner was liable even although the pursuer's injuries were the result of the acts of another: two children played with the door of a shed on waste ground and it fell on another as a result of its insufficiency.[2] It would not have fallen if the boys had not climbed up the door and lifted a drop bar. On the other hand where the goods were intrinsically safe, there was no liability.[3] An interesting case showing the state of the Scots law at the turn of the nineteenth century is *Gordon v. McHardy*.[4] The pursuer sued for the death of his son. It was said he had died as a result of eating tinned salmon. His wife bought it from the defender in an unmarked dented can. The action, brought in delict, was held relevant in the sheriff court. It was unanimously held to be irrelevant in the Inner House. The Lord Justice-Clerk (MacDonald) noted that to examine the contents would be to destroy the condition established by the manufacturer. He held that "a grocer who gets a quantity of tins of preserved food and sells them to the public as he got them, cannot be liable for the condition of the contents of the tins if he buys from a dealer of repute".[5] If there had been a dent in the tin (signifying a break in the preservative vacuum) he thought it might be different but of course the pursuer or his wife ought to have noticed that. Lord Moncreiff, ahead of his time, said that if there had been any averment that the defender was asked to disclose the name of the manufacturer and refused, he would have allowed an inquiry.

Cases are then brought against manufacturers. In the first noticeable **15–2** cases[6], the Inner House, despite proof that there had indeed been dead mice found in aerated water bottles, rejected claims by a consumer against a manufacturer. The pursuer relied mainly on English authority but put the argument on principle and relied on the fact that Scots law had already accepted that the servant of a tenant could sue a landlord for negligence.[7] It

---

[1] *Campbell v. Ord* (1873) 1 R. 149.
[2] *Findlay v. Angus* (1887) 14 R. 312.
[3] *Duff v. National Telephone Co.* (1889) 16 R. 675.
[4] (1903) 6 F. 210.
[5] *ibid.* at 212.
[6] *Mullen v. A.G. Barr & Co.* and *McGowan v. Barr & Co.*, 1929 S.C.461.
[7] *Kennedy v. Bruce*, 1907 S.C. 845, distinguishing *Cameron v. Young*, 1907 S.C. 475 on the basis that *Cameron* was a contract cases (although Lord Ardwall's reading of the Session papers noted a reference to fault).

was also accepted as good law at that time that a manufacturer would be liable for products he knew to be dangerous or which were *per se* dangerous such as explosives. Lord Ormidale on principle would have considered agreeing that there was a duty but felt constrained by persuasive authority from England. Lord Hunter, influenced by *Heaven v. Pender*[8] did think there was a duty and that it had been breached. In the United States, another mighty manufacturing nation, liability had already been fixed on the manufacturer.[9] That was the immediate background to *Donoghue v. Stevenson* which marks the beginning of the modern common law.

THE NEIGHBOUR PRINCIPLE AND PRODUCT LIABILITY

The Product Liability Rule

15–3 The product liability[10] ratio of *Donoghue v. Stevenson*[11] can be said to be found in the following passage:

> "a manufacturer of products, which he sells in such a form as to show that he intends them to reach the ultimate consumer in the form in which they left him with no reasonable case in the preparation or putting up of the products will result in an injury to the consumer's life or property, owes a duty to the consumer to take that reasonable case".[12]

Intermediate examination

15–4 In *Donoghue* the seller of the ginger beer could not be expected to open the bottles to check for decomposed snails. This explains why the fact that the bottle was opaque is such a material fact. *Gordon v. McHardy*[13] discussed above[14] shows the Scottish courts appreciating that a retailer cannot be expected to examine a vacuum sealed can and that as a result, *per* Lord Moncreiff, the identity of the manufacturer had to be revealed. As *Donoghue* arguably unified the law in the United Kingdom it is now appropriate to consider some English authority as well.

15–5 Very soon after *Donoghue* the concept was tested in *Grant v. A.K.M. Ltd.*[15] In *Grant* a retailer took goods from their packaging and placed them

---

[8] (1883) L.R. 11 Q.B.D. 503.

[9] *MacPherson v. Buick Motor Co.*, 217 N.Y. 382, 11 N.E. 1050 (1916); and see also the case noted by D. Powles, "Product Liability—A Novel Dimension in Scots Law" in A.J. Gamble (ed.), *Obligations in Context* (1990, W. Green) at p. 33: *Lyons v. Coca Cola Bottling Works* (1927) III So. 305 (glass in the bottle). See also A. Rodger, "Lord MacMillan's Speech" (1992) 108 L.Q.R. 236.

[10] Product liability as a generalised phrase may have come to the fore as a result of its adoption in the 1960s in the work of the American Law Institute; indeed it may well be the Restatement of Torts, Second that "founded" the statutory law discussed below: Fleming, *Product Liability*, Paisley Papers, p. 119.

[11] 1932 S.C. (H.L.) 31.

[12] *ibid.* at 57.

[13] (1903) 6 F. 210.

[14] See para. 15–1 above.

[15] [1935] All E.R. 209.

on shelves. This would allow him to detect the presence of dead mice, snails and the like. In this case the injury came from chemicals on the product and it was accepted by the Privy Council that the possibility of intermediate examination did not deprive the plaintiff of success so long as the defect remained "hidden and unknown".[16] In *Kubach v. Hollands*[17] the second defendants who had purchased chemicals from the third party were met by the defence that the third party's invoice stated that the chemicals should be "examined and tested by user before use". The chemicals had not been examined and tested and when used caused harm to the pursuer. The second defenders lost because they "had ample and repeated opportunity of intermediate examination, and, if they had taken the simple precaution which the invoice warned them to take, no mischief would have followed". In a more recent authoritative exposition of the law in the House of Lords, the principle of intermediate examination was restated as part of the essence of *Donoghue* liability.[18] It has been asked, "but what is the house purchaser to do once the defect ceases to be latent? None can afford to throw away a defective house as one would a contaminated bottled drink".[19]

The Common Law and Defective Products

The chapter title being product liability, the scope is not limited by the type **15–6** of damage caused. *Donoghue* liability is in relation to dangerous products. Safe but disconform products do not fall within its ratio. At common law a safe but disconform product raises a liability for economic loss and the relevant principles are canvassed above.[20] In such cases the role of contract becomes ever more important for if it is contract that brings parties into a relationship, the contract has to be respected so far as the defender is concerned.

Complex Structures and the Common Law

The so-called complex structure theory was abandoned in *Murphy v.* **15–7** *Brentwood District Council*[21] That theory indicated that in complex structures, like houses, one product could destroy the whole product and thus be the cause of property damage instead of economic loss. While the theory has gone, if the facts clearly reveal a product destroying a bigger product there is room for *Murphy* to be distinguished. In *Stevenson and Stevenson v. Stephen (Builders) Ltd and Stevenson*[22] the pursuers bought a house and it burned down. A fire started in the garage and spread to the house. "It was able to do so because there was no separating wall or fire stop between the

---

[16] Although it did not have to be decided it was considered that the presence of phenol in a bottle of Irn Bru would not have been reasonably detectable in a translucent but labelled bottle and if it had it would not have indicated danger: *Lockhart v. Barr*, 1943 S.C. (H.L.) 1; (Inner House) 1941 S.L.T. 416.

[17] [1937] 3 All E.R. 907.

[18] *Murphy v. Brentwood District Council* [1990] 3 W.L.R. 414.

[19] Heuston, *Overview of the Law of Negligence*, Paisley Papers 65.

[20] See Chap. 10. See *Muirhead v. Industrial Tank Specialties Ltd* [1986] Q.B. 507; *Simaan General Contracting Co. v. Pilkington Glass Ltd (No. 2)* [1988] Q.B. 758.

[21] *Murphy, ibid.*

[22] Unreported, May 3, 1995.

house and the garage in the roof space to prevent or at least to retard the passage of fire". It was alleged a proper fire stop would have held back the fire till the fire brigade arrived. It was also averred that the work was not carried out according to the building warrant. It was held the case was relevant despite the fact that the amount sued for was rebuilding in terms of a title condition. The claim was not for the defective house but the house destroyed because of the foreseeable danger to the property of omission to build the fire barrier.

Proof of the common law liability

15–8 In the United States strict product liability was reached through the use of the approach to evidence. Here it came close but ultimately the burden almost always remains with the pursuer. The case of *Grant* was an example of *res ipsa loquitur* being applied.

In this context the most important Scottish case is *Lockhart v. Barr*.[23] Lord Justice-Clerk Cooper described the case before him as being:

> "midway between *Grant v. Australian Knitting Mills* and *Mullen v. Barr*. In *Grant* the matter knew that all the articles in question had been deliberately impregnated with sulphite, and that this sulphite must be rendered innocuous. In *Mullen v. Barr* a priori grounds for believing that a ginger-beer bottle had been chosen as a habitat for a mouse were relatively slender, for such a thing had never happened in over fifty years. In the present case every bottle was potentially contaminated by some deleterious substance which might vary from microbe bearing dirt to the most virulent poison, and every bottle was supposed to be treated in the cleaning plant on this footing. "[24]

The really mysterious thing about the case is that the Lord Ordinary had found no proof that there was anything in the bottle sufficient to cause harm; the injuries were "something of a mystery". The Lord Justice-Clerk was able however, to review the evidence and find that it was caused by contaminants sufficient to cause the injuries. He held that the "so-called maxim" *res ipsa loquitur* did not apply but did not say why. Liability was established on the basis that on the evidence the only explanation was that an employee had taken an unwashed bottle and put it on the filling side of the plant, even although no direct evidence was available of this.[25] In *Donoghue v. Concrete Products (Kirkcaldy) Ltd*,[26] *Lockhart* was applied to allow the pursuer not to have to prove precisely how a defective slab came to be worked upon by him. The defenders had alleged that they had an excellent system and the only way in which the slab could have come into circulation was an isolated act of negligence by an employee for which they

---

[23] 1943 S.C. (H.L.) 1; (Inner House) 1941 S.L.T. 416.
[24] *ibid* at 417.
[25] *ibid*. at 418 there is an amusing indication in the report that Health and Safety staff at the plant were not all they might be: the sample which both sides sent for analysis had been severely depleted by three of the defenders' employees tasting the bottle to see if it were really poisoned!
[26] 1976 S.L.T. 58.

should not be liable. The Lord Ordinary (Wylie) held that as the case was not an employers' liability system case but a product liability case this explanation was no defence.[27] In *Carroll v. Fearon*[28] the English Court of Appeal upheld a finding that once a tyre burst and it was established that there had been a defect in the manufacturing process, liability was established. The defenders' argument that the pursuer had failed to show the respects in which the manufacturing process had failed was rejected. This is an important exposition of the law applicable as much in Scotland as in England. The fact that Scottish pleadings require specification does not mean that the pursuer must be called on to specify more than the law requires.

The Scope of the Common Law Rule

The protection of the law expanded beyond food.[29] Not only the person **15–9** who has consumed the product but the ultimate user has been protected.[30] It also applies to persons in the vicinity of the product.[31] The duty extended to the packaging of the product.[32] Directions and instructions are subject to the duty.[33] Simply having been in possession of the goods as an importer is not sufficient to establish liability at common law.[34]

STATUTORY LIABILITY

The nature of liability

The Consumer Protection Act 1987 is based upon harmonisation of laws by **15–10** the European Directive 85/374/EEC.[35] It is expressly stated in the Act that it has to be construed to comply with the Directive.[36]

---

[27] *ibid.* at 60.

[28] [1998] T.L.R. 31.

[29] *Brown v. Cotterill* [1934] 51 T.L.R. 21 (tombstone); *Vacwell Engineering Co Ltd v. BDH Chemicals Ltd* [1971] 1 Q.B. 88 (Chemicals); *Herschtal v. Stewart & Ardern* [1940] 1 K.B. 155 (motor vehicle).

[30] *Grant v. A.K.M. Ltd* [1935 All E.R. 209.

[31] *Brown, ibid.* and see also *Stenett v. Hanock* [1939] 2 All E.R. 650.

[32] *Barnes v. Irweell Valley Water Board* [1938] 2 All E.R. 650.

[33] *Watson v. Buckley* [1940] 1 All E.R. 174, *Holmes v. Ashford* [1950] 2 All E.R. 76. *Vacwell, op. cit.*

[34] *Thomson v. Sinclair*, 1992 G.W.D. 8–439.

[35] See generally Clark, *Product Liability* (Sweet & Maxwell, 1989); J. Blaikie "Product Liability" (1987) 32 J.L.S. 325; A. Clark, "Liability for Defective Products" (1981) 26 J.L.S. 398; A. Clark, "Product Liability: The New Rules", 1987 S.L.T. (News) 257; A. Clark, "Conceptual Basis of the Product Liability" (1985) 48 M.L.R. 325; A. Clark, "U.S. Product Liability" (1982) 27 J.L.S. 514; W.C.H. Ervine, "Product Liability and Part 1 of the Consumer Protection Act 1987" (1988) SCOLAG 21; P.R. Ferguson, "Pharmaceutical Products Liability", 1992 J.R. 226; P.R. Ferguson, "Compensation for Alleged Vaccine Injury" (1994) 39 J.L.S. 80; C. Newdick, "The Future of Negligence in Product Liability" (1987) 103 L.Q.R. 288; C. Newdick, "The Development Risk Defence" 1988 C.L.J. 455; J. Stapleton, "Products Liability Reform—Real or Illusory", 1986 6 O.J.L.S. 392; D. Powles, "Product Liability—A Novel Dimension in Scots Law", in A.J. Gamble (ed.), *Obligations in Context* (1990, W. Green) at p. 33.

[36] s. 1. This saved the Act from an attack in the European Court.

"Products"

15–11 "Product" is specially defined as meaning any goods or electricity and includes a product which is comprised in another product, whether by virtue of being a component part or raw material or otherwise.[37] "Goods" is defined as including "substances, growing crops, and things included in land by virtue of being attached[38] to it and any ship, aircraft or vehicle."[39]

There is no liability in respect of any game or agricultural produce.[40] There is a new European Union directive proposed to apply to agricultural produce too.[41]

"Defective"

15–12 The common law of negligence has normally been concerned with dangerous products and the concept of defectiveness more a matter of contract. Happily the legislation directs the courts to the issues to be considered by way of laying down a general principle and guidelines.[42] There is a defect in a product if the safety of the product is not such as persons generally are entitled to expect; and "safety", in relation to a product shall include safety with respect to products comprised in that product and safety in the context of risks of damage to property, as well as in the context of risks of death or personal injury.[43] In determining what "persons generally are entitled to expect" in relation to a product all the circumstances must be taken into account, including: (a) The manner in which, and purposes for which, the product has been marketed, its get-up, the use of any mark in relation to the product and any instructions for, or warning with respect to, doing or refraining from doing anything with or in relation to the product,[44] (b) What might reasonably be expected to be done with or in relation to the product; and (c) the time when the product was supplied by its producer to another.[45] It might be of interest to note that at the end of the twentieth century the contractual test of the nineteenth century "merchantable quality" was changed to "satisfactory quality".[46]

Who is liable?

15–13 The focus of the legislation is upon the producer. A "producer", in relation to a product means (a) the person who manufactured it; (b) in the case of a substance which has not been manufactured but has been won or

---

[37] s. 1(2) and (3). See also J. Stapleton, "Software, Information and the Concept of Product" (1989) 9 Tel Aviv Stud. in Law 47; R. Colbey, "Personal Injury Claims Arising out of Food Poisoning" [1994] J.P.I.L. 294.

[38] For Scotland this means becoming heritable by accession: s. 45(5).

[39] s. 45(1).

[40] Defined as produce of the soil or stock farming or fisheries so long as it has not undergone an industrial process at the time of supply. See generally, D. Crichton, R. Mays and S. Middlemiss, "Liability for CJD Deaths", 1998 J.R. 89.

[41] "Extension of Product Liability Directive" (1998) 43 J.L.S. 45.

[42] See A. Stoppa, "The Concept of Defectiveness in the Consumer Protection Act 1987: A Critical Analysis" (1992) 12 L.S. 210.

[43] s. 3(1).

[44] The huge increase in litigation in the U.S. is attributed to design defect and failure to warn cases: Fleming, *Product Liability*, Paisley Papers, 126.

[45] s. 3(2).

[46] *Stair Memorial Encyclopedia*, Vol. 20 "Sale". See *Thain v. Anniesland Trade Centre* 1997 S.L.T. (Sh. Ct) 102.

abstracted, the person who won or abstracted it; (c) in the case of a product which has not been manufactured, won or abstracted but essential characteristics of which are attributable to an industrial or other process having been carried out (for example; in relation to agricultural produce), the person who carried out that process.[47]

But not only these persons are liable. Section 2 of the Act extends the **15–14** ambit of liability. The range of persons liable are: (a) the producer of the product; (b) any person who, by putting his name on the product or using a trade mark or other distinguishing mark in relation to the product, has held himself out to be the producer of the product; (c) any person who has imported the product into a Member State from a place outside the Member State in order, in the course of any business of his, to supply it to another.[48]

A further and defeasible liability is placed upon another category of **15–15** person. Where any damage is caused wholly or partly by a defect in a product, any person who supplied the product (whether to the person who suffered the damage, to the producer of any product in which the product in question is comprised or to any other person) is liable for the damage if—(a) the person who suffered the damage requests the supplier to identify one or more of the persons (whether still in existence or not) who produced or imported it; (b) that request is made within a reasonable period after the damage occurs and at a time when it is not reasonably practicable for the person making the request to identify all those persons; and (c) the supplier fails, within a reasonable period after receiving the request, either to comply with the request or to identify the person who supplies the product to him.[49]

The extensions of liability do not apply to a person in respect of any **15–16** defect in any game or agricultural produce if the only supply of the game or produce by that person to another was at a time when it had not undergone an industrial process.[50] Where two or more persons are liable by virtue of the Act for the same damage their liability is joint and several.[51]

Who can sue?

The Act deals with this issue from the point of view of the defences and **15–17** restrictions upon liability. Theoretically anyone can sue. But as will be seen below most consumers will be able to sue and most non-consumers will not—but that is not precisely the law for the reasons that become clear below.

Defences

A defect is not to be inferred from the fact only that the safety of a product **15–18** which is supplied after the product complained of is greater than the safety of the product in question.[52]

---

[47] s. 2(2).
[48] s. 2(2). For a common law case against an importer see *Thomson v. Sinclair*, 1992 G.W.D. 8–439.
[49] s. 2(3).
[50] s. 2(4).
[51] s. 2(5).
[52] s. 3(2).

Compliance with community law

15–19 It is a defence to show that the defect is attributable to compliance with any requirements imposed by or under any enactment or with any Community obligation.[53]

Non-supply

15–20 It is a defence to show that the person proceeded against did not at any time supply the product to another.[54]

Non-commercial supply

15–21 It is a defence to show that the only supply of the product to another by the person proceeded against was otherwise than in the course of a business of that person's.[55]

No defect

15–22 It is a defence to show that the defect did not exist in the product at the relevant times.[56]

The development risks/state of the art defence

15–23 It is a defence to show that the state of the scientific and technical knowledge at the relevant time was not such that a producer of products of the same description as the product in question might be expected to have discovered the defect if it had existed in his products while they were under his control.[57] The Directive provided that the Commission would review in 1995 whether Member States should be allowed to continue to permit this and other provisions.[58] There was concern during the passage of the legislation that the United Kingdom's form of the defence narrated above did not properly implement the Directive.[59] Article 7(e) of the Directive provides a defence that "the state of scientific and technical knowledge at the time when he put the product into circulation was not such as to enable

---

[53] s. 4(1)(a).

[54] s. 4(1)(b).

[55] s. 4(1)(e). See Blaikie, "Product Liability" (1987) 32 J.L.S. 325 at 328.

[56] s. 4(1)(d).

[57] s. 4(1)(e). See Goldberg, "The Development Risk Defence and Medicinal Products" (1991) 36 J.L.S. 376; P. Spink, "The Consumer Protection Act 1987—The State of the Art Defence" (1997) 42 J.L.S. 416.

[58] Nothing has been done as a result of the review at the time of writing. The other two provisions are a limitation on maximum damages never adopted by the U.K. and the option to include primary agricultural products and game within "product", an option not taken up by the U.K.. See C. Hodges, "The European Commission's 1995 Review of the Product Liability Directive" [1996] J.P.I.L. 135.

[59] See, *e.g.* A. Clark, *Product Liability* (Sweet & Maxwell, 1989), Chap. 8; J. Blaikie, "Product Liability" (1987) 32 J.L.S. 325; W.C.H. Ervine, "Product Liability and Part 1 of the Consumer Protection Act 1987" (1988) SCOLAG 21; C. Newdick, "The Future of Negligence in Product Liability" (1987) 103 L.Q.R. 288; J. Stapleton, "Products Liability Reform—Real or Illusory" (1986) 6 O.J.L.S. 392.

the existence of the defect to be discovered."[60] Eventually this divergence led to a challenge by the commission before the ECJ in *Commission v. United Kingdom*.[61] The ECJ treated the Commission's argument as being that the United Kingdom had converted the intended strict liability regime into a negligence liability. The United Kingdom did not challenge the submission that the Directive set out an objective test but argued instead that read together the United Kingdom's version interpreted in the light of section 1(1) of the Act did not infringe the obligation to deliver the directive. The ECJ agreed. In so doing the court accepted that the directive defence (and thus the United Kingdom's defence) required it to be shown that the producer had complied with the most advanced knowledge available on an objective analysis, but the producer would be able to argue that the knowledge was not accessible. This is nowhere near saying that the court agreed with a negligence standard. Instead it is allowing some practical room for a defence where objectively the knowledge exists printed by a John Bull printing set in Mongolia or perhaps an obscure internet site but is not yet printed in the respected journals, or, to take the example of the internet—located on an established and recognised site. This is not the place to canvass this point but the internet was developed for scientific use and many pieces of information appear on the internet before they appear anywhere else. They are searchable in ways in which obscure published papers are not.[62] Most people familiar with the way in which United Kingdom's courts construe United Kingdom legislation will be surprised that the ECJ thought that the United Kingdom's courts would ignore the generous words of the United Kingdom's defence to impose a liability based on section 1(1). Semantically, the United Kingdom defence seems to allow more room for danger than the E.C. Directive even as more liberally explained by the court, especially in cases where information was reasonably accessible but a reasonable producer did not find it. United Kingdom courts in all fairness ought of course now to interpret the United Kingdom statute, not according to the semantics of United Kingdom statutory interpretation but by the hermeneutics of the United Kingdom in Europe. It is still open to a pursuer denied a remedy by a United Kingdom interpreter of the Act to take a Eurorep case[63] based on a failure to apply section 1(1) to give effect to Directive Article 7.

Component/design

It is a defence to show that the defect (i) constituted a defect in product **15–24** ("the subsequent product") in which the product in question had been comprised; and (ii) was wholly attributable to the design of the subsequent

---

[60] Note the comments in W.A. Wilson, "The Product Liability Directive", 1980 S.L.T. 1 which suggests that the final U.K. version was one which had been rejected even before the directive came into being.

[61] C–300/95; [1997] All E.R. (E.C.) 481.

[62] Thus the comment of the Attorney General is well-phrased enough to deal with such concepts where he says: "The state of knowledge must be construed so as to include all data in the information circuit of the scientific community as a whole, bearing in mind, however, on the basis of a reasonableness test the actual opportunities for the information to circulate.".

[63] See Chap. 11.

product or to compliance by the producer of the product in question with instructions given by the producer of the subsequent product.[64]

Contract

15–25 The liability of a person by virtue of the Act to a person who has suffered damage caused wholly or partly by defect in a product, or to a dependant or relative of such a person, cannot be limited or excluded by any contract term, by any notice or by any other provision.[65]

Damage recovery

15–26 A person is not liable in respect of any defect in a product for the loss of or any damage to the product itself or for the loss of or any damage to the whole or any part of any product which has been supplied with the product in question comprised in it.[66]

15–27   A person is not be liable for any loss of or damage to any property which, at the time it is lost or damaged, is not (a) of a description of property ordinarily intended for private use, occupation or consumption; and (b) intended by the person suffering the loss or damage mainly for his own private use, occupation or consumption.[67] No damages shall be awarded to any person in respect of any loss of or damage to any property if the amount which would fall to be awarded to that person and any liability for interest, does not exceed £75.[68]

15–28   Section 1 of the Congenital Disabilities (Civil Liability) Act 1976 has effect if (a) a person were answerable to a child in respect of an occurrence caused wholly or partly by a defect in a product if he is or has been liable in respect of any effect of the occurrence on a parent of the child, or would be so liable if the occurrence caused a parent or the child to suffer damage.[69]

15–29   Where any damage is caused partly by a defect in a product and partly by the fault of the person suffering the damage, the Law Reform (Contributory Negligence) Act 1945 and section 5 of the Fatal Accidents Act 1976 has effect as if the defence were the fault of every person liable for the damage caused by the defect.[70]

Related Claims

15–30 Just as it is sometimes a nice question whether a contract is one of sale or one for work and materials, some cases appearing to be product liability cases may turn equally, alternatively or exclusively on the principle of "professional" liability.[71] In the case of employees injured by their tools, the common law already implies a duty of reasonable care.[72] The common law

---

[64] s. 4(1)(f).
[65] s. 7.
[66] s. 5(2).
[67] s. 5(3).
[68] s. 5(4).
[69] s. 6(3).
[70] s. 6(4).
[71] See for example *McNeill Estates v. Faulds of Girvan*, 1992 G.W.D. 1–42.
[72] See Chap. 14.

protection was enhanced by the Employer's Liability (Defective Equipment) Act 1967.[73] While that was intended to mean that the worker would be able to sue his employer if injured by equipment, it has not had that clear cut effect. In Scotland it is submitted that the word "fault" in the 1967 Act should be construed as encompassing a breach of the 1987 Act.

---

[73] See Chap. 14.

CHAPTER 16

TRANSPORTATION

Introduction

The boat is nearly as old as man and many references to shipping will be **16–1**
found in Stair. The train was one of the technological advances of the
eighteenth and nineteenth centuries. The automobile and the aeroplane
assumed dominance in the twentieth. All four have to do with interconti-
nental travel as much as domestic travel. They have in common the ability
to harm anything in their path and their own contents.[1] Legally they tend to
be treated differently presumably because to the legislator they seem like
quite different things.[2] It might be thought unnecessary to discuss such
cases at all in a book of some limited scope. There are two reasons why this
chapter appears. First anyone reading the general negligence chapter can
find very many day to day examples of the application of general principles
herein. Secondly, the practitioner and student ought to be aware of special
rules of which there are some in relation to each mode of conveyance.

ROADS AND FOOTPATHS

The decision of the Second Division in *Gibson v. Strathclyde Regional* **16–2**
Council[3] has the benefit of crystal clarity. It is fair in the sense that the case
is not a rule of general exculpation for roads authorities and admits the
possibility of action in certain circumstances. The case is also very useful by
way of guidance because it overruled a very pro-pursuer decision in *King v.
Strathclyde Regional Council*.[4] The following practical propositions can be
extracted:

(1) liability is for fault;

(2) the general rule applies that a pursuer's personal injury case should
    not be dismissed on relevancy unless it is bound to fail if proved, the
    onus of establishing that, in argument, being on the defender[5];

---

[1] R. Mayou, "Psychological, Quality of Life and Legal Consequences of Road Traffic
Injury" [1995] J.P.I.L. 277; C.N. Simkins, "Mechanism of Traumatic Brain Injury Resulting
from Rear End Car Crashes" [1997] J.P.I.L. 35.
[2] Italy is apparently the only country to combine air law and maritime law in the one body
of law "Il Codice della navigazione". Diederiks-verschoor, *An Introduction to Air Law* (6th ed.,
Kluwer Law, 1997).
[3] 1993 S.L.T. 1243.
[4] Glasgow Sh. Ct, Jan. 8, 1991, unreported.
[5] 1993 S.L.T. 1243, *per* Lord Justice-Clerk Ross at 1245H–K.

(3) a daily inspection case cannot normally be supported by a bald averment that it would be reasonable and practicable to do that[6];

(4) it is possible to establish a daily inspection case without averments of proper practice giving rise to an inference of negligence although the circumstances should be, on one view special, exceptional and obvious,[7] or perhaps better, the subject of averment.[8] There is no need as is sometimes suggested to specify which particular authority follows which particular practice—that is a matter of proof rather than averment.

The arguments often made by pursuers were made in this case and largely rejected, particularly the point that the pursuer seldom has the knowledge of what is reasonable or practicable, the daily burden of roads administration being beyond their knowledge and in the absence of private or public funding, that of their professional advisers. In a case where a woman slipped on an ungritted road she failed because although a 12-hour delay could have been due to slackness, she had to aver that.[9] Pursuers are seldom successful.[10] It is essential to bring evidence before the court of what would be reasonable in an inspection case although this can come down to fairly technical matters. Thus in *McLaughlin v. Strathclyde Regional Council*[11] the following exposition of the evidence illustrates how these cases proceed:

"The only evidence as to the standard of maintenance which might be expected of an authority came from Mr Green, who said that the authority would not normally take action to repair a hole in the road surface until it reached about 75mm in depth, while one in a footway would be attended to when it reached 40mm. Those are obviously only rules of thumb but do give some indication of what the practice of the defenders, at least, is. Mr Cheeseman said that he would expect an authority to remedy the state of affairs which he found on his inspection, but I think that in giving that evidence, he was referring primarily to the state of the tarmac as it was when he saw it, that is after erosion had had some effect. He did say that a hole of one inch in depth could pose a hazard, but also agreed that most people would veer round a drain gully. He did not really deal with any question of general practice. On the evidence, the differences in the levels of the tarmac and the kerbstones are not shown to have exceeded 1 inch to 1½ inches, or 25 to 35mm. The difference in level of the tarmac was in the vicinity of a grating, where it might be expected that members of the public would take some care to look where they were placing their feet, and it was in part of the roadway, not in a footway. Similarly, it might be expected that members

---

[6] *ibid., per* Lord Justice-Clerk Ross at 1246A and Lord Weir at 1248B.

[7] *ibid., per* Lord Weir at 1248A.

[8] *ibid., per* Lord Justice-Clerk Ross at 1246H.

[9] *Gordon v. Inverness Town Council*, 1957 S.L.T. (Notes) 48. See also *Carr v. Geddes*, 1992 G.W.D. 8–441.

[10] See, *e.g. Tulloch v. Lothian Regional Council*, 1992 G.W.D. 18–1074; *McLaughlin v. Strathclyde Regional Council*, 1992 S.L.T. 959.

[11] 1992 S.L.T. 959.

of the public would take some care in stepping over or onto a kerb. Even though, on Mr Cheeseman's evidence, it may be inferred that the defects had existed for some time, I do not think that it is possible to draw the inference that the defenders were, at the date of the accident, in breach of any duty of reasonable care."[12]

The authority must, however, take care of infirm pedestrians such as blind or partially blind people who have no one to see them along the streets.[13] It is helpful and sometimes essential to show that a defect in a pavement has been reported because then the case is one of a known danger. It has been held in one case that the report can be made to a councillor rather than a paid official.[14]

Because public authorities are involved, it should not be forgotten that **16–3** general principles of liability apply, although the important cases from public authority immunity in negligence are not cited and discussed.[15] Once a scheme is in place it must be a reasonable scheme.[16] The power to mark roads and the like and the existence of foreseeability of injury is not itself sufficient to create a duty to mark roads, although it might be possible to make a case if there is evidence of special risks known to the authority.[17]

There will be liability for a dangerous obstruction allowed to be on the **16–4** road.[18] In *O'Keefe v. Edinburgh Corporation*[19] it was also said: "It may be, and I think it is very likely, that, under certain circumstances and in accordance with due road administration, the defenders will be bound to remove the snow from the roads."[20] Liability has been said to depend upon knowledge and there being time for them to remedy the hazard of which they are aware.[21] It has also been decided that the duty is owed to all road users and the authority cannot be expected to remedy all problems immediately.[22] In one case nothing was done to a street in days but this was not negligence in the context of the range of work to which the authority had to attend as low priority work could be left until high priority work had been completed.[23] In *Kemp v. Secretary of State for Scotland*[24] it was held

---

[12] *ibid.* at 961. Other cases dealing with precise measurements are *Macmillan v. Lord Advocate*, 1991 S.L.T. 150 where the pursuer tripped over a metal strip set in the floor at the doorway of a canteen. It was no more that half an inch in height. On the evidence the Lord Ordinary (Weir) found that the strip represented an appreciable risk. In *McClafferty v. British Telecom*, 1987 S.L.T. 327, it was found that a three-quarters of an inch raise in a paving slab did not pose a foreseeable risk of injury.

[13] *McKibben v. Glasgow Corporation*, 1920 2 S.L.T. 51. See also "Duty to the Blind", 1964 S.L.T. (News) 41; "Duty to the Blind—The Final Word", 1964 S.L.T. (News) 185.

[14] *McLaughlin v. Strathclyde Regional Council*, 1996 Rep.L.R. 179.

[15] *Stovin v. Wise* [1996] A.C. 923, although an English House of Lords case is still important but is not in point where there is already a duty of care recognised in Scotland on an authority. See *Forbes v. Dundee District Council*, 1997 S.C.L.R 682.

[16] See *Grant v. Lothian Regional Council*, 1988 S.L.T. 533; *O'Keefe v. Edinburgh Corporation*, 1911 S.C. 18. This is in the sense of the effect of the scheme rather than its *Wednesbury* reasonableness which might be more significant if the *Stovin v. Wise* line of cases are in play.

[17] *Murray v. Nichols*, 1983 S.L.T. 194.

[18] *O'Keefe v. Edinburgh Corporation*, 1911 S.C. 18 (*obiter*).

[19] 1911 S.C. 18 (*obiter*).

[20] *O'Keefe v. Edinburgh Corporation*, 1911 S.C. 18 (*obiter*).

[21] *O'Keefe v. Edinburgh Corporation*, 1911 S.C. 18.

[22] *Cameron v. Inverness County Council*, 1935 S.L.T. 281.

[23] *Grant v. Lothian Regional Council*, 1988 S.L.T. 533.

[24] 1999 Rep. L.R. 110.

that the roads authority were liable for having a raised kerb at the edge of a footpath which caused the pursuer to fall into the path of traffic. There was evidence from a police office and a consulting engineer that the design was a hazard.[25]

16–5 However, most important is the case of *Carr v. Geddes*.[26] In this case a driver skidded on black ice. The roads authority tried to have the case dismissed. The pursuer had alleged that the authority knew or ought to have known that the road was liable to flooding and black ice which would form later. The pursuer had not averred a failure in a system of priorities. A proof before answer was allowed because the key facts would be within the knowledge of the defenders. Add to this *Kozikowska v. Kozikowski*,[27] in which a proof before answer was allowed. The authority had averred that the road had been gritted on two occasions, an averment that it should have been gritted early in the morning was not irrelevant on the ground that it was going beyond the obligation to act reasonably.[28] Further, the averment that the locus was a well known black spot was held to be relevant for inquiry (in the context of detailed averments of the locus) and it was not essential that previous accidents be narrated to support the "black spot" argument. The approach in both of these cases is borne out by the Inner House authority of *McGeouch v. Strathclyde Regional Council*,[29] in which a failure to grit case was allowed on the understanding it was not a challenge to the policy of the authority but a complaint as to its operation. It was held in *McKnight v. Clydeside Buses Ltd*[30] that the roads authority were under an obligation to mark low bridges where they knew or ought to have known it constituted a danger such as in this case where there had been many accidents before.

16–6 Although the wording of the Roads (Scotland) Act 1984 seems more helpful requiring the authority to take steps, it has been held to reflect the common law.[31]

16–7 Railway operators must take care to run their operation at level crossing to prevent harm,[32] to the extent that it is permissible to allege that they failed to slow down their trains without specifying the precise speed at which they should have run it.[33] The law was set out in *Smith v. LMS Railway*[34] as being that as a result of many authorities discussed therein that a railway company has a duty at every level-crossing where members of the public have a right to be, and where there is reason to expect them to be, to take all reasonable precautions in train operation (and perhaps in other respects) to reduce the danger to a minimum, the nature of the precautions which are required and the question whether the duty has been fulfilled depending upon the circumstances of each case.[35]

---

[25] There was one-third contributory negligence as the pursuer was drunk.

[26] 1992 G.W.D. 8–441.

[27] 1996 S.L.T. 386.

[28] Considering *Cameron v. Inverness County Council*, 1935 S.C. 493; *McGuffie v. Forth Valley Health Board*, 1991 S.L.T. 231.

[29] 1985 S.L.T. 321.

[30] 1999 S.L.T. 1167.

[31] *Grant v. Lothian Regional Council*, 1988 S.L.T. 533.

[32] *Smith v. LMS Railway*, 1948 S.C. 125.

[33] *Bain v. British Railways Board*, 1964 (Notes) 92.

[34] 1948 S.L.T. 235.

[35] *ibid.* at 239.

Roadworks affect the safety of roads. The authority have to mark these. **16–8** The duty, except in so far as set out in statute, is to take reasonable care. *Storey Bros v. Stirling County Council*[36] has to be read with care. Some considerable reliance was placed on English authority. The finding of liability seems to have been based on a finding of a continuing duty to mark the works. The evidence was that they were marked before and after an accident but not around the time of it. The finding is justified on the facts because it seemed most probable that the marks were removed by the authority rather than a contractor or vandals. Many cases raise the issue of the intervention of vandals, the pursuer's only hope is to argue, based on sufficient averment, that the criminal third party intervention is within the duty. [37] Where possession and control is in a contractor he may be sued as where the works, narrowing the road to the extent that two cars could not pass, he failed to institute a one-way system.[38]

AUTOMOBILES AND OTHER ROAD ACCIDENTS

Roads have been in use well before the internal combustion engine. Thus **16–9** there has in the past been held to be liability for entrusting a difficult horse to a child unused to horses,[39] for walking behind a cart instead of actually driving it,[40] or for sitting on the shaft instead of the box preventing a good view being obtained.[41] Driving too fast easily inferred negligence.[42] Even in the nineteenth century "too fast" meant "faster than is reasonable" because it was appreciated even then that the majority of people often drive "too fast". Easier modern analogies can be seen with cases of driving without lights[43] in which the duty was held not to be absolute but a precaution which ought usually to be taken, or driving too close to the vehicle in front.[44] The "rule of the road", to drive on the left hand side, is said to originate in custom. The General Turnpike Act made it an offence not to drive on the left, the driver to forfeit and pay a sum over and above the damages occasioned. The same statute prohibited the use of the footpath to vehicles. The rule was explained by Lord Justice-Clerk Moncrieff as being dependent upon the vehicles keeping each other on the whip or right hand side. In further explaining the rule it was stated that a slower vehicle should draw to the side to let the faster vehicle pass.[45] This rule was originally applicable only to a beast of burden under the control of man.

In early cases involving horses the view was taken that there was a duty **16–10** on drivers to avoid pedestrians. Early cases support the view that there is a prima facie case of fault where a pedestrian is run down and it is for the driver to explain his conduct.[46] Cars, unlike horses, do not "have a life of

---

[36] 1974 S.L.T. (Sh. Ct) 92.
[37] See Chap. 10.
[38] *Cloggie v. J. O'Donoghue (Reinstatements) Ltd*, 1981 S.L.T. (Sh. Ct) 10.
[39] *Brown v. Fulton* (1882) 9 R. 36.
[40] *Baird v. Hamilton* (1826) 4 S.790.
[41] *Grant v. Glasgow Dairy Co.* (1882) 9 R.182.
[42] *ibid.*
[43] *Gibson v. Milroy* (1879) 6 R. 890.
[44] *Auld v. McBey* (1881) 8 R. 495.
[45] *Ramsay v. Thomson* (1881) 9 R. 140 at 145.
[46] *McKechnie v. Couper* (1887) 14 R. 345; *Anderson v. Blackwood* (1886) 13 R. 443.

their own". One early case involving a horse may have some modern analytical value. The owner of a horse was held not liable for the horse suddenly bolting.[47] This may suggest the driver of a car which goes out of control due to a spontaneous hidden mechanical defect should have no liability. Indeed, in early cases involving carriages the view was that there was a presumption that an accident occurring from the breakdown of a public conveyance was due to the fault of the proprietor or hirer and that he had to show that all that could be done to provide against accident had been done.[48] Traction engines and locomotives on the roads, the forerunners of the modern car were treated as dangerous machines. A person injured was able to recover without proof or fault in terms of an Act of 1861. Looking at the matter from the point of view of the pedestrian, Guthrie Smith states[49]: "A man suffering from old age, deafness or other infirmity, is entitled to assume that drivers will take care for his safety". However, this may be limited to having no need to fear of contributory negligence.[50] It is however, important to realise when referring to older cases that every case depends upon its facts and the facts of motoring have changed. [51]

16–11   Consonant with general principle, it is not fault if the bad driving is not in any sense voluntary as where a driver crashes because he has a sudden subarachnoid haemorrhage,[52] but it is fault to drive through a red light.[53] The opinion has been expressed that to cross against an amber light is negligent, being against the Highway Code. This is subject to the proviso in the Code as was then current that it would be permissible to cross into the junction if to pull up might cause an accident.[54] Accidents following upon a skid raise difficult issues. Although it can in the abstract be said that a skid is neutral,[55] a skid at a speed greater than walking pace has been said to be evidence of negligence where it occurs on icy roads.[56] Perhaps the most accurate statement is that a skid is merely one of the items to be taken into account.[57]

16–12   Simply having run down a pedestrian is not *per se* negligence. It may be that the pedestrian has been the author of his own misfortune and there

---

[47] *Shaw v. Croall & Sons* (1885) 12 R. 1186.

[48] *Lyon v. Lamb* (1838) 16 S. 1188. Glegg was of the contrary view, again ignoring the authorities cited by Guthrie Smith and citing no Scots authority for his view.

[49] *The Law of Damages*, p. 138.

[50] *Clerk v. Petrie* (1879) 6 R. 1076.

[51] In *Ramage v. Hardie*, 1968 S.L.T. (Notes) 54, Lord Robertson said: "In view of the development of motor traffic, and in particular the increase in the volume of traffic, the development of motorways and other fast main roads, the greater speeds, and the improvement in driving skills and greater appreciation of the rights and duties of drivers, some of the observations and dicta in early reported cases read somewhat strangely today". At the time of writing the same caveat must be issued as certainly the cars have become safer in the sense that many are fitted with advanced braking systems.

[52] *Griffen v. McGill's Executors*, 1983 S.L.T. 498; *Penny v. McGill's Executors*, 1983 S.L.T. 498. See *Waugh v. James K. Allan Ltd*, 1964 S.C. (H.L.) 102 discussed in Chap. 2 for the idea of the antecedent negligence in driving at all.

[53] *Bell v. Glasgow Corporation*, 1965 S.L.T. 57. See also *McNeil v. Clelland*, 1993 S.L.T. (Note) 662.

[54] *Bell v. Glasgow Corporation*, 1965 S.L.T. 57 at 61.

[55] *Laurie v. Raglan Building Co.* [1942] 1 K.B. 152.

[56] *Gibson, Mercer & Co. v. Partridge*, 1957 S.L.T. (Sh. Ct) 56.

[57] *McGregor v. Dundee Corporation*, 1962 S.C. 15 at 22; *Thomson v. Brankin*, 1968 S.L.T. (Sh. Ct) 2.

was nothing a careful driver could have done.[58] Knocking down a pedestrian when the vehicle is on the wrong side of the road indicates fault.[59] A failure to keep a good look out and driving at excessive speed can constitute fault.[60] A driver can even be held liable where a pedestrian is either drunk or the worse for drink if the driver has not kept a good lookout, although the condition of the pedestrian may amount to contributory negligence.[61] Crossing in front of a bus after disembarkation is not a complete bar where a person is run down by a driver going too fast and not keeping a good lookout.[62] The driver of a car entering a major road is not excluded from making a claim. Much depends upon the circumstances and if the car on the main carriageway should have seen the car joining the main road then there will liability upon the driver on the main road, although there may be an element of contributory negligence.[63] This approach is set out by Lord Hunter as follows:

"I agree there may be circumstances in which a driver on a major road may be justified in assuming that a vehicle on a minor road will give him the right of way, but it seems to me that the question is always one of circumstances. One thing is certain and that is that a driver on a major road is not entitled to assume that, as he has the right of way, he can approach any junction on the basis that all traffic from side roads is going to give way to him. Nor, in my opinion, is a driver on a major road entitled to assume that other vehicles will not emerge from minor roads on to the major road in such a way as to make it necessary for him to moderate his speed. Indeed, I think in modern road conditions drivers are usually bound to take into account the risks which may be created by the negligence of others".[64]

A full review of the law in Scotland and in England at the time appears in **16–13** *Ramage v. Hardie*.[65] Here a Ford Prefect emerging from a side road collided with a Jaguar "of the fastest kind" which was going rather fast. The question was whether the Jaguar driver was in a sense to blame for not taking into account the possibility of a car emerging from the minor road. It was accepted that often a driver on a main road has to take account of the possibility of a car emerging from a minor road but his Lordship disavowed any notion that there was a legal duty for the main road driver always to be able to pull up for a grossly negligent driver. There has to be something in the conduct of the minor road driver that puts the main road driver on alert: "if the aggression becomes manifest too late, and the driver of the vehicle on the major road is by that time committed to his course to such an extent that slowing up or stopping is of no avail, then the latter is not at

---

[58] *Muir v. Walker*, 1991 G.W.D. 1–48.
[59] *Purcell v. Johnston*, 1991 G.W.D. 15–946.
[60] *Garland v. Fairnington*, 1993 S.L.T. 711.
[61] *Cavin v. Kinnaird*, 1994 S.L.T. 111.
[62] *Gigli v. Taylor*, 1992 G.W.D. 39–2341.
[63] *Malcolm v. Fair*, 1993 S.L.T. 342.
[64] *Cockburn & Co. Ltd v. Scottish Motorbus Co. Ltd*, 1964 S.L.T. (Notes) 7 (O.H.). See also *Brown v. Central S.M.T. Company*, 1949 S.L.T. 66.
[65] 1968 S.L.T. (Notes) 54.

fault".[66] In another case a driver who was pushing his broken down car backwards from a main road into the mouth of a farm road was allowed to recover from a driver on the main road who collided with him—the basis being that a careful driver ought to have seen the motorist in difficulty.[67] In an earlier case a passenger in a gritting van succeeded when he was struck by a car heading in the same direction. The vehicle was well lit and the driver should have seen his vehicle and him, even although his hazard warning lights were not on.[68] In another case the pursuer failed to show that his colleague was negligent when he drove through a red light in their fire engine.[69] The driver of a motor car crashing into a stationary lorry after dark was allowed a proof before answer.[70] A driver should look ahead even when turning and looking at other traffic.[71] A motorcyclist has been held to be at fault for weaving in and out at speed overtaking other cars and then colliding with an oncoming driver.[72]

The location of the centre of the road is important. A mechanical digger crossing the centre line of the road (although in this case it was not marked) to pass parked cars and collided with an oncoming vehicle. Neither driver saw the other. The collision took place near the centre line of the road. With care both vehicles could have passed. The driver of the digger was at fault[73] however there was contributory negligence on the part of the other driver. A driver succeeded in full where he collided with a bus which was on his side of the road. However, he succeeded against the owners of a lorry. The lorry encroached sufficiently far over the centre to create an emergency and the actions of the bus in taking evasive action were thus neutral.[74] Running into the rear of a vehicle raises a considerable inference of negligence.[75] This is but an application of a dictum of Lord Cooper: "The following driver is in my view bound so far as reasonably possible, to take up such a position, and to drive in such a fashion, as will enable him to deal successfully with all traffic exigences reasonably to be anticipated."[76] This dictum was found helpful as recently as 1990 to make a finding of contributory negligence against a driver whom it was held had not kept sufficiently aware of traffic behind.[77] An averment by a passenger in a car that two vehicles had collided on a bend in a road was held relevant on the basis that the defender could not establish that one or both was not at fault—proof, would of course be a different matter.[78] An averment that a motor cyclist involved in collision as a result of which he died was

---

[66] *ibid.* at 56.
[67] *Morrison v. Laidlaw*, 1994 S.L.T. 359.
[68] *McLeod v. Cartwright*, 1981 S.L.T. (Notes) 54.
[69] *Chalmers v. Strathclyde Fire Board*, 1999 G.W.D. 14–657.
[70] *Crawford v. Peter McAinsh Ltd*, 1962 S.L.T. (Notes) 26.
[71] *Coull v. Lothian Regional Council*, 1994 S.L.T. 377.
[72] *Mokwa v. Partridge*, 1992 G.W.D. 28–1663.
[73] *Young v. Roche Services Group*, 1989 S.L.T. 212.
[74] *Macdonald v. Harvey*, 1993 G.W.D. 19–1225.
[75] *Thomson v. Brankin*, 1968 S.L.T. (Sh. Ct) 2. The sheriff put it as saying there was a prima facie case of negligence against the party running into a car in front and proof of a skid in itself would not be sufficient to discharge the prima facie case.
[76] *Brown & Lynn v. Western SMT*, 1945 S.L.T. 329 at 332.
[77] *Joliffe v. Hay*, 1991 S.L.T. 151.
[78] *Barrow v. Bryce*, 1986 S.L.T. 691.

inexperienced and the holder of only a provisional licence was held to be relevant as being a matter which the finder of fact would be entitled to take into account depending on the circumstances.[79] Where road conditions demand it may be necessary to drive at a walking pace and not as fast as 15mph where for example there is a risk of injury to workmen working on road works.[80] Cases involving buses are similar but there are often cases by passengers complaining of the bad driving, which is more likely to cause injury in view of the need for passengers to board and disembark.[81] In England a passenger in a taxi sued the driver for letting him off on the wrong side of the road from his destination when the driver, knowing the passenger had been drinking, knew he would be endangered.[82] It was held that there was no duty in the absence of the insistence of the passenger to be deposited at a specific point. In any event fixing a specific duty would be too difficult involving an assessment of conditions of the roads and the passenger. In *Penman v. Blue Cap Logistics*[83] the pursuer crashed into the defender's vehicle which had broken down. A case based on the failure to take steps when the vehicle broke down failed. However, a case based on the fact of the breakdown itself succeeded.[84] A site foreman who stepped back into the path of an oncoming car was successful although with 75 per cent contribution.[85]

Causation

A man was unsuccessful in suing a chief constable in respect of the driving **16–14** of officers because it was held that if the pursuer had been driving at a reasonable speed the accident would not have occurred. This suggests that the case turned on the fact that the actions of the police car were not the legal cause of the accident.[86] The driver of a bus was considered not to be in any way the cause of an accident where the bus had been merely stationary in its bus bay.[87] Although something like black ice may seem to be natural and thus the true cause of a collision, this need not be the case. Where a driver became aware of black ice but instead of slowing down continued on through a narrow passage in the road even although he must have been aware that there might have been bodies on the road, this was held on appeal (reversing the Lord Ordinary), to constitute fault.[88] It must often be averred and proved why travelling at speed constitutes fault.[89] A failure to put on hazard warning lights has been held not to have broken the causal connection between injury and the defender's wrong, although this was in a case where the pursuer's vehicle had a revolving light on its top.[90]

---

[79] *Armstrong v. Glasgow Corporation*, 1965 (Notes) 83.
[80] *Davidson v. Scott*, 1987 S.L.T. 480.
[81] See *Fraser v. W. Alexander & Sons (Northern) Ltd*, 1964 S.L.T. (Notes) 79; *McCorriston v. Grampian Regional Council*, 1995 S.C.L.R. 170.
[82] *Griffiths v. Brown* [1998] T.L.R. 649.
[83] 1999 S.L.T. 1246; 1999 Rep. L.R. 91.
[84] Under reference to *Binnie v. Rederij Theodoro DV*, 1993 S.C. 71.
[85] *Bryce v. McKirdy*, 1999 S.L.T. 988.
[86] *Grieve v. Chief Constable, Fife Constabulary*, 1991 G.W.D. 21–1247.
[87] *Cairns v. Irving*, 1993 G.W.D. 1–54.
[88] *McAtear v. Lewis*, 1992 G.W.D. 5–352.
[89] *Colborne v. Wallace*, 1993 G.W.D. 17–1121.
[90] *McLeod v. Cartwright*, 1981 S.L.T. (Notes) 54.

Evidence

16–15 In cases where parties are alleging contrary stories, for example that it was the other person who crossed the centre line, the evidence of a "traffic accident expert" can assist the court based on dynamics and impact damage.[91] On the other hand the English Court of Appeal in *Liddell v. Middleton*[92] has held that it is rarely that experts would be needed in car crash cases. They can be helpful in determining questions of primary fact but not in drawing conclusions. The same must be the case in Scotland. The location of an injured pedestrian after the accident is of assistance.[93] In one case it seemed that the evidence of a police officer as to the point of collision combined with that of a doctor as to the nature of the injuries was a major influence in choosing which of two sets of eye-witness testimony should be accepted.[94]

The Highway Code

16–16 As will be seen from some of the cases already noted the Highway Code is used as a guide to what the reasonable man should do when driving a car.[95] It has been said "No doubt the fact that there is a Highway Code is within judicial knowledge."[96] Not only that the use of the stopping distance figures as an adminicle to be used with caution has been approved.[97] The stopping distance figures were used to evaluate evidence actually given, although it was said that only the figures actually given could be used and they could not be extrapolated to speeds under 20mph nor those over 70mph.[98] It was held not to be possible to use the stopping distances in the code to substitute for the inculpatory evidence given by a party himself.[99]

Defences

16–17 General defences apply and reference is made to the chapter on defences, especially contributory negligence, *volenti* and *ex turpi causa*. Note should be taken of the special statutory exclusion of the defence of *volenti non fit injuria* discussed below.

RAILWAYS

16–18 Centuries of railway technology have meant that accidents are now rare but the nineteenth century reports are full of law on the topic. Nonetheless, head on collisions still happen.[1] Recent developments in the law in the

---

[91] *Anderson v. Redden*, 1991 G.W.D. 28–1690; and see also the evidence of "an accident investigator" in *Young v. Roche Services Group Plc*, 1989 S.L.T. 212.

[92] [1996] P.I.Q.R. P36, CA.

[93] *Garland v. Fairnington*, 1993 S.L.T. 711.

[94] *Connell v. Campbell*, 1993 G.W.D. 20–1260.

[95] *Bell v. Glasgow Corporation*, 1965 S.L.T. 57. In *Rosser v. Lindsay* [1999] T.L.R. 137 it was held that the code's injunction to use mirrors frequently was only of use as guidance in the case of a vehicle on a construction site. The edition current at the time of writing is that published on Feb. 25, 1999.

[96] *Cavin v. Kinaird*, 1994 S.L.T. 111 at 113.

[97] *ibid.*

[98] *Callaghan v. Glasgow District Council*, Glasgow Sh. Ct, Nov. 20, 1979, unreported, as noted and explained in *Cavin, ibid.*

[99] *Cavin*, at 113.

[1] July 21, 1991: *McMahon v. British Railways Board*, 1995 S.L.T. 590; March 6, 1989: *McManus v. British Railways Board*, 1994 S.L.T. 496.

United Kingdom dividing responsibility for rolling stock, stations and the permanent way might mean that in those few cases which might still sadly arise there will be litigation not only by injured passengers but between defenders as to responsibility.[2] An example from the past is *Smyth v. The Caledonian Railway Co. and the Glasgow Iron and Steel Co.*[3] in which a man was injured due to the failure of equipment but on the premises of another. It might be of assistance in the new order and so is quoted at some length. The Lord President (Robertson) said:

"The accident occurred through the failure on the part of the switch apparatus to operate effectively. Now, the railway and the switch apparatus are, according to the pursuers, the property of the Caledonian Railway. Further, the operations which miscarried were operations with the plant of the Caledonian Railway and conducted by the servants of the Caledonian Railway. All that goes far to show prima facie a case against the Caledonian Railway . . . When I turn to the case against the Glasgow Steel Company, I enter upon an entirely different character of statement. The keynote there is that while the Caledonian Railway are the proprietors of this railway, and the using Company, the duty assigned to the Steel Company in cond. 7 is merely this: that, in as much as their railway passes through their works, and, it may be said, is used for the transit of their traffic, there is a resulting duty on them to supervise and examine the proceedings of the Caledonian Railway and their plant and apparatus. That is the essential part of cond. 7. Now, the importance of that statement must be judged by its relation to the context, and it seems to me to have no more importance than belongs to an anecdote or illustration of the text. I could quite have understood its being said: 'I, the pursuer, was a platelayer engaged in the maintenance of these lines and the keeping of the apparatus, and the footing on which I was employed was this, that the Company, my employers, were the maintainers, and as such specially charged with responsibility.' But nothing is said to connect this statement of practice with the essential charge against the Company, which is not that they were bound to do the thing, but to see that it was well done. Now, can it be held that it results from the averred facts, which are these: that this railway was the property of the Caledonian Railway, passing doubtless through the works of the other Company, but still run and managed by the Caledonian Railway—can it be held that there results from these facts an obligation on the Glasgow Steel Company in a question with their employees to see that the Caledonian Railway do their work properly? The argument would be equally applicable to the case where there was a mere local proximity of the works to the railway. Suppose a manufacturer had his establishment close to the railway, so close that an accident with great impulse might drive wagons on to his land, would he be liable if there were an accident due to the fault of the railway company's servants, merely because he did not go into their premises to see if they were doing their duty? I cannot

---

[2] A hint of this can be seen in the occupier's case *Todd v. British Railways Board*, 1998 G.W.D. 11–568.

[3] (1896) 4 S.L.T. 303.

distinguish that case from the present, and the conclusion I have come to is, that the case against the Steel Company is irrelevant, and the action must be dismissed against them."[4]

16–19 There will be statutory duties which ought first to be investigated in cases of liability. Injuries to employees are now dealt with under employers' liability. In a recent case there was no liability where a worker fell and hit his head on the permanent way.[5] Injuries at stations and in relation to persons crossing the line tend to be considered under Occupiers' Liability.[6] Older cases naturally do not refer to the Act and depend upon their own facts. In *Anderson v. British Railway Executive*,[7] the family of a deceased man was successful even although he had taken an unauthorised but commonly used route (with trespassing warnings posted). However he was held 80 per cent in contribution.

16–20 Cases of carriage of goods are dealt with under the contract of carriage which may be found in documents incorporated by reference or international conventions.[8] Cases involving level-crossings are treated above under roads. Cases of carriage of passengers are now more commonly dealt with as delict cases especially as the Unfair Contract Terms Act has precluded the use of contract terms to limit or exclude liability.[9] In *McGinty v. London, Midland and Scottish Railway Company*.[10] the earlier authorities both Scots and English were reviewed.[11] The facts were that a train overshot the platform. The pursuer opened the carriage door and being under the impression that she was at the platform she fell to the ground and was injured. The law was stated as being:

> "Where liability has been affirmed against a railway company in this class of case it has been on the ground that the passenger has been deceived by something done or omitted to be done by the railway company's servants; that something amounting to negligence, into thinking that he was at the place at which it was intended that he should alight when he was not; and that he himself has not been guilty of contributory negligence. So far as a rule can be extracted from the authorities, that appears to me to be the rule. Cases where the passenger knows that his carriage is not at the platform and there is an invitation to alight may involve other considerations."[12]

---

[4] *ibid.* at 303–304.

[5] *Carswell v. British Railways Board*, 1991 S.L.T. 73.

[6] See *McGlone v. British Railways Board*, 1966 S.L.T.; *Titchener v. British Railways Board*, 1984 S.L.T. 192; *Todd v. British Railways Board*, 1998 G.W.D. 11–568. Older cases depending upon the licensee category of English law are accordingly of very limited value or at least require care in their use, *e.g. Tough v. North British Railway Company*, 1914 1 S.L.T. 121.

[7] 1955 S.L.T. (Notes) 46.

[8] See, *e.g. Robert Hutchison & Co. Ltd v. British Railways Board*, 1971 S.L.T. 84.

[9] For the law before see *Gray v. London and North-Eastern Railway Company*, 1930 S.L.T. 759.

[10] 1939 S.L.T. 353.

[11] *e.g. Potter v. North British Railway Co.* (1873), 11 M. 664; *Anthony v. Midland Railway Co.*, 1909, 100 L.T. 117; *Sharpe v. Southern Railway Co.* [1925] 2 K.B. 311; *Muirheads v. North British Railway Co.* (1884) 11 R. 1043; *Neilson v. North British Railway Co.*, 1907 S.C. 272.

[12] McGinty, *per* Lord Justice-Clerk (Aitchison) at 358. The strong dissent in this case needs to be considered as well where the facts are, as is likely in contemporary conditions, to be different.

In *Henderson v. London, Midland, and Scottish Railway Co.*[13] it was held that the carrier did not have to take account of unusual passengers such as Sir Frederick Ness Henderson, shipbuilder, Ayrshire, over seventy years of age and over twenty stones in weight. Years of legislation making provision for the disabled and the cultural changes which have resulted, at the time of writing, have resulted in many ramps and the like being required by planning departments and effected by local authorities.

A train is a product and following the enactment of the Consumer Protection Act 1987 that theory of liability might well be applicable.[14]

SHIPS

There are many special rules relating to the damage done by or to ships. So **16–21** much so this must be considered to be a speciality. However, the injured person or a small ship owner may well consult the general practitioner or the non-specialist and if nothing else the following should sound a warning as to the need to consider a number of special substantive and procedural issues. Only a large scale map can be offered of the subject here. As shall be seen international conventions often apply. Jurisdictional and conflicts matters arise beyond the scope of this text. A good example is *De Mulder v. Jadranska Linijska (Jadrolinija)*[15] in which the pursuer's yacht, registered in London, collided with the defenders' ferry, the *Trogir*, registered in Rijeka, Yugoslavia, in Trogir harbour. The pursuer raised an action in Scotland against the defenders, the owners of the *Trogir*, establishing jurisdiction by arrestment to found jurisdiction of another of the defenders' ships. In most jurisdictions there is the procedural complexity that actions involving ships may be actions *in rem* rather than simply *in personam*—the action can be brought against the owner of the property, namely the ship. That is the position in Scots law.[16] It is, however, also the case that an action can be brought *in personam* but it is still an admiralty action.[17]

There is another speciality, all the more significant because at the time of **16–22** writing jury trial is becoming more popular. The Nautical Assessors (Scotland) Act, 1894, provided that in any action or proceeding in the Court of Session arising out of, or relating to collision at sea, salvage, towage, or any other maritime matter, the Court could and on the application of any party, had to, summon to its assistance at the trial one or more persons of nautical skill and experience.[18] The 1894 Act has been

---

[13] 1935 S.L.T. 553.

[14] See Chapter 15.

[15] 1989 S.L.T. 269.

[16] Rules of Court, Chap. 46.

[17] See for a case under the then applicable Rules of Court 135, 136, 144 and 145, *Baird v. Aberdeen Coal and Shipping Co. Ltd*; *Shepherd v. Aberdeen Coal and Shipping Co. Ltd*, 1975 S.L.T. (Notes) 50.

[18] s. 2. In *Williamson v. Richard Irvin & Sons Ltd*, 1960 S.L.T. (Notes) 34, a fireman in a trawler which was at sea in heavy weather was injured when thrown into the scuppers whilst emptying buckets from the boiler room. He sued the owners averring that the accident was caused by the fault of the skipper in not seeing that lifelines were rigged when the ship was in heavy seas, and in failing to detail a man to warn the pursuer of the advent of a particularly

repealed in its application to the Court of Session which now has power to summon an assessor in any case or it may do so on the motion of a party but is not obliged to have an assessor. Nautical cases are still specially provided to the extent that there is an official list of nautical assessors.[19]

16–23   Ordinary principles of negligence can require to be applied. Thus it was a matter for the ordinary law where the question was directed to the duty of care owed by the ship owners to owners of an oil rig and overseers of diving operations involving questions of foreseeability of liability of owners and overseers in consequence of failure by safety ship owners to pick the diver out of water.[20] It works both ways with shipping cases shaping the general law. The *"Boy Andrew" v. Owners of S.S. "St Rognvald"*[21] is one of the principal cases in the general law of causation in Scots law. Where there is no speciality under the collision regulations next considered ordinary principles apply and there is no strict liability at sea: an error of judgement or a wrong decision is not necessarily negligence in the circumstance.[22] As Lord Stormonth Darling said, "It is not, however, the practice to judge by a very strict standard the conduct of seamen in what has been termed 'the agony of the collision.'"[23]

16–24   The actual decision in many collision cases may well turn on the Collision Regulations. In reading older cases it must be appreciated that at various times the rules provided for presumptions of fault.[24] The source of the rules has usually been international conventions but these are often brought into force by statutory instrument. The present regime is under the Merchant Shipping (Distress Signals and Prevention of Collisions) Regulations 1996 made under and in terms of the Merchant Shipping Act 1995.[25] Unlike the Highway Code which it resembles, discussed above, breach of the Collision Regulations is a criminal offence; but like the Highway Code there is no civil liability imposed either by the principal Act nor the regulations. However, the rules are likely to be used as showing what ought to be done.[26]

---

heavy sea. Lord Cameron said at 35, "There may be and no doubt are many matters of seamanship which are easily understood, but the fact that they must be easily understood by persons without maritime experience does not make them any the less matters of seamanship, and in my opinion this is an action which very clearly arises out of a maritime matter and the decision of which turns upon questions of what is good seamanship in relation to the safety of the ship's company. In these circumstances the motion which counsel for the defenders has made for the appointment of a nautical assessor cannot be resisted in view of the terms of section 2 of the 1894 Act. As a necessary consequence of that the inquiry into the averments of parties can only be by way of proof, as it has been repeatedly laid down that you cannot have a jury trial in the presence of a nautical assessor for reasons which are manifest." See also *Prior v. Kelvin Shipping Co. Ltd*, 1954 S.L.T. (Notes) 11 in which Lord Strachan considers the meaning of "maritime matter".

[19] Rules of Court, Chap. 12.
[20] *Comex Houlder Diving Ltd v. Colne Fishing Co. Ltd (No. 2)*, 1992 S.L.T. 89 (Outer House).
[21] 1948 S.L.T. 83.
[22] *Henderson v Noble* (1897) 5 S.L.T. 177.
[23] *ibid*. at 178.
[24] *e.g.* Merchant Shipping Act 1894, s. 419(4).
[25] *ibid*, ss. 85 and 86.
[26] See *e.g. The Campbeltown and Glasgow Steam Packet Joint Stock Co. Ltd v. William Denny & Brothers*, (1907) 15 S.L.T. 756 on the then applicable regulations and to be read subject to

Various statutes may apply to ships, either as ships in themselves, or **16–25** because they fit some other statutory object. Thus the Occupiers' Liability (Scotland) Act 1960 applies to ships. Although the question as to who is responsible may not always be obvious and may require proof before answer as where those indemnifying operators of a ship were unsuccessful in arguing for dismissal of an occupier's case.[27]

An example the other way under a law now no longer in force was that a **16–26** ship was not a "steel structure" in terms of the Construction (Working Places) Regulations 1966,[28] reg. 28(1) and the Engineering Construction (Extension of Definition) Regulations 1960[29]. Ordinary principles of damages apply unless the special limitation rules apply.

Special Limitation Rules

To make insurance affordable and thus more likely to be in existence it has **16–27** been the case for a long time that limitation has been allowed. It still is and the general practitioner now accustomed to the applicability of the Unfair Contract Terms Act 1977 must appreciate this special regime. The Merchant Shipping Act 1995 is the United Kingdom statute presently giving effect[30] to the Convention on Limitation and Liability for Maritime Claims 1976.[31] It defines the structures to which it applies which are broadly ships whether seagoing or not, with special rules depending on tonnage.[32] Under United Kingdom law vessels constructed for drilling and engaged in drilling are covered if they are within the definition of ships.[33] Limitation is open to the shipowner being the owner, charterer, manager or operator of a seagoing ship and salvors.[34] Claims in damages including now breach of contract cases falling within Article 2 of the Convention can be limited, the most relevant to this work being claims in respect of loss of life or personal injury or loss of or damage to property occurring on board or in direct connection with the operation of the ship or with salvage operations, and consequential loss resulting therefrom[35]; and claims in respect of other loss

---

the abolition in 1911 of the presumption of fault rule. See also the Inner House consideration in *Moatschappij Hoek-van-Holland v. Clyde Shipping Co. Ltd. (the "Aranmore")* (1902) 10 S.L.T. 612 showing a divergence on the same facts and the same regulations. Another case is *The Humber Steam Trawling Co. Ltd v. Brink* (1895) 3 S.L.T. 210. The absence of other reported cases may be due to cases not being reported as being thought too specialised or more sadly that the business goes by choice of laws clauses to the English Courts. There are a huge number of English cases sufficient for the learned editors of Marsden to produce an annotated version of the rules to which readers of this text are respectfully referred.

[27] *Hawkins v. Northern Marine Management Ltd (No. 2)*, 1997 G.W.D. 37–1795.

[28] S.I. 1966 No. 94.

[29] S.I. 1960 No. 421. See *Shepherd v. Pearson Engineering Services (Dundee) Ltd*, 1981 S.L.T. 197.

[30] s. 185.

[31] Cmnd. 7035.

[32] There are special rules made by the U.K. for hovercraft: Hovercraft Act 1968. Passengers' luggage is covered by the Carriage by Air Act 1961.

[33] In this regard a derogation from the international position.

[34] Art. 1(2) and (3).

[35] Art. 2(1)(a). The present Article no longer restricts the limitation to "any person being carried in the ship" as was the case under the Merchant Shipping Act 1894, s. 503 and so the decision in *Innes v. Ross*, 1957 S.L.T. 121 that an injured crew member fell within that phrase is no longer important.

resulting from the infringement of rights other than contractual rights, occurring in direct connection with the operation of the ship or salvage operations;[36] and claims in respect of the removal, destruction or the rendering harmless of the cargo of the ship.[37] Certain claims by virtue of Article 3 cannot be limited including salvage or general average claims, oil pollution cases, nuclear cases and most importantly employers' liability cases to the extent that under national law limitation is precluded or restricted. Limitation has been seen as a privilege rather than an absolute right. Under the previous legislation it was necessary to prove that a collision was not as a result of the actual fault or privity of the person claiming limitation. The burden was on the party seeking to limit.[38] Now if it is proved that the loss resulted from the defender's personal act or omission committed with the intent to cause such loss, or recklessly and with the knowledge that such loss would probably result, then there will be no bar to the limitation defence.[39] The burden is now placed on the claimant.

16–28   At the time of writing there are no cases on the new wording.[40] It might be hazarded that a different decision might be arrived at on the facts of the *Aberdeen Venturer*,[41] a case of a drunken engineer. The critical issues appear in the following passage from the opinion of Lord Grieve:

> "the defenders' system in so far as it was designed to prevent men joining their vessels in a drunken condition, or taking alcohol on board their vessels, or both, was as good a system as could be operated having regard to the fact that the union concerned denied them the right of search, and the fact that the quays were not enclosed. The defenders' system, however, in so far as it was designed to ensure that their employees were at all times in a fit state to carry out their duties at sea, was deficient in certain respects. The defenders knew that some of their employees might well have had a drink before joining, albeit they might not be drunk, and could not be stopped from sailing. They also knew that there was a real possibility of drink being smuggled on board, and thereafter consumed on board. Further, they knew that it was the practice of their skippers to make an issue of beer of two to three cans to all crew members, whether on watch or not, shortly after their vessels left harbour for the fishing grounds. In these circumstances the defenders should have appreciated that there was a risk of one or more men who, though apparently sober when the vessel put to sea, might become intoxicated when it was time for them to go on duty or after they had gone on duty. It was for the defenders to form a policy designed to avoid crew members being on watch in an unfit condition and to make that policy known to their employees, especially their officers who were

---

[36] Art. 2(1)(c).

[37] Art. 2(1)(e).

[38] See for a Scottish example *Richard Irvin & Sons Ltd v. Aberdeen Near Water Trawlers Ltd*, 1983 S.L.T. 26.

[39] Art. 4.

[40] But see the same words in other conventions for guidance as suggested in Marsden at p. 544 fn. 53.

[41] *Richard Irvin & Sons Ltd.*

responsible for discipline once the vessels left harbour. Instead of issuing general directions such as are contained in paras 11 and 12 of the Instructions to Skippers, they should have given more positive directions regarding (a) the necessity of ensuring that no one went on watch or on duty when his sobriety was in doubt, and (b) that an issue of alcohol should not be made to anyone about to go on duty, whether his sobriety was in doubt or not. These were matters which the defenders were not entitled to leave to the unfettered discretion of their skippers. These were things which the defenders did not do and which they should have done. They were therefore in fault in not doing them. Had they been done the defenders have failed to show that they had no bearing on the casualty which occurred. They have accordingly failed to show that it was not contributed to by their actual fault, and they cannot limit their liability."[42]

It would be more difficult to treat this as a personal act and while careless it would perhaps be hard to characterise it as reckless.

Oil Pollution

The Merchant Shipping (Oil Pollution) Act 1971 imposes strict liability **16–29** upon ship owners for pollution caused by oil escaping from ships carrying a cargo of oil and provides for actions to be raised directly against the ship owner's insurers. The Merchant Shipping Act 1974 makes the International Oil Pollution Compensation Fund liable to persons suffering damage in the event that the ship owners or their insurers are unable to meet their liabilities. Provision is also made for the liability of ship owners, insurers and the fund to be limited and, in the event of the total of all claims exceeding the limit, for those claims to rank rateably.[43] Claims for secondary economic loss are excluded.[44]

Statutory Duty of Safety

Section 100 of the Merchant Shipping Act 1995 provides that it is the duty **16–30** of the owner of a ship to take all reasonable steps to secure that the ship is operated in a safe manner. The equivalent provision under the previous legislation, section 31, was considered in a Scottish case, *Littlejohn v. Wood & Davidson*.[45] The pursuer was injured when he was working on a ship moored at port. He fell into a cavity there being a hole in a floor resulting from the removal of a hatch. It was argued for the owners that the ship was not at the time being operated as it was in port and that the section did not infer civil liability. Lord Johston held that "operate" was habile to cover all the forms of maritime activity relating to a ship whether she be in port or at sea with the exception of the ship being in dry dock or perhaps if laid up.[46]

---

[42] *ibid.* at 33.

[43] See, *e.g. Anderson v. The Braer Corporation*, 1996 S.L.T. 779; *Black v. Braer Corporation*, 1999 S.L.T. 1401; *Eunson v. Braer Corporation*, 1999 S.L.T. 1405.

[44] *Landcatch v. International Oil Pollution Compensation Fund; Landcatch v. Braer Corporation*, 1999 S.L.T. 1208.

[45] 1997 S.L.T. 1353.

[46] *ibid.* at 1355I.

It was also held that the section could infer civil liability because the legislation envisaged the protection of a specific class: "here the class is enormous, namely all those at sea, including those on board a ship in port, but it is nevertheless a specific and definable class totally akin to those who work in factories wherever they may be."[47]

A ship is a product and following the enactment of the Consumer Protection Act 1987 that theory of liability might well be applicable.[48]

AIRCRAFT

16–31 An aircraft is premises for the purposes of occupiers liability. The basic principles of employers liability apply. Jurisdiction and conflicts problems are likely to arise. Aircraft can cause a nuisance or a trespass and these topics are dealt with elsewhere in this book.[49] Military aviation has its own rules beyond the scope of this book. An aeroplane is a product and following the enactment of the Consumer Protection Act 1987 that theory of liability might well be applicable.[50]

Despite the existence of many international conventions it seems that a collision between two aircraft governed by Scots law so far as the claim for damage to one of the planes is concerned would be decided according to general principle.[51]

Carriage by Air Act 1961 and The Warsaw Convention

16–32 Where passengers are injured on an aircraft the case would normally be treated as a contractual claim. Such cases are regulated by international convention incorporated into United Kingdom law by the Carriage by Air Act 1961, by which effect was given to the Convention concerning international carriage by air known as "The Warsaw Convention".[52] Both that scheme and the domestic scheme derived from it have the benefit for the pursuer of strict liability but the burden of a low pecuniary limitation.[53] The scheme provides that a ticket is given which includes a notice to the effect that, if the passenger's journey involves an ultimate destination or stop in a country other than the country of departure, the Warsaw Convention may be applicable and that the Convention governs and in most cases limits the liability of carriers for death or personal injury and in

---

[47] *ibid.* at 1355L.
[48] See Chap. 15.
[49] See Chap. 5.
[50] See Chap. 15.
[51] See Diederiks-Verschoor, *An Introduction to Air Law* (6th ed., Kluwer Law, 1997), pp. 122–123.
[52] See generally N. Taylor, "Limitation of Liability of Aircarriers to Aircrash victims—Has the Warsaw Convention Reached its Retirement Age?" [1994] J.P.I.L. 113.
[53] In an exercise of French linguistic imperialism the law in international travel cases is that section 1(1) of the Act read together with Schedule 1 sets out the provisions of the Convention. Part I of the Schedule sets out the English text of the Convention, and Part II sets out the French text. Section 1(2) provides that, if there is an inconsistency between the text in English and Part I of Schedule 1 and the text in French in Part II of that Schedule, the text in French shall prevail.

respect of loss of or damage to baggage. In a Scottish appeal to the House of Lords, *Abnett v. British Airways Plc. (Scotland), Sidhu v. British Airways Plc.*[54] it was held on a contractual case that the convention applied. Mrs Abnett had been on her way to Malaysia and stopped off in Kuwait. While refuelling she and the other passengers were captured by the invading Iraqui forces, a stage in what became the Gulf War. She sued at common law for the neglect of the airline in running the flight when they knew or ought to have known of the deteriorating relations between Iraq and Kuwait. Her claim was strictly for breach of the implied term to take reasonable care which she argued was implied in the contract of carriage. The associated *Sidhu* claim was in negligence. It was accepted that the Convention should always receive a purposive construction.[55] In *Abnett* Lord Hope pointed out that the Convention was a partial codification only:

"Nothing is said in this Convention about the liability of passengers to the carrier, for example. Nor is anything said about the carrier's obligations of insurance, and in particular about compulsory insurance against third party risks. It is clear from the content and structure of the Convention that it is a partial harmonisation only of the rules relating to international carriage by air."[56]

On analysis of the history of the convention it was seen to be a compromise whereby the carrier's freedom to contract out of liability was surrendered for the right to limit liability in cases covered by the provisions. Lord Hope concluded:

"Were remedies outside the Convention to become available, it would encourage litigation in other cases to restrict its application still further in the hope of obtaining a better remedy, against which the carrier would have no protection under the contract. I am in no doubt that the Convention was designed to eliminate these difficulties. I see no escape from the conclusion that, where the Convention has not provided a remedy, no remedy is available."[57]

At the time the case was argued a French court had come to the opposite conclusion on the Convention.[58]

A different case came before the House of Lords around the same time: **16–33** *Herd v. Clyde Helicopters Ltd.*[59] Police Sergeant Herd was a member of the Police Helicopter Unit of the Strathclyde Police Force. His duties were to carry out aerial surveillance and detection. The helicopters used by the Unit were supplied by the defenders, Clyde Helicopters Ltd, in terms of a

---

[54] 1997 S.L.T. 492.
[55] Under reference to *Fothergill v. Monarch Airlines Ltd* [1981] A.C. 251. The same case was authority for resort to preparatory works available to the public, *i.e.* the minutes of the International Conference on Private Aeronautical Law at Warsaw, 4–12 October 1929.
[56] *Abnett*, at 499.
[57] *ibid.* at 504.
[58] *Ismail A. Mohamed v. British Airways*, Unreported, November 8, 1995, Tribunal de Grande Instance de Paris.
[59] 1996 S.L.T. 976.

contract. During the fatal flight a snow storm came up and the pilot, an employee of the defenders became lost and an engine failure occurred. The helicopter collided with a block of flats as a result of which Sergeant Herd died. The defenders argued that by the Carriage by Air Acts (Application of Provisions) Order 1967[60] their liability was confined to liability under that Order. In the Outer House and the Inner House the defenders succeeded.[61] This case unlike *Abnett* but like *Sidhu* was a delict case. It was also a domestic case rather than an international transport case. The pursuers argued on appeal that the Order did not operate to limit the respondents' liability because the regional council contract was not a contract of carriage and that the deceased neither accepted nor consented to the terms of the regional council contract. Accordingly, he was not on board the helicopter as a passenger and neither was he a party to any contract of carriage. The defenders argued that they had agreed to the carriage of Sergeant Herd on a contractual basis namely the instructions of the chief constable. On a reading of the order it was held that the order should apply preventing the common law claim for negligence. Lord Hope delivering an opinion of his own, (the other Lords concurring with Lord Chancellor McKay) found two aspects troubling. His two concerns were not abstract but derived from his broad understanding of the overall legislative pattern both international and local. There was no contract between Sergeant Herd and the respondents to which the rules in the Order of 1967 could be said to have become statutory terms, and the contract between the respondents and the police authority by which he was a passenger on the helicopter did not provide for a place of departure or destination or any agreed stopping places—two features for Lord Hope at the heart of the convention schemes. He carefully rehearsed the well-researched argument based on French cases that the conventionist interpretation to local legislation need not apply to persons on a plane other than as ordinary passengers such as a student pilot on a flying lesson,[62] or a person taking aerial photographs,[63] or a case in which a person was injured while taking a person from a skiing accident.[64] In the end Lord Hope agreed with the Lord Chancellor that the words of the Order meant what they said and although the result would seem harsh the pursuer got the benefit of strict liability. *Herd* does seem to be unfair or illogical in one sense because the widow would have succeeded (subject, as Lord Hope points out to proof of fault) had he been assigned to a squad car rather than a helicopter to carry out his police duties. Most people, even the ordinary package tourist, knows that insurance is required to go to Malaga but most workers go where they are sent. That may be the fault of the legislation rather than the absence of bold spirits in Westminster.

In *Hammond v. Bristow Helicopters Ltd*[65] three different pursuers each sued for PTSD as a result of crashes or near crashes in helicopters. They claimed under the Warsaw Convention as applied by the 1961 Act. On

---

[60] S.I. 1967 No. 480, especially paras 3 and 4 of and Schedule 1 to, that Order.
[61] *Herd.*
[62] *St Mutuelle d'Assurance Ariennes v. Gauvain* (1967) 21 R.F.D.A. 436.
[63] *Ortet v. Georges* (1976) 30 R.F.D.A. 490.
[64] *Barnes v. Service Arien Francais* (1993) 47 R.F.D.A. 343.
[65] 1999 S.L.T. 919.

careful interpretation "bodily injury" in this context did not include PTSD although one of the pursuers who alleged that the stress brought about a peptic ulcer was, it is submitted, properly allowed a proof.

The two year limitation period is a year less than that normally expected by the Scottish practitioner in personal injury cases.

CHAPTER 17

ANIMALS

Introduction

This chapter deals with a person's liability for animals. Liability in respect **17–1**
of killing or detaining animals is properly an aspect of interference with
moveable property.[1] Historically, the law has treated animals specially. This
is unsurprising when most legal systems have their historical roots in
essentially agricultural communities: animals constitute both stock and
machinery in such communities. Some animals clearly and notoriously can
be so harmful to person or property that taking reasonable care that they
do not cause harm is not perceived as being sufficient for the welfare of the
community. Thus there is a tradition of the imposition of stricter forms of
liability—a tradition which continues to the present day. Animals in law are
things, but things capable of considerable independent action—perhaps
only slaves, and robots raise similar problems for the law.[2] At the time of
writing the law applicable to cases coming before the court is very likely to
be that applied by the Animals (Scotland) Act 1987. However, cases might
still arise, unlimited or unprescribed, under the old law which is now
discussed both for that practical reason and to show the development of the
law, but briefly, the more esoteric aspects being developed in the periodic
literature for those interested.[3] Lord Hunter's review of the development of
strict liability in Scotland in the case of *Henderson v. John Stuart (Farms)
Ltd*[4] is instructive. He noted that liability for animals is found in Stair,[5]
which placed liability on the master of a pushing ox if he knew that the ox
was accustomed to do so but, if not he was free from liability. Such failure,
his Lordship noted, rendered the master liable in reparation, on the ground
of culpa—but the fault was not in the failure to take reasonable care, but in
failure to restrain or confine.[6] Whereas Stair makes reference to the civilian
Actio de pauperies, the English law was built on a Scienter action.[7] The

---

[1] Chap. 6.
[2] The Germans have gone so far as to recast the BGB to provide a separate section for
animals: See Blackie, "The Provoking Dogs Problem 2" 1993 J.L.S. 148; See also P. Handford,
"The Dog Act in the New South Wales Court of Appeal" 1995 Tort Law Rev. (Note), p. 5.
[3] See D.L. Carey Miller, "A Statutory Substitute for Scienter" (1973) J.R. 61; D.L. Carey
Miller, "The Scottish Institutional Writers on Animal Liability" (1974) J.R. 1; Blackie, "The
Provoking Dogs Problem 2" 1993 J.L.S. 148.
[4] 1963 S.C. 245.
[5] I, ix, 5.
[6] *Henderson*, at 249.
[7] D.L. See Carey Miller, "A Statutory Substitute for Scienter" (1973) J.R. 61; D.L. Carey
Miller, "The Scottish Institutional Writers on Animal Liability" (1974) J.R. 1.

result was often the same but the basis of liability was different as can be seen in a dictum of Lord President Cooper in *McLaughlan v. Craig*[8]:

> "If a man were to keep a tiger and failed to confine it effectually with the result that it devoured a passing pedestrian, the inference of culpa would, in most circumstances, be practically irrebuttable. Nevertheless under the law of Scotland, I would not think that a pursuer would necessarily succeed in proving culpa even in such a case, if it were established, for example, that the animal had escaped as a result of an act of God or of the queen's enemies, or through the wrongful act of a third party, or if the effective cause of the accident was the meddling and rash act of the injured person himself. Here again the law of England may reach broadly similar results, but by a different route, namely, the recognition of certain limited and well defined defences to the scienter action, which, although the authorities have wavered, apparently have some similarity to the defences recognised as being open in cases where the doctrine of *Rylands v. Fletcher* applies."[9]

However, for some time it seems that the law in Scotland was considered to be very much identical to the law of England. This phase of the law is best illustrated by the decision of the second division in *Burton v. Moorhead*.[10] The pursuer was attacked by a dog established to have bitten others before. It had been secured by a chain bought as sufficient and new two years prior to the accident. The chain broke when the dog attacked. The Lord Justice-Clerk (Moncrieff) said:

> "the dog has a privilege of one worry. But when the ferocity of the dog is quite well known to the owner his obligation is not one of reasonable care, but not to keep the dog at all, unless he does it in such a way as to make it perfectly secure. The distinction is most clear, and therefore the owner of the dog keeps it entirely at his own risk."[11]

Both the Lord Justice-Clerk and Lord Young accepted the main point of the English distinction that the "one worry" only applied to domestic animals and that in relation to wild animals strict liability applied. Despite occasional civilian revisionism[12] that was the received view.[13] Similarly in *Fraser v. Pate*[14] Lord Justice-Clerk Alness considered that the law in Scotland and England was the same in relation to the allegation of negligence in keeping animals from the highway.

---

[8] 1948 S.C. 599.
[9] *ibid.* at 610–611.
[10] (1881) 8 R. 892.
[11] *ibid.* at 895.
[12] Lord President Cooper (above); The Law Reform Committee for Scotland 1963 (Cmnd. 2185)
[13] Although reluctantly at times; see Lord McDonald in *Gallacher v. St. Cuthbert's Co-operative Association Ltd*, 1976 S.L.T. (Notes) 25.
[14] 1923 S.L.T. 457.

THE CURRENT COMMON LAW

The common law of negligence applies to a person's control or lack thereof, **17–2** of his animals as much as his motor car or his dynamite. In that the common law of negligence applies the analogy of dynamite and a tiger is a useful one when read in the light of the dictum of Lord President Cooper quoted above. Thus a result very much like strict liability could apply to a person looking after a notoriously dangerous animal irrespective of the 1987 Act. In *Henderson v. John Stuart (Farms) Ltd*[15] Lord Hunter said:

> "If this case were to be considered against the background of the modern law of Scotland relating to the duty of care owed by employers to employees, uncomplicated by authorities on the subject of liability of owners for injury caused by their animals, I do not think that its decision would present any serious difficulty. One example of the employer's duty to take reasonable care for the safety of the employee is his duty to take reasonable care to provide and maintain a safe system of work. It is on breach by the defenders of such a duty that the pursuers found the present action."[16]

The employer was culpably careless in letting the workman enter without protection. The fact that there was a bull in the pen as opposed to dynamite and illuminated candles could make no difference. The *obiter* statement as regards non-employees is equally, it is submitted, correct:

> "There may, in the case of a stranger suing on the ground of failure to confine, be something to be said for providing a remedy on a rather arbitrary basis . . . but the existence of a remedy on a somewhat strict or even arbitrary basis for breach of the duty to confine an animal does not, in my opinion, deprive a stranger of his right to sue an action on the ground of failure to take reasonable care. That an action on the ground of negligence in respect of injury caused by an animal is available to a stranger under the law of Scotland is, in my opinion, well vouched by authority . . . I would not shrink from the proposition that averments such as the pursuer makes in the present case would, in appropriate circumstances, be relevant even in the mouth of a stranger."[17]

There may be cases, where the statute is not clear that a case based on negligence may be useful on its own or in the alternative, taking into account that in the past inferences of fault may be made and that the doctrine of *res ipsa loquitur* may apply.[18] A postman attacked by a dog succeeded on the basis of the liability for animals *mansuetae naturae* with vicious propensities.[19] At common law there may be difficulties in establishing that an owner is fixed with knowledge of propensities of a beast.[20]

---

[15] 1963 S.C. 245.
[16] *ibid.* at 245.
[17] *ibid.* at 253.
[18] *Snee v. Durkie* (1903) 6 F.42; *Hendry v. McDougall*, 1923 S.C. 378.
[19] *O'Connor v. McRobb*, 1975 S.L.T. (Sh. Ct) 42.
[20] *Maclean v. Forestry Commission*, 1970 S.L.T. (Notes) 23 (I.H.).

Where fault is required it is not so easily inferred from the happening of an incident as where a bull escaped unexplained.[21] It was held, however, in *Hill v. Lovett*[22] that at common law and under the Occupier's Liability (Scotland) Act 1960 there was liability for the lack of care in allowing a person to enter a garden in which there were two territorially defensive dogs.

17–3   It has often been accepted that as in the law of England the presence of an animal on the road does not infer liability.[23] But reasonable care must be taken and cases can succeed or be allowed to go to proof before answer.[24] The presence of animals on the road has raised interesting questions both in Scotland and England. In *Fraser v. Pate*,[25] Fraser, a motor-cyclist, sued the farmer said to have allowed his sheep to stray on to the highway. Considerable reliance was placed on an English case *Heath's Garage Ltd v. Hodges*.[26] The court accepted the Lord Ordinary's analysis that there was no liability because there was no duty. It may however be observed that there was a curious examination of the domestic/wild animal dichotomy which in the circumstances is of doubtful relevance. While the distinction is a valid one so far as the conduct of animals by way of biting, goring or otherwise injuring people according to their nature is concerned it can hardly be said that a man eating tiger equally infers liability to its keeper should it decide instead to throw itself upon someone's motor cycle. On the actual point the case may well have been properly decided on the law of negligence on the facts of the use of roads at the time. It is an open question how far animals may be allowed to stray without inferring negligence in today's conditions where many people expect to be able to drive without even seeing a horse. Lord Anderson it should be noted concurred on the basis that "nothing we are deciding in this case is to be taken as encouraging carelessness on the part of farmers in the discharge of their duty of taking all proper precautions to ensure their gates and fences are sufficient to confine bestial to their grazings."[27] In *Sinclair v. Muir*[28] the Second Division allowed a proof before answer on appeal in the case of a motor cyclist knocked over by a charging bull on the road. In *Gardiner v. Miller*,[29] the pursuer collided with a horse that had escaped, the basis of the case, however, being the failure to have a gate which could not easily be left open by strangers. A proof before answer was allowed. In *Wark v. Steel*,[30] the pursuer was a pedal cyclist who collided with a horse, the sheriff substitute followed *Fraser* and dismissed. On appeal the sheriff allowed a proof before answer and the pursuer succeeded at the proof. There is a careful practical imposition of

---

[21] *Dobbie v. Henderson*, 1970 S.L.T. (Sh. Ct) 27.
[22] 1992 S.L.T. 994.
[23] *Clark v. Armstrong* (1862) 24 D. 1315; *Milligan v. Henderson*, 1915 2 S.L.T. 156; *Fraser v. Pate*, 1923 S.L.T. 457 and *Anderson v. Wilson's Trs*, 1965 S.L.T. (Sh. Ct) 35 in which it was held that darkness did not constitute a special circumstance attracting liability.
[24] *Sinclair v. Muir*, 1933 S.N. 42, 62; *Colquhoun v. Hannah*, Unreported October 31, 1942; *Gardiner v. Miller*, 1967 S.L.T. 29.
[25] 1923 S.L.T. 457.
[26] [1916] 2 K.B. 370.
[27] *ibid.* at 460.
[28] 1933 SN 42, 62.
[29] 1967 S.L.T. 29.
[30] 1946 S.L.T. (Sh. Ct) 17.

the effect of that decision and the sheriff substitute correctly, it is submitted, distinguishes between the "great unfenced areas in the high-lands" and the "populous country" where there is regularly fencing to be found. The most recent discussion which usefully reviewed the authorities was *Swan v. Andrew Minto & Sons*,[31] where the pursuer collided with one of two black cows belonging to the defenders which had strayed on to an A-road from adjacent land. The cows were grazing on opposing grass verges and so blocked the whole road. It was alleged, *inter alia*, that the defenders ought to have erected a stockproof fence and inspected it and to have taken care that it should have remained so. The defenders averred, *inter alia*, that the cows jumped over the fence and the pursuer while denying that, said that the fence should then have been higher, these not being olympic cows or related to the cow kingdom as Pegasus to the horse.[32] The sheriff founding on the cases after *Fraser*, correctly it is submitted, allowed a proof before answer.

THE ANIMALS (SCOTLAND) ACT 1987

The Act is a product of the efforts of the Scottish Law Commission.[33] The **17–4** legislation accordingly needs to be read as a whole before any attempt is made to construe any particular part of it. The attractive feature of this kind of legislation is that it is often possible to locate a specific answer to many practical problems.[34]

Who to sue

A person is liable to be sued for any injury or damage caused by an animal **17–5** if at the time of the injury or damage complained of, he was a keeper of the animal.[35] A person is a keeper of an animal if he owns the animal or has possession of it or if he has actual care and control of a child under the age of 16 who owns the animal or has possession of it.[36] However, a person is not regarded as having possession of an animal by reason only that he is detaining it under section 3 of the Act or is otherwise temporarily detaining it for the purpose of protecting it or any person or other animal or of restoring it as soon as reasonably practicable to its owner or a possessor of it.[37] If an animal has been abandoned or has escaped, a person who at the time of the abandonment or escape was the owner of it or had it in his possession shall remain its owner or shall be regarded as continuing to have possession of it.[38] The Crown does not acquire ownership of an animal on

---

[31] 1998 Rep.L.R. 42.

[32] *inter alia*, the defenders relied on Walker. *Delict*, pp. 632–634; on *Clark v. Armstrong* (1862) 24 D. 1315 and of course *Fraser, op. cit.* They also relied on *Milne v. Macintosh*, 1952 S.L.T. 84 which was a droving case and *Fraser v. Lyle*, Unreported, Paisley Sheriff Court, February 3, 1998.

[33] Scot Law Com. No. 97.

[34] It is perhaps a pity that instead of an offer to extend the English Act to Scotland, a U.K. Act could not have been arrived at.

[35] s. 1(a).

[36] s. 5(1)(a) and (b).

[37] s. 5(2)(a).

[38] s. 5(2)(b)(c).

its abandonment for the purposes of the act, but presumably does so as a matter of the law of property.[39]

Strict Liability

17–6 The Act provides for strict liability.[40] However, it only does so to the extent that "the animal belongs to a species whose members generally are by virtue of their physical attributes or habits likely (unless controlled or restrained) to injure severely or kill persons or animals, or damage property to a material extent."[41] The practical approach of the Act is evidenced by the fact that it then goes on to deal with specific types of damage caused by specific animals. These are deeming provisions and the effect of them is that reference to the general rules is unlikely to occur frequently. The categories of strict liability created by these deeming provisions are as follows:

Dogs

17–7 Dogs are deemed to be likely (unless controlled or restrained) to injure severely or kill persons or animals by biting or otherwise savaging, attacking or harrying. Thus there is strict liability for a dog bite.[42] Note that they are not deemed to be likely to eat crops and a turnip eating dog would not attract strict liability upon his master. In *Fairlie v. Carruthers*,[43] notable as one of the first cases on the 1987 Act, the defender's dog ran into the pursuer. The defender was the keeper. It was held the conduct of the animal in this case did not fall within this statutory phrase. The phrase "attack and harry" has within it the notion of intent and there will be a limit to how far the court will enquire into the mind of a beast but *Fairlie* was more of a collision than an attack.

Dangerous wild animals

17–8 Dangerous wild animals within the meaning of section 7(4) of the Dangerous Wild Animals Act 1976, shall be deemed to be likely (unless controlled or restrained) to injure severely or kill persons or animals by biting or otherwise savaging, attacking or harrying.[44]

Damaging Foragers

17–9 Any of the following animals in the course of foraging, namely, cattle, horses, asses, jules, hinnies, sheep, pigs, goats and deer, are deemed to be likely (unless controlled or restrained) to damage to a material extent land

---

[39] s. 5(2)(c).
[40] s .1.
[41] s. 1(b).
[42] *O'Neil v. Coyle*, 1995 G.W.D. 21–1185.
[43] 1996 S.L.T. (Sh. Ct) 56.
[44] The list of dangerous animals includes: wolf, jackal, foxes and dogs, except the domestic dog and the common red fox, a cassowary, the old world monkey, a mangabey, baboon or mandrill, an alligator, the emu, a cobra or a mamba, lions, tigers, cheetahs, gibbons and gila monsters, orang-utans and chimpanzees, ostriches and grizzly bears, vipers and rattlesnakes. Note that the common names, such as those listed, are not definitive—that is only the case with the zoological terms listed in the Schedule. See the Dangerous Wild Animals Act 1976 (Modifications) Order 1984 S.I. 1994 No. 1111.

or the produce of land, whether harvested or not. Thus there is probably no strict liability for goat bites. In *Foskett v. McClymont*[45] the other logical case was tested—whether a bull, of the species cattle and thus making its keeper strictly liable for property damage, attracted strict liability for personal injury. The pursuer had general authorisation from the defenders to deploy radar systems on the defenders' land. While doing so he ended up being attacked by a bull that tossed him over a wall on to some nettles. It was argued that the strict liability case made out by the pursuer had to fail in this case because there were insufficient averments to allow the pursuer to lead evidence that the bull in question belonged to a species falling within section 1(1)(b). By amendment at the bar the pursuer had added what some might call the bald averment that a bull was indeed of the species of animal narrated in the section. To an extent there is a pleading point there and with respect the defender probably had a good point—the species ought to have been identified to give fair notice to the defenders' zoological experts of which beasts were to be considered. At the level of ordinary knowledge both sides and the judges seemed to accept there are docile bulls and nasty bulls. It was never clear whether this is a result of temperament or genetics. While the defenders will know the species of their bull it is not within the traditional approach to pleading to compel them to specify and expend money in ultimately proving the point unless it is squarely raised by the pursuer. On the substance of the case and on the assumption that it is fair to say that cattle are a species and a bull is a species as defined by being identifiable by sex then the case was indeed relevant. It should, however, be noted that the Dangerous Wild Animals Act which by reference defines some of the deemed animals is written in terms of zoological species. The Lord Ordinary considered that the pursuer was putting the case that all bulls fell within the Act and that in looking at the Act he was entitled to adopt that position, although this was likely to generate considerable factual controversy. The much weaker point that because cattle appeared in s. 1(3)(b) (likely to damage crops, etc.) that meant they could not fall within s. 1(1)(b) was correctly rejected. Equally weak was the argument that the Act had intended to simplify rather than radically change the previous law and that too was rejected by Lord Osborne. He was entirely certain, and rightly so it is submitted, that any vestige of the former distinction between animals *ferae naturae* and *mansuetae naturae* had been abolished.

Causation

In all cases, whether general or deemed, the injury or damage complained of need only be directly referable to the physical attributes or habits of the animal. **17–10**

Defences and Derogations from Strict Liability

Unlikely means

In respect of the first two categories of deemed liability above, there is no strict liability in respect of any injury caused by an animal where the injury consists of disease transmitted by means which are unlikely to cause severe **17–11**

---

[45] 1998 S.C. 96.

injury other than disease.[46] Nor does it apply to injury or damage caused by the mere fact that an animal is present on a road or in any other place.[47]

Contributory Negligence

17–12 For the purposes of the Law Reform (Contributory Negligence) Act 1945, any injury or damage for which a person is liable under the strict liability provisions shall be treated as due to his fault as defined in that Act.

Sole Fault and Volenti

17–13 A person shall not be strictly liable under the Act if—(a) the injury or damage was due wholly to the fault of (i) the person sustaining it; or (ii) in the case of injury sustained by an animal, a keeper of the animal; (b) the person sustaining the injury or damage or a keeper of the animal sustaining the injury willingly accepted the risk of it as his.[48]

Trespassers and Guard dogs

17–14 A more complicated exemption to the civil liability established by the Animals (Scotland) Act 1987, designed to cover, *inter alia*, situations involving trespassers and guard dogs, is that where the injury or damage was sustained on, or in consequence of the person or animal sustaining the injury or damage coming on to, land which was occupied by a person who was a keeper, or by another person who authorised the presence on the land, of the animal which caused the injury or damage; and either

    (i) the person sustaining the injury or damage was not authorised or entitled to be on that land; or (as the case may be)

    (ii) no keeper of the animal sustaining the injury was authorised or entitled to have the animal present on that land.

A person is not, however, exempt from liability by virtue of this rule if the animal causing the injury or damage was kept on the land wholly or partly for the purpose of protecting persons or property, unless the keeping of the animal there, and the use made of the animal for that purpose was reasonable, and if the animal was a guard dog within the meaning of the Guard Dogs Act 1975, unless there was compliance with section 1 of that Act. That Act requires that a person must not use a guard dog at any premises unless the handler who is capable of controlling the dog is present

---

[46] As where my panther gives you rabies by licking your cut hand. A bite might be expected to transmit disease: see the facts of *Hill v. Lovett*, 1992 S.L.T. 994, *per* Lord Weir at 998E, "It may be thought remarkable that a small bite from a terrier should have had these terrible consequences, but it is not in question that on occasion, according to the medical evidence, a dog bite can lead to the production of organisms which are highly resistant to therapy and this is the case as regards this injury."

[47] Thus the owner of a sleeping dog over which you trip need not fear strict liability though he may have to answer in negligence, or under the Occupiers Liability Act 1960 or indeed the Factories Acts 1961. For the common law see *Anderson v. Wilson's Trs*, 1965 S.L.T. (Sh. Ct) 35; *Gardiner v. Miller*, 1967 S.L.T. 29; 1966 (Notes) 80.

[48] For a consideration of this provision as a defence in the case of a pursuer (or his dog) provoking the defender's dog see Blackie, "The Provoking Dogs Problem 2" (1993) J.L.S. 148.

on the premises and the dog is under the control of the handler at all times while it is being used except while it is secured so that it is not at liberty to go free about the premises.[49] There must also be a notice clearly exhibited at every entrance to the premises warning that a guard dog is present.[50]

---

[49] Guard Dogs Act 1975, s. 1(1).
[50] Note that the Guard Dogs Act itself does not lay down civil liability: s. 5(2)(a).

CHAPTER 18

DAMAGES FOR WRONGS

Introduction

There are rules that apply to damages no matter what area of the law **18–1**
triggers the remedy. An example is the rules applying in cases of fatal
accidents where the same rules apply to cases of delict or breach of
contractual duties. As the law of damages is a subject in its own right it
would accordingly be possible to omit all treatment of damages from this
book,[1] but academics might want to study the subject in the round and
practitioners might well expect to find guidance on the end result of a
reparation claim in this book. Aquilian liability depends upon damage and
so the existence of an actionable head bears upon liability itself.[2] No
attempt is made to track current awards even indicatively.[3]

PRINCIPAL THEMES

It cannot be said that each and every case of damages is an application of a **18–2**
single general principle. Various questions about damages have to be
answered in different ways. In the context of most cases founded on delict,
damages is pressed into service as a form of substitutional redress: *e.g.* a leg
is missing and money replaces it. The normal fundamental principle is often
to say that damages are to bring about *restitutio in integrum*. But that cannot
be right. If I run over your leg I have nothing to restore and if money is
taken from me I am poorer than at the start of the story.[4] Even if money
substitutes for your leg it cannot be said your leg represented money to me
unless the delict was intentional and I am a sadist who would have paid for
the pleasure on the market.[5] It is better to say that damages for a wrong are
normally compensatory and seek to restore the status quo *ante*.

---

[1] So far as personal injuries are concerned, there is an excellent looseleaf practitioner text:
McEwan and Paton on Damages for Personal Injuries in Scotland (W. Green) and see also the
more compact S.A. Bennett, *Personal Injuries Damages in Scotland* (Barnstoneworth, 1999).
There is only one treatise on the subject as a whole: D.M. Walker, *The Law of Damages in
Scotland* (W. Green, 1955).

[2] For an exposition of that important relationship see Stapleton "The Gist of Negligence"
(1988) 104 L.Q.R. 213.

[3] See *McEwan and Paton, Greens Reparation Bulletin* and *Greens Reparation Law Reports*.

[4] See *Admiralty Commissioners v. SS Valeria* [1922] A.C. 248.

[5] Economic and legal theorists work on such analyses: *e.g.* "To illustrate from tort law, the
demand for clean air and water, and hence the contours of nuisance doctrine, may vary
depending on whether the question is posed as whether the victim of pollution would be
willing to "sell" his "right" to be free from pollution for a price that the polluter would be
willing to pay or as whether the victim would offer to "buy" the right to clean air or water

This approach may be contrasted with contract damages which are designed to compensate by giving substitutional effect for the failure in the expectations engendered by the promises. It is not generally appropriate to cross-cite contract and delict cases unless the contract case is in relation to a directly equivalent obligation, namely to take reasonable care of something, or where the contract case would assist in valuation of a particular item. Scots law makes things more complicated by awarding damages for solatium—affront, pain and suffering. These did not exist before (*ante*) and so do not really restore any status quo *ante*. Thus damages cannot be regarded as simply compensation.

Compensatory Damages

18–3 Damages awarded for a wrong may seek to compensate the pursuer for the wrong. This is said to be by way of *restitutio in integrum*—restoring the situation, so far as money can, to where it was before the wrong was committed. There are innumerable dicta on this matter.[6] One often cited is: "The dominant rule of law is the principle of *restitutio in integrum* and subsidiary rules can only be justified if they give effect to that rule".[7] However, the result in that case has not always been followed and indeed has been rejected.[8] Scots courts, in what may be either a demonstration of a love of principle or a reluctance to grapple with the difficulty of formulating logical rules, often declare themselves against specific rules. Another oft-cited passage[9] is Lord Dunedin's four propositions in the "*Susquehanna*"[10]:

"(1) There is no difference in this matter between the position in Admiralty law and that of the common law, and the common law says that the damages due either for breech of contract or for tort are damages which, so far as money can compensate, will give the injured party reparation for the wrongful act and for all the natural and direct consequences of the wrongful act. (2) If there be any special damage which is attributable to the wrongful act that special damage must be averred and proved. . . . (3) If the damage be general, then it must be averred that such damage has been suffered, but the quantification of such damage is a jury question. (4) For a jury question no rigid rules, or rules that apply to all cases, can be laid down, but in each set of circumstances certain relevant considerations will arise which, were the matter before a judge, it would be the duty of the judge in the case to bring before the jury."[11]

from the polluter at a price the latter would be willing to accept . . . I want to prescind from these "baseline" problems and examine wealth maximisation in the more common tort situations in which such problems are not acute": R.A. Posner, "Wealth maximization and Tort Law: A Philosophical Inquiry." in Owens (ed.) (Oxford, 1995), pp. 99–100.

[6] Commentators have added little, with the exception of the complete theoretical overhaul in J. Stapleton, "The Normal Expectancies Measure in Tort Damages" (1997) 113 L.Q.R. 257.

[7] *Liesbosch Dredger v. S.S. Edison* [1933] A.C. 449, *per* Lord Wright at 463.

[8] See below.

[9] See, *e.g. Hutchison v. Davidson*, 1946 S.L.T. 11.

[10] [1926] A.C. 655, at 661.

[11] At 661.

The Scottish courts generally like to keep the issue open. A good example **18–4** is the following hypothesis from Lord Normand in *Hutchison v. Davidson*[12]:

> "The law of damages ought not, it has been said, to be reduced to a mere rule of thumb, and, whatever subordinate rules may be formulated, there must be some cases which cannot fairly be brought within them. If the garage of a country house is destroyed, and it would cost £300 to replace it, it would in my view be less than just to award £100 because a garage could be bought for that sum in a neighbouring town. The defender's counsel conceded that in such a case the reasonable cost of restoration was the proper measure of damages, and I think that this concession was in no way rash, for a garage in the neighbouring town is not comparable as regards the proprietor's convenience with a garage which is an adjunct of his country house."

It can be seen that in the Scots courts attempts are made to do justice (in the juridical sense of treating like cases alike), *e.g.* by formulating subsidiary rules. See for example the treatment of an obvious harm, damage to property, in the following opinion of Lord Jamieson in *Pomphrey v. James A. Cuthbertson Ltd*:[13]

> "The owner of an article which has been damaged through the fault of another is entitled to reparation for the wrongful act and for all the natural and direct consequences of the wrongful act. He is entitled to *restitutio in integrum*. To give effect to that general principle of law certain rules have been evolved in practice. If the article can be economically repaired the measure of damages is the cost of the repairs, together with any consequential damage naturally and directly flowing from the wrongful act. If on the other hand the article is totally destroyed or cannot be economically repaired, and is an article which has a marketable value, the measure of damages is in the general case its value immediately before it was damaged. The owner of a damaged article must therefore decide whether the article is capable of being economically repaired or is to be treated as a constructive total loss. If he makes a wrong decision, he may lay himself open to the charge by the wrongdoer that he has failed in his duty to minimise the damage. The test is: What would a prudent owner, who had himself to bear the loss, do in the circumstances?"[14]

Restitutionary Damages for Wrongs

This heading denotes the area sometimes described as "restitution for **18–5** wrongs". It is a more familiar concept in England where a doctrine known as "waiver of tort" allows the plaintiff to sue for value surviving with the

---

[12] 1946 S.L.T. 11 at 19.
[13] 1951 S.L.T. 191.
[14] At 196–197. For an example which makes a practical point, see *McQueen v. Hepburn*, 1979 S.L.T. (Sh. Ct) 38 which considers some of the older dicta.

defendant.[15] The principle that there are two kinds of damages, compensatory and restitutionary, has been recognised by the English Court of Appeal.[16] If no one suffers a loss but the wrongdoer makes a gain from the wrong, compensatory damages do not make the wrongdoer pay for the wrong. It is possible to say that the pursuer requires to be compensated, if that is taken to mean not *restitutio in integrum*, but having his hurt assuaged—in other words some form of solatium could be awarded. But recognised principles of justice might demand that instead the wrongdoer should give up the gain. That meets the same prophylactic aims that delict normally meets—if a wrongdoer has to give back the gain there will be a deterrent effect. By stripping only the gain there is still no conflict with the principle against punitive damages.

18–6 As there has not been a recognised phrase in the Scots law of delict for this kind of claim, it is not surprising that these cases cause problems. Worse, the ill-developed law of restitution in Scotland is only now coming to address these issues.[17] For the Scots lawyer wrongs seems to equate to delict and any such cases are treated like delict cases. It is inevitably a hybrid exercise unless the law of unjustified enrichment takes over the "wrong" inquiry traditionally conducted within delict, a step which may be both unnecessary and undesirable. As Blackie points out, there is one strong authority against restitutionary damages. In *Teacher v. Calder*[18] a partner withdrew capital from a business in breach of agreement and employed it profitably elsewhere. The measure of damages was the loss of profit that could have been made had the money remained in the business, instead of the profits made in the "diverted" business. However, this was a case of breach of contract and was argued in the Court of Session on analogy with trust and partnership. In a delict case, *Exchange Telegraph v. Giulianotti*,[19] the defender used information obtained from the pursuers' contracting party. The defender knew that it was valuable information, having previously subscribed to the information service. That was the wrong of inducing a breach of contract.[20] The pursuers were granted interdict. Interestingly, the claim was put forward as one of recompense and was disposed of on the basis of the lack of subtractive enrichment: there was no actual loss to the pursuer which he could be compensated for, although there was obviously a gain to the defender. If the theory of restitution for wrongs is accepted then such a decision should not be followed. Professor Blackie argues that "the decision seems incorrect and is a striking example of where the gain should have been recoverable."[21] Blackie also explores what he calls *auctor in rem suam* cases, coming to the conclusion that the

---

[15] See Goff & Jones (4th ed.), pp. 714–734; Clerk & Lindsell, para. 27–73.

[16] *Ministry of Defence v. Ashman* (1993) 66 P. & C.R. 195. See generally M. Gething, "The action in unjust enrichment to recover the proceeds of a tort" (1995) Tort L. Rev. 123.

[17] See Stewart, *Restitution in Scotland* (1992); J. Blackie, "Enrichment and Wrongs" (1992) *Acta Juridica* 23; Stewart, *Restitution Supplement* (1995); J. Blackie, "Enrichment, Wrongs and Invasion of Rights in Scots Law" in D. Visser (ed.), *The Limits of the Law of Obligations* (1997, Juta), at p. 284; A.J.M. Steven, "Recompense for Interference in Scots Law", 1996 J.R. 51.

[18] (1899) 1 F. (H.L.) 39, affirming the Court of Session.

[19] 1959 S.C. 19.

[20] See Chap. 7; *BMTA v. Gray*, 1951 S.L.T. 247.

[21] J. Blackie, "Enrichment and Wrongs" (1992) *Acta Juridica* 23.

English rules have been adopted into Scots law. The result is that one category of case that might be described as restitution for wrongs is clearly recognised in Scots law.[22]

One very important case which has often been overlooked or underesti- **18–7** mated (or indeed cited for its support of the compensatory principle) is *Watson Laidlaw & Company Ltd v. Pott, Cassels & Williamson.*[23] It is submitted that this dictum represents the key to open the door to restitutionary damages for wrongs in Scots law. For that reason it is quoted at length, with emphasis added at the critical passage. The appellants challenged a finding that they should pay £3,000 damages for the infringement of a patent in respect of the buffer bearing of a centrifugal machine. There was no question as to the validity of the patent, nor was it denied that it had been infringed. The main point of dispute was the question whether there was to be an award in respect of machines sold in Java. It was argued that it was the energy of the appellants that had generated sales of the machines and not the fact that they were selling machines which infringed the patent. It was ultimately held that a large proportion of the Java sales would have gone to the holders of the patent (60 per cent). The importance of the case is in the analysis of the principle to be applied by Lord Shaw of Dunfermline:

"In the case of damages in general, there is one principle which does underlie the assessment. It is what may be called that of restoration. The idea is to restore the person who has sustained injury and loss to the condition in which he would have been had he not so sustained it. In the cases of financial loss, injury to trade, and the like, caused either by breach of contract or by tort, the loss is capable of correct appreciation in stated figures.

In a second class of cases, restoration being in point of fact difficult— as in the case of loss of reputation—or impossible—as in the case of loss of life, faculty, or limb—the task of restoration under the name of compensation calls into play inference, conjecture, and the like. And this is necessarily accompanied with those deficiencies which attach to the conversion into money of certain elements which are very real, which go to make up the happiness and usefulness of life, but which were never so converted or measured. The restoration by way of compensation is therefore accomplished to a large extent by the exercise of a sound imagination and the practice of the broad axe. . . . In all these cases, however, the attempt which justice makes is to get back to the *status quo ante* in fact, or to reach imaginatively by the process of compensation a result in which the same principle is followed.

In patent cases the principle of compensation is in all instances to some extent, and in many instances to the entire extent, dependent upon the same principle of restoration. The patentee may show that the trade done by the infringer would have been his (the patentee's) trade, and he is entitled in such cases to be restored against the action of the infringer;

---

[22] See *Aberdeen Railway Co. v. Blaikie* (1853) 1 Macq. 461; *Magistrates of Aberdeen v. University of Aberdeen* (1877) 4 R. (H.L.) 48.
[23] 1914 1 S.L.T. 130.

and he may adopt, in liquidating that principle in money, an alternative course. He may say, 'I shall accept the profits which have been made by the infringer in this trade which ought to have been my trade'; or he may take the other head of the alternative and say, 'The illicit opposition to and interference with my own trade caused me damage. I lost profit which I would have otherwise made in it; I lost business connection; the development of my business on its natural lines was interrupted by my being driven by these acts of piracy out of sections of my own trade.' These and other things may be heads of damage. And it is well settled that a patentee may choose his course of measuring his loss either by the profits which the infringer made, or by items of damages such as those referred to, but that in respect of the same matter he cannot have both his own damages and the infringer's profits.

In the course, however, of deciding cases, certain expressions have been used by learned judges, which, according to the contention, are to the effect, or truly mean, that if the patentee chooses the latter course, namely, to reckon up his claim under heads of damage, he is limited, so to speak, by the principle of restoration. Phrases, for instance, have been used which it is said imply that the entire measure of his damage is the loss which he has incurred of the trade in the pirated articles. And then comes in an astute argument, that in all cases where the infringer can establish that the trade in the machines which happened to contain the patented article or part would under no circumstances have ever reached the patentee himself, no claim can be admitted. To take an instance such as the present case affords, the patentee was not in a position to carry on business in a certain part of the world exclusively possessed for commercial purposes by the energies of the infringer and his agents.

It is said in such a case: Where is the damage which the patentee has incurred? On the other heads of the case he has obtained his damages; but on this part, which covers a section of trade which in no circumstances he could have touched, he can have sustained no damage, because he would never have sold his patented articles within that section. The duty of an infringer is covered by the principle of restoration, and the patentee has surely been restored to as good a position as he was in before the infringement, or would have been in but for it, if he has been put into the same financial position as he would have occupied in that region of trade where alone he would have been operating.

It is at this stage of the case, however, that a second principle comes into play. It is not exactly the principle of restoration, either directly or expressed through compensation, but it is the principle underlying price or hire. It plainly extends—and I am inclined to think not infrequently extends—to patent cases. But, indeed, it is not confined to them. For wherever an abstraction or invasion of property has occurred, then, unless such abstraction or invasion were to be sanctioned by law, the law ought to yield a recompense under the category or principle, as I say, either of price or of hire. If A., being a liveryman, keeps his horse standing idle in the stable, and B., against his wish or without his knowledge, rides or drives it out, it is no answer to A. for B. to say: 'Against what loss do you want to be restored? I restore the horse. There is no loss. The horse is none the worse; it is the better for the exercise.' I confess to your Lordships that this seems to me to be precisely in principle the kind of question and retort which underlay the argument of the learned counsel for the appellants about the Java trade. . . .

In various cases—of which the present is a good example—it is only by this combination of actual damage on the principle of restoration, with, in another section of these operations the principle of royalty, that a full and adequate response can be made to the cardinal question which remains always to be answered in these infringement suits, the question put by Vice-Chancellor Page Wood in *Penn* v. *Jack* (1867, L.R. 5 Eq. 81), viz.: 'What would have been the condition of the plaintiff if the defendants had acted properly instead of acting improperly? That condition, if it can be ascertained, will, I apprehend, be the proper measure of the plaintiff's loss.' To apply the principle: The appellants did this Java trade improperly. Had they done it properly they would have done it under royalty. That royalty the respondents would have obtained."[24]

There are a number of other cases involving wrongs where the issue has **18–8** been considered or raised. Most significant are the trespass cases discussed above.[25]

There are many other cases where conduct the pursuer might well **18–9** describe as wrongful are met with an award against the defender, *i.e.* where the pursuer has not had property extracted and has suffered a loss only in the sense of having lost the opportunity of a gain—not of course itself a bar to a claim in delict. The cases are those where either in respect of moveable or heritable property, the defender has taken—or continued in—occupation. It is quite difficult to analyse these problems and indeed they do not necessarily constitute a type.[26] Sometimes the answer can be that there is a proper contract implied by fact and circumstance. Where that is not possible there is a gain in the hands of the defender. The question is whether this constitutes a subtractive loss to be met traditionally by the law of recompense or whether it is better seen as a wrong to the pursuer's property interests. Sometimes it seems to be a practical matter of mensuration. These cases too are theoretically important because (1) some may (as Steven argues) support a lost *Eingriffskondiktion* in Scots law—an action for interference with a right; and (2) they involve the kind of case which was influential in England.

In *Rochester Poster Services Ltd* v. *A.G. Barr plc*[27] the pursuers sought **18–10** payment in respect of the defenders' occupation of an advertisement site for a period of 17 months after an agreed lease had expired. The sheriff dismissed the case. The Sheriff Principal held that the case should be allowed to proceed because it was alleged that there was no intention of donation and thus the pursuers were entitled to a reasonable payment in respect of the use. On the authority of *Glen* v. *Roy*,[28] it was for the party in

---

[24] *ibid.* at 137–139.

[25] In Chap. 5. See *Graham* v. *The Duke of Hamilton* (1868) 6 M. 965; *Ramsay* v. *Blair* (1876) 3 R. (H.L.) 41, affirming 3 R. 25; *Lord Advocate* v. *Glengarnock Iron and Steel Company Ltd,* 1909 1 S.L.T. 15; *Davidson's Trs* v. *Caledonian Railway Co.* (1895) 23 R. 45.

[26] See Steven, 1996 J.R. 51 for a possible explanation.

[27] 1994 S.L.T. (Sh. Ct) 2.

[28] (1882) 10 R. 239.

occupation to show that he was in occupation for nothing or less than its real worth. In *G.T.W. Holdings Ltd v. Toet*[29] the defenders admitted to occupying the pursuers' subjects for five years. The pursuers were unsuccessful before the sheriff who dismissed the case on the basis that the defenders were not enriched by the occupation, but succeeded before the Sheriff Principal. There are many cases and the facts will determine whether implied contract or recompense may apply.[30]

18–11   "Real worth" appeared to be a useful test but its inherent ambiguity had to be confronted in *Secretary of State for Defence v. Johnstone*.[31] The facts were agreed between the parties. The defender was the wife of a serving airman. They separated in 1990. For some months she occupied the former marital home on terms agreed. After that she remained without agreement. The pursuer claimed entitlement to charge an open market rent; the defender argued that only the amount which would be charged to service personnel should be charged. It was a matter of admission that if the defender had not occupied the property, it would have been occupied by a member of the services. While the defender accepted that the cases turned on the "real worth" of the property, it was argued by the defender that the proper measure was the pursuer's loss. Decree was granted to the pursuer and it was held that the proper measure was the real worth to the defender. The case is therefore authority for restitution for a wrong and applies Lord Shaw's restoration principle. The usual measure in Scots law in a recompense case is in *quantum lucratus est* the defender.[32] This is a *lucratus* decision but one where the gain exceeds the loss. It has been argued that these cases are evidence of an unnoticed *Eingriffskondiktion* in Scots law.[33] The same principle would apply to moveables.[34]

18–12   Finally, Blackie points out that while fraud is usually about compensation for a loss, *Fraser & Co. v. Reid*[35] might be different. The pursuers were fraudulently led to believe they were getting a bargain buying at the price the fraudster himself had paid. He had in fact made a profit. There was no evidence that they could have bought cheaper.

Penal, Punitive and Exemplary Damages

18–13 There is no single principle under this head. Scots law appears to have given up the idea that whether or not there is compensation there can be damages to punish the wrongdoer.[36] So far as English law is concerned, the

---

[29] 1994 S.L.T. (Sh. Ct) 16.

[30] See, *e.g. Shetland Islands Council v. B.P. Petroleum Development*, 1990 S.L.T. 82.

[31] 1997 S.L.T. (Sh. Ct) 37.

[32] I have suggested before that there is no reason why some cases recorded under the rubric *quantum meruit* should not in fact be regarded as restitution cases, thus allowing a different measure, and not implied contract cases: *Restitution Supplement*, 12B.

[33] For an analysis of cases based upon the idea of a neo-civilian *Eingriffskondiktion* see A.J.M. Steven, "Recompense for Interference in Scots Law", 1996 J.R. 51.

[34] *Chisholm v. Alexander* (1882) 19 S.L.R. 835, although it is possible to analyse this as an implied contract case; and see a hybrid—a ship, in law moveable but being used as a warehouse: *Aktieselskabet "Heimdal" v. Noble*, 1907 S.C. 249.

[35] (1888) 5 Sh. Ct. Rep. 216.

[36] *Gibson v. Anderson* (1846) 9 D. 1; *Muckarsie v. Dixon* (1848) 11 D. 4; *Black v. NB Rly*, 1908 S.C. 44.

position is that "exemplary damages theoretically can be given in actions of negligence but they are virtually unknown."[37]

The criminal law now makes up for this by punishing all sorts of trivial **18–14** anti-social behaviour. Violent profits, which is an almost defunct remedy, can on one view be said to be partly penal.[38]

Mitigation

Mitigation is a principle of the law of damages and thus applies to damages **18–15** for delict.[39] In practice it is found very seldom in personal injuries cases, where the plea is usually that the sum sued for is excessive, and the pursuer is put to proof of his losses.[40] In personal injuries cases it may be suggested that the pursuer could have gone back to work sooner, could have found other work, has not tried to find other work or is malingering. So while the phrase "mitigation" can be found in some delict cases, it is often used in the sense of a plea in mitigation—to lower the penalty otherwise properly imposed. This is consonant with theory. In *actio injuriarum* cases loss is not the gist of the delict and mitigation is required. In aquilian cases as the loss is the gist of the wrong then two purposes are served by putting the pursuer to proof of actual loss. Nonetheless, theoretically it should be the position that once some loss is proved the remoteness rules apply, which themselves involve a mitigation aspect.

Although abortion in the United Kingdom has arguably become a form **18–16** of *ex post facto* birth control, in cases of wrongful birth it is not a failure to mitigate to refuse an abortion in the absence of health grounds.[41]

Remoteness

The pursuer can only recover damages which are not too remote. This is **18–17** often seen as an aspect of liability itself, or confused as such. It is best thought of separately and is treated separately above.[42]

---

[37] Charlesworth, *Negligence* (9th ed., 1997), p. 384; McGregor on *Damages* (16th ed., 1997), Chap. 11. "In the United States punitive damages are an established institution, widely regarded as having an important function and hitherto resistant to constitutional challenge (but see *Honda Motor Co. v. Oberg*, 129 L.Ed. 2d 336; 114 S.Ct. 2331 (1994)). The huge sums occasionally awarded by juries are very commonly reduced by the judge; see G. Schwartz, 'Mass Torts and Punitive Damages: A Comment', 39 Villanova L. Rev. 415 (1994). The federal government has protected itself from liability for punitive damages, and their award is restricted in various ways in different states": T.A. Weir, *Casebook on Tort* (8th ed.), p. 346, n. 6.

[38] See para. 19–15.

[39] A particular problem touching on mitigation is considered below and should be read in conjunction with this section.

[40] For a theoretical discussion which also takes this view of mitigation in tort see J. Stapleton, "The Normal Expectancies Measure in Tort Damages" (1997) 113 L.Q.R. 257.

[41] *Emeh v. Kensington Area Health Authority* [1985] Q.B. 1012. This was accepted in the Scottish case of *McFarlane v. Tayside Health Board*, 2000 S.L.T. 154.

[42] Chap. 10.

Causation

18–18 Damage not caused by the wrong is not generally recoverable.[43] Properly this issue is addressed as a remoteness issue where there is at least some actionable damage.[44] In an aquilian case, if there is no head of damage caused by the fault there can be no liability.

Once and for all

18–19 The general rule is that all loss must be recovered in one action.[45] A further extension of this is that all heads of loss are assumed to have been sought in any action raised (although that is wider and more debatable).[46] The main justification for the rule is that there is a public interest in concluding litigation, even if it results in injustice to a particular pursuer whose injuries become much worse after the action, or it may cause injustice to a defender who has disbursed a huge sum for future wage loss only to see the pursuer skip from the court having made a miraculous recovery.[47] The practical effect of the rule is that cases should never be concluded unless and until all loss and damage is known, or may with reasonable certainty be estimated. Thus a clear prognosis in a medical report is essential. The general rule is subject to exceptions. In personal injury cases, and perhaps in any other case where the damages incorporate an attempt to measure future loss, it is possible to alter what is claimed for even if it has the effect of opening up a proof or requiring further proof. This was decided by a court of seven judges in *Rieley v. Kingslaw Riding School*[48] in which, pending appeal on liability, the pursuer's leg required to be amputated. The Lord Ordinary had indicated that a higher award would have been appropriate had the leg needed to be amputated. The Inner House in these circumstances agreed to hear the additional proof. The English rules then in force were thought to be most helpful by way of guidance. Such cases are exceptional, however.

Renewed claims

18–20 A possible exception to the once and for all rule is that a further claim (*e.g.* after conclusion of a first action or after a time limit) may be regarded as being so different that it constitutes a new claim. Such cases are likely to be found under either (i) prescription and limitation—it being too late to include a new head—or (ii) *res judicata.* Theoretically both should be treated the same.

It submitted that the proper approach is the *res judicata* approach—if the *media concludendi* are exhausted, no new action is possible. Whether or not *litis contestatio* is a contract (as it has often been described, with justifica-

---

[43] Chap. 10.
[44] See Chap. 10.
[45] See para. 2–1.
[46] See Chap. 22 below.
[47] It is submitted that this is the true defender's public interest point rather than that expressed by Lord Davidson: "it may be highly inconvenient for defenders to be obliged to keep their files open on a case for many years against the possibility that such a further claim may be presented": *Paterson v. Costain Mining Co.*, 1988 S.L.T. 413 at 414.
[48] 1975 S.L.T. 61.

tion), the joining of issues on pleadings makes clear what has or has not been brought within the contract or, less contentiously, brought before the court. Thus if an action is raised for £1,000 solatium, a claim for £9,000 patrimonial loss should still be competent. The public interest and the defender's interest in avoiding stale claims is met by prescription and limitation. More difficult is where an omnibus sum is sought in one crave. Even then the *media concludendi* are in the condescendences and it ought to be possible to unravel the true position. The pursuer who does not adopt a schedule of damages or equivalent takes the risk that a claim will be construed as an omnibus claim. The onus, however, always remains on the defender to show that an otherwise competent claim has been lost in this way. Claims which are not brought under new heads but are in fact renewed versions of previous claims will normally be defeated by the plea of *res judicata*. In prescription cases the renewed claims point must be dealt with under the statutory code.

Interim Damages

By virtue of special rules a pursuer may get an advance payment.[49] This is **18–21** not so much an exception in spirit but in the letter, in that the pursuer obtains damages "twice or more and for all".[50] There is a balancing exercise at the end, and the pursuer might have to repay in certain circumstances.[51] The application of the rule has been settled to a considerable degree by *Cowie v. Atlantic Drilling*,[52] in which the Division upheld a finding of interim damages (in terms of rule 89A of the 1965 Rules) in favour of a workman injured on a North Sea oil rig. There were a number of alleged breaches of duty and a plea and averments of contributory negligence. There were two issues: (1) Would the pursuer succeed on liability to any extent? The court considered this matter well settled by an existing line of authority[53]: the test is whether the pursuer will succeed, or will certainly succeed, or will almost certainly succeed. In this case the accident was admitted; an absolute duty was applicable and the court was satisfied that the test was met. (2) Would the pursuer succeed without any substantial finding of contributory negligence? Here the court settled a divergence of view on the proper interpretation. View 1 was that substantial meant anything more than *de minimis*.[54] View 2 was that it meant "considerable" or "big" which was defined as more than a quarter or a third.[55] The court rejected view 1 and preferred view 2. The Lord Ordinary had thought contributory negligence would not exceed a third. The First Division found

---

[49] There is a full treatment in McEwan & Paton, Chap. 1. For a general discussion, albeit regarding English law, see S. Ashcroft, "Law Commission Paper No. 224: Structured Settlements and Interim and Provisional Damages—A Practitioner's Review" [1995] J.P.I.L. 3.

[50] The practice is governed by rule 43.9 of the 1994 Rules of Court and the new Sheriff Court Rules, rule 36.8–10. The payment may itself be by instalments: Damages Act 1996, s. 2.

[51] See observations in *Walker v. Infabco Diving Services Ltd*, 1983 S.L.T. 633.

[52] 1995 S.L.T. 1151.

[53] *Douglas's C.B. v. Douglas*, 1974 S.L.T. (Notes) 7; *Walker v. Infabco Diving Services Ltd*, 1983 S.L.T. 633; *Nelson v. Duraplex Industries Ltd*, 1975 S.L.T. (Notes) 31 and *Reid v. Planet Welding Equipment Ltd*, 1980 S.L.T. (Notes) 7.

[54] *Nelson v. Duraplex Industries Ltd*, 1975 S.L.T. (Notes) 31; *Noble v. Noble* 1974 S.L.T. (Notes) 75 and *Herron v. Kennon* 1986 S.L.T. 260.

[55] *McNeil v. Roche Products Ltd*, 1988 S.L.T. 704.

it impossible to come to an estimate; however, that operated in the pursuer's favour as the court was therefore unable to say that there would be a considerable finding.

Provisional Damages

18–22 The public policy arguments that cases should finish or that people should not be troubled too often by the same action has less force when the defender is a public authority or an insured body. On that assumption United Kingdom legislation provides for provisional damages.[56] This is still, as will be seen from the text following, not a true exception to the common law,[57] but practically it is a huge divergence. Section 12 of the Administration of Justice Act 1982, which applies in Scotland, provides:

"(1) This section applies to an action for damages for personal injuries in which—

(a) there is proved or admitted to be a risk that at some definite or indefinite time in the future the injured person will, as a result of the act or omission which gave rise to the cause of the action, develop some serious disease or suffer some serious deterioration in his physical or mental condition; and

(b) the responsible person was, at the time of the act or omission giving rise to the cause of the action,
   (i) a public authority or public corporation; or
   (ii) insured or otherwise indemnified in respect of the claim.

(2) In any case to which this section applies, the court may, on the application of the injured person, order—

(a) that the damages referred to in subsection (4)(a) below be awarded to the injured person; and

(b) that the injured person may apply for the further award of damages referred to in subsection (4)(b) below, and the court may, if it considers it appropriate, order that an application under paragraph (b) above may be made only within a specified period.

(3) Where an injured person in respect of whom an award has been made under subsection (2)(a) above applies to the court for an award under subsection (2)(b) above, the court may award to the injured person the further damages referred to in subsection (4)(b) below.

(4) The damages referred to in subsections (2) and (3) above are—

(a) damages assessed on the assumption that the injured person will not develop the disease or suffer the deterioration in his condition; and

---

[56] There is a full treatment in McEwan & Paton, Chap. 2. See generally J. Blaikie, "Provisional damages: A Progress report", 1991 36 J.L.S. 109; J. Blaikie, "Provisional damages: Please may I have some more?", 1995 S.L.P.Q. 65 and albeit regarding English law, S. Ashcroft, "Law Commission Paper No. 224: Structured Settlements and Interim and Provisional Damages—A Practitioner's Review" [1995] J.P.I.L. 3.

[57] See Lord Weir in *Potter v. McCulloch*, 1987 S.L.T. 308 at 310.

(b) further damages if he develops the disease or suffers the deterioration.

(5) Nothing in this section shall be construed—
    (a) as affecting the exercise of any power relating to expenses including a power to make rules of court relating to expenses; or
    (b) as prejudicing any duty of the court under any enactment or rule of law to reduce or limit the total damages which would have been recoverable apart from any such duty.

(6) The Secretary of State may, by order, provide that categories of defenders shall, for the purposes of paragraph (b) of subsection (1) above, become or cease to be responsible persons, and may make such modifications of that paragraph as appear to him to be necessary for the purpose."[58]

There have been a number of illuminating cases. In *Potter v. McCulloch*,[59] the issue was whether such cases were suitable for a jury; the answer was that they are not.[60] However, the opinion suggested a number of issues of interpretation that might arise. In *White v. Inveresk Paper Co. Ltd (No.2)*,[61] as anticipated in *Potter* the word "serious" in section 12 (1) (a) had to be considered. Lord Murray, accepting there was a 5–10 per cent risk of osteoarthritis, found this to be material and not *de minimis* and did not consider this to be serious deterioration. "Serious" qualifies "deterioration" rather than "effects". The persuasive factor seems to have been the argument that was put by counsel that a clear line needed to be drawn in such cases. Lord Murray pointed out that "the deterioration in question does not provide a clear cut and severable threshold of the kind which is really needed to enable the reservation to be properly applied in future. The line between permanent minor residual restrictions of the knee and the onset, probably gradually, of osteoarthritic symptoms would be difficult or impossible to draw".[62] In *Paterson v. Costain Mining Co.*[63] the pursuer's claim was held to be irrelevant because the deterioration feared would result from subsequent exposure to noise and not from the act or omission bringing about the action. However, it was held that the pursuer could, subject to contributory negligence and *volenti non fit injuria*, sue again under the continuing harm exception. In *Prentice v. William Thyne Ltd*[64] the risk of deterioration was considered more of a certainty; the pursuer's condition had already deteriorated to such an extent that its course was clear and directly related to the original act. Lord Dervaird approved the recognisable threshold approach in *White*.[65] In *Meek v. Burton's Gold Medal Biscuits Ltd*,[66] Lord Prosser rejected the idea that the Act could not be used

---

[58] The section came into force by virtue of S.I. 1984 No. 1287.
[59] 1987 S.L.T. 308.The case involved an allegation of future arthritis or metatarsalgia.
[60] Such cases may however utilise the optional procedure.
[61] 1988 S.L.T. 2.
[62] At 5; see also *McMenemy v. Argyll Stores Ltd*, 1992 S.L.T. 971.
[63] 1988 S.L.T. 413.
[64] 1989 S.L.T. 336.
[65] At 337.
[66] 1989 S.L.T. 338.

where the subsequent claim would depend upon a subsequent triggering event—such an approach was not required by the decision in *Paterson*. However, in this case an award was not made. Although there was a risk of serious deterioration, even then there might not be serious consequences. This again seems like a threshold case. In *McColl v. Barnes*,[67] there was a risk of post-traumatic epilepsy which started at about 10 per cent and declined over time. An order was made under section 12 (2) (b) to cover seven years after the accident—about three years after the decision. It is submitted that to be sure of deferment the pursuer ought to be able to draft a clear interlocutor indicating when the fresh application is appropriate.

One criticism of structured settlements is that insurers have inserted clauses in agreements to exclude the right to seek provisional damages. The English Law Commission is seeking to remedy this.[68]

Excursus: Alleviation: mitigation and remoteness in context.

18–23 The term "alleviation" has been made use of to describe the situation where a party other than the party with a duty to mitigate has alleviated the loss. This is not a matter likely to arise in contract because loss is not essentially the gist of contractual liability.[69] It arises sharply in aquilian cases where at the time of the proof the pursuer has no loss through the intervention of another alleviating the loss caused by the wrongdoer. For the Scots lawyer the principle is clear: *res inter alios acta, aliis neque nocet, neque prodest*.[70] There is a huge practical exception to the rule and that is in relation to state benefits, where the state may oblige the compensator to repay certain amounts of certain benefits and to deduct these from the damages payable to the victim. However, that does not affect liability itself, although it may extinguish the damages payable. Mitigation may eliminate the liability completely. The situations to be considered are where a benefit accrues to the victim before proof. The possible distinction is between benefits payable as a result of the wrongdoing and cases where it is entirely collateral—*i.e.* it would have happened regardless of the wrong. An important case on this point arose in personal injuries and in England. In *Parry v. Cleaver*,[71] Reginald Parry, a police officer, was badly injured in a car crash with another driver, Anthony Cleaver who admitted liability. The plaintiff was discharged from the service due to ill health resulting from the accident and this allowed him to receive his service pension to which he had made compulsory contributions. It seems to have already been well-established that insurance and charitable payments were excluded from consideration.[72] Lord Reid said that the common law has always treated the

---

[67] 1992 S.L.T. 1188.

[68] S. Ashcroft, "Law Commission Paper No. 224: Structured Settlements and Interim and Provisional Damages—A Practitioner's Review" [1995] J.P.I.L. 3; S. Eden, "Structured Settlements", 1996 Rep.B. 11–3; R. Redmond-Cooper, "Structured Settlements and Provisional Damages: Harmonisation Perspectives" [1995] J.P.I.L. 12.

[69] Unless otherwise provided for in the contract itself.

[70] "A thing done or a transaction entered into between certain parties cannot advantage or injure those who are not parties to the act or the transaction": Trayner, *Latin Maxims* (4th ed., 1894, reprinted 1993), p. 552.

[71] [1970] A.C. 1.

[72] *per* Lord Reid at 13G. Indeed he cites an old Scottish case, *Forgie v. Henderson* (1818) 1 Murray 410 in support at 14F.

matter as one of justice, reasonableness and public policy.[73] The fact that wrongdoers would get the benefit of charitable payments would be revolting to the ordinary man's sense of justice.[74] Lord Reid decided that in this respect a compulsory pension was no different from voluntary insurance.[75]

So far as reparation is concerned a most interesting point is the **18–24** application of the *res inter alios* principle in cases other than personal injury. As discussed below in some detail, in the context of damages for negligent valuation, there is an established rule of assessing loss—the difference in the value given and the true value, imagining that the defect which has emerged did not exist. The same issues arise. In *Gardner v. Marsh and Parsons*[76] the plaintiffs obtained a survey prior to taking a long lease. The survey was admittedly careless. They discovered the defect years later. The basic assessment of damages made was in accordance with the traditional formulae set out above. One of the points taken on appeal was that the landlords had, in terms of the lease, repaired the damage, which meant that the valuation was too low. It was argued that accordingly there was no loss.[77] Existing authority in England meant that the plaintiffs could accept that it might in some circumstances be possible for the defendant to have this kind of windfall defence: where the loss-avoiding conduct flows inexorably from the original transaction and can be seen as part of a continuous course of dealing with the actionable situation.[78] Thus where the wrong, while causing a loss, also causes a profit, there may be an argument for the diminution of the loss, but that will not prevail where there is no continuous transaction.[79] In any event some cases can be dealt with simply

---

[73] At 13H; Lord Wilberforce is less happy with any form of words: see at 39F.

[74] *per* Lord Reid at 14D.

[75] At 16. Even Lord Pearson, dissenting, seems to have accepted that there has to be a causal link between the benefit and the wrong; but his dissent was addressed to the fact that despite other factors coming into play the wrong had to be at least one of the causes of the benefit; the charitable cases can be accounted causally by saying that the bounty comes from the charitable motives of the donors rather than the accident. See the review of authorities by Lord Pearson at 50–51. He argues that the charitable motive is certainly more proximate in time than the accident but the accident is still at least *sine qua non*. This kind of thinking sees the charitable giving as the *causa causans* or a *novus actus interveniens*. As Lord Reid discovered, the basic principle had in fact been expressed in Scotland as long ago as 1818. In *Forgie v. Henderson* (1818) 1 Murray 410, a jury case for assault, the pursuer claimed damages for his medical costs. He was entitled to payments for a time from a friendly society. In charging the jury the Lord Chief Commissioner said at 418: "There are, 1st, special damages, consisting of the surgeon's account, and the pursuer being kept from his work; but in calculating this loss at the sum proved, you must consider whether it is probable he would have wrought every day, and also whether you will give it for the weeks he was confined to bed, or the months he was partially laid aside. I do not think you can deduct the allowance from the Society, as that is of the nature of an insurance, and is a return for money paid." The same rule applies in property damage cases: see the statement by Lord President Robertson on behalf of the court, adopting Lord Kyllachy's view in *Port-Glasgow & Newark Sailcloth Co. v. Caledonian Railway* Co. (1892) 19 R. 608. The reasoning in *Parry v. Cleaver* was followed in Scotland in *Davidson v. UCS Ltd*, 1990 S.L.T. 329 in a fatal case. That case was followed in *Campbell v. Gillespie*, 1996 S.L.T. 503 (the headnote says that *Parry* was distinguished. This was because the Scots case turned on statute rather than any departure from its reasoning). See also *Lewicki v. Brown and Root Wimpey Highland Fabricators Ltd*, 1996 S.L.T. 1283, *per* the Lord Justice Clerk.

[76] [1997] 1 W.L.R. 489.

[77] *per* Hirst L.J. at 503A.

[78] Hirst L.J. noting counsel's argument at 503D.

[79] *Hussey v. Eels* [1990] 2 Q.B. 227; Pill, L.J.; *Gardner* at 514.

because they do involve *res inter alios acta*, such as *Gardner* where it was the collateral agreement of lease with the landlords that caused the diminution in loss.[80] The other reason why courts are keen to protect the pursuer from the diminution of loss argument is that the defender benefits from the "cap" in the general valuation rule, *i.e.* he will not normally be liable for the cost of repair. Thus this fixing of the loss at a given time is said to represent "sauce for the goose" which necessitates that it also be "sauce for the gander".[81] In a sheriff court case, *Lawson v. McHugh*,[82] these English cases were reviewed. The defenders were sued for an allegedly negligent survey. At the heart of the fault was a failure to notice that there was a river running by the end of the garden which was undermining the property. The key point at debate related to the fact that the council caused works to be done which the defenders alleged had cured the undermining problem. The defenders sought dismissal on the basis that the sum sued for was not properly specified, the pursuers having failed to take into account the works done. The pursuers sought deletion of the defenders' averments anent the repair of the river bank as being *res inter alios acta*, founding on the *Parry v. Cleaver* principle and the decision of the Court of Appeal in *Gardner v. Marsh*.[83] The defenders founded on the general compensatory principle and the decision of the Court of Appeal in *Kennedy v. Van Emden*.[84] The learned sheriff favoured the general compensatory principle and the dissenting opinion in *Gardner*. The averments were allowed to stand. Essentially the sheriff favoured the less complicated Scottish approach which is often to allow matters to be heard first.

Structured Settlements

18–25 In particularly serious personal injury cases both sides may seek the tax advantages that come from making periodical payments to the pursuer.[85] The Damages Act 1996 provides that the necessary policy must be purchased from an authorised insurer under the Policyholders Protection Act 1975. In such cases the Policyholders Protection Board indemnify the beneficiary by 100 per cent in the event of the insurer defaulting.[86] In cases

---

[80] *per* Hirst L.J. at 503H: "Furthermore, these repairs undertaken by Guidedale at the plaintiff's insistence were *res inter alios acta* and therefore collateral to Mr. Dyson's negligence." Indeed it is worth noting that in *Hussey v. Eels* [1990] 2 Q.B. 227, the earlier decision of the Court of Appeal applied in *Gardner*, the plaintiffs who had bought at an undervalue more than two years later obtained planning permission for the land and sold at a profit. This diminution of loss was not taken into account although clearly the causal connection was strong—the passing of time and their own initiative made the gain remote.

[81] *per* Bristow in *J. Daisley v. B.S. Hall* (1972) 225 E.G. 1553 at 1557.

[82] 1998 G.W.D. 31–1618.

[83] [1997] 1 W.L.R. 1618.

[84] [1996] P.N.L.R. 409.

[85] There is a full treatment in McEwan & Paton, Chap. 17. See the Income and Corporation Taxes Act 1988, s. 329AA; Finance Act 1996, s.150 and Sched. 26; S. Eden, "Structured Settlements", 1992 37 J.L.S. 207 and, regarding English law, S. Ashcroft, "Law Commission Paper No. 224: Structured Settlements and Interim and Provisional Damages—A Practitioner's Review" [1995] J.P.I.L. 3; R. Redmond-Cooper, "Structured Settlements and Provisional Damages: Harmonisation Perspectives" [1995] J.P.I.L. 12.

[86] 1996 Act, ss. 4, 5.

where the pursuer is incapax the curator bonis will require the authority of either the Accountant of Court or the court itself.[87] The court may then allow the structured settlement to take place, as it did in *Bell's Curator Bonis, Noter*.[88]

Interest on Damages

In most ordinary actions interest is claimed from the date of citation in the **18–26** action. The Interest on Damages (Scotland) Act 1958, as amended, allows the court a complete discretion to award interest from the date when the right of action arose which in an accident case will be the date of the accident.[89] Interest on solatium is permitted too.[90] A judicial tender, to be successful, must take into account the awards of interest which may be made.[91] Compensation recovery[92] has raised and may yet raise difficult questions as to whether interest is to run on the sum awarded or the sum under deduction of compensation recovery.[93] However, the 1997 Act provides that in assessing damages the amount of listed benefits is to be disregarded.[94] That seems to go against the approach in *Cavanagh*.[95]

The issue also arises in cases not involving personal injury. In *Boots the* **18–27** *Chemist Ltd v. G.A. Estates Ltd*[96] the Second Division had to consider the issue. An action of damages based on negligence and nuisance and arising out of flood damage suffered in 1984 was signeted in 1987 and settled in about March 1991. Under a joint minute agreement was reached on various heads of loss sustained on particular dates. The parties submitted to the determination of the court the matter of interest on the various sums. It was argued for the pursuers that section 1 (1) of the 1958 Act permitted the court to award interest from the date when the right of action arose, being when *damnum* and *injuria* occurred, and that the amendment made by the Interest on Damages (Scotland) Act 1971 had altered the emphasis of the section, which now required the court to ascertain if there was a reason not to award interest from the date when the action arose. They argued that the expenditure of money by the pursuers was like a loss of use case in a property damage or destruction case. The defenders argued that the rate of interest and the period for which it was awarded should be restricted. No judicial demand had been made until the summons called in 1988. Despite requests, the defenders had not been provided with the full detailed claim until five years after the event. The defenders argued that any award should be at less than the judicial rate and that interest should not run until, at earliest, the date of citation and in fact not until the amount of loss had been established by the joint minute. The Lord Ordinary awarded interest on loss of stock from the date of citation to the date of decree, and on the

---

[87] Judicial Factors Act 1849 (as amended).
[88] 1999 S.L.T. 33.
[89] s.1. For a full treatment in the context of personal injuries see McEwan & Paton, Chap. 3.
[90] s. 1A.
[91] s. 1B.
[92] See para. 18–45.
[93] See *Morrison v. Laidlaw*, 1994 S.L.T. 359; *Cavanagh v. BP*, 1995 S.L.T. 1287.
[94] s. 17.
[95] 1995 S.L.T. 1287.
[96] 1993 S.L.T. 136.

remaining items from the dates on which the expenditure had been incurred, at the judicial rate prevailing at the time. The Second Division held that a pursuer might recover interest by way of damages where he was deprived of an interest-bearing security or a profit-producing chattel, or where money had been wrongfully withheld, and that even if damages had not been quantified, interest might reasonably be held to run from a date when the damages might reasonably be regarded as quantifiable or capable of ascertainment, because from that date the wrongdoer could reasonably be regarded as wrongfully withholding the damages. In the absence of special circumstances, inordinate delay in prosecuting an action should not result in a pursuer being deprived of interest on items of damages which were capable of being ascertained and in respect of which expenditure had been incurred by the injured party. The reclaiming motion was refused.

HEADS OF CLAIM

18–28 In this section the main heads of claim are set out for the benefit of the student and comparatist wanting to know what it is the reparation pursuer seeks to recover. Practitioners will resort to the specialist looseleaf text in respect of personal injuries,[97] but will find here a comprehensive survey of some value in noting other heads too.[98] The term "patrimonial" is often used for financial claims through habit. It is another of those terms that makes Scots law look civilian—perhaps more than it is. Some have urged a return to the concept,[99] albeit in a different context, others have suggested it is a rather out of date expression which might not assist in determining rights.[1] Scots reparation practitioners regularly deal with English insurers where there is a distinction between general and special damage.[2]

Out of Pocket Expenses

18–29 Money spent by the pursuer as a direct result of the wrong is usually recoverable. Common examples are taxi fares to the hospital, broken glasses and damaged clothing. More debatable instances include the excess on an insurance policy covering the cancellation of a holiday resulting from an accident, which has been held recoverable.[3] The cost of cure has long been an accepted expense which is recoverable, and the future cost of medical treatment is routinely awarded.[4]

---

[97] McEwan & Paton.

[98] In respect of all cases Professor Walker's work, *The Law of Damages in Scotland*, albeit dated (1955) is still valuable not only because of the range of cases covered—extending over contract and most of the nominate contracts—but also because of the discussions of some perennial topics.

[99] G. Gretton, "Trust and Patrimony" in H.L. MacQueen (ed.), *Scots Law into the 21st. Century* (W. Green, 1996), p. 182.

[1] *Gunstone v. SWAA*, 1987 S.L.T. 611 at 614K, *per* Lord Prosser.

[2] For a tangential discussion of those terms which incidentally illustrates that they are widespread in Scottish practice see *Irving v. Hiddleston*, 1998 S.C.L.R. 350.

[3] *Whyte v. University of Dundee*, 1990 S.L.T. 545.

[4] Awards are recorded in McEwan & Paton and in Bennett, *Personal Injury Damages in Scotland* (Barnestoneworth, 1999), Chap. 7.

Loss of Earnings

The pursuer here seeks the money he could not make up to the proof **18–30** because of the accident and the money he will not make in the future because of it.[5] It is often necessary to check the earnings of comparable workers. Casual earnings are recoverable, although it has not been decided in Scotland whether this may include earnings made while claiming benefits (a claim allowed in an English case).[6] Illegal earnings such as those made but not declared to the DSS while claiming state benefit might be disregarded as they have been by the English Court of Appeal.[7]

The self-employed face difficulties as a result of decisions which rightly exclude partnership profits[8] and company profits[9] on the basis of remoteness. Providing suitable evidence can be adduced, it seems that a sum for general labour and pains might be established, as indeed was envisaged in the leading recent case.[10] However, there are difficulties in proof and there may be other difficulties in relation to services and employability claims.[11] The First Division has recently taken a liberal view of the problems of some workers. In *Anthony v. Brabbs*[12] the pursuer owned a company with his wife. Its main asset was the renting out of his services. He sued for loss of the salary from the company and his dividends. An attack was made on the claim on the basis of remoteness but Lord Rodger correctly noted that this was not a remoteness of injury case—a secondary economic loss case— which would have to fail, but a remoteness of damage case in which, the pursuer having clearly suffered a personal injury, a proof before answer was necessary to determine the appropriate losses.

Past Loss

This is normally easily computed where the job and the pay were essentially **18–31** stable. There should, however, be investigation of what has actually been earned by comparable workers—perhaps showing bonuses or promotions or upgradings (or vice versa), because the court is being asked to value something which has not actually happened.

Future wage loss: Multipliers and Multiplicands

The basic approach is to multiply a multiplicand by a multiplier.[13] The **18–32** multiplicand is usually the wages the pursuer would get in a year. The multiplier is a figure which very roughly tries to produce a sum which if sensibly invested would, while itself being depleted over the term of future

---

[5] This topic is extensively treated in McEwan & Paton.

[6] *Duller v. S.E. Linc Engineers* [1981] C.L.Y. 585.

[7] *Hunter v. Butler* 1995 T.L.R. 715. See *Young v. Roche Services Group*, 1989 S.L.T. 212 for earnings not declared by the employer.

[8] *Vaughan v. GGPTE*, 1984 S.L.T. 44.

[9] *Fulleman v. McInnes's Exrs*, 1993 S.L.T. 255.

[10] *Vaughan v. GGPTE*, 1984 S.L.T. 44 at 46.

[11] G. Junor, "Loss of earnings—What about the Self-employed?", 1996 Rep. L.B. 12–6.

[12] 1998 S.L.T. 1137.

[13] This topic is treated fully in McEwan & Paton. See also R. Milligan, "Approaching Future Wage Loss", 1995 S.L.T. (News) 173; " Multipliers for Future Wage Loss", 1998 S.L.T. (News) 291.

loss, produce the necessary annual return.[14] Until recently it was fixed by the judge based on his experience and assisted by decided cases. There have, however, been remarkable recent developments. In *O'Brien's C.B. v. British Steel*[15] the traditional multiplier/multiplicand was approved but it was accepted that rather than simply take a broad brush approach to the multiplier the Scottish courts could take cognisance of the "scientific" evidence in the arithmetical and actuarial tables known as the Ogden Tables.[16] So far as the Ogden Tables are concerned, the House of Lords recently decided in *Wells v. Wells*[17] that the previous assumption that the pursuer would invest the damages on the stock market instead of safe gilts was wrong. The pursuer does not require to be a risk taker. The money is thus assumed to be invested in the safer gilts and thus a bigger multiplier is needed to produce a bigger award to take into account the lower rate of return. Now the Ogden Tables will be the starting point instead of a cross-check. Practical application can prove difficult, however.[18] The Ogden Tables provide only for the contingency of mortality and judicial experience is still needed to enhance or discount multipliers from the tables.

Employability and Disadvantage on the Employment Market

18–33 Someone who is injured and who does not fully recover may be disadvantaged in their ability to find work. Where economic conditions are such that people may be expected to seek jobs many times in their working lives, this constitutes a disadvantage. Even where a workman still has a job at the time of the proof, his chances of working may well be diminished for the future. The Scottish courts take account of this and make awards accordingly.[19] The clearest case is *Kirkpatrick v. Scott Lithgow Ltd.*[20] There was cogent analysis of the various heads of damage. The pursuer's legs were both amputated. He was still employed by the defenders who had provided him with other work. Even then it was not clear that the company would be able to do so far into the future. Lord McCluskey called the head of damage "future loss (or prejudice to earning capacity)."[21] He assessed the award in two stages. The immediate future was until the end of the foreseeable future, which was when the order book of the company dried up. This was an easy arithmetical exercise. Lord McCluskey did not

---

[14] It is applied in personal injury cases from the date of the proof: *Will v. Charles Will Ltd*, 1980 S.L.T. (Notes) 37. In death cases it is applied from the date of the death: *Dingwall v. Walter Alexander & Sons Ltd*, 1981 S.L.T. 313. See generally P. Haberman, "The Changing world of Multipliers", 1996 J.P.I.L. 41 (English law).

[15] 1991 S.L.T. 477.

[16] 3rd ed., 1998. Reproduced in Bennett, *Personal Injury Damages in Scotland* (Barnstoneworth, 1999), App. 1A.

[17] [1998] 3 W.L.R. 329.

[18] See *e.g.* R.L. Denyer, "Loss of Earnings and the Badly Injured Child" [1997] J.P.I.L. 244 (English law).

[19] See McEwan & Paton, Chap. 6. One of the earliest cases where the point is clear is *McNee v. G.R. Stein & Co*, 1981 S.L.T. (Notes) 31. The defenders were assoilzied but if an award had been made it would have included a sum in respect of the small but material loss of future employment prospects: *ibid. per* Lord Murray. The residual effect was upon the appearance of the pursuer's hand rather than its function.

[20] 1987 S.L.T. 654.

[21] At 661.

consider that the calculation could be made in this case simply by applying a multiplier either to his pre-accident salary or the gap between the pursuer's pre- and post-accident salaries. Lord McCluskey explained the position as follows:

> "The pursuer might well work a good deal longer with the defenders, if they have work. On no view is he likely to be able to continue to a normal retiring age having regard to the effort involved in simply getting about. Obviously his prospects in the open labour market would be rather poor. On the other hand because he is a skilled tradesman, they cannot be dismissed as negligible. Furthermore, although his earnings with the defenders—had he remained in full employment with them as a maintenance electrician—would undoubtedly have been high, the uncertainty over the long term future for the employees of the defenders places a substantial question mark against using [the pre-accident wages figure]."[22]

Ultimately Lord McCluskey awarded one-half of the sum produced by applying a multiplier of six years and halving it for contingencies.[23] The concept was applied in unusual circumstances in the case of an active businessman who was sequestrated through the negligence of solicitors.[24] The case is significant because in this case the pursuer's pre-wrong earnings were not usually by way of income but by way of realising capital gains on the sale of companies. He had been, and would be for some time, disadvantaged in doing this. It is clear that "employability" is not the essence of the award.

An award for disadvantage on the labour market[25] can be made in **18–34** addition to future loss of earnings.[26] There is no doubt that this is a more effective approach in cases where it would be difficult to show loss of earnings, *e.g.* where a pursuer had been made redundant.[27] The existence of the award means that loss of earnings itself, the well-known paradigm, turns out to be part of a wider head of claim which is well described by Lord McCluskey as "prejudice to earning capacity". It can be assessed by a particular sum to which a multiplier is attached or by an overall lump sum. It has been held that an averment stating "The pursuer's future employability has been affected by said accident" was entitled to go to proof where although the pursuer was still at work she was finding it more difficult to carry out her work and might need an operation.[28] Naturally if the matrix of working conditions and the victim's skills is such that there is no disadvantage, there will be no award.[29] The Inner House gave practical guidance in

---

[22] At 661.
[23] At 661.
[24] *Mill v. Iain Smith and Partners*, 1989 S.L.T. 319.
[25] See generally A. Ritchie, "Smith v. Manchester Awards: How do Courts Assess Loss of Capacity on the Labour Market?" [1994] J.P.I.L. 103.
[26] *Hughes v. British Railways Board*, 1992 S.L.T. 97.
[27] *Marshall v. Bertrams Ltd*, 1985 S.L.T. 80.
[28] *Cooper v. S.R.C.*, 1993 G.W.D. 31—2014.
[29] A clear case was *Hempsey v. Inverclyde D.C.*, 1985 S.L.T. 348. A plumber was blinded. He was still employed. Lord Cowie thought that there was no disadvantage for this man in this trade at that time: "Even if the pursuer were to lose his present employment, he is still a qualified plumber, and there is nothing in his present condition to suggest that he would be unable to carry on his trade successfully and compete with other plumbers in the labour market. There is another one-eyed plumber in the employment of the defenders": at 348.

Robertson's C.B. v. Anderson[30] that where it is not too speculative a loss of future earnings claim should be allowed rather than a loss of employability claim. In *Robertson's C.B.* itself this meant that the more generous multiplier approach was used for an unemployed man with a poor work record and a criminal record, raising the employability element of the award from £25,000 to £80,000.[31]

Services

18–35 Claims under this head, once thought rather notional, are now potentially substantial.[32] They are founded on sections 8 and 9 of the Administration of Justice (Scotland) Act 1982. Section 8 provides *inter alia* that where necessary services have been rendered to the injured person by a relative in consequence of the injuries in question (unless the relative has expressly agreed, in the knowledge that an action for damages has been raised or is in contemplation, that no payment should be made in respect of those services), the responsible person is liable to pay to the injured person by way of damages such sum as represents reasonable remuneration for those services and repayment of reasonable expenses incurred in connection therewith. The payments for past services are to be held in trust for the person who rendered the services.[33] Future loss of services must also be compensated.[34] The relative has no direct action.[35] Section 9 provides *inter alia* that a wrongdoer shall be liable to pay to the injured person a reasonable sum by way of damages in respect of the inability of the injured person to render personal services to his relatives, being services which were or might have been expected to have been rendered by the injured person, are of a kind which when rendered by a person other than a relative, would ordinarily be obtainable on payment, and are services which the injured person but for the injuries in question might have been expected to render gratuitously to a relative. Put simply, the pursuer is paid under section 8 for the services others have rendered or will render to him and under section 9 for the services he or she cannot render that will have to be obtained from elsewhere, possibly on a long-term basis. While sometimes it might be appropriate to take a broad brush and deal with all of these claims in a lump sum, the better approach was set out in *Low v. Ralston*.[36] A mother and her two children were injured in a car accident. The claim included a claim under section 9 of the Administration of Justice Act 1982 for loss of services of the mother and a claim under section 8 of the 1982 Act for necessary services rendered to the mother. The pursuer said that since the accident she had suffered pain in her neck when carrying out household tasks such as ironing or cooking and required assistance

---

[30] 1996 S.L.T. 215.

[31] See also *Barker v. West Lothian Health Service Trust*, 1996 S.C.L.R. 768.

[32] McEwan & Paton, Chap. 12. See generally D. Kinloch, "Section 8 Claims", 1997 Rep.B. 15–2; J. Blaikie, "Personal Injury Claims: the Valuation of Services", 1994 S.L.T. (News) 167; D. Gardiner, "Market Value of Needed Services as the Fair and Reasonable Value" (1993) 1 Tort L. Rev. 233 (English law).

[33] Section 8(2); see A. Reed, "Carer's Recompense held on Trust", 1994 J.I.P.L. 215.

[34] Section 8(3).

[35] Section 8(4).

[36] 1997 S.L.T. 626.

from her husband and her mother. She used to carry out home decorating prior to the accident, but was no longer able to do so. She required to employ a decorator to redecorate her home and further plans for redecoration had required to be shelved. She sought, as is not uncommon, an award for loss of services in terms of section 9 of the Act of 1982. Lord Osborne said:

"I recognise that, in a number of cases, the court has made lump sum awards covering claims under both sections 8 and 9 of the Act of 1982. However, it appears to me that there is an obvious disadvantage in following that course. It stems from the differing provisions of the two sections. In particular in s. 8(2) it is provided that: 'The injured person shall be under an obligation to account to the relative for any damages recovered from the responsible person under subsection (1) above. . . . It is to be observed that there is no equivalent provision in s. 9, which is what one would expect having regard to the differing nature of the two types of claims. The result of this state of affairs is that, in relation to damages awarded in response to a claim under s. 8(1), the injured person is under legal obligation to account to the relative concerned. Where one is dealing with damages awarded under s. 9, the injured person is beneficially entitled to the damages awarded. If the court, when faced with claims under both sections, makes a lump sum award, in which no distinction is drawn between the amount awarded in respect of one claim as opposed to the other, in my opinion, it is obvious that difficulty may arise in relation to the operation of the provisions of s 8 (2) of the Act of 1982. The injured person will have no means of knowing the extent of their obligation to account to the relative concerned. In my opinion, that would be a most unsatisfactory situation. Therefore I consider that the proper course is for the court to make a separate award under each section."[37]

It has been held in Scotland[38] that one spouse injured by another spouse cannot make a section 8 claim as the money recovered would go back to the wrongdoer. This was foreshadowed by a similar decision in the House of Lords in an English case based on the English common law but commenting on the position under the Scottish legislation.[39]

Accommodation

In some cases the principle of *restitutio* will require that a pursuer be given **18–36** sufficient money to acquire necessary accommodation, *e.g.* where he or she has been rendered tetraplegic and cannot use an ordinary house.[40]

Congenial Employment

This is a head recognised in England where for example a painter and **18–37** decorator is redeployed as a clerk.[41] However, it has not found favour in Scotland. In three cases in which it was raised it has been treated as an

---

[37] At 628.
[38] *Kozikowska v. Kozikowski*, 1996 S.L.T. 386.
[39] *Hunt v. Severs* [1994] 2 A.C. 350.
[40] *Martin v. James & Andrew Chapman (Haulage Contractors) Ltd*, 1995 G.W.D. 2–77; following *Roberts v. Johnstone* [1989] 1 Q.B. 878.
[41] *Kennedy v. Burke*, unreported, July 24, 1994, Manchester County Court.

aspect of solatium. It is submitted that so long as the solatium award is clearly enhanced as a result of this being established, there is no need for it to be treated as a separate head, although it is clearly essential to aver and prove it in support of solatium.[42] In *Lenaghan*, giving the opinion of the court, Lord Mayfield said that there may be "circumstances, in an exceptional case, such as where the pursuer's loss of congenial employment is a major factor in the claim, where a separate claim would be appropriate."[43]

Pensions

18–38 When a person is injured and cannot work the current economic world is such that he is likely to lose a pension or be unable to maintain the contribution necessary to make it worthwhile. This is not a remote loss— although perhaps at one time it might have been thought to be—and is now a difficult practical point.[44]

Property: Destruction and Loss of Use

18–39 These issues are seldom litigated. Loss of use of heritable or moveable property is generally recoverable subject to general principle. The basic rule is that where goods can be economically repaired the measure of the damages is the cost of the repair together with any consequential damage naturally and directly flowing from the wrongful act. If the article is totally destroyed or cannot be economically repaired then where the goods have a market value the measure is generally the market value immediately before the damage.[45] An example, in relation to heritage, is *Co-operative Wholesale Society Ltd v. Motherwell District Council*.[46] In this case the pursuers' heritable subjects were damaged by fire. The same day the council started demolishing them. The pursuers sought to recover damages from the local authority for demolishing the subjects without authority. In quantifying their loss they referred *inter alia* to the additional cost of reinstating the building imposed upon them by the actings of the local authority and to the market value prior to the fire, but they made no reference to the market value immediately prior to the demolition. It was held that because the fire-damaged building remained in its pre-demolition condition for only a few hours, it might be impractical to place an open market value on it and that the cost of reinstatement and the market value prior to the fire might prove to be relevant factors in quantifying the pursuers' loss. This shows the

---

[42] *Stark v. Lothian & Borders Fire Board*, 1993 S.L.T. 652; *Lenaghan v. Ayrshire & Arran Health Board*, 1993 S.L.T. 544; 1994 S.L.T. 765; *MacLean v. Lothian and Borders Fire Brigade*, 1999 S.L.T. 702.

[43] 1994 S.L.T. 765 at 769G–H.

[44] McEwan & Paton. See generally *Auty v. NCB* [1985] 1 W.L.R. 784; *Mitchell v. Glenrothes Development Corporation*, 1991 S.L.T. 284; J. Blaikie, "Assessment of Pension Rights in Personal Injuries Claims", 1995 J.R. 40; R. Bolton, "Other Approaches to Valuing Loss of Pension Benefits" [1995] J.P.I.L. 216; J.J. Rowley, "An Updated Guide to Pension Loss Calculation", 1995 J.P.I.L. 212; "A Guide to Pension Loss Calculation", 1995 J.P.I.L. 107.

[45] *Pomphrey v. James A. Cuthbertson Ltd*, 1951 S.C. 147; *Hutchison v. Davidson*, 1946 S.L.T. 11.

[46] 1985 S.L.T. 89.

desire to compensate without giving a windfall gain. It also shows that the general broad proposition of *restitutio in integrum* is of little help in answering practical problems. In *Calvey v. Eastern Scottish Omnibuses*,[47] the pursuer claimed storage, bus fares and inconvenience. It was argued the storage costs should have stopped when the insurers agreed the vehicle was a write off and that he should have bought a car, avoiding incurring the bus fares. The learned sheriff restricted the storage charges to the shorter period but did not find that the pursuer had failed to mitigate. He accepted that *The Liesboch*[48] was not universally applied.[49] Subject to the duty to mitigate replacement goods may be hired and it does not matter that the hire has been arranged such that the victim does not have to pay as he uses,[50] but he must be legally liable for the hire and not, for example, entitled to avoid his actual liability in the actual transaction due to the illegality of the transaction.[51]

"Pure" economic loss

These cases of course raise fundamental issues about liability.[52] Much of the **18–40** development in this area is recent. However there are two cases which suggest that the law will deal with these cases as others. *White v. Jones*,[53] where it was held that there was liability, brought the loss within the duty, logically precluding any role for the law of damages—the solicitors sent the whole estate to the wrong person and had to send the same amount to the right person. A prime example of the success of the substitutional redress approach is in cases of negligent valuation. In the case of a negligent valuation the loss is economic—the pursuer has paid more for something than it is worth. Prior to the law of delict being so evidently applicable to these cases there was a body of law in contract on the measure of damages. It would be open in principle to argue different measures in delict and contract but these differences narrow where the duties are essentially co-extensive. It is theoretically (and practically) better to start with liability and proceed to mensuration. In *Martin v. Bell Ingram*[54] the court accepted that there could be liability for a primary economic loss caused by a defective, but not dangerous, exercise of professional advice contained in a statement, but did not necessarily say what that liability would be. In fact the point was decided in the absence of any argument:

"It was not disputed that where the negligence consists of the failure of surveyors to detect a defect in the building, the proper measure of

---

[47] 1991 G.W.D. 705.
[48] *Liesboch (Dredger) v. Edison SS* [1933] A.C. 449.
[49] Following in this respect *Carson v. McDonald*, 1987 S.C.LR 415. See also and generally *Iver v. Judge*, 1994 S.C.L.R. 735, *Diamond v. Lovell* [1999] 3 W.L.R. 561.
[50] *Gillespie v. Aziz*, 1993 S.L.T. (Sh. Ct) 63.
[51] *Diamond v. Lovell* [1999] 3 W.L.R. 561. For a discussion of credit hire costs and liabilities as a head of recoverable loss see N. McKenzie, "No Such Thing as a Free Lunch", 1999 S.L.T. (News 279; C. Fletcher, "Free Lunch — Credit Where Credits Not Due", 1999 S.L.T. (News) 169.
[52] See 10–2 *et seq.*
[53] [1995] 2 A.C. 207. See 10–18.
[54] 1996 S.L.T. 575.

damages is the difference between the price paid as representing the market price of the subjects on the basis of the report, and the market price which the subjects should have fetched on the basis of their actual condition."[55]

In view of this point not being disputed it would be possible to argue it in another case, although it seems likely that if it had been argued Lord Justice-Clerk Ross would have been in favour of the basic approach.[56]

18-41   The leading Scots authority referred to in *Martin* was *Stewart v. H.A. Brechin & Co.*,[57] in which the passage above quoted was stated to be the law, but with the additional refinement that the notional sale was one between a willing buyer and a willing seller. The case was on the face of it probably one of contract, the surveyors being instructed by solicitors instructed by the pursuers. The case lays down the proper point that the cost of repair is a guide in calculating damages but its value depends upon the case. English cases make that allusion easier to understand. So far as English law is concerned the point was decided, again as a matter of the law of damages, some time ago in *Phillips v. Ward*.[58] That case sets the same measure as the later Scots case but it is much more clearly based on the expectations of contract.[59] It also established an important point of principle that even if the repairs cost more than the loss of value the defender is immunised against that greater and real loss. The most significant English case prior to *Martin* is *Perry v. Sidney Phillips & Son.*[60] It emphasised the point in *Phillips* by reversing a decision allowing repair costs. It also allowed, in contract, damages for the inconvenience which such surveys engender. The decision in *Martin* could not have been arrived at unless, albeit not argued to the death, it were accepted as the law that this was the correct mode of valuation and that it applied to delictual cases—for that is without any doubt what *Martin* was. It was the *ratio decidendi* of the case. However, because a part of the case was agreed it may be attacked before the Inner House on that point.[61]

18-42   Difficult questions arise in relation to cases where the loss resulting is greater than might have been expected because of a fall in the market—for example, where solicitors fail to obtain a title and where surveyors overvalue property causing a lender to be over-exposed. The leading case is now *South Australia Asset Management Corporation v. York Montague Ltd*[62]

---

[55] *per* L.J.-C. Ross at 584.

[56] at 584H.

[57] 1959 S.C. 306.

[58] [1956] 1 W.L.R. 471.

[59] *per* Denning L.J. at 473: "I take it to be clear that the proper measure of damage is the amount of money which will put Mr Phillips into as good a position as if the surveying contract had been properly fulfilled."

[60] [1982] 1 W.L.R. 1297.

[61] In England *Ward* and *Perry* have been followed time and time again. Peter Gibson L.J., in a dissent in an important English Court of Appeal case (*Gardner v. Marsh & Parsons* [1997] 1 W.L.R. 489, imposing liability on surveyors based on both contract and tort), noted at 505F that it had not been suggested that there was any difference in the measure of damages.

[62] [1996] 3 All E.R. 365 and other related cases The case is sometimes known as the *Banque Bruxelles Lambert* appeal because that decision in the Court of Appeal was the leading decision. It settled before getting to the Lords. See P.J. Wade, "High Valuations versus Bad Lending", 1995 Rep.B. 4–2 and *Leeds Permanent Building Society v. Fraser & Steele*, 1995 S.L.T. (Sh. Ct) 72, both ante-dating *South Australia Asset Management*.

and the associated appeals. The present position is most easily seen in the decision in the *Nykredit* associated appeal. The lenders on March 12, 1990 advanced £2.45 million on the security of a property valued by the defendants at £3.5 million. The correct value had been said by the judge to be between £2 and £2.375 million. The price obtained at auction in February 1993 when the market had taken a fall was £345,000. The judge quantified the damages at £3,058,555. On appeal the House of Lords said the figure should be the difference between £3.5 million and the true value at the date of the valuation. So the negligent surveyors escaped the consequences of the fall of the market. The Court of Appeal tried to establish a more sophisticated scheme based on differentiating between successful transactions and no-transaction cases.[63] The case in question was a no-transaction case—it would not have taken place had the property been properly valued. The surveyor is protected from loss if the market rises and so he should suffer from a fall. The Court of Appeal did not say that the surveyor was to guarantee the value of the property, merely that when he got it wrong on the day of the valuation he was responsible for the consequences of so doing, the possibility that the market might fall being reasonably foreseeable. The reasoning of the House of Lords appears to be based on limiting the scope of the duty—the surveyors were not advising on a course of conduct but relaying information upon which the pursuers would act. The test in tort was: how much worse off were the pursuers because the information was wrong? Lord Hoffmann explained the reasoning by way of the doctor and mountaineer analogy. The mountaineer, who is worried about his knee, goes to the doctor who says it is OK. He goes mountaineering and is injured but not through anything wrong with his knee. The doctor cannot be liable to the mountaineer. This does have the look of a causal inquiry. In the case of the doctor the mountaineer can say "but for your mistake I would not have gone on the mountain". But the proximate cause of his injury is the fall. In the case of the surveyor the proximate cause of the loss is the bad advice. The cases are not, it is submitted, the same.[64]

SOLATIUM

Solatium is different from a patrimonial award. The term was formerly used **18–43** in Scotland in fatal cases for the award to the family for their grief but as will be seen in the next section that term is no longer used, having been replaced successively by loss of society and now the relatives' non-patrimonial award. Its roots are not entirely clear. Most likely the sum we call solatium, representing pain and suffering, derives either from our own custom based on that of other European states or is taken from the civilian tradition in respect of the *lex aquilia* which, although historically and doctrinally was against such an award, came as a result of custom and practice to allow it by the 17th and 18th centuries.[65] The term "solatium"

---

[63] Derived from *Hayes v. James & Charles Dodd (a Firm)* [1990] 2 All E.R. 815.

[64] For an examination of the causation aspects see W.V.H. Rogers, "Causation and Falls in the Market", 1997 Tort L.R. 12.

[65] Zimmerman, p. 1026. Markesinis reports that the Great Senate decided for Germany that damages for pain and suffering have a dual function, providing compensation for damage but also indicating that the wrongdoer owes satisfaction—this will include pain and loss of amenity: pp. 682–683. They also take into account the relative wealth of the parties and whether the wrongdoer is insured. Case 83, pp. 705–718.

might be borrowed from the law of the true *actio injuriarum* where a solatium to make up for the insult or affront was awarded. Professor Walker suspects that solatium was taken into the Scottish action for damages based on the *lex aquilia* via assythment.[66] It has chiefly been associated with personal injury but in recent years, as liability for economic loss has expanded, it has appeared in such claims, especially those for professional negligence. An award for intangible inconvenience and distress arising from the incompetent performance of a service is well established in contract, the line of authority for the common law world originating in Glasgow Sheriff Court.[67] This is justifiable on the expectation principle of contract—in these contracts peace of mind or a happy holiday can be said to be what was bargained for. Delict is about restoration rather than expectancies and so although the solatium award in personal injury and the inconvenience award in holiday and service cases look the same, they are not. However awards are made in delict cases and this was done without argument in *Martin v. Bell-Ingram*[68] and held to be the law, albeit in default of full argument in *Lawson v. D.M. Hall.*[69] If an award were not appropriate in delict then there would be a practical distinction between suing in contract and suing in delict. It is submitted that the contract-based holiday/service cases are not authority for an intangible award in delict, but that economic loss is now a well-recognised head of claim compensating a recognised interest, and the intangible harm done by the economic loss requires to be assuaged or satisfied in precisely the same way as in traditional cases. It is thus an extension of the law which has not yet been fully argued but, it is submitted, solatium in economic loss cases is quite rightly allowed.

18–44   Much of a reparation lawyer's time is given over to investigation, estimating, negotiating and arguing the correct level of solatium.[70] It cannot be an exact science. It is expected that advocates on each side will proffer guidance where the case is before a judge alone. As some of the pain and suffering may relate to the past and some to the future it is necessary to apportion these elements to properly compute interest on the damages. The practitioner will consult a practitioner looseleaf text or electronic database[71] to gain a feeling for the appropriate level of award. In England the Judicial Studies Board have published "Guidelines for the Assessment of General Damages in Personal Injury Cases".[72] General damages is the English version of solatium and it is quite legitimate to refer to English cases and the Guidelines to assist the court in coming to a decision on what is essentially a jury matter based on impression. The CICA tariff,[73] if used

---

[66] *Delict*, p. 23. It may be, however, that it may simply have come over with the aquilian action and Scots lawyers used the word solatium because of its common non-pecuniary connotations. At a practical level see *Irving v. Hiddleston*, 1998 S.C. 759.

[67] *Diesen v. Sampson*, 1971 S.L.T. (Sh. Ct) 49; *Jarvis v. Swan Tours* [1973] Q.B. 233.

[68] 1986 S.L.T. 575.

[69] 1998 G.W.D. 1618.

[70] See, *e.g.* A.P. Moriarty, "Ophthalmic complications of Whiplash, Head Injury and Blunt Trauma", 1998 J.P.I.L. 65; C. Morris-Coole, "Epilepsy: Litigation Considerations and the Claim for General Damages" [1996] J.P.I.L. 215.

[71] V. Walker, citing *Brown v. MacGregor*, Feb. 26, 1813, FC in which the term solatium is used.

[72] 4th ed., 1998, reproduced in McEwan & Paton.

[73] See para. 19–23.

at all, ought to be considered as a cross-check average figure in the very simplest of cases, with no extra features for the pleader to ensure that researches have produced the right kind of figure but not something to be presented to the court.

Solatium may now include, as mentioned above, a sum for loss of employability or loss of congenial employment if these do not appear as substantial heads in their own right.

Recoupment and non-recoupable benefit

It is thought to be unfair for a victim to recover damage both from the **18–45** wrongdoer and the state. There have been various schemes and approaches. The regime under the Law Reform (Personal Injuries) Act 1948 was not generous enough to the state. The scheme under the Social Security Administration Act 1992 introduced a system involving compensation recovery, administered by the Compensation Recovery Unit. It was perceived to be unfair mainly because it allowed recoupment from the solatium award, so the public coffers gained from the pursuer's pain and suffering for which the state itself had not compensated him. The current scheme builds on the 1992 scheme but is a fresh version under and in terms of the Social Security (Recovery of Benefits) Act 1997.[74] It applies to all cases where the case had not been determined or settled by October 6, 1997. The defender compensator is made liable to the Secretary of State.[75] The pursuer will appreciate that the defender has this liability and must know the extent of the clawback to enable decisions as to settlement or continued conduct of the litigation to be made. The compensator is allowed to deduct the payments he is obliged to make from the pursuer.[76] The Act provides how this is to be done, the principle being "like for like".[77] Deductions from each category of damages awarded may only extend to those paid over the relevant period—normally five years from the accident.[78] A full and final settlement brings the relevant period to a premature end.[79] Compensation has to be broken into three heads from which associated benefits are recoverable: (1) Earnings lost during the relevant period;[80] (2) Cost of care incurred during the relevant period;[81] (3) Loss of mobility during the relevant period.[82] Courts must now specify in their orders the amount of any compensation payment which is attributable to

---

[74] And the associated 1998 Regulations. See generally, A. Dismore, "Social Security (Recovery of Benefits) Act 1997 and Regulations", 1998 J.P.I.L. 14. There is a full treatment, updated by regular supplements, in McEwan & Paton, Chap. 16.

[75] s. 6.

[76] s. 8.

[77] Sched. 2.

[78] In the case of disease it is five years from the first listed benefit claim.

[79] s. 3(4).

[80] Benefits recoverable are: Disability working allowance; Disablement pension payable under s. 103 of the 1992 Act; Incapacity benefit; Income support; Invalidity pension and allowance; Jobseekers allowance; Severe disablement allowance; Sickness benefit; Statutory Sick pay; Unemployability supplement; Unemployment Benefit.

[81] Recoverable benefits are: Attendance allowance; Care component of disability living allowance; Disablement pension increase payable under s. 104 or s. 105 of the 1992 Act.

[82] Recovered from Mobility allowance; mobility component of disability living allowance.

each of these three heads over the relevant period.[83] Settlements and tenders will have to be arranged to take account of recoupment.[84] Recoupment and interest has raised problems of interpretation.[85] The 1992 scheme gave rise to a claim of damages known as "loss of non-recoupable benefit".[86] This arose where the pursuer's pre-accident benefit, which could not have been subject to recoupment, was replaced by a recoupable benefit as a result of the accident. A similar sort of situation is still conceivable but probably less likely with the like for like provisions.[87] The 1992 scheme allowed for a small settlements figure of £2,500. The 1997 Act permits this but it has not been reintroduced at present.

DAMAGES ON DEATH

18–46 The fact of causing death is treated no differently from causing injury so far as the defender's liability is concerned. Thus whether a defender is liable at all is dealt with under the general law of delict or indeed the general law of contract. However, the issues of remoteness and title to sue which arise in delict cases based on the death of a relative, have been resolved by statute—the Damages (Scotland) Act 1976 as amended. (One of the main purposes of the Act was to abolish assythment which had been held not to have been lost by desuetude.[88] It did.[89]) The actual award that will be received by a person in respect of the death of another will also be affected by general issues of the law of damages dealt with above, such as the use of the multiplier and the multiplicand to compute damages. The law on recovery for nervous shock could fall within the title of this chapter, in that the pursuer in such a claim may be founding on the effect of a death on another party, but that topic is treated separately. Nonetheless the similarities between the terms of the Act and some nervous shock judgments ought to be taken into account. The category of "immediate family" might be expected to be utilised in common law cases where the relationship is in question—or at least to be taken into account.

18–47 The Damages (Scotland) Act 1976 itself has been amended most notably in 1982 and in 1993. The 1993 Act is one of the very few which had retrospective effect. As a result of one of the campaigners for reform having died of injuries while the legislative process was underway, some of the provisions applied to deaths after July 16, 1992, the date of introduction of the Bill to Parliament.[90] It is likely that other reforms will be debated

---

[83] ss. 15. See *Mitchell v. Laing*, 1998 S.L.T. 203.

[84] For difficulties see A. Paton, "Tenders and Recovery of Benefits: Further Developments", 1998 Rep.B. 22–4.

[85] *George v. George C. Peebles & Son*, 1998 S.L.T. 685; *Spence v. Wilson*, 1998 S.L.T. 688.

[86] *Hassall v. Secretary of State* [1995] All E.R. 909, accepted in Scotland in *Arnott v. Bristol-Myers Co. Ltd*, 1998 S.L.T. 110.

[87] A claim under the 1997 Act was allowed following *Hassall* (above) and *Arnott* (above) in *McKenna v. Chief Constable, Strathclyde Police*, 1998 S.L.T. 1161.

[88] *Mckendrick v. Sinclair*, 1972 S.L.T. 110.

[89] s. 8. See Robert E. Mackay, "The Resuscitation of Assythment?", 1992 J.R. 242.

[90] And see Scot. Law Com. Report No. 134 of 1992 upon which the Act was based. For some of the context and debate before, during and after the Act see W.J. Stewart, *A Casebook on Delict* (2nd ed., 1997), Chap. 1. Note the comments of Lord McCluskey in the Extra Division in relation to Scot. Law Com. Reports Nos 30 and 31 in *Hamilton v. Fife Health Board*, 1993 S.L.T. 624 at 627.

over the years.[91] One of the features of the legislation is that it makes practical procedural provisions to avoid a multiplicity of claims and allows remoter relatives to be ignored in the process.[92]

To what cases does the Act apply?

The Act applies where a person dies in consequence of personal injuries **18–48** sustained by him as a result of an act or omission of another person, being an act or omission giving rise to an obligation to pay damages to the injured person or his executor. It has been held to apply to a foetus injured while still *in utero* but subsequently born alive.[93] Subject to the Act the person liable to pay the damages is also liable to pay damages in terms of section 1 of the Act to any relative as defined in the Act.[94] There is no liability if liability has been excluded or discharged whether by antecedent agreement or otherwise by the deceased before his death or if liability is excluded by another enactment.

Who is a "relative"?

The following are within the definition of relative: any person who **18–49** immediately before the deceased's death was the spouse of the deceased[95]; any person not being the spouse of the deceased, who was immediately before the deceased's death living with the deceased as husband and wife[96]; any person who was a parent or child of the deceased, including any person who had been accepted into the family as a child of the deceased; any person who was an ascendant or descendant (other than a parent or child) of the deceased; any person who was, or was the issue of, a brother, sister, uncle or aunt of the deceased; and any person who, having been a spouse of the deceased, had ceased to be so by virtue of a divorce. Any relationship of affinity is to be treated as consanguinity and any relationship of the half blood is to be treated as a relationship of the whole blood. The stepchild of any person is to be treated as his child.[97] In addition section 1(1) of the Law Reform (Parent and Child) (Scotland) Act 1986 applies so that the fact that a person's parents are not or have not been married to one another is to be left out of account in establishing the legal relationship between the person and any other person. The relationship is to have effect as if the parents had been married to one another. The Act does not especially mention adopted children but in principle they are children of the adopter and not of the natural parents.

The relative's executor

The 1993 Act provided for the transfer of a relative's vested claim to the **18–50** deceased relative's executor. In determining the amount of damages payable to an executor by virtue of this provision the court is to have regard

---

[91] See, *e.g.* L.G. Moodie, "The Effect of Death on Damages", (1993) 38 J.L.S. 212.

[92] See Rules of the Court of Session, Chap. 43, Pt 1. See also *Henderson v. Occidental Petroleum (Caledonia) Ltd*, 1990 S.L.T. 315.

[93] *McWilliams v. Lord Advocate*, 1992 S.L.T. 1045; *Hamilton v. Fife Health Board*, 1993 S.L.T. 624.

[94] s. 1(1).

[95] This is so even where the pursuer knew that the deceased would die at the time of marriage: *Phillips v. Grampian Health Board*, 1988 S.L.T. 628, IH; 1992 S.L.T. 659 (proof).

[96] This provision was inserted by the Administration of Justice Act 1982, s. 14(4).

[97] ss 1 and 10(1) and Sched. 1.

only to the period ending immediately before the relative's death.[98] The executor can bring an action or if appropriate be sisted as a pursuer. An action is not to be considered concluded while an appeal is competent or remains undisposed of.[99]

Who is a member of the "immediate family"?

18–51 The definition in the Act[1] is by reference to the definition of "relative" set out above. Subject to the same extensions for stepchildren and those whose parents were not married, the category comprises any person who immediately before the deceased's death was the spouse of the deceased; any person not being the spouse of the deceased, who was immediately before the deceased's death, living with the deceased as husband and wife[2]; and any person who was a parent or child of the deceased, including any person who had been accepted into the family as a child of the deceased. Thus brothers and sisters are excluded. The death of a child as a result of antenatal injuries is included.[3] A daughter-in-law or son-in-law is a member,[4] as is a mother-in-law or father-in-law.[5]

Loss of Support

18–52 The damages payable are to be such as will compensate *a relative* for any loss of support suffered since the date of the deceased's death or likely to be suffered as a result of the act or omission in question, together with any reasonable expense incurred in connection with the deceased's funeral.[6] In calculating loss of support no account is to be taken of any patrimonial gain or advantage which has accrued or which will or may accrue to the relative from the deceased or from any other person by way of succession or settlement or any insurance money,[7] benefit,[8] pension[9] or gratuity which has been or will be or may be paid as a result of the deceased's death.[10] In *Bews v. Scottish Hydro-Electric plc*[11] it was held that a payment by employers under a policy referring to death was not paid "as a result of the deceased's death" but as a matter of their discretion. However it was an *ex gratia* payment and thus not deductible.[12] Where the deceased was awarded a

---

[98] s. 1A.

[99] s. 2A.

[1] s. 10(2).

[2] This provision was inserted by the Administration of Justice Act 1982, s. 14(4).

[3] *McWilliams v. Lord Advocate*, 1992 S.L.T. 1045; *Hamilton v. Fife Health Board*, 1993 S.L.T. 624.

[4] *McAllister v. ICI plc*, 1997 S.L.T. 351.

[5] *Monteith v. Cape Insulation*, 1998 S.L.T. 456.

[6] s. 1(3). See the full treatment in McEwan & Paton, Chap. 13.

[7] This includes a return of premiums. See also *Davidson v. UCS*, 1990 S.L.T. 329.

[8] This means any benefit under the Social Security Act 1975 or the Social Security (Northern Ireland) Act 1975 and any payment by a friendly society or trade union for the relief or maintenance of a member's dependants.

[9] This includes a return of contributions and any payment of a lump sum in respect of a person's employment.

[10] s. 1(5).

[11] 1992 S.L.T. 749.

[12] Following *Dougan v. Rangers FC Ltd*, 1974 S.L.T. (Sh. Ct) 34.

provisional award of damages under section 12(2) of the Administration of Justice Act 1982, the making of that award does not prevent liability arising, but the loss of support award must take into account any part of the provisional award relating to future patrimonial loss as was intended to compensate the deceased for a period beyond the date on which he died.[13]

To establish loss of support it is not essential for a claimant to show that the deceased was, or might have become, under a duty in law to provide or contribute to the support of the claimant. If however that is established it can be taken into account.[14] The prospect of dependency on a retirement pension is taken into account[15] as is loss of accommodation provided by the deceased's employer.[16] In the ordinary case the deceased's net income is established and the amount used to support the family determined.[17] Possible pay rises and other factors are taken into account.[18] Identifying the loss of support from a partnership in a business can involve more difficult questions but in some cases average salary and/or drawings can provide the basis of a calculation.[19] By virtue of section 9(2) of the Administration of Justice Act 1982 the loss of personal services is a head of damage within the loss of support claim. The personal services must be such as (i) were or might have been expected to be rendered by the deceased, (ii) of a kind which when rendered by a person other than a relative would ordinarily be obtained on payment and (iii) such that the deceased might have been expected to render gratuitously. This extends to cases where a deceased husband was an energetic handyman and gardener about the house.[20] But the usual claim is for the many unpaid services of the housewife such as childcare.[21] Such awards may be calculated on a multiplier/multiplicand basis and produce quite substantial awards.[22]

Contemplation, Grief and Non-Patrimonial Benefit Award

Alternatively or in addition to a loss of support claim there is the **18–53** "contemplation, grief and non-patrimonial benefit award" or an amended section 1(4) award.[23] In legislation passed or made before the Damages (Scotland) Act 1993 the phrase "loss of society award" is to be construed as an amended section 1(4) award.[24] To call this a loss of society award would be to risk confusion with cases under the unamended Act and to call it the non-patrimonial award might risk leaving out of account the other ele-

---

[13] s. 1(5A).

[14] s. 1(6).

[15] *Davidson v. UCS*, 1990 S.L.T. 329.

[16] *Hatherley v. Smith*, 1989 S.L.T. 316.

[17] *ibid.*

[18] *Worf v. Western SMT Co. Ltd*, 1987 S.L.T. 317.

[19] *Prentice v. Chalmers*, 1984 S.L.T. 63.

[20] *Worf v. Western SMT Co. Ltd*, 1987 S.L.T. 317.

[21] See *Brown v. Fergusson*, 1990 S.L.T. 274; *Spittle v. Bunney* [1988] 1 W.L.R. 847.

[22] *e.g. Worf* above. More than £51,000 was awarded in *G's C.B. v. Grampian Health Board*, 1995 S.L.T. 652. See J. Blaikie, "Personal Injury Claims: the Valuation of Services", 1994 S.L.T. (News) 167.

[23] There is no short form for this in use. "Grief" would be too narrow and cause problems for mistaken cross-referencing to nervous shock.

[24] 1993 Act, s. 7(1).

ments. Such an award is competent only to relatives who are members of the deceased's immediate family.[25] The three elements to such an award, being such damages as the court thinks just, are: (1) distress and anxiety endured by the relative in contemplation of the suffering of the deceased before his death; (2) grief and sorrow of the relative caused by the deceased's death; (3) the loss of such non-patrimonial benefit as the relative might have been expected to derive from the deceased's society and guidance if the deceased had not died. The court may take a broad brush to this award and need not ascribe particular sums to any head. The last part is essentially the same as the loss of society award previously provided for and decisions on that will be useful in relation to subsection (3) cases.[26] Note that the transfer provisions noted above mean that if a wife dies shortly after her husband who died as a result of the defender's negligence, her section 1(4) claim, having vested, will transmit to her executor. However, of the various heads it is more likely that the grief and sorrow element will transfer than the non-patrimonial element because of the restriction on the transfer to the position before the death of the relative. The new phrasing of the award was not intended by the Commission to change but to clarify the law so previous decisions are still relevant— nonetheless, the general view of pursuers' agents, now supported to an extent by the courts, is that the Commission intended to allow the courts to award the higher sums which the 1976 Act might have envisaged.[27] Thus while by statute marriage or prospects of remarriage are excluded as relevant factors, subsequent cohabitation does have to be taken into account. This seems anomalous in policy though sound in principle.[28]

Funeral Expenses

18–54 Relatives are entitled to recover any reasonable expense incurred in connection with the deceased's funeral.[29]

The executor's claim

18–55 The rights to damages in respect of personal injuries, including solatium, sustained by and vested in the deceased immediately before his death, are transmitted to the executor.[30] No right to patrimonial loss attributable to any period after death is transmitted: thus only loss of earnings to the date of death is in issue, not future loss of earnings. So far as solatium is concerned only the period up to the death is counted. Where the injury was a verbal injury then in respect of non-patrimonial loss the executor cannot raise an action but can only continue it if it had been raised by the deceased

---

[25] See above. A child *in utero* is a child for these purposes—*Cohen v. Shaw*, 1992 S.L.T. 1022.

[26] See *Dingwall v. Walter Alexander & Sons*, 1981 S.L.T. 313; *Donald v. SPTE*, 1986 S.L.T. 625.

[27] A.M. Hajducki, "Death Payments—A New Approach", 1999 S.L.T. (News) 77. See *McManus v. Babcock Energy*, 1999 G.W.D. 21–1013.

[28] *Morris v. Drysdale*, 1992 S.L.T. 186.

[29] s. 1(3). This includes a headstone: *Prentice v. Chalmers*, 1985 S.L.T. 168; 1984 S.L.T. 63; *Porter v. Dickie*, 1983 S.L.T. 234.

[30] s. 2(1); s. 2 was amended by the 1993 Act.

and not concluded. The executor can bring an action or if appropriate be sisted as a pursuer. An action is not to be considered concluded while an appeal is competent or remains undisposed of. Section 3 of the 1976 Act, which prevented loss of society claims transmitting, was repealed by the 1993 Act.[31] It should be noted that the executor's claim does not exclude the relatives and vice versa.[32]

The Awards: Pro-rating

Where the award is limited by contract or statute damages are limited on a **18–56** pro rata basis.[33]

---

[31] S. Forsyth, "Transmissible Solatium After Death", 1999 S.L.T. (News) 45.
[32] s. 4.
[33] s. 6.

CHAPTER 19

OTHER REMEDIES

This book is only about reparation for delict. That by definition means that **19–1** the remedy is usually damages. However, in a wider sense, other remedies can compel the defender to make reparation.

Interdict[1]

Rather than wait for a person to breach their obligation and sue for **19–2** damages, the apprehended wrong allows the conduct to be restrained in advance. This is certainly economically efficient. Relevant cases do not always involve a detailed examination of the law of delict because a broad approach is taken to the idea of wrongdoing. Sometimes it is possible that interdict is being granted as a remedy to a rightholder, which right may be *in rem* rather than *in personam*. It is also possible that the law can recognise a right not to have an interest infringed without deciding that an infringement of that interest is actionable in damages. Interdict may be granted on an interim basis as a matter of discretion rather than right. The essential requirements are title and interest to sue, a prima facie case and the balance of convenience being in the applicant's favour.[2]

In cases involving wrongs to the person there is little difficulty. Interdict **19–3** will be granted against, for example, apprehended assault.[3] In the same way molestation[4] will be interdicted. In the case of parties who are married, a matrimonial interdict—which restrains or prohibits any conduct of one spouse towards the other or a child of the family or prohibits a spouse from entering or remaining in a matrimonial home or in a specified area in the vicinity of a matrimonial home—can be fortified by a power of arrest.[5] Conduct which amounts to harassment[6] is restrained by a special statutory remedy.[7]

Economic delicts[8] may be restrained. Many cases involving economic **19–4** delicts involve trade unions and account must be taken of their immunities in delict.[9] Unless the immunity applies, strikers, sitters-in and illegal

---

[1] The "standard" text that has served and still serves is Burn Murdoch which is now out of date in many places. Professor Walker's *Civil Remedies* (1974) is still an important source. There is full contemporary coverage of the subject in S.S. Robinson, *The Law of Interdict* (2nd. ed., 1994, Butterworths/Law Society of Scotland).

[2] *Deane v. Lothian Regional Council*, 1986 S.L.T. 22.

[3] paras 4–3 *et seq.*

[4] In the contemporary sense of harassment rather than the traditional sense of troubling of possession in lands: see Stair I,9,26 which also imported a right to obtain an order ordering the wrongdoer to persist.

[5] Matrimonial Homes (Family Protection) (Scotland) Act 1981, s. 14(1); s. 15(1)

[6] See Chap. 4 above for a discussion of the right.

[7] See below.

[8] See Chap. 7.

[9] See Chap. 2. See also K. Ewing, "Interdicts in Labour Law", 1980 S.L.T. (News) 121.

picketers will be restrained.[10] An important rule is that interdict cannot be granted in absence if the defender claims or is likely to claim that he acted in contemplation or furtherance of a trade dispute.[11]

19–5   An anticipated breach of confidence will be restrained.[12]

19–6   In relation to heritage, interdict operates as a possessory remedy as well as preventing wrongs. It is best to see these cases as adjuncts of the rights conferred by the law of property rather than as wrongs to property.[13] Nuisance is a problem and illustrates clearly the tension between rights and remedies. The issue is seen in *RHM Bakeries v. Strathclyde Regional Council,*[14] discussed above.[15] While from the standpoint of interdict nuisance incurs a strict liability, so far as damages are concerned culpa must be averred and proved, albeit by inference.[16] A fear of repeated trespass can be restrained.[17]

19–7   So far as moveables are concerned, it is clear from *Leitch & Co. v. Leyden*[18] that where appropriate, wrongs to moveables will be interdicted.[19]

19–8   Passing-off is a delict which is regularly restrained by interdict: by its nature, if it continues irreparable damage may be done.[20] The nature of this wrong tends towards the use of interdict and the balance of convenience in interim interdict applications will normally favour an established trader.

19–9   Abuse of process is discussed above.[21] It may be interdicted.[22] Wrongful diligence may also be restrained.[23] Powers similar to interdict are provided by statute in the Debtors (Scotland) Act 1987.

19–10   Normally interdict cannot be granted against the Crown and instead declarator needs to be sought.[24] Where it is sought to prevent a breach of European Union Law interdict may be appropriate.[25]

---

[10] See dicta in *Galt v. Philp* 1984 S.L.T. 28; *Phestos Shipping Co. v. Kurmiawan,* 1983 S.L.T. 388; *Timex Electronic Corporation v. AEEU,* 1994 S.L.T. 438; the ACAS and governmental code limit of six picketers seems to have been accepted.

[11] *Scotsman Publications Ltd v. SOGAT,* 1986 S.L.T. 646.

[12] Indeed that is the best way of implementing the obligation. The topic is dealt with in Chaps 4 and 7. See *A Family v. BBC,* The Scotsman, Nov. 6, 1992.

[13] See, *e.g. Calquhoun v. Paton* (1859) 21 D. 996; *Maxwell v. GSW Railway Co.* (1866) 4 M. 447. And for a third party enforcing a real burden see *Lees v. North East Fife District Council,* 1987 S.L.T. 769. See also *Wills Trs v. Cairngorm Canoeing and Sailing School Ltd,* 1976 S.L.T. 162; *Cowie v. SRC,* 1985 S.L.T. 333; *Nicol v. Blott,* 1986 S.L.T. 677; *Burton's Trs v. Scottish Sports Council,* 1983 S.L.T. 418.

[14] 1985 S.L.T. 214.

[15] See Chap. 5 and *Banks v. Fife Redstone Quarry Co.,* 1954 S.L.T. (Notes) 77; *Hugh Blackwood (Farms) Ltd v. Motherwell D.C.,* 1998 G.W.D. 1290; *Noble's Trs v. Economic Forestry Ltd,* 1988 S.L.T. 662; *Wemyss Bay Caravan, Petitioners,* 1990 G.W.D. 3–141; *Forth Yacht Marina Ltd v. Forth Road Bridge Joint Board,* 1984 S.L.T. 177.

[16] See Chap. 5.

[17] *Hay's Trustees v. Young* (1877) 4 R. 398; *Stuart v. Stephen* (1877) 4 R. 873; *Colquhoun and Cameron v. Mackenzie* (1894) 22 R. 23; *Wallace-James v. Montgomerie & Co.* (1899) 2 F. 107.

[18] 1931 S.C. (H.L.) 1.

[19] See also Chap. 6.

[20] See Chap. 7.

[21] Chap. 9.

[22] *Ormiston v. Redpath Brown & Co.* (1866) M. 488; *Rhind v. Kemp & Co.* (1893) 21 R. 275.

[23] *McCarroll v. Mackinstery,* 1926 S.C. (H.L.) 1.

[24] Crown Proceedings Act 1947, s.43(a), s 21(a); *Lord Advocate v. SRC,* 1990 S.L.T. 158.

[25] *R. v. Secretary of State for Transport, ex p. Factortame Ltd (No 2)* [1991] 1 A.C. 603.

Declarator

A litigant may ask the court to declare that a certain course of conduct is a **19–11** civil wrong. In such a case the law of delict is truly at work. A simple declarator might well be sufficient when dealing with a responsible body which would follow the decision of the court. Indeed, before the enactment of the Crown Proceedings Act 1947 this process was necessary in ordinary reparation cases. Most frequently declarator comes before the court with interdict but as most interdict cases resolve after the interim stage, the declarator is seldom decided.

Judicial Review

The basic purpose of the remedy of judicial review is to control the **19–12** administrative function. The jurisdiction lies with the Court of Session. It was the introduction of new procedures in the latter part of the nineteenth century which encouraged frequent resort to the remedy. While it is usually used to reverse a decision improperly arrived at, the procedure also allows for a claim for damages and for restitution. It is thus arguable that this is a remedy for a civil wrong and within the scope of a work on reparation. Scots law does not, however, restrict judicial review to public law cases.[26] Thus to the extent that there is a procedure for complaining about a decision of a private law body which may result in damages this remedy properly appears in this book. The test of wrongfulness in this context has nothing to do with the tests of wrongfulness in the common law. Normally what needs to be shown is a failure to comply with natural justice or *Wednesbury* unreasonableness or irrationality.[27] The courts are neither a debating club nor an advisory service.[28] Thus the absence of a live issue which could be constituted by a remaining claim for damages will result in a petition for review being dismissed.[29] So far as the potential reparation claim is concerned the courts are not enthusiastic. In *McDonald v. Secretary of State for Scotland (No. 2)*[30] the pursuer sought *inter alia* damages in a case complaining of illegal searches. Because on one view the apparent delict would be justified by the prison rules this meant that the reparation action was effectively challenging the prison rules. It was held that the action, challenging the substantive merits rather than alleging procedural impropriety, was incompetent.

In *Shetland Line (1984) Ltd v. Secretary of State for Scotland*,[31] two **19–13** shipping companies had submitted erroneous projections for three financial years which were based on wrong information from the Scottish Office. Other companies had submitted projections which had been made on the

---

[26] *West v. Secretary of State for Scotland*, 1992 S.L.T. 636.

[27] See, *e.g. Associated Picture Houses v. Wednesbury Corporation* [1948] 1 K.B. 223; *Council of Civil Service Unions v. Minister for the Civil Service* [the GCHQ case] [1985] A.C. 374; *Shetland Line (1984) Ltd v. Secretary of State for Scotland*, 1996 S.L.T. 653. For the substantive grounds see Finch & Ashton, *Administrative Law in Scotland* (1997, W. Green); *Stair Memorial Encyclopaedia*, Vol 1, *sub voce* "Administrative Law".

[28] *MacNaughton v. Macnaughton's Trs.* 1953 S.L.T. 240, *per* L.J.-C. Thomson at 244.

[29] *Marco's Leisure Ltd v. West Lothian District Licensing Board*, 1994 S.L.T. 129.

[30] 1996 S.L.T. 575.

[31] 1996 S.L.T. 653.

correct basis, and this resulted in the two companies' subsidies under the scheme being less than if their projections and relevant invoices had been correctly submitted. There is a foreseeable but-for loss in such a case. The companies sought *inter alia* damages. Lord Johnston held *inter alia* that damages were not awardable in respect of the consequences of a decision of a Minister of the Crown in the absence of misfeasance or an abuse of power amounting to bad faith, although a duty of care might arise in respect of the manner in which a power was exercised; even if there were a claim in negligence, in the circumstances it should be pursued in a separate action for reparation and not by continuing the petition for judicial review. He said:

> "Counsel was not very specific as to how a duty of care would arise when the minister was simply exercising a statutory power which did not in itself create an obvious tort, but his submission was that it was perfectly possible as a matter of law for a minister in the exercise of a statutory decision making power to owe a duty of care in negligence to an ultimate recipient or beneficiary of that decision, and would be liable if that duty was breached causing loss to the latter. In the present case the negligence was said to be the failure on the part of the minister or his officials properly to investigate the basis upon which the second respondents' claims were being made. That amounted to a negligent act by omission, giving rise to a potential liability in damages to the petitioners as being directly affected as a result of the negligence. Not surprisingly counsel could not produce a direct authority with this proposition other than pointing to the numerous cases in the footnote of the passage from *Halsbury* to which he had referred me. Furthermore, it would appear that the balance of the academic view, as epitomised by Professor Wade [*Administrative Law* (6th. ed.)] at p. 780, is that a court would not award damages against public authorities merely because they had made some order which turns out to be *ultra vires* unless there was malice or conscious abuse. Thus it was apparent that counsel was seeking to extend the long established view that ministers could be responsible in damages for misfeasance or abuse of office involving, in the latter case, bad faith, to the additional context of simple negligence as admitting a further claim for damages if the facts fitted."[32]

Lord Johnson then expanded upon the reasons why reparation, even if there were a claim in negligence, could not be sought in this judicial review:

> "Even if there was a claim in negligence, in my opinion, it should not be pursued in an action relating to judicial review. At the end of his submissions counsel for the petitioner was effectively arguing that he might have an action for reparation giving rise to a claim for damages. If so, it is clear to me that he should make that by way of separate action and not as an addendum to a petition for judicial review which started seeking a wholly different remedy, namely reduction of certain ministerial decisions. I appreciate that the Rules of Court permit damages to

---

[32] At 657.

be awarded in proceedings for judicial review and that does appear to have happened on at least one occasion (*Kelly v. Monklands District Council* [1986 S.L.T. 169]). In my opinion, however, in this case, to allow the petition to be continued for such claim to be first averred and then quantified would create a procedural shambles. There is presently no prejudice to the petitioners in this context as regards passage of time. If therefore the claim sought by counsel can be substantiated, the appropriate action will enable the very complex legal questions to be ventilated and also require quantification of damage. By the appropriate action I mean a separate action for reparation indicating the existence and breach of an alleged duty of care, between the parties. Despite counsel's submissions I do not consider that any decision as to the lawfulness of the decision itself turns on this question, which must relate to how the minister went about arming himself with the requisite knowledge."[33]

Restitution

Depending on the wrong, the easiest way for a wrongdoer to make the **19–14** matter good again is to make restitution. If I steal your book the wrong is redressed by ordering its return. Although there has been a wrong there has been no damage, although there may be some element of loss of use or consequential loss where a car is stolen (as opposed to most books). The case where there is no loss but a gain in the hands of the defender is met by what is called an award of restitutionary damages for the wrong which is discussed elsewhere in this book.[34] One of the most prominent indigenous legal wrongs is spuilzie[35]—the primary remedy for taking of the property of another was to restore the property.

Violent Profits

The rationale of violent profits is not entirely clear. Erskine speaks of all **19–15** profits that might have been made.[36] Bankton speaks of profits that could have been made.[37] Stair speaks of the profits that the greatest industry could procure.[38] Erskine speaks of full profits, whether by the owner possessing or by letting.[39] Stair referred to the remedy as being partly penal.[40] On balance it seems to be a primitive way of dealing with consequential loss. The attempt is to compensate for the loss of use by setting the highest possible figure in respect of usable assets and leaving the wrongdoer the burden of trying to make the complicated argument. While the view has been expressed elsewhere in this book that some form of exemplary or punitive damages is the kind of thing that a system may

---

[33] At 658.
[34] Chap. 18.
[35] See Chaps 1 and 6.
[36] III.7.6.
[37] I,276.
[38] IV,29,2.
[39] II,6,54.
[40] IV,29,2.

properly adopt, it is submitted that violent profits ought to be formally abolished, perhaps in a consultation exercise considering the related issues. Courts are now well able to estimate the various financial issues.

Self-Help

19–16 Self-help is the first port of call of the client and now the last resort of the system. It is economically efficient and empowering. It eliminates transaction costs and delay. So far as infringements with interests are concerned which do not cause damage then self-help can be most effective.

19–17 Taking nuisance as an example, where there is a festering dungheap in a person's neighbour's garden, the easiest way of putting an end to this wrong (assuming it to be a nuisance) would for the person to shift it and charge his neighbour for any expense thereby incurred—abatement. It immediately mitigates consequences such as illness from the noxious fumes. Can this be done? The difficulty is that a trespass would be needed to do so.[41] Should the wrongs be balanced? Is there a general modern principle that the "rule of law" also requires a "process of law"? In principle self-help should be permissible. In the case of moveables, A takes B's ball. B sees it in A's garden. Why should he not take it back?[42] Is it better if it is lying in his garden or just outside in the street? The same arguments seem to apply as set out above. The civil courts exist to allow these matters to be thrashed out expensively and peacefully. One solution seems to have vanished—the possessory interdict which allowed the restoration of the relatively recent status quo. What could encourage self-help is the attitude of the law towards the self-helper. If self-help recapture is carried out without breach of the civil law—as where a car is re-possessed from the street in broad daylight—it is very difficult to suggest an action for spuilzie, especially if met by a counterclaim from the owner for breach of contract or wrongful use. An illuminating historical analysis appears in *Rae & Cooper v. Davidson*[43] in relation to agricultural holdings. Apparently in the 19th. century the *brevi manu* remedy had resulted in so many actions for wrongful eviction that it was difficult to persuade a sheriff officer to carry it out.[44] It was a matter of concession in the vitriolic and expensive neighbourhood dispute in *Rae & Cooper* that if a party had a right of access he could not *brevi manu* build his own road.[45]

State Systems

(i) Workmen's Compensation

19–18 The title of this section is deliberately archaic. It is helpful to show that for a very long time the common law system has not been thought sufficient to meet the need for accident compensation. The Workmens Compensation Act 1897 can be taken as the first significant intervention of the state in

---

[41] See *Giels v. Thomson* (1872) 10 M. 327.
[42] See Bell, Comm., II, 70 and *Guthrie v. Morren and Guthrie*, 1940 S.L.T. (Sh. Ct) 33.
[43] 1955 S.L.T. 25.
[44] *ibid.*, *per* L.J.-C. Thomson at 29.
[45] *per* Lord Wylie at 750.

compensating other than through the delict system. That model has stayed in place, although an over-arching welfare state which grew up in the twentieth century provides a large range of benefits for many occasions which can often be seen as compensating claimants as much as, or in addition to, redistributing wealth. The 1897 Act was extended in 1900, repealed in 1906, re-enacted in 1923 and consolidated in 1925.[46] Unlike modern state benefits which are dealt with administratively, the courts had a role by way of arbitration and could deal with interpretation by way of appeals on points of law. There were detailed provisions as to who was or was not a workman. Compensation was for injury by accident and not fault. There were many decisions on this point; the key concept was that of an unlooked-for mishap or untoward event which was not expected or designed.[47] Compensation was by way of weekly payments rather than a lump sum, unless the workman died, in which case members of his family obtained a lump sum based on his pay but subject to a maximum. This system co-existed with delictual claims through the courts.

At the time of writing people injured by accident at work still receive **19–19** compensation that those injured at home do not. The current scheme is the payment of industrial injuries benefit.[48] The claimant has to show that he sustained a personal injury as defined and cases under the previous schemes are relevant. There must have been an industrial accident arising out of and in the course of the employment. An accident does not include a process and there are other schemes covering prescribed diseases.[49] The employment test is broadly in line with the same test in the context of vicarious liability. The phrase "arising out of" negates a number of difficult causal questions while keeping the scheme tied to a kind of accident. Poynter and Martin[50] state that an accident is deemed to arise out of and in the course of the employment if the worker is helping people in an emergency or trying to save property at or near where the person is employed. For example, a milkman was covered by the scheme when he was trying to put out a fire at a customer's bungalow. Finally, an accident may also trigger a claim for disablement benefit. The effect is that many people injured at work or suffering disease as a result of it will receive state compensation. This is usually paid by a pension except in the more trivial cases. This helps explain why there are detailed recoupment provisions for cases where the worker exercises the right to sue in an ordinary delict action—it is to

---

[46] Hepple has recently explained that this legislation was actually at the time seen as something of a turning point between individualism and collectivism and cites D.G. Hanes, *The First British Workmens Compensation Act 1897* (1968) at p. 105 where the Act is described as "some sort of historical watershed".

[47] *Fenton v. Thorley* [1903] A.C. 443; *Raeburn v. Lochgelly Iron Co.*, 1927 S.C. 21.

[48] For full details, including full references to the unreported administrative decisions required to advise upon the scheme see R. Poynter and C. Martin, *Rights Guide to Non-Means-Tested Benefits* (Child Poverty Action Group, issued annually). "Industrial" is really a misnomer in this context as the scheme extends to most workplaces and work.

[49] The diseases are set out in Pt 1 of Sched. 1 to the Social Security (Industrial Injuries) (Prescribed Diseases) Regulations 1985 as amended and include, by way of illustrative examples only, repetitive strain injury, deafness, contraction of anthrax, tuberculosis, lead poisoning, pneumoconiosis, allergic rhinitis, some asthma and silicosis. It is however necessary for the illness to be linked to the type of employment specified in the column opposite to it and indeed for the illness to be caused by the employment.

[50] See n. 48 above.

restrict the double compensation that would result. In discussion of whether
the present delict system ought to be replaced by a system of state
compensation, this fully functioning model, which in some form has been in
existence for a very long time and which has perhaps successfully compensated many more individuals than the entire legion of delict cases both
reported and unreported, ought to be recalled.

(ii) Motor Insurers Bureau

19–20 Third Party insurance is compulsory for drivers in the United Kingdom.
Many drivers do not buy policies. Therefore, some people injured by
impecunious uninsured drivers have no redress through the delict system. It
would have been possible to establish a government fund. However, for the
moment this mischief is met by the Motor Insurers Bureau ("MIB"). The
involvement of the state in this scheme is shadowy.[51] The MIB is run and
funded by the insurance industry. It was set up in 1946. Membership is
compulsory for all insurers under the Road Traffic Act 1974. The scheme
operates under two agreements between the MIB and the Secretary of
State.[52] They cover three categories: (1) the identified uninsured motorist;
(2) an identified motorist where insurance cover is legally avoidable at the
instance of the insurers or where the risk is not one precisely covered; and
(3) untraced drivers (who may or may not be insured). Since 1988 property
damage is recoverable except under the untraced drivers scheme. Even then
the comprehensively insured driver will not recover repair costs and thus
will not recover his no claims bonus (the additional premium is recoverable
if it can be properly established). These agreements constitute the first
aspect of the state's involvement. The other is the general background: if
the insurers had not set up this scheme, there might have been compulsory
legislation. As matters stand, in law, a person who establishes liability
cannot sue the board—they have done no wrong and there is no contractual
nexus. Even though the MIB founders are insurers they are not legally
insurers for the purposes of interim damages.[53] *Ius quaesitum tertio* might
be the answer if it were not for the fact that beneficiary is not defined. Lord
Dilhorne complained that it was wrong that the court was required to give
judgment against a person not liable in law.[54] However, because the scheme
covers expenses, the court should not reduce to nil a legally-aided
defender's liability for expenses where the defence has in fact been run by
the MIB.[55] Campbell indicates that 1,250,000 drivers in the United Kingdom are driving without insurance.[56]

---

[51] Atiyah, pp. 247 *et seq.*
[52] See E. Campbell, "The Uninsured Driver, the MIB and the Insurance Disk System"
(1994) 39 J.L.S. 170 for a full exposition of the practical aspects of the scheme.
[53] *Martin v. McKinsley*, 1980 S.L.T. (Notes) 15; See also *Fergusson v. McGrandles*, 1993
S.L.T. 822.
[54] *Albert v. MIB* [1972] A.C. 301.
[55] *Douglas v. Cunningham*, 1966 S.L.T. (Notes) 7.
[56] E. Campbell, "The Uninsured Driver, the MIB and the Insurance Disk System" (1994)
39 J.L.S. 170, n. 1.

The present scheme in force[57] provides as follows. The principal obliga- **19–21** tion is for the MIB to pay the relevant sum[58] to or to the satisfaction of the claimant or cause the sum to be paid to the claimant where the claimant has obtained judgment against any person in a court in Great Britain.[59] This obligation applies whether or not the person liable to satisfy the judgment is in fact covered by a contract of insurance and whatever may be the cause of the failure to satisfy the judgment.[60] There are many conditions precedent to the MIB accepting liability. The application must be in proper form as defined.[61] Notices which are required must be by recorded delivery to the MIB with receipt or by fax with fax transmission report produced.[62] Notice must be given of proceedings within 14 days[63] to the insurer—where there is an insurance contract and the insurer can be ascertained—or otherwise on the MIB.[64] The scheme defines notice rather onerously as including notice that proceedings have been started, a copy of the writ and the execution of service, a copy or details of any insurance policy, copies of all correspondence with the claimant or his solicitor relevant to the loss, injury or damage or the insurance contract and any other information which the MIB may reasonably specify.[65] Notice must be given within seven days of the filing of a defence or any amendments or productions or the fixing of a proof and any supplementary matter required thereanent.[66] Notice must be given of the intention to apply for judgment.[67] Importantly for routine practice the MIB incurs no liability unless the claimant has as soon as reasonably practicable demanded the information to which he is entitled under section 154(1) of the Road Traffic Act, and in the event of not receiving it has reported the matter to the police and in addition has used all reasonable endeavours to obtain the name and address of the registered keeper of the vehicle, or if asked by the MIB has done as they say.[68] The MIB are not liable if the claimant does not allow them to run a case in his name or to allow them to be joined as a party.[69] There is no liability unless the claimant assigns the unsatisfied judgment or undertakes to repay to the MIB any sum recovered himself.[70] The MIB does not pay a claim under the excess of £300.[71] It is not liable beyond £250,000.[72]

---

[57] New Supplemental Agreement dated August 13, 1999, effective October 1, 1999.

[58] A sum payable or remaining payable under an unsatisfied judgment, including an amount payable or remaining payable in respect of interest on that sum, and either the whole of the costs awarded by the court as part of that judgment or, where the judgment includes an award in respect of a liability which is not a relevant liability, such proportion of those costs as the relevant liability bears to the total sum awarded under the judgment: see para. 1.

[59] para. 5(1). The obligations of the MIB may be carried out by agents: para. 22.

[60] para. 5(2). An unsatisfied judgment is one not satisfied in full within seven days from the date upon which the claimant became entitled to enforce it: para. 1.

[61] para. 7.

[62] para. 8.

[63] Time limits are specially defined in para. 2.

[64] para. 9(1). Nervous lawyers should do both.

[65] para. 9(2). The rules are very tight in England and Wales—see para. 10.

[66] para. 11.

[67] para. 12.

[68] para. 13.

[69] para. 14.

[70] para. 15.

[71] para. 16(2), para. 1.

[72] para. 16.

Compensation from other sources may be deducted as from the Policy-holders Protection Board or any other source.[73]

This obligation is subject to many exceptions all of which must be very carefully examined by practitioners[74]: (a) a claim incurred by the user of a vehicle owned or in the possession of the Crown,[75] unless responsibility for the existence of a contract of insurance under the Road Traffic Act in relation to the vehicle had been undertaken by another person (whether or not the person liable was in fact covered by a contract of insurance)[76] or the relevant liability was in fact covered by a contract of insurance;[77] (b) a claim arising out of the use of a vehicle which is not required by virtue of section 144 of the 1988 Road Traffic Act unless the use is in fact covered by such a contract[78]; (c) a claim by or for the benefit of a person other than the person suffering death, injury or other damage which is made either in respect of a cause of action which has been assigned[79] or pursuant to a right of subrogation or contractual or other right[80]; (d) a claim in respect of damage to a motor vehicle or losses arising therefrom where at the time the damage was sustained there was not in force in relation to the use of that vehicle a contract of insurance as is required by the Road Traffic Act and the claimant either knew or ought to have known that that was the case[81]; (e) a claim which is made by a claimant who at the time of the use giving rise to the liability was voluntarily allowing himself to be carried in the vehicle and before the commencement of his journey in the vehicle or after such commencement he could reasonably be expected to have alighted from it and knew or ought to have known that—(i) the vehicle had been stolen or unlawfully taken[82]; the vehicle was being used without there being in force in relation to its use a contract of insurance required by the Road Traffic Act[83]; the vehicle was being used in the course or furtherance of a crime[84]; or the vehicle was being used as a means of escape from or avoidance of lawful apprehension. In relation to this the burden of proof is on the MIB but in the absence of evidence to the contrary, proof by the MIB of any of the following matters will be taken as proof of the claimant's knowledge that the vehicle was driven without insurance, namely that the claimant was the owner or registered keeper of the vehicle or had caused or permitted its use[85]; or that the claimant knew the vehicle was being used by

---

[73] para. 17.
[74] A vehicle which has been unlawfully removed from the possession of the Crown shall be taken to continue in that possession whilst it is so removed (para. 1(5)(a)). References to a person being carried in a vehicle include references to his being carried upon, entering, getting on to and alighting from the vehicle (para. 1(5)(b)). "Owner" in relation to a vehicle which is the subject of a hiring agreement means the person in possession of the vehicle under that agreement (para. 1(5)(c)).
[75] para. 6(1)(a).
[76] para. 6(1)(a)(i).
[77] para. 6(1)(a)(ii).
[78] para. 6(1)(b).
[79] para. 6(1)(c)(i).
[80] para. 6(1)(c)(ii).
[81] para. 6(1)(d).
[82] para. 6(1)(e)(i).
[83] para. 6(1)(e)(ii).
[84] para. 6(1)(e)(iii).
[85] para. 6(3)(a).

a person who was below the minimum age at which he could be granted a licence authorising the driving of a vehicle of that class[86]; that the claimant knew that the person driving the vehicle was disqualified from holding or obtaining a driving licence[87]; or that the claimant knew that the user of the vehicle was neither its owner nor registered keeper nor an employee of the owner or registered keeper of any other vehicle.[88] Disputes are to be resolved by the Secretary of State.[89]

The Supplementary Agreement does not cover cases where the owner or driver is untraced. Such cases are dealt with under the following scheme.

The MIB provide for cases of untraced drivers formerly under a 1972 **19–22** Agreement and now under a 1996 agreement. There must be an untraced driver responsible for death or personal injury. It must be a case such that on balance of probabilities the untraced person would be liable to pay. The liability needs to be one which ought to be covered by compulsory insurance. Cases where the car is used as a weapon—*e.g.* to run down the applicant—are not covered. The application must be made within three years of the accident.[90] The agreement does not apply where the vehicle was a Crown vehicle; where the applicant knew the car was taken without lawful authority unless he reasonably believed the owner would consent; or where it would have been unreasonable for him to bale out on discovering the vehicle was stolen or where he knew the vehicle was uninsured.[91] The incident has to have been reported to the police within 14 days or as soon as the applicant could reasonably do so and the applicant must co-operate with the police.[92] The amount the MIB pay is to reflect a court award. It does not include property damage or loss of earnings if the earnings have in fact been paid.[93] Complex provisions exist in cases of contribution but the important effect is that if any finding is made against a joint wrongdoer, the MIB are liable for the balance.[94] An award is subject to co-operation with the MIB's inquiries. They can require a statutory declaration to be made. The decision must be notified with reasons setting out the circumstances of the decision and reasons for any refusal. There is a right of appeal to an arbitrator.

The MIB has been involved in many reported Scottish cases; involvement may be assumed in many cases not in the reports. Sometimes the MIB is convened as a defender and sometimes it enters by minute of sist.[95]

---

[86] para. 6(3)(b).
[87] para. 6(3)(c).
[88] para. 6(4). For the purposes of para. 6(1)(e) knowledge which the claimant has or ought to have includes knowledge of matters of which he could reasonably be expected to have been aware had he not been under the self-induced influence of drink or drugs: para. 6(4).
[89] para. 19.
[90] Untraced Ag. para. 1. There is no delay provision for non-age as in common law cases.
[91] Untraced Ag para. 1(2).
[92] para. 1(1)(g).
[93] cl. 4.
[94] Untraced Ag. para. 5(4) and for appeals Untraced Ag. para. 5(5).
[95] See, *e.g. Clark v. McLean*, 1995 S.L.T. 235; *Paterson v. Hampton*, 1994 S.L.T. 1231; *McFarlane v. Breen*, 1994 S.L.T. 1320; *Fergusson v. McGrandles*, 1993 S.L.T. 822; *Ashcroft's C.B. v. Stewart*, 1988 S.L.T. 163; *Sloan v. Triplett*, 1985 S.L.T. 294; *Kay v. Morrison's Reps*, 1984 S.L.T. 175; *Meanan v. MIB*, 1971 S.L.T. 264.

(iii) The Criminal Injuries Compensation Scheme

19–23 The Criminal Injuries Compensation Scheme ("CICS")[96] began in 1964 and was designed to assist victims of crime who will normally find a delict action against the wrongdoer worth little. The ad hoc, political, nature of the scheme means that it has changed with the times and with the prevailing political feeling. It lacks the development of the common law but the courts have helped to shape it through judicial review applications. At first the term "crime of violence" was not defined in the scheme but cases required it to be tightened up to deal with "proper" crime.[97] In 1994 major changes were attempted by the Government to apply a tariff, not seen in Scots law since the *Quoniam Attachiamenta*.[98] This was partly as a response to the fact that many considered the Criminal Injuries Compensation Board to be failing to operate the scheme successfully. Cost may also have been a factor as the tariff compensation is often much less than common law damages, upon which CICS awards were originally based. The new scheme was successfully challenged by a number of trade unions,[99] but the government reintroduced the tariff while putting the scheme on a statutory footing with the Criminal Injuries Compensation Act 1995 ("CICA").

19–24 Claims are handled by the Criminal Injuries Compensation Authority ("CICA").[1] A basic outline of the CICA and its place in the overall scheme of things is set out above.[2] As explained in Chapter 1 the scheme is now under the statutory authority of the Criminal Injuries Compensation Act 1995. Decisions taken by claims officers are subject to review and appeal to adjudicators, but not to the Secretary of State.[3] Once the process is exhausted the CICA can be judicially reviewed on ordinary principles.[4] An application must be made in writing on an official form. It "should be made" as soon as possible after the incident and must be *received* by the authority within two years although the claims officer may waive this time limit where he considers that, by reason of the particular circumstances of the case, it is reasonable and in the interests of justice to do so.[5] It is for the applicant to make out his case; the CICA will not pay for his legal representation.[6] The standard of proof is balance of probabilities.[7] The officer can arrange for medical examination and the applicant's reasonable expenses must be met.[8] A guide to the scheme is published by the CICA. It

---

[96] At the time of writing the applicable scheme is that issued on Dec. 12, 1995. See generally P. Duff, "Criminal Injuries Compensation, Nervous Shock and Secondary Victims", 1992 S.L.T. (News) 311 and "The 1996 Criminal Injuries Compensation Scheme", 1996 S.L.T. (News) 221 at p. 239; A.S. Pollock, "Criminal Injuries Compensation: the Tariff" (1996) 40 J.L.S. 93. See also Atiyah, Chap. 13.
[97] See para. 19–26.
[98] For a trenchant and well argued critique see I. Walker, "Criminal Injuries Compensation: A government betrayal" [1994] J.P.I.L. 47.
[99] *R. v. Secretary of State for the Home Department* [1995] 2 W.L.R. 464.
[1] para. 1.
[2] Chap. 1.
[3] paras 2 and 3. There are detailed rules on appeals in paras 50–82.
[4] Under the old scheme see *S v. CICB*, 1997 G.W.D. 5–172.
[5] para. 17.
[6] para. 18.
[7] para. 19.
[8] para. 20.

sets out where appropriate the criteria by which decisions will normally be reached.[9] Its status is therefore most uncertain but it should obviously be consulted in connection with any application for judicial review. "Appropriate" and "normally" are debatable concepts in this context.

No compensation is payable where the criminal injury was sustained **19–25** before October 1, 1979 and the victim and assailant were living together at the time as members of the same family.[10] Criminal injury is defined to mean one or more of the following: "personal injuries" sustained in Great Britain and directly attributable to a crime of violence (including arson, fire-raising or an act of poisoning)[11]; or an offence of trespass on a railway[12]; or the apprehension or attempted apprehension of an offender or a suspected offender, the prevention or attempted prevention of an offence, or the giving of help to any constable who is engaged in any such activity.

"Personal injury" includes physical injury (including fatal injury), mental **19–26** injury (that is, a medically recognised psychiatric or psychological illness) and disease (that is, a medically recognised illness or condition). Mental injury or disease may either result directly from the physical injury or occur without any physical injury, but compensation will not be payable for mental injury alone unless the applicant was put in reasonable fear of immediate physical harm to his own person[13]; or (b) had a close relationship of love and affection with another person at the time when that person sustained physical (including fatal) injury directly attributable[14] to conduct within categories noted above[15] and that relationship still subsists,[16] and the applicant either witnessed and was present on the occasion when the other person sustained the injury or was closely involved in the immediate aftermath; or was the non-consenting victim of a sexual offence (which does not include a victim who consented in fact but was deemed in law not to have consented)[17]; or as defined in detail and more widely, persons such as train drivers running down trespassers on the railway.[18] It is not necessary for the assailant to be convicted or even identified and conduct counts as a criminal injury, even if it could not on the basis of non-age or diplomatic immunity form the basis of a criminal prosecution.[19] To avoid becoming entangled in road traffic law and overlapping with the MIB scheme, the CICA scheme does not apply to cases where the injury is attributable to the use of a vehicle except where the vehicle is used so as to deliberately inflict or attempt to inflict injury on any person.[20] Accidental injuries incurred

---

[9] para. 21.
[10] para. 7(b).
[11] para. 8(a).
[12] para. 8(b). This is presumably for the benefit of train drivers.
[13] para. 9(a).
[14] In *W. v. CICB*, 1999 G.W.D. 14–631 a judicial review was successful where the applicant had been refused a claim based on the applicant's psychological distress after finding out about her husband's prolonged sexual abuse of their daughters. The basis of rejection had been that the injury was not "directly attributable" to a crime of violence. The Lord Ordinary held that this meant a link in time and space in a common sense way and not as in common law causation.
[15] para. 9(b).
[16] para. 9(b)(i)—unless the victim has since died.
[17] para. 9(c).
[18] para. 9(d).
[19] para. 10.
[20] para. 11.

while preventing crime do not attract compensation unless the person was taking an exceptional risk, which was justified in all the circumstances.[21] While these extended definitions seem over-cumbersome it is probably hoped that they allow the paid officials to deal with claims swiftly and cheaply instead of there being difficult questions of interpretation and legal science evidenced in *Gray v. CICB*[22] and the cases therein referred to, which were decided under the previous Criminal Injuries Compensation Scheme, paragraph 4(a).[23]

19–27	An award may be reduced or withheld if the claims officer considers that: the applicant failed to take, without delay, all reasonable steps to inform the police—or other body or person considered by the authority to be appropriate for the purpose—of the circumstances giving rise to the injury;[24] or the applicant failed to co-operate with the police or other authority in attempting to bring the assailant to justice[25]; or the applicant failed to give all reasonable assistance to the CICA or other body or person in connection with the application[26]; or the conduct of the applicant before, during or after the incident giving rise to the application makes it inappropriate that a full award or any award at all be made[27]; or the applicant's character as shown by his criminal convictions (excluding spent convictions) or by evidence available to the claims officer makes it inappropriate that a full award or any award at all be made.[28] These exclusions apply in death claims.[29] An award will only be made if the claims officer is satisfied that there is no likelihood that an assailant would benefit if an award were made,[30] or that it would be against the interests of an applicant under the age of 18 for an award to be made.[31] In cases of violence in the family arising after October 1, 1979 an award will be withheld unless the assailant has been prosecuted in connection with the offence, except where the claims officer considers that there are practical, technical or other good reasons why a prosecution has not been brought[32]; and in a case between adults an award will be withheld unless the officer is satisfied that the applicant and the assailant stopped living in the same household before the application was made and are unlikely to share the same household again.[33] A man and woman living together as man and wife are treated as members of the same family.[34]

19–28	Previously damages were based on the common law with all its diffi-culties. To save cost in administration, if not also in actual payments, the present scheme introduces a tariff which sets out the amount of payment

---

[21] para. 12.
[22] 1992 S.C.L.R. 777. See also *C v. CICB*, 1999 G.W.D. 21–985.
[23] See too *P's C.B. v. CICB*, 1997 S.L.T. 1180 (under the 1969 scheme).
[24] para. 13(a).
[25] para. 13(b).
[26] para. 13(c).
[27] para. 13(d). "Appropriate" is a question-begging concept in this context.
[28] para. 13(e).
[29] para. 14.
[30] para. 15(a).
[31] para. 15(b).
[32] para. 16(a).
[33] para. 16(b).
[34] para. 16.

under an award.[35] There are provisions for cases for which there is no provision[36] and for using the tariff in trickier cases such as where there are multiple injuries and the rules differ according to whether multiple injuries are serious or minor. Serious multiple injuries are compensated by awarding the tariff for the highest rate and by adding 10 per cent of the second highest and 5 per cent for the third highest.[37]

Loss of earning is recoverable but only from 28 weeks after the date of **19–29** the applicant's incapacity for work.[38] Past loss is computed on the applicant's emoluments and what they would have been; any emoluments actually received; any changes in pension rights and social security clawback provisions; and any pension payable whether or not as a result of the injury.[39] Detailed provisions exist for calculating future loss based on a multiplier laid down in the scheme.[40] The officer may choose a lump sum instead.[41] The multiplicand is not permitted to exceed one-and-a-half times the gross average industrial earnings as published by the Department of Education and Employment.[42] Special expenses may be recovered where the applicant has been incapacitated for more than 28 weeks, whether or not that person has been working.[43] The award may also cover NHS costs; costs of physical aids; private medical costs where reasonable; accommodation costs; equipment costs; or residential costs provided where these are considered necessary as a direct consequence of the injury. Unpaid care provided at home by a relative or friend will be compensated by assessing the carer's loss of earnings or earning capacity. Future cost of care is also compensatable.[44]

Death claims have separate rules. The estate only gets funeral expenses **19–30** and does not inherit the applicant's claim.[45] This arrangement prevents the state's bounty being available for the deceased's credit card bills but does allow the claim in effect to transmit to a certain extent. A qualifying claimant is the spouse of the deceased being for these purposes a person who was living with the deceased as husband and wife in the same household immediately before the date of death and who if not formally married had been so living throughout the two years before that date, or a spouse or former spouse of the deceased who was financially supported by the deceased immediately before the date of death; or a parent of the deceased whether or not the natural parent, provided that person was accepted by the deceased as a parent of the family or a child of the deceased or an accepted child.[46] Tariff compensation is paid with an additional amount if dependency is established, but dependency is not

---

[35] para. 22(a). The tariff appears as an appendix to the scheme. It will no doubt change from time to time and so is not set out here.

[36] paras 28 and 29.

[37] para. 26.

[38] para. 30.

[39] para. 31.

[40] para. 32.

[41] para. 33.

[42] para. 34.

[43] para. 35.

[44] para. 36.

[45] para. 37; para. 44.

[46] para. 38.

established where the deceased's only normal income was from social security benefit.[47] Dependency is calculated on the same basis as past and future loss of earnings.[48] A claim for parental services is available to persons under 18 at a tariff level with a multiplier to cover the years until that person reaches 18.

Actions of Harassment

19–31 An actual or apprehended breach of the right to be free from harassment can be the subject of a civil claim.[49] In such an action the court can, without prejudice to any other remedies, award damages[50] or grant interdict or interim interdict.[51]

If the court is satisfied that it is appropriate for it to do so in order to protect the person from further harassment, it can grant a non-harassment order requiring the defender to refrain from such conduct in relation to the pursuer as is specified in the order for such period, including an indeterminate period as is specified.[52] An application can be made at any time to have such an order varied or revoked.[53] A person who is found to be in breach of a non-harassment order is guilty of an imprisonable offence.[54]

---

[47] paras 39 and 40.
[48] para. 41.
[49] Protection from Harassment Act 1997, s. 8(1)(2).
[50] s. 8(5)(a). The damages can include damages for anxiety and any financial loss arising from it (s. 8(6)), as where a high earner is frightened to go to work.
[51] s. 8(5)(b)(i). See *Furber v. Furber*, 1999 S.L.T. (Sh. Ct) 26 (appeal against granting of interim anti-harassment order).
[52] s. 8(5)(b)(ii).
[53] s. 8(7).
[54] s. 9.

CHAPTER 20

DEFENCES

Introduction

There are many things a defender may seek to do to avoid being found **20–1**
liable. Many of these strategies are not defences but non-constitutive
factors. Other defences are considered in what it is hoped is their proper
context. The following list is intended to be a comprehensive list of
defences which may be available in Scots law and will act as a useful
checklist for the practitioner and a map to the location of the law on each
topic in this book. Because nearly every case raised by the ordinary
practitioner is met by a plea of contributory negligence this is treated in
some detail. While the opposite is the case with *volenti non fit injuria* it is of
some theoretical interest and so is given an extended treatment here. As
well as defences a defender may be fortunate enough to find himself
entitled to some form of immunity.[1]

The following are the main defence arguments: No duty[2]; no cause[3]; no **20–2**
harm[4]; no breach of any duty[5]; denial of the facts; statutory authority;
damnum fatale; Act of God[6]; contributory negligence[7]; sole fault[8]; *res
judicata*[9]; *volenti non fit injuria*[10]; assumption of risk[11]; *veritas*[12]; privilege[13];
qualified privilege[14]; fair comment[15]; the defender is immune[16]; the pursuer
does not have title and interest to sue[17]; self-defence[18]; necessity[19]; and
disclaimers and exemptions.[20]

---

[1] Chap. 2.
[2] Chap. 10.
[3] Chap. 10.
[4] Chap. 10.
[5] Chap. 10.
[6] para. 6–22.
[7] para. 20–3.
[8] Chap. 10.
[9] Chap. 3.
[10] para. 22–1.
[11] paras 20–15 *et seq.*
[12] Chap. 8.
[13] Chap. 8.
[14] Chap. 8.
[15] Chap. 8.
[16] Chap. 2.
[17] Chap. 2.
[18] Chap. 4.
[19] Chap. 4.
[20] Chap. 10.

CONTRIBUTORY NEGLIGENCE

20-3 People should take care for their own safety. Potential defenders are entitled to take into account that potential pursuers will look after themselves. Today contributory negligence reduces the value of the pursuer's claim. Its history is not at all as clear as one might expect. The case which established that the law of Scotland was in happy consonance with the prevailing law of England, *McNaughton v. Caledonian Railway*[21] was rather special in being a decision only on whether a jury verdict did actually meet the issue. Yet hardly any time at all before that, in the middle of the nineteenth century, Lord President Boyle had charged a jury in terms that were very similar to those which would be used today. The facts of *Hislop v. Durham*[22] were that a young girl fell into an unfenced coal pit. It was strongly argued that she had either tried to kill herself or at the very least it seems to have been obvious, on the evidence, that she was very drunk. The Lord President charged on this point as follows:

> "If you are satisfied that the defender is liable, you will give fair and reasonable damages with reference to what has occurred, the injured feelings of the relatives, and the proved industrious habits of the deceased. But you will also take into consideration the state of the deceased, which in some measure led to this dreadful catastrophe."[23]

So it is at least arguable that a wrong turn, perhaps influenced by English cases, took place in the mid-nineteenth century only to be fixed in the mid-twentieth. Even then it has to be appreciated that the doctrine did not mean that any mistake by the defender lost him his damages:

> "It is not sufficient to disentitle to damages that there has been fault on the pursuer's part, that he had been doing something which strictly he ought not to have done, and without which having been done the injury would not have occurred. The fault must be such as to have directly conduced to the injury suffered, and not merely remotely connected with it; for, in that case, it is not to be considered as contributory to the injury within the principle that fault or negligence on the part of the individual injured shall afford a good answer to a claim by him for damages against a defender who has also been guilty of fault or negligence . . . In a legal view, it, in the question of the abstract right to damages, forms no part of the case, the negligence of the defenders alone being held to have caused the injury, whatever weight it may be entitled to in assessing the amount of the damages. But, on the other hand, if while there was fault on the part of the defenders, directly conducing to or causing the injury, there was at the same time fault on the part of the individual injured, by rashness, or want of the care which he was bound to exercise, which also directly contributed to the injury, then damages cannot be recovered by him."[24]

---

[21] (1858) 21 D. 160.
[22] (1842) 4 D. 1168.
[23] *ibid.* at 1171.
[24] *McNaughton* at 166–167.

The agony rule and the dilemma principle

The law was changed so that contributory negligence is not a complete **20–4** defence, but the language of the law is still such that it is said that the pursuer has been *guilty* of contributory negligence. Doctrines developed to avoid the rigour of the rule and two—the agony rule and the last opportunity rule—are still referred to.[25] The agony rule demands that the court should not take a strict view of the pursuer's behaviour when the defender has put him in a difficult situation. The agony rule is a phase of the dilemma principle which latter applies where there is time for a choice.[26] It is submitted that the same result would apply now, the modern reformulation of the reasonable man test being one of defender objectivity. In *Windram v. Robertson*[27] the Lord President pointed out that sometimes being in a dilemma (which implies having some time to think) means that the right thing to do is follow the well-known rules:

" But if a person, through no fault of his own, is in a state, from the circumstances of the case, in which he cannot tell what is the right and proper manoeuvre, then more than ever, it seems to me, he is absolutely bound to stick to the rules and to leave them at his own peril."[28]

In *McNair v. Glasgow Corporation*[29] the agony rule was held not to be applicable to a road accident. Lord Sands said that the maritime rule of maintaining course and speed until a stage of agony is reached does not apply to a main-road driver.[30]

---

[25] The last-opportunity rule has already been discussed and the softening of contributory negligence has resulted in its fading away in negligence cases. In *Calder v. Simpson*, 1994 S.L.T. 32 the sheriff principal said (at 33): "In the present case if the defender were to prove all of his averments it is perfectly possible that a reasonable sheriff might take the view that the pursuer showed a negligent disregard for his own safety in crossing the road where he did and further in running from a place of safety into a position of danger. With regard to the latter point it is not legitimate to argue as the pursuer's agent did, or to hold as the sheriff did, that the pursuer's actings can be excused by the 'agony rule'. In the first place as the pleadings stand the pursuer's case is not that he ran into the offside lane in the agony of the moment but that he was already in the offside lane when the defender's car approached and, in any event, the level of emergency in which he was placed depends upon disputed facts concerning the defender's speed and the parties' mutual visibility."

[26] See *Henderson v. Noble* (1897) 5 S.L.T. 177. The schooner Thames and the fishing boat Pilgrim were lying at anchor. The launch belonging to the Thames was returning from the shore with her skipper and boy and five of the Pilgrim's men when a hurricane blew up. The skipper of the Thames could not reach his own vessel without a rope, and the first bit of rope he tried was found too short. He was then hauled back to the Pilgrim, and a second rope was joined to the first. Before it could be used the anchor of the Pilgrim broke and it crashed into the Thames. It was held that the Pilgrim was not liable in damages. Although the defenders were not bound to anticipate the breaking of the anchor, they were bound to know that in a gale their boat might drag its anchor, or the chain might break. Lord Stormoth-Darling said (at 178): "It is not, however, the practice to judge by a very strict standard the conduct of seamen in what has been termed 'the agony of the collision,' and it cannot be said here that, on the whole, the 'Pilgrim' was to blame for the collision."

[27] (1905) 13 S.L.T. 157; (1906) 14 S.L.T. 178.

[28] *ibid.* at 159.

[29] 1923 S.L.T. 171.

[30] *ibid.* at 177. See also *McLean v. Bell*, 1932 S.L.T. 286.

Law Reform (Contributory Negligence) Act 1945

20–5 The Law Reform (Contributory Negligence) Act 1945 allowed the apportionment of responsibility which had been allowed in maritime cases since the Maritime Conventions Act 1911, as opposed to allowing the defence to completely exculpate the defender. The 1945 Act provides:

> "Where any person suffers damage[31] as the result partly of his own fault[32] and partly of the fault of any other person or persons, a claim in respect of that damage shall not be defeated by reason of the fault of the person suffering the damage, but the damages recoverable in respect thereof shall be reduced to such extent as the court thinks just and equitable having regard to the claimants share in the responsibility for the damage."[33]

The statute is a U.K. statute and so English cases are usefully considered. There, "just and equitable" has been construed as allowing negligence to be ignored in one case[34] but not so in another.[35] The fault in question is fault which causes the loss or damage not the fault causing the damage.[36] The issue is one of responsibility—it must be the operative cause. The English cases have canvassed whether allocation is by cause or blameworthiness.[37] The English Court of Appeal has expressed the view that small percentages, below 10 per cent, are not to be found.[38]

Children

20–6 While it is clear that there are difficulties with the ascription of responsibility to children as defenders, children have been held to be contributorily negligent for a long time.[39] It is easier to justify a complete exculpation based on the child being the sole cause of its injuries and not the fault of the defender than reducing the damages of a child for being childish. The main issue is the awareness of the child. In *Campbell v. Ord and Maddison*,[40] it was said:

> "Negligence implies a capacity to apprehend intelligently the duty, obligation, or precaution neglected, and that depends to a large degree

---

[31] Including loss of life or personal injury: s. 4.

[32] Negligence, breach of statutory duty or other act or omission which gives rise to a liability in tort or would, apart from this Act give rise to the defence of contributory negligence.

[33] s. 1.

[34] *Boothman v. British Northrop Ltd* (1972) 13 K.I.R. 112.

[35] *Hawkins v. Ian Ross (Castings) Ltd* [1970] 1 All E.R. 180.

[36] *Davies v. Swan Motor Co.* [1949] 2 K.B. 291.

[37] *Smith v. Bray* (1939) 56 T.L.R. 200; *Collins v. Hertfordshire C.C.* [1947] K.B. 598; *Weaver v. Commercial Process Co. Ltd* (1947) 63 T.L.R. 466.

[38] *Johnson v. Tennant Bros Ltd*, CA, Nov. 19, 1954, unreported.

[39] *Cass v. Edinburgh Tramways Co.*, 1909 S.C. 1068 (an important decision of the Inner House); *Frasers v. Edinburgh Street Tramway Co.* (1882) 10 R. 264; *Plantza v. Glasgow Corp.*, 1910 S.C. 786.

[40] (1873) 1 R. 149.

on the nature of that which he has neglected, as well as on the intelligence and maturity of the person said to have neglected it. The capacity to neglect is a question of fact in the individual case, as much so as negligence itself, which is always a question of fact."[41]

It should be remembered too that these decisions were taken when contributory negligence was a complete bar. There will not be contributory negligence by a child where the conduct is the very conduct that the pursuer had a duty to prevent. In *Wylie v. Lilley*[42] the Inner House rejected the argument that a child setting off a detonator which had essentially been left lying around was contributorily negligent under reference to the Privy Council advice in *Yachuk v. Oliver Blais Co. Ltd.* [43] It is perhaps interesting to note that in the famous *Hughes v. Lord Advocate*,[44] Lord Wheatley, at first instance, commented *obiter* that he did not consider the pursuer to have been contributorily negligent under reference to *Wylie*. The point which had been pled was not taken further. *Brogan's Tutors v. Glasgow District Council*[45] is another landmark. A child was electrocuted by an appliance installed by the defenders. The argument was that although the child could not himself be in any way contributorily negligent his parents could. Lord Wylie, utilising to an extent the passing of the 1945 Act, declined to follow a passage in Glegg[46] and dicta in *Hastie v. Edinburgh Corporation*.[47] He held that the negligence of the parents in allowing the child access to the appliance did not affect the pursuer's claim. He did this noting that the contrary rule, once applicable in England had been swept aside there.[48] He appreciated too that where a right of relief was unlikely to fall to the defender this was in a sense inequitable for having been only partially to blame, he carried the whole burden of damages.

The modern cases apply the same principles but apportionment is **20–7** possible. In *McKinnell v. White*[49] a child aged five was injured in a road accident. Liability was apportioned 50/50. In *Harvey v. Cairns*[50] a child aged six stepped into the path of a vehicle travelling at a speed which was normal for that particular stretch of road but excessive. The driver was unqualified and unsupervised. Lord Osborne considered that the child's conduct in running in front of the car was the main cause of the accident. Liability was held to fall two-thirds on the pursuer. In the same way, in *Banner's Tutor v. Kennedy's Trustees*,[51] a child aged five got out the back of a minibus and ran

---

[41] *ibid.*, *per* Lord Justice-Clerk Moncreiff at 153.
[42] 1961 S.L.T. (Notes) 33.
[43] [1949] A.C. 386.
[44] 1962 S.L.T. 90.
[45] 1978 S.L.T. (Notes) 47.
[46] *Reparation* (4th ed., 1955).
[47] 1907 15 S.L.T. 194. In *Hastie*, L.P. Dunedin (at 195) thought it is not expedient to lay down in general terms the precise duties lying on persons who have care of public places. He thought the proximate cause was not the existence of the pond but the fact that the child was unattended. If "parents cannot afford nurses to look after children, it is one of the results of the world as we find it." The problem was lack of proximate cause, not contributory negligence. The Lord Ordinary (Salvesen) had cited *Ross v. Keith* (1888) 16 R. 86 (Lord Young) with approval on the lack of any duty to fence.
[48] *Oliver v. Birmingham and Midland Omnibus Co.* [1933] 1 K.B. 35.
[49] 1971 S.L.T. (Notes) 61.
[50] 1989 S.L.T. 107.
[51] 1978 S.L.T. (Notes) 83.

into a lorry. She had been expressly warned by the minibus driver not to go out until he opened the door but he didn't take any actual steps to prevent her getting out. The court held that she was a girl of usual intelligence. She had had parental guidance about roads and had seen heavy traffic. She was held to be 20 per cent liable for the accident.

Roads

Roads

20–8 These case should be considered against the basic liability position set out above.[52] In *Buchanan v. Allan*[53] the passenger of a driver with a provisional licence was held one-third in contribution. The pursuer had not often driven with the defender and could not have had confidence in his driving ability. This seems unfair. A passenger should be entitled to assume that a driver properly in possession of the appropriate licence will drive safely, albeit perhaps cautiously and on quieter roads.[54] This also appears to be a case of inoperative negligence, if negligence it be at all. The negligence was not in any sense a cause of the injuries it only put the pursuer in the place where the operative negligence took effect. In *Morris v. Pirie*[55] a car broke down. The driver did not seek help to push it off the road which would have been easy to do. A lorry driving too fast came upon it and swerved into a second car. The relatives of the lorry driver sued the driver of the broken-down car. The defender was liable but the pursuer was 60 per cent responsible. In *Malcolm v. Fair*[56] a pedestrian and driver were found equally responsible. Lord Cameron did not consider that the mere fact that the pursuer was intoxicated ruled him out of court:

> "I conclude from the evidence that he had not taken proper care for his own safety as he moved out onto the carriageway, that he failed to observe the approach of the defender's car although this must have been obvious to him if he had been keeping a proper lookout. This failure is consistent with his being under the influence of drink at the time. Furthermore, and in particular, I hold that the pursuer failed to carry out the appropriate drill for ascertaining whether traffic was approaching towards him from the north, namely by looking again for such traffic once he got to the offside of the cars parked on the kerb. If he had done so I hold that there was nothing to prevent his observing the approach of the defender's car and for himself to have taken steps to avoid moving into its path. On a broad view of the matter I have reached the conclusion that each party was equally to blame for the accident. In the circumstances I shall sustain the first plea in law for the pursuer and the fourth plea in law for the defender and assess the degree of contributory negligence on the part of the pursuer at one half."[57]

---

[52] Chap. 16.
[53] 1994 G.W.D. 35–2088.
[54] See generally *Nettleship v. Weston* [1971] 2 Q.B. 691.
[55] 1985 S.L.T. 365.
[56] 1993 S.L.T. 342.
[57] *ibid.*

This point crops up frequently in practice, sometimes by chance, when the defenders get the medical records under a specification, and it is important that pursuers appreciate that a few drinks or more will not rule a pursuer out of court.

There are a huge number of seat-belt cases.[58]

A pedestrian who crossed against the pedestrian light at 6 a.m. was not **20–9** contributorily negligent.[59] Nor was a pedestrian who said he had nearly crossed the road when he was hit by a car that did not slow down or swerve.[60] Allowing oneself to be driven by a person later convicted of drunk driving was not contributory negligence where there was no evidence that the pursuer should have been aware of the defender's condition.[61] Pedestrians should look around when crossing and failure to do so is likely to constitute contributory negligence.[62] A failure to cross at a pedestrian crossing when there is one available is not of itself a bar to action but such a course is likely to attract a finding of contributory negligence.[63] In some circumstances it may be contributory negligence not to show rear lights.[64] It may be contributory negligence to cross in front of a bus after disembarkation where a pedestrian walks in front of a car.[65] A pedestrian who looks at the road when setting off between parked cars but who does not keep a good lookout may well have a finding of contributory negligence made against him: it is not a matter of look right, look left and look right again — it is a matter of continued awareness.[66] A pursuer who ran into a vehicle which had admittedly crossed the notional centre line of a narrow road was held to have been contributorily negligent.[67] It is not always the case that any conduct in an emergency will not amount to contribution. The pursuer must still take such care as is reasonable. In *BOC Ltd v. Groves*,[68] a drunk driver came to a halt on a motorway contra-flow. The pursuers' tanker driver started braking some 300 yards before the locus but decided to drive on to a slip road rather than braking further. A pedestrian ran across the slip road to try to warn others. The driver then had to brake but it was too late. Obviously every case depends on its own facts and there might be circumstances where the pedestrian's conduct would amount to a *novus actus*.[69]

Workers

These cases ought to be considered against the background of liability **20–10** where the practical duties tend to take into account the proclivity of the traditional agricultural or industrial worker to work so hard that he

---

[58] *Greally v. Russell of Denny Ltd*, 1975 S.L.T. (Sh. Ct) 3; *Douglas's C.B. v. Douglas*, 1976 S.L.T. (Notes) 4; *Smith v. Donald McLaren Ltd*, 1977 S.L.T. (Notes) 51; *Mitchell v. Hutchison*, 1983 S.L.T. 392; *Belford v. Jones*, 1973 S.L.T. (Notes) 85; *Mackay v. Borthwick*, 1982 S.L.T. 265; *Sloan v. Triplett*, 1985 S.L.T. 294; *Barker v. Murdoch*, 1977 S.L.T. (Notes) 75; *Hanlon v. Cuthbertson*, 1981 S.L.T. (Notes) 57; *Hill v. Chivers*, 1987 S.L.T. 323.
[59] *Purcell v. Johnston*, 1991 G.W.D. 15–946.
[60] *Garland v. Fairington*, 1993 G.W.D. 38–2510.
[61] *McColl v. Barnes*, 1992 S.L.T. 1188.
[62] *Coull v. Lothian Regional Council*, 1994 S.L.T. 377.
[63] *ibid.*
[64] *Morrison v. Laidlaw*, 1994 S.L.T. 359.
[65] *Gigli v. Taylor*, 1992 G.W.D. 2341.
[66] *Cavin v. Kinaird*, 1994 S.L.T. 111.
[67] *Young v. Roche Services Group*, 1989 S.L.T. 212.
[68] 1993 S.L.T. 360.
[69] Lord Penrose expressly reserved his opinion on this point.

disregards his own safety. It is possible even in statutory duty cases to make a finding of contributory negligence against a workman. In statutory cases it must be considered whether Parliament intended such a defence would be available. In all cases where it is sought to use the defence the workman is entitled to organise his behaviour on the basis that everyone else has carried out their obligations.[70] This is illustrated in the case of *Arbuckle v. A.H. McIntosh Co. Ltd*[71] in which it was argued that the employee was also in breach of his duties under regulations applying to the use of a saw. Lord Abernethy said:

"There remains the question of contributory negligence. It was argued by counsel for the defenders in his closing submissions that in terms of [the Woodworking Machines Regulations 1974] reg 14(1)(a) . . . there was strict liability on the part of the pursuer as an employee to comply with the regulations. The relevant part of that regulation provides: 'Every person employed shall, while he is operating a woodworking machine (a) use and keep in proper adjustment the guards and devices provided in accordance with these Regulations'. Accordingly, said counsel, if the regulations were breached, the pursuer must himself accept a degree of contributory negligence. Counsel did not refer to any authority for this proposition. I am unable to accept it. In the first place the defenders have no pleadings to support such an argument. But secondly, and more importantly, the saw with the guard in the setting I have held it was in was handed over to the pursuer like that by Mr Wilson who had himself by way of demonstration cut the first two plinths with the guard in that position. Furthermore, Mr Wilson said that from time to time in the course of his duties as foreman he would have observed the pursuer working at the saw and he said nothing about the position of the guard. In that situation it seems to me impossible to say that the pursuer was contributorily negligent . . . The employee's duty in terms of reg. 14(1)(a) only arises when the employers have provided a saw with a guard which is properly adjusted. The saw which the employers provided here did not have such a guard. It follows, therefore, that there is no room for a finding that this accident was caused to any extent by a breach of reg 14(1)(a) on the part of the pursuer."[72]

20–11 In *Scott v. Kelvin Concrete Ltd*[73] the pursuer entered a mechanical pressing machine and accidentally set it off. As is not uncommon the various safety devices fitted to the machine had been disabled to allow work to be proceeded with more easily and swiftly. The pursuer was experienced and knew of the dangers. Lord Coulsfied said:

"It is true that the immediate occasion of the machine being live was the pursuer's inadvertence, and the defenders argued that that was the cause of the accident and that the pursuer was, at least to some extent, to

---

[70] *Grant v. Sun Shipping Co. Ltd*, 1948 S.C. (H.L.) 73.
[71] 1993 S.L.T. 857.
[72] *ibid.* at 858.
[73] 1993 S.L.T. 935.

blame. This is, perhaps, not the sort of situation of repetitive work or fatigue in which inadvertence is most commonly regarded as something which does not amount to contributory negligence. Nevertheless, in the particular circumstances of this case, in view of the defenders' gross failures in proper care and the fact that the pursuer was required to do his best to make and keep operational a machine which lacked elementary safety features, it seems to me that, if the pursuer did fail to operate the isolator button, his failure can properly be regarded as falling within the principles of cases such as *John Summers & Son Ltd v. Frost* and therefore not amounting to contributory negligence. In these circumstances, I have no hesitation in holding that the accident was entirely due to fault and breach of statutory duty on the part of the defenders."[74]

In *McIntyre v. Strathclyde Regional Council*[75] a joiner was instructed by his foreman to remove shuttering. Both knew that for the work to be carried out safely the erection of trestles or a scaffold would be required in order to provide a working platform. The foreman left the site and the joiner was left to look for such material. None was readily available and he carried out the job in a less safe manner and was injured. Lord Penrose said:

"On the other hand I consider that the pursuer failed to have regard for his own safety in the way he proceeded to carry out the task. He himself did not support in evidence his case on record that the method was inherently dangerous. He denied that the method was extraordinary. He resisted the suggestion that it involved an absence of control. He maintained that he was in control of the piece of timber being used and in removing the shutters. He said that one would not expect the shuttering to fall on top of one. He said that he could see everything that was happening. He had done the operation in the same way before and did not think it was dangerous. The plywood had fallen on him on this occasion because he was not quick enough in getting his batten out of the way. It did not occur to him at the outset that the procedure was dangerous ... Mr Johnston, who had seen the method used by Mr McIntyre, said, in answer to a general question, that the method used "would have been another way of doing the job, to be truthful" as against the normal method of using trestles ... In my opinion Mr McIntyre could have sought out Mr Steel and, if necessary, have waited for his return to the site and must be regarded as having adopted the method he did as an expedient which involved unnecessary personal risk for himself."[76]

Others

Cases of tripping, slipping and falling on the highway are many in practice. **20–12** It is common for the defenders to say that the pursuer should have taken care of his own safety. The Lord Justice-Clerk (Ross), sitting in the Outer

---

[74] *ibid.* at 937.
[75] 1994 S.L.T. 933.
[76] *ibid.* at 938.

House, would have sustained such a plea against a pursuer for her failure to keep a good look out and for failing to watch where she placed her feet.[77] While in theory this is certainly open, the law should not want its citizens to be walking, stooped downward, looking for the careless handiwork of public authorities. Lord Ross would have found the parties *equally* to blame.[78] It is perhaps reasonable to expect a general observation which would reveal uncovered manholes but perhaps asking too much to notice minor projections or depressions, as is daily suggested in pleadings but seldom supported after proof. Sheriff Morrison made a finding of 20 per cent contributory negligence in a pothole case.[79] Here at least it can be said that there was a finding that the defender knew it was an area with potholes and so this fact can be said to make the citizen have to stoop streetward. The level of the finding also seems fair.

20–13 As shall be seen below *volenti non fit injuria* is often used as a defence in sports cases. Where it does not succeed, or is otherwise inapplicable, there is an argument for contribution. It is seldom, however, that mere participation in a sport shows a lack of care for one's own safety but in the case of an intrinsically dangerous sport this might well be argued. Bullfighting would seem to be one of the few examples of such a sport. Most other sports are organised in such a way that the reasonable person taking reasonable care for their own safety can participate safely—this ought to include hang-gliding, mountaineering and recreational downhill skiing. On the other hand, the more intrinsically dangerous the sport the less room there is for permissible lack of care by the participating pursuer. So the hang-glider who wants to loop the loop or buzz a passing car would be at risk of a finding as would the blindfold ski racer.

20–14 Just as children will be held liable in contributory negligence so might the infirm but this is subject to the point that in a system type of reasonable care the pursuer can seldom be said to have contributed. In *McKibben v. Glasgow Corporation*[80] the Pursuer was nearly blind and was injured when she stepped into an uncovered water toby in the street from which there had been left protruding a T shaped key and pipe to a height of 2½ feet. She was successful at jury trial with no contribution and the appeal by the defenders unsuccessful. The Lord Justice-Clerk, commenting that there was ample evidence for the verdict arrived at by the jury and said:

> "I think that the public authorities in a burgh or city such as Glasgow are bound to have the streets in an ordinarily safe condition for those who are using them and I confess I demur to the view that blind people are not entitled to walk about the streets unless accompanied by some person in charge of them."[81]

The council knew that there were many unaccompanied blind people about. Lord Dundas put it thus: "I think in each case the jury would have to consider, in the case of a blind person, whether that blind person was in the

---

[77] *McClafferty v. British Telecommunications plc*, 1987 S.L.T. 327.
[78] *ibid.* at 328.
[79] *Brown v. Edinburgh City Council*, 1999 S.L.T. (Sh. Ct) 43.
[80] 1920 2 S.L.T. 51.
[81] *ibid.* at 52.

circumstances fairly and reasonably treated by the corporation or other defenders—whether he had or had not been duly warned and reasonably guarded."[82] The accident appears to have happened when the street was busy.

VOLENTI NON FIT INJURIA

Literally, a legal wrong is not done to one who is willing. It is a maxim from **20–15** Aristotle and was used by the Roman lawyers to personally bar a free man who had himself sold by a confederate into slavery to be released and pocket the sale fee.[83] If established it is a complete defence. It is used less often now, partly due to its definition being narrowed and partly because contributory negligence allows the court to mark disapproval of the conduct of some pursuers by reducing their award rather than removing it.

At one time it was thought that a workman taking a dangerous job was **20–16** willing to be injured, or that a tenant accepted the dangers in let premises by staying in the premises.[84] However, as early as *Burns v. Kinnear, Moodie & Co.*[85] it did not put pursuers out of court easily. In *Burns* the pursuer was a workman in the employment of the defenders. His duties were to attend to two lucigen lights on a new quay under construction in Leith Harbour. One of the lucigen lights went out. The quay was not fenced, and there was no other light. The pursuer fell. The defenders argued that the pursuer had known and accepted the risk as to the lamp going out, and the defenders were not bound to fence the quay. It was held[86] that the admission as to knowledge of the defective state of the lighting apparatus did not bar the pursuer from his right of action—there was not a sufficient averment of knowledge and acceptance of danger to exclude the pursuer from going to a jury. In *Jeffrey v. Donald*[87] Lord Low said:

> "It was argued that the maxim *volenti non fit injuria* applied, because although the danger was obvious, the pursuer's daughter had continued in the defender's service for two months prior to the date of the accident. I doubt whether the maxim would, in the circumstances, have applied even to a servant of full age, because I think that it is now settled that the mere fact that a servant continues in the employment although he knows that the condition of the premises is such as to create the risk of an accident, is not sufficient to bar a claim upon his part in the event of an accident actually happening (*Smith v. Baker & Sons*, L.R. 1891, App.Cas. 325). But, however that may be, I think that it is plain that the

---

[82] *ibid.* at 54.

[83] It is also noted in *Buchan v. Melville* (1901) 9 S.L.T. 459 that: "Under the Roman law, a person might submit to his opponent the determination of a question between them, on the ground that no wrong was done to a person who, willingly and with full knowledge, consented to this. '*Non enim volenti, scienti, ac conscienti, potest injuria videri facta.*'" See generally Ingman, "A History of the Defence of *volenti non fit injuria*", 1981 J.R. 1; Tan, "*Volenti Non Fit Injuria*: An Alternative Framework", 1995 Tort L.R. 208.

[84] *Sheilds v. Dalziel* (1894) 24 R. 849.

[85] (1894) 2 S.L.T. 60.

[86] Following *Smith v. Baker* (1891) A.C. 325; *Wallace v. Culter Paper Mills* (1892) 19 R. 915.

[87] (1901) 9 S.L.T. 199.

maxim does not apply in this case. Assuming that the defender was guilty of negligence, I think that it is out of the question to say that because a girl of thirteen did not leave his employment on account of the risk which she was called upon to run, the defender is relieved from all liability."[88]

In *Wallace v. Culter Paper Mills Co.*,[89] Lord President Robertson considered the phrase "accepting the risk":

"Much of the difficulty which has gathered round this legal question has arisen from the ambiguity of the terms 'risk' and 'accepting the risk'. If 'risk' means simply 'danger', and 'accepting the risk' means 'encountering the danger', then every workman who is sciens of a dangerous defect in machinery, and goes on working, accepts the risk in that sense, for he exposes his life and limbs to the danger of loss or injury. But about such a workman, there remains over the question whether he 'accepts the risk' in this other sense, that he agrees to relieve his master of the consequences of any injury caused by what, *ex hypothesi*, is the master's fault, and insures himself against the risk."[90]

20–17 The trend of rejection in employment cases has been relentless.[91] *Steel v. Glasgow Iron and Steel Co. Ltd*[92] is important as a Scottish case showing generosity to rescuers and a review of English and other authority up to the time of the case. The deceased tried to uncouple his train while it was moving to avoid an imminent collision. The Lord Justice-Clerk took the following from the evidence: (1) that the deceased, if he had so chosen, could have escaped injury; (2) that he deliberately attempted to split his train, and in so doing necessarily incurred some risk; (3) that, if he had

---

[88] At 200. In *Smith v. Forbes & Co.* (1896) 4 S.L.T. 206 the sheriff said (at 206, 207): "These cases, I think, decide that, where such averments are made as in this case, that is to say, where it is admitted that the danger was known to the pursuer, but where there is nothing to lead to the conclusion that the pursuer agreed to relieve his masters from liability for any injury caused through their fault beyond the mere averment that he went on working after he had asked that safeguards against the known danger should be provided, then the law is that the question whether the workman was merely 'sciens' or was also 'volens' when he so continued working, is a question of fact which must be decided by the judge or the jury, as the case may be, on the evidence led in the cause."

[89] (1892) 19 R. 915.

[90] *ibid.* at 918.

[91] *Thos. W. Ward Ltd v. Revie & Co.*, 1945 S.L.T. 49 contains *obiter* observations by Lord Moncrieff in the Inner House to the effect that the foundation of the defence infers a recognition that a man may legitimately and without negligence expose himself to the risks incidental to his employment (at 53): "If this were not so, and negligence were open to be inferred from every acceptance by the workman of the risks incidental to the locus where his master has set him to work, the plea would neither have been devised nor be required, seeing that in all cases the sufficient defence of contributory negligence would have been open. I hold it to be entirely clear, on the contrary, that there are risks which, as matter of daily occurrence, a workman must accept, and so may accept without negligence. It is clear that much industrial work can only be carried on in dangerous surroundings; and that a workman (unless indeed he is to be encouraged to be obstructive at every turn) must thus be entitled, without incurring a charge of negligence, to leave it to his master, when deciding where to set him to work, to charge himself with the duty of making proper provision for his safety."

[92] 1945 S.L.T. 70.

been able to split the train, the effects of the collision would probably have been materially reduced, and that in any event there were good grounds for his entertaining such an expectation; (4) that the emergence of imminent danger and the deceased's response were in substance one transaction; and (5) that there was no evidence to show that the deceased was trying to rescue the engine crew, or that his efforts, if successful, could have had any appreciable effect in lessening the danger to them. The case was actually argued on *novus actus interveniens*. Lord Mackay who dissented, seemed to do so, on the basis that the deceased was the author of his own misfortune. As late as *Stewart's Executrix v. Clyde Navigation Trustees*[93] the plea was sustained in the Outer House but was rejected in the Inner House, on the basis of the authorities mentioned above. An averment[94] directed towards *volenti* was allowed to stand in *Keenan v. The City Line Ltd*[95] by Lord Hill Watson because the averment, followed "by a further averment that the pursuer was well aware that if he expressed unwillingness to drive the said truck on the said day because of his incompetence, he would not have been required to do so but would have received further tuition," was a relevant averment to support the defenders' plea.[96] Jury trials becoming more common it might be appropriate to note that an issue was allowed based on the defence in *Rowand v. Saunders & Connor (Barrhead) Ltd*[97] in the following terms: "Whether the pursuer willingly and knowingly undertook the risk of said accident and consequent loss, injury and damage?" In *Kirkham v. Cementation Co. Ltd*[98] matters were such that a plea could be repelled for want of averment: "It is essential before a plea of *volenti non fit injuria* could be upheld that there should be relevant averments not only to the effect that the pursuer knew of the risk of danger but that he voluntarily agreed to take that risk on himself and not hold his employer liable for any injury."[99]

A plea was repelled in *Smith v. McKenna*[1] where the pursuer was injured **20–18** when a pillion passenger on a motorcycle driven by a learner as he well knew. Lord Robertson said:

"In the present case no averments are made which reflect upon the defender's ability to drive the scooter safely. It may be inferred, from the averments that he was an apprentice, that he was young, but no facts are averred from which a lack of experience and skill in driving can be inferred. There might he many reasons why the driver of a vehicle was an 'L' driver, which did not reflect on his ability to drive safely. This situation is in marked contrast to the cases (where the defence of volenti was held relevant) in which a passenger rode in a vehicle with a drunk

---

[93] 1946 S.L.T. 302.
[94] "Further, esto the pursuer was incompetent to drive the said truck on the date of the accident (which is denied) he knew it and he voluntarily agreed to accept the risk of the consequences of driving the said truck while he was in the said state of incompetence as a driver".
[95] 1953 S.L.T. 128.
[96] *ibid.*
[97] 1953 S.L.T. 265.
[98] 1964 S.L.T. (Notes) 33.
[99] *ibid.* at 34.
[1] 1967 S.L.T. (Notes) 26.

driver (e.g. *McCaig v. Langan, Lampert v. Hefer,* 1955 2 S.A. 507). It was implicit in these cases that the driver was to the knowledge of the pursuer (the passenger), so drunk as to be unable to drive the vehicle safely. It is not said in the present case that the defender was so unskilled, so inexperienced or otherwise so incompetent in driving that he—to the knowledge of the pursuer—was unable to drive the scooter safely. In the absence of such averments, I do not see how it could be proper to draw the inference that the pursuer must have appreciated that the driver was incapable of exercising reasonable care and so consented to the lack of it."[2]

The plea was successful against a workman where he jumped from a mine train contrary to a statutory prohibition and his employer's instructions with other men. He blamed the employer primarily, or as being vicariously liable, but both cases were lost because of the maxim.[3]

20–19   A fireman resisted the plea in *Flannigan v. British Dyewood Co. Ltd*[4] there being insufficient averment that the pursuer agreed to relieve the master of the consequences of injury. However, when reclaimed, the case was lost on other grounds and the Lord Justice-Clerk (Grant) expressed the view that if the case had otherwise proceeded a proof before answer would have been appropriate with hesitation.[5] The Inner House even reversed a dismissal on the ground of a workmans' *volenti* —the issue would often be one of fact and so the issue should be allowed to go to the jury.[6] *Grant v. McClafferty*[7] narrowed the scope for the landlord to rely on continued occupation particularly where, as in that case, it was said there had been a complaint which the landlord had not fixed.[8] The plea is still taken at the time of writing. It was argued in *Lewis v. Buckpool Golf Club*.[9] The second defender averred: "The risk of being hit by a golf ball in the circumstances of the accident was one incidental to the pursuer's participation in the game of golf and to which he impliedly acceded." It was not argued that simply by taking part in the game the pursuer impliedly consented to assume the risk of any injury which might be caused by flying golf balls. The argument was that by going on to a putting green when he could see that the second defender was about to drive off from an adjacent tee the pursuer voluntarily assumed the risk that the second defender might mis-hit the ball and cause him injury. It was argued that the pursuer knew that the members of the party were not first class golfers, but members of a cricket club on a day's outing. The pursuer could have kept back from the green until the second defender's party had driven off and left the adjacent tee. On analysis the court did not accept the plea.[10] In *Devlin v. Strathclyde Regional Council*[11] a child jumped on to a skylight during a game of tig

---

[2] *ibid.* at 26, 27.
[3] *Hugh v. NCB*, 1972 S.L.T. (Notes) 56.
[4] 1969 S.L.T. 223.
[5] 1970 S.L.T. 285 at 289.
[6] *Robertson v. Primrose*, 1909 S.L.T. 409.
[7] (1906) 14 S.L.T. 571.
[8] See also *Murphy v. D.Y. Stewart & Co. Ltd* (1906) 14 S.L.T. 129, 336 (an occupiers case).
[9] 1993 S.L.T. (Sh. Ct) 43.
[10] *ibid.* at 46.
[11] 1993 S.L.T. 699.

when on the roof of a school building where he should not have been. It was held *obiter* that the statutory defence of assumption of risk would have been made out against the child if there had been liability.

Volenti and duty

Henderson v. London, Midland & Scottish Railway Co.[12] shows that the issue **20–20** of *volenti* is not relevant if there is no duty. But it is often difficult to differentiate no duty from *volenti*. The essence of the defence had to be considered in some detail and with rigour in *Winnick v. Dick*,[13] The reason for precise analysis was the terms of the Road Traffic Act 1972, s. 148(3).

> "Where a person uses a motor vehicle in circumstances such that under section 143 of this Act there is required to be in force in relation to his use of it such a policy of insurance or security as is mentioned in subsection (1) of that section, then, if any other person is carried in or upon the vehicle while the user is so using it, any antecedent agreement or understanding between them (whether intended to be legally binding or not) shall be of no effect so far as it purports or might be held—(a) to negative or restrict any such liability of the user in respect of persons carried in or upon the vehicle as is required by section 145 of the Act to be covered by a policy of insurance; or (b) to impose any conditions with respect to the enforcement of any such liability of the user; and the fact that a person so carried has willingly accepted as his the risk of negligence on the part of the user shall not be treated as negativing any such liability of the user. For the purposes of this subsection references to a person being carried in or upon a vehicle include references to a person entering or getting on to, or alighting from, the vehicle, and the reference to an antecedent agreement is to one made at any time before the liability arose."

The facts were that a passenger in a motorcar injured in an accident, raised an action of damages against the driver, who had been convicted of an offence under the 1972 Act. The men had been drinking together for most of the day and when the pursuer entered the defender's car to return home, he knew that the appellant was drunk. The important argument for this discussion is that it was suggested that *volenti ab ante* excluded any obligation to take reasonable care. The following passages represent the received view of the defence:

> "This argument of the defender seems to be based on an observation of Asquith J. in *Dann v. Hamilton* [1939] 1 K.B. 509 where his Lordship said at p. 512: 'As a matter of strict pleading it seems that the plea volenti is a denial of any duty at all, and, therefore, of any breach of duty, and an admission of negligence cannot strictly be combined with the plea'. I pause to observe that the same might be said about an

---

[12] 1935 S.L.T. 553.
[13] 1984 S.L.T. 185. See generally, Kidner, "The Variable Standard of Care, Contributory Negligence and *Volenti*", 1991 L.S. 1; Jaffey, "*Volenti non fit injuria*" [1985] C.L.J. 87.

admission of duty. In *Bankhead v. McCarthy,* 1963 SLT 144; 1963 S.C. 263 Lord Walker expressed an *obiter* view to the effect that he was not at all clear that the plea of volenti in England operates in the same way as it does in Scotland, and quoted the above passage in the opinion of Asquith J. as illustrative of the English view. He went on to say that in Scotland the plea of volenti has never been regarded as being a denial of the duty, but rather as a consent to accept the consequences of a breach of duty. For my part I am content to examine the Scottish view on the matter for the decision in this case . . . From these expressions of view as to what is involved in the maxim so far as the law of Scotland is concerned, I can find no support for, but rather refutation of, the contention that its effect here is to establish that on this journey there never was any duty on the defender as the driver of the car to take reasonable care quoad the pursuer; that consequently there could never be any liability on the defender at all; and that consequently there could be no liability which fell within the purview of s. 148(3) of the Road Traffic Act 1972. In my opinion the effect of the maxim was not to relieve the defender from any duty to take care quoad his passengers. On the contrary the maxim proceeds on the basis that there is duty to take care and not be negligent, but the successful establishment of the maxim means that the pursuer has accepted the risk of the defender's negligence in the exercise of his legal duties and has absolved the defender from the consequences arising from that negligence. So even apart from the technical difficulty of accepting it at all, to which I referred earlier, I am of the opinion that the defender's first argument fails."[14]

20–21 Two House of Lords cases give support to the continued existence of the defence and take the view that it is the same as the statutory formulation in the Occupiers Liability (Scotland) Act 1960. In *Titchener v. British Railways Board,*[15] *inter alia* a girl was injured by a train as she took a short-cut across the line requiring her to climb over a fence which had been brought down by vandals. Lord Hunter said:

"As Lord Reid said in *McGlone,* s. 2(3) merely puts in words the principle *volenti non fit injuria.* That principle is perhaps less often relied upon in industrial accident cases at the present time than formerly, but so far as cases under the 1960 Act are concerned, the principle is expressly stated in s. 2(3) and there is no room for an argument that it is out of date or discredited."[16]

Another interesting aspect of the defence which arose in that case was that it proceeded upon the basis that the train was run properly. She admitted that she was fully aware that the line was one along which trains ran, and that it would be dangerous to cross the line because of the presence of the trains. She said in cross-examination "it was just a chance I took".[17]

---

[14] *ibid*. at 188.

[15] 1984 S.L.T. 192.

[16] *ibid*. at 196.

[17] Differing in this respect from the boy in *McGlone v. BRB*, 1966 S.L.T. 2, who did not have a proper appreciation of the danger from live wires: see Lords Reid at 10 and Pearce at 12.

"The appellant did not suggest that the train which injured her had been operated in an improper or unusual way. The importance of that is that the chance which she took was no doubt limited to the danger from a train operated properly, in the "ordinary and accustomed way"—see *Slater v. Clay Cross Co. Ltd* [1956] 2 Q.B. at p. 271, per Denning L.J. Had there been evidence to show that the train which injured the appellant was driven negligently, like the train in *Slater,* the risk which materialised would not have been within the risks that the appellant had accepted. But there is nothing of that kind here. In my opinion therefore the defence under s. 2(3) is established."[18]

While having no effect in that case the *Slater* point is one which ought to be kept in mind in cases where on the face of it the pursuer has "asked for it" by being in a dangerous place.

The position of children in contributory negligence has already been **20–22** discussed and it is clear from *McGlone* as discussed in *Titchener* that the need for acceptance rather than simple awareness is enough to protect most young people from the effect of the defence. A more subtle point arose in *Hughes' Tutrix v. Glasgow District Council.*[19] A tenant raised an action for her child injured by catching her hand on a broken toilet bowl against the landlords.[20] The defenders pled *volenti non fit injuria* that by continuing to reside in the premises while knowing of the condition of the toilet bowl, the pursuer had accepted the danger and thereby barred her child from maintaining her claim for damages. Sheriff Gordon rejected the argument. He reviewed the authorities[21] and concluded:

"[I]n my view, the only defence open to the landlord is the defence of volenti non fit injuria as it is expressed in s. 2(3), and not only does s. 2(3) specifically equate the defence of volenti in such cases with the defence of volenti in other cases, it specifically refers to risks 'which *that* person has willingly accepted as his' (my emphasis), and it is quite impossible to suggest that the child in this case willingly accepted the risk of the state of the bowl."[22]

Volenti non fit injuria is often mentioned in sports cases, especially in regard **20–23** to spectators, but it is seldom that a spectator can actually be said to have assumed a risk of injury.[23] So far as participators are concerned the defence does seem to be appropriate for known risks meaning those within the rules

---

[18] *Titchener v. BRB,* 1984 S.L.T. 192, *per* Lord Fraser at 196.
[19] 1982 S.L.T. (Sh. Ct) 70.
[20] On the basis of the Occupiers' Liability (Scotland) Act 1960, s. 3(1).
[21] *Lord Salvesen in Hardie v. Sneddon,* 1916 2 S.L.T. 197 (distinguished) (contributory negligence); *Davidson v. Sprengel,* 1909 S.C. 566 (distinguishable) (father's own action not on behalf of child); other cases he thought were cases where a plea of *volenti* against a parent succeeded but which the learned sheriff thought "a little difficult to evaluate, since it is not clear whether they were taken in contract or in delict, and in some cases it is not very clear whether, although the injury was sustained to the child, the pursuer was suing for damages due to himself in respect of that injury to his child."
[22] *Hughes' Tutrix v. Glasgow D.C.,* 1982 S.L.T. (Sh. Ct) 70 at 75.
[23] *Murray v. Haringay Arena* [1951] 2. K.B. 146; see especially *Wooldridge v. Sumner* [1962] 2 All E.R. 978.

of a game or the normal practice of a sport. So there is no action for a dislocated shoulder charge in football. The defence does not apply where one footballer headbutts another or where there is an unexpected hole round the bend of a pisted ski run. The formula one racer takes the risk of death by going too fast through a corner but not by being shunted off by another driver. *Volenti* does not apply to ordinary neighbour negligence.[24] A person injured by a risk not inherent in a sport is unharmed by neglect and does not waive a duty which otherwise exists. However, the position may vary from duty to duty and, for example, the legislature was correct to include a specific defence in the Occupiers' Liability (Scotland) Act 1960 because that Act itself laid down a duty which arguably would not exempt inherent risks.

20–24 *Volenti* does not apply to conduct after the fault and so a woman who had sex after a failed sterilisation could not be *volenti* re the sterilisation albeit she was *volenti* re the sex.[25]

CRIMINALITY: THE *EX TURPI CAUSA* RULE

20–25 The maxim *ex turpi causa non oritur actio* is more usually encountered in the law of contract.[26] It has been considered a defence to delict or tort claims in many jurisdictions. Courts are understandably reluctant to award damages to one wrongdoer caused by another wrongdoer. Such cases range from the safeblower who blows up his confederate acting as look-out to a case where a person injures a passenger when infringing an obscure traffic regulation. The question has been regularly debated in England.[27] Australian cases have shown something of a lead in moving away from a rigorous application of the maxim.[28] There are two recent Scottish cases one of which reconsiders much of the authority. In *Duncan v. Ross Harper & Murphy*[29] the pursuer was one of a group of men who took part in the theft of a motorcar, it being inferred from the fact that the pursuer was found in the car shortly after it was stolen that he was implicated. Lord Kirkwood did not become involved in any extensive jurisprudential analysis:

> "[I]t was a matter of admission that, even if the defenders had raised an action on his behalf against Chalmers, the principle ex turpi causa non oritur actio would have applied and the action would have been bound to fail. If the action was bound to fail, then the pursuer has failed to establish that he has suffered any loss in consequence of the defenders' breach of contract."[30]

20–26 In *Weir v. Wyper*,[31] the pursuer was a 16–year-old girl who went on a trip with two men and another girl. One of the men and the other girl left the

---

[24] *Wooldridge, ibid.*
[25] *Sabri-Tabrizi v. Lothian H.B.*, 1998 S.L.T. 607.
[26] See McBryde, *Contract.*
[27] *Pitts v. Hunt* [1991] 1 Q.B. 24. *Ashton v. Turner* [1981] Q.B. 137 takes a firm line.
[28] *Jackson v. Harrison* (1978) 138 C.L.R. 438; *Progress and Properties v. Craft* (1976) 135 C.L.R. 651; retreating from *Smith v. Jenkins* (1970) 119 C.L.R. 397. The Australian position was analysed in *Weir v. Wyper*, 1992 S.L.T. 579.
[29] 1993 S.L.T. 105.
[30] *ibid.* at 107.
[31] 1992 S.L.T. 579.

car leaving the pursuer with the defender. The pursuer knew that the defender held only a provisional licence. She asked for a lift home. The defender began showing off—driving very fast and braking violently when it was necessary to stop. The car left the road and overturned. Lord Coulsfield examined many cases in a careful analysis:

"In my opinion, the Scottish authorities, far from supporting the contention of counsel for the defender that Scots law has adopted a firm rule that participation in any type of criminal conduct, however minor, disables an injured party from recovering damages, indicate that the matter is one of the particular facts. That view is also, in my opinion, consistent with the Australian and English cases to which I was referred. In *Jackson v. Harrison* the High Court of Australia held, by a majority of four to one, that where a passenger was injured through the negligent driving of a person who was disqualified from holding a driver's licence, to the passenger's knowledge, the passenger was not disabled from recovering damages. Three of the judges in the majority held that illegality did not bear on the standard of care reasonably to be expected of the driver and the fourth held that the relevant statutory provisions did not require recovery of damages to be denied and the driver exempted from liabilityIt therefore appears to me that the only judge who has been prepared to adopt the absolute rule contended for by counsel for the defender in the present case is Barwick C.J. in *Jackson v. Harrison* and, as I have observed, even he did so with qualifications. It follows, in my view, that these two authorities support the view that the proper course is to examine the whole facts and circumstances before attempting to arrive at a conclusion.

I would add that it is, in my view, easy to envisage circumstances in which the denial of a right to recover damages to a person driven by an unqualified driver would be plainly wrong: take, for example, the case of an unqualified driver conveying a nurse who is not herself a qualified driver, to attend to a person who is seriously ill. In the present case, the pursuer, a 16 year old girl, found herself alone with the defender late at night on a country road. She may not have been prudent in allowing herself to be placed in that situation but that is not the issue. I find it hard to see that, given this situation, it could be said that in allowing, or even asking, the defender to drive her home she was participating in any significant criminal activity or that any reasonable application of public policy would deny her a right to recover damages for injuries caused by negligent driving on the part of the defender. Nevertheless, for the reasons I have indicated, the question is, in my view, one depending on the particular facts and circumstances and the proper course is to allow a proof before answer."[32]

It is submitted he correctly concluded that the maxim was not to be rigorously applied. He considered that if the defence was restated or explained as an aspect of public policy it need not be a complete bar to claims. The proper course was to take each case on its merits and it is

---

[32] *ibid.* at 581, 582.

probably only in cases of significant criminal activity (such as the safeblower example) that the defence would have a chance of success.[33] It should be mentioned that such cases and cases like them are sometimes argued on the basis of a public policy against recovery and yet others are argued on the basis that, in negligence cases, it is impossible to fix a standard of duty of care: for example, as between the safeblower and his look-out—the court will not try to fix the standards of the reasonable man choosing to become a thief. This latter argument seems unnecessary and may well have been a way out of the otherwise draconian effect of subscribing fully to the *turpis causa* rule.

20–27   *Ex turpi causa non oritur actio* is a defence in relation to intentional wrongs as much as cases pled in negligence. It was successful in *The Bile Bean Manufacturing Co. v. Davidson*.[34] In that case the petitioners sought interdict against rival traders selling bile beans. However, in the course of the case it was discovered they were both charlatans.[35]

STATUTORY AUTHORITY

20–28 Parliament can authorise conduct otherwise wrongful. It is a matter of interpretation in each case. Simply because some acts are authorised does not mean that the defender can carry out the work without any care: "common-law remedies remain both for the purposes of interdict and reparation unless they be excluded or impaired by statute."[36] The burden is on the defender: "It is clear that the burden lies on those who seek to establish that, the Legislature intended to take away the private rights of individuals, to shew that by express words, or by necessary implication, such an intention appears."[37] A clear example is *Lord Advocate v. North British Railway Co. Ltd*,[38] in which the defenders carried manure under a statutory obligation but they left it so as to constitute a nuisance for the army in their barracks. The Lord Kyllachy said:

"The Railway Company say that they are protected by the Act from all complaints against the character of the manure; and, as to the unloading, they say that they are not responsible, because the unloading is performed by the consignee. The answer to that contention is that, when a railway company undertakes or has imposed upon it the duty of conveying an offensive substance from one of its stations to another, it is obliged to provide reasonable arrangements for loading and unloading."[39]

---

[33] See the cases considered in *Weir. Sloan v. Triplett*, 1985 S.L.T. 294; *Ashcroft's C.B. v. Stewart*, 1988 S.L.T. 163; *McLean v. Ross Harper and Murphy*, 1992 G.W.D. 667, 687; *Wilson v. Price*, 1989 S.L.T. 484; *Winnick v. Dick*, 1984 S.L.T. 185.

[34] (1906) 14 S.L.T. 294.

[35] *ibid.* at 296. In fact the name was not even original: "Even this was not in a true sense original, the word beans having been in several cases applied to boluses in an oval form, and the words 'Bile Beans' having formed part of a trade mark taken out so early as 1887 by one Smith."

[36] *Hanley v. Edinburgh Mags*, 1913 1 S.L.T. 420, *per* Lord Shaw at 425.

[37] *Metropolitan Asylums District Managers v. Hill* [1881] A.C. 193, *per* Lord Blackburn at 208.

[38] (1894) 2 S.L.T. 71.

[39] *ibid.* at 71.

In *Hanley v. Magistrates of Edinburgh*[40] building work authorised by the authority resulted in a culvert being narrowed and flooding of the pursuer's lands. Lord Shaw of Dunfermline reviewed the law and applied it meticulously to the statutory provisions in question in a speech which is as valid and useful today.

"I am humbly of opinion that no part of this section, which was a section for the protection of the proprietors of Craigentinny, imports any repeal of the right at common law that those lands should be protected against the inundation nuisances which have occurred, and imports, neither by implication nor by its terms, any repeal of the imperative obligations resting upon the Corporation under the Municipal Act of 1879 to make the sewers of the burgh such as shall effectually drain every portion of it. It would no doubt be possible to figure a case in which a protection clause was so framed as to work out to the injury of the person assumed to be protected by Parliament, but nothing of the sort is in this case to be inferred. I do not doubt that all the protection afforded the Craigentinny irrigation works can be continued alongside of the proper and effectual draining of the burgh, and I should myself have had little doubt that Parliament would not, except by extreme inadvertence, have permitted the protection of one riparian owner's rights to operate as a title to stoppage of the general and effective drainage of the city of Edinburgh—a stoppage which might involve serious consequences in the production of disease or in patrimonial loss."[41]

While many cases seem to be about nuisance, the same principle applies across the law. In *Lundie v. MacBrayne*[42] the question was whether a statute allowed what would otherwise be the wrong of wrongful detention.[43] Again in *Percy v. Glasgow Corporation*,[44] in the House of Lords, the question was whether a man arrested on a tram by council officers was precluded from suing by the power vested in the officals by byelaws. In relation to moveable property in *Bell v. McGlennan*,[45] a radio investigation officer had statutory authority to hold a television set for six months but the period after that was not authorised. There has been a tangential discussion in relation to the economic delicts.[46]

This defence may also be taken to include the statutory defence to product liability which applies where the defender has designed the product to comply with a Community obligation.[47] Because European Union law has direct applicability, and sometimes direct effect, an Act may be permitted by way of this legal authority albeit it has not been expressly adopted by Parliament.

---

[40] 1913 1 S.L.T. 420.
[41] *ibid.* at 426, 427.
[42] (1894) 21 R. 1085.
[43] Chap. 6.
[44] 1922 S.L.T. 352.
[45] 1992 S.L.T. 237.
[46] *D. & J. Nicholl v. Dundee Harbour Trs*, 1914 2 S.L.T. 418.
[47] Chap. 15.

JUSTIFICATION

20–29 Where there are conduct delicts there has to be an escape from liability for those who carried out the conduct with good reason. So in the case of conspiracy, the conduct can be justified by the predominant purpose being non-harmful[48]; in the case of interference in contract justification is possible too.[49] The reasonable chastisement of children[50] and self-defence[51] can be seen as sub-sets of this principle. The actions of police officers arresting and searching persons[52] and seizing goods[53] would come under this defence.

NECESSITY

20–30 There are few Scottish sources.[54] The police may trespass in the execution of their duty.[55] A farmer may recover his straying animals.[56] Chasing foxes may allow trespass[57] but picketing does not.[58] The High Court has recently reviewed the defence of necessity as a form of coercion and allowed it in principle.[59] That might, and indeed ought to, make the defence available at least in cases of intentional harm.

SELF-DEFENCE

20–31 Defending oneself or one's property is a defence. So far as defence of the person is concerned the subject is treated above.[60] So far as property is concerned the sheep-worrying dog cases are sufficient authority for the commission of delicts against property in the defence of property.[61]

DAMNUM FATALE (VIS MAJOR)

20–32 A *damnum fatale* is a loss which could not have been anticipated by human foresight sometimes also called an Act of God. It is a defence which is seldom needed. The requirement for foreseeability in negligence itself excludes many a *damnum fatale*. Causation may also exclude liability—it was the wind not the workmanship that caused the tile to fall on the

---

[48] Chap. 7.
[49] Chap. 7.
[50] Chap. 4.
[51] Chap. 4.
[52] Chap. 4.
[53] Chap. 6.
[54] For England, see *Cope v. Sharpe* [1912] 1 K.B. 496; *Leigh v. Gladstone* (1909) 26 T.L.R. 139.
[55] *Shepherd v. Menzies* (1900) 2 F. 443.
[56] *Earl of Morton v. McMillan* (1893) 1 S.L.T. 92.
[57] *Colquhoun v. Buchanan* (1785) Mor. 4997.
[58] *Merry and Cunninghame v. Aitken* (1895) 22 R. 247.
[59] *Moss v. Howdle*, 1997 S.C.C.R. 215.
[60] Chap. 6.
[61] *Leven v. Mitchell*, 1949 S.L.T. (Sh. Ct) 40; *Farell v. Marshall*, 1962 S.L.T. (Sh. Ct) 65.

pursuer. It is relevant in delicts where foreseeability is not a requirement of liability. Where there is strict liability at common law, it is a defence. There is a dictum of Lord Watson in *Countess of Rothes v. Kirkcaldy Waterworks Co.*[62] that a fall of rain could be so exceptional as to amount to *damnum fatale*. But it would have to be exceptional.[63] The re-reading of the law of nuisance in *RHM Bakeries (Scotland) Ltd v. Strathclyde Regional Council*[64] means that the defence of *damnum fatale* is less likely to ever be considered and that the older cases which appear to allow such a defence may well be explicable on the basis that the event negates a finding of *culpa*, rather than the existence of a discreet defence.

CONSENT

In certain delicts consent provides a full defence. In cases of intentional **20–33** harm or conduct delicts the defence may be called *volenti non fit injuria*. The most significant instance is assault where the delictual nature of the act is avoided by the pursuers consent. This defence is dealt with where it is most relevant.[65] The principle should apply to all delicts where the complaint is of intentional harm. It has been submitted above that, in cases of negligence, the requirement for foreseeability of harm means that there is no need to treat non-contractual consent as a defence—if there is any implicit agreement between the parties that obviates the duty as between those parties. Such agreements, or even unilateral accpetances, are subject to the controls discussed below.

CONTRACT

Volenti non fit injuria and consent have already been discussed. These **20–34** defences involve consideration of the voluntary acceptance of the possibility of harm on the part of the pursuer. They are strictly speaking independent of contract albeit they are acts of the will. In Scots law for there to be a contract there must be an act of the contracting will—an intention to have one's intentions brought within the legal rules that bring with them sanctions. In such cases where a pursuer has accepted a risk or disclaimed the defender's liability for it, the defender is properly utilising one branch of the law of obligations to overcome another. Contractual obligations are the laws that parties choose for themselves and they may well choose to contract out of the obligations imposed, or which would in the future be imposed by circumstances by the law of delict. So in principle the defender can obtain contractual exemption or restriction of liability from any delictual obligation whether based on the defender's intentional conduct or his negligence. Further investigation of this is strictly within the law of contract,[66] especially since the obligation upon which the pursuer is likely to

---

[62] (1882) 9 R. 113.
[63] *Greenock Ry v. Greenock Corp.*, 1917 S.C. (H.L.) 56.
[64] 1985 S.L.T. 214, discussed in Chap. 5.
[65] Chap. 4.
[66] See McBryde, *Contract*.

be founding in a bilateral contract is probably one based on an implied term of the contract to take reasonable care rather than, strictly speaking, a delictual obligation, although concurrent liability is accepted in Scotland. Some notice is given here, however, of the restrictions on contract as a defence to delictual claims. First there is the common law control of the incorporation of terms by reference—ticket cases. In *Taylor v. Glasgow Corporation*,[67] the Second Division made the distinction between vouchers and true documentary incorporation to prevent the defenders using their "contractual" terms. In *McCutcheon v. MacBrayne*,[68] the House of Lords refused to allow defenders to rely on terms which had been advertised on their vessels and which had been signed by the pursuer on some previous occasions—the defenders had failed to establish a course of dealing. Secondly, there is the rule of interpretation which prohibits a party's exclusion of his own liability, unless clearly expressed. A fully worked out example is *Golden Sea Produce Ltd v. Scottish Nuclear plc*.[69] The pursuers, proprietors of a fish hatchery business, were tenants at the defenders' electricity generating station. A large number of the pursuers' fish died as a result of the presence of an excessive level of chlorine pumped from Hunterston "A" power station. The excessive level of chlorine was averred to have occurred when a valve in a chlorination plant, owned by the operators of the power station, was opened by mistake. *Inter alia* the defenders argued an exemption clause which was held not to exclude negligence.[70]

20–35   Section 16 of the Unfair Contract Terms Act 1977 provides:

"Subject to subsection (1A) below where a term of a contract or a provision of a notice given to persons generally or to particular persons purports to exclude or restrict liability for breach of duty arising in the course of a business or from the occupation of any premises used for business purposes or from the occupation of any premises used for business purposes of the occupier, that term or provision (a) shall be void in any case where such exclusion or restriction is in respect of death or personal injury; (b) shall in any other case, have no effect if it was not fair and reasonable to incorporate the term in the contract, or as the case may be, if it is not fair and reasonable to allow reliance on the provision. (1A) Nothing in paragraph (b) of Subsection (1) above shall be taken as implying that a provision of a notice has effect in circumstances where apart from that paragraph, it would not have that effect. (2) Subsection (1) (a) above does not affect the validity of any discharge and indemnity given by a person on or in connection with the award to him of compensation for pneumoconiosis attributable to employment in the coal industry, in respect of any further claim arising from his contracting that disease; (3) Where under subsection (1) above a term of a contract or a provision of a notice is void or has no effect, the fact that a person agreed to, or was aware of, the term or provision,

---

[67] 1952 S.C. 440.
[68] 1964 S.C. (H.L.) 28.
[69] 1992 S.L.T. 942.
[70] *ibid.* at 946–948.

shall not of itself be sufficient evidence that he knowingly and voluntarily assumed any risk."

This is the version of the Act resulting from amendment by the Law Reform (Misclellaneous Provisions) (Scotland) Act 1990. The previous version did not deal with non-contractual notices in this way.[71] It is not merely of historical interest to note two of the cases under the unamended Act. *Robbie v. Graham & Sibbald*[72] was a surveyors negligence case based on delict. The defenders founded on a disclaimer in the form of application for the loan, which explained that the type of survey requested was the basic service which might not reveal defects that a more detailed survey would discover. The form further stated that neither the building society nor the surveyors gave any warranty of the accuracy of the report and that the surveyors did not accept responsibility to applicants or to any other person. Lord Weir said:

"The disclaimer by the defenders in this case was not a notice having contractual effect and there was no contractual relationship between the pursuers and the defenders. The pursuers are therefore not in the advantageous position of a purchaser of property in England of being able to argue that the defenders' disclaimer of liability fell foul of the provisions of Part I of the Act of 1977. Counsel for the pursuers conceded that her clients enjoyed no protection from the Act in the circumstances of this case."[73]

This did seem like the correct decision at the time and one which justified **20–36** the amendment of the 1977 Act. In a remarkable decision after the Act was amended but based on the law previously in place, *Melrose v. Davidson and Robertson*,[74] Lord President Hope speaking of a similar factual arrangement said:

"In my opinion the effect of that part of the declaration which relates to the report and valuation to be obtained by the society was to create a contract between the pursuers and the society, and this was a contract of the kind to which s. 16 of the 1977 Act applies by virtue of s. 15(2)(c) of that Act. The opening of this part of the declaration states that the applicants 'accept that the Society will provide me/us with a copy of the report and mortgage valuation which the Society will obtain in relation to this application'. At the end of the declaration there is a statement that the applicants enclose the inspection fee, according to the appropriate entry in the scale of charges for inspection of the property including

---

[71] The unamended version was as follows: "Where a term of a contract purports to exclude or restrict liability for breach of duty arising in the course of any business or from the occupation of any premises used for business purposes of the occupier, that term—(a) shall be void in any case where such exclusion or restriction is in respect of death or personal injury; (b) shall in any other case, have no effect if it was not fair and reasonable to incorporate the term in the contract."

[72] 1989 S.L.T. 870.

[73] *ibid.* at 872.

[74] 1993 S.L.T. 611.

VAT which, it is stated, the society has to pay to the valuer. It seems to me that there is here an offer by the building society to provide a copy of the report and mortgage valuation to the applicants, which the pursuers in this case accepted by signing the declaration and returning the application form to the society ... In my opinion a contract by the society to provide the applicants with a copy of the report and mortgage valuation was a contract relating to the services to be provided by the valuer in the preparation of that report. There is a simple and obvious relationship between the provision of these services and the valuer's wish to have the benefit of the disclaimer in order to exclude or restrict his liability for negligence in the provision of them. The effect of s. 15(2) is that, to this extent, s. 16 applies to the contract which was created when the pursuers signed and returned the application form to the society. That is sufficient to enable them to obtain the benefit of s. 16(1) to defeat the application of the disclaimer since, for the reasons given by Lord Griffiths in *Smith v. Bush* at [1990] 1 A.C., pp. 858–860, it cannot be disputed that it would not be fair and reasonable for the defenders as professional valuers to exclude their liability to the purchasers of this dwellinghouse.

For these reasons I consider that the defenders are not entitled to the benefit of the disclaimer and that we should adhere to the interlocutor of the Lord Ordinary. I would refuse this reclaiming motion."[75]

While this must have been a very welcome decision for the pursuer, it is by no means clear that the obligation to pay for the survey report was enough to have the effect the court gave to it. The amended version of the Act will avoid the need for these rather strained analyses. *Robbie* is authority for adopting the *Smith v. Bush* approach to fairness and reasonableness.

It may at first sight seem strange that there are no cases on section 16(1)(a) but that is like many excellent provisions which are so clear and unambiguous that no one would seek to argue against them.

PRESCRIPTION

20–37 Prescription and limitation are pled as defences. Prescription truly extinguishes an obligation by operation of law. Limitation is more of a bar against a particular pursuer which must be pled. The law was extensively and usefully overhauled by the Prescription and Limitation (Scotland) Act 1973. The Act is a complex piece of legislation, but with amendments that have taken place since, and a body of case law, it is now reaching maturity as something of a workable and rational code.[76]

"Reparation" defined

20–38 The word must be defined because the word is used in the Act. In this particular context the Inner House has taken a narrow interpretation of the word.[76] Reparation it was said is pecuniary remedy for loss caused by a wrong, not a remedy for breach of contract.[78]

---

[75] *ibid*. at 614 and 615.

[76] See generally D.M. Walker, *The Prescription and Limitation (Scotland) Act 1973* (5th. ed., 1996).

[77] *Miller v. Glasgow D.C.*, 1989 S.L.T. 44.

[78] Contrary to the view expressed in Gloag & Henderson (9th. ed.); applied in *Middleton v. Douglass*, 1991 S.L.T. 726.

A five year period

The primary prescriptive period is a continuous period of five years. That **20–39** applies to various obligations but for the purposes of this work the most relevant is the application to "any obligation arising from liability (whether arising from any enactment or any rule of law) to make reparation".[79] The time runs from the time when the obligation becomes enforceable which in terms of the Act is the time when the loss occurs.[80]

Discoverability

The legislation provides, albeit in obscure language, that the clock does not **20–40** start running until the claim is discovered.[81] Houses were built between 1970 and 1971. Cracks and bulges appeared, it was said, in 1988 and an action raised in 1989. A prescription plea was taken on the basis that the pursuer was aware of the damage earlier in 1972 when complaints had been made. Complaints were made in 1977 as well, but they did not raise any major issues. The prescription plea was repelled on the basis that neither event indicated that damage was evident or discoverable, preventing the concurrence of *damnum* and *injuria* required for an *aquilian* reparation action. Nor had it been established that the damage sued for was the same as had emerged previously.[82] This contrasts with *Dumfries Labour and Social Club and Institute Ltd v. Sutherland, Dickie & Copland*,[83] in which cracks were noticed in 1979 and professional advice was that there was no major problem. In 1980 more cracks were noticed and the professionals advised monitoring the situation. Cracks were noticed again in 1983 and a major investigation commenced in 1984 which revealed the unknown existence of a public sewer. The pursuers' argument that no cracking (after the first) was obvious until after summer 1983, the court held on the evidence (of experts) that further cracking would have taken place and would likely have been noticed by the end of 1981. This seems a harsh decision in view of the fact that the pursuer instructed experts early on but there may be a common-sense view that says if the experts have to be called back then there is enough to be considering a claim. In *Glasper v. Rodger*,[84] the Inner House reversed a sheriff principal's upholding a plea of prescription to allow a proof before answer. The basis of the pursuer's case was that the defenders, their Scottish solicitors, took title in the wrong name. It was admitted that loss arose on registration of the wrong title. It was admitted that the action was raised outwith five years from that date. However, the action had been raised within five years from the date when the pursuers discovered that the title was allegedly wrong—when the title had to be used

---

[79] Prescription and Limitation (Scotland) Act 1973, s. 6(1) and Sched. 1, para. 1(d).

[80] s. 11. It should be noted that in Scotland the prescriptive period for reparation for damages cases is the same whether or not the case is based on delict or contract. See correction 1994 Rep.B. 5–3.

[81] See on this issue: MacQueen, "Latent Defects, Collateral Warranties and Time Bar", 1991 S.L.T. (News) 77, 91, 99.

[82] *Sinclair v. MacDougall Estates Ltd*, 1994 S.L.T. 76.

[83] 1993 G.W.D. 21–1314.

[84] 1996 S.L.T. 44.

in the context of other transactions. The case is important because it is an authoritative interpretation of section 11(3) of the 1973 Act. The court accepted the reasoning of Webster J. in *Peco Arts Inc. v. Hazlitt Gallery Ltd*[85] to hold that reasonable diligence does not necessarily mean doing everything possible, and indeed may involve doing nothing at all.

The long negative and imprescriptible reparation obligations

20–41 The long negative prescription of 20 years[86] is a long-stop mopping up obligations otherwise limping along. In *McMurtrie v. George Wimpey & Co. Ltd*,[87] it was held that the long negative prescription applied to personal injury cases regardless of whether the victim was unaware, and could not reasonably have been aware, that he had suffered loss injury or damage. However, it was still the case that there had to be a concurrence of *damnum* and *injuria* and so in a case such as *McMurtrie*, where the *damnum* was a disease, the critical date would be when the earlier exposure resulted in the disease.[88]

Certain obligations do not prescribe at all. Any obligation of a trustee to make reparation or restitution in respect of any fraudulent breach of trust to which the trustee was a party or was privy does not prescribe. The context suggests that this category is designed for proper trusts or perhaps also resulting trusts. Whether or not it applies to constructive trusts might be a debateable point, at least until there is some unanimity as to the precise location of constructive trust in Scots law.[89] It is recognised in various writings and cases, and it is submitted, that a fraudulent breach of a constructive trust would, probably, be imprescriptible.

Relevant claim

20–42 A relevant claim interrupts the prescriptive period. In *Middleton v. Douglass*,[90] the purchaser of a house sued a property agent and an architectural technician for damages when the house he bought was demolished three years later. The action began in delict within the prescriptive period. A contractual claim was added later and after the prescriptive period had elapsed. It was held that the delictual claim was not a relevant claim sufficient to interrupt prescription. In *G.A. Estates Ltd v. Caviapen Trustees Ltd (No. 2)*,[91] a counterclaim was raised and then averments about certain warranties were deleted. More than five years after the counterclaim was made, but within five years of the deletion, it was sought to add the averments again. Lord Coulsfield held:

> "The choice between the possible constructions is, in my view, not an easy one, but, on balance, I have come to the view that the argument of

---

[85] [1983] 1 W.L.R. 1315.
[86] Prescription Act 1617; Conveyancing (Scotland) Act 1924.
[87] July 2, 1998.
[88] Note, it was also held that that the burden of averment was on the defender to set up the *de quo*: see also *Strathclyde Regional Council v. W.A. Fairhurst and Partners*, 1997 S.L.T. 658; *Strathclyde Regional Council v. Border Engineering Contractors Ltd*, 1998 S.L.T. 175.
[89] See generally Wilson, "The Constructive Trust in Scots Law", 1993 J.R. 99.
[90] 1991 S.L.T. 726. This applied the approach of the Inner House in a contract/restitution claim: *NV Devos Gebroeder v. Sunderland Sportswear Ltd*, 1990 S.L.T 473.
[91] 1993 S.L.T. 1045.

the defenders in the present case should be sustained. The words of s. 6(1), so far as material, are 'If, after the appropriate date, an obligation . . . has subsisted for a continuous period of five years—(a) without any relevant claim having been made in relation to the obligation'. It seems to me that, so long as an action seeking to enforce the obligation is in court, a relevant claim is being made; and that it cannot be said that a continuous period of five years has elapsed 'without a relevant claim having been made' if, at any point during that period, a relevant claim was being made. It is true that, on that reading of the section, there may be cases in which there is uncertainty as to the date on which the new prescriptive period is to start, and that the period may be prolonged, but, like, I think, Lord Kissen in *British Railways Board v. Strathclyde Regional Council* [1982 S.L.T. 55], I am not unduly impressed by these arguments. In the whole circumstances, therefore, I have come to the view that, in the present case, the relevant period did not commence until 21 March 1991, so that the 1992 amendment came well within it."[92]

Thus the present balance of authority, correctly it is submitted, is in favour of the existence of an action which itself was a relevant claim prevent the time-bar from running. This would appear to be prejudicial where a case is sisted for a lengthy period of time but the defender can always move to recall the sist.

Relevant acknowledgment

In *Richardson v. Quercus Ltd*[93] it was held that the sheriff had been right to **20–43** hold that the prescriptive period had been interrupted by a relevant acknowledgment in terms of section 10(1) of the 1973 Act. This was on the basis that the insurers wrote a letter "without prejudice to liability" stating *inter alia* that reasonable repairs could be carried out and the circumstances of the case. This met the condition in section 10(1)(a) of "performance" which was given a wider definition than might have been expected, that of the defender perhaps being more in accord with the literal meaning of the phrase in its context. Even with the phrase noted, which was more emphatic than the usual "without prejudice", it was held that in any event the letter could meet the condition in section 10(1)(b)—an unequivocal written admission.

Product liability cases

The obligation to make reparation in respect of damage caused by breach **20–44** of the Consumer Protection Act 1987 prescribes in 10 years.[94] Section 22A does not of course apply to a product liability claim at common law based on *Donoghue v. Stevenson*,[95] and *Grant v. Australian Knitting Mills*,[96] the

---

[92] *ibid.* at 1049. See also *BRB v. Strathclyde Regional Council*, 1982 S.L.T. 55; *Hood & Co. v. Dumbarton District Council*, 1983 S.L.T. 238.
[93] 1999 S.L.T. 596.
[94] s. 22A.
[95] 1932 S.C. (H.L.) 31.
[96] [1936] A.C. 85.

long-stop for such claims, if not affected by the three year limitation, or five year prescription. If an action has started before the end of the 10 year period then the obligation does not prescribe until the action is over.

LIMITATION

Personal injuries

20-45 Personal injuries in this connection includes a claim in respect of distress and inconvenience.[97] The same phrase where it appears in the Damages (Scotland) Act 1976 has recently been subject to judicial interpretation which might be relevant in the context of prescription.[98] In England, the results of a failure to carry out a sterilisation properly have been held to be personal injuries under English limitation legislation.[99]

The starting date

20-46 The basic limitation period in personal injury cases is three years. As in most prescription and limitation cases the starting date and finishing date for the period are the crucial issues. If necessary a preliminary proof will be ordered. In *McArthur v. Strathclyde Regional Council*,[1] it was held that generally it is for the person arguing that time should run from a later date to aver when the facts allowing that came to his knowledge. In *Hunter v. North of Scotland Hydro-Electric Board*,[2] notes in a medical report put the commencement date back further than the testimony of the injured person. In another case, even although doctors testified to keeping the true serious state of the now deceased's health from him, it was held that he could have pressed his doctor for a diagnosis, he having already submitted an application for industrial disablement benefit outwith the three year period.[3]

Non-age and unsoundess of mind

20-47 The statute itself excludes the period of non-age and unsoundness of mind. It has been held that non-age includes both pupillarity and minority under the law before the Age of Legal Capacity (Scotland) Act 1991.[4] Unsoundness of mind does not mean insanity but an inability through mental state

---

[97] *Fleming v. Strathclyde Regional Council*, 1991 S.C.L.R. 646.
[98] *Hamilton v. Fife Health Board*, 1993 S.L.T. 624.
[99] *Walkin v. South Manchester Health Board* [1995] 4 All E.R. 132. For a discussion and an application of Scots law see Blaikie, "Failed Sterilisations: Some problems of time bar", 1997 S.L.P.Q. 287. See also Sutherland, "Is Pregnancy a Personal Injury", 1996 Rep.B. 8–10. In the appeal in *McFarlane v. Tayside Health Board*, 1998 S.C.L.R. 126 decided after the article was written the analysis was in terms of *damnum* and *injuria* making the application of limitation easier, assuming that analysis to be correct. In *Anderson v. Forth Valley Health Board*, 1998 S.C.L.R. 97 Lord Nimmo Smith considered the case one of personal injury but would in any event have allowed an economic loss case.
[1] 1995 S.L.T. 1129.
[2] 1989 G.W.D. 15–645.
[3] *Ford v. Union Insulation Co. Ltd*, 1989 G.W.D. 16–696.
[4] *Fyfe v. Crudace Ltd*, 1986 S.L.T. 443; *Forbes v. House of Clydesdale*, 1988 S.L.T. 594.

to manage affairs as the reasonable man would do, which, in the case in which the phrase was first considered, was indicated by the pursuer having a vocabulary of only 20 to 30 words. On the other hand, her solicitors had managed to raise actions on her instructions other than the one in question.[5] However, in one case on this "extension", the interesting question was raised whether there need be any causal link between the section 17 factor and the delay—the answer was in the affirmative! In *Bogan's Curator Bonis v. Graham*, it was held that the unsoundness of mind was not the cause of the delay and thus the extension would not apply. This raises the equally interesting practical point of what must be done when consulted by a very young injured pursuer (or his representative). The answer, following the logic of *Bogan*, must be that it is not possible to wait until three years after the expiry of non-age before raising an action for then the non-age has not caused the delay. However, this view was rejected in *Paton v. Loffland Brother's North Sea Inc.*[6] In this case Lord Marnoch was of the opinion that there was no need for a causal connection between the delay and the incapacity. The intention was to provide a blanket immunity to those disabled from litigating. On balance it is submitted Lord Marnoch's view is to be preferred. It does reflect that there is no "causal" language in the section. On the other hand, the idea that knowing of a claim a very bright, very rich, child could willingly delay raising an action until out of non-age is unsatisfactory from a defender's point of view. Nonetheless cases of the rich able child are rare and in the absence of clear statutory language the interpretation that favours protection should be followed. Lord Marnoch's view was followed by Lord Philip in *Jardine v. Lord Advocate*.[7] That the protection in appropriate cases has been held to extend to almost 18 years by the First Division is also support for the blanket protection interpretation: in *McCabe v. McLellan and Donnelly*,[8] the action was one based on medical treatment given, or not properly given, almost immediately after birth. It is clear from the opinions in the Inner House that it was thought that the period of non-age was a blanket immunity. No thought of an action had been contemplated until a television programme on the topic.[9]

Sufficiently serious injury

The limitation period does not begin to run until the pursuer is aware that **20–48** the injuries are sufficiently serious to justify the bringing of a court action. This provision prevents people having to sue for every little knock to protect their position. However, the issue is one of interpretation and the rule must still be "it is never too early to see your solicitor", and for the solicitor: if in doubt, sue. The reason can be seen in *Blake v. Lothian Health Board*.[10] The event took place in 1986 and an action was raised in 1990. The

---

[5] *Bogan's C.B. v. Graham*, 1992 S.C.L.R. 920.
[6] 1994 S.L.T. 784.
[7] Unreported, December 18, 1997.
[8] 1994 S.L.T. 346.
[9] Although based on English law, see generally Allison, "Limitation of Actions in Child Abuse Cases" [1996] J.P.I.L. 19.
[10] 1993 S.L.T. 1248.

pursuer argued for a date in October 1987. The defenders sought an earlier commencement because after the accident the pursuer had been diagnosed as suffering acute lumbar backache. The limitation plea was repelled. The correct test was said to be based on the reasonable claimant. In this case that meant that the earlier incidence of back pain was not sufficiently serious to start the time-clock running. This was in contrast to the earlier case of *Mackie v. Currie*,[11] In this case the pursuer was struck by a car and bruised on the hip but made no claim at the time. It was only when he began to suffer from arthritis more than three years later that he sued. The Lord Kirkwood followed a gloss on the statute by Professor Walker to state that only if injuries were *de minimis* should the clock be prevented from running. In *Mackie*, as the pursuer had been taken to hospital in an ambulance this took him outside the notion of *de minimis*. It is submitted that the use of the phrase *de minimis* is an unfortunate gloss on the statute and should not be taken too literally, and that the hardy, robust, uncom-plaining, phlegmatic people (favoured by the law of delict in relation to nervous shock) should not be penalised by losing their claims.[12] In *Ferla v. Secretary of State*,[13] it was held that having taken advice from a solicitor and his union, and having made a CICB claim, the pursuer was aware that his injuries were sufficiently serious to raise an action.[14]

Knowledge of material facts

20–49 If there are material facts outwith the knowledge of the pursuer then the period may be allowed to start when he came to know the material facts.[15] In a section 18 case, raised by relatives, it was said that the delay in raising an action timeously had been that the cause of the accident which resulted in the death of the pursuer's husband remained unexplained until a fatal accident inquiry, at which time it became clear that there might be a case of absolute statutory duty. The defender argued that as there was and always had been the case of absolute statutory duty there had been no need to delay to investigate cause.[16] A preliminary proof was allowed. In *McArthur v. Strathclyde Regional Council*,[17] Lord Abernethy said that section 17 was for the benefit of the pursuer, which meant that the onus was on the pursuer to explain why he did not have the critical knowledge. This was followed in *Steel v. Begg Cousland & Co. Ltd*,[18] in which a deafness case was lost on time-bar. The case was raised because the pursuer, whose hearing was deteriorating, was told by a co-worker that he might be able to sue for deafness. It was held that the onus on the pursuer was to lay down sufficient averments from which it could be established that it would have been reasonably practicable for him to become aware of the "delaying" facts. With respect it is submitted that the only onus on the pursuer in an "own

---

[11] 1991 S.L.T. 407.
[12] It should be noted that no attempt was made to ask the court to exercise the discretion in this case.
[13] 1995 S.L.T. 662.
[14] See also *Shuttleton v. Duncan Stewart & Co. Ltd*, 1996 S.L.T. 517.
[15] *Paton v. Loffland Brothers North Sea Inc.*, 1994 S.L.T. 784.
[16] *ibid.*
[17] 1995 S.L.T. 1129.
[18] 1999 S.L.T. (Sh. Ct) 74.

knowledge" case is to raise the issue. Thereafter it is for the defender to counter with the facts that made it reasonably practicable for the pursuer to have found out the key fact. Reasonable practicability is usually inserted as a counter-proviso. The reason is the obvious one, that to make it a matter for the pursuer is to ask him to prove what he, on his averment, does not know. The defenders who are often large employers or their insurers will often know when the news about the key fact became public having received other claims. The purpose of the reasonable practicability proviso is to give the defender a locus to contradict the pursuer where he tries to succeed on the basis of his own lack of knowledge.

The discretion

The discretion is that given to the court to allow an action brought out of **20–50** time to proceed if it is equitable to do so. Its operation can be seen in the following examples.[19] A man was injured on November 3, 1975 and an action was begun on February 13, 1981.[20] There was a letter written by representatives of the proposed defender saying that for certain purposes they accepted the writ as having been served on February 7, 1977. A plea having been taken and upheld, the court, on appeal, refused to allow the pursuer to get back into the action since he had a claim against the insurers of the solicitors who had not raised the action on time. This is an important case giving the informal guidance that a strong case against solicitors means that the discretion need not be exercised.[21] In the case of *Elliot v. J. & C. Finney*[22] the court, although refusing to extend on the basis of time in hospital, did allow an extension on the equitable ground, for although an action for negligence against the solicitors might well be successful, it was not thought to be completely straightforward and the pursuer did not have the benefit of legal aid. In *Pritchard v. Tayside Health Board*,[23] another case where there were strong grounds for allowing a preliminary proof on a section 17(2)(b)(iii) claim, an equitable extension was not allowed: the pursuer was held to have known that her injuries were moderately severe from an early stage.[24] She was aware of pain and swelling in January 1982, but only in August 1983 became aware the injury was more than minimal. It may well be, that if the action had been quickly raised then the discretion would have been allowed. Even if there is a good case against solicitors who have missed a date, the discretion can be exercised where, for example, the innocent pursuer's health would be prejudiced.[25] Where the solicitor's delay means that the case is quite stale it may be that, if it has been intimated informally and there is no real prejudice to the defenders, the case can go ahead rather than delay recovery for the pursuer longer.[26] Even very long

---

[19] See generally Wade, "Time-bar in Disease Cases", 1995 Rep.B. 6–2.

[20] *Donald v. Rutherford*, 1984 S.L.T. 70.

[21] This is especially so if any delays are unexplained. *Beaton v. Strathclyde Buses Ltd*, 1993 S.L.T. 931; *Wilson v. Telling (Northern) Ltd*, 1996 S.L.T. 380; *McFarlane v. Breen*, 1994 S.L.T. 1320; *McLuskey v. Sir Robert McAlpine & Son Ltd*, 1994 S.C.L.R. 650.

[22] 1989 S.L.T. 208, 605.

[23] 1989 G.W.D. 15–643.

[24] Accident, Oct. 30, 1981; action raised, July 1986.

[25] *Johnson v. Thomson*, 1995 S.C.L.R. 554.

[26] *Oliver v. KCA Drilling Ltd*, 1995 S.C.L.R. 554. The issue of prejudice arises on both sides and was considered an important factor in *Carson v. Howard Doris Ltd*, 1981 S.C. 278. See also *Kidd v. Grampian Health Board*, 1994 S.L.T. 267; *McLaren v. Harland and Wolff Ltd*, 1991 S.L.T. 85.

periods between the accident and the case will not prevent the discretion being exercised. In *Comber v. Greater Glasgow Health Board*,[27] the alleged incident was in 1973, and the action was raised in 1987. Perhaps the most important factor is that the defenders did not aver, nor lead evidence at the preliminary proof that they would be at a disadvantage. The pursuer had made attempts to complain by writing to the board and the Secretary of State but only put lawyers on to the task in 1983, after consulting a victims' organisation. In another case, this raised by a widow, the time-limit was missed by 19 days and the discretion was exercised. The defence took the plea very late on—only after they had the deceased's evidence on commission. Doctors admitted delaying informing the deceased of the full seriousness of his condition.[28] A case was allowed to proceed with all pleas standing in 1992 in respect of a motor accident in 1983. The action was eight months late, even taking into account the fact that the pursuer had been under 18 at the time of the accident. The pursuer was the defender's girlfriend and had delayed seeking legal advice out of sympathy for the defender.[29] However, it was held on appeal that the case should not have been allowed to proceed with all pleas standing—the discretion had not been exercised at all. In this case the Inner House was then able to apply its own view which was that there was a very good case against the solicitor who had actually advised that the time was up, when there was in fact nine days left to run. The discretion was not exercised in the Division. A man who had been exposed to the carcinogenic effects of asbestos between 1933 and 1944, was diagnosed in June 1987 as suffering from cancer. An action passed signet before the expiry of the three year period but the defenders had been struck off the register. Legal aid had to be applied for to make an application to get the company put back on the register. After sundry procedure the action was served in 1990. The court allowed a proof before answer. The defenders had known the claim was coming, the pursuer's solicitors had done nothing obviously wrong and the pursuer was 75.[30] A case which was a few days late, was allowed.[31]

Amendment

20–51 Strictly this is part of the law of procedure. However, the rule is that amendment which raises matters not properly interrupted by the action will not be allowed, as that would be a way of circumventing the law on prescription and limitation. An important case is *Boyle v. Glasgow Corporation*.[32] This case was based on the now repealed Law Reform (Limitation of Actions, etc.) Act 1954, s.6(1), but the principle remains valid. A minute of amendment including averments relating to the alleged negligence of the defenders' foreman, for whom they were vicariously liable, was allowed to

---

[27] 1989 S.L.T. 639.
[28] *Ford v. Union Insulation Co. Ltd*, 1989 G.W.D. 16–696.
[29] *Clark v. McLean*, 1995 S.L.T. 235, following *Comber v. Greater Glasgow H.B.*, 1989 S.L.T. 639.
[30] *Griffen v. George MacLellan Holdings Ltd*, 1994 S.L.T. 336; this was before the Damages (Scotland) Act 1993 which might affect the strength of the "aged pursuer" point.
[31] *Cunningham v. Western Automobile Club Co. Ltd*, 1998 G.W.D. 28–1446.
[32] 1978 S.L.T. (Notes) 77.

be received before the time-bar. Answers to the pursuer's minute of amendment were allowed, and later an interlocutor was pronounced allowing the closed record to be amended in terms of the pursuer's minute of amendment and the defenders' answers thereto all after the time-bar. The defenders contended that the averments added to the record by the amendment and answers should be excluded from probation being time-barred. It was held that if the case were not to be treated as a new case the matter would not have raised problems, confirming the general rule, but holding that intimation of the minute of amendment was sufficient notice. This rule has the practical benefit of avoiding a multiplicity of actions. There are many examples of debated amendments on time-bar and the following is one. In *Jones v. McDermott (Scotland)*[33] an employee slipped on ice. He averred breaches of the Factories Act 1961, s. 29, and of the Occupiers Liability (Scotland) 1960 Act, s. 2(1). Shortly before proof the pursuer moved to amend to introduce a case based on the fault of a supervisor. This was opposed on the basis that: (a) it was time-barred; and (b) there would be prejudice. It was held that this did not amount to a new case and there was no prejudice. The averments against the supervisor were virtually identical to those pleaded under section 2(1) of the 1960 Act. The pursuer was only bringing the case into sharper focus. The occupiers' liability case, though technically a statutory case was "an appropriate expression of the common law duty of care owned by an occupier of premises to someone lawfully resorting there".[34]

---

[33] 1986 S.L.T. 551.
[34] *ibid., per* Lord Weir at 552F.

CHAPTER 21

CONTRIBUTION AND RELIEF

While many delict cases in the reports are actions between two people, **21-1** multi-party problems arise. Sometimes these are submerged in the reports as where there are causation or remoteness problems. As we have seen normally parties with a joint interest can sue or be sued together. Contribution and relief govern the position of the defenders among themselves. Contributory negligence is of the same family of concepts where the defender shares responsibility with the pursuer. For practical reasons contributory negligence is treated as a partial defence.[1]

Common law

If matters were once doubtful, it was decided in *Palmer v. Wick and* **21-2** *Pulteneytown Steam Shipping Co. Ltd*[2] that liability among joint wrongdoers, certainly in cases not involving intentional wrongdoing, is pro rata, so that the joint wrongdoer who paid the victim in full could recover a share from the other wrongdoer. Where a decree has been pursued against only one co-wrongdoer, relief is still possible against the non-appearing wrongdoer.[3] A voluntary payment, as opposed to a settlement, could not found relief.[4]

Law Reform (Miscellaneous Provisions)(Scotland) Act 1940

Section 3(1) of the Law Reform (Miscellaneous Provisions) (Scotland) Act **21-3** 1940 deals with actions by a pursuer against joint wrongdoers in a single action. Section 3(2) deals with actions where a contribution is sought by one joint wrongdoer from another who was not sued by the victim. The action on which the statutory claim is founded must be one raised in the Scottish courts.[5] The person who is sued for relief must be a person who if sued relevantly competently and timeously might also have been found liable.[6] Procedurally a defender can call a co-wrongdoer as a third party allowing the court to make any appropriate apportionment in the same proceedings. It may also apply to certain contractual claims.[7] Apportionment is probably founded on causation; it can also be based on blameworthiness.[8] Where an action against one wrongdoer has failed on the

---

[1] Chap. 20.
[2] (1894) 21 R. 39.
[3] *NCB v. Thomson*, 1959 S.C. 358.
[4] *Gardiner v. Main* (1894) 22 R. 100.
[5] *Comex Houlder Diving Ltd v. Colne Fishing Co. Ltd*, 1987 S.L.T. 443.
[6] *Singer v. Gray Tool Co. (Europe) Ltd*, 1984 S.L.T. 149.
[7] *Engdiv Ltd v. G. Percy Trentham Ltd*, 1990 S.L.T. 617.
[8] *Drew v. Western SMT Co. Ltd*, 1947 S.L.T. 92; *Christies Tutor v. Kirkwood*, 1991 S.L.T. 805.

merits another wrongdoer has a difficulty in suing for contribution on the basis of the doctrine *res judicata*.[9] Contribution may be sought from any person who may have been competently, relevantly and timeously sued, at the time the action was raised against the person seeking contribution.[10] The section does not apply to a third party alleged to have been liable to a defender rather than the pursuer.[11] In *Hardy v. British Airways Board*,[12] the pursuer tried to abandon against the second defender, the case against the first defender being time-barred. The second defender opposed the pursuer's abandonment on the basis of the Act. It was argued they would lose their right of apportionment under section 3. The argument based on section 3(1) failed because, as the claim had been extinguished, there was no possible finding of joint and several liability. It was then accepted that a separate action of relief might be raised under section 3(2) and that the argument was one of convenience. The Inner House could see no convenience—quite the contrary, the first defender would be held unnecessarily in the pursuer's process. If the court cannot apportion liability it may resort to a finding of equal sharing. At least this is what happened, by a majority, in *Drew v. Western SMT Co. Ltd*[13] where the sheriff's finding that one party was entirely to blame was rejected. Although it seems anomalous in an era of concurrent liability, it is essential for the application of the statute that the parties are jointly and severally liable as "wrongdoers". While a joint and several decree can pass against parties liable under different heads[14] that does not affect the statute. In *National Coal Board v. Knight Brothers*,[15] a third party's contention that section 3(2) of the Act was only applicable in a case where there were joint wrongdoers and was not applicable in a case where the basis of the pursuers' case against the defenders was a contractual indemnity was upheld. The parties should be found, or be able to be found, to contribute to the same injury and *damnum*.[16] Each wrong need only materially contribute to the loss.[17] It does not matter that one wrongdoer is more to blame than another.[18] In a later case it was held that although one obligation was statutory and another contractual the liability of both pursuers and defenders was of the same nature and to the same extent, and there was a common liability giving rise to a right of relief.[19] It has been suggested that *Knight Brothers* was wrongly decided.[20]

---

[9] *Singer* (n. 6 above); *Dormer v. Melville, Dundas & Whitson Ltd*, 1990 S.L.T. 186.

[10] *Taft v. Clyde Marine Motoring CDO Ltd*, 1990 S.L.T. 170; *Dormer*, above.

[11] *R. & W. Watson Ltd v. David Traill & Son Ltd*, 1972 S.L.T. (Notes) 38.

[12] 1983 S.L.T. 45.

[13] 1947 S.L.T. 92.

[14] *Belmont Laundry v. Aberdeen Steam Laundry* (1898) 1 F. 45; *Rose Street Foundry and Engineering Co. v. Lewis and Sons*, 1917 S.C. 341; *Duthie v. Caledonian Ry* (1898) 25 R. 934.

[15] 1972 S.L.T. (Notes) 24.

[16] *Glasgow Corp. v. John Turnbull & Co.*, 1932 S.L.T. 457 at 460, assuming of course it is a *damnum injuria datum* case?

[17] *McGillvray v. Davidson*, 1991 G.W.D. 31–1876.

[18] *Ellerman Lines v. Clyde Navigational Trs*, 1910 2 S.L.T. 323.

[19] *B.P. Petroleum Development Ltd v. Esso Petroleum C. Ltd*, 1987 S.L.T. 345.

[20] Young, "Rights of Relief", 1992 S.L.T. (News) 225, citing *NCB v. Knight Bros*, 1972 S.L.T. (Notes) 24.

Res Judicata

Res judicata, discussed in detail below,[21] is a plea which arises in considera- **21–4** tions of contribution and relief. Because the Act envisages and permits two actions out of the same incident it already comes close to infringing the basic rationale of *res judicata*. What takes some cases out of the idea is that the new defender was not a party to the original case. In *Anderson and Others v. Wilson*[22] the defenders were a bus company and the pursuers were five injured passengers. The defenders called a third party, the judicial factor of the estate of a car driver called Sterrick. The pursuers amended to treat the third party as an additional defender jointly and severally. Wilson pled that there had been a previous action by a sixth pursuer called Morris. In that case Sterrick's J.F. and Wilson had been sued as defenders jointly and severally. The case was fought out and the defenders held liable jointly and severally—Wilson to the extent of one-third and Sterrick's J.F. to two-thirds. Wilson tried to argue he should only be liable for one-third in this action as well—but this argument was rejected.

Settlement

Most reparation cases settle. Where there are co-delinquents there is **21–5** always a concern that the party not in process will complain that the defence could have been better taken or that the settlement is far too generous. The Act refers to a party "found liable". In the absence of such a finding the common law would not protect a party making a wholly extra-judicial offer.[23] However, the House of Lords held in *Comex Houlder Diving Co. v. Colne Fishing Co. Ltd*[24] that a right of relief under the Act could follow upon a Scottish decree based on a settlement. A party in any doubt as to the position is probably still well advised to take an assignation when settling with the victim,[25] but that right it should be noted prescribes or is limited in its own right and accordingly cannot always be a proper substitute for a right of relief. The correct view is that a right can be assigned even if there has been payment—the payment being the purchase price of the assignation. *Purden's Curator Bonis v. Boyd*[26] allowed the fact of payment to be treated as relevant albeit on the basis that the assignee should not recover more than the assignor.[27] In *Widdowson v. Hunter*[28] the action was between the purchasers of a business and the sellers. The defenders argued among other things, that the action should be dismissed, as they had been prejudiced by the pursuers settling extra-judicially a separate action arising out of the same matter which they had raised against the pursuers' former solicitors. They argued that they had lost any right of relief which they had against the solicitors under section 3(2) of the Act.

---

[21] Chap. 22.
[22] 1972 S.L.T. 170.
[23] *NCB v. Thomson*, 1959 S.C. 358.
[24] 1987 S.L.T. 443.
[25] *NCB*, n. 23 above.
[26] 1963 S.L.T. 157.
[27] See also *The Shoe Co. (Edinburgh) Ltd v. Laidlaw (Edinburgh) Ltd*, 1990 G.W.D. 30–1752.
[28] 1989 S.L.T. 478.

Lord Sutherland held that the defenders had not lost any right of relief under section 3(2) and accordingly were not prejudiced by the pursuers settling their other action extra-judicially.[29] The facts read short of *Elf Caledonia (Enterprises) Ltd v. London Bridge Engineering Ltd*,[30] were that an oil platform, the Piper Alpha, exploded with enormous loss of property and loss of life. The owner occupiers settled damages actions with the various claimants on the owner occupiers. The owner occupiers then sought indemnity from the 146 sub-contractors for the payments made by their insurers and underwriters. The complex litigation was dealt with by way of seven test cases being conjoined. On the 381st day of a 391 day proof, it was argued that six of the actions were irrelevant. The owner occupiers in terms of the contracts of indemnity were entitled only to recover their losses. It was said that the owner occupiers had largely not suffered any loss as the claims were met by insurers and underwriters. Lord Caplan dismissed the six cases. It was said that because the contractors by their indemnity and the insurers by their contracts covered the same loss they were co-debtors and the insurers would be able to sue for a proportion of their losses by way of contribution. It was also said that the insurers could have proceeded by subrogation and the owners would have had to have transferred their rights against the contractors to the insurers. Subrogation and the difficulties with this decision are treated below.[31] A settlement taking into account the possibility of an award of damages in a foreign court which is later relied upon as a claim of indemnity is not a matter of asking a Scottish court to award foreign damages and is permitted.[32]

Reform

21–6 It should be noted that there is a Scottish Law Commission Report and draft Bill seeking to reform the law.[33] Detailed legislation is envisaged.

Prescription and limitation

21–7 A party has two years from the payment of the principal liability to claim from the co-wrongdoer.[34] As above noted this applies only to the independent right of relief—a claim based on an assignation will be affected by the prescription or limitation of the underlying obligation.

---

[29] Following *Singer v. Gray Tool Co.(Europe) Ltd*, 1984 S.L.T. 149, overruling *Travers v. Neilson*, 1967 S.L.T. 64.
[30] 1998 G.W.D. 33–1665.
[31] Chap. 22.
[32] *Elf Caledonia (Enterprises) Ltd v. London Bridge Engineering Ltd*, 1998 G.W.D. 33–1661—overturned on appeal: 2000 G.W.D. 2–87.
[33] Scot. Law Com., No. 115.
[34] Prescription and Limitation (Scotland) Act 1973, s. 8A(1).

CHAPTER 22

EXTINCTION AND TRANSFER OF LIABILITY

Decree and *res judicata*

Decree brings the right to pursue the wrongdoer to a close and makes **22–1** liquid the monetary value of the claim. The corollary to the rule that all loss should be recovered in the one action suggests that decree of absolvitor extinguishes liability, certainly to the extent of the *media concludendi* of the action.[1] The same applies to a decree in favour of the pursuer. The issue most commonly arises in relation to the doctrine of *res judicata* which operates as a defence but is essentially that the cause of action has been extinguished by the granting of a prior decree. Macphail says: "The rule may be stated thus: when a matter has been the subject of a judicial determination in *foro contestioso* by a competent tribunal, that determination excludes any subsequent action in regard to the same matter between the same parties or their authors, and on the same grounds."[2] An acquittal in a criminal matter is not *res judicata* and a victim of crime, or their family if the victim is deceased, may raise a civil action to vindicate the wrong.[3] Common law negligence and breach of statutory duty are in most circumstances not different *media concludendi*[4] but it depends on the nature of the negligence and the terms of the statutory duty. It is possible to escape the effect of *res judicata* by a plea of *res noviter veniens ad notitiam*.[5] In *Maltman v. Tarmac Civil Engineering Ltd*[6] a workman was successful in his damages claim against his employers. It should be recalled that this was before the reform in relation to corroboration in civil evidence effected by the Law Reform (Miscellaneous Provisions) (Scotland) Act 1968 and the workman could not therefore succeed without corroboration. The defenders enrolled a motion for a new trial on the grounds *inter alia* that their records showed that one of the defenders' witnesses had been paid off four days before the accident. His testimony was not corroborative of the actual incident but was very significant in establishing that he himself had spilled oil on the ground where the pursuer slipped later that day. The court unanimously allowed a new trial. It was not necessary that the new evidence would lead to a different verdict but that it was of crucial importance. Subject to the point that this case was decided in the context of

---

[1] *Stevenson v. Pontifex* (1887) 15 R. 125; *Shields v. N.B. Ry* (1874) 2 R. 126. See Chap. 23 for discussion on the detailed application of the "once and for all" rule.

[2] Macphail, *Sheriff Court Practice*, para. 2.104.

[3] *Mullan v. Anderson*, 1996 Rep.L.R. 47; see Chap. 1.

[4] *Matuszczyk v. NCB*, 1955 S.C. 418.

[5] Macphail, *Sheriff Court Practice*, paras 2.109, 2.110.

[6] 1967 S.L.T. 141.

the rules of court it is a valuable review of the authorities and demonstrates a quite proper brake on the effect of *res judicata*.[7] In *Sawers and Racal Insurance Service Ltd v. Ablestart Ltd t/a M.J. Banks Ltd*[8] it was held impossible to substitute a first pursuer for a second pursuer to sue for another head of loss after settlement. In *Margrie Holdings Ltd v. City of Edinburgh District Council*[9] the pursuers sought to recover the cost of borrowing incurred by them whilst the defenders failed to pay out instalments of a grant. An earlier action to enforce payment of the grant had been successfully pursued and settled extra-judicially. The defenders *inter alia* argued unsuccessfully that the action was *res judicata*. It was held that the *media concludendi* were not the same.[10]

22-2   There is a divergence of authority on the common practical point which arises where accidents cause both personal injuries and property damages. In *Mcphee v. Heatherwick*[11] a motorcyclist sued the driver of a motorcar in the small debt court, on the ground of his negligent driving, for damages consisting of the excess on his insurance policy and the value of his crash helmet. The driver admitted liability and consented to decree. The motorcyclist's insurers, who were unaware of the small debt action, raised a summary action against the driver in the name of the motorcyclist, on the same ground, for the cost of replacing the motorcycle. The defender pleaded *res judicata*. This was upheld by Sheriff McPhail. As there is an apparent divergence of opinion it is perhaps important to see what it was that the learned sheriff actually decided:

> "What was litigated and what was decided? (See *Grahame v. Secretary of State for Scotland,* 1951 S.L.T. 312, 1951 S.C. 368, Lord President Cooper at p. 321.) In my opinion, what was litigated in the small debt action was the question whether the pursuer entitled to reparation from the defender for patrimonial loss sustained through the alleged fault of the defender in causing the accident on 15 November 1975. What was decided was that the pursuer's contentions were correct and that the defender should pay the pursuer the sum sued for plus expenses. In the present action the pursuer raises exactly the same question and invites the court to make exactly the same decision. It makes no difference that in the small debt action the pursuer sued for his 'excess' and the value of his crash helmet, while in the present action he sues for the cost of the repair of his motorcycle. In each case he sues for pecuniary loss caused by the same infringement of his patrimonial interests; and the rule is that the damages which arise from one and the same cause of action must all be assessed and recovered in one action (*Stevenson v. Pontifex and Wood* (1887) 15 R. 125, Lord President Inglis at p. 129; and see Professor D. M. Walker's *Civil Remedies*, at pp. 405–406, 529–530 and 878). The rule may be thought to be particularly apt in a case such as this, where the damages claimed in the second action

---

[7] "Res Noviter", 1967 S.L.T. (News) 201.

[8] O.H., April 29, 1997, unreported.

[9] 1996 S.L.T. 871.

[10] Note the adverse comments in the First Div. on the use of *media concludendi* in *Short's Trs v. Chung (No. 2)*, 1999 S.L.T. 751.

[11] 1977 S.L.T. (Sh. Ct) 46.

could have been claimed at the time when the first action was raised. To put it in another way: the subject-matter of the action in the small debt court was the right of the pursuer to obtain reparation from the defender for patrimonial loss sustained as a result of the accident. So also in the present action, and the grounds of action are the same in both cases because in each the ground on which the pursuer has founded his claim is the fault of the defender in driving his vehicle in a negligent manner and so causing the accident."[12]

The most important point to notice about this case, which on some points appears not to have been fully argued before the learned sheriff, is that both actions were for ordinary financial losses, so while decided on the basis of the wider general principle, the sort of issue which challenges the general dicta did not arise for decision. The point in *McSheehy v. MacMillan*[13] was different. The pursuer raised a small claim against the defender for damages consisting of the excess on his insurance policy, loss of a vehicle and non-reclaimable insurance. The defender admitted the claim and decree was granted of consent. The pursuer's insurers subsequently raised a summary cause against the defender in the name of the pursuer in respect of the same collision for the cost of repairing the vehicle. The defender pleaded *res judicata*. The sum sued for in the action of £798 represented the sum paid by the pursuer's insurance company to the pursuer in settlement of his claim under his policy. In terms of the policy there was a right of subrogation to the insurance company to use the pursuer's name in an action to recover their outlay. It should be noted that for the purposes of this case it was accepted that the *media concludendi* were the same—the negligent driving. That may not be the case where different claims are put forward but whatever the case this was not argued out in *McSheehy*. Instead Sheriff Lockhart considered that the subject-matter was different and on that basis he came to a different result. It is submitted he came to the correct result but the two rubrics are confused— the subject-matter was the same but the *media concludendi* were different. It is also the case that the fundamental reason for the decision in *McSheehy* was that the insurers were *dominus litis*—a fair point to make but perhaps not one which taking account of subrogation should be decisive. In the most recent reparation case, *Irving v. Hiddleston*,[14] the facts and legal background are different although all the same authorities were canvassed. The pursuer's first solicitors settled her claim for damages. A sum was accepted in respect of *solatium*. Payments were also made in respect of her excess and loss of use. The pursuer's condition got worse and she sued in the Outer House. It was accepted that the claim for *solatium* was ruled out. However, no claims had previously been put forward for loss of wages or employability or for services. The actual ruling in this case was that the compromise did not encompass the new claims. Thus it is essentially a contract case deciding the meaning of certain terms agreed between the parties. Accordingly, it is submitted that the comments following *McPhee*

---

[12] *ibid.* at 47 and 48.
[13] 1993 S.L.T. (Sh. Ct) 10.
[14] 1998 S.C.L.R. 350.

and not following *inter alia McSheehy* are *obiter*. And for the reasons set out above, perhaps unnecessary. Nonetheless Lord Macfadyen's remarks on the general principle will be noted.

Death

22–3 The maxim *actio personalis moritur cum persona*[15] appears in Trayner.[16] He went on to say: "All penal actions are of this character, as well as those in which the cause of action arises from delict." However, that is not now the law. In *Milne v. Gauld's Trustees*[17] a wife was allowed to raise an action for damages and *solatium* (for wrongful diligence) after the death of her husband on the basis that it passed to her as *jus mariti*. To allow this was to hold as was indeed accepted that the damages claim vested at the time of the wrong. The *actio personalis* rule was not followed. It was made clear that there was nothing penal about the action.[18] The same applies where the defender dies.[19] Claims by relatives of deceased persons are now treated under the Damages (Scotland) Act 1976. Defamation of the dead has been dealt with elsewhere.[20]

Discharge by agreement

22–4 The general rule is that the settlement is the end of the matter and it would have to be reduced before any more could be sought.[21] There are now special provisions in relation to young people.[22] While very many cases are settled by formal discharges often prepared by insurance companies, some are settled when in court by formal minute of tender and acceptance. Any settlement must be amenable to challenge on grounds vitiating the agreement—such as fraud. Juridical policy is in favour of the security of transactions but settlements can be reopened. The decision in the law of restitution in *Morgan Guaranty Trust Co. of New York v. Lothian Regional Council*[23] that a payment in error of law may be recovered is available to parties entering into arrangements fundamentally null. It is submitted that the provisions recently formulated after much thought in relation to young people give a hint of the true issues which underlie settlement.[24] If a court is appraised of an issue and all parties are called then the court process itself as a matter of policy, if not reality, is enough to ensure procedural and, probably, substantive justice. But the fact that a lawyer signs a joint minute based on lies and deceit should not be the end of the matter. Agreements with one of a multiplicity of defenders will not normally now

---

[15] A personal right of action dies with the person.
[16] *Latin Maxims and Phrases* (4th ed., 1894).
[17] (1841) 3 D. 345.
[18] Any remaining doubt is removed by the House of Lords decision in *Purden's C.B. v. Boyd*, 1963 S.L.T. 157
[19] *McNaughten v. Robertson*, 17 Feb. 1809, F.C.; *Morrisson v. Cameron*, 25 May 1809, F.C.; *Bourhill v. Young's Trs*, 1942 S.C. (H.L.) 78.
[20] Chap. 2.
[21] *N.B. Ry v. Wood* (1891) 18 R. 27.
[22] Chap. 2.
[23] 1995 S.L.T. 299.
[24] Chap. 2.

provide the party agreeing with a discharge as against the pursuer. Nor will the doctrine of *res judicata* affect a person who is not a defender but who could be called as such.[25]

Tenders

Many agreements are given effect by a formal minute of tender and **22–5** acceptance thereof in process.[26] The tender has the effect of putting the recipient (usually the pursuer) at risk for all expences from the date of the tender.[27] The court, however, retains an overall discretion.[28] The tender must offer the expenses of the action to the date of the action and take account of interest accruing on the principal sum.[29] The pursuer has a reasonable time to consider a tender, which is considered to be something, which should be regarded as urgent.[30] Multi-party actions raise some difficulties. A Williamson[31] tender is an offer made by one defender to the other defenders or third parties, to accept liability on the basis of a particular apportionment of liability. A Houston[32] tender is made by one defender to the other defenders and the pursuer. At the time of writing there are no provisions for a pursuer's tender. There had been a scheme[33] made under the Court of Session Act 1988 but it was revoked (without retrospective effect) two months later. However, it was later held that the scheme was in fact *ultra vires* and had not been in effect for the two months between regulations.[34] It is likely that a new scheme may be devloped. In the meantime a pursuer can write a letter stating that it will be founded upon in the event of an argument about expences and in appropriate circumstance can expect such a Morrison[35] letter to be given serious attention.

Prescription and limitation

Prescription extinguishes liability and limitation by preventing the pursuer **22–6** taking action has the same practical effect in most cases.[36]

Personal bar

Leaving aside statutory prescription and limitation, delay in the knowledge **22–7** of a claim may be argued to suggest an implied waiver—the common plea is one of *mora*, taciturnity and delay, depending for its success on some

---

[25] See Chap. 21 for settlement in conjunction with contribution and relief.

[26] For a full discussion, see *McEwan and Paton on Damages for Personal Injuries in Scotland*, Chap. 18.

[27] See, *e.g. Hodge v. British Coal Corp. (No. 3)*, 1992 S.L.T. 1005.

[28] *Bhatia v. Tribax Ltd*, 1994 S.L.T. 1201.

[29] See, *e.g. Fleming Bros (Structural Engineers) Ltd v. Ford Motor Co. Ltd*, 1969 S.L.T. (Notes) 54.

[30] See, *e.g. Kenny v. L.A.*, 1993 S.L.T. 372.

[31] *Williamson v. McPherson*, 1951 S.C. 438.

[32] *Houston v. British Road Services Ltd*, 1967 S.L.T. 329.

[33] A.S. (Rules of the Court of Session Amendment No. 4) (Miscellaneous) 1996 (S.I. 1996 No. 2168).

[34] *Taylor v. Marshall's Food Group* [1998] T.L.R. 571.

[35] *Morrison v. Barton (No. 2)*, 1994 S.L.T. 685. See also *Cameron v. Kvaerner Govan*, 1999 S.L.T. 638.

[36] Chap. 20.

prejudice to the defender.[37] It is a matter of fact in any case, but the existence of the modern prescription and limitation code may support the view that pursuers are entitled to wait the length of the period and so something out of the ordinary would need to be shown to bar a claim. Indeed it has always been the case that *mora* has been prohibited from being a kind of back-door prescription. In *MacKenzie v. Cattons Trustees*,[38] Lord Deas, said: *"Mora* is not a good *nomen juris.* There must either be prescription or not. We are not to rear up new kinds of prescription under different names."[39] There have been no instances since the new code.[40] In *Woods v. A.C.S. Motors Ltd*,[41] Lord Hunter said:

> "The plea of *mora* cannot be *de plano* sustained and indeed *mora* and taciturnity is not a proper plea in law at all. Short of the lapse of the prescriptive period of time there has been delay in bringing the action; but the inferences to be drawn from the evidence led would be, because of the delay, considerably different from what these would have been if the action had been timeously brought."[42]

A concise summary of the present position is given by Sheriff Principal Reid in a contract case.[43] The sheriff dismissed the action after a four year sist. This was reversed by the sheriff principal:

> "It is now well settled that the effect of mora is to increase any onus of proof on the party responsible for it in respect of matters whose proof has been prejudiced by it (*Rutherford v. Harvey & McMillan*, 1954 S.L.T. (Notes) 28). Mora alone can never form the basis of a dilatory plea. If accompanied by taciturnity and acquiescence, duly pled and proved, it may have effect as a plea to the merits of an action (*Assets Co. Ltd. v. Bain's Trustees* (1904) 6 F. 692 at pp. 705, 711). It has been said that mora is not to be used to rear up prescriptions under different names (*Mackenzie v. Catton's Trustees* (1877) 5 R. 313, at p. 317). It appears to me that the effect of affirming the learned sheriff's interlocutor would resemble rearing up a prescription against a claim which has been made the subject of an action against which prescription does not operate. There can, in principle, be no difference between the effect of mora in raising an action and mora in the conduct of an action and it could not be suggested that mora in raising an action short of prescription should entitle the court to refuse to entertain it on the view that the pursuer had impliedly abandoned his claim."[44]

Perhaps too this is best seen as a defence because if two persons are wronged and one acquiesces the right of action remains for the other—the

---

[37] *Auld v. Shairp* (1874) 2 R. 191.
[38] (1877) 5 R. 313.
[39] *ibid.* at 317.
[40] See, *e.g. Munro v. Jarvey* (1821) 1 S. 161.
[41] 1930 S.L.T. 717.
[42] *ibid.* at 718. See also L.P. Clyde in *Halley v. Watt*, 1956 S.L.T. 111.
[43] *Church Of Scotland Home Board v. J.C. Mcgeagh & Co. Ltd*, 1980 S.L.T. (Sh. Ct) 75.
[44] *ibid.* at 76.

obligation thus not being extinguished so far as the defender is concerned. *Mora* is relevantly argued as special cause why a jury trial should not be allowed—the main point usually being that by leaving a case for its full time before litigation the memory of witnesses may be affected and a jury, unlike a judge, might not be able to compensate properly for that.[45]

In English materials reference will be found to waiver of tort allowing a restitutionary claim where for example there has been no loss. There is no need for such language in Scotland where a restitutionary action may be taken in its own right.[46]

Assignation

This topic is discussed elsewhere in this book.[47]   **22–8**

Insolvency

The liability of the bankrupt estate is with the estate rather than the **22–9** individual whose estates are now sequestrated. Actions against a liquidator have to be considered very carefully. The title to sue of the bankrupt has been considered above.[48] A defender must take care in settling with a trustee that there is not some liability to the bankrupt which must also be discharged.

Subrogation

The House of Lords in a Scottish appeal reviewed the law of subrogation **22–10** whereby in appropriate circumstances on one party paying damages to another (the victim of a wrong) that paying party is entitled to sue the wrongdoer. *Esso Petroleum Co. Ltd v. Hall Russell & Co. Ltd*[49] was a reparation case arising out of an incident where a tug caught fire and cast off her line while taking part in berthing an oil tanker at a jetty. The fire on the tug was caused by a coupling blowing out of a hydraulic pipe above the starboard engine exhaust. The tanker then collided with the jetty causing damage to the tanker and the jetty and an escape of bunker oil. The oil polluted the shore causing loss to crofters. The owners of the tanker raised an action against the builders of the tug. The builders averred that they had properly fitted the coupling, and convened four third parties, one of whom were the islands council as harbour authority, who it was averred were vicariously liable for the negligence of the pilot on the bridge of the tanker when the accident occurred. The pursuers admitted and adopted the averments made by the builders against the third parties. The pursuers sought *inter alia* to recover sums which they had paid out in settling claims

---

[45] *Davidson v. Chief Constable, Fife Police*, 1995 S.L.T. 545 (jury allowed); *Summers v. North Of Scotland Hydro-Electric Board*, 1975 S.L.T. (Notes) 35 (jury allowed); *Mcdermid v. Underhill Heating Engineering Ltd*, 1971 S.L.T. (Notes) 12 (proof before answer but not because of *mora*).

[46] Chap. 5.

[47] Chap. 2.

[48] Chap. 2.

[49] 1988 S.L.T. 874.

made by persons who had suffered loss as a result of the oil pollution. These liabilities were said to have arisen out of an agreement ("Tovalop") entered into by major oil companies as owners of oil tankers. It provided that if before the owner satisfied in full his liability under the agreement he paid compensation or another person provided insurance for that payment, such person acquired by subrogation all the rights of the person compensated under the agreement. The Inner House held that the averments of the owners in support of their claim to recover the sums paid by them to the crofters and the terminal operators under and in terms of Tovalop were irrelevant. It was held that the doctrine of subrogation did not entitle the shipowners to recover in their own name sums paid out by them in terms of Tovalop, nor could the shipowners recover sums paid out by them under and in terms of Tovalop directly as a head of damage suffered by them. The following explanation of the role of subrogation was given by Lord Goff:

"There can of course be no direct claim by Esso against Hall Russell in restitution, if only because Esso has not by its payment discharged the liability of Hall Russell, and so has not enriched Hall Russell; if anybody has been enriched, it is the crofters, to the extent that they have been indemnified by Esso and yet continue to have vested in them rights of action against Hall Russell in respect of the loss or damage which was the subject matter of Esso's payment to them. All that is left is the fact that the crofters' rights of action against Hall Russell continued to exist (until the expiry of the relevant limitation period), and that it might have been inequitable to deny Esso the opportunity to take advantage of them—which is the classic basis of the doctrine of subrogation in the case of contracts of indemnity (see *Castellain v. Preston* (1883) 11 Q.B.D. 380). In normal cases, as for example under contracts of insurance, the insurer will on payment request the assured to sign a letter of subrogation, authorising the insurer to proceed in the name of the assured against any wrongdoer who has caused the relevant damage to the assured. If the assured refuses to give such authority, in theory the insurer can bring proceedings to compel him to do so. But nowadays the insurer can short circuit this cumbrous process by bringing an action against both the assured and the third party, in which (1) he claims an order that the assured shall authorise him to proceed against the third party in the name of the assured, and (2) he seeks to proceed (so authorised) against the third party. But it must not be thought that, because this convenient matter of proceeding now exists, the insurer can without more proceed in his own name against the third party. He has no right to do so, so long as the right of action he is seeking to enforce is the right of action of the assured. Only if that right of action is assigned to him by the assured can he proceed directly against the third party in his own name (see, *e.g., Compania Colombiana de Seguros v. Pacific Steam Navigation Co.* [1965] Q.B. 101; [1964] 2 W.L.R. 484; [1964] 1 All E.R. 216). I have no doubt that the like principles apply in the present case. It follows that Esso could only proceed directly in its own name against Hall Russell in respect of the crofters' claims against Hall Russell if, on paying the crofters, it received from them a valid and effective assignation of their claims. I cannot think that, in practice, Esso would have met with difficulty if it had, at the time of payment to the crofters,

asked each of them for a receipt which operated either as an assignation
or as an authority to proceed against the third party in the name of the
crofters concerned; if any such practical difficulty should exist, it could
surely be overcome in future by an appropriate amendment to Tovalop.
For these reasons, which are substantially the same as those expressed by
the Lord President in his judgment, I would reject Esso's claim based
upon subrogation."[50]

This doctrine based on unjust enrichment and enforced by a fused form of
equity is not the same as a statutory assignation. An assignation should
always be obtained before any subsequent action is raised.[51] While the
English references seem to suggest a procedure for compelling the indemnified person to allow his name to be used, no such actions appear in the
Scots cases.

It has been said in a Scots appeal to the House of Lords[52] that the
terminology of assignation and subrogation should not be confused:

"It appears to me further that the decision of the Court must be arrived
at on all the facts of the case. I cannot agree that we may disregard the
fact of the real plaintiffs being underwriters in England, who sue in the
name of the assured by reason of their right of subrogation. Its exact
weight is another matter. In this particular case I do not think it carries
their case much further. They have been described, I think rather
loosely, as mere assignees. If, as I expect was the case, that term was
used for the purpose of stating that they stood in the shoes of their
assured and had no better rights than theirs, there is nothing to be said
against it; but the case is not one of assignment. Under an old equity,
now a statutory right, they sue in the name of their assured, and the right
to pursue the rights and remedies of the assured against third parties is
one to which they are subrogated. Both in terms of the statute and in
terms of long usage I think that the word 'subrogation', as used in
section 79, subsection (1), of the Marine Insurance Act, ought to be used
in preference to the term "assignment," which is provided for in section
50, subsection (2), and involves different incidents."[53]

There are of course a number of cases which while not raising subrogation
directly raise similar questions either under the law of contract or restitution arising from cases where one party has settled another's liability.[54]

Subrogation was considered in *Elf Enterprises (Caledonia) Ltd v. London
Bridge Engineering Ltd*,[55] in which the insured sued for (mainly) the

---

[50] *ibid.* at 878. Lord Jauncey (a Scots Lord of Appeal) said: "My Lords, the foregoing
authorities leave me in no doubt as to the existence of a general rule in both English and Scots
law that where an indemnifier is subrogated to the rights of someone whom he has
indemnified he can only pursue those rights in name of that person."

[51] See *Goodyear Tyre and Rubber Co. Ltd v. Gillies*, 1944 S.L.T. (Sh. Ct) 13 where
subrogation crops up as part of a defence. It is truly a simple case of title to sue where there
had been an actual transfer of the property to the indemnifying insurers.

[52] *Société du Gaz de Paris v. SA de Navigation; Les Armateurs Français*, 1926 S.L.T. 33.

[53] *ibid.*, per Lord Sumner at 36.

[54] See, *e.g. Halliday v. Lyall and Scott Ltd*, 1995 S.L.T. 192; *Norwich Union Fire Ins. Soc. Ltd
v. Ross*, 1995 S.L.T. (Sh. Ct) 103.

[55] 1998 G.W.D. 33–1661. See para. 22–10—overturned on appeal: 2000 G.W.D. 2–87.

insurers' losses in honouring the insurance contract, against the sub-contractors under indemnity contracts. It was held that the bulk of the actions should be dismissed. The insurers had made the payments. The pursuers therefore had no loss. It was said that the insurers could recover their outlay by way of subrogation but for that to happen the pursuers would have had to transfer their enforceable right against the sub-contractors to their insurers. One of the points made was that the pursuers could not recover twice. It is not clear that that is what they intended to do nor that, necessarily, this is what would have happened. Gow, citing English authority says that if the the insured has been paid himself and recovers from a third party then he must account to the insurer.[56] Generally the court is not concerned that a pursuer is insured.[57] Once the case is (if ever)[58] fully reported this aspect will require careful scrutiny as it would for any practitioner faced with a similar problem. The safest way is always to take assignations before action.

Statutory transfer

22–11 Certain statutory provisions transfer liability. The Third Parties (Rights Against Insurers) Act 1930 allows a pursuer to sue an insurer directly where the insured has become bankrupt or otherwise unable to meet the loss of the pursuer. In the case of a company, liquidation or receivership, will trigger the right.[59] There is no direct right of action. Liability must be established against the insured.[60] The insurer can plead the insolvent person's defences.[61] But it has been held in England that unpaid premiums cannot be deducted.[62] The rules must be followed carefully although in one case advertisement of the summons was held sufficient instead of intimation to the insurers, which should be done to be on the safe side.[63] Bolstering this safety net for the pursuer are provisions to deal with the insolvency of the insurers of the insolvent defenders. There is a Policy-holders Protection Board to whom liability will be transferred in certain cases of insurance companies themselves in liquidation in terms of the Policyholders Protection Act 1975. These rights are practically meaningful because of the existence of compulsory insurance. As explained above there is a conflict of authority on whether directors who do not take out the compulsory insurance are liable for breach of statutory duty.[64]The Road Traffic Acts have for some time made third-party insurance in respect of death and personal injury, compulsory.[65]

For some time[66] provision has been made for the "compulsory" insurer to meet unsatisfied judgments.[67] The requirement for notice was considered

---

[56] *Mercantile and Industrial Law of Scotland* (1964), p. 345.
[57] *Port Glasgow Sailcloth Co. v. Caledonian Railway* (1892) 19 R. 608.
[58] The transcript of the judgment (not the evidence!) extends to 1,453 pages.
[59] See Insolvency Act 1986.
[60] s. 1(4); *Post Office v. Norwich Union* [1967] 2 Q.B. 363; *Bradley v. Eagle Star* [1989] 2 W.L.R. 568.
[61] *Firma C-Trade SA v. Newcastle Protection & Indemnity Ass.* [1991] 2 A.C. 1.
[62] *Murray v. Royal and General* [1970] 2 Q.B. 495.
[63] *Saunders v. Royal Ins.*, Aug. 25, 1998.
[64] See para. 11–8.
[65] See Road Traffic Act 1988, s. 143.
[66] Road Traffic Act 1934, s. 10.
[67] See Road Traffic Act 1988, s. 151.

in *Orme v. Ferguson.*[68] The pursuer pled that his solicitor had in a telephone discussion told the insurers that an action had been raised. Proceedings were commenced the following day. The sheriff principal, upholding the sheriff held that the inaccuracy of saying that proceedings had commenced when they were not in fact commenced until the following day was slight.[69] An action against the insurers is a special statutory claim and not, despite the fact that a delict started the problem, a matter relating to tort, delict or quasi-delict in terms of the Civil Jurisdiction and Judgments Act 1982, Sched. 4, Art. 5(3) and (4) such as to allow the insurers to be sued in the court of the locus of the accident.[70]

---

[68] 1996 S.L.T. (Sh. Ct) 2.
[69] See the English cases and Commonwealth cases discussed: *Herbert v. Railway Passengers Assurance Co.* (1938) 60 Ll.L.Rep. 143; *Weldrick v. Essex and Suffolk Equitable Ins. Soc. Ltd* (1949) 83 Ll.L.Rep. 91; *Ceylon Motor Ins. Ass. Ltd v. P.P. Thanbugala* [1953] A.C. 584; *Harrington v. Link Motor Policies at Lloyds* [1989] 2 Lloyd's Rep. 310; *McGoona v. Motor Insurers Bureau* [1969] 2 Lloyd's Rep. 34.
[70] *Davenport v. Corinthian Motor Policies at Lloyds*, 1991 S.L.T. 774. See Chap. 23.

CHAPTER 23

ASPECTS OF JURISDICTION AND CHOICE OF LAW

Private international law is now comprehensively dealt with in specialist **23–1** texts.[1] Nonetheless it is appropriate to set out the main principles and rules required by a Scots lawyer in considering (i) whether the Scottish courts may deal with the issue and (ii) whether it is the rules of law set out in this book which apply to the dispute.

JURISDICTION

The Civil Jurisdiction and Judgments Act 1982 provided a statutory scheme **23–2** for all jurisdictional matters in relation to delict. It had a European Union provenance but the opportunity was also taken to bring the rules of jurisdiction among the U.K. jurisdictions into a similar harmony.[2] So far as delictual claims are concerned the following provisions are relevant.

Article 5 of Schedule 4 to the 1982 Act provides that a person domiciled **23–3** in a part of the United Kingdom may be sued in another part of the United Kingdom, "in matters relating to tort, delict or quasi-delict, in the courts for the place where the harmful event occurred",[3] and "as regards a civil claim for damages or restitution which is based on an act giving rise to criminal proceedings, in the court seised of those proceedings, to the extent that that court has jurisdiction under its own law to entertain civil proceedings".[4]

There are special rules of interpretation.[5] The U.K. rules are brought as closely as possible into harmony with the international rules and the same special rules of interpretation apply.[6] The basic rule is in Schedule 4 which provides in Article 2 that "Subject to the provisions of this Title, persons

---

[1] A.E. Anton and P.R. Beaumont, *Civil Jurisdiction in Scotland* (2nd. ed., 1995); A.E. Anton, *Private International Law* (2nd. ed., 1990).

[2] See Beaumont, "Jurisdiction in Delict in Scotland" (1983) J.L.S. 528; Black, "Styles for Averring Jurisdiction under the 1982 Act", 1987 S.L.T. (News) 1.

[3] Art. 5(3).

[4] Art. 5(4).

[5] "3(1) Any question as to the meaning or effect of any provision of the Conventions shall, if not referred to the European Court in accordance with the 1971 Protocol, be determined in accordance with the principles laid down by and any relevant decision of the European Court; (2) Judicial notice shall be taken of any decision of, or expression of opinion by, the European Court on any such question; (3) Without prejudice to the generality of subsection (1), the . . . reports . . . reproduced in the Official Journal of the Communities . . . may be considered in ascertaining the meaning or effect of any provision of the Conventions and shall be given such weight as is appropriate in the circumstances."

[6] s. 16(1), (3).

domiciled in a part of the United Kingdom shall . . . be sued in the courts of that part." Then in Article 5 it is provided *inter alia* that a "person domiciled in a part of the United Kingdom may, in another part of the United Kingdom, be sued: (1) in matters relating to a contract, in the courts for the place of performance of the obligation in question; . . . (3) in matters relating to tort, delict or quasi-delict, in the courts for the place where the harmful event occurred or in the case of a threatened wrong is likely to occur; (4) as regards a civil claim for damages or restitution which is based on an act giving rise to criminal proceedings, in the court seised of those proceedings, to the extent that that court has jurisdiction under its own law to entertain civil proceedings".

23–4 There has only been one significant consideration of the provisions in Scotland. In *Davenport v. Corinthian Motor Policies at Lloyds*[7] the issue was whether a claim based on a statutory right of recovery against insurers, based on an action based on delict fell within the Civil Jurisdiction and Judgments Act 1982, Sched. 4, Art. 5(3). It was held in the Inner House, it is submitted correctly that it did not—it was not based on delict. The ground of the action after all was the statutory right. It was said in this case that Article 5 created a series of exceptions to the general rule contained in Article 2 that persons should be sued in the courts where they were domiciled and that the exceptions had to be strictly construed. This legislation does of course have to be construed according to the rationale of the European law.[8] Lord Milligan made the practical point:

"I add only a note of regret in that there seems to me much to be said for there being jurisdiction to pursue an action such as the present in a court where there was jurisdiction in the delictual action, and rather less to be said against this being so, at least within the United Kingdom."

The European cases support the view that the pursuer has a choice of where to sue, at least where the event giving rise to the event directly produced harmful effects upon the person who is the immediate victim of that event.[9] Similar U.K. legislation applying before the 1982 Act although dealing with the same concepts and ideas is of general interest, but the new legislation needs to be interpreted in a communitaire fashion.[10]

23–5 In the tricky case of international defamation the European Court of Justice has held that the courts of every jurisdiction where a defamatory statement is disseminated have jurisdiction under Article 5(3), limited to the harm actually caused.[11]

---

[7] 1991 S.L.T. 774.

[8] In *Davenport* the court applied *Kalfelis v. Schröder, Münchmayer, Hengst & Co.* (189/87) [1988] E.C.R. 5565; and considered *Peters v. ZNAV* (34/82) [1983] E.C.R. 987; and *Six Constructions Ltd v. Humbert* (32/88) [1989] E.C.R. 341.

[9] *Bier v. Mirres de Potasse d'Alsace* (21/76) [1976] E.C.R. 1735.

[10] Law Reform (Jurisdiction in Delict) (Scotland) Act 1971, s. 1; *Kirkcaldy D.C. v. Household Manufacturing Ltd*, 1987 S.L.T. 617. And see *Longworth v. Hope* (1865) 3 M. 1049.

[11] *Shevill v. Presse Alliance SA* [1995] 2 A.C. 18, ECJ; [1996] 3 W.L.R. 420, H.L. See generally Reed, "A To Chill a Mocking Word (Multistate Defamation)" [1997] Tort L.R. 3.

Forum non conveniens

Forum non conveniens remains a part of the law of jurisdiction, although **23-6** the 1982 Act restricts the applicability of it in international cases between Convention countries.[12] In *Foxen v. Scotsman Publications*,[13] the plaintiff was allowed to sue for defamation in England despite the fact that only 10 per cent of the copies of the newspaper concerned were sold outside Scotland. *Forum non conveniens* was held not to be applicable. In *Cumming v. Scottish Daily Record and Sunday Mail*,[14] a Scottish student said he had been defamed by the *Sunday Mail*. Less than 10 per cent of the copies of the newspaper were sold in England. The same judge who decided *Foxen* changed his mind to find that *forum non conveniens* was open in intra-U.K. cases.[15] *FMC v. Russell*[16] arose out of an accident. The defender's paramour was working on an oil rig when a bolt came out of an assembly and killed him. The defender in *this* action was pursuer in another action in Aberdeen Sheriff Court against the U.K. owners, employers and product producers. She also sued six companies in the United States. The parties and grounds of claim both differed. The U.S. companies obtained interim interdict to prevent her continuing her action in the United States. On a motion for recall Lord Bonomy accepted the legal position as being set out in *Societe Nationale Industriale Aerospatiale v. Lee Kui Jak*.[17] The petitioner had to establish that Scotland was the natural forum for the case and that it would be vexatious and oppressive to litigate in a foreign jurisdiction. It is not enough that the foreign case is conducted under different rules or provides different remedies. Lord Bonomy noted that in the leading House of Lords case *Spilada Maritime Corporation Ltd v. Cansulex*[18] Lord Goff considered the Scots cases on *forum non conveniens*.[19] The search was for a real and substantial connection. The petitioners were concerned that in the United States they would be exposed to greater damages and exemplary damages. Lord Bonomy after a meticulous consideration of the issues recalled the interim interdict. An important factor was that the Texas court had power to stay proceedings on the basis of *forum non conveniens*. As the petitioner had not established the plea there, there was no reason to apply it in Scotland. Forum shopping is an inevitable consequence of differing liability regimes.[20]

---

[12] But not in extra-convention cases: *Re Harrods (Buenos Aires) Ltd* [1992] Ch. 72.

[13] [1994] T.L.R. 84.

[14] [1995] T.L.R. 333.

[15] See Amodeo, "Conflicts of Jurisdiction within the U.K." (1995) J.L.S. 321.

[16] Unreported, Outer House, February 27, 1998.

[17] [1987] A.C. 871.

[18] *The Spilada* [1987] A.C. 460.

[19] See, *e.g. Sim v. Robinson* (1892) 19 R. 655; *Clements v. McCauley* (1866) 4 M. 583; *Societe du Gaz de Paris v. Armateurs Francais*, 1926 S.C. (H.L.) 13.

[20] See generally Tippler and Christensen, "The Possibility of Bringing a United States Lawsuit for Product Liability Damages Arising in the United Kingdom" [1995] J.P.I.L. 185; Williams, "Bringing Proceedings in the US for English Plaintiffs: The Obstacle of *forum non-conveniens*" [1996] J.P.I.L. 2.

CHOICE OF LAW

23-7 Prior to the legislation which will next be examined the law was that the law of the pursuer's domicile was irrelevant.[21] The defender's domicile was equally irrelevant.[22] The claim had to satisfy both the *lex fori* and the *lex loci delicti*. For a long time the rule known as the double actionability or double delict rule applied. It will still apply to delicts committed before the new Act and to defamation actions.[23] It thus merits some short attention here. It was emphatically approved in *Mitchell v. McCulloch*[24] an action in which the pursuer claimed damages from the defender for personal injuries sustained in a shooting incident in the Bahamas. An element of the claim was the loss of the pursuer's services to his practice, a claim considered to be possible under the law of the Bahamas but not under Scots law.[25] It was held that the claim must be actionable under both systems.[26] Exceptions developed.[27] The rule was applied to an interdict action for passing off.[28] The rule was criticised in England[29] and by Scots lawyers.[30] This resulted in a joint report of the two law commissions[31] and legislation.[32] This led to the passing of the Private International Law (Miscellaneous Provisions) Act 1995. The general rule is that the applicable law is the law of the country in which the events constituting the tort or delict in question occur.[33] Where elements of these events occur in different countries there are three rules: in cases of personal injury[34] or death the applicable law is that of the territory where the individual was when the injuries were sustained[35]; for damage to property it is the place where the property was when it was damaged[36]; and for all other cases the territory where the "most significant element or elements of the events" complained of occurred, failing that, the law of the territory with which the subject matter has the "most real and substantial connection".

---

[21] *Convery v. Lanarkshire Tramway Co.* (1905) 8 F. 117.

[22] *Naftalin v. L.M.S. Railway*, 1933 S.C. 259.

[23] s. 13(1). This is defined as any claim under the law of any part of the U.K. for libel or slander of title, slander of goods or of malicious falsehood and any claim under the law of Scotland for verbal injury (s. 13(2)(a)) and to claims of the same nature under the law of any country (s. 13(2)(b)).

[24] 1976 S.C. 1.

[25] Applying *Young v. Ormiston*, 1936 S.L.T. 79; *Gibson v. Glasgow Corp.*, 1963 S.L.T. (Notes) 16.

[26] Applying *Rosses v. Sir Bhagrat Sinjie* (1891) 19 R. 31; *Evans v. Stein* (1904) 7 F. 65; *Naftalin v. L.M.S. Ry*, 1933 S.C. 259; and *McElroy v. McAllister*, 1949 S.C. 110.

[27] Some were suggested in *Boys v. Chaplin* (1971) A.C. 356 and another arose in *Red Sea Insurance Co. v. Bouygues* [1995] 1 A.C. 190, PC. See Rodger, "Bouygues and Scottish Choice of Law Rules in Delict", 1995 S.L.P.Q. 58.

[28] *James Burrough Distilleries Plc. v. Speymalt Whisky Distributors Ltd*, 1989 S.L.T. 561.

[29] See, *e.g.* Carter, "Choice of Law in Tort and Delict" (1991) 107 L.Q.R. 405.

[30] Black, "Delict and the Conflict of Laws", 1968 J.R. 40.

[31] Law Com., No. 193; Scot. Law Com., No. 129.

[32] Blaikie, "Foreign Torts and Choice of Law Flexibility", 1995 S.L.T. (News) 23; Blaikie, "Choice of Law in Delict and Tort: Reform at last", 1997 Edin.L.R. 361; Rodger, *op. cit.*

[33] s. 11(1). See generally Williams and Mead, "Abolition of the Double Actionability Rule: Questions still to be answered" [1996] J.P.I.L. 112.

[34] This includes disease or any impairment of physical or mental condition: s. 11(3).

[35] s. 11(2)(a).

[36] s. 11(2)(b).

The general rule may be displaced. If it appears, in all the circumstances, **23–8** from a comparison of (a) the significance of the factors which connect a tort or delict with the country whose law would be the applicable law under the general rule; and (b) the significance of any factors connecting the tort or delict with another country, that it is substantially more appropriate for the applicable law for determining the issues arising in the case, or any of those issues, to be the law of the other country, the general rule is displaced and the applicable law for determining that issue or issues (as the case may be) is the law of that other country. The factors which may be taken into account as connecting a tort or delict with a country for the purposes of this section include, in particular, factors relating to the parties, to any of the events which constitute the tort or delict in question or to any of the circumstances or consequences of those events.[37] Collisions between vessels are dealt with by the law and custom of maritime law.[38]

---

[37] s. 12.
[38] *Currie v. McKnight* (1896) 24 R. (H.L.) 1.

CHAPTER 24

PROOF

A review of the significant features involved in proof is not out of place in **24–1**
this book: it completes the structure of liability because to read this book
not knowing of proof would be to distort the view of the law given. It can
be said that rules of liability take into account rules of proof—thus a system
might not adopt strict liability if there were a fault system with strong
presumption in favour of a pursuer, or if the standard of proof were very
low. In the same way if proof is very difficult, rules on liability might be
eased.

Standard of proof

Generally the standard is proof on the balance of probabilities. This **24–2**
contrasts with the criminal law where the standard is proof beyond a
reasonable doubt. The civil standard applies even if some criminal matter is
in issue as part of the civil investigation.[1] Some factual situations may be
such as to make it difficult to establish a certain fact as probable as where a
person tries to say that an object dropped from a roof top fell upwards.
Such cases are rare ordinarily and care must always be taken that a rule of
law is not being developed where it ought not to be.

Inference, prima facie negligence and *res ipsa loquitur*

Seldom are all the facts known in reparation cases (as in many other areas **24–3**
of law) as matters of *primary* fact. Very often an intellectual step has to be
taken of making up a fact to fit the existing facts. This "making up" clearly
must be controlled or the law would soon become arbitrary. Inference in
this sense is the limit on the way in which such facts may be made up.
Inference is a logical process but there is no evidence of inference being
used in any technical logical fashion. On one view it has become a woolly
notion of "appropriate common-sense surmise". A leading case is *Inglis v.
London, Midland, and Scottish Railway Co.*[2] A child fell from a train when a
carriage door opened during a journey. The pursuers claimed the guard had
not checked the doors were closed when the train left Glasgow and the
defenders that the door was interfered with from inside during the journey.[3]
The pursuers claimed that the happening was instructive of negligence.[4]

---

[1] *e.g. Sloan v. Triplett*, 1985 S.L.T. 294; *Wilson v. Price*, 1989 S.L.T. 484.
[2] 1941 S.L.T. 408.
[3] The cases relied on are instructive: *Mars v. Glasgow Corp.*, 1940 S.C. 202; *Connelly v.
L.M.S. Ry*, 1940 S.C. 477.
[4] *Richards v. G.W. Ry* (1873) 28 L.T. 711; *Cassidy v. N.B. Ry* (1873) 11 M. 341; *Cooper v.
Caledonian Ry* (1902) 4 F. 880; *Burns v. N.B. Ry*, 1914 S.C. 754.

The Inner House accepted that on the basis of authority the opening of a door was prima facie evidence of negligence.[5] *Res ipsa loquitur*[6] did not apply. Lord President Normand explained:

> "[T]his maxim has a certain utility when an accident occurs at a moment when the thing which causes the injury is outside immediate human control. When that condition is not present, it is better to avoid the expression *res ipsa loquitur*, and to consider whether the facts and circumstances proved are prima facie evidence of negligence and affect the onus of proof. It may be that this is merely a matter of phraseology, but the truth is that the words *res ipsa loquitur* are sometimes used as if they possessed a magical power to solve difficult questions of negligence. The learned Sheriff-Substitute has not erred in substance, but I think that if he had relied less on the Latin maxim he would have seen the necessity of an express finding of negligence in that the defenders had failed to close and properly fasten the door or to see that it was properly closed and fastened before the train left St Enoch's Station, as it was their duty to do. That finding is clearly implied by the Sheriff's note, and it should find a place in the interlocutor."[7]

Lord Moncreiff was even more analytical:

> "I do not however find myself able to adopt the reasoning which bases that decision on an application of the doctrine of *res ipsa loquitur*. It may indeed now be regarded as settled that the unexplained opening of a railway carriage door in course of travel affords prima facie evidence of negligence on the part of whoever may have been responsible for the closing of the door . . . Even in such a case, however, there will be at most an analogy with, and not a proper example of, an application of the maxim [*res ipsa loquitur*] . . . In a case such as the present, in which the defenders ceased to be in control of the door before the commencement of the journey, the unexplained opening of the door, while still relevant prima facie to infer negligence, is thus in no way relevant even prima facie to infer negligence for which the defenders are responsible. The res, or if it be preferred the res ipsa, is thus unavailing to transfer the onus of proof; the doctrine or maxim does not apply; and the pursuer must, as in other cases, undertake the whole burden of proving his case. In discharging that burden he may however rely, as part of his proof, on the opening of the door as affording prima facie evidence of negligence; and may complete his proof, and either bring that negligence directly home to the defenders or in turn charge them to acquit themselves of negligence, by having resort to the familiar method of exclusion. It is this method which the pursuer has followed in this case."[8]

The same idea is seen in *O'Hara v. Central Scottish Motor Traction Co. Ltd.*[9] A driver swerved. It was held that this was prima facie evidence of

---

[5] *Gee v. Metropolitan Ry* (1873) L.R. 8 Q.B. 161; *Richards v. G.E. Ry* (1873) 28 L.T. 711; *Burns v. N.B. Ry*, 1914 S.C. 754.

[6] *Inglis* at 411–412.

[7] *ibid.*

[8] *ibid.*

[9] 1941 S.C. 754.

negligence requiring the defender to provide full legal proof of an explanation. Of course, it must be appreciated that since that case the requirement of full legal proof has been eased.[10] In *Mathison v. McNeill*[11] it was held that averments that a steering wheel had not worked were insufficient to allow the defender a proof against a case of prima facie evidence. If he meant to prove a latent defect that had to be averred.

Res ipsa loquitur translates as the thing speaks for itself. Like many latin **24-4** maxims in Scots law the incantation of the words still has a magical quality. Nonetheless the courts have now divested the maxim of any force beyond that which it is entitled by reason of it denoting a special category of cases where inference may be made.[12] The thing said to be the *res* must be the cause of the accident for the doctrine to apply.[13] It was seen in *Inglis* that the doctrine can only apply where the thing in question is within the control of the defender. The leading Scots case is *Devine v. Colvilles*.[14] A workman was injured when he jumped from a platform about 15 feet above ground. He stated that his action in jumping from the platform was the result of his having been put in a state of alarm by a very violent explosion which occurred a short distance from the place where he was working. After proof before answer it was established that following a violent explosion or series of explosions panic amongst the workers in the steel works ensued. The employers were operating new plant which had been purchased from a reputable firm some months before. The cause of the explosion was unexplained but the evidence established that it occurred as the result of an outbreak of fire in a flexible oxygen hose. The pursuer maintained that the maxim *res ipsa loquitur* applied and that the employers had not discharged the onus of negativing negligence on their part. The House of Lords adhered to the finding of *res ipsa loquitur* which had been upheld by a majority in the Inner House. It is clear from *Devine* that although the law of evidence is quite different in both jurisdictions authorities on *res ipsa loquitur* in England are used in Scotland. Indeed once it has become a matter of logic rather than law it ought to be equally valid in any jurisdiction. While Scots courts are generally, it is submitted, receptive to arguments based on logical inference they are no longer so swayed by a general argument of *res ipsa loquitur*.[15] Thus where a member of the public sustained injuries the nature of which were undisclosed by the report in using a lavatory in public baths, it was held that *res ipsa* did not apply because other members of the public might well have misused the lavatory pan.[16] The maxim did not apply where a workman sued a joiner when he was injured in a hut. The roof blew off. The walls fell in. The joiner defender built the hut but he did not fix the sleepers nor felt the roof.[17] A typical decision is *Fleming v. C. & W. West*,[18] in which it was averred that

---

[10] The 1988 Act should allow the defender to escape without the need for corroboration.

[11] 1948 S.L.T. (Notes) 24.

[12] See generally, D. Kinloch, "Liability in Damages Where Cause of Accident Unknown", 1998 Rep.B. 22–2.

[13] *Binnie v. Rederij Theodoro BV*, 1991 G.W.D. 26–1523.

[14] 1969 S.L.T. 154.

[15] Perhaps as a result of Lord President Cooper's comments in *Elliot v. Young's Bus Services Ltd*, 1946 S.L.T. 145 at 150.

[16] *McLeod v. Glasgow Corp.*, 1971 S.L.T. (Notes) 64.

[17] *Booth v. Macmillan*, 1972 S.C. 197.

[18] 1976 S.L.T. (Notes) 36.

the defender electricians had been asked to check an immersion heater. About an hour after they did so the area associated with the immersion heater went on fire. It was held that whether or not the maxim applied the inference was such that even in the absence of specification of the cause a prima facie case arose.[19] It is submitted that this is the state of Scottish practice.[20] At the time of writing the only problem is that the "contra *res ipsa*" school has carried the day but the "prima facie inference" line has rather been forgotten.[21]

24-5   The *res ipsa loquitur* doctrine can apply in any kind of case. Cases under the Occupiers' Liability (Scotland) Act 1961 are prime candidates for application of the doctrine because by statute the foreseeability of harm or remoteness of injury issue is no longer live. Nonetheless, causal issues and breach of reasonable care issues remain to which issues *res ipsa* may be directed successfully or not.[22] More recently in *McQueen v. Glasgow Garden Festival (1988) Ltd*[23] the pursuer was injured by fragments of a firework tube, but because the injury was due to the shell inside the tube exploding, the injury had not been caused by the *res*, which was the shell, and so the doctrine could not be used. The doctrine could not in any event apply, as against the organisers of the firework display, as the accident was not unexplained—there was an explanation that it was caused by the shell.[24] It was also accepted that the defect was latent. In *Borris v. Lord Advocate*,[25] the pursuer was hit on the head by a piece of wood which fell from a dry dock. The defenders tried to have the case dismissed because the doctrine did not support the case as others were also present who might have been responsible. It was held that the maxim was a presumption of fact and was only of value after proof. Thus a proof before answer was allowed. It was only in exceptional cases that the issue could be decided against a pursuer on relevancy.[26] That statement depends of course on the particular pleadings. Some may be so doomed that there could be no *res ipsa* argument.

McGhee causation

24-6 It can be difficult to establish that a breach of a duty caused a loss. The case of *McGhee v. National Coal Board*[27] made this an easier exercise and so the rules of liability in relation to causation should be seen in the context of that decision. However, the use to which the ruling in *McGhee* can be put must be carefully circumscribed. There must be a basis in evidence for the

---

[19] Lord Stewart in this case considers the various views of the maxim despite having declared he had no wish to "attempt to wrestle with the complexities of the concept" (at 36).

[20] In *Johnston v. Ayrshire and Arran H.B.*, Nov. 11, 1998, unreported, a medical negligence case failed despite reference to an English case which relied on the doctrine: *Bentley v. Bristol and Weston H.A. (No. 2)* [1991] 3 Med.L.R. 1. which Temporary Judge Coutts held was not applicable to an occurrence under direct human control.

[21] Not by all see Kinloch, *op. cit.*

[22] *McQueen v. Ballater Golf Club*, 1975 S.L.T. (Notes) 39.

[23] 1995 S.L.T. 211.

[24] This was what prevented the doctrine applying in *Bolton v. Stone* [1951] A.C. 850.

[25] 1993 G.W.D. 6–435.

[26] However, it was appreciated that there was a special case where the issue had been decided as a matter of relevancy: *Booth v. MacMillan*, 1972 S.C. 197.

[27] 1973 S.C. (H.L.) 37.

relaxation to apply.[28] The ambit of *McGhee* was carefully stated and it may be said constrained in the English decision of *Wilsher*.[29]

No evidence

The onus being upon the pursuer in nearly all reparation cases—it is open **24-7** to the defender to cross examine to discredit the case and to lead no evidence at all. However, the defender must be very sure. In *O'Donnell v. Murdoch McKenzie & Co. Ltd*[30] the House of Lords considered this issue in a statutory case. By a majority of 3 to 2 it found for the pursuer reversing the Inner House. The pursuer was left to make his own scaffolding. It was suggested that even if there had been safe scaffolding the pursuer would have taken a less safe course. Lord Upjohn said:

"This case is far removed from those familiar cases where employers have failed to provide safety equipment (belts, helmets, goggles, boots, etc.), and prove by evidence that the employee would not have used it if provided, so their breach did not cause the accident. The defenders called no evidence and in such cases, as was established in your Lordships' House in *Ross v. Associated Portland Cement Manufacturers* [1964] 1 W.L.R. 768, only the most favourable inferences should be drawn from the pursuer's evidence. If my summary of the effect of the evidence as to the pursuer's movements between the scaffold and sill is correct then, in my opinion, it is not right to draw the inference that on the balance of probabilities he would at the time of the accident have left the safety of the scaffold even to square the corners . . . In my opinion it does not lie in the mouth of the defenders, who were in breach of their obligations and who called no evidence, to point to the very vague evidence of McGarvie and McGinley and invite the Court to draw the inference that he would have done so."[31]

The accepted proposition from this case is that where no evidence is led by the defender if inferences are to be drawn from the pursuer's evidence, they should be those favourable to him. However, this cannot be taken too far. The Inner House considered the rule in *Johnstone v. City of Glasgow District Council*.[32] A visitor to a tenement sued the proprietors on the basis that they had not maintained the stair. After proof it was established that the pursuer fell because of a defect which had existed for about three months. No evidence was led as to what would be done by a person in the position of the defender. Thus the Lord Ordinary's decree of absolvitor was upheld. The opinion was expressed in relation to dicta in two leading cases[33] that in considering the evidence of a pursuer in a case in which a defender has led no evidence the court is not entitled to indulge in

---

[28] *Kay's Tutor v. Ayrshire and Arran Health Board*, 1987 S.C. (H.L.) 145.
[29] [1988] 2 W.L.R. 577.
[30] 1967 S.L.T. 229.
[31] *ibid.* at 232.
[32] 1986 S.L.T. 50.
[33] *Ross v. Associated Portland Cement Manufacturers* [1964] 1 W.L.R. 768; *O'Donnell v. Murdoch MacKenzie & Co. Ltd*, 1967 S.C. (H.L.) 63.

speculation. The evidence led must be capable of giving rise to any inference drawn from it, and such an inference must be a reasonable one. "Looking at all the circumstances we sense a whiff of declining interest in the premises by the landlords and their agents, but it is not sufficient to allow an inference of negligence on their part to be drawn from it. To draw such an inference would be merely speculative."[34]

Evidence

Corroboration

24–8 Until the Civil Evidence (Scotland) Act 1988 the general rule in civil proceedings was that the pursuer had to prove his case by corroborated evidence. That of course did not mean that there had to be two eye-witnesses—indeed any eye-witnesses.[35] However, it did mean that a truthful and reliable pursuer who was an eye-witness and who had no other evidence had to fail. This was perceived generally as unfair and certainly so in relation to industrial accidents. The then relatively new Scottish Law Commission put forward proposals.[36] These resulted in section 9 of the Law Reform (Miscellaneous Provisions) (Scotland) Act 1968. Section 9 provided that "the court . . . if they are satisfied" could find a fact proven notwithstanding that the evidence was not corroborated. On the face of it these are simple words which seem to have a simple aim. The case is still to be proved on balance of probabilities and "satisfied" is not on the face of it the same as "totally convinced" for example. In an early case considering the 1968 Act[37] the decision of a Lord Ordinary was reversed. The apparently neutral phrase in the Act "satisfied that [the] fact has been established" was glossed to become a "relatively high" test hardly likely to be satisfied if corroborative evidence was available but not produced or if there was a strong body of contradictory evidence.[38] It should be noted that the precise ground for reversing the Lord Ordinary was on more fundamental grounds always applicable to appeals—that it was not at all clear why the Lord Ordinary had accepted the pursuer's evidence and rejected that of the defenders' witnesses.[39] It is thus arguable that the case is no more than *obiter* so far as section 9 is concerned. So far as it decided that an appellate court could still apply the principles of *Thomas* it was probably right. It was however, hugely influential and has continued to be so even well after the passing of the 1988 Act. The main influence has been in saying when a first instance judge should be "satisfied" and even Lord Guthrie's more moderate approach to the legislation led him to state that the presence or absence of corroboration remained an important consideration as did the absence of corroborative testimony when it was available.[40] It is probably

---

[34] *Johnston*, above, *per* Lord Grieve at 53.

[35] *Cleisham v. British Transport Commission*, 1964 S.C. (H.L.) 8.

[36] Scot. Law Com., No. 4 (1967).

[37] *Morrison v. J. Kelly & Sons Ltd*, 1970 S.C. 65.

[38] *per* L.P. Clyde at 203.

[39] *Thomas v. Thomas*, 1948 S.L.T. 2; *Jordan v. Court Line Ltd*, 1947 S.L.T. 134; *McCusker v. Saveheat Cavity Wall Insulation Ltd*, 1987 S.L.T. 24.

[40] At 204. He also mentioned *mora* which has not been pre-eminent in the subsequent cases but it is discussed in *McLaren v. Caldwell*, 1973 S.L.T. 158 at 166.

acceptable to say that although corroboration is not needed, if it is present a judge is more likely to be satisfied than in a case where it is not. The "absent witness" point is more difficult because if corroboration is not needed the pursuer should not be worse off because there is another witness. The defender can always locate and call that witness. In employment cases defenders can more easily than the pursuer identify and take statements from the workmates of the man in hospital. It cannot reasonably be presumed that the "absent witnesses" must be hostile.

Lord President Clyde toughened the gloss in *McGowan v. Lord Advo-* **24–9** *cate*[41] to go so far (with the Division) as to reverse a jury verdict on the basis that there was no corroboratory evidence from three other potential witnesses. One of the witnesses for the pursuer gave a contradictory account unchallenged. In *McLaren v. Caldwell's Paper Mill*,[42] Lord Milligan in the majority said that the pursuer could not be blamed for not calling the driver of the lorry because he was actually blaming him. In the absence of evidence that other people in the vicinity must have seen what happened he did not attach much importance to their absence.[43] This is an important dictum from one of the significant early cases for it is submitted that it makes it clear that the pursuer is not under any duty as such to call all witnesses who may have seen something, although that is what is still often done "to be on the safe side". It is also the case that there needs to be a foundation in the evidence for the absent witness to be significant—that may be something which the defender has to do either by leading evidence of his own or taking it in cross-examination of the pursuer. Lord Stott's dissenting opinion in this *McLaren* is often cited and discussed. He accepted that when the Act was being used a judge required to exercise some care where evidence is uncorroborated. It was nonetheless clearly stated that there was no onus on the pursuer to call potentially contradictory witnesses.[44] He disagreed with the interpretation sought to be placed on Lord President Clyde's words but would in any event have disagreed with them. The following passage has often been discussed:

"The terms of the section do not suggest that it was intended to benefit only the man working alone. They are general and comprehensive, and appear to have been chosen not with reference to any special set of circumstances but as a general remedy for the anomaly and injustice arising from a rule of law whereby the court, convinced that an injured man had given a truthful account of his accident were nevertheless bound to reject it from lack of corroboration. The Act now requires to be read subject to the ratio of the decision in *Morrison v. Kelly*. But it is one thing to say, as was said in *Morrison*, that the evidence of a single witness should not have been accepted when there was a weight of evidence the other way. It is quite another to say, as counsel for the reclaimers appears to say, that the evidence of the pursuer should have been rejected because there was an uncalled witness whose evidence might have been contradictory."[45]

---

[41] 1972 S.C. 68.
[42] 1973 S.L.T. 158.
[43] *ibid.* at 164.
[44] *McLaren*, at 168.
[45] *ibid.* at 169.

There were two Outer House cases decided before *McLaren*: in *Mason v. SLD Olding Ltd*[46] the pursuer failed for not calling a co-worker in a case of vicarious liability which depended on that co-worker's evidence; in *McDougall v. James Jones & Sons*[47] the pursuer failed being unable to use the Act on the view that the pursuer if of doubtful credit had to lead other evidence even if likely to be hostile. Where the pursuer did lead evidence to corroborate which was not accepted that did not preclude the applicability of the Act.[48]

24–10   After *McLaren* there was a jury verdict which was allowed to stand where there was no direct contradiction of the pursuer by the only other witness to the material fact.[49] The "contradiction" point appeared again in *McCallum v. British Railways Board*[50] where it was held that the contradictions that did appear were only as to detail. That does again suggest that cases of contradiction are much more difficult for the pursuer but that can or should only be in a practical rather than a legal way. The case is, however, authority for saying that the pursuer need not bring into the witness box every person who was in the vicinity even if only to say they knew nothing about it.[51] *McCallum* would have been decided in the knowledge that the law had been reviewed and restated in the 1988 Act. *McArthur v. Organon*,[52] is of interest because it does give an idea of what "satisfied" means if it is not a relatively high test. The question was whether a rat kicked and caused an injury or whether the accident was the pursuer's fault. Lord Ross was faced with two witnesses of credit. In a situation like that clearly it would be difficult to be satisfied. In the end he preferred the defenders' witness so the matter did not arise. In *Commerford v. Strathclyde Regional Council*[53] Sheriff Bell, preferring Lord Stott's approach, considered he could be satisfied by the evidence of the pursuer albeit he was contradicted by a fellow employee eye-witness. He believed the pursuer and not the other man. He certainly did not think that the Act only applied to cases where a man was working on his own.[54]

24–11   Section 9 was repealed by the Civil Evidence (Scotland) Act 1988 which in general terms and subject to many restrictions removed the need for corroboration from all civil claims. The new rule provided by section 1(1) is that in any civil proceedings the court, or as the case may be, the jury, if satisfied that any fact has been established by evidence in any proceedings, is entitled to find that fact proved by that evidence notwithstanding that the evidence is not corroborated. The new wording does not include the word "they" which Lord President Clyde used to justify interference with a lower court in *Morrison*. This may mean that this newer Act will preclude interference from above except on the more usual basis of demonstrable

---

[46] 1982 S.L.T. 385 (decided June 14, 1972).

[47] Nov. 27, 1970 unreported.

[48] *Thomson v. Tough Ropes Ltd*, 1978 S.L.T. (Notes) 5; *Commerford v. Strathclyde R.C.*, 1987 S.C.L.R. 758.

[49] *Ward v. Upper Clyde Shipbuilders Ltd*, 1973 S.L.T. 182.

[50] 1991 S.L.T. 5.

[51] *ibid., per* Lord Sutherland at 8.

[52] 1982 S.L.T. 425.

[53] 1987 S.C.L.R. 758.

[54] *ibid.* at 763. The case was appealed but not on this point and indeed it seems not to have been disputed on appeal.

error as in the *Thomas* line of cases. Some attempt has been made to apply the old gloss to the new rule.[55] However, Lord Rodger in *Laing v. Tayside Health Board*,[56] made it plain that the wording of the 1988 Act was different from he 1968 Act, although it is impossible to trace through *Hansard* how this wording came in.[57] There he merely notes the different wording but the actual decision is in line with the more liberal interpretation. The Scottish Law Commission cited Lord Stott with approval and that may be taken as a statement of the law at the time the 1988 Act was passed. If "satisfied" is thought to be ambiguous then a *"Pepper v. Hart"* reference to *Hansard* shows that the Government in answering questions on the possibility of a *Morrisson* approach being taken favoured the Stott approach.[58]

It might be thought that the revolutionary nature of the 1988 Act—in **24–12** allowing hearsay—would mean that the older authorities bringing in corroboration by the back door could be forgotten. The rationale of the 1988 Act is to hear the case and weigh up the evidence. *Laing* did not require the old authorities formally to be discussed but it is a decision in line with the attitude of the legislation. *Gordon v. Grampian Health Board*[59] is an unsatisfactory consideration of the new legislation. It seems the sheriff and the defenders' counsel were surprised by the fact that the pursuer who had a witness at court, did not call that witness. Thus arguments were perhaps not as full as they might be. There seems to have been no citation of contrary authority. It is understandable how the decision was arrived at but the pursuer did not want to call a hostile witness. Proceedings continued instead on the basis of hearsay. On one view that is using two relaxations of the law and should be discouraged. On another it is perfectly in accord with the new law of evidence. The defenders immediately chose not to give evidence albeit they could have called the witness who was hostile and was within the precincts of the court. The sheriff could then have evaluated the evidence. It is also long established that the defender who does not call evidence may have any reasonable inference drawn against him.

At the time of writing no reparations cases have gone to the Inner **24–13** House. In *K v. Kennedy*,[60] a case was won on the basis of a hearsay statement of a witness who testified to the opposite effect! The court it must be said brushed aside the cases on section 9 of the 1968 Act saying they did not apply to a case such as the one they were considering under the Social Work Act. So *K* is not conclusively in favour of a more liberal interpretation but nonetheless the precise terms of the 1988 Act were those applicable to the case. In *M v. Kennedy*[61] it was held to be perfectly acceptable not to call two other witnesses (albeit expert witnesses) where it was thought they were simply going to say the same thing as the witness

---

[55] *Mckay v. Yarrow Shipbuilders Ltd*, July 4, 1991, unreported.

[56] 1996 Rep.L.R. 51.

[57] And see *M v. Kennedy*, 1993 S.C.L.R. 69 which supports the view that no evidence need be called to support a credible and reliable witness although the case being in childrens' proceedings might be distinguished.

[58] *Hansard*, H.L., Vol. 490, col. 773.

[59] 1991 S.C.L.R. 213.

[60] 1992 S.C.L.R. 386.

[61] 1993 S.C.L.R. 69.

who was called.[62] In *Aimes v. Chief Constable, Strathclyde Police*,[63] a woman testified that a policeman punched her in the face. The sheriff believed her. On appeal it was complained that, as was the case, corroboration was available and was not called. The sheriff principal, while not commenting on the older cases accepted that the coming into force of the 1988 Act meant the court could take a decision in these circumstances in favour of the pursuer. Indeed at one stage he describes the 1988 Act, correctly it is submitted, as altering the law. In coming to that view he took account of the fact that the sheriff had been careful to scrutinise the uncorroborated testimony and to express a view on the unsatisfactory nature of the officer's testimony. Then in a non-reparation case *Lynch v. Lynch*,[64] Lord Coulsfield held that the enactments which rendered corroboration unnecessary in civil cases entailed that evidence of a single witness is always sufficient. He commented, in very strong terms, about "the so-called rule that failure to lead corroborative evidence which appears to have been available should lead a judge to regard evidence which has been led with special care and attention." He considered that if it were ever important and the point were argued the old cases might be open to reconsideration.

In a reparation case in the Outer House, *Rae v. Chief Constable, Strathclyde Police*,[65] Lord Marnoch said:

> "[I]t would, I believe, be wrong to say that a single witness' evidence should always be looked at, as it were, askance. But the Weight to be attached to evidence is, in my opinion, a different matter and where, without any attempt at explanation, someone who, on the face of matters, is a crucial witness is not led to substantiate a party's position that, in my opinion, is clearly a situation in which the Court may be disinclined to give maximum weight to the uncorroborated testimony."[66]

With respect, this is smuggling the old cases back into account. It is open to the defender to call the missing witness and put the evidence before the court if it is bad for the pursuer—it is just not fair, the law having been changed to assume that the uncalled evidence is against the party not calling the witness. Another point which has not been expressly explained by the judges is when and by whom the explanation for the absence of the witness is to be explained—one possibility is to take it in a rather contrived way from the pursuer; another is to make it a matter of submission. It is best to do both given the present state of the law.

Hearsay

24–14 Hearsay is admissible in terms of statute but there are rules of court which must be followed.[67] In *Davies v. McGuire*,[68] hearsay was admitted (although on the facts it did not require to be relied upon) in a Damages (Scotland)

---

[62] *ibid., per* L.P. Hope at 73.
[63] 1998 S.L.T. (Sh. Ct) 16.
[64] 1997 G.W.D. 30–1501.
[65] 1998 Rep.L.R. 63.
[66] *ibid.*
[67] *Lenaghan v. Ayrshire and Arran Health Board*, 1994 S.L.T. 765.
[68] 1995 S.L.T. 755.

Act case in the form of a police officer's testimony as to what was said to him by many of the pursuer's witnesses at the time and that was used to contradict their actual testimony. In an employers' liability case, *Anderson v. Fraser & Co.*,[69] it was held that a solicitor could give evidence of a statement given to her by a witness, and that this was not a precognition. This allowed rebuttal of the evidence given by the defenders' solicitor and their insurance investigator that the same witness had given a statement unfavourable to the pursuer.[70] In *Stevenson v. Chief Constable, Strathclyde Police*,[71] evidence was admitted of statements made to a precognition-taking private detective so that these could be put to the people who made them as previous inconsistent statements. The questions and answers had been sufficiently carefully noted so as not to make this a case of using a precognition.

---

[69] 1992 S.C.L.R. 417.
[70] See also *McAvoy v. Glasgow D.C.*, 1993 S.L.T. 859.
[71] 1998 G.W.D. 18–935.

INDEX